AIRBORNE

A Combat History of American Airborne Forces

Lt. Gen. Edward M. Flanagan Jr., USA (Ret.)

PRESIDIO
PRESS

Ballantine Books • New York

To the superb airborne troopers of the U.S. Army
Past Present and Future

A Presidio Press Book
Published by The Random House Publishing Group

Copyright © 2002 by Edward M. Flanagan Jr.
Maps copyright © Mary Craddock Hoffman

All rights reserved under International and Pan-American Copyright
Conventions. Published in the United States by The Random House Publishing
Group, a division of Random House, Inc., New York, and simultaneously in
Canada by Random House of Canada Limited, Toronto.

Presidio Press and colophon are trademarks of Random House, Inc.

www.presidiopress.com

Library of Congress Control Number is available
upon request from the publisher.

ISBN 0-89141-833-4

Manufactured in the United States of America

First Hardcover Edition: January 2003
First Trade Paperback Edition: January 2004

1 3 5 7 9 10 8 6 4 2

Contents

Acknowledgments

Writing a book covering a period of military history spanning the years from before World War II to the present requires the assistance of people who have contributed their time, expertise, specific information, and guidance. I am deeply indebted to all of them. And some of them deserve special recognition.

Donna Barr Tabor is the XVIII Airborne Corps historian. She helped me with maps, photographs, and summaries of the history of XVIII Airborne Corps and answered many specific questions about personalities and events.

Colonel Robert V. Kane, publisher emeritus of Presidio Press, edited my manuscript with close attention to detail and singular expertise. He found a number of glitches that needed correction.

Lieutenant General Jack Mackmull (retired), commander of the XVIII Airborne Crops from 1 September 1981until 7 April 1984, and the Joint Task Force commander for Urgent Fury in Grenada was kind enough to review my account of the operation.

Lieutenant General William P. Yarborough (retired) gave me a copy of his oral history collected in interviews by members of the U.S. Army Center of Military History. His remarks and memories were of great assistance in covering the early development of the airborne concept and the combat operations of the 509th Parachute Infantry Battalion. General Yarborough was one of the founding fathers of airborne and special operations. Having graduated from West Point in 1936, in 1940 he was one of seventeen officers who volunteered to command the original Parachute Test Platoon. But on the day in 1940 when he was to take the written examination used to select the platoon commander, he was suddenly ordered to Camp Jackson, South Carolina, for a new assignment. Lieutenant Bill Ryder, a West Point classmate, got the coveted command, instead. But Bill Yarborough was not to be denied: a couple of months later he became a paratrooper, a parachute company commander, and a test officer for parachute equipment. In that job, he designed the U.S. paratrooper wings and jump boots and, later, the famous jump jacket and trousers worn in World War II airborne combat operations. Years later, he played a leading role in persuading the Department of the Army to authorize the red beret for wear by qualified paratroopers in airborne units and the green beret by qualified troopers in Special Forces units. He has been gracious and generous enough to write the foreword for this book.

John J. O'Brien, the installation historian for Fort Campbell, Kentucky, and with the Don. F. Pratt Memorial Museum, was very helpful in providing many photos and maps from the museum's archives.

Gerard M. Devlin, author of *Paratrooper,* very generously offered photos for use in my book.

E. J. McCarthy, executive editor of Presidio Press, used his outstanding expertise to guide me in producing the final version of this book.

Robert P. Anzuoni, director of the 82d Airborne Division Historical Society was very helpful and generous in supplying me with photos of the division in World War II combat.

First Sergeant Daniel Bennett, of the 82d's Advanced Airborne School at Fort Bragg answered many detailed questions about the organization of the division and the capacity and range of today's air transports.

In the bibliography is a list of the officers and men who sent me letters covering their parts in the various airborne operations recorded herein. I have tried to weave their personal stories of bravery, misfortunes, complications, and operations planning into the text to give it a strong heartbeat. I am indebted to them for their help, especially to their accomplishments in many operations, combat and otherwise.

And I would be remiss if I failed to mention the support given me by the current (2002) XVIII Airborne Corps Commander, Lt. Gen. Dan K. McNeill.

Foreword

Lieutenant General Edward "Fly" Flanagan is notable and outstanding among those who have collected, preserved, written, and been themselves an important part of U.S. airborne history. As both a veteran paratrooper and pilot himself, Fly writes with the skill of a historian and the experience of a seasoned professional soldier.

From his pages the sounds, the misery, and the triumphs of many battlefields emerge with a realism that warriors understand.

The airborne saga began during a period of history in which even the sight of an airplane in flight was something of a curiosity. In 1942, the ten-hour, 1,500-mile flight of the 509th Parachute Infantry Battalion from Land's End in England to Algeria in North Africa was in some respects akin to the voyages of Leif Erikson and Christopher Columbus. This may be hard to understand in an era of universal air travel with its giant aircraft that carry hundreds of passengers and incredibly heavy loads—which include main battle tanks, artillery, and motor vehicles—and that fly routes literally spanning the globe, but the very audacity of that airborne assault achieved one of the most important goals of military operations—strategic surprise.

Even then, enthusiasm for the burgeoning U.S. airborne institution was put to an extreme test by a series of circumstances that threatened to bring the whole movement to a halt. As a prime example, on the night of 9–10 July 1943, twenty-three aircraft carrying paratroopers of the 504th Parachute Infantry Regiment to drop zones in Sicily were shot down by friendly antiaircraft artillery. Eventually, a board of inquiry reached the conclusion that inexperienced planners and not the airborne concept itself deserved the blame.

Although more than six decades separate the airborne of 2002 from its beginning, and innumerable technical developments and changes have served to mold today's institution, one factor remains constant—the airborne spirit.

The intangible but very real end product that stems from an individual's evaluation of himself is perhaps the most precious result of the process that produces parachute soldiers. A warrior who will bail out at night onto a battlefield deep in enemy country while carrying fifty pounds of equipment, weapons, and ammunition is not likely to perform poorly in combat. Fly Flanagan's research corroborates this thesis in a most convincing way.

—LT. GEN. WILLIAM P. YARBOROUGH

Introduction

The "airborne" concept began long before the early days of World War II when, for example, on 20 May 1941, the Germans launched a mammoth parachute and glider assault on Crete. Although the Germans captured the island, it was with catastrophic loss. Of the some 13,000 paratroopers who jumped on the island, 5,140 were killed or wounded, and 350 troop transport planes were destroyed. Hitler was completely devastated by the casualties and decided, then and there, that any large-scale airborne operation in the future was a waste of manpower. Crete was the last large airborne assault by the Germans.

Over the past several centuries, airborne pioneers have gazed into the future. In 1784, Benjamin Franklin theorized: "Where is the prince who can afford to cover his country with troops for its defense, as that ten thousand men descending from the clouds, might not, in many places, do an infinite deal of mischief before a force could be brought together to repel them?"

Others put their dreams into reality. As early as 1785, men were experimenting with parachutes of one sort or another. That year, Jean Pierre Blanchard, a balloonist, dropped his dog from the balloon with an improvised parachute. The drop was successful, but the dumbfounded dog landed and ran away. In 1837, Robert Cocking jumped from a balloon with what was a huge umbrella. Unfortunately, on descent, after the umbrella opened properly, its ribs became entangled, and Cocking experienced what was probably the first fatal parachute "streamer." On 30 January 1887, Tom Baldwin made a leap from a balloon over Golden Gate Park in San Francisco. He and his brother Sam, both high-wire walkers, had developed a parachute that deployed from a container. Tom jumped from 5,000 feet. In five seconds his chute opened, and he landed safely before a gawking and amazed crowd in the park.

With the development of the airplane and the increase in deaths from plane crashes, it became clear that a parachute was necessary to save the lives of pilots in mal-functioning planes. Leo Stevens, who had jumped a number of times from a balloon, developed a parachute that could be packed and stored on the bottom of a plane. On 12 March 1912, at Jefferson Barracks, Missouri, he successfully demonstrated his parachute with a drop from a moving plane at 1,000 feet. It was the first parachute jump from a moving airplane.

In World War I, Germany was the only nation to provide its aircraft pilots with parachutes. They were static-line activated chutes. In one air to air fighter plane fight, Capt. Eddie Rickenbacker, the ace of aces in the U.S. Air Service, shot down a German Fokker. In his book, *Fighting the Flying Circus*, he wrote:

> It was an easy shot I could not have missed. I was agreeably surprised, however, to see that my first burst had set fire to the Hun's fuel tank and that the machine was doomed. I was almost equally gratified the next second to see the German pilot level off his blazing machine and with a sudden leap overboard into space let the Fokker slide safely away without him. Attached to his back and sides was a rope which immediately pulled a dainty parachute from the bottom of his seat. The umbrella opened within a fifty foot drop and lowered him gradually to earth within his own lines. . . . Not unmixed with my relief in witnessing his safe jump was the wonder as to why the Huns had all these human contrivances and why our own country could not a least copy them to save American lives.

In the fall of 1918, Col. William P. "Billy" Mitchell was the chief of all the AEF air units and was the air component adviser to Gen. John J. "Black Jack" Pershing, the commander of all U.S. forces in Europe in World War I. Mitchell was an outspoken, flamboyant, self-confident thrity-nine-year-old aviator who tried unsuccessfully to have developed a parachute for his pilots. Even though frustrated, his energy and far-sightedness did not stop there.

He is probably the originator of the concept of vertical mass envelopment. In his *Memoirs of World War I*, he wrote of a meeting he had had with General Pershing on 17 October 1918:

I also proposed to him that in the spring of 1919, when I would have a great force of bombardment airplanes, he should assign one of the infantry divisions permanently to the Air Service, preferably the 1st Division; that we should arm the men with a great number of machine guns and train them to go over the front in our large airplanes, which would carry ten or fifteen of these soldiers. We could equip each man with a parachute, so that when we desired to make a rear attack on the enemy, we could carry these men over the lines and drop them off in parachutes behind the German position.

General Pershing approved the concept and told Mitchell to begin planning.

Mitchell happily told one of his staff officers, Maj. Lewis H. Brereton, Pershing's decision. Well, the war was over before Mitchell had a chance to pursue his radical idea. But it was not lost in Brereton. In World War II, he would command an Allied airborne army.

Between the wars, the Russians grasped the "airborne" concept and decided to do something about it. In the United States in the early twenties, Leslie L. "Sky High" Irvin had developed a rip-cord, "free-fall" parachute and had jumped it successfully before circus crowds many times. In 1931, the Russians bought several thousand of the free-fall parachute developed by Irvin and organized a parachute test outfit. In 1933, forty-six Russian paratroopers dropped from two bombers and established a record for mass jumps. They even went so far as to drop a small tank with a huge parachute. By 1935, the Russians had formed battalion-sized parachute units and were making mass jumps.

Other European nations followed the success of Russia in developing parachute units. In 1935, the French established a jump school at Avignon, and in 1937, formed their first parachute units, the 601st and 602d Air Infantry Groups. In 1938, the Italians opened their jump school in Libya. And in 1937, the Germans opened their jump school at Stendal near Berlin.

But between the wars, the United States was far behind in adopting Billy Mitchell's concept. America was in an isolationist mood. In the fall of 1939, the German war machine had overrun Poland, and Hitler had gone to war with England and France. The United States military establishment had a wake-up call. In January 1940, Maj. Gen. George A. Lynch, chief of Infantry, designated Maj. William C. Lee to study in depth the possibility and feasibility of transporting infantrymen by air.

Major Lee was a forty-three-year-old infantryman who had served in
World War I as a platoon leader and company commander. He had had
twenty-one years of active service. But he took on General Lynch's assignment with enthusiasm, competence and energy. He went through
many months of struggle with the Air Corps who wanted to control the
airborne units, with died-in-the-wool army leaders who would fight
World War II with World War I tactics, and with the War Department for
improved chutes and transport aircraft. Lee finally succeeded in establishing the Army's Parachute Test Platoon. Finally, on 16 August 1940,
Lt. William T. Ryder, the commander of the Parachute Test Platoon,
made the first jump from a Douglas B-18 bomber. He was "America's first
paratrooper."

Major Lee worked relentlessly to develop the tactics, organizations,
and equipment of the army's airborne forces. Throughout the army's airborne establishment, he would become known as the "Father of American Airborne."

Eventually, in 1944, he became the commanding general of the 101st
Airborne Division. But on 9 February 1944, in England, in preparation
for the invasion of France, he suffered a massive heart attack and had to
return to the States for treatment.

This book attempts to chronicle the history of U.S. airborne forces
from the early, difficult, inventive days of the test platoon through airborne combat operations from World War II to the present.

What has developed through these years of airborne forces in many
different types of combat and peace-keeping operations, in a vast variety of countries and situations, and with expansive technology and rad-
ically improved equipment is an airborne force that is superbly well-
trained and available for a variety of missions

Today, the XVIII Airborne Corps epitomizes that force. It is America's
Contingency Corps. Each unit in the corps is trained to deploy by air with
as little as eighteen hours of notification. For example, division and corps
assault command posts can land in an objective area in 29 hours, given
the appropriate airlift.

The mission of XVIII Airborne Corps: "To maintain the XVIII Airborne Corps as a strategic crisis response force, manned and trained to
deploy rapidly by air, sea and land anywhere in the world; prepared to
fight upon arrival and win."

"War to the XVIII Airborne Corps comes in the shape of contingency
operations," reads the corps handbook. "The Corps provides command

and control (C2) for the Army's crisis response forces. This mixture of force capabilities is as versatile and lethal as it is deployable and expansible. It is not a fixed force, but can be tailored to any contingency worldwide based on factors of METT-T (mission, enemy, terrain, troops and time available).

"Likewise, the Corps missions range from a simple show-of-force (Honduras 1988) to providing a deterrent force against a major and immediate threat (Saudi Arabia 1990). The Corps often operates in undeveloped, austere environments without in-place logistic and communication infrastructures. Further, the most likely contingencies require the Corps simultaneously to fight in the objective area while deploying additional forces to amass the combat power necessary for decisive operations."

The XVIII Airborne Corps is the end result of some sixty years of airborne force development through bloody, deadly wars and lengthy, widespread peace-keeping missions. This book hopes to convey that story.

On 31 May 2001, Lt. Gen. Dank McNeill, Commanding General of XVIII Airborne Corps, took control of all U.S. and coalition forces in Afghanistan as commander of Joint Task Force 180 (Afghanistan). The main elements of XVIII Airborne Corps headquarters began arriving in late April 2002. Brigadier General Stanley A. McCrystal was the first staff officer to arrive to organize Combined Joint Task Force 180. About 400 officers and men from the corps were deployed to support the headquarters. In the summer of 2002, some 3,000 82d Airborne Division soldiers were deployed to Afghanistan.

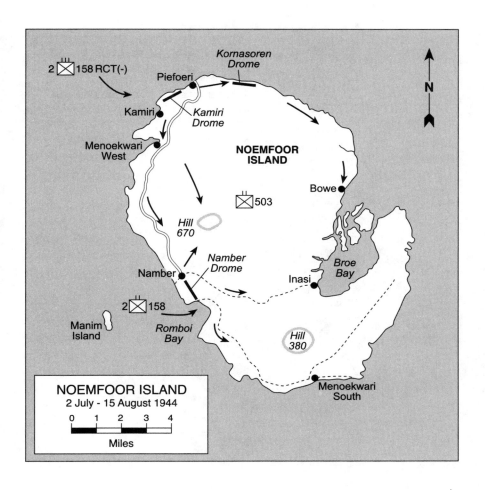

NOEMFOOR ISLAND
2 July - 15 August 1944

0 1 2 3 4
Miles

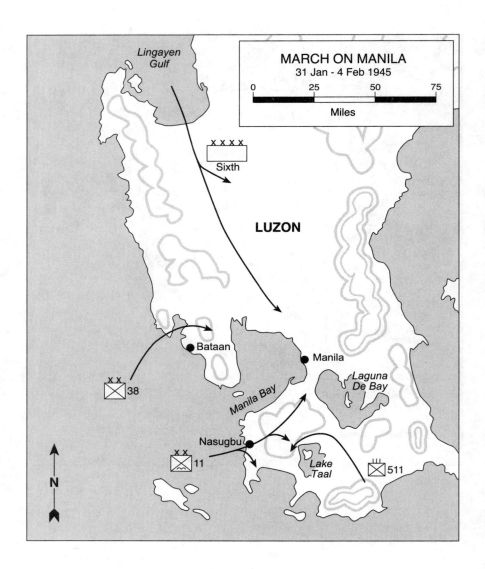

MARCH ON MANILA
31 Jan - 4 Feb 1945

0   25   50   75
Miles

Lingayen
Gulf

XXXX
Sixth

LUZON

Bataan

XX 38

Manila

Laguna
De Bay

Manila Bay

Nasugbu

XX 11

Lake
Taal

III 511

N

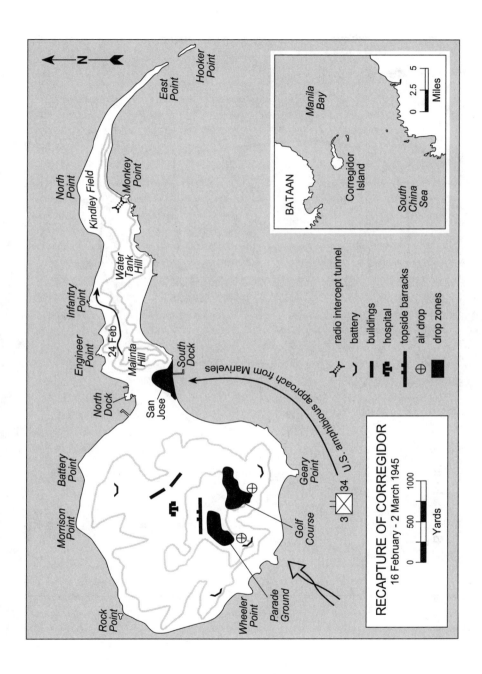

RECAPTURE OF CORREGIDOR
16 February - 2 March 1945

radio intercept tunnel
battery
buildings
hospital
topside barracks
air drop
drop zones

3   34   U.S.

Yards
0   500   1000

N

Hooker Point
East Point
North Point
Monkey Point
Kindley Field
Water Tank Hill
Infantry Point
24 Feb
Engineer Point
Malinta Hill
South Dock
North Dock
San Jose
amphibious approach from Mariveles
Battery Point
Morrison Point
Rock Point
Geary Point
Golf Course
Wheeler Point
Parade Ground

BATAAN
Manila Bay
Corregidor Island
South China Sea
Miles
0   2.5   5

xix

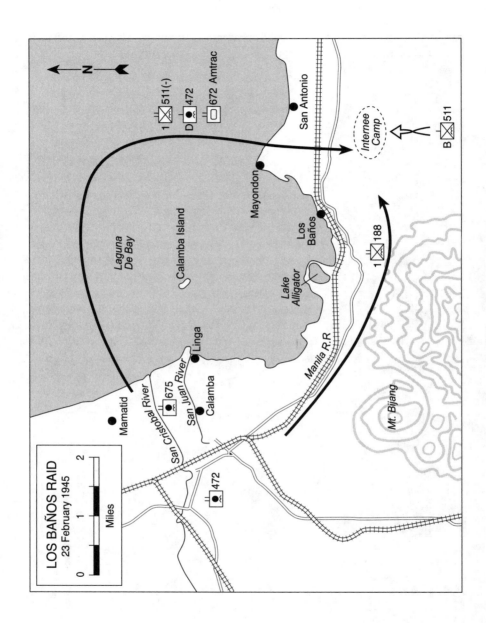

LOS BAÑOS RAID
23 February 1945

Miles
0   1   2

Mamatid

San Cristobal River

675

San Juan River

Linga

Calamba

472

Laguna
De Bay

Calamba Island

Mayondon

Lake
Alligator

Los
Baños

Manila R.R.

1 511(-)

D 472

672 Amtrac

San Antonio

Internee
Camp

B 511

1 188

Mt. Bijang

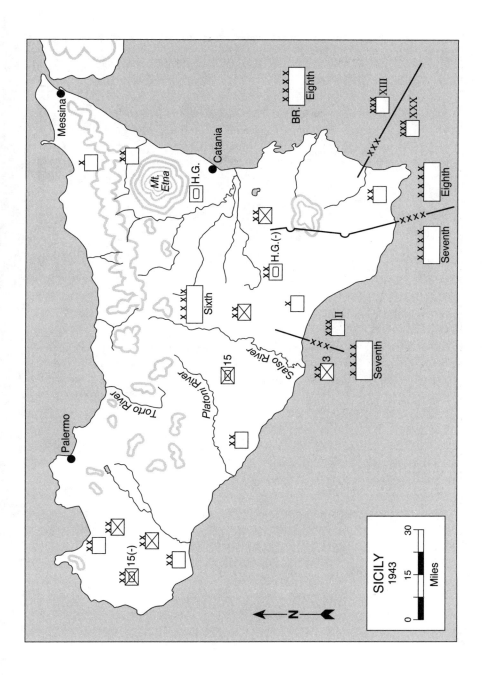

SICILY
1943

Miles

0   15   30

N

Messina

Mt. Etna

Catania

H.G.

H.G.(-)

Palermo

Torto River

Platoni River

Salso River

Sixth

Seventh

Seventh

Eighth

Eighth

BR.

XIII

II

3

15

15(-)

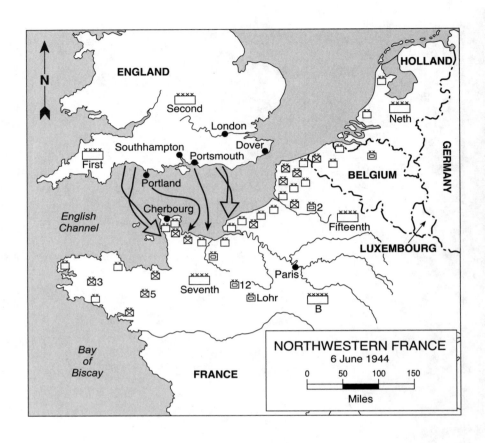

NORTHWESTERN FRANCE

6 June 1944

Miles

0   50   100   150

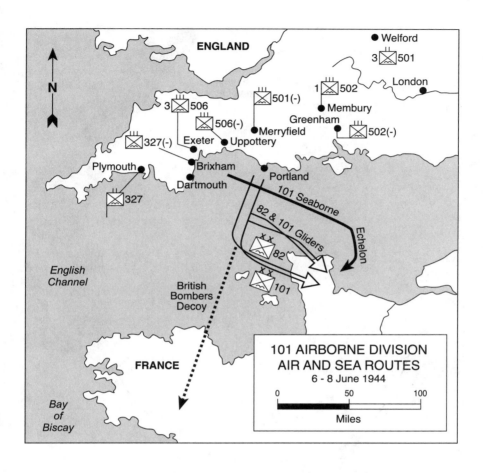

**101 AIRBORNE DIVISION
AIR AND SEA ROUTES**
6 - 8 June 1944

ENGLAND

N

Welford

3 ⊠ 501

1 ⊠ 502   London

3 ⊠ 506   501(-)   Membury

506(-)   Greenham

327(-)   Exeter   Uppottery   Merryfield   502(-)

Plymouth   Brixham   Portland

Dartmouth   101 Seaborne

327   82 & 101 Gliders   Echelon

English
Channel

British
Bombers
Decoy   XX 82

XX 101

FRANCE

Bay
of
Biscay

0   50   100

Miles

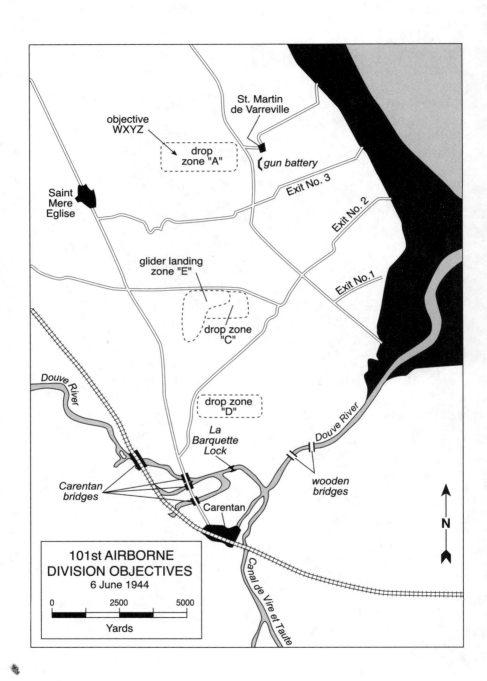

St. Martin
de Varreville

objective
WXYZ

drop
zone "A"

(gun battery

Exit No. 3

Saint
Mere
Eglise

Exit No. 2

glider landing
zone "E"

Exit No.1

drop zone
"C"

Douve River

drop zone
"D"

La
Barquette
Lock

Douve River

Carentan
bridges

wooden
bridges

Carentan

N

**101st AIRBORNE
DIVISION OBJECTIVES**
6 June 1944

0   2500   5000

Yards

Canal de Vire et Taute

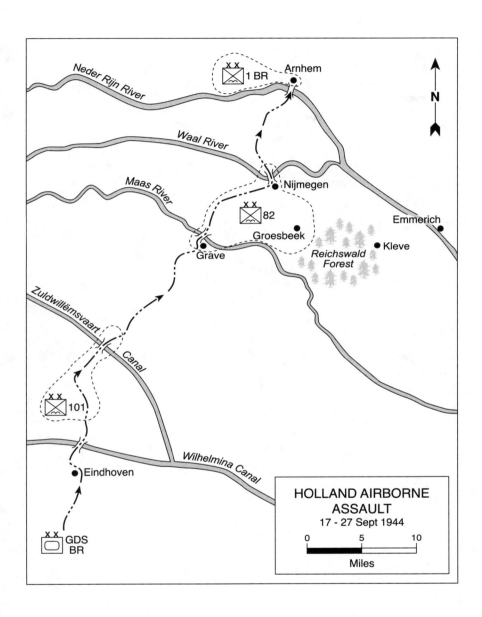

Neder Rijn River

Arnhem

XX 1 BR

Waal River

Maas River

Nijmegen

XX 82

Groesbeek

Emmerich

Grave

Reichswald Forest

Kleve

Zuldwillemsvaart

Canal

XX 101

Wilhelmina Canal

Eindhoven

XX GDS BR

N

HOLLAND AIRBORNE
ASSAULT
17 - 27 Sept 1944

0   5   10

Miles

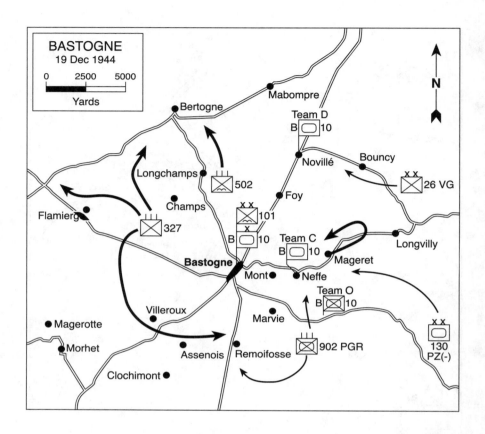

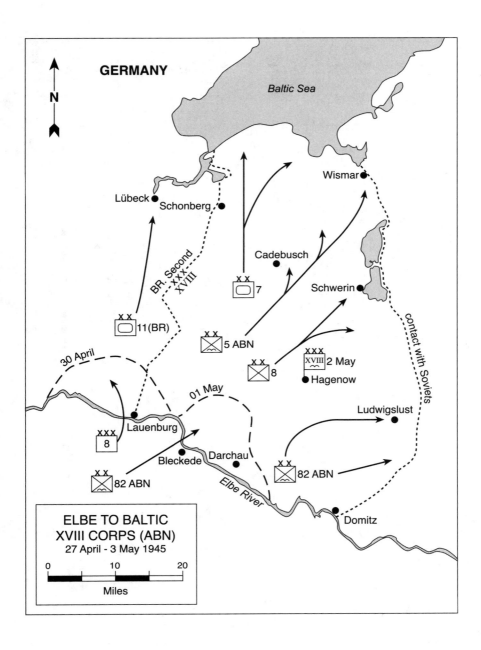

GERMANY

Baltic Sea

N

Lübeck

Schonberg

BR. Second
xxx
XVIII

Wismar

Cadebusch

7

Schwerin

11(BR)

5 ABN

8

XVIII 2 May
Hagenow

30 April

Ludwigslust

01 May

contact with Soviets

8

Lauenburg

Darchau

Bleckede

82 ABN

Elbe River

82 ABN

Domitz

ELBE TO BALTIC
XVIII CORPS (ABN)
27 April - 3 May 1945

0   10   20
Miles

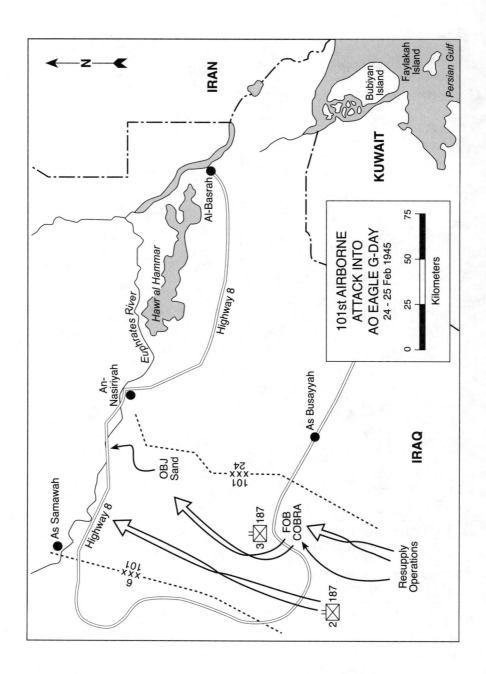

101st AIRBORNE
ATTACK INTO
AO EAGLE G-DAY
24 - 25 Feb 1945

Kilometers

0   25   50   75

1: Airborne: The Beginning

Lieutenant William T. Ryder crouched in the open cargo door of a C-33 transport aircraft flying at an altitude of about 1,500 feet over an open field just to the south of Fort Benning's Lawson airfield. It was 3 August 1940, a calm, warm summer day. Lieutenant Ryder was strapped into a T-4, a twenty-eight-foot backpack parachute whose rip cord was attached by a static line to an overhead anchor cable that ran the length of the cargo compartment of the plane. On his chest, attached to his main harness, was a smaller twenty-two-foot parachute in a rectangular canvas pack. This was his reserve, which, if his main chute failed to open properly, he could activate by pulling a handle sticking out of the right-hand side of the parachute. He wore an Army Air Corps one-piece twill coverall, what looked like a soft, old-fashioned football helmet strapped under his chin, and shin-high, laced brown boots with straps across the instep. Kneeling beside Lieutenant Ryder on the floor of the plane was W. O. Harry "Tug" Wilson, the Army Air Corps' most experienced jumper, a parachute expert who, with a team of four other Air Corps riggers and trainers, had been working with Lieutenant Ryder and his Parachute Test Platoon for the previous two months. Wilson leaned far out of the plane's door, his face rippling in the 110-mile-an-hour wind, looking for the "go point," red panels on the forward edge of the drop zone (DZ). As the plane neared the drop zone, the pilot throttled back to the jump speed of about ninety miles per hour and flew directly above the go point. Wilson tapped the lieutenant's left leg sharply, and Ryder thrust himself out the door, an exhilarating event he had been thinking constantly about during the preceding few months. Just below the plane, two seconds later, as his static line pulled the parachute silk out of his backpack, Ryder felt the welcome jolt of the parachute's opening shock (common to the T-4 and its successor, the T-5, widely used throughout World War II). He floated down, landed safely with his feet apart to the width of his hips, and did a front roll—standard landing procedure in those days. Bill Ryder had just made U.S. Army airborne history by being the army's first paratrooper and leading the army's first parachute unit, the Parachute Test Platoon, on its first jump. General Ryder wrote years later:

> although Tug was jumpmaster, I wanted to be at the door with him as each man made his first jump. This would not only give me a chance to observe closely each man's reactions and performance, but somehow it seemed proper and fitting to do so. Accordingly, it was arranged that after I'd jumped, the plane would land and pick me up so that I could be with each jumper as planned . . . the plane landed, and I re-embarked to join the first jump unit. As we climbed and circled for the next jumper, I conveyed to the men as best I could, the elation, satisfaction and confidence I'd experienced from my jump. As we headed towards Lawson, I joined Tug by the door and, with eager anticipation, awaited the historic occasion of the first enlisted man's qualifying "parachutist" jump.

The man who would become the U.S. Army's first enlisted paratrooper earned that distinction by a fluke. In the Parachute Test Platoon's barracks the night before the initial jump, the forty-eight men of the platoon (nine more than the standard thirty-nine-man infantry platoon of 1940, to compensate for expected casualties and dropouts) drew numbers from a steel helmet to determine who would become the army's first enlisted paratrooper.

"Tug called the man to the door," General Ryder wrote:

> He stood up and moved quietly to join us. Properly he hooked up, checked equipment, and calmly crouched in the door, awaiting Tug's command. But when it came, he remained immobile. Tug again shouted, "Go!" and slapped his backside, thinking perhaps that the first command had not been heard. But the man remained fixed and made no move. Quietly, we moved him from the door and placed him in a rear seat. It was vital that every parachutist jump willingly and with determination, on his own volition. A hesitant or balky jumper in combat could be a disaster.

• • •

Then Wilson motioned the number two man, Pvt. William M. "Red" King, to the head of the line. "Red King," wrote General Ryder, "one of the men who had taken a 'bust' from rank of corporal to be an eligible volunteer, had drawn the No. 2 position. Red was a flamboyant, devil-may-care type whose enthusiasm and vitality boosted morale throughout our training. He moved smartly to the door when called and, on Tug's command, leaped immediately and vigorously from the door, thus earning the distinction of becoming the first U.S. Army soldier to jump as a parachutist."

The Parachute Test Platoon's first two jumps were individual, "tap-out" jumps. General Ryder writes further that

> during the next six weeks we managed a jump per week, except for a week in early September, when we underwent a concentrated demolitions course. These included both mass and individual jumps made from lower altitudes. We were relieved from the 1,500-foot altitude constraint prescribed for Air Corps training jumps, and allowed to jump at 750 feet to obtain tighter landing patterns in our mass jumps. Accordingly, by late September 1940, Test Platoon members had completed five individual/mass jumps that were to become the qualification standard for a parachutist's rating.

In his outstanding book on U.S. airborne forces, *Paratrooper,* Gerard M. Devlin writes about the source of the paratroopers' most famous cry, "Geronimo!" On the night before the Parachute Test Platoon's first mass jump, Privates Eberhardt, Ward, McLaney, and Brown went to a movie at Fort Benning's main post theater. The movie featured troopers of the U.S. Cavalry chasing Indian braves. Eberhardt remarked casually and confidently that the mass jump the next morning would be no more difficult than the "tap-outs" of the first two jumps. One of the other neophyte jumpers suggested sarcastically that Eberhardt would be so scared that he wouldn't even be able to remember his own name. Eberhardt's reaction was typical of the novice jumpers. He told them that he was not scared and, to prove it, he would shout "Geronimo" as he leaped out of the plane.

By jump time the next morning, word of Eberhardt's boast had spread throughout the platoon. When Eberhardt's plane came over the DZ, some of the men who had jumped from another plane were already on the ground. Eberhardt's plane flew directly over them, and the men in Eberhardt's stick began their first mass jump. When Eberhardt jumped, he shouted "Geronimo!" and followed it with an Indian war whoop so loud that the men on the ground and beside him in the air heard him clearly. Eberhardt did not realize it at the time, but he had just created a slogan thereafter associated with army paratroopers. There was even a song written about it: "Geronimo, Look Out Below."

Lieutenant Ryder and his Parachute Test Platoon had arrived at this unique status, the actual forerunner of the army's many parachute units, along a path strewn with difficulties, doubts, and uncertainties. The army's airborne concept had developed very gradually, and at times almost faded from reality just before and during the early years of U.S. involvement in World War II. One major impediment was that some senior officers, educated and nurtured in the "lean years" between World Wars I and II, still had visions of massive World War I ground attacks supported by battalions of artillery, horse cavalry for reconnaissance and raids, some tanks and, in the minds of some of the more advanced thinkers, a few support aircraft. In 1945, in fact, cadets at the U.S. Military Academy at West Point were still learning to ride horses in the school's massive riding hall. Some of the older army leaders could not imagine that paratroopers were useful for any other missions than small, daring, and almost suicidal raids on enemy headquarters, bridges, ammunition dumps, or communications centers. Gliders in combat and the German heavy drop capability were simply beyond credibility.

John Keegan, in *Six Armies in Normandy*, writes about the lethargy of the Allied armies in developing parachute units. He mentioned that, in 1936, British and French observers had witnessed a Soviet maneuver in which paratroopers had been dropped, however primitively and dangerously, from a giant Tupolev aircraft. The paratroopers clung "desperately to the rail along its fuselage as they breasted the chord of its monstrous wing and then, at a signal, releasing their grip in unison to be wheeled away like needles from a mountain pine in the first storm of winter."

The Soviets were probably the first to develop military airborne units. In 1931, they sent a delegation to the United States to purchase several thousand parachutes of the kind used by such stunt jumpers as Leslie L. "Sky High" Irvin, famous for his jumps at circuses and on small-town airfields. The parachutes, Model A types, had rip cords rather than static lines for hooking up to an anchor cable in the plane. On 18 August 1933, the Soviets had forty-six paratroopers jump from two bombers in an attempt to break the world record for mass jumps, and at the same demonstration dropped a small tank with a large parachute, probably performing the first heavy equipment drop. In 1935, they achieved a military distinction when, on maneuvers witnessed by astonished foreign observers, they dropped two battalions of infantry on an airfield. The paratroopers held the field until reinforcements, armed with sixteen artillery weapons, were flown in.

The Germans quickly followed the initiative of the Soviets in developing airborne forces. Although the Treaty of Versailles prohibited the Germans from rearming, Hermann Göring formed a police detachment whose main purpose was to eliminate communist cells in Berlin. Part of the detachment consisted of paratroopers who would parachute onto the suspected cells' locations. Two years later, Göring, now the chief of the German Luftwaffe, brought the parachute detachment into his air service and expanded it into the 1st Parachute Rifle Battalion. On 1 July 1938 he appointed Maj. Kurt Student to command the parachute forces of the Luftwaffe.

One of the earliest U.S. proponents of parachute forces was Brig. Gen. William P. "Billy" Mitchell, Army Air Corps; in 1918 he had been Gen. John J. Pershing's air service advisor in France. Mitchell felt that the trench warfare, in which thousands of men rose out of their dugouts and trenches on command and threw themselves at each other in mass attacks, had squandered millions of lives and made little impact on the outcome of the war. In October 1918, in a detailed briefing he had proposed to General Pershing that, on a given date in the near future, he collect all available U.S. bombers (some 1,200 planes), load each of them with two machine guns and ten men from the 1st Infantry Division strapped into parachutes, and drop them en masse on a target area behind the German lines. These men would be supported by fighter aircraft until they were dug in. He also proposed to Pershing that simultaneously with the parachute attack a massive U.S. forces assault be launched from the trenches to link up with the paratroopers of the "Big Red One."

General Pershing, an old horse cavalryman, much to Mitchell's surprise, actually approved development of the plan. Mitchell returned to his own office and he and Maj. Lewis H. Brereton, his assistant, who would in World War II command the First Allied Airborne Army, began planning to launch the airborne attack near the "fort-studded" city of Metz, France, in the spring of 1919. But, of course, the Armistice interfered with this bold and radical operation, and the Big Red One did not achieve the distinction of being the army's first airborne division.

The German paratroopers *(fallschirmjäger)* were first organized into a regiment and then expanded into divisions. During the early morning hours of 10 May 1940, the Germans used both parachute and glider forces in combat for the first time to spearhead the German attack on the Netherlands. From later reports of the attack on the Dutch defenses, one might have assumed that the Germans used massive airborne forces. In actuality, the forces employed were fairly modest but, at that stage of the war and with the weakness of the Dutch defenses, proved over-whelming. (Undoubtedly, U.S. airborne pioneers thought that the German effort was "massive" given the paucity of the airborne effort at the time in the United States.)

In the German attack on the Netherlands, Kurt Student, by now a major general, used four parachute battalions and a regiment of air-transported infantry to seize the bridges at Moerdijk, Dordrecht, and Rotterdam on the main road network from the south and into the heart of the Netherlands to pave the way for the follow-up ground forces. In another phase of the operation, Student deployed one parachute battalion, followed by two air-landed regiments, to land on the airfields near The Hague to seize the main government buildings.

The attacks on the bridges were successful; the attack on the airfield near The Hague was not, but it did cause widespread confusion. Three days after the attack Queen Wilhelmina and her government fled to Britain, and the next day Gen. H. G. Winkelman, the Dutch commander in chief, sued for peace. The battle for the Netherlands was over.

Another phase of the initial German strategy to outflank the Maginot Line in France, by attacking through the Low Countries, was the assault against the fortress of Eben Emael, an underground, concrete and steel fortress near the juncture of the Meuse River and the Albert Canal along the Dutch-Belgian border, about fifteen miles north of Liege. Eben Emael was manned by a force of some 780 men in a structure that the Dutch and the Allies thought invulnerable to attack. It was Belgium's most modern fort and reputedly the strongest in the world.

In a maneuver allegedly conceived by Hitler himself, a contingent of seventy-eight German soldiers, the Fallschirm-Pioniere Abteilung (Parachute Engineer Unit) led by Lt. Rudolf Witzig, soared silently in nine gliders from their release point and landed relatively quietly on top of the fort in the dark, predawn hours of 10 May 1940. The principal weapons of the glider troops were six 110-pound explosive devices that could blast six-inch holes through solid steel. The power of the explosive derived from its "shaped charge," a device invented by an American scientist, C. E. Monroe, and later perfected by the Germans. The glider troops quickly dropped their explosives into the fort's guns and exits, not only knocking out the armament of the fort but also trapping its soldiers in what was now an immense blasted, wrecked building. Twenty-eight hours later, the helpless garrison surrendered to the small band of German glidermen.

In 1939, even though it was obvious that the Germans were pioneers in the airborne effort, the U.S. Army was still far behind in this field because of the mindset of some of the senior officers. Fortunately, however, for the airborne concept to become a reality in the combat philosophy of the U.S. Army, there was one senior officer who had an open mind, the sagacity to recognize the potential of airborne forces, and the power to do something about it. He was George C. Marshall, the army chief of staff.

General Marshall became the army's chief of staff on 28 April 1939, jumping from two to four stars over twenty more senior generals. Marshall was a brilliant and decisive leader who would develop, organize, equip, train, and expand the U.S. Army from its 1939 level of some 160,000 men to its wartime peak strength of about 8,000,000. He was a man who could visualize trends in warfare and would seek to adopt the best for the army.

In 1938 and 1939, the army's military attachés were reporting that a number of major powers, including France, Italy, Germany, and the Soviet Union, were experimenting with airborne troops—delivered by both parachute and air-landing techniques. The U.S. attaché in Germany reported that the Germans' development of parachute, glider, and air-landed troops was especially well conceived and organized under Student's expert leadership and that, for what it was worth, the airborne troops remained under the command of the air force (Luftwaffe). Marshall decided to explore this unique concept of dropping and landing troops behind enemy lines.

In April 1939 he directed his G-3 officer, Maj. Gen. R. M. Beck Jr., to send a memorandum to the chief of infantry, Maj. Gen. George A. Lynch, requesting that he "make a study for the purpose of determining the desirability of organizing, training and conducting tests of a small detachment of air infantry with a view to determine whether or not our Army should contain a unit or units of this nature." The memorandum also said: "It is visualized that the role of this type of unit will be, after being transported in airplanes, to parachute to the ground a small detachment to seize a small vitally important area, primarily an air field, upon which additional troops will later be landed by transport airplanes. The air infantry unit or units will in all probability be small and lightly equipped. Their training should include a considerable amount of athletic drills, utilization of parachutes, demolitions, and exercises in security functions." And, finally, the document concluded in the peculiar, unnecessarily polite, yet demanding jargon of staff officers: "It is believed desirable that the study referred to be initiated without delay." The last rejoinder was unnecessary; the chief of infantry had been doing preliminary spadework for some months.

In five days, Lynch had back on Marshall's desk a lengthy study that outlined the Soviet and French use of airborne forces on maneuvers; the U.S. potential to mobilize airplanes to carry cargo, soldiers, and artillery units; and a 1934 Fort Benning test that proved that an entire infantry battalion and all its equipment could be flown great distances during both day and night. He concluded with a recommendation for extensive tests to prove or disprove his proposal. His airborne concept went far beyond the small-unit, hit-and-run raid idea then prevalent among senior officers.

It was seven months before General Lynch heard from the army staff. Marshall had passed the Lynch study to Gen. Henry H. "Hap" Arnold, the Army Air Corps chief, who in turn passed it to his Air Corps Board at Maxwell Field, Alabama. Colonel Walter Weaver, commandant of the Air Corps Tactical School at Maxwell Field, speaking for the Air Corps, replied:

> I recommend that we create in the Air Corps an organization similar to what the Marines are in the Navy, that this organization perform such functions as the following:
>
> Man antiaircraft equipment . . . for the protection of airdromes.
> Be charged with the neutralization of gassed airdromes.
> Provide the guard for the protection of . . . airdromes and supply centers.
> Perform such military ceremonies as have heretofore been customary at army posts, such as firing of salutes and rendering of honors for distinguished persons.
> Provide the guard for prisoners.
> Furnish the guard for aircraft forced down in the vicinity.

Be so organized and equipped as to perform the functions of parachute troops on landing parties from air transports.

It is believed that there is a real need for such an organization within the Air Corps. It might be well to consider building up such an organization under the existing Military Police, now found at most of our large stations. As a suggestion of a name for this organization, it might be called "The Air Grenadiers" or "The Air Corps Grenadiers."

Lieutenant Colonel Carl "Tooey" Spaatz took a different view of the matter. He wrote the Air Plans Division study and reported to General Arnold that the Army Air Corps had more important projects to worry about than "air infantry" and that at any rate, the Air Corps had no extra air transports to support the project. General Arnold bought that position and sent Spaatz's report on to Marshall who agreed, at least temporarily, with the Spaatz view. The project lay dormant until January 1940, when Arnold reported to Marshall that he could spare a few transport aircraft for the project. Marshall then directed Lynch to give the "air infantry" top priority and to assume responsibility for the program.

General Lynch immediately assigned the project to Maj. William C. Lee, forty-three years old, one of his smartest and most dedicated staff officers, and who had been a platoon and company commander in combat in World War I. Lee's first and most important problem was planes and parachutes. He contacted the Air Corps and asked for transport aircraft, the development of a static line–activated parachute, the loan of two riggers and two experienced parachute jumpers, and several equipment chutes for tests by the Infantry Board at Fort Benning. In three weeks, the Air Corps sent the planes, the men, and some of the equipment to Lawson Field at Fort Benning. By May 1940, the Air Corps test center at Wright Field, Ohio, had developed the T-4, a backpack, static line–activated personnel chute, twenty-eight feet in diameter, and a smaller, rip-cord-activated reserve chute. By June 1940 the Infantry Board was ready to start live jump tests.

In the summer of 1940, Marshall had not yet decided to which branch the paratroopers belonged. Major General Eugene Schley, the chief of engineers, thought that his branch should adopt them because he believed paratroopers would require extensive training in the use of explosives; General Arnold felt that the Air Corps should have them because of their dependence on aircraft to get them to their objectives; and

General Lynch felt that they were clearly an adjunct of the infantry. He was so incensed at the other branch chiefs' attempts to embezzle the developing airborne battle force that he requested a meeting with Marshall to settle the matter. The three branch chiefs met with the chief of staff in his office. Generals Arnold and Schley presented their cases first, but then General Lynch had his moment. "Once on the ground," he reasoned, "the parachutist becomes an infantryman and fights like an infantryman." As a clincher, he added that the Parachute Test Platoon was already in training at Fort Benning and that the inevitable increases in the airborne effort be under the chief of infantry and that Fort Benning be the seat of future paratrooper training.

Marshall, as was his wont, listened quietly to the three generals. Then he said, "Gentlemen, you've all presented convincing arguments as to why your particular branch should take charge of this vital project now underway at Benning. I want you to know that we are in fact going ahead with plans to form a parachute battalion. The first one will be activated in just a few weeks. It is my decision to place the formation and development of that battalion under the control of the Infantry at Fort Benning. Thank you for coming here today, gentlemen. Good day."

The original Parachute Test Platoon had been activated at Fort Benning on 1 July 1940. Among the thirty officers who had volunteered to lead the platoon were Lts. William T. Ryder and William P. Yarborough, both from the West Point class of 1936 and both assigned to the 29th Infantry Regiment at Benning. Ryder had had an interest in airborne and paratroopers long before General Lynch decided to form a Parachute Test Platoon. He had studied the use of airborne forces by the Soviets and the Germans, had seen some of the equipment drops at Benning, had studied everything he could find on the subject, and had written and submitted to the Infantry Board a number of papers on the use of airborne forces in combat. He wrote that "he logged quite a few observer hours by soliciting flights with Air Corps classmates" when he was stationed in the Philippines shortly after graduation from West Point.

When the day finally arrived for the Infantry Board to test the officers to select the platoon leader, Lieutenant Yarborough was not there; he had been ordered to Camp Jackson, South Carolina, but he would be back soon as a full-fledged paratrooper. Bill Ryder passed the board's test with flying colors, and he walked out of the board's test room a full hour before any other candidate. He won the job of platoon leader easily even though, as he wrote, "I was married and the father of a baby daughter!"

(Because of the potential hazards of the parachute training, only single men were supposed to be allowed to volunteer.)

The 200 soldiers who initially volunteered for the Parachute Test Platoon also came from the 29th Infantry Regiment. Members of the platoon would receive flying pay of $30 a month while in training. In short order, Ryder selected some forty-eight men and divided the platoon into four squads. The platoon moved from permanent barracks at Benning to a tent camp near Lawson Field and began a period of daily, intensive physical fitness training including three-mile runs, calisthenics, tumbling, and hand-to-hand combat.

"Belief that personal packing enhanced jumper respect for, and confidence in, the parachute led us to require each man to pack his own chute for jumps," wrote Brig. Gen. William T. Ryder. "This entailed over 40 hours instruction on panel folding, line stowing, twist removals, pack sewing and closing, tacking, harness adjustment, etc. Such practice was later abandoned (but when I went through jump school in June of 1943, we were still packing our own chutes) and supplanted by 'rigger' packing. But it did serve its purpose of instilling great confidence in the parachute as a reliable means of transport among our early parachute units."

In July, the platoon flew up to Maguire Field next to Fort Dix, New Jersey, in three B-18 bombers. Fort Dix was near Hightstown, New Jersey, where Major Lee had discovered that the Safe Parachute Company had erected two 150-foot parachute jump towers similar to the ones used at the 1939 World's Fair in New York City. Lee obtained the necessary authority and funds for the platoon to use the towers. One tower had vertical steel cables to guide the parachute from the top of the tower's extended wings to the ground. The other tower was without the guide cables and permitted the jumper to flow with the wind once he was released at the top. Below each tower, the paratrooper's chute was attached to a large metal circle that was in turn suspended from a cable that ran to the top of the tower. When ready, the paratrooper was pulled to the top of the tower. Once at the top, the tower operator pulled the entire rig up and bumped it against the extended arm of the tower, a move that caused the chute to snap clear of the metal circle to which it had been clipped. Later that year, the Ledbetter Construction Company of Birmingham, Alabama, would build 250-foot parachute training towers at Fort Benning for the training of future paratroopers.

During the training at Hightstown General Lynch paid a surprise visit to the platoon. Even though he was in his early sixties and would retire the following year, he took a ride on the controlled parachute rig and landed safely, to the ardent applause of the cheering platoon. He proved that at least one senior army general was totally in favor of the airborne concept and that he would do all that he could to foster its growth and development.

After the platoon finished its ten days of training on the towers at Hightstown, it returned to Benning for the final phases of its training. By the sixth week, the platoon was physically fit, well disciplined, enthusiastic, and motivated. Each man, under the tutelage of Tug Wilson and his four-man rigger team from Chanute Field, Illinois, had learned to pack his own chute, a skill that would be learned by all paratrooper trainees during the war years.

The Parachute Test Platoon's fifth and final jump on 29 August 1940 was scheduled as a mass jump of the entire platoon from three aircraft. Once on the ground, the platoon's mission was to attack an "enemy" position on the edge of the DZ using weapons, ammunition, and equipment that would be dropped with them in separate parachute bundles. So significant was this first mass jump that the War Department brass decided to come to Fort Benning to watch it. First to arrive at Lawson Field was General Lynch, accompanied by Major Lee and several staff officers from the infantry branch chief's office. The next plane carried not only General Marshall but, unannounced, Secretary of War Henry L. Stimson.

The jump went off with only two minor flaws. One involved Pvt. Steve Voils, who had the distinction of having the first "Mae West," and pulled his reserve chute rip cord to slow his descent. (A "Mae West" parachute is one in which one of the suspension lines drapes across the top of the parachute causing it to form two huge bulges.) The other involved Pvt. Leo Brown, one of the last men to jump. During his descent he was caught in an updraft and drifted over the heads of the VIPs on the edge of the DZ. He landed on top of a hangar at Lawson Field and needed a ladder to get down. Later, Ryder said that he was "pleasantly surprised to hear that some visiting South American officers who observed the exercise went away doubly impressed by the accuracy of U.S. parachutists who could land men on top of buildings."

The men of the platoon carried out the army's first airborne tactical operation with well-drilled precision. They double-timed through all their maneuvers, assembled their weapons and gear, and attacked the objective with enthusiasm. The VIPs were duly impressed with the demonstration. General Marshall told the men later at lunch that the army would activate whole battalions of paratroopers and that they would have a major role in training them. But the vision of airborne divisions and corps was still not clear.

Many years later, in retrospect, Gen. Matthew B. Ridgway wrote: "To no individuals do our Army Airborne Forces, both parachute and glider, owe more than to General of the Army, George C. Marshall, and General of the Air Force, Henry H. Arnold. It was their early and sustained support that brought our airborne forces into being for the large scale combat operations in Europe and Asia in World War II, and subsequently in Korea, Vietnam, Grenada and Panama."

After the successful demonstration of its tactical competence, the platoon split into two teams. One, under 2d Lt. James A. Bassett, a 1938 West Point graduate, who had joined the platoon as second in command on 11 July 1940, went to Chanute Field for a comprehensive and exacting course in parachute maintenance and rigging. The other team under Ryder stayed at Fort Benning and would eventually perform two functions: the establishment of the parachute school and the development of the cadre for the army's first parachute battalion. When Bassett returned to Benning some seven weeks later, he was surprised to find that the Parachute Test Platoon's original four squad tents had grown into a large tent city and that construction crews were hard at work building World War II–type wooden barracks nearby. He soon learned that the scores of enlisted men he saw swarming through the area were the volunteers for the army's first parachute battalion—the 501st.

On 16 September 1940, the army staff issued a War Department order that stated in part: "The 1st Parachute Battalion is constituted and will be activated at the earliest practical date at Fort Benning, Ga." On 26 September 1940, the War Department issued an amendment to that order changing the unit designation from the 1st Battalion to the 501st Parachute Infantry Battalion. This was because the Marine Corps was also forming parachute battalions and its first battalion also had the number 1. To avoid confusion, the army elected to number battalions in the 500 series, giving the Marines 1 through 499. On 1 October 1940, the 501st Parachute Infantry Battalion was activated at Fort Benning under the command of the recently promoted Maj. William M. Miley, West Point class of 1918. Miley had been a champion gymnast while a cadet and, later, as an officer, the master of the sword at West Point. In keeping with the incredible slowness of officer promotions between the wars, it had taken him twenty-two years to move from second lieutenant to major. But two and a half years later, Major General Miley would become the commander of the 17th Airborne Division, the army's fifth World War II airborne division.

Even though Miley was still gathering recruits and officers, putting them through jump training, and watching the battalion's barracks and mess halls rise rapidly, in November 1940 the War Department issued orders to form three more parachute infantry battalions in 1941. He was ordered to furnish cadres and supervise the training of the new battalions. With some foresight, he recognized that he would have a difficult training problem if he were ordered to train his own battalion and also furnish cadres and training for three more parachute battalions. He recommended that the chief of infantry establish a special organization with the mission of parachute-training each new battalion and furnishing jump-qualified replacements to the new battalions as required. The chief of infantry concurred and forwarded his recommendation to the War Department. On 10 March 1941, the Provisional Parachute Group was activated at Fort Benning. All junior officers and men came from Miley's battalion. Recently promoted Lieutenant Colonel Lee became its commander. Lee was the officer who had done so much work in the earliest days of the airborne development that he became known as the "Father of Airborne." His mission: jump-train each new battalion, develop tables of organization and equipment (TO&Es), and develop doctrine for the use of airborne troops.

In July and August of 1941, the 502d, under Maj. George P. Howell Jr. (class of 1919), the 503d, under Maj. Robert F. Sink (class of 1927), and the 50th, under Maj. Richard Chase (Syracuse University class of 1927) were activated. In addition to the three parachute battalions activated in 1941, two air-landed battalions came on board: the 550th and 88th Airborne Infantry Battalions. At the same time the Air Corps began experimenting with gliders at Wright Field in Ohio.

Colonel Lee, commander of the Provisional Parachute Group, helped develop the various devices at Benning that generations of paratroopers have come to remember with respect, if not fear. There were the 250-foot towers on which paratrooper trainees made their first controlled jumps, some with the benefit of the four cables that kept the trooper in bounds, and some without the cables and only the wind to guide them to their landings. There were the thirty-four-foot jump towers that gave the trooper a sense of the opening shock of the twenty-eight-foot canopy.

(For some reason, there were more washouts on the thirty-four-foot towers than on the 250-foot towers or from aircraft actually in flight. It may be that the towers, only thirty-four feet above the ground, gave the fledgling jumper a heightened sense of acrophobia.) Mockups of the passenger compartment of the C-47 transport plane trained the recruits in the proper techniques of exiting. Landing trainers taught the neophyte jumper how to land safely without breaking a leg or an arm. And a suspended harness contraption taught a trooper how to guide his parachute while in the air. He found out later, on actual jumps, that it was easier to control the parachute in the air than it was to manipulate the suspended harness in the mock-up shed.

There was no lack of volunteers for parachute duty even though both the standards and the washout rates were high. In June 1941, the army authorized parachute pay for all qualified paratroopers on jump status: initially officers received $100 per month and enlisted men $50. The disparity was presumably because officers had the more difficult jobs—jumpmastering, DZ selection, and responsibility for all phases of the operation—before and after the jump.

Lieutenant William P. Yarborough (retired in 1971 as a lieutenant general) was one of the first officers to join the ranks of the paratroopers and was a company commander in the 501st Parachute Battalion in 1940. He remembers his first association with jumping out of an airplane.

I remember the smell of the airplane varnishes, the grease and the oil, and the smell of the engine exhausts which were particularly intriguing, somehow different, even pleasing. Then, too, there is the recollection of wonder mixed with some uneasiness upon being belted into the seat of an apparatus which carried me aloft for the first time to see below a world which appeared more vast and different than I had ever dreamed it would be.

To contemplate stepping from the relative security of a flying vehicle into thin air while depending completely upon a parachute system which was far from "idiot proof" aroused an emotion that few of us ever took lightly. It tested enzymes and hormones which would later be identified as important assets for producing a superior breed of warrior. These are facts which are well known to all airborne soldiers.

The challenge of jumping from an airplane in flight or descending onto a hostile landing zone in an aircraft without an engine would be paralleled later by life or death situations for which airborne soldiers had already prepared themselves by identifying and strengthening their own psychological assets.

The collective discipline inside the aircraft would be translated into personal discipline, courage and staying power on the battlefield.

The original Parachute Test Platoon spawned a group of instructors who were the envy and the idols of the paratroopers-to-be. Soon after their own training ended, and as soon as they took on the mantle of leaders and trainers, the test platoon veterans took on an air of competence, self-confidence, and expertise, characteristics that imbued the trainees with their own self-confidence. In their singular uniform of white T-shirts, fatigue trousers, spit-shined jump boots, and baseball caps, the instructors were models for the fledging paratroopers.

Even young officers going through the paratrooper course were completely intimidated and impressed with the instructor cadre. At calisthenics, for example, the very muscular instructor had a disconcerting habit of starting the classes doing thirty or more push-ups in the sawdust pits while, he, on the platform above them, did the push-ups with one arm while counting cadence with the other. But no matter what the class—parachute packing, tumbling, tower jumps, mock-up door training, rope climbing, or long-distance running the "paratrooper shuffle" (by which the runner moved fairly slowly, not lifting his feet far off the ground, so that he could move long distances carrying mortar plates or machine guns on his shoulders)—the student showed total respect.

And so the U.S. airborne effort came into being. As Bill Yarborough put it: "From the essence drilled by Bill Ryder's Parachute Test Platoon in the early 1940s, a tradition for extraordinary daring, leadership and accomplishment spread to the fledgling American parachute battalions, then to the regiments which received cadres linking them to a common origin. From the regiments, the genes were passed to the divisions, corps and even to an Allied airborne army. Their numbers were different, but each American airborne unit was and remained a blood brother of the others. The triumphs of one were celebrated by all without jealously or envy."

2: The Buildup

The German invasion of Crete sent a significant signal to the Germans and the Allies on the future of their airborne forces. For the Germans it was a negative signal; for the Allies, a positive. Crete is a case study of a successful, though extremely costly, airborne operation. Its lessons were not lost on the Allies whose military senior leaders were in 1941 still debating the size, composition, and missions of their airborne forces.

Crete was the first major airborne operation in military history. It followed the rapid German conquest of Yugoslavia and Greece in April 1941. The Greek army surrendered on 23 April, but British and Commonwealth forces, in addition to Greeks who had refused to surrender, continued to fight to the south in Greece. On 26 April German parachute and glider troops, in a brief, explosive firefight, seized the Corinth Canal bridge to block the retreat of these forces. The Germans removed preset demolition charges from the span and carelessly left them lying on the bridge. An unknown Greek or British soldier fired one fortuitous rifle round into the stacked demolitions and blew them up, dropping the bridge into the canal, slowing the German pursuit for two days, and permitting the bulk of the Greek and British troops, already across the canal, to escape. Some 34,000 troops were evacuated by sea from Greece, the majority of whom landed on Crete.

Hitler decided that possessing Crete was of vital importance for two reasons: one, it would deny the island to the Allies, thus cutting off their ability to interdict Axis shipping over a large part of the Mediterranean and blocking Royal Air Force (RAF) bombers from attacking the Rumanian oil fields; two, it would give Hitler a base from which he could secure a large part of the Mediterranean and launch air attacks against the large Royal Navy Base at Alexandria, Egypt.

On 20 May 1941 Hitler launched Operation "Mercury," the German invasion of Crete, a combined-arms assault that involved all three branches of the Wehrmacht, but one in which the airborne forces of the Luftwaffe had the major role. Units of the German 7th Parachute Division jumped near their objectives—the Maleme, Retimo, and Herakleion airfields. The New Zealand defenders, previously alerted by British spies to the probable airborne attack and therefore heavily armed with machine guns, mortars, and grenades in their camouflaged defensive positions around the airfields, inflicted heavy casualties on the German paratroopers who, after landing, were unarmed until they could reach their personal weapons, scattered in bundles that had been parachuted separately. Nonetheless, the rest of the 7th Parachute Division jumped in the next day and, in spite of heavy casualties, secured the Maleme airfield. The next morning, part of the German 5th Mountain Division flew in from Greece. The Allies shot down many of the transports, but enough men survived to assist the 7th Parachute Division in securing the airfields. On 21 and 22 May, the rest of the 5th Mountain Division attempted to land by sea transport. But the Royal Navy, in complete control of the waters around the island, repulsed both attempts with heavy German losses. Eventually, however, the Germans began to overrun the airfields, and by 28 May they had succeeded in their mission of taking Crete. On 31 May the British and Commonwealth troops, who couldn't be evacuated from Sfakia, surrendered to the Germans.

The German losses had been high: of the 13,000 German paratroopers who landed on the island, 5,140 were killed or wounded; 350 planes were shot down. But Crete demonstrated that the Germans were far ahead of the Allies in the airborne effort, even to including the dropping of heavy artillery pieces and antitank guns, each with five or more large parachutes.

The Crete operation taught the Allies some valuable lessons in airborne tactics. If the operation is near the sea, control of the air and the sea is essential. And the command channels must be clear and simple. The German chain of command was simple and direct; the British chain was not. For example, on 27 May when New Zealand's Maj. Gen. Bernard C. Freyberg, the commander of the Commonwealth forces on Crete, started to evacuate his troops, Churchill tried to countermand the operation by sending a futile message to his commander in chief, Middle

East: "Victory in Crete is essential at this turning-point in the war. Keep hurling in all you can." Other valuable lessons learned by the Allies in the Crete operation were that surprise is vital; that airborne commanders must be flexible and adapt their tactics to rapidly changing situations; that large airborne units, of division size or larger, are effective and employable, given the necessary aircraft support; and that strong reserves ready to be committed by air or sea are basic necessities.

For the Germans, Crete ended their major World War II airborne operations. It was so costly in manpower and aircraft that Hitler lost confidence in his airborne forces and did not commit them again in their primary role. After October 1941, the shortage of trained German ground units forced the German high command to use its trained airborne forces as regular infantry in the campaign against the Soviet Union that followed Crete. Even though Gen. Kurt Student felt that the Crete operation, the capture of a well-defended strategic island by airborne forces without naval or heavy ground support, proved the value of large airborne forces, he admitted in a postwar interview that Crete "was the graveyard of German parachutists." (After Crete the Germans made minor combat jumps in some ten operations. The largest drops involved battalion-sized forces and were used as reinforcements or attacks on a rear area. On 16 December 1944, for example, before the Battle of the Bulge an "ad hoc" German battalion of some 900 men dropped on Belle Croix in Belgium.)

That Crete gave a needed impetus to the U.S. effort to activate airborne divisions is without question. Thus the five airborne divisions that eventually made up the U.S. World War II contingent owed their existence to the German demonstration of the potential of massed airborne forces, valuable in operations far more significant than small raids on isolated headquarters, bridges, or supply dumps. And the U.S. Army high command must be given credit for having the foresight to upscale its airborne forces from battalions to airborne divisions in less than eighteen months after the Crete operation. In June 1941 Major Miley received orders to move his 501st Parachute Infantry Battalion to Fort Kobbe, near Howard Field, Panama, to conduct air-landing and parachute operations with the 550th Airborne Infantry Battalion (an air-landing battalion) soon to be activated in Panama. The 550th was commanded by Lt. Col. Harris M. Melasky (class of 1917). Miley and his 501st arrived in Panama in September. On 10 October 1941, the army formed the 88th Airborne Infantry Battalion under the command of Lt. Col. Eldridge G. Chapman, who would later command the 13th Airborne Division in France in 1945. On 15 June 1942 the 88th became the 88th Airborne Infantry Regiment, and on 21 September 1942 the 88th was reorganized as the 88th Glider Infantry Regiment.

But before airborne divisions were activated, airborne regiments came on board. It was the Japanese attack on Pearl Harbor on 7 December 1941 that removed all restrictions on the army's limited troop strength. The War Department ordered the quickest activation possible of four parachute regiments using the existing battalions at Fort Benning as their cadres, but this was to be just the start of the army's development of parachute units. By the end of World War II, there would be fourteen parachute infantry regiments, four separate infantry battalions, many battalions of support forces, including artillery, and five airborne divisions. In addition to this lineup during the war there were some ten glider infantry regiments, fifteen glider field artillery battalions, and numerous other branch glider outfits.

On 2 March 1942, the 502d Parachute Infantry Regiment was formed at reduced strength from the 502d Parachute Infantry Battalion. The commander was the newly promoted battalion commander, Lt. Col. George P. Howell Jr. On that same date, two battalions of the 503d Parachute Infantry Regiment were formed from the 503d and 504th Parachute Infantry Battalions, the 3d Battalion coming from graduates of the Parachute School. Newly promoted Colonel Miley, who had been in Panama for six months with the 501st, returned to become the commander of the 503d. He turned the 501st over to his executive officer, Maj. Kenneth Kinsler, who would later command the 503d Parachute Regimental Combat Team in the Pacific Theater of Operations.

William "Bud" Miley was beginning an extensive career as an army paratrooper. At West Point he was an intercollegiate tumbling champion, as well as a master of the rings and parallel bars. He was the first officer in the grade of captain, major, lieutenant colonel, colonel, and general officer to qualify as an army parachutist. He commanded the first parachute battalion (501st), the first parachute regiment (503d) and the 1st Parachute Brigade. He served as the deputy commanding general of the 82d Airborne Division and later commanded the 17th Airborne Division in combat. After World War II he commanded the 11th Airborne Division in Japan, making him the only officer to have commanded two airborne divisions.

Meanwhile, on 21 March 1942 the Provisional Parachute Group became the Airborne Command, and Col. William C. Lee assumed command. His command consisted of the Command Headquarters Company, the 501st, 502d, and 503d Parachute Infantry Regiments and the 88th Airborne Infantry Battalion. The Airborne Command was based initially at Fort Benning, but on 9 April 1942 it moved to Fort Bragg, North Carolina, and then on 4 April 1943 to its new training area, Camp Mackall, North Carolina, a World War II camp hewn out of a pine forest and rapidly studded with barracks, mess halls, theaters, separate latrines outside the barracks, bachelor officers' quarters, orderly rooms, headquarters buildings, warehouses, and assorted maintenance sheds made of pine and tar paper sidings nailed together astonishingly fast. The troops would soon refer to their barracks as "tar paper shacks."

The Parachute School remained at Fort Benning but still under the Airborne Command, converted volunteers into paratroopers, and sent them to the new battalions at Fort Bragg for tactical training and testing by the Airborne Command.

In April 1942 the Air Corps took steps to keep up with the army's rapidly expanding airborne effort. It established the Air Transport Command at Stout Field near Indianapolis, with Col. Fred C. Borum as its commander, and had the mission of training pilots to fly the planes and gliders used by the airborne soldiers. (The Air Transport Command became I Troop Carrier Command and then, until the end of the war, Troop Carrier Command.)

The initial concept of U.S. gliders may be attributed to Gen. "Hap" Arnold who in early 1941 had sent a memo to Maj. Gen. G. H. Brett, acting chief of the Army Air Corps, suggesting that he would like to see developed a two-man jeep with wings, that could take off and land as a glider and then shed its wings on the ground for its primary role. He may have gotten this idea from the Soviets, who allegedly had fitted a tank with wings and flown it in 1930. True or not, the Air Corps fortunately got on with its glider program without developing flying, gliding jeeps.

On 5 June 1941, the Air Corps sent six pilots to the Elmira, New York, Soaring School and six to the Frankfort Sailplane School in Joliet, Illinois. Their mission was to become familiar with gliders and provide the leadership and training for the hundreds of glider pilots who were to follow.

Douglas W. S. Wilmer, a World War II glider pilot, wrote recently that in June of 1941 it had been reported that Germany had over 50,000 trained glider pilots. Early estimates for the American Glider Corps was for 30,000 men. This figure was never met and in a few months was lowered to about 10,000. The best information we have today is that 6,000 Glider "G" Wings were issued in World War II. Wilmer wrote:

Within the Air Corps Command there was a great deal of concern that the Glider program not conflict with either the flying cadet program or the acquisition and manufacturing of regular airplanes. Orders were issued that only non-airframe manufacturers could bid on glider projects and a large number of household names with wood-working shops, beer companies, pickle plants, piano companies, automobile, streetcar and casket plants (it may be that this is where the sardonic term "flying caskets" for gliders came from) reported in. Of these, the Ford Motor Co.'s station wagon plant at Iron Mtn., Michigan became a major supplier.

To head up the glider pilot training program, General Arnold named Richard DuPont, one of the nation's leading sport glider pilots. In an interesting aside, Doug Wilmer notes an order issued on 28 December 1931 that "the Army Air Corps before February 1943 had strict regulations that no pilot was allowed to fly in a glider or ride a motorcycle." According to Wilmer:

For the most part, the early glider pilot fledglings were men who had flying experience, some with just a little and others with a lot. He may have already been in the service or still a civilian. In any case, he was volunteering to fly gliders for the Army Air Corps. He would have rather flown fighters, but for one reason or another he could not pass the physical or educational standards required for flying cadets.

The Glider Program of that day seemed to be a "catch all" for anyone with flying experience for whom the Air Corps could not find an immediate assignment. . . .

Most of the Glider flying schools (Deadstick, Light Glider, and Early Cargo Glider) were all civilian contract schools and later when we began to receive "B" students we had civilian flying instructors, and these flying efforts were spread all over the country in small towns and a few were in Universities. Local women would cook and the students would live in dormitories or hotels. You must remember that America was just attacked at Pearl Harbor and the effort to produce flyers for all the services was an unbelievable "can of worms," every business man was trying to get his share of the war, and every flight instructor had a half dozen job offers from all over.

The future glider pilots "soon became proficient in flying airplanes without power and [were] moved to schools that trained in flying the light two- and three-place gliders. The army operated the Advanced Glider Schools that flew the large cargo-type CG-4A Waco gliders after which he received his 'G' wings. . . . Some who knew the glider pilot during World War II thought that the 'G' in his wings stood for 'guts,' but to the glider pilot these wings meant that he had completed a long and difficult flying course and that this was his badge of graduation. They were awarded once, but they were his to keep forever."

Wright Field in Ohio developed a number of prototype gliders and finally settled on the Waco CG-4A, a box-like contraption with wings, whose small-gauge steel-tubing skeleton was covered with canvas. It had a wingspan of eighty-four feet, a length of forty-nine feet, and a capacity of 3,750 pounds. That equated to two pilots and either thirteen fully combat-loaded soldiers, a jeep, or a pack 75mm howitzer and six men. The passengers entered the CG-4A through a side door in the rear. The nose of the glider and the pilots' cockpit was a compartment hinged at the top so that, when raised, jeeps and howitzers could be loaded and unloaded underneath it from the front. The CG-4A became the glider workhorse of World War II.

In a very short time, enthusiasm for the glider ran high in both the U.S. Army and Army Air Corps. In the army, Colonel Lee and his staff envisioned the glider's easily providing the paratroopers with artillery, antitank guns, jeeps, miniaturized engineer bulldozers, and a large number of reinforcing soldiers who would need no special training—except perhaps a dose of psychological indoctrination to make them somewhat at ease in the cramped, dark innards of the awkward, oversized kites. At about this time, Lt. Gen. Lesley J. McNair, commander of the Army Ground Forces, suggested that all standard infantry divisions undergo aircraft and air-landing training before going overseas. Soon, however, he concluded that such training was too time consuming and dropped the idea.

Eventually, the Air Corps Materiel Command expended some $500 million on the glider program and built a number of experimental and limited-production models. It was a substantial undertaking that had to develop a large fleet of combat gliders almost from scratch.

"One of the companies building CG-4A's charged the government a million dollars for the only one they built and 'Cost Plus' was the name of the game for everybody," wrote Wilmer. "The procurement of the WW II Combat Glider was a nightmare for every one involved. But the biggest problem was delivery and this was not solved until Henry Ford got into production. . . . The 4,190 CG-4A's built by Ford for about $17,300 (apiece), was the largest producer; and the Northwestern Co., of Minneapolis . . . with 1,509 was second; however, altogether there were 13,909 Waco CG-4A's produced at an average cost of $18,800."

The glider program was beset with more than the manufacturing scandals. On 1 August 1943, for instance, a manufacturer in St. Louis was demonstrating a Waco glider in a flight over the city. Aboard the glider were the company's chairman, the mayor, other local luminaries, and some military representatives. Midway through the flight the glider's fabric began to tear. The glider vibrated, rattled, and swayed out of control; one wing began to fold slowly backward and then collapsed. The glider, unhooked from the tow plane, cartwheeled to earth. There were no survivors.

If the glider riders of the various airborne units being formed had been aware of the structure of the glider, the variety of its manufacturers, or the St. Louis crash, they might have been even more cautious about riding in it, especially with no flight or jump pay and no right to refuse. They were not volunteers as were the paratroopers. And the glider accident rate was especially alarming. In 1943, the Airborne Command reported the training loss of three to six gliders daily. One poster at Laurenburg, Maxton Army Air Base, North Carolina, summed up the glider riders' feelings: Beneath a series of photos showing glider wrecks, one glider man had written: "JOIN THE GLIDER TROOPS! No flight pay; no jump pay; BUT Never a Dull Moment." Such was the birth of the glider program and the glider soldier—"Those who were roped in."

By 1942, the Army Air Corps was in need of a center where the rapidly expanding airborne force pilots could be trained. Lieutenant Colonel George A. Larson, U.S. Air Force (Ret.) wrote that:

the AAF [Army Air Force] announced a training base was to be built east of Alliance (Nebraska), at an estimated cost of three million dollars . . . which escalated to 15 million dollars. . . . The base would come under the control of the Troop Carrier Command, training paratroopers, airborne infantry, Waco CG-4A glider pilots, and Douglas C-47 Skytrain crews on airborne tactics and combat operations. . . . Contractors hired every man or woman to work at the airfield construction site as day laborers, cooks, clerks, and a hundred other skills. . . . Hills were cut down to level the ground for runways by earth scrapers and bulldozers. . . . In September 1942, the first AAF officers arrived, dressed in light-weight cotton Summer uniforms, not suitable for the Fall and Winter months. After the first heavy snow, the AAF commander at Alliance dispatched an empty C-47 to Denver, Colorado to pick up Winter weight Army issue uniforms. . . . By 1943, thousands of glider infantry, paratroopers, glider pilots, and C-47 pilots filled the base. By January 1944, over 14,000 paratroopers were at Alliance, rehearsing for the June 1944, Normandy D-Day invasion of German occupied France.

In 1941, Capt. James M. Gavin (class of 1929) was a tactical officer at West Point. "Tactical officers," he wrote, " concern themselves more with the discipline of the Corps of Cadets than with teaching. However, I became deeply interested in tactics that could be learned from the European war. . . . I also read avidly the Germans' conquest of Europe and their use of a new arm—parachute-glider troops—and I taught as many classes as possible on the new and evolving reports from our military attaché in Cairo, Colonel Bonner Fellers."

In August 1941 Captain Gavin volunteered for jump school and completed his training unscathed but, he remembered, "banged around a bit." He was assigned as a company commander in the 503d but in a few weeks was moved to the Provisional Parachute Group where, as the plans and training officer, he wrote that he had an "exciting opportunity to experiment and develop new techniques for large-scale parachute-glider operations. The whole concept of vertical envelopment was an exciting one, and it would seem to offer a new dimension of tactics if we entered the war. . . . The Germans saw the possibility of combining parachutes and gliders into large organizations on a division scale. As a beginning they organized hundreds of sports glider clubs as a means of circumventing the Versailles Treaty. They then organized the first airborne combat division."

In the spring of 1942, Gavin and General Lee went to Washington to discuss the creation of the United States' first airborne division. The army staff was not wholeheartedly in support and listed certain restrictions on the formation of a first airborne division: it must have completed its basic training, it could not be a regular or a National Guard division, and it must be stationed where the weather was generally good and near one or more airfields. After more research, Lee and Gavin determined that the 82d Infantry Division at Camp Clairborne, Louisiana, reactivated on 25 March 1942 and commanded by Brig. Gen. Omar Bradley (class of 1915) filled the bill. The assistant division commander was Brig. Gen. Matthew B. Ridgway, a 1917 graduate of West Point. In 1939, Ridgway had been promoted to lieutenant colonel and was in Washington in the War Plans Division of the General Staff. He was well known to General Marshall, was promoted to brigadier general—skipping colonel—and transferred to the 82d Infantry Division.

The 82d Airborne Division began its illustrious career as the 82d Division, activated at Camp Gordon, Georgia, on 25 August 1917 (in World War I, there was only one kind of an army division; designation of a division as infantry, armor, airborne, or mechanized started in World War II). Initially, the division was made up of men from Alabama, Georgia, and Tennessee, but a few months later the 82d began to receive men from New England and Mid-Atlantic states and almost everywhere else in the Union. Because the 82d's men came from almost all the 48 states, it was given the nickname "All-Americans," reflected in its "AA" shoulder patch.

The original World War I 82d Division had two infantry brigades of two regiments each (325th, 326th, 327th, and 328th) and an artillery brigade of three artillery regiments (319th, 320th, and 321st). The division also had an engineer regiment (307th), three machine gun battalions (319th, 320th, and 321st), an ordnance battalion, and a medical battalion. It is interesting to note that the division artillery of today's 82d Airborne Division is the 319th Airborne Field Artillery Regiment.

In World War I, the 82d Division fought in three campaigns: the Marbache sector, the St. Mihiel offensive, and the Meuse-Argonne offensive. It spent 105 days in the front lines, advanced over eleven miles (this was of course the war of the trenches), and captured some 845 prisoners. Men in the division won 3 Medals of Honor and 75 Distinguished Service Crosses. It suffered 1,413 men killed in action and 6,664 wounded. During World War I the division was commanded by such stalwarts as Maj. Gen. Eben Swift, Brig. Gen. James Erwin, Brig. Gen. William P. Burnham, and Maj. Gen. George B. Duncan.

Probably one of the most famous heroes of World War I was Alvin C. York, a member of G Company, 328th Infantry, 82d Division. He described himself as "just a blacksmith from Cumberland Hill, Tenn." When he registered himself in his hometown of Pall Mall, he declared himself a conscientious objector, but his petition was denied. He reluctantly entered the army of World War I.

On 4 October 1918, on the Meuse-Argonne front, Pershing's First Army renewed the offensive after the initial attack that, while not overwhelming, had caused a collapse within the German high command and caused the German chancellor to cable President Wilson for an armistice. The French and the British did not wish to accept any unilateral action by Wilson. Meanwhile, German General Ludendorff felt that, given the current situation, he could withdraw behind his own lines and resist unwelcome peace proposals.

In the Meuse-Argonne offensive, on 8 October 1918 Corporal York was part of a seventeen-man patrol whose mission was to destroy German machine gun positions that had slowed the 82d's advance. The patrol stole behind enemy lines and had taken several prisoners when hidden German machine guns cut down several men of the patrol, including three top noncommissioned officers (NCOs). The intense fire drove the patrol under cover where it defended itself and guarded its prisoners. York, the senior NCO present, assumed command of the patrol and with several other men charged the nearest enemy machine gun. The Germans kept up their fire and drove the Americans into gun emplacements or behind rocks and stumps in front of their trenches. York crawled away.

Now alone, York, the Tennessee sharpshooter, shot out the German machine gun crew one by one, quickly forcing the German commander to surrender. On the patrol's return from enemy territory, York repeatedly broke off from what was left of the patrol to capture still more Germans until he and the survivors of the patrol returned to the 82d's lines with 132 prisoners.

York was promoted to sergeant on 1 November, and on 18 April 1919 his division commander, Maj. Gen. George B. Duncan, awarded him the Medal of Honor.

In the early days of the developing airborne force, the U.S. Army necessarily concentrated on the infantry. So it was not until the summer of 1942 that a Parachute Artillery Test Battery came into being at Fort Benning under the command of 2d Lt. Joseph D. Harris. His mission was to develop a system of dropping artillerymen, their weapons, and ammunition simultaneously with the infantry, ready to provide direct artillery support. (That the army of 1942 would assign a second lieutenant such a task is evidence that the "old army" believed in giving a man a job and letting him do it.)

Harris's major problem was that the standard direct-support artillery piece was the 4,980-pound 105mm howitzer, so large that it could not be dropped by any existing parachutes. Harris turned to the pack 75mm, a small, lightweight (1,268 pounds) howitzer. The pack in its name meant that it could be broken down into seven pieces each weighing about 180 pounds, light enough for transportation over rugged terrain on the backs of mules. Harris knew that a 180-pound load could be parachuted safely to the ground. With this hint of a solution he and his test battery went to work.

Harris worked with the Troop Carrier Command to develop a rigging system whereby a C-47 could drop a total of nine loads, each weighing about 200 pounds, including the parachute and the container. The nine loads would include the front trail assembly, the rear trail, the bottom sleigh and recoil mechanism, the cradle and top sleigh, the tube, the breech ring, the wheels, and ammunition and ammunition cart. The Troop Carrier Command and the test battery finally developed a system by which the C-47s were rigged with six "bomb" racks under the main fuselage. The other three loads became "door bundles." Early on a problem arose because, after the nine loads were dropped, they scattered over large areas of the DZ, and it became time consuming for the cannoneers to locate all the pieces of their own howitzers, reassemble them, and move them into firing positions.

Colonel John B. Shinberger, of the Airborne Command at Fort Bragg, came up with an ingenious solution to the problem of keeping all the pieces of each howitzer close together on the ground. He developed a system that linked together all the nine loads on a "daisy chain" of a long nylon strap. When the green light was on by the door of the C-47, the jumpmaster standing in the door would shout "Go!" At that command, two men near the door would throw out the three door bundles and then follow them out the door. Simultaneously, the jumpmaster, using a toggle switch, would push a button to release the six loads in the bomb bay under the C-47. Meanwhile, the rest of the cannoneers were to jump out the door. The jumpmaster was then to follow the last man out. Once the nine loads of the howitzer and its ancillary equipment were in the air, the static lines of the parachutes would pop the chute open. Because the guidelines of the loads were all looped to the daisy chain, the loads were free to move along the daisy chain and not become tangled with each other. And because they were all linked together, the loads landed fairly close together on the ground.

After the parachute test battery completed its experiments and had developed a reasonably practical method for dropping artillery pieces, it evolved into the first Parachute Field Artillery Battalion, the 456th, activated at Fort Bragg on 24 September 1942.

Lieutenant Lou Burris was one of the original artillery paratroopers. He wrote of that experience:

> In the first class of artillerymen to go through jump school at Fort Benning, Ga., in 1942, in a sweating formation, in one-piece coveralls, at the double, shouting cadence was Major Douglass Quandt, Lts. Norman Martin, Nick Stadtherr, Lou Burris and others. We grumbled together, swearing we would kill some of those instructors if they ever came to a unit of ours. All movements were at the double and infractions were punished with pushups, starting at 50.
>
> All artillerymen from that class, and those immediately following, went to the Test Platoon at Fort Bragg, to devise ways of packing and dropping the 75mm Mountain Howitzer. The test platoon became a battery and then a battalion as the officers and men flowed in. The battalion was designated the 456th Field Artillery Battalion, a part of the new 82d Airborne Division.

The War Department made immediate plans to convert the 82d to the army's first airborne division. For a brief period in July 1942 the 82d was, in fact, a motorized division. But at a full-dress parade of the division on 15 August 1942, General Ridgway, forty-seven years old at the time, informed the troops that the 82d was to become the army's first airborne division and would cadre the second, the 101st Airborne Division.

The War Department assigned to the 82d the 504th Parachute Infantry Regiment and the 325th and 326th Glider Infantry Regiments. The 504th, activated on 1 May 1942, was commanded by Col. Theodore L. Dunn and later by the regiment's executive officer, Lt. Col. Ruben Henry Tucker. But because of the shortage of CG-4A gliders, the War Department on 12 February 1943 changed the division organization from one parachute–two glider configuration to two parachute–one glider by dropping the 326th and adding the 505th Parachute Infantry Regiment, activated at Fort Benning in July 1942 and commanded by thirty-five-year-old Col. James Gavin. To balance this change and permit the formation of parachute and glider combat teams, Company B, 307th Engineers joined Company C of the 307th as parachute troops. And the 456th Parachute Field Artillery Battalion joined the 376th Parachute Field Artillery Battalion, already in the division. The 505th moved to Fort Bragg on 9 March 1943.

Early in 1943, while the 505th was still at Fort Benning, Colonel Gavin received a call from the post commander, who was very interested in selling a lot of war bonds and who wanted a 505th representative to report to post headquarters. Colonel Gavin sent his public information officer, Capt. Barney Oldfield. The post commander announced that he wanted to have an Easter Sunday–morning breakfast during which he would try to sell a lot of war bonds. So Oldfield came up with what he thought was a great idea. He said that he knew Gypsy Rose Lee, the famous exotic dancer, who was then appearing in *Star and Garter* in New York, and that he would be happy to call her and invite her to come to Benning for the breakfast. He suggested that they have the affair in the post gymnasium because a lot of men would show up. His plan was that before the breakfast, she would take off all her clothes and then be covered with war bonds of various denominations with the higher priced bonds strategically placed on her anatomy. The audience would then bid on the bonds, with each bond being removed from her body as it was bought. The idea met with a lot of enthusiasm, in some quarters.

Oldfield called Gypsy Rose Lee and she accepted the invitation. The news spread around the post "like wildfire" wrote Gavin. "All went well until about a week before the affair, when the Post Commander got wind of it. 'What is this?' he demanded. 'A strip tease artist attending an Easter morning breakfast in the Post Gym?' He stopped it at once. It fell to Oldfield to call Gypsy Rose Lee and explain that they were withdrawing the invitation. She seemed to understand. . . . But that was our last brouhaha with Post Headquarters at Fort Benning." On 9 March 1943 the 505th moved to Fort Bragg and joined the 82d Airborne Division.

Determined that the 505th would be outstanding in combat performance, absolutely his top priority, Colonel Gavin became a tough taskmaster. He set up and personally ran the regiment's personnel through mock combat exercises and long, tough road marches under heavy loads of individual weapons and gear. He was a "hands on" leader, one who gave an order and then made sure that it was carried out. He tried to learn the names of as many of his men as possible, and he was with them on and off duty. He listened to his men's problems and took action, and even made a number of free-fall parachute jumps, just to be the first to do it. Eventually, he would be known far and wide as "Slim Jim" Gavin, the young, slender, active, "out in front" charger in training and in combat. His men would come to respect and have faith in him. One of his troopers said: "I'd follow Slim Jim into hell—and pay for the coal to keep the fires stoked."

"He was hardest on his officers," wrote T. Michael Booth and Duncan Spencer in *Paratrooper—The Life of Gen. James M. Gavin.* "In the 505th officers were required to be 'the first out of the airplane door and the last in the chow line.' Gavin thought he had the finest infantry on earth in the ranks of his battalions, and if properly led, trained, respected, and treated, they would be the instrument to prove his ideas correct." And so they would.

Many years later, General Ridgway remembered that "having just acceded to command of the 82d Infantry Division, I vividly recall first having been told the 82d would become a mechanized division and then suddenly being informed in secrecy that it would be an Airborne division. Asked if I would like to have it, my reply was 'Fine! I would like to have it, though I have never heard of one.' I must have forgotten Crete and Germany's airborne success."

Both the 82d and the 101st Divisions became "airborne" on 15 August 1942. General Bradley had left the 82d to assume command of the newly activated 28th Division, and Ridgway, according to General Marshall's plan, became the new commander. His deputy was newly promoted Brig. Gen. William M. Miley. The division artillery commander was Brig. Gen. Joseph M. Swing (class of 1915), who would later activate and command the 11th Airborne Division and lead it through bloody battles on Leyte and Luzon. Ridgway's chief of staff was Col. Maxwell D. Taylor (class of 1922). These first senior airborne commanders would become famous during the war.

It was only appropriate that the "Father of Airborne," Gen. William C. Lee, should become the commander of the 101st Airborne; Brig. Gen. Don F. Pratt was assistant division commander; and Brig. Gen. Anthony C. McAuliffe was the division artillery commander.

The 82d trained at Camp Clairborne, Louisiana, from 25 March 1942 until 1 October 1942. On 14 October it began its airborne training at Fort Bragg.

In February of 1943, the War Department selected the 82d Airborne Division for deployment to Africa, there to get ready for the invasion of

Sicily. And thus on 20 April 1943, just some eight months after it became "airborne," the 82d found itself moving from Fort Bragg to Camp Edwards, Massachusetts, in preparation for its movement to the European Theater of Operations. "On the 27th of April," wrote Steven Mrozek, "the troopers boarded the trains that would take them to a pier in the Port of New York. Loaded down with heavy barracks bags, they boarded the transport. Early on the morning of 28 April 1943, the troopship slipped its moorings and began the journey that would take the division to nine countries, from Fort Bragg to Berlin."

General Gavin remembered that after an uneventful Atlantic crossing it was off to Casablanca on 10 May, and the first man stepped ashore at 3:15 P.M.

The division moved to a staging area north of the city, where it remained for three days. That was followed by a move by truck and rail to Oujda in western Algeria, near the Spanish Moroccan border. . . . A day or so after our arrival, General Matthew Ridgway, the Division Commander of the 82d Airborne Division, told me that we were to parachute into Sicily. Since there was sufficient airlift for only one reinforced regimental combat team, he had decided to give the mission to the 505th Parachute Infantry. It would have with it the 456th Parachute Artillery Battalion, the 3d Battalion of the 504th Parachute Infantry, and B Company of the 307th Airborne Engineers.

And so began the 82d's path to fame. But not yet.

3: Airborne Torch

In the summer of 1941 the United States was nervous but not yet committed to the war. The Great Depression was fading, and the industrial might of the United States was beginning to break out of the doldrums of the 1930s. On 16 September 1940, President Roosevelt had signed into law the Selective Service Act authorizing the induction of 900,000 men for a year, raising the regular army's strength to 500,000. As recently as the fall of 1939 the army had consisted of 190,000 men, divided into three half-strength, "square" infantry divisions in the United States, a half-strength division in Hawaii, and the Philippines Scout Regiment of 3,500 men in the Philippines. (The square division had four infantry regiments; the triangular [today] has three infantry regiments.) The only division near full strength was the 1st Cavalry Division at Fort Bliss, Texas, consisting of 12,000 men and 6,000 horses. Knowing that in October 1941 the Selective Service Act was due to expire, Gen. George Marshall and Secretary of War Henry L. Stimson mounted a vigorous campaign to renew the draft: this passed by one vote in the Congress. New draftees and those already in uniform would serve for eighteen months. Marshall could now get on with building a formidable army in spite of high-level government officials, including the president, who felt that air and sea power were enough to defeat Germany.

On 22 June 1941 the German Wehrmacht launched Operation *Barbarossa,* a gigantic surprise attack on the Soviet Union. To have the bulk of his forces available for this campaign, Hitler withdrew a large part of his combat troops from France and the Low Countries, leaving only enough force to ensure those countries' continued German occupation and massive fortification of their coastlines. Thus, for employment in

Barbarossa, Hitler could have 150 combat divisions in a mammoth, three-pronged drive along a 2,000-mile front. During the first ten weeks of fighting, in the northern part of the Soviet Union the Germans blasted their way to the outskirts of Leningrad; in the middle the German forces, heavy in armor, crunched 400 miles into the heart of Russia; in the south the Wehrmacht drove 700 miles to the Dnieper River bend. In ten weeks, they killed or captured over 1 million Red Army personnel. Luckily, the early arrival of a brutally cold winter helped the Soviets slow and even block the German assault, which was further hampered by the lack of equipment and clothing for the frigid, almost arctic conditions.

"In the spring of 1942, the world-wide strategic situation of the Allied Powers looked bleak," wrote Lt. Gen. William P. Yarborough in his book, *Bail out Over North Africa.*

> Virtually all of the Western European area was either in the hands of the Axis Forces, or was dominated by them. The Germans were on the outskirts of Moscow—halted for the moment, but not lacking in equipment, reserves or will to win.
>
> In the Libyan Desert, the British defeat at Tobruk was added to the list which already included Dunkirk, Hong Kong and Singapore. Rommel's Afrika Korps had not yet begun to worry too much about Montgomery's British Eighth Army. After all, stretching all the way across the North African Continent to the Atlantic Ocean, was Axis territory.

The Axis forces had virtual control of the Atlantic Ocean and the Mediterranean Sea. In March 1942, some half-million tons of Allied shipping was sunk by Axis submarines. And British convoys entering the Mediterranean through the Straits of Gibraltar were pounded by German and Italian planes based in Italy, Sicily, and North Africa. The Luftwaffe was blasting the British homeland, the British were fighting desperate battles in Asia, and the German Afrika Korps was in command in Egypt and Libya. The United States was still in shock over Pearl Harbor and was just beginning to mobilize its armed forces and crank up its industrial might.

In the spring of 1942 Stalin appealed to the British and the United States to launch, as soon as possible, an attack across the English Channel on France to relieve the Soviets of some of the formidable power and presence of the Wehrmacht. The British and American press quickly took up the appeal and started the clamor for a "second front." The pressure on the United States and Great Britain from a number of directions for such action became enormous.

In April 1942 the British and U.S. governments agreed upon a cross-Channel strategy. But the fact that British forces were spread around the world and that the Americans were far from totally mobilized either industrially or militarily for any "second front" precluded any substantial assault on Hitler's Europe in 1942, or even in 1943, as it turned out. But with all the cries for a second front, President Roosevelt ordered his joint chiefs of staff to come up with a plan to quiet the tumult and "do something."

On 11 June 1942, "General Marshall told me definitely that I would command the European theater," wrote General Eisenhower in *Crusade in Europe*. "General [Mark W.] Clark and I, with a few assistants, left Washington in late June 1942. . . . Our party landed in England without incident and I immediately assumed command of the European Theater of Operations, United States Army, which then comprised only the United Kingdom and Iceland. . . . The United States theater in Europe was established for the purpose of preparing the American part of the invasion of the Continent, agreed upon between the British and American governments as the main strategical effort in defeating Germany."

But because of the need for time to build up the U.S. logistics and military forces, "the invasion of the Continent" was still two years away. "But consider the picture in June 1942," wrote Eisenhower. "The United States was just getting into its stride in the mobilization and training of its armies, navies, and air forces. Only the 34th Division, the 1st Armored Division, and small detachments of the United States Air Forces had arrived in northern Ireland.

"They were still only partly trained. The great bulk of the fighting equipment, naval, air, and ground, needed for the invasion did not exist. Some of the landing craft were not yet in the blueprint stage."

Meanwhile, Stalin kept up his "insistent" demand for an offensive by Great Britain and the United States in 1942. And Roosevelt, under pressure, had ordered his chiefs of staff to launch some kind of offensive ground action in the European zone in 1942.

General Eisenhower and his staff came up with three possible courses of action: (1) reinforce the British armies fighting the forces of Gen. Erwin Rommel in Libya; (2) conduct a limited operation (codenamed Sledgehammer) on the northwest coast of France as a bridgehead for the future; or (3) prepare amphibious forces to seize northwest Africa with the ultimate goal of attacking to the east and thus grinding Rommel and his forces in a giant vise.

Admiral Ernest L. King was the chief of U.S. naval operations. Eisenhower, Marshall, and King, with his emphasis on the Pacific Theater, were all opposed to a North African landing. They felt that a 1942 North African campaign would set back a cross-Channel operation in 1943. The Allied Combined Chiefs of Staff, including British Adm. Sir Dudley Pound, could not agree on a possible scenario. Roosevelt, who was under pressure after having promised Soviet Foreign Minister Vyacheslav Molotov that there would be some sort of a diversionary operation in 1942, entered the discussion.

After considerable study and talk between the British and U.S. chiefs of staff, General Eisenhower wrote: "On July 24 it was determined to proceed with the planning for the invasion of northwest Africa with an Allied force of all arms, to be carried out under an American commander. The operation received the name Torch." The president approved the plan on 25 July, and both the British and the Americans agreed that the operation should have "a completely American complexion," wrote General Eisenhower. "The hope was that French North Africa would receive the invading troops with no more than a nominal show of resistance, and the chances of this favorable development were to be considered to be much brighter if the operation was advertised as purely American. British standing in France was at low ebb because of the Oran, Dakar, and Syrian incidents, in which British forces had come into open conflict with the French. In his headquarters in the Claridge Hotel on July 26, General Marshall informed me that I was to be the Allied commander in chief of the expedition." General Clark became his deputy for Operation Torch.

Seizing the North African coast would open the Mediterranean, relieve Malta, and was to give some U.S. forces experience in combat and logistics before the major event of the war—Operation Overlord, the future invasion of Europe.

Operation Torch had as its objective the capture of five North African ports, three in Morocco and two in Algeria. The Western Task Force, 35,000 troops commanded by Maj. Gen. George Patton, would mount up in the United States, land in Morocco on three beachheads: Port Lyautey, Safi, and Fedala, eventually to subdue Casablanca; the Center Task force, comprising 39,000 U.S military personnel would sail from

Britain under the command of Maj. Gen. Lloyd L. Fredendall and would capture Oran, Algeria; the Eastern Task Force, with 33,000 U.S. and British troops under the command of Maj. Gen. Charles W. Ryder, would land at Algiers and take that city.

In June of 1942, Lt. Col. Edson Duncan Raff (class of 1933) and his 2d Battalion of the 503d Parachute Infantry Regiment (on 2 November 1942 redesignated the 2d Battalion, 509th Parachute Infantry, and hereafter referred to as the 509th Parachute Infantry Battalion) arrived in England aboard the converted luxury liner, *Queen Mary.* Shortly thereafter, the paratroopers moved by train to the estate of American-born Lady Ward at Chilton Foliat, near Hungerford in Berkshire, where they immediately moved into Nissen huts. There they began an intensive training program, adopting some British techniques and equipment. They ran the difficult British obstacle course in record speed. "From the Tommies," wrote General Yarborough, "the Americans learned the secret of rapid and sustaining stiff-legged marching. They fired high explosives from their mortars and threw live grenades, many of them for the first time. Little by little, they were making up for the realism which had been lacking in their training in the United States." And the battalion made a number of jumps in Devonshire.

Lieutenant Colonel Raff was a short, physically fit, hard-driving commander, known to his troops as "Little Caesar." "Ed Raff was a superb soldier," wrote General Yarborough. "I had known him first at West Point where we had been on the swimming team together. I had seen a lot of him at Fort Benning in the early airborne days when new parachute battalions were being formed in rapid succession. He was a tough disciplinarian, fearless, aggressive and tenacious. He always kept himself in top physical condition and in the stamina department was more than a match for any man in his unit. . . . He was to prove his worth repeatedly under some of the most difficult combat situations." General Eisenhower called him "a gallant American."

The battalion had some lighter moments. "By the end of July," wrote Colonel Raff in his *We Jumped to Fight,* "morale began to sag."

> The battalion seemed to be going stale. . . . To help ease the situation, we had frequent movies at night, a couple of British ENSA shows and one show with Al Jolson, supported by various other famous Hollywood movie stars.

Just before the latter performance, our paratroopers staged a jump for the actors far more spectacular than anything the actors themselves did later. A series of normal jumps [was] highlighted by an accidental low altitude mass jump from 150 feet without casualties. The less said about it the better. But truthfully, as I saw those soldiers pouring out of the transport so close to the ground my first gray hair sprouted. Mr. Irvin, who designed the particular chute we use, would be interested to know that all chutes functioned perfectly and that there were no casualties. And in the States we worried about low jumps from 800 feet!

Colonel Raff became so proud of his battalion that a number of times he asked the headquarters in London to send a general to inspect his troops—who would be in formation, fully geared up for a combat jump. "I shall always believe that some officer in London remembered my vain request for a general to inspect us," Raff wrote, "because one day out of a clear blue sky someone from the American Embassy phoned. 'Mrs. Roosevelt is visiting your camp tomorrow at 10 a.m.,' he said. We all keenly appreciated the honor our small unit was paid by her presence. She, in turn, seemed to enjoy her task."

By the spring of 1942 Maj. William P. Yarborough was a qualified parachutist, had commanded a parachute infantry company, and had served as an intelligence officer of the Airborne Command. While in the latter job, he was asked by the War Department to go to the Soviet Union as a military attaché to gather all possible information on the Red Army parachute troops. While waiting for the attaché job, he received word from General Clark that he wanted him to come to England as his airborne planner. With enthusiasm, he accepted this job instead, arriving in England in July 1942, and went to work in Norfolk House, General Eisenhower's command post (CP).

For a couple of months, Yarborough spent his time going through the British jump school near Manchester, making several jumps from captive balloons and out the circular jump hatches of British Whitley bombers. He studied the "overall environment of the United Kingdom." He also gained access to the part of the British intelligence system involved with British airborne operations. He considered this contact "invaluable" later when he started U.S. operational planning.

In early September of 1942 Yarborough was summoned by Clark to the general's office in Norfolk House, so he duly arrived, saluted, and reported (up until this time he had been working on the airborne phases of Sledgehammer). Clark was by now the chief planner for Operation Torch. He got up from his chair and pulled open a curtain behind his desk, revealing a large wall map of North Africa. On the map were three large arrows that showed the direction of the three task forces involved in Torch. He briefed the major on each task force: the western one was to sail from the United States and take the port of Casablanca and then occupy French Morocco; the center one was to take Oran; and the eastern force, in a predominantly British effort, to capture Algiers and then drive on to Tunis.

He talked to Yarborough specifically about the Center Task Force, the CTF. He pointed out that within the tactical area of the CTF were two French airfields, Tafaraoui and La Senia. They were of particular importance because they were the only good airfields in all of western Algeria, and Tafaraoui was the only hard-surfaced airfield between Morocco and Algiers. La Senia was five miles south of Oran, and Tafaraoui about ten miles farther south. Both were too far inland to be early objectives for amphibious forces.

"Bombing La Senia and Tafaraoui in order to interrupt their use by hostile forces would serve to convince the French garrisons that we did not come as allies but as enemies," wrote General Yarborough. "Destruction of the ground facilities would make our own air operations from the two fields more difficult. To General Clark, the use of paratroops to seize, immobilize, and hold La Senia and Tafaraoui, seemed a logical and legitimate application of the skills and potential of airborne forces. It was my advice as his Airborne Planner, that he now sought."

General Clark added, "It's important, Major, that we grab these two airfields as soon as possible on D Day. With them in our hands, we can prevent French fighters from taking off to oppose our amphibious landings at daylight." He also told Yarborough that he wanted two airborne plans: one if the French were friendly—a no-jump, air-landing at La Senia; the other, it they resisted, combat jumps at both La Senia and Tafaraoui to destroy French planes parked at both fields. "We're going to try to convince the French that they should come to our side and fight the Germans. . . . But if they refuse, we'll fight the French as we would the Germans."

Clark in essence asked Yarborough what he thought Colonel Raff's paratroopers could do. Yarborough could only reply that he needed time to think it over and, if the general agreed, that he would be back in the morning with his answer. Clark gave him an okay.

At 0830, Yarborough was back in Norfolk House and briefed Clark on the plans he had developed during a sleepless night. One was Plan Peace, the battalion air-landing at La Senia in broad daylight on D day; the other was Plan War, the battalion parachute assaulting at midnight of D minus 1 directly onto Tafaraoui airfield with the mission of destroying the French fighter planes before they could attack the amphibious landings at daylight. In Plan War one company would march north to La Senia to knock out the fighter planes there. In Plan War, Yarborough recommended landing the Allied aircraft, which would be almost out of gas, on the rock-hard mud flats east of Oran, there to wait for fuel from the amphibious forces landing at daylight. General Clark approved the plans.

On the following Sunday at 1000, Colonel Raff got a call from Yarborough. "Raff," he said, "you've got to come to London right away. No, can't postpone it. It's the most important thing in your life."

"Life and death?" asked Colonel Raff.

"Well, almost" replied Yarborough. "You'd better get a plane right away."

"The next morning I reported to General Clark who, much to my surprise, was not at European Theater Headquarters," wrote Colonel Raff.

"Dispensing with formalities, he said, 'Raff, we've got a job for you and your outfit to do. Look over the plans, then tell me if you can do it. If I'm not here, leave me a note.'

"Two hours later. I left him this note:

'There is not doubt in my mind but that we can accomplish the mission, provided: (1) we get a break by the Air Corps and (2) by the weather. And provided, (3) I am permitted to command my paratroopers when we hit the ground.'"

The days following General Clark's approval of Major Yarborough's plan and Colonel Raff's reply were filled with top secret preparations. Clark approved the creation of a Paratroop Task Force under the command of Col. William C. Bentley, U.S. Army Air Corps. Bentley had had some experience with northwest Africa because he had been the U.S. military attaché in Tangiers prior to his assignment to London in early 1942. Under Bentley's command were the Air Corps' 60th Troop Carrier Group and Raff's 509th Parachute Battalion. The planning staff of the Paratroop Task Force was made up of officers from both commands, the British providing numerous aerial photos and voluminous data on the target area.

Raff established a war room just outside his sleeping quarters in Berkshire. An armed guard blocked anyone without a pass. Inside, Raff and his planners made scale models of the terrain around the two airfields, even including miniature airplanes and antiaircraft gun emplacements. The walls of the room were covered with photographs "from every conceivable angle and under innumerable conditions of lighting." Raff brought small groups of his men to the war room, sometimes a company commander and his senior NCOs, sometimes a squad leader and his men, and had them briefed in specific detail about their missions. Eventually, each paratroop "saboteur" knew exactly where he would slash the tail surfaces or where he was to place his incendiary grenades in order to immobilize the Vichy airplanes which were his personal targets.

General Yarborough wrote that:

> as the invasion plan took shape, it became firm that the paratroops would invade Africa as part of the Center Task Force or "CTF" under Maj. Gen. Lloyd L. Fredendall. Their specific job was to capture Tafaraoui Airdrome with the Parachute Battalion, less one company, and to send that company north through Valmy to La Senia Airdrome, there to immobilize Vichy French combat aircraft. The aircraft destroyed, or otherwise immobilized, the Parachute "Saboteur" company was then to withdraw to Tafaraoui, where it would join the remainder of the Battalion in an active defense of the Airdrome until the arrival of sea-landed Combat Command "B" of the American 1st Armored Division.

One major problem facing both the Air Corps and Raff's planners was finding the DZ in North Africa in complete darkness after a flight of some 1,500 miles from England because, General Yarborough wrote, "many paratroopers knew by experience that finding a drop zone on the first pass, even in daylight, was often a very difficult task." The solution to this problem rested on a recently developed British system consisting of what were called Rebecca and Eureka, two highly secret devices by which a pilot, through his receiving unit—Rebecca—could home in on the radar beam emitted from the sending unit—the Eureka, a portable suitcase-sized device. The catch was that someone had to put the sending unit—the Eureka—on the spot that needed to be found.

PATHFINDERS

Obviously, someone with the Eureka had to be sent to the correct location in North Africa—no easy task. Major Yarborough found 2d Lt.
Norman Hapgood, a young army Signal Corps officer who had been sent
to England to study the Rebecca-Eureka radar system. Hapgood "looked
like a scientist," wrote General Yarborough. "He habitually wore civilian
clothes of indifferent tailoring.... But he guarded the two brown suitcases
holding the precious gadgets like crown jewels." Yarborough continues:

> The problem of getting Hapgood and his wonderful machines
> into North Africa was no small one in itself. Its solution involved
> first a discharge from the Army, and an airplane ticket back to
> America to throw enemy agents off the scent. Back in the United
> States, Hapgood would be taken in tow by our Intelligence Service,
> which would arrange for his clandestine entry into Algeria. We bade
> him goodbye one afternoon about three weeks before D-day. Our
> last glimpse of him until we met again in Algiers was of his tall,
> stooped figure, bent a little more under the weight of his two suit-
> cases, struggling along Regent Street until he was finally picked up
> by a taxicab. Before he left the office, he had proudly showed us
> the little devices on each suitcase which, if activated, would blow
> Eureka to bits. Even the Gestapo could not put the machines to-
> gether again once the destruct mechanisms had done their jobs.

In addition to the radar devices, the Royal Navy planned to furnish a
navigational aid, a radio signal transmitted from the *Alynbank*, a merchant ship that was to sail an elliptical course in roughly a two-mile oval
in the western Mediterranean about twenty-five miles off the Algerian
coast. The incoming planes, theoretically, would pick up the radio signal about 200 miles from the African Coast and ride it in to the radar
signal from Eureka. Then Hapgood's Algerian "underground" helpers
would light ground flares to mark the exact location of the drop zones.

D day for Operation Torch was set for 7 November 1942. But as the
days wore on, Raff did not yet know whether Plan Peace or Plan War was
in effect.

Robert D. Murphy had long been stationed in North Africa as the senior U.S. State Department officer. He had been in secret contact with
some French generals who were sympathetic to the Allied cause and arranged a meeting between Clark and Gen. Charles Emmanuel Mast, the
chief of staff of the French XIX Corps in Algeria. The meeting was sched-

uled for 21 October at Cherchel, about ninety miles west of Algiers. General Clark made the journey "accompanied by a small staff," wrote General Eisenhower. "The trip was made by airplane and submarine and was carried out exactly as planned except that local suspicion finally was aroused and the French conspirators were forced to escape very hurriedly, while General Clark and his group had to hide until they could reembark in their submarine."

Finally, the group got down to business. General Clark explained that the Allies were planning an operation in North Africa shortly but refrained from spelling out the details—an important one being that General Patton and his Western Task Force were already on the Atlantic and steaming east. General Mast promised to provide whatever assistance he could after the Allied landings and he would order the French soldiers to avoid resistance. "The idea that we might land unopposed was further strengthened after General Clark's historic submarine voyage to North Africa," wrote General Yarborough, "where he kept his appointment with General Charles Emmanuel Mast." But by the night of 7 November 1942, D day minus 1, neither Major Yarborough nor Colonel Raff knew whether they would parachute in or air-land.

By D day minus 1, Colonel Raff had moved his battalion of 556 paratroopers by railroad from its training base, Camp Foliat, to the two departure airfields, Saint Eval and Predannack, on the southern tip of England known as Land's End. If General Clark could persuade the French not to resist the Allied invasion, Plan Peace would be in effect, and the 509th would take off after dark on 7 November and air-land during daylight at La Senia. If the French opposed the landing, then Plan War would be in effect, and the 509th in thirty-nine C-47 airplanes would take off at 1730 during daylight, fly some 1,600 miles at a speed of about 135 miles per hour, and twelve hours later make a night combat jump on Tafaraoui airfield. Colonel Bentley, the Paratroop Task Force commander, had been told that if Plan War was in effect he would receive a coded message from Gibraltar: "Advance Napoleon"; if Plan Peace were in effect, he would receive the message, "Advance Alexis."

Colonel Raff wrote,

An hour before dark we changed to jump suits, then everyone checked ammunition, loaded clips in carbines, Tommy guns or Garand rifles, safety-taped grenades before putting them in the lower jacket pockets, settled two days of K-rations in pouches of the trousers, and arranged parachutes in the planes to form a pillow to lean against. We hoped blankets already spread on the floor of the C-47s would encourage men to sleep on the journey.

At 1700 hours, we were standing by our airplanes in the gathering dusk. At 1710, from Gibraltar came the words "Advance Alexis." The Peace Plan was in effect!

Their adrenalin pumping, the thoroughly keyed up paratroopers and the young aircrews now had to delay departure for four hours—long enough to permit our formations to arrive over North Africa in daylight rather than under cover of darkness. Accordingly, the first aircraft took off at 2105 and by 2145 all were in the air in formation and on the way to the battle area. As our wheels raced along the runways for takeoff, I thought of the mighty ocean armada filled with Allied troops which for weeks had been approaching Africa closer and closer, and were now almost within striking distance.

"The takeoff was without incident," wrote Colonel Raff. "All thirty-nine planes climbed off, not one being forced to return because of mechanical difficulties." But shortly thereafter, flight difficulties began in earnest.

The flight plan scheduled the C-47s to assemble in the air over Portreath, fly westward over the Scilly Isles, and then turn south toward the Bay of Biscay. Later, the formation at 10,000 feet would fly over neutral Spain and toward the British signal ship *Alynbank*. If all went well, the *Alynbank*'s homing signal, simulating an Italian beacon, would permit the formation to home in on Eureka manned by Lieutenant Hapgood near Tafaraoui.

Another problem, unknown to Colonels Bentley and Raff, was that Marshal Henri Pétain had unexpectedly, and at the last possible moment, issued orders from Vichy, France, to put all French troops in North Africa on full combat alert. He had become highly suspicious after he found out about the approaching Allied convoys. Plan War was now in effect. But the troop commanders did not know it.

On 6 November, General Eisenhower and a small staff had left London as surreptitiously as possible and headed for Gibraltar, where he set up a CP in the deep bowels of the Rock. When he learned of Pétain's order, he had messages sent to the approaching fleet that the French were prepared to fight.

On the *Alynbank,* its radio operators were desperately trying to send the "Play Ball" message to the Paratroop Task Force planes, notifying them that Plan War was now in effect. The message did not get through. *Alynbank* was transmitting at 460 kilocycles instead of the agreed on 400 kilocycles.

Colonel Raff was riding in the second plane of the first flight, and Major Yarborough was in the lead plane of Flight B that had taken off from Saint Eval. Lieutenant Colonel Tom Schofield, the 60th Group commander, was his pilot. During the long flight from England the troopers slept as best they could on the floor or on the canvas seats. About dawn, Major Yarborough was awake and standing behind Colonel Schofield, looking out the plane's windshield. "I saw the first faint light of dawn illuminate the sky," Yarborough wrote. "I knew that we should be over Africa. We had been in the air for seven hours. Tensely we peered into the gloom below. A dense ground haze seemed to stretch interminably obscuring everything from view. None of our other planes was in sight."

What I did not know until later was that during the flight over the southern part of the Bay of Biscay our formation had already begun to scatter. Not more than two planes in any element or three in any flight had been able to stay together. . . . The navigators generally had become confused to the extent that most had fallen back on "dead reckoning."

The strong easterly wind, which had not been predicted in the preflight weather report, blew most of the aircraft off course to the west 50 miles or more from their expected landfall.

Silhouetted against the dazzling whiteness below, our lone airplane filled with mildly uneasy paratroopers circled looking for a hole in the clouds. "Rebecca" was dead as a mackerel and it looked as though we were invading Africa alone!

Suddenly I noticed with a start that there was a small black speck moving toward us from a great distance. It was coming fast. . . . I tried to keep my voice calm. "All right, men, take the plugs out of the windows and put the muzzles of your weapons through. If this is an enemy fighter, wait until he's close enough before you fire—he won't think this flying banana has any armament. Maybe we can fool him."

The plane came closer and closer. Finally, the dark speck grew large enough to be identified—it was a C-47. "I'll bet that son of a bitch is lost, too," one of the paratroopers cracked. The troops laughed nervously. The second plane joined Major Yarborough's.

Finally, a rift appeared in the clouds and Schofield flew lower. To Yarborough and Schofield's surprise, they recognized some terrain feature and realized that they were over Spanish Morocco, 240 miles west of Oran. And beneath them, on the ground, they saw one of the C-47s. Schofield pulled back on his yoke and zoomed out of the area toward the Mediterranean. Then they saw another plane on the ground trying to take off, followed by horsemen trying to catch the plane. It finally made it and joined the other two planes. Schofield flew low over the Mediterranean, and Yarborough searched for other planes. Soon he spotted several flying in the same direction. The formation began to grow. "I strained my eyes toward the panorama which was unrolling ahead as we turned inland," wrote Yarborough. "I could see the vast outline of the Sebkra d'Oran, a long oval shaped salt desert which stretched from Oran to the east for thirty miles.

"Suddenly I grabbed Schofield's arm and pointed to the ground ahead. There on the extreme western edge of the Sebkra were ten or twelve of our aircraft on the ground. To the north of them, scattered among the rocks of some high ground, were forty or fifty parachutes marking the spot where some of the troopers evidently had dropped."

"What do we do?" yelled Schofield. "Land here or go into Tafaraoui?"

Major Yarborough made a quick decision. "Land here!" He yelled back. Yarborough went back into the plane and told the troops, "Take your chutes off, get your weapons ready and let's be prepared to bail out of this crate if we have to." Schofield had landed just in time. As the wheels of his plane touched the surface of Sebkra, the fuel gage hit empty.

When Major Yarborough got out of the plane, he saw that a number of C-47s were on the ground with paratroopers lying under the wings of some of them. He asked one of the pilots, "What's the score? What the hell gives?"

"Damned if I know," he said. "We were flying toward Tafaraoui when some ack-ack opened up on us. Things began to happen fast. The first thing I knew, the ship ahead of us slowed down and its load bailed out. Four or five other ships did the same thing. We came in here and landed.

Our load is up there in the rocks chasing snipers." Major Yarborough had one thought: "Something was badly snafued—that was obvious." Plan War was obviously in effect.

At about 0810 on the morning of 8 November, and before Major Yarborough and his three planes had landed, Colonel Raff was in a flight of six planes that flew down the north edge of the Sebkra near the town of Lourmel. As his plane flew over the area, Colonel Raff saw opposite the town on the dry lake bed some twenty-four C-47s, with propellers stopped and troops deplaning. His plane and the other five circled the area ready to land. But at that moment an excited voice cried on the plane's radio, "The troops on the ground are digging in! They are being pinned down by fire from those armored cars on the road." Raff looked down, could see the armored cars, but could not pick up any flash of fire from weapons. Raff turned to his pilot and said, "Well, Ober, this is it! We're going to jump to knock out the armor and give the troops on the ground a chance to do something. Pick out a drop zone north of the road and ring the bell when you're ready." Back in the cabin, he ordered, "OK, let's get going. Chutes on!"

Colonel Bentley was aboard Raff's plane. They decided to jump all six plane loads to fight the tanks. Raff asked Bentley to radio the other pilots to jump their paratroopers when they saw Raff jump from the lead plane. As his plane came over the hastily selected DZ, Raff leaped out. But as he got closer to the ground, he realized that the terrain was hilly and rocky. His landing was not routine, he wrote:

> A rock or piece of equipment, or something else, had struck into my lower ribs. With some effort and spitting of blood, I moved my carcass sufficiently to undo the harness.
>
> Captain Morrow and Lieutenant Birkner assembled their men behind a rock wall. Then, with anti-tank men leading, the assembled paratroopers moved out using approved methods of creeping and crawling. It was slow going. In half an hour, the foremost anti-tank man stopped, stood up, and yelled back in a disappointed voice, "Those vehicles have stars! They're American!"
>
> It was true. They were part of the American Armored Force which had broken through early that morning. Well, at least we were among friends. But what an undramatic ending to the first combat jump!

To add to his troubles, though, Raff had cracked two ribs and was in great pain, but stayed alert and active.

The tanks belonged to Lt. Col. John K. Waters's Combat Command B of the 1st Armored Division pushing inland from the landing near Oran.

Shortly after his three planes landed, Yarborough found Raff lying behind a pile of boulders. A medic was putting strips of adhesive tape along his rib cage. "What happened, Ed?" Yarborough asked. Through bloody lips, Raff said, "I think I've busted a rib." He then went on to explain that he had jumped his men after one of his planes had been fired on, and he was worried about where all his planes were. He could not account for nine planes and 135 of his paratroopers.

In actuality, one plane had landed at Gibraltar after becoming lost over Spain. Two had tried to land at La Senia but were driven off by antiaircraft fire and landed on the other side of Oran, the men aboard being captured by the French. Two other planes had landed in French Morocco at Fez airport and were taken prisoner by the French. The four other planes were down in Spanish Morocco. Some three months later the Spanish allowed the men to leave without their planes or equipment.

About an hour after Major Yarborough had found Colonel Raff, they decided that because Plan War was in effect, they had to get the battalion to Tafaraoui. Raff met with his company commanders, told them the situation, and ordered them to move out along the Sebkra toward Tafaraoui. Major Yarborough got a jeep from the armored force for Raff to ride in across the desert.

"In about an hour, the battalion was moving slowly across the Sebkra," wrote Yarborough. "Each step was a task in itself. Just under the dry upper crust of the lake's surface was a type of plastic mud that would have immobilized a dinosaur. Our feet picked the stuff up until each shoe felt like it weighed fifteen pounds. Raff, looking green around the gills, inched past us in the jeep. Distances in North Africa are deceptive to the eye. The Sebkra was at least eight miles wide. We were tired when we reached the south shore."

On the south shore, one of Raff's communications sergeants handed Yarborough a message he had picked up from a friendly airman who had landed at Tafaraoui. The report said that a few enemy machine guns were still firing and that the U.S. tankers on the field had rounded up a lot of prisoners. They needed troops to guard them.

Yarborough showed the message to Raff. "How about it, Ed?" he said. "If you give me the OK, I can slip a company in there."

"The planes are out of gas."

"Not all of them. Ours may have half an hour left even though she reads empty. If I could get three ships, we could haul about eighty men."

"OK, go ahead." He spat a blob of blood. "Let me know by radio when you get there."

Yarborough sent a message to the planes parked on the desert floor, and shortly afterward Lt. Joe Beck landed three C-47s near the battalion assembly area. Raff picked Capt. John Berry's company and some battalion headquarters men to fly to Tafaraoui. The plan was to fly at about 100 feet for the thirty-five- mile flight. No parachutes were necessary, and Yarborough jammed the planes as full as possible. The short flight would end in disaster.

Once airborne, Yarborough stood behind Lieutenant Beck so that he could pick out a spot on the field where he wanted to land. Suddenly, Yarborough caught a movement of some sort in the air to the right front of the plane.

"What kind of planes are those, Joe?"

"Joe didn't answer," wrote Yarborough.

He became a whirlwind. He slid into a steep bank and cut the motors. The copilot pumped the flaps down, throwing shudders through the whole ship. My heart jumped into my throat and stayed there. I could feel the impact as the Vichy machine gun bullets hit our ship broadside. The fuselage began to leak light as the rounds poured into the defenseless mass of men seated on the floor. The noise was deafening. Each shot cracked so loud that I had the sensation of feeling it as well as of hearing it. I made my body as thin as I could by pressing my back against the bulkhead. We smashed into the ground going 130 miles an hour and slewed to a violent halt.

The French Dewoitine 520 fighters made a number of passes over the downed plane and forced the other two planes to crash land in the desert. Then they made repeated strafing runs over the downed planes and the helpless paratroopers and airmen. Finally, they flew off, leaving the three planes riddled with bullets and dead and wounded paratroopers strewn across the area. Yarborough, who had used his helmet to dig as deeply as he could into the desert floor, stood up. One of the first dismal sights he saw was a paratrooper hanging lifeless from the open door of his plane, with blood dripping from his fingertips.

Another wounded trooper staggered toward Yarborough with his hands stretched out as if he were blind. Yarborough yelled over and over for an aid man until finally the wounded man told him that he was the aid man. Yarborough pulled a tourniquet from his pouch and twisted it around his elbow. Then Yarborough saw Capt. William Muir, one of the battalion's two doctors, holding his hand against the side of his head.

"How do you feel, Doc?" Yarborough asked him. "I think I'm hit pretty badly," he said. "I have two in the head and one through the shoulder. The one in my shoulder hurts like hell. They got Lieutenant Kunkle." He pointed toward the plane. "Look at Lieutenant Beck. He was on top of that wing trying to check his antenna even before the last strafing run hit us."

Despite his severe head injuries, Captain Muir hobbled from plane to plane, trying to take care of the wounded, even as the French fighters continued to strafe the area. Later he was awarded the Distinguished Service Cross for his heroism under fire. "Likeable Lieutenant Joe Beck, C-47 troop carriers pilot," wrote Colonel Raff, "also received the Distinguished Service Cross for his coolness and bravery under fire in this action."

One of the more seriously wounded paratroopers was Pvt. John "Tommy" Mackall, a twenty-two-year-old soldier from Wellsville, Ohio. He was evacuated by air to Gibraltar where, four days later, he died of his wounds. He was first buried by the British with full military honors at the base of Gibraltar. (On 8 February 1943, the War Department published General Order Number 6, which officially changed the name of Camp Hoffman, North Carolina, a new airborne training center a few miles to the west of Fort Bragg, to Camp Mackall. And on 25 February 1943 the 11th Airborne Division was activated at Camp Mackall.)

The sun was beginning to set on D day, 8 November. Captain John Berry, the company commander, was sitting on the ground sobbing angrily and damning the French. Yarborough saw Lieutenant Crosby crawl painfully from the door of one of the other planes. Some of the lightly injured men were making the wounded more comfortable by opening parachutes and setting them up to ward off the last rays of the sun.

The attack by the French fighters had killed seven and wounded twenty men of Yarborough's small eighty-man force, basically, Capt. John Berry's E Company. Yarborough decided to leave the wounded with Doc Muir and press on with the sixty men, some walking wounded, still left in his small task force. The long flight from England, the arduous march through the heat of the desert of Sebkra, the strain of their baptism of fire, had left their marks on even the physically fit paratroopers. The men "grunted with the effort as they quickened their steps to catch up after weariness had caused them to lag behind a step or two. Every trooper was carrying some item of equipment. Men silently passed machine guns when a bearer would stumble or falter," wrote Yarborough. "At the end of two hours, we halted. The troopers slumped to the ground without speaking."

Yarborough tried to figure out where he was. With his compass and his memory of the terrain models in London, he deduced that he was in the Sebkra d'Oran fifteen or twenty miles southwest of Valmy. He knew then that he had to march to the east, hit the Valmy–St. Barbe-de-Tiélat Road, and then move on to Tarafaoui Airdrome. Yarborough put out a point guard of six men with Tommy guns. Then he and the rest of the troopers followed, stumbling along the road, numb with fatigue. At 0205 Yarborough checked his watch and decided to call a halt, letting the men rest for an hour. Then he got them up and started the long trek, eventually of thirty-eight miles. They all walked like zombies, but not a man lost his weapon or any ammunition. About midmorning, Yarborough and his exhausted men staggered into Tafaraoui.

The remainder of the battalion, some 300 men, along with Colonel Raff, moved out after dark from Sebkra d'Oran. Arabs along the way were curious, and to them some of the paratroopers gave their useless, heavy underwear, and parts of their K-rations. The Arabs supplied them with water. At dawn a French plane came over and the troops spread out, but nothing came of that alarm.

"The march to Tafaraoui continued," wrote Colonel Raff. "It ended, for a time, at another farm, this one owned by a Spanish Loyalist, who permitted us to rest in his hay stacks. . . . About noontime our route of march joined the main road. In a short time, Major Yardley had started a bus service deluxe to Tafaraoui. He first rode to the airport in a civilian car, then commandeered a bus to take all the paratroopers there. . . . The aging charabanc lasted four trips."

When the 509th reached Tafaraoui on 9 November, D day plus 1, Colonel Raff learned that the airfield was already occupied by a U.S. armored force. He felt that the worst was over. He also found out that Algiers had fallen and that Casablanca and Oran would soon capitulate. British Spitfires were knocking out enemy tanks and installations. Colonel Waters and his armored force were about to make the final assault on La Senia and Oran. Raff's job, as it turned out, was to defend the airfield and provide security for General Doolittle and his staff who had set up their CP on the field.

In addition, Raff readied his battalion for any future action. He set up a salvage section of parachute riggers and supply men that sent out small parties of men to the abandoned planes where they picked up parachute materiel, ammunition and weapons loads, and other equipment and hauled them to salvage dumps on Tafaraoui field. The riggers repacked the chutes, and the supply troops combed through the gear and salvaged anything worth saving. Raff had each man turn in all equipment except for his helmet, boots, and jump suit. The supply sergeants eventually made up 300 sets of equipment for the next operation, whatever and whenever that would be. The C-47s were repaired within the limits of available tools.

Colonel Raff took time to assess his situation. He had seven men killed, twenty or more wounded, and eighty-eight missing. His operation, the first U.S. airborne operation of the war, was in fact a disappointing "no show." About all that could be said was that it was valuable to him and his troops mostly for training and undergoing the reality of combat.

On 10 November 1942 the French surrendered Oran, two days after Torch began. On that same day, General Patton and his force encircled Casablanca. Early on the morning of 11 November the French admiral, Jean Darlan, after some discussions with General Clark, decided to come over to the Allied side. And by the next day, all fighting west of Algiers ceased just before Patton was about to make a final assault on Casablanca.

On 10 November, Colonel Hewitt from the operations section of the II Corps staff came to see Raff in his improvised CP in a hangar at Tafaraoui. He told Colonel Raff that the 509th was being placed under the operational control of Gen. K. A. N. Anderson, the commander of the British First Army, charged with seizing the roads leading to Tunis. Colonel Hewitt wanted to know when the battalion could be ready for another jump and how many men would be ready. As events developed, Raff replied that he could have 150 ready by 13 November, 300 ready by 15 November, and another 150 on 16 November.

For Colonel Raff and the 509th Parachute Infantry Battalion the war was just beginning. By 1100 hours on 12 November, 150 men, with full equipment, that included repacked parachutes, left Tafaraoui to travel

250 miles east to Maison Blanche Aérodrome, the chief airport of Algiers, near General Anderson's headquarters that was aboard a ship in Algiers harbor. Two days later, another 170 fully equipped paratroopers, under the 509th's executive officer, Maj. Doyle Yardley, followed. The 509th was gearing up for another mission one day away.

4: On to the East

The sight of Maison Blanche as we glided in for a landing made one whistle in amazement," wrote Colonel Raff. "On it was the greatest concentration of aircraft I ever expect to see. . . . Over and above almost every type of American military plane, from P-38's to B-24's, there were British Walruses, Beaufighters, Hurricanes, Spitfires, wingtip to wingtip around the rim. Two or three hangars had slim, speedy-looking Dewoitine 520's crowded around their entrances. Alongside them were Potez bombers, Renaults, Caudrons and other strange looking craft with French markings. There was even a Nazi twin-engine Heinkel on the field."

After his arrival on the field on 12 November, Raff moved the battalion into hangar 3. In hangar 2, two companies of the British Parachute Brigade, commanded by Brigadier Flavell, were preparing for their mission the next morning. Raff talked to the officer in command, and was told that there was no need of his assistance in the brigade's mission. Flavell said that he was to jump two companies into Bône, contact the French garrison there, and then move on to Tunis.

On the night of 12 November Major des Veaux, the French liaison officer with the British airborne troops, escorted Raff to Algiers and to General Anderson's shipboard CP. Raff was surprised to find that General Clark was also there. Clark congratulated him on the success of the England-to-Oran operation. Raff quickly told him that it was anything but a success with five men dead, sixteen wounded, and eighty-eight missing—without any combat. He added that Tafaraoui had been taken by U.S. armor without any help from the 509th. But by nightfall, he said, he would have over 300 paratroopers ready to jump in and fight wherever he was ordered to go.

The next morning, General Anderson's operations officer called Raff to the headquarters in Algiers. "General Anderson wants you to go to Tébessa," the brigadier told him.

"Fine, when?" asked Raff.

"On the fifteenth."

"What's the mission?"

"To deny the aerodrome there to the Axis. Here's the only map we have. Look it over. Remember, Tébessa's cold and high. Carry enough food and ammunition to last six days." Raff looked at the map. Tébessa was near the Tunisian border, some 300 miles to the east. And no one was certain that the Germans had not already taken the airfield, or whether the French were friendly.

Raff hurried back to Maison Blanche, assembled his commanders and staff, and outlined the mission. He told them that Captain Morrow's D Company, Captain Berry's E Company, and elements of the Headquarters Company would jump directly onto the airfield at Tébessa.

On the day before the jump, just by chance, Raff had talked to a pair of Frenchmen at Maison Blanche who had just come from Tunis, and had asked them about Tébessa. One of them mentioned a nearby airfield at Youks-les-Bains that was used by French bombers, and told Raff that the field was three times larger than Tébessa. Raff had a French flying map, and the Frenchman marked a square on a spot on the road from Tébessa to Constantine. That was Youks-les-Bains. And that map, Raff noted, was the only information Major Wanamaker, his Air Corps flight leader, would have to find the DZ at Youks-les-Bains. Raff got in touch with General Anderson's headquarters and his mission was changed to seizing Youks-les-Bains and then sending a company on foot to take Tébessa. Raff thought to himself, what a change from the details, maps, and photos he had had on hand in England before the invasion jump!

The British again came to his aid. Brigadier Flavell gave the battalion wicker baskets with parachutes attached to use for dropping equipment and supplies. The panniers were just the right size for pushing out the door of a C-47. Major Marshall, Flavell's second in command, handed Raff an envelope containing 25,000 francs "for good will and intelligence purposes." The francs had supposedly been left in an Algiers bank by the German-Italian Armistice Commission. Raff guessed that the 509th would use the francs more for fresh eggs and other food than intelligence.

Late in the afternoon of 14 November the last of the 509th arrived from Tafaraoui. Major Yarborough and Jack Thompson, an American war correspondent, were with them. Thompson, said Raff, was "colorful, with his full black beard and mustache, [and] soon became known in the Algerian-Tunisian sector as the 'man with the beard.' His presence as one of my most trusted friends, as a member of my skimpy staff who pitched in as telephone orderly, runner, and journal clerk made him a concrete part of the adventure." And he would make his first jump the next day.

That afternoon Raff learned that the British paratroopers had landed at Bône, taken the airfield, allied themselves with the French in the city, and sent patrols east toward Tunis. But they had not yet run into any Germans.

To Raff, 0400 in the dark of the next morning came quickly. His cooks had been up much earlier, getting breakfast for the troops, some of whom were about to make their second combat jump in eight days. Squad leaders were rousing their men, sometimes not too gently. Take-off was scheduled for 0730. In the interim, the troops shaved, put on their jump suits and boots, ate breakfast, and checked weapons and ammunition. Some smoked one cigarette after another, "manifesting that something must be on their minds besides breakfast," thought Raff. In hangar 2, British paratroopers of Flavell's brigade were also up and getting ready for a "do," as they called it, a combat jump at Souk el Arba. "That day," wrote Raff, "the Allies planned to have their greatest combat parachute assault to date."

At 0530 on 15 November, 350 of the original 556 troopers of the 509th who had left England marched from hangar 3 to the parachute issue point, where they drew their mains and reserves, and then filed back to the hangar to "gear up" for the jump. After strapping on their chutes and personal equipment, they lined up in plane order and were given a safety inspection by their NCOs. Then in single file they marched out, clumsily, because of all their heavy, strapped-on gear, to their designated planes.

Major Wanamaker gave the signal for the troopers to climb aboard; on each plane, they loaded in reverse jumping order. On Raff's plane, Major Yarborough went first, followed by Jack Thompson, enlisted men from Headquarters Company, and finally the jumpmaster, Colonel Raff, last aboard and first to jump.

At 0730 sharp, the first of the twenty-two C-47s roared down the runway and headed east. Aloft, the planes formed into a V of V's and, es-

corted by British Spitfires and Hurricanes, flew down the coast instead
of going through thick clouds near the mountain peaks. After about two
hours the planes headed inland. The weather was still a problem, with
clouds hanging over the landscape, so Wanamaker ordered the other
planes to spread out to avoid a crash. The mist was so thick that Raff
thought they would have to turn back. Finally, though, the planes flew
out of the clouds, reformed in a V of V's, and flew past the white-walled
city of Constantine, a place that Raff thought looked like a Tibetan
lamasery.

Soon, to the right of the road the planes were following, Youks-les-
Bains appeared, close to the mountains. But a DZ was still uncertain.
Wanamaker led the planes in a 180-degree turn and flew north of the
road. Shortly after, Wanamaker said, "There it is," pointing to a clearing
near the airfield, and led the formation down to an altitude of 350 feet.
Someone in Raff's plane yelled, "There are soldiers in those trenches below." "It's too late now," Raff thought. He gave the crew chief the prearranged signal, a nod of his head, yelled "Go! Go!" and leaped from
the plane followed rapidly by the rest of his stick.

In the other planes the red lights came on, and the jumpmasters
opened the planes' doors and gave the commands to stand up and hook
up, check equipment, sound off for equipment check, and close in the
door. At the green light, the jumpmaster threw out the door bundles and
followed them out the door. Right behind him came the rest of his stick.
In a few minutes the entire 509th was in the air and then made their landings, some on very hard ground. One of the jumpers was Cpl. Lester C.
McLaney, a member of the original Parachute Test Platoon. He spotted
some troops standing on high ground, and, from their helmets and uniforms, he knew that they were French soldiers—not Germans. The
Americans had beaten the Nazis to Youks-les-Bains.

The DZ was covered with white personnel chutes and red, yellow, and
blue equipment chutes. Around the field some fifteen men had been
seriously injured, the most severely hurt being Capt. John Berry, whose
leg was broken in several places. Doc Alden fractured three bones in his
foot; two other men had compound fractures of their legs; and many
more had bumps and scratches. But Jack Thompson, who landed near
Major Yarborough, was surprised that on his first jump he had landed
unscathed, after only some twenty minutes of airborne instruction the
day before, including "now this thing is a parachute." Raff's men
streamed in from the far ends of the DZ and assembled under their com-

pany commanders. Raff found out that the jump injuries had resulted from three planes loads' jumping early and landing on a rocky rise short of the DZ. Doc Alden, in spite of his injury, tended the injured men while they waited for ambulances to come from Tébessa; he was later aided by French medical officers.

Raff moved the battalion off the DZ and had Captain Morrow's D Company dig a perimeter defense. Later Morrow coordinated his defense with the French. Raff sent Major Yardley and E Company, now under Lt. Archie Birkner, a total of 150 men, on foot to seize the airport at Tébessa, nine miles away. Raff looked around the area and saw that the French infantrymen defending Youks-les-Bains were well sited and entrenched, and supported by 75mm guns. On a rise to the east of the field, Raff also noted that the French could have fired on the DZ with all types of weapons; he realized that the 509th would have been slaughtered if the Germans had occupied those same positions.

Shortly afterward, a small group of French officers and men walked up to Raff at his impromptu DZ on some high ground by the DZ. One of the officers was Colonel Berges, the commander of the 3d Zouave Regiment, whose troops were defending Youks-les-Bains. "From the group of soldiers, a figure detached itself and walked toward Colonel Raff," wrote Yarborough. "Cautiously the French commander extended his hand. Raff took it. In an instant tension relaxed. The French surrounded us, patted us on the backs, offered to roll up our chutes and haul them to a safe place before 'les Arabes' got to them."

"French and American soldiers-in-arms encircled the small American flag we had carried in a knapsack from England for just such an occasion as this one," Raff wrote. "To serve as a memento, the red fouragere of the 3rd Zouaves, won by the unit after many citations in battle, was hung around my left shoulder by a private of the regiment. Needless to say, I was never without it during the long months that followed. I, in turn, presented an American flag to Colonel Berges."

After that meeting on the DZ, Raff, Thompson and Yarborough piled into Colonel Berges's Renault and headed for his command post in Tébessa. In the French mess, Raff presented him with an American flag that Berges hung on the same staff with the Zouave banner, heavy with battle honors. Berges, through his interpreter, Capt. Chauppard-Lallier, told Raff that the Germans were expected at any time—their patrols had been seen in the vicinity. Over a glass of red wine Berges said with emotion in his voice, "Now we will fight together. Now we will turn our guns toward the Boche. Together we will drive him from Tunisia and from France." The group drank to that. Then Berges unpinned his badge of the 3d Zouaves and fixed it to Raff's blouse. "From this day, our regiment is your regiment. You and your battalion are welcome at any time wherever the Troisieme Zouaves may be." The motto on the badge was in French: "J'y suis–j'y reste"—"I'm here, and here I stay."

At Tébessa Major Yardley and his men found no Germans on the ground, but they did find some in the air. The day after they arrived on the field at Tébessa, the men looked up and saw a German Ju 88 in a long glide about 600 feet off the ground, attempting to strafe the lone U.S. C-47 on the field. The troopers in the slit trenches around the field opened up with a withering blast of rifle fire, and the German plane, riddled with bullets, disappeared over the hills to the south, trailing a plume of smoke. That afternoon, Arabs brought in some of the wreckage and told a jubilant Major Yardley that the pilot had died in the crash.

In the old Roman fort where Colonel Berges had his headquarters in Tébessa, he gave Raff and his staff sleeping quarters and a room for his battalion CP. There Raff had telephones connected to Youks-les-Bains, the Tébessa airport, and General Clark's headquarters in Algiers. Sitting with his battalion simply dug in on the defensive was not the type of combat that the aggressive Raff wanted for his paratroopers, who were still untried in combat.

At Berges's CP, Raff was briefed on the enemy situation in the area, learning that many German transports and glider units were landing near Tunis. On a map, Berges showed him the mountain passes leading into Tébessa and pointed out the Gafsa-Gabès road as the easiest way for the Germans to come from Tripolitania to the west. Raff asked what French troops were available at Gafsa to stop the Germans. "Just a little group of thirty men with old-type armored cars and a few motorcycles. Really nothing," he said. Berges also told him that Colonel Schwartz was now the French commander in Tébessa. At lunch Raff talked to Schwartz, a crippled but very energetic commander, according to Raff, about the likelihood of Raff's going to Gafsa. Schwartz assured Raff that it would be very helpful to the French. Raff reasoned that from Gafsa he could reconnoiter to the southeast and, if permitted, move from there southeast to Gabès. That evening Raff called General Clark, who told him: "No, Raff, your mission is quite clear. A reconnaissance patrol forward to Gafsa would be all right. But don't—get this now—don't go one mile beyond Gafsa." Well, thought Raff, at least he could go to Gafsa.

"Raff was a human dynamo," according to Yarborough, who had returned to Tébessa from Clark's headquarters. "He told me, 'We're going right into Gafsa after the bastards.' The fact that his little force was operating without support or without certain re-supply bothered him none at all. He wanted Nazi hides and he was going after them as fast as he could."

For the reconnaissance trip to Gafsa, Colonel Schwartz turned over two buses to Raff, which he loaded with twenty of his paratroopers, each with sufficient food and ammunition for three days. On the top of each bus in the baggage rack, he posted two men with light machine guns. He planned to send one bus ahead and follow it an hour later with the other. After a lot of difficulty in getting reliable bus drivers, Raff and his reconnaissance force finally pushed along the eighty miles from Tébessa to Gafsa over narrow, twisting mountain roads, through defiles, a fir tree forest, and onto a flat plain.

At the entrance to the Gafsa compound Raff found French soldiers guarding the gate. When he met Commandant Manceau Demiau, the French officer in charge of the Chasseur d'Afrique patrols who were reconnoitering beyond Gafsa, he realized that he had run into a problem when Demiau asked him to set up his CP at the airport rather than in Gafsa. Shortly afterward, Raff and Demiau settled their differences and in time "became close friends." Demiau and his staff were a source of considerable intelligence that Raff was able to pass on to Clark's CP in Algiers.

Raff learned that the situation to the north was changing. Enemy armor and great numbers of Germans and Italians, reported by a Chasseur d'Afrique patrol, had moved into Kairouan—a Muslim holy city in Tunisia. Raff thought that he might have to move from Gafsa. His total strength there was two French armored cars, some French motorcyclists, 100 U.S. paratroopers (he had added sixty from Tébessa with Allied Force Headquarters permission), and fifteen armed British sailors who had come from vessels sunk in the Malta convoys.

Yarborough had flown back to Algiers and reported to Clark, who showed him a message from Tébessa saying that Raff had commandeered transportation and pushed over 150 kilometers southeast to Gafsa. "I'm sending Raff some help," Clark said. "I think he can probably use some infantry and some tank destroyers."

But before the U.S. tank destroyers could get to Raff's force, a column of Italian tanks started for Gafsa. Raff decided to withdraw to Feriana.

But before he left he had his men blow up a 40,000-gallon gasoline dump, his signal for his withdrawal. "Thus," said Raff, "Central Tunisia was abandoned to the Axis."

General Clark sent more U.S. troops to Raff's force, now called Raff's Tunisian Task Force. At about the same time Raff was promoted to full colonel. In addition to the 509th he had a battalion of the 26th Infantry under Lt. Col. Johnny Bowen, a company of Algerian Tirailleurs, a British antimine engineer detachment, and B Company, 701st Tank Destroyer Battalion under Capt. Gilbert Ellman. Major Yardley now became the commander of the 509th.

Local native intelligence indicated that Germans and Italians were in a defensive position at the Faid Pass. Raff decided to attack even though he had orders not to go beyond Gafsa. Supported by U.S. P-38 fighters, Raff's Ruffians, as they became known, battled the Germans and Italians for two weeks in a series of forays across the Algerian border into Tunisia. On the night of 1 December 1942, the force headed through Sidi-bou-zid and Kasserine and attacked Faid Pass. In an all-day battle, Raff's troops collected over 130 German and Italian prisoners of war (POWs) and left scores of enemy dead.

Since the three amphibious landings of Operation Torch, the Allies had been pushing to the east toward Tunisia's western border and by late November were within twenty miles of Tunis. But then, on 28 November, a German force under Gen. Jürgen von Arnim counterattacked and regained lost territory. By the middle of December 1942, the Allies were on a line in northern Tunisia fifty miles to the west of Tunis. In the south, General Rommel halted his retreat at Mareth in southern Tunisia , where the "Desert Fox" built a fortified line to block the advance of Gen. Bernard Montgomery's veteran British Eighth Army out of Egypt.

General Eisenhower had been impressed with the operations of Raff and his Ruffians. In his book, *Crusade in Europe,* he wrote: "Up to this time the only protection we had been able to establish in all the great region stretching from Tébessa southward to Gafsa had been provided by French irregulars reinforced and inspired by a small United States parachute detachment under the command of a gallant American, Colonel Edson D. Raff. The story of his operations in that region is a minor epic in itself. The deceptions he practiced, the speed with which he struck, his boldness and aggressiveness, kept the enemy confused during a period of weeks."

5: El Djem Bridge Raid

Within a week the 509th had had two combat jumps in North Africa, and a third was yet to come inside a month. It would be another disaster.

The Germans and Italians in North Africa were in a precarious situation. All of their equipment, vehicles, ammunition, and fuel had to be shipped in from Italy either by air or sea. Consequently there was a great deal of message traffic between Italy and North Africa. The Germans felt that their Enigma was the very best encoding machine and totally unbreakable. But the British, through their superb Ultra system, intercepted and decoded the German and Italian messages and knew when the enemy sea convoys would leave Sicily and attempt to make the thirty-six-hour trip to North Africa. With this foreknowledge, at least half the seaborne supplies meant for Rommel's forces in southern Tunisia ended up at the bottom of the Mediterranean Sea. To make matters worse, on 20 November Rommel learned that of fifty transport planes carrying fuel for his tanks, forty-five had been shot down. During a walk in the desert with one of his battalion commanders, Maj. Hans von Luck, Rommel said, "Luck, that's the end." But he had to fight on.

Hitler was aware of Rommel's desperate need for supplies and men and attempted to reinforce him through the port cities of Bizerte and Tunis, 100 miles from Sicily; both cities had all-weather airports. On 9 November, Luftwaffe transports and gliders began landing soldiers on the Tunis runway at the rate of 1,000 men per day. Tanks and artillery were ferried across by water. The men and equipment were then loaded on trains and reached Rommel and his Afrika Korps at the Axis defensive Mareth Line in southern Tunisia by way of the north-south Tunisian coastal railroad.

General Anderson realized that he had to stop the flow of men and supplies over this railroad by knocking out a vital railroad bridge near the village of El Djem. "The bridge had been bombed by the collective bombers of the air forces and, at least once, by Major Cochran in his P-40," wrote Colonel Raff. "Although much effort had been expended for no damage done by these attacks, the French insisted they were all a waste of time; that the railroad was not being used." Nonetheless General Anderson's staff decided that the bridge had to go.

Three weeks after the 509th's jump at Youks-les-Bains, all Raff's paratroopers, less an eighty-five man detachment commanded by Capt. Archie Birkner, had returned to Boufarik near Algiers. Raff was using Birkner's men to patrol and to help him defend the Thelepte airfield. After Raff's promotion to full colonel, Maj. Doyle Yardley took over command of the bulk of the 509th at Boufarik.

"I hadn't heard much about the third parachute mission until three C-47's, two of them loaded with paratroopers and one with supplies, flew into Thelepte with orders to proceed that night to a drop zone north of El Djem," wrote Colonel Raff. As soon as he found out the details of the mission, he tried to delay the operation for twenty-four hours so that he could arrange to have a C-47, protected by all of Major Cochran's fighters, land somewhere near the bridge the morning after the drop and pick up his paratroopers safely and quickly. However, he wrote that "Malta and other agencies had already sent word that the much-postponed mission would take place that night. I knew that a drop at the exact spot, even in partial moonlight, required considerable skill in night navigation and familiarity with terrain around the drop zone. Therefore, I talked Major Cochran into flying the mission as co-pilot of the lead troop carrier plane. He had been over the bridge so many times during past weeks in daylight, that if anyone could find it, he could. Cochran consented to try."

The parachute attack was set for the night of 26 December.

Cochran and his P-40s had been attacking the bridge in vain for a number of days. They had fired rockets and strafed the guard shacks at each end of the bridge, but the steel-girdered railroad bridge would not collapse.

Colonel Raff held Major Cochran in high esteem. He had watched Cochran and his squadron of P-40 Warhawks operating from the Thelepte airfield against the Luftwaffe in the air above that part of Tunisia and against enemy forces on the ground where Cochran's unit gained a reputation as the best fighter squadron in North Africa. Cochran was a "fighting Irishman who cooperated with us 1000 percent," wrote Colonel Raff. Later, Phil Cochran was the role model for Flip Corkin, the fighter pilot hero in "Terry and the Pirates," a popular comic strip at the time.

Second Lieutenant Dan A. DeLeo, a twenty-four-year-old who had enlisted in the Illinois National Guard in 1937 as a private and had then been commissioned, was not one of the original members of the 509th. He was one of 180 replacements who had come to Africa by boat after Operation Torch forces had landed and was in Captain Birkner's company at Thelepte airfield. After Raff found out that he could not postpone the parachute jump, he told DeLeo that he was to lead the attack to blow up the bridge, and to accomplish that mission, he would have a team of thirty-two men and 400 pounds of TNT. Included in his party, were five demolition experts from 509th's Headquarters Company, twenty-five men who had come with DeLeo from England, and two French paratroopers, 1st Sgt. Jean Guilhenjouan and Cpl. Paul Vullierme, both of whom had lived in the area and spoke Arabic fluently. The Frenchmen's main challenge was to guide the party about ninety miles back to friendly lines during hours of darkness after the raid. Raff told DeLeo that the C-47s would drop him and his party at night just north of the bridge in a wide open area, and then he and his team would hike south along the railroad tracks about five miles until they found the bridge. Then, still in darkness, they would blow the bridge with their hand-set explosives and make their way back to U.S. lines. If they ran into enemy opposition, Raff told DeLeo he was to split his team into small groups and infiltrate back to U.S. lines.

At 2130 hours on 26 December 1942 DeLeo and his men got ready for the drop. In addition to routine gear—weapons, ammunition, K-rations, main and reserve chutes, jump helmets, jump suits, and boots—each man had a pocket-sized, black plastic escape kit containing a small saw blade, some tough fishing line, a tiny magnetic compass, and about a dozen wooden matches. In a hangar near the airstrip, the men strapped on their parachutes and some sixty pounds of other equipment, shuffled to the three C-47s on the loading area, and climbed aboard. At 2230 the planes roared down the runway and lifted off in bright moonlight.

About an hour into the ninety-mile flight Cochran was having difficulty finding the objective. To make certain of his location, his and the other two C-47s circled El Djem. Inside the blacked-out planes the men were smoking their last cigarettes before the jump. After circling El Djem Cochran led the formation north, parallel to, and just east of the railroad track. When Cochran thought he was over the selected DZ, he switched on the red light just to the right of the jump door. In his plane, DeLeo, the jumpmaster, gave the usual commands to "stand up, hook up, check equipment, and close in the door." When he switched on the green light, DeLeo leaped out the door, followed rapidly by his stick of jumpers. The other planeloads followed; two of the C-47s parachuted the TNT loads that had been hooked up under the planes.

In the darkness the men could not see the ground. But they landed, most with jarring impacts. Privates Charlie Doyle and Roland W. Rondeau were two of DeLeo's men and, like the rest of the team, they experienced blacked-out rides to the uneven ground and rough landings near the railroad tracks. Lying on the ground, they heard the planes droning off in the night and the landings of the rest of the team.

DeLeo quickly found the railroad tracks and his predesignated assembly point, and turned on a dim signal light. Within a half-hour he assembled all his men—but it took another hour to find both bundles of explosives. The demolitions team broke up the bundles and passed blocks of the explosive to the men detailed to blow the bridge. When they were ready, DeLeo and his men started moving south along the tracks, confident that the bridge was just a short distance ahead.

A couple of hours later, back at Thelepte, Raff watched the three C-47s return safely and park. He walked out to one of the planes and talked to the airmen, becoming convinced that the planes had dropped the paratroopers at the preselected DZ. In reality, though, DeLeo and his men had been dropped about a mile south of the bridge.

DeLeo and his paratroopers trudged southward along the tracks, confident that shortly they would find the bridge. For a couple of hours, they stumbled stealthily along the railroad, not certain that the drop had been undetected by the Germans in the area. Finally, after another hour of walking, DeLeo called a halt. His weary men, burdened with their heavy packs, took a break in an orchard that turned out to be only a mile from the Axis-occupied town of El Djem.

By then DeLeo was becoming apprehensive; he knew that he should have already reached the bridge. Two men he sent south to find it came back a half-hour later and reported that the bridge was nowhere in sight. DeLeo was greatly alarmed, now calculating that the C-47s had dropped his team far more than five miles to the north of the bridge. So he kept up the march to the south.

At daybreak he called a halt. Studying the terrain around him, he saw that he was standing in wide-open land with some hills in the distance. He dug his map and compass out of his pocket and, with some back azimuths penciled on his map and the help of his two French guides, learned the rotten truth: his team was twenty miles south of the bridge. He had been marching all night in the wrong direction.

He realized that he could not go back twenty miles to the bridge, given the daylight, the exhausted condition of his troops, and the possibility of enemy forces in the immediate area. As an alternative, he decided to blow a building that he saw some two hundred yards away, beside the tracks. One of his men had inspected it and found that inside was a lot of electrical equipment that apparently controlled switches on the railroad. He also decided to blow up as much of the railroad track as his TNT loads would permit. He told his demolition men to put explosives in the building and along about a hundred yards of track as fast as they could. All explosives were hooked to one detonator.

As the demolition troops were getting ready to set off the explosives, one of the DeLeo's lookouts to the south ran back and said that he had spotted what looked like a platoon of Germans about a mile away moving up the tracks toward them. Another lookout to the north raced in and reported that some Germans were approaching from the north. Apparently, the Arabs he had seen on the DZ earlier collecting parachutes had reported their presence to the Germans. Seeing that he and his men were in a trap, DeLeo gathered his troops around him and gave them the bad news. Then he told all the men not involved with the demolitions to take off in small groups immediately, head across country about ninety miles west to U.S. lines, and travel only at night. He told the demolition men to detonate the explosives and then take off. A few minutes later, 400 pounds of TNT blasted the area, a hundred yards of track went spilling across the ground, and debris from the control building filled the sky.

Lieutenant DeLeo, Pvt. Roland Rondeau, Sgt. John Betters, and Pvt. Frank Romero, along with the two French guides, formed one group and headed west. They hid out during the day and trudged on the next night. The next morning, they hid in a thicket along a road, slept a few hours, and ate what little food they had left. Occasionally they heard a truck

pass by on the road, headed west. DeLeo, aware that there was a long
foot march from friendly lines, decided to high-jack a vehicle. He waited
patiently for the right one to pass by. As luck would have it, the next vehicle was just what he wanted—a small pickup truck with only a driver
in the cab and the bed covered with a canvas tarpaulin—perfect place
to hide the men with him.

DeLeo took off his helmet, held his pistol behind him, walked out on
the road, and flagged down the vehicle. The Italian driver stopped, stuck
his head out the window, and stared into DeLeo's .45 Colt. DeLeo
climbed into the cab, and his men scrambled from the woods and
jumped into the back of the pickup under the tarpaulin. In fluent Italian DeLeo told the driver to head west and to do nothing foolish. In the
cab DeLeo found a white scarf that he wrapped around his head, to look
somewhat like an Arab, he thought.

A few miles down the road, DeLeo was startled to see a column of German soldiers marching on both sides of the road, toward the truck. He
told his men about the enemy troops on the road and to get their
weapons ready. He pushed his pistol into the side of the driver who got
the message—no shenanigans. The truck moved on through the Germans who paid it no attention. DeLeo breathed a sigh of relief.

But after a couple of hours the truck's engine began to rattle and rumble, and with a final loud bang, the vehicle chugged to a halt. The scared
driver tried unsuccessfully to restart the motor. Finally, one of DeLeo's
men inspected the engine and found that it had thrown a rod. Still fifty
miles west of U.S lines, DeLeo decided to take the driver along so that
he could not report them to the Germans. The six men trudged through
the countryside by night and hid in the bushes along the road during
the day. They bartered with the Arab villagers for food and, on a couple
of occasions, were almost captured. Four days later, DeLeo and his team
found a French outpost, and some three weeks after their ill-fated jump
made it safely back to U.S. lines. Of the thirty paratroopers who made
the jump only six returned.

One of them was Pvt. Michael P. Underhill, a rifleman who was hik-
ing to the west with two demolition men. He was armed with his M1
Garand rifle, sixty rounds of ammunition, and four hand grenades. The
demolition men had only their Colt .45 pistols. On the trek west, he took
the point and led them up a small hill. To their horror, they soon found
that they were being scouted after by what looked like a platoon of enemy soldiers. What turned out to be Italian troops fired at the three

paratroopers, and Underhill returned the fire. He told the demolition men to move out while he held off the enemy. Later that night the three were able to reassemble in nearby woods. The demolition men decided that the danger was too great and that they were going to surrender, but Underhill would have none of it, saying, "Not me. I'm going home." They split up. The demolition men walked into the Italian lines with their hands up, while Underhill walked around the Italians, threw a grenade into an enemy truck, killing or wounding two soldiers, and took off.

He hiked to the west, mostly at night, hiding in bushes from Axis patrols. He fed himself on the remains of his K-rations and some eggs and water he bought from friendly Arabs. "They cost too much, but I had to buy them," Underhill told Colonel Raff later at his command post in Feriana.

"Behind the Allied lines, he kept right on walking," wrote Colonel Raff.

> Fortunately, for the end of the story, there was a little town called Hadjeb el Aioun through which he had to pass to continue his westward trek, otherwise it might have ended at the Atlantic Ocean. French troops occupying the town told Captain Roworth about "an American parachutist who had come in the night before." Roworth gave him a lift in a jeep to Feriana.
>
> The stirring part of the whole story is that mighty Underhill, though much of a man, is a slight, modest youth barely 18 years old. He had learned to be self-reliant on a Pennsylvania farm which he managed himself.
>
> To my way of thinking, Corporal Underhill is the man every soldier ought to be. The determination and tenacity he displayed, I like to feel, is innate in every American paratrooper.

The 509th had no more combat jumps in Africa but continued to fight as straight infantrymen with Anderson's forces. For a number of months, bitter fighting continued in North Africa. In February of 1943 Rommel, the Desert Fox, launched a desperate and vicious surprise attack against the unprepared U.S. ground forces defending the Kasserine Pass. Rommel's seasoned Axis forces fought through the pass until they butted up against Eisenhower's well-organized Allied defenses of armor, artillery, and air power. The 509th was a part of those defenses. Once Rommel recognized that his offensive was being overpowered he withdrew, but taking over 2,000 U.S. prisoners with him.

The Axis domination of North Africa ended in May 1943, when all their forces had been forced into a small area in northeastern Tunisia. Any escape by Rommel's forces to Italy was blocked by the Allied naval blockade. During the last few weeks of combat the Germans and Italians lost some 248,000 men, including the remnants of Rommel's Afrika Korps. An ill Rommel was evacuated to Germany for hospitalization before the end of the battle. His successor, Col. Gen. Jürgen von Arnim, and Italy's Field Marshal Alessandro Messe were captured.

When the fighting ended in North Africa, the 509th reassembled and moved by train back to Oujda, French Morocco, "the place that God forgot," according to the 509th troopers. There they moved into a hastily built tent camp—Camp Kunkle, named for Lt. David Kunkle, who had been killed in action on Torch D day.

What to do next was the obvious question that faced the Allied High Command after Rommel's defeat in North Africa. On 13 January 1943 the Allies had held a summit conference at Hotel Anfa, near Casablanca, to answer that specific question. Present at the conference were President Roosevelt, Prime Minister Winston Churchill, Gen. George Marshall, Gen. Sir Alan Brooke, and other top military brass from the Combined Chiefs of Staff.

In spite of the fact that by the spring of 1943 the United States had thousands of troops in Africa and Britain, the top planners decided that an invasion of France, as the major offensive against Germany, was impossible for at least another year. Churchill wanted to strike at the "soft underbelly" of Europe, the Balkans. The Americans were opposed to that because Marshall wanted to wait until the Allies were fully prepared for the maximum blow against the Axis. Churchill's idea did not carry. Political considerations, particularly Stalin's urgent request for a massive offensive against Germany, were also important at this stage of the war. Thus came the decision to invade Sicily and, if that went well, to invade Italy. Another decision of the joint conference was Roosevelt's and Churchill's agreeing to appoint Eisenhower as supreme commander in the Mediterranean Theater, Gen. Sir Harold R. L. G. Alexander as deputy and commander of all ground troops, and Air Chief Marshal Sir Arthur Tedder to direct all air operations.

On 23 January, Eisenhower received a top secret message: "The Combined Chiefs of Staff have resolved that an attack against Sicily will be launched in 1943 with the target date as the period of the favorable July moon."

In a May 1943 Trident Conference in Washington, D.C., the Americans and British agreed to go from Sicily to Italy, designated 1 May 1944 as the firm date for the cross-Channel invasion, and agreed to build up forces for the major assault in England.

Operation Husky, the code name for the invasion of Sicily, was the next platform for the use of U.S. airborne forces.

6: Operation Husky

In late April 1943 the 82d Airborne Division troopers, disguised as ordinary soldiers with no jump wings, jump boots, or division insignia, boarded troop trains at Fort Bragg and headed for Camp Edwards, Massachusetts. They spent a week there in isolation and then again boarded trains that took them to ships for a twelve-day trip across the Atlantic. At 1515 hours, on 10 May, the first paratrooper of the 82d stepped ashore at Casablanca. For three days the division bivouacked in a staging area north of the city. The troops sweltered in the heat and wondered what would come next. What came next was a rough ride by truck and rail to Oujda, the same place where the veteran troopers of the 509th, proud of their being the first U.S. paratroopers to be used in combat, had found themselves in a primitive tent camp licking their wounds, recuperating, reequipping, remanning, and wondering "what went wrong."

Much to the disgust of Maj. Doyle Yardley, the 509th's new commander, and his troops, the veteran and proud troopers of the 509th were attached tactically and administratively to the 82d. The cocky 509th considered itself far superior to the green, untested 82d and told the 82d troopers in many a fist-fight in Oujda dives that the 82d was attached to the 509th. The glider regimental combat team of the 82d moved on about twelve miles east of Oujda to Marina under the command of Brig. Gen. Charles L. Keerans Jr., a forty-four-year-old West Pointer (class of 1919); the 82d's assistant division commander. Major General Matthew B. Ridgway, a forty-seven-year-old graduate of West Point (class of 1917), and the brilliant division artillery commander, Brig. Gen. Maxwell D. Taylor, a forty-two-year-old West Pointer (number four academically, class of 1922), remained at Oujda with the bulk of the division.

For the next seven weeks, the paratroopers and glidermen of the 82d
spent their time in rigorous training in the broiling desert heat, endured
long day and night hikes with full field equipment, fired their weapons
in live-fire exercises, made parachute jumps and glider landings, fought
hand-to-hand combat drills, and soldiered through a full division review
for the brass, including Generals Eisenhower, Bradley, Patton, Clark, and
Spaatz, as well as the sultan of Morocco and the high commissioner of
Spanish Morocco. At this parade, as the erect and proud troops were
passing in military review on the ground, paratroopers were jumping behind them and gliders were landing off to the side.

Life in Africa in the bivouacs of pup tents was not ideal by any stretch
of the imagination. Dysentery was common. The food was filled with dust
and sand, and the coffee speckled with flies. The troopers began to realize that combat might be easier and talked endlessly of where that
would be.

On 14 May, General Ridgway called Col. James M. Gavin, a thirty-six-
year-old graduate of West Point (class of 1929), to his makeshift 82d Airborne Division squad tent CP and told him that his regiment, the 505th
Parachute Infantry, reinforced by the 456th Parachute Field Artillery Battalion, the 3d Battalion of Col. Reuben H. Tucker's 504th Parachute Infantry, and B Company of the 307th Engineer Battalion—some 3,406 paratroopers—would parachute into Sicily sometime in the future. Ridgway
mentioned that there was enough airlift for only one regimental combat
team on D day and that the jump was scheduled for a night under a full
moon—with the jump close to midnight. Ridgway did not mention it, nor
did he need to remind Colonel Gavin, that this operation would become
the first major night massed parachute jump in history. When Colonel
"Tommy" Tucker (class of 1935) learned that the 505th, not the 504th,
would make the initial jump, he was unhappy because he hated to "play
second fiddle." In the battles to come, though, he would have the chance
to prove time and again his superb, out-front combat leadership.

Preparations for Operation Husky began in earnest immediately after the Casablanca Conference of January 1943 at which General Eisenhower was named supreme Allied commander. His three deputies for
air, land, and sea were British. General Sir Harold Alexander was the
principal deputy and the actual commander of the Allied land forces,
the 15th Army Group consisting of Gen. George S. Patton's U.S. Seventh
Army and Gen. Bernard Montgomery's British Eighth Army. When General Ridgway learned that Maj. Gen. G. F. "Hoppy" Hopkinson, com-

mander of the British 1st Airborne Division, was to be in charge of the airborne phase of the operation, he was decidedly provoked. To balance matters, he sent General Taylor to the Allied headquarters in Algiers to represent him and to ensure that U.S. airborne forces were properly deployed.

With the operation scheduled for 10 July 1943, Eisenhower's planners moved rapidly ahead. They considered three important factors: the island's terrain, the location of the major airfields and major ports, and the size and location of the enemy forces.

Sicily is triangle-shaped, slightly larger than Vermont, and encompasses some 10,000 square miles, a "mountainous, inhospitable land, the steppingstone between Africa and Europe," in Gavin's words. "Too small in size and resources to be an independent nation, yet too large to be ignored, it has played a key role in the affairs of the Western world since the dawn of history. 'Always raped but never loved' was the way one writer described it." Mount Etna, at 10,000 feet, is the island's most prominent feature. The port of Messina, then heavily defended, in the northeastern corner of the island is the primary transit point between Sicily and Italy, and thus it became the strategic objective of the campaign. Unfortunately Messina, with its rugged terrain and narrow beaches, was beyond the range of North Africa–based fighter aircraft. Therefore, Allied planners had to rule it out as the initial objective. The widest and most accessible beaches for amphibious landings are along the island's southeastern and western shores. Sicily's other major ports—Palermo, Catania, Augusta, and Syracuse—are in the northwestern and southeastern corners of the island, along with most of the island's thirty major airfields.

On the island were twelve Italian divisions, six in fixed coastal positions and six with mobility, altogether some 240,000 troops. Two of the mobile divisions, Livorno and Napoli, "very good divisions" according to Gavin, were in the area of possible Allied assault landings. On the island, the Germans had the Hermann Göring Tank and understrength 15th Panzer Grenadier Divisions, about 30,000 men. Field Marshal Albrecht Kesselring promised two more divisions to the commander of all the Axis ground forces, Italy's General of the Army Alfredo Guzzoni, a sixty-six-year-old veteran called out of retirement to organize the defenses of Sicily, a land he had never before set foot on. His command was the Italian VI Army. Many of his Italian units were short of equipment, training, and morale; many Italian soldiers were fed up with Mussolini's disastrous war and could surrender easily.

The Germans and the Italians had, of course, no positive idea of the Allied strategy, or where the Allies would strike next. The Italians felt that since it was closest to the strong Allied forces in North Africa, Sicily would be the target, with landings on the southeastern shores of the island. The Germans, however, were undecided. They knew that the British had sent reinforcements to Greece in the spring of 1941, and Hitler's staff had seemed to divine, with some accuracy, that Churchill wanted to hit Europe's "soft underbelly," the Balkans, from command and logistic bases near Cairo.

To give some credence to the German suspicions, the British devised an elaborate hoax. They wrapped the body of a dead British soldier who had died from pneumonia (dubbed "Major Martin") in the uniform of a Royal Navy courier, and handcuffed to his wrist an attaché case containing a number of sealed envelopes addressed to key British diplomats in Cairo. The correspondence cleverly made clear Allied intentions to land in Greece and possibly Sardinia. On 20 April 1943 the British launched the body from a submarine about a mile off Huelva, Spain, where the tide would wash it ashore. Three days later, some Spaniards picked up "Major Martin" and turned the body over to the Spanish Ministry of Marine. The British naval attaché in Madrid duly requested the return of the body and papers. When he received them he discovered that, as planned, the papers had been extracted and photographed and turned over to the Germans, who accepted them as genuine.

The Italians, however, were unconvinced. In spite of the bogus evidence, they still believed that the Allies must land in Sicily from bases in North Africa. On 12 May Adm. Karl Dönitz, who had just returned from a meeting with Mussolini, reported the Duce's opinion to Hitler. Later Dönitz recorded in his diary: "The Führer does not agree with the Duce that the most likely invasion point is Sicily. Furthermore, he believes that the discovered Anglo-Saxon order confirms the assumption that the planned attack will be directed mainly against Sardinia and the Peloponnesus." So convinced was Hitler by the British hoax that on 25 July, two weeks after the Sicilian invasion, he sent his favorite general, Rommel, to take command of all German forces in Greece. He moved the 1st Panzer Division from France to the town of Tripolis in Greece, ordered his navy to lay three new minefields off Greece, and, in early June, sent a group of German torpedo boats from Sicily to Greece.

The strategic Allied objective in Sicily was, obviously, the port city of Messina, three miles from the Italian mainland across the Strait of

Messina. The invasion plan called for over seven Allied divisions to wade ashore along a 100-mile front in southeastern Sicily. On the right, Gen. Bernard Montgomery's Eighth Army of four divisions, an independent brigade, and a commando force would land on the southeast side of Sicily along a forty-mile front stretching from the Pachino Peninsula north along the Gulf of Noto to a point just south of Syracuse. To the west, Patton's Seventh Army of three divisions would land along a wide front in the Gulf of Gela. Once ashore, the Eighth Army would fight to the north, seizing in succession Augusta, Catania, and the airfields at Gerbini before making the final thrust on Messina. The Seventh Army would seize several airfields between Licata and Comiso and then advance inland about twenty miles, to protect the western flank of the Eighth Army's beachhead. Unfortunately, General Alexander never gave any detailed plans for the campaign beyond the initial amphibious landings. This oversight paved the way for disagreement between Montgomery and the volatile Patton once the battle for Sicily was under way.

Patton arranged his forces with Maj. Gen. Troy Middleton's 45th Infantry Division landing near Scoglitti and then moving northeast toward Comiso and Ragusa to link up with Montgomery's left flank. In the center, Maj. Gen. Terry de la Mesa Allen's 1st Infantry Division, reinforced with two Ranger battalions under the command of Lt. Col. William O. Darby, would secure Gela and its airfields and then push north to Niscemi. On Allen's left was Maj. Gen. Lucian K. Truscott's 3d Division, reinforced by a Ranger battalion and Combat Command A of the 2d Armored Division, with orders to land at Licata and protect the left flank of the U.S. beachhead. Patton grouped the 45th and 1st Divisions under Lt. Gen. Omar Bradley's II Corps and kept the 3d Division under Seventh Army. In reserve, he had the rest of the 2d Armored Division, the 9th Infantry Division, a regiment from the 1st Infantry Division, and a battalion of French Moroccan troops. All of the amphibious landings were scheduled to go ashore at 0245, 10 July 1943.

The airborne phase of Operation Husky was developed by a combined U.S.-British team working at the Allied headquarters in Algiers. The senior U.S. airborne advisor was Maj. Gen. Joseph M. Swing (class of 1915, and classmate of General Eisenhower), called temporarily from his new command, the recently activated 11th Airborne Division at Camp Mackall, North Carolina. The British advisor was Maj. Gen. F. A. M. Browning.

Elements of two airborne divisions were to land behind enemy lines in four separate U.S. and British operations, both parachute and glider. Leading the attack during the hours of darkness on 9–10 July was Operation Ladbroke, 1,600 men of the British 1st Air Landing Brigade under Brigadier P. H. W. "Pip" Hicks, landing by gliders just below Syracuse to seize key terrain, including the Ponte Grande Bridge needed by Montgomery's troops to reach Syracuse. About one hour after Ladbroke came Husky 1, in which Gavin's 505th Airborne Regimental Combat Team would parachute onto the Piano Lupo heights north and northeast of Gela, on Sicily's southern shore. His mission was to block all roads leading to Patton's beachhead near Gela, to confuse the enemy about the main amphibious effort, tie up Axis communications, and secure the DZ for Husky 2, Tucker's 504th on the night of 11 July. The fourth airborne operation, Fustian, was a parachute landing by the British 1st Parachute Brigade on the night of 13 July to capture the Primasole Bridge north of Lentini, paving the way for Montgomery to move rapidly across the flatlands of Sicily's eastern shore to capture Messina.

Gavin, of course, prepared himself for the operation. One month before D day, on the night of 9 June he, two of his battalion commanders, and two Air Corps troop carrier wing commanders managed to get a flight to Malta and there join five RAF fighter pilots for a nighttime reconnaissance of their assigned flight routes and drop zones. As the planes skirted the south coast of Sicily, the airborne passengers were delighted to note that their ground checkpoints showed up clearly in the moonlight. After the flight, Gavin wrote that "knowing the exact date of our mission gave a tremendous stimulation to our desire to train, but we soon learned that there was little time available for training."

On 26 May Gavin had a meeting with Patton, and on the next day he and Ridgway visited General Bradley's headquarters in Relizane. On 6 June he met with the 1st Division staff for a final briefing. "I was looking forward to hearing the seasoned and legendary Terry Allen tell us what to do," wrote Gavin. "When his staff got through explaining what was expected of us, he concluded by saying, 'I don't want any God-damned bellyaching. I want you to do your job and let me know what you are doing.' So much for the five-paragraph field order."

By 4 July, the division's two parachute regimental combat teams and the attached 509th had been shuttled eastward in wobbly old boxcars (known as "40-and-8s"—forty troops or eight mules) hundreds of miles across Algeria from French Morocco to ten airfields around the city of Kairouan. The division's array of pup tents was dispersed in a thirty-mile arc because the bivouacs were well within range of Axis planes flying out of Italy and southern France. Once again the troops, still unaware of their next move—combat or endless training in the North African heat—began to think that combat might be a welcome relief. Their evenings were highlighted occasionally by USO shows including, among other stars, Bob Hope and Frances Langford.

Finally, on the morning of 7 July, the unit commanders of the division received their orders—within forty-eight hours many of them would parachute into Sicily during the hours of darkness, preceding the amphibious landings. The last paragraph of Gavin's operations order to his commanders emphasized one point: all paratroopers and their gear would be dropped onto the island of Sicily even if the C-47 pilots had not found the proper DZs in the dark. The planes would return to Africa empty of paratroopers.

The 226 C-47s carrying his troopers belonged to Brig. Gen. Harold L. Clark's 52d Troop Carrier Wing, based on airstrips around Kairouan. In briefings at the strips the day before the invasion, the pilots got their missions and flight paths. They were warned that, because of Allied ships moving toward Sicily, their flight route would not be direct route of 350 miles. After assembling over Kairouan, said their briefers, they would fly a 415-mile dogleg course across the Mediterranean, southeast to Chergui Island then east to Malta, then north to the southeast corner of Sicily, then west to the Gela area, and then north to the DZ. Near the DZ, the planes would climb from 200 feet, their low flight altitude over water to avoid enemy radio-directional finders to 600 feet for the drop. The large pond north of the Acate River was the "go point" where the pilots would turn on the green jump lights, thus completing their 3.5-hour flight. The pilots listened with great interest, leaning forward on their ammunition box seats to catch every word and map direction. Even with the lack of experience for most of them, they knew that this was not a routine training mission.

"The fateful day of July 9, 1943, seemed to rush upon us," wrote Gavin, "so busy were we with last-minute preparations, and almost before we realized it, we were gathered in small groups under the wings of our C-47s ready for loading and takeoff. . . . " Because of security restrictions, it had not been possible to inform every trooper of his destination until just before take-off. Then each was given a small slip of paper written by Gavin which read (in part): "You will spearhead the landing of an American Force upon the island of SICILY. . . . You have been given the means to do the job and you are backed up by the largest assemblage of air power in the world's history.

"The eyes of the world are upon you. The hopes and prayers of every American go with you. . . ."

Two hours before the 505th took off, 144 British Horsa and U.S. Waco gliders towed by U.S. C-47s and British Albermarle bombers and carrying the British 1st Air Landing Brigade, took off for Ponte Grande, a bridge south of Syracuse. When the airplane pilots sighted the Sicily shore they began climbing to 1,500 feet, their release altitude. Almost simultaneously, shore batteries opened fire. The pilots took evasive action but, in the darkness and in a tangled formation, they cut the gliders loose too soon, resulting in one of the worst glider disasters of the war. Some ninety gliders, loaded with combat soldiers, fell into the sea. The rest of the gliders crash-landed along the coast. Only twelve gliders actually made it to the designated landing zone near the bridge, but, unbelievably, eighty-three roughed-up British stalwarts in those gliders grouped together and took the bridge.

Back at the airstrips Colonel Gavin's paratroopers strapped on their parachutes and individual gear. Each man carried either an M1 Garand rifle, a submachine gun or carbine rifle; a spring-loaded jump knife in a chest-high zippered pocket of his jump suit—easy to get at if he needed to cut a strangling parachute riser cord; bandoliers of ammunition across his chest; grenades in his jump suit's reinforced pockets; and, in addition, a fold-up entrenching tool, gas mask, canteen, first aid packet, K- and D-rations (the latter a concentrated chocolate bar), field bags with extra clothing, steel jump helmet, and jump boots. Each trooper was loaded down with 80 to 90 pounds of gear.

As the "load up" command was relayed across the airfields, the single files of troopers shuffled to the planes, one by one climbed up the four steps to the cabins, and step by step struggled to their assigned bucket seats in the C-47s. They had been waiting for this moment during months of training, parachuting, running, crawling under barbed wire with machine guns firing over their heads, hurling grenades, rushing through squad and platoon exercises, hauling themselves over barricades, firing hundreds of rounds down range, sweltering in the North African heat, and being indoctrinated with their superiority as airborne soldiers. Their final test was 415 air miles across the Mediterranean.

"The pilots were revving up their engines and we were ready to roll down the runway when an airman from the weather station ran up to the door of the plane yelling for me," wrote Colonel Gavin. "'Colonel Gavin, is Colonel Gavin here?' 'Here I am,' I answered, and he yelled, 'I was told to tell you that the wind is going to be thirty-five miles an hour, west to east.' He added, 'They thought you'd want to know.'"

"Well, I did, but there was nothing I could do about it. Training jumps had normally been canceled when the wind reached about fifteen miles an hour. But we couldn't change plans now."

In unison, the C-47 pilots revved their motors, taxied slowly to take-off positions, and then one by one took off in the fading light, forming a V of V's in the darkening sky, and heading for Malta, their first checkpoint. But the high winds blew the armada far off course and broke up the formation. Some of the pilots found themselves headed up the east coast of Sicily rather than along its southern shore but they recognized their error and headed west. Others simply headed inland and dropped their paratroopers where they thought the DZ was. Only one-eighth of the 505th Regimental Combat Team was dropped as planned in front of the 1st Division. The remainder landed all around the U.S. 45th Division, the Canadians, and the British. But at least they were in Sicily, albeit scattered some sixty miles across the island, all the way from Cap Moto to Licata. The last man parachuted onto Sicily at about 0100 on 10 July.

Several planeloads of troopers from the 3d Battalion and regimental headquarters dropped in front of the British army. When they assembled they found that they had an unusual problem. The U.S. challenge was "George" and the countersign, "Marshall." The British had a different code of recognition. "To the dismay of the American paratroopers," remembered Colonel Gavin, "they found that 'George' was greeted with a fusillade of fire. One big, burly Irishman, well over six feet tall, in the Regimental Demolitions Platoon, talked to me about his experience afterward. When first challenged, he was shot at, so he decided to hide and grab any British soldier he could get close to and explain his predicament. Soon a British soldier came by. He jumped out and pinned his arms to his sides and told him who he was. Thus he learned the British countersign and survived. That detachment fought side by side with the British for several days, but was finally put aboard a boat and sent to the American landing beaches near Gela."

The 2d Battalion of the 505th, commanded by Maj. Mark Alexander, landed far to the east, about fifteen miles from Gela, near the town of San Croce Camerina. Alexander's jump had not been easy. As his plane crossed the Mediterranean, he had been at the door looking for land-marks. The red warning light came on and his troops stood up, hooked up, and closed in the door, right behind him. Suddenly the green light came on. The men behind him tried to push him out the door, but he fought them off, knowing full well that they were still over the sea. Then he unhooked, went up to the pilot, and yelled at him over the noise of the motors, "What in the hell are you doing?" All the pilot could say was that "the co-pilot was in too much of a hurry." Alexander hurried back to his position at the door. Soon the plane crossed the coast, it took some tracer fire, but the battalion jumped—and landed on solid ground among a number of huge pillboxes several stories high. Fortunately, most of the troopers landed close to one another.

Once Alexander had assembled enough men, they got into a firefight with the Italians in the pillboxes but soon learned to neutralize the pill-boxes by firing at the slits and then throwing in grenades when they could crawl close enough. The action was not without casualties. Lieu-tenant Norman Sprinkle and five of his men were killed by machine gun fire as they raced across open ground against one of the bunkers. In a short time, though, Alexander's men had subdued the Italians in the bunkers. And soon thirty-six survivors came out of the pillboxes with arms raised overhead to surrender.

The battalion fought through most of the night and, by daybreak, Ma-jor Alexander had assembled the majority of his men, 455 in all. The bat-talion then moved two miles south toward the coast near the town of Ma-rina di Ragusa. En route, he ran into Lt. Col. Harrison Harden Jr., commander of the 456th Parachute Field Artillery Battalion, and twenty-one of his men pulling a 75mm pack howitzer and thirty-one shells. Near Marina di Ragusa he found some coastal forts with coast artillery guns aimed seaward. With some bravado he had Colonel Harden's pack 75 lob a few rounds at the fort; in a short time, the white flags flew over the fort and some 100 Italians surrendered.

Later his battalion moved north using donkeys, carts, and wheelbar-rows to carry their weapons and ammunition. By late afternoon, the bat-talion had captured San Croce Camerina and then the town of Vittoria. By sundown of D day, the 2d Battalion of the 505th was in control of a large section of the beachhead in front of the 45th Division's landing zone. (Alexander and his men rejoined the 82d on 12 July.)

Lieutenant Colonel Art "Hardnose" Gorham (class of 1938) com-manded the 1st Battalion of the 505th. The targeted DZ for his battalion was at Objective Y, the Piano Lupo, a hill about 172 meters high that dominated the approaches to the Ponte Olivo airfield. His mission was to block Axis forces from moving southward, to control the Ponte Olivo airfield by fire, and to assist in taking Objective Y. Shortly after the operation, Capt. Edwin A. Sayre, commander of A Company, 1st Battalion, 505th, wrote:

A Company took off at 2030 hours for the first check point at Malta. I do not know whether or not we saw Malta as I had never seen it before, but when we were to arrive there I thought I saw a light. In any event, we continued and about fifteen minutes before the scheduled jump time we could see flashes of gunfire through the door of the plane, on the left. This surprised me, because I had expected to see Sicily appear on the right. There was considerable firing, and the pilot turned to the right away from the island. We figured out later that we had hit the coast of Sicily somewhere between Noto and Siracusa.

We circled to the right, going out to sea, and came back in toward the southern coast. We followed along the shore until we saw the lake, which was a check point. The squadron then turned in toward the island. About one minute after the turn, we met with heavy ack-ack, apparently coming from the Ponte Olivo airdrome. The squadron turned to the right to avoid this fire and shortly thereafter the green light was given. It was about 0035.

Planes were under heavy machine gun fire when we jumped, and there was a lot of firing on the ground. By 0230 I had assembled fifteen men from the company and contacted the battalion executive officer. Company A was to attack a point from which about four machine guns were firing. We first attacked at 0400. The point from which the machine guns were firing was a garrison surrounded by pillboxes and was pretty strong. The attack was held up until about 0530 at which time fifty more men had been assembled. The attack was resumed and the garrison was killed or captured by 0615. It was held by one hundred Italians, with German noncoms from the Hermann Goering Panzer Division. We could hear a lot of fire in the valley—up toward Niscemi and down toward the beach. At about 0630, Lieutenant Colonel Gorham, the battalion commander, arrived with about thirty troopers from headquarters.

By this time, Gorham had gathered about a hundred troops in the valley astride the road from Niscemi south to Objective Y and was in the process of consolidating his position. But at about 0700 his outpost spotted a German armored force about 4,000 yards away—the western column of the Hermann Göring Panzer Division—led by two motorcycles and a Volkswagen command car. The troopers on the perimeter stayed low and out of sight and let the vehicles move into their position, where they killed or captured the German soldiers in them. When the commander of the armored column heard the firing, he stopped about 3,000 yards down the road and deployed his infantry—two companies, or about two hundred men. Gorham told his troopers to hold their fire, lie low, and let the Germans get within 100 yards of their position. When the Germans got close he gave the command to fire. His two machine guns and two 60mm mortars opened fire across the open terrain, killing fifteen enemy soldiers. Shortly thereafter, they captured forty Italian and ten German infantrymen. Even though the German tanks continued to rumble forward, Alexander's bazookas knocked out two of them and damaged two more. The German commander ordered a withdrawal.

Gorham felt that it was time to move on to his objective, Piano Lupo, the high ground off to his left. He moved out, using about fifty prisoners to carry his wounded, and set up a defensive position on the high ground that controlled both the road and the airfield. Then, well aware of his mission, he sent Captain Sayre and a squad to attack Objective Y, a fork in the road surrounded by Italian pillboxes. As he approached the Y, U.S. naval gunfire began to fall 100 yards north of the pillboxes. So Sayre sent one Italian prisoner to demand the surrender of the pillboxes or, he threatened, he would bring in heavy naval gunfire. The Italians were unaware that Sayre had no communications with the U.S. Navy, but the ruse worked, and his small detachment occupied the pillboxes at about 1045. A few minutes later four German tanks appeared. Sayre's troops fired from the pillboxes and the tanks withdrew. Later that night, Gen. Paul Conrath, the Hermann Göring Division's commander, relieved the armored column commander for his inept attack and charged him with cowardice.

At about 1130 scouts from the 1st Division's 16th Infantry Regiment came on the scene. For a short time Sayre attached his detachment to the 16th and, through 1st Division radios, called General Ridgway, who had come in by boat after dawn and set up the 82d's CP near Gela. Sayre reported to his commanding general: "All missions accomplished."

"Actually, Colonel Gorham and his small group of troopers and the lieutenants from the 3d Battalion, 504th, accomplished all the missions assigned to the entire Regimental Combat Team," wrote Colonel Gavin. "It was a remarkable performance, and I know of nothing like it that occurred at any time later in the war."

By the evening of D day, 10 July, the Allies were firmly ashore on Sicily. Later that evening Italian General Guzzoni ordered a second armored attack against Gela. Colonel Gorham and his 100 paratroopers were eating their breakfast when then heard the rumble of the second wave of tanks. One of the tanks fired a round at Gorham's defensive lines of foxholes but missed. Then four other tanks came on line. Gorham's men fired all the bazooka rounds they could find, but these were no match for tanks that were heavier than the ones encountered the day before. After a tank shattered one of his bazooka teams Gorham ran over, picked up the bazooka, and knocked out the tank—but another tank cut down "Hardnose" Gorham. His medical officer, Capt. William Comstock, raced to him, but he himself was seriously wounded by a round exploding nearby. Lieutenant Dean McCandless, with the help of some other troopers, managed to haul Gorham's body and the wounded Comstock back to relative safety. After about a half-hour the German tanks withdrew, leaving a score of dead paratroopers and tankers on the battlefield.

On their jump, Colonel Gavin and his headquarters men had been scattered over the area like the rest of his combat team. Gavin was uncertain of his location. After they landed, he and some six of his men holed up in a ditch after a brief firefight in an olive orchard. The next day he picked up some more men. "It had been a long day," he wrote.

We waited and waited for the setting sun. Soon the Sicilian sun was low in the sky and quickly disappeared like a ball of fire into a cauldron. . . . We began to get things together so as to be able to move out. Water was the first need; it was almost gone. . . . I felt that I had been a failure on my first day in combat and had accomplished nothing. I was determined to find my regiment and engage the enemy wherever he might be. We went into the Sicilian night, heading for what we hoped was Gela, somewhere to the west. . . .

After about an hour we were challenged by a small group of wounded and injured of the 505th under the command of Lieutenant Al Kronheim. . . . At about 2:30 we were challenged by a ma-

chine-gun post of the 45th Division, and at last we had reentered
our own lines. We learned that we were about five miles south of
Vittoria. In about another mile we came to the main paved road
from the beach to Vittoria, passing a number of foxholes and dead
Italian soldiers. By then I had about eight troopers with me. . . . We
then went to the edge of Vittoria where I borrowed a jeep. I continued on toward Gela, and to my surprise came across the 3d Battalion of the 505th, in foxholes in a tomato field and just awaken-
ing. The battalion commander, Lt. Col. Edward Krause, whose
nickname was "Cannonball," was sitting on the edge of a foxhole,
dangling his feet. I asked him what his battalion was doing. He said
that he had been reorganizing the battalion and that he had about
two hundred and fifty present. . . . I asked him about his objective,
several miles to the west near Gela, and he said that he had not
done anything about it. I said we would move at once toward Gela
and told him to get the battalion on its feet and going. In the mean-
time, I took a platoon of the 307th Engineers, commanded by Lt.
Ben L. Wechsler.

Gavin gathered some more men—cooks, orderlies, clerks, and
parachute riggers—and, with Wechsler's platoon, formed a skirmish line
of about seventy men. He put himself in the center. When they were
ready, he gave the command to move out. He also sent word to "Cannonball" to bring his battalion forward as fast as possible. The high
ground they were about to attack was Biazzo Ridge. The dug-in Germans
opened fire first and killed three of Gavin's lead scouts. The paratroopers reacted as they had been trained during lengthy, grueling maneuvers in the United States and North Africa. They hit the ground, firing
as fast as they could from the prone position. During the shooting, Maj.
William J. Hagen, the executive officer of Krause's battalion, arrived with
part of the battalion and joined in the fight along with a lost platoon from
the 45th Division and some sailors who had come ashore. Somehow,
from scattered troops from various units Gavin had gathered about 250
men who fought in close combat, some of it hand-to-hand, for a small
piece of Sicily.

By the middle of the afternoon, they had gradually built up their fire
superiority and charged the German lines, forcing them to withdraw
from the ridge. As Gavin's troops went over the top, the enemy firing
became more intense. Mortar and artillery fire exploded around them,

and heavy machine gun fire began to rake the ridge. And Gavin's men had found German tanks on the other side.

"The first wounded began to crawl back over the top of the ridge," wrote Gavin.

> They all told the same story. They fired their bazookas at the front plate of German tanks, and then the tanks swiveled their huge 88-mm. guns at them and fired at the individual infantrymen. By this time the tanks could be heard, although I could not see any because of the smoke and dust and the cover of vegetation. Hagen came in, walking and holding his thigh, which had been badly torn by fire. Cannonball had gone forward to command the attack. It did not seem to be getting anywhere, however, as the German fire increased in intensity and our wounded were coming back in greater numbers. . . . The first German prisoners also came back. They were from the Hermann Goering Parachute Panzer Division. I remember one of them asking if we had fought the Japanese in the Pacific; he said he asked because the paratroopers had fought so hard.

Gavin gave his attacking troopers a well-deserved break atop the ridge. Shortly, they were joined by a forward observer from a 155mm howitzer battalion and a pack 75 from the 456th. Then Gavin gave the order to move out along the road behind the withdrawing Germans. Moving cautiously around a bend in the road, the lead scouts came face to face with a Mark VI Tiger tank, a mammoth land dreadnaught. The men deployed, and the bazooka gunners fired their rockets. They watched as the rounds bounced off the four-and-a-half-inch-thick steel hide of the Tiger. Then the artillerymen used their pack 75 as an antitank gun and managed to force the tanks to withdraw.

In the middle of the fighting, German Messerschmitt fighters roared overhead but, fortunately, did not attack the paratroopers, concentrating instead on a small railroad gatekeeper's house, assuming perhaps that it was a CP. During the fight, Capt. Al Ireland, a member of Gavin's staff, suggested that he go back to the 45th Division and get some help. Gavin replied that that was the best idea he had heard all day.

At about six that evening, Lt. Harold H. Swingler and a number of troops from Gavin's Headquarters Company arrived on the scene. About an hour later Ireland arrived at the battle scene with half a dozen Sherman tanks. Gavin ordered a counterattack. "I wanted to destroy the German force in front of us and to recover our dead and wounded," he wrote. "Our attack jumped off on schedule; regimental clerks, cooks, truck drivers, everyone who could carry a rifle or a carbine was in the attack." With the help of the Shermans, pack 75mm fire, and artillery concentrations brought in by the 155mm battalion forward observer, Gavin and his makeshift band of fighters beat back the Germans on Biazza Ridge. Near the top of the ridge Swingler and two men had crawled up on a cut through which a paved road ran, but then an enemy machine gun killed Swingler's two troopers. Swingler crawled to the top of the crest and saw a German Tiger tank with the crew outside looking at it. He threw a grenade, killed the crew, and captured the paratroopers' first Tiger tank.

With the Germans pushed off Biazza Ridge, Gavin's force captured twelve artillery pieces, two trucks, loads of ammunition, and piles of equipment and supplies. But the price was high for blocking a veteran German Panzer *kampfgruppe* from driving into the 45th Division coming across the beaches. The 505th had scores of wounded, including Colonel Gavin. Fifty-one paratroopers had been killed in action and were buried along the ridge. Captain George B. Wood, an Episcopal priest and chaplain of the 505th, wrote about the burial. "While the wounded were being tended, I had a shortened burial rite after the bodies were reverently placed in the ground, their dog tags and personal effects having been removed. We had fashioned crude wooden crosses out of k-ration crates. Only when the grisly task on Biazza Ridge was completed, came the recognition of the horror of it all."

While Gavin and his troopers were storming and taking Biazza Ridge, General Patton ordered General Ridgway to commit Colonel Tucker's 504th Regimental Combat Team as planned in Operation Husky 2. And that operation almost spelled the demise of the airborne division as an entity.

7: The Airborne Division Crisis

The second day of the Allied Sicily invasion, 11 July, was the U.S. Seventh Army's most difficult day in the campaign. Early in the morning, General Guzzoni renewed his ground attack, infantry and armor, against the relatively shallow center of the U.S. lines—Piano Lupo, Gela, and the beachhead—with two divisions, the Hermann Göring and the Italian Livorno. The Axis ground forces assault was supported by over 500 sorties of German and Italian planes operating from Italy. The first air strike by twelve Italian planes hit at dawn; another attack at 0635 forced ships offshore to weigh anchor and take evasive action. At 1530 thirty Ju 88s attacked the Gela area, and at 2150, a large flight of German planes blasted the same area and forced more of the unloading ships to disperse. One ammunition ship, the USS *Robert Rowan,* took a direct hit and sank. The British hospital ship HMS *Talambia* was struck by a German bomber, had a hole torn in her side, and sank later in the day. Only the fast work of her Indian crew members, who lowered the lifeboats rapidly, saved most of the patients. During the day U.S. antiaircraft fire, both ashore and afloat, and especially in the Seventh Army area, was intense.

The unloading of ships on the beach and the Axis planes strafing the shoreline created congestion in front of the beach that prevented Bradley from sending his tanks into battle and left only naval gunfire and artillery to support the 1st and 45th Division infantrymen. To shore up the front lines Patton pressed all available troops—infantrymen, paratroopers, Rangers, engineers, tankers, and artillerymen, and even cooks, clerks, and navy shore personnel, into a multifaceted force to defend the beachhead. By the end of the day the Seventh Army had suffered over 2,300 casualties—the greatest one-day loss during the campaign. But by dark the Seventh Army still held and, in some areas, had expanded its narrow footprint; Axis troops never quite reached the beachhead. Ships' guns added to the firepower on shore and helped drive the German tanks into the hills.

Patton decided to reinforce his beleaguered troops. He ordered General Ridgway to commit Tommy Tucker's 504th Parachute Regimental Combat Team (RCT) on the night of 11 July to its predesignated DZs on an airfield already in U.S. hands, Farello, three miles east of Gela. Tucker's RCT consisted of the 1st and 2d Battalions of the 504th, Lt. Col. Wilbur M. Griffith's 376th Parachute Field Artillery Battalion, and C Company of the 307th Engineer Battalion. The drop had originally been scheduled for the night of D day, but it would now be twenty-four hours later, which would prove disastrous.

On the morning of 11 July, General Ridgway sent a coded message to Brig. Gen. Charles L. "Bull" Keerans, the 82d's assistant division commander, whose mission in North Africa was to supervise the shipment of men and supplies to the 82d on Sicily. The message told Keerans to commit the 504th. After Tucker got the mission from Keerans, he knew that the DZ was already in friendly hands and he therefore expected no particular difficulties—just a routine training jump. Keerans, who was not a qualified paratrooper, decided to ride along as an observer.

Ridgway was nonetheless deeply concerned about the safety of his second wave of troopers, given the extent and ferocity of the German and Italian air attacks on the beachhead and the Allies' reciprocal use of heavy antiaircraft fire. He did not want his planeloads of paratroopers flying over antiaircraft guns and heavily armed Allied ships whose gunners were extremely active and alert, firing at every airplane that flew near them. Ridgway convinced the Air Corps to alter the flight route and carry his paratroopers around the shipping lanes to the far western end of the beachhead and then fly thirty-five miles inland, over friendly territory to the DZs. At 0845 on 11 July, Patton sent out a top priority message to all subordinate commanders informing them of the change of flight path: "Notify all units, especially antiaircraft, that parachutists of the 82d Airborne Division will drop."

But by the evening of 11 July Patton was still most apprehensive about the safety of Tucker's RCT. That very evening he wrote in his diary: "Went to the office at 2000 to see if we could stop the 82d Airborne lift, as enemy air attacks were heavy (during the day) and inaccurate Army and Navy anti-aircraft gunners were jumpy. Found we could not get contact by radio. Am terribly worried."

That same evening, at the Kairouan airfields Tucker and his men prepped for their first combat jump, checking equipment, adjusting parachute straps, loading weapons, getting their plane and jump stick assignments, and exchanging quips. The mood was grim, but the troops felt ready. Just before 1900, Tucker's 2,304 heavily loaded men boarded 144 C-47s. Forty-five minutes later the last of the C-47s roared down the runway. The pilots formed the flight into a V of V's and headed for their first checkpoint at Malta. Shortly afterward the last rays of sunshine faded from the night sky, and the 504th RCT was on its way to its first run-in with destiny.

At 2032 hours, the lead planes of Tucker's 504th crossed the coast of Sicily near Sampieri, flew for some thirty-five miles over the beachhead to the DZ at Farello, and at 2040 the first stick bailed out, precisely as planned. The rest of the paratroopers in the first flight landed as if it were a training mission back home. But there the similarity ended. A few minutes later, just as the second flight crossed the shoreline, a lone machine gunner on the ground opened fire. Other nervous gunners heard the firing, assumed that the Axis enemy had renewed its air attacks, and started blazing away with ferocity at the shadowy C-47s churning through the dark sky. The pilots turned on their lights in the hopes of identifying themselves and dissuading the antiaircraft gunners, but to no avail. The firing spread like an epidemic throughout the area, and ships offshore caught the disease. The sky was ablaze with tracers and flares, bullets from hundreds of machine guns, and 20mm cannon rounds from the offshore ships. It looked like a Fourth of July celebration—only seven days late. In the second flight, a plane carrying the lucky Lt. Col. Bill Yarborough and his staff from the 2d Battalion of the 504th managed to avoid the blazes in the sky and being shot down. The remainder of the flight was not so fortunate.

The intensity of the firing broke up the column of C-47s, some twenty-three of these shot down and lost and thirty-seven severely damaged. Some troopers, hanging in their chutes, were killed by ground fire. Eight planes at the tail of the column turned and headed back to Africa without dropping their troopers. Other planes dropped their men into the adjacent British zone and onto far-flung areas throughout the beachhead.

Tucker's plane headed the third wave, which was pummeled with the same intensity of fire. Tucker's S-4 officer, Maj. Julian A. Cook, was wounded in Tucker's plane. But Tucker directed the pilot to fly back along the coast and then inland, and Tucker finally recognized the DZ at Farello. He led his men out the door, and they landed near some U.S. tanks that were firing at the planes. He got out of his parachute harness, raced over to the tanks, banged on the turrets with his helmet, and yelled at the tankers to stop the firing.

By 0715 on 12 July, Tucker had assembled on the DZ only one rifle company and four howitzers of one pack 75 artillery battery. By night-fall, he could account for only 550 of the 2,000 men who had mounted up in Africa.

When Tucker's planes returned to Kairouan, some with hundreds of bullet holes in their fuselages, General Taylor, who had been left there to help launch Tucker's RCT, went out to inspect them. He was as-tounded at what he found. Some badly shot-up planes, with blood across their floors, carried dead and wounded troopers. Aircrews and medics were frantically trying to get them to aid stations. Some planes would re-quire months of repair; others would never leave the ground again. When the final count was in, Operation Husky 2 was, without a doubt, a disaster. The 504th had 81 men killed, 132 wounded, and 16 missing. General Hal Clark's 52d Troop Carrier Wing had 7 killed, 30 wounded, and 53 missing.

Ridgway was beside himself with fury at the loss of his men to friendly fire (an oxymoronic term if there ever was one). When he became aware of the catastrophe, he sent a recommendation to General Patton saying that unless "fire of all troops ashore against all aircraft was stopped, fur-ther troop movement by air be canceled indefinitely." Patton accepted the recommendation.

General Bull Keerans did not return with the planes to Kairouan, and his disappearance was a mystery. One report had it that his plane was one of the twenty-three shot down, and that he was killed. William B. Breuer, author of *Geronimo,* investigated what happened to Keerans. He wrote that Sgt. Fielding Armstrong, who had been the crew chief on Gen-eral Keerans's plane, was scouring the shore looking for Lt. John Gib-son, the pilot, and Raymond Roush, the copilot. Although Armstrong had thought that they were dead, both Gibson and Roush were only in-jured and had survived. Armstrong said that "along the shore line I ran into General Keerans. He apparently had escaped the ditching and subsequent machine-gun shooting unscathed. While we were talking, the general spoke to a number of passing people he apparently knew. He asked me to go inland with him, and I said no, that I was going to try to get back to my outfit (in Tunisia)."

Breuer wrote that "since World War II, the US Army had thought that General Keerans had been killed when his plane crashed that night. But the author [Breuer] contacted the pilot of Keerans's C-47, John Gibson, and was shown statements from two crew members that Keerans was alive and well on the following morning." Later Keerans apparently went inland and disappeared, eventually being listed as killed in action. Whatever the circumstances, General Keerans was the first U.S. general officer to be killed in combat in World War II.

On the morning of 12 July, Col. Harry Lewis and his 325th Glider Infantry Regiment were in Kairouan ready to mount up in gliders and make the bumpy towed flight to Sicily to reinforce the paratroopers. But the disaster that had struck Tucker's 504th caused the cancellation of Lewis's mission.

But that calamity did not deter the British paratroopers. Just before midnight on 13 July the British 1st Parachute Brigade, under Brigadier Gerald Lathbury, took off from Tunisia in Operation Fustian, the last large-scale parachute operation of the Sicilian campaign. Lathbury's objective was the capture of the Primasole Bridge north of Lentini and behind German lines. By sheer coincidence German paratroopers landed on the same DZ as the British, and only minutes apart. The Germans were assembling on the DZ when the British descended on them. The result was a shootout almost face to face. But at dawn the British were in command of the DZ and the bridge.

This operation, too, was not without its tragedy. Eleven of the 124 U.S. planes carrying the British paratroopers were shot down and fifty were severely damaged by the combined antiaircraft fire of the Axis and the Allies. Some twenty-seven planes at the end of the column turned back without dropping their troops.

General Eisenhower was distraught over the airborne tragedy. On 13 July, Patton wrote that he received a "wire from Ike, cussing me out" because of the tragedy during the night of the 11th. "He demanded an investigation and statement of punishments for those guilty of firing on them."

General Patton went on that "it is my opinion that every possible precaution was taken by this headquarters to obviate firing on our own airborne troops and that the failure to do so was an unavoidable incident of combat."

As far as I can see, if anyone is blamable, it must be myself, but personally I feel immune to censure.

Perhaps Ike is looking for an excuse to relieve me. I am having full report made but will not try anyone (by court martial). If they want a goat, I am it. Fortunately, Lucas, Wedemeyer, and Swing are here and know the facts. . . . Men who have been bombed all day get itchy fingers.

Ike has never been subjected to air attack or any other form of death. However, he is such a straw man that his future is secure. The British will never let him go.

It was difficult to assess blame for the airborne disaster. Ridgway later wrote that "the responsibility for loss of life and materiel resulting from this operation is so divided, so difficult to fix with impartial justice that disciplinary action is of doubtful wisdom. Deplorable as is the loss of life which occurred, I believe that the lessons now learned could have been driven home in no other way, and that these lessons provided a sound basis for the belief that recurrences can be avoided. The losses are part of the inevitable price of war in human life."

By the morning of 13 July the Allies were firmly ashore in Sicily. By 15 July the Seventh Army had gradually forced its way out of the beachhead and into the hills surrounding it. General Guzzoni withdrew to more defensible terrain in the northeast. Heavy fighting continued.

General Ridgway had under his command some 3,883 of the 5,307 paratroopers who jumped into Sicily. Patton backed up the 82d Airborne Division with heavy-artillery support units, and the 82d continued the campaign as straight infantry. The 82d's part in the Sicily operation ended on 22 July when the 505th captured Trapani, a port on the westernmost tip of Sicily. Five thousand Italian troops were dug in around the area, but they were not in a fighting mood. Captain Al Ireland, Gavin's S-1 officer, volunteered to ride a jeep into Trapani under a white flag. With the luck of the Irish, he returned shortly with Adm. Giuseppe Manfredi, the port commander, who surrendered the port to Ridgway and Gavin.

For the rest of July and into August the Axis forces, bolstered by reinforcements from France and Italy, put up a stiff fight in the eastern part of the island. But it was useless. On 8 August Guzzoni began the evacuation of the island and, under heavy Allied pressure from the south, withdrew some 40,000 Germans and Italians and most of their equipment across the Straits of Messina. On 17 August, elements of the 3d Infantry Division's 7th Infantry Regiment entered Messina just hours after the last Axis troops had sailed for Italy. Patton brought reinforcements into the port city so that, in the words of Brig. Gen. William Eagles, the 3d Division's assistant commander, "the British did not capture the city from us after we had taken it." Patton had won the race. Colonel Gavin summed up the Sicily campaign: "The battle for Sicily pitted Patton and his newborn Seventh Army against Montgomery and his veteran British Eighth Army." The rivalry would continue during many more campaigns. As Patton put it: "Of course, had I not been interfered with . . . by a fool change of plans, I would have taken Messina in ten days."

On 17 August, when Messina was occupied by the Allied forces, the 82d returned to North Africa to get ready for the Italian invasion.

In the aftermath of the Sicily campaign it was apparent that the U.S. soldiers, previously untested in combat, had done well. After landing they had repulsed heavy counterattacks, forced the Axis to withdraw, and pursued the enemy relentlessly over the sun-scorched hills of Sicily. In thirty-eight days, the Allies had killed or wounded some 29,000 enemy soldiers and captured some 140,000. The U.S. losses totaled 2,237 killed and 6,544 wounded and captured. The British suffered 12,843 casualties, including 2,721 dead. But during the first seventeen days of August, the Axis had been able to evacuate over 100,000 men and 10,000 vehicles from Sicily because of the failure of the Allied air and naval forces to interdict the Strait of Messina. Eisenhower and his principal commanders had not developed a coordinated plan to prevent the withdrawal of Axis forces from Sicily.

The U.S. airborne operations in North Africa and Sicily gave rise to major actions and reactions. The widely scattered drop of the 504th drove General Ridgway to organize trainers, develop better assault techniques, and organize pathfinder units made up of experienced paratroopers and pilots who would, on future airborne operations, drop ahead of the main body with electronic homing devices and lights to mark the DZs and guide the incoming planes.

The reaction of General Conrath of the Hermann Göring Division and Field Marshal Kesselring, the commander of German forces in Italy, was not what the U.S. planners could have hoped for in their wildest dreams. The confusion of the 82d's drop indicated to the enemy that swarms of paratroopers were dropping from the skies all over Sicily, and the resulting overestimation of the number of paratroopers caused the German higher command to hold back the Hermann Göring Division from seriously threatening the U.S. Seventh Army.

After the war, Kesselring wrote that "the paratroopers effected an extraordinary delay in the movement of our own troops and caused large losses." General Kurt Student, the father of the German airborne effort, said that "it is my opinion that if it had not been for the Allied airborne forces blocking the Hermann Goering Armored Division from reaching the beachhead, that division would have driven the initial seaborne forces back into the sea."

But the most serious and scathing Allied reaction to the use of airborne forces in Sicily was General Eisenhower's. He was concerned about the future of airborne forces and angry at the commanders who had not foreseen the difficulties that resulted in the Sicily debacle. He sent an after-action report to General Marshall in which he stated:

> I do not believe in the airborne division. I believe that airborne troops should be reorganized into self-contained units, comprising infantry, artillery, and special services, all of about the strength of a regimental combat team. Even if one had all the air transport he could possibly use, the fact is that at any given time and in any given spot only a reasonable number of air transports can be operated because of technical difficulties. To employ at any time and place a whole division would require a dropping over such an extended area that I seriously doubt that a division commander could regain control and operate the scattered forces as one unit. In any event, if these troops were organized into smaller, self-contained units, a senior commander, with a small staff and radio communications, could always be dropped in the area to insure necessary coordination.

General Eisenhower's report to General Marshall caused in the army's high command grave doubts about the wisdom of pursuing the airborne division concept and very nearly prompted the army chief of staff to abandon the idea and to disband the five airborne divisions already in existence (82d, 101st, 11th 13th, and 17th). Even some of the army's small cadre of airborne enthusiasts were divided among themselves. One confident and optimistic group was planning for an airborne corps (which, of course, came to pass eventually in the European Theater) while another group, far less committed to large airborne formations, felt that battalions, for quick in-and-out raids, made sense. Even Lt.Gen. Lesley J. McNair, the tough and demanding commander of the Army Ground Forces, who was originally in favor of airborne troops and large airborne units, was disillusioned by the bungling and misfortunes of the Sicilian airborne campaign. General Ridgway was also disillusioned about the value of airborne divisions after the Sicilian campaign, but changed his mind later.

Colonel Gavin had a different view. "When I learned of this exchange of views, I was puzzled by the fact that no senior officers from higher headquarters were present at any of the airborne operations in Sicily. Their views therefore were based on impressions gained from Eisenhower's headquarters hundreds of miles away. . . . In a later study of this subject, both American and British Combined Staff planners saw nothing in the combat experience of the British or the Americans which indicated that the division was not a proper organization for airborne troops."

Before General Marshall would take final action on the matter, however, he directed the convening of a special board to study the problem and to determine the War Department policy on the mission and scope of the U.S. airborne programs and operations.

The first board was headed by Brig. Gen. Albert E. Pierson, then the assistant division commander of the 11th Airborne Division. "I was ordered to the Pentagon to study the matter," he wrote in a letter to the author. "I saw Mr. Stimson, the Secretary of War, and then reported to Gen. Thomas T. Handy, Operations Division, to head a board of officers with Air Corps and Marine Corps members. We concluded that division organization for airborne troops could be supported in combat and recommended that the division be retained." His board also concluded that "an airborne division could be sustained by air for 3–5 days" but, General Pierson added, "some of my supporting documents were rather sketchy. . . . However, not much came of this report, but the Swing Board which followed became the all-important doctrine."

The War Department selected General Swing to preside over a second board of officers to investigate the same matter. General Swing (class of 1915 and a classmate of General Eisenhower) was an obvious choice for the job because he had been present in Sicily as Eisenhower's airborne advisor, had watched the 82d's miscarried operation, and was currently the 11th Airborne Division commander. "As you know," Swing wrote in an 11 October 1975 letter to Dick Hoyt, the editor of the 11th Airborne's *Voice of the Angels*, "General Ike sent for me at Mackall to come to Algiers as his A/B Advisor, Why? Because Alexander's A/B Commander Browning was also technically responsible for the planning of the British 1st Airborne Division and the 82d. Browning did not want the 82d in the operation at all. There was hardly enough equipment to lift one division."

In September 1943 the Swing Board met at Camp Mackall, the home of the 11th Airborne Division. The board members included experienced paratrooper and glider officers, artillerymen, and Air Corps troop carrier and glider unit commanders and staff officers. For a couple of weeks, the board reviewed both the Axis and Allied airborne operations to date, studied the organization of the airborne division, and analyzed problems encountered by the Air Corps troop carrier units in the North Africa and Sicily operations. They reviewed navigational problems, interservice communications, and command and control of airborne forces before and after commitment. By the end of September, the board had finished its deliberations and recommended that the War Department publish a training circular that would define the relationships between the airborne and troop carrier commands, their several responsibilities, and the details of airborne operations from takeoff to drop and assembly. In short order the War Department published *Training Circular 113*, which became the "bible" for subsequent airborne operations.

Training Circular 113 did not, however, satisfy Generals Marshall and McNair that airborne divisions were here to stay in spite of the fact that the 82d, less the 504th still fighting in Italy, and the 101st, under the command of the "Father of Airborne," Maj. Gen. William C. Lee, had already been deployed to England and were in the throes of getting ready for an invasion of the Continent. McNair and Marshall wanted proof beyond the shadow of a doubt that an airborne division could function in combat as conceived. McNair ordered General Swing to plan a division maneuver for December 1943, making it clear that the future of the airborne division as an entity depended on the success or failure of that maneuver.

Secretary of War Stimson was also concerned about the airborne division concept and its place in the tactics and strategy of winning World War II. He decided to see for himself. He came to Camp Mackall on

23–24 November 1943. On 23 November the 11th staged an infantry-artillery, parachute-glider maneuver that was a success. But this was not done by an entire division, and it was not staged under the trying circumstances of long flights over water, as in the Husky Operations. The coming December performance would have to examine that total picture.

General Pierson remembered Stimson's visit:

> I recall a vivid night glider exercise at Mackall where a number of very senior individuals came down to observe night glider landings. I was present at a glider landing field with a group consisting of General Arnold and Mr. Stimson, observing gliders come in for perfect landings on this particular field. After several gliders came down, we heard music coming from the sky. It was some time afterward a glider came down for a landing and approached the treeline where the observers were standing. It rolled up abreast of us, the nose of the CG-4A opened and out came an Air Force orchestra complete with their instruments.

There were, of course, other landings that proved that gliders could be operated at night.

In a 27 November 1943 letter to General Swing, Secretary Stimson wrote: "I believe I got more of value from this particular inspection trip than from any trip I have made. . . . The Airborne Infantry Division will play a great part in our future successes, and I know that the 11th Airborne Division will render outstanding service to our country on some not too far distant D Day."

But Marshall and McNair were still not convinced. The Knollwood maneuver in December would have to answer that doubt.

The objective of the December operation was the capture of the Knollwood Airport in North Carolina. Headquarters, Army Ground Forces directed that the maneuver be conducted according to the recently published *Training Circular 113*, designing the maneuver to provide practical and straightforward answers to the following questions: Could an airborne division fly a three- to four-hour instrument course, at night, across a large body of water and arrive on schedule at precisely selected drop and landing zones? Could such a force land by parachute and glider without sustaining excessive landing casualties? Could the division then wage extended ground combat? Could the division so landed be resupplied totally by parachute and plane and glider landings?

By December 1943 the 11th Airborne Division was a functioning, well-trained, combat-ready, and highly disciplined division able to enter combat by parachute, glider, and amphibiously if the occasion so demanded. Starting on 4 December 1943, the Knollwood maneuver would test the combat and airborne readiness of the division.

On 4 December, after intensive planning and preparation, the units of the division moved out of Camp Mackall in a series of truck convoys. The troopers were carrying their individual packs and weapons. The men wore their jumpsuits and brown jump boots; the glider riders wore fatigues and canvas leggings. The ride was dusty but, for a change, not hot. December in North Carolina can be cold, and the troops would remember this particular operation for a lot of things—one of which was the freezing-cold weather. The truck convoys moved to five airfields in North and South Carolina: Pope Field at Fort Bragg; the airstrips in a triangle at Mackall; the air base at Florence, South Carolina; and the army air bases at Lumberton and Laurinburg-Maxton in North Carolina. Most of the officers and NCOs were aware that the results of the Knollwood maneuver would determine the future of the airborne division as a unit; that foreknowledge added a tension to their preparations, above and beyond the normal anxiety before a drop.

Army Ground Forces designed the Knollwood maneuvers to test the feasibility of loading an airborne division in its jump transports and gliders, flying a four-hour triangular course—for the most part over water—hitting the drop and landing zones at night under blacked-out conditions, assembling the units into combat formations speedily, and then attacking the defending forces aggressively. The test results would answer two questions: Is the 11th Airborne Division combat ready? Is the airborne division a valid and practicable concept?

On 5 December, the Army Ground Forces test team deployed a composite combat team from the 17th Airborne Division plus a battalion from Col. Duke McEntee's 541st Parachute Infantry Regiment around the objective, the Knollwood Airport and several other critical points.

The 11th Airborne Division, with the 501st Parachute Infantry Regiment attached, was originally scheduled to take off on the night of 5 December, but adverse weather forced postponement for twenty-four hours. Under Secretary of War Robert Patterson and General McNair were on hand for the scheduled takeoff on 5 December, but, with the postponement, they flew back to Washington. The importance of the maneuver to the army was so critical that they came back again to watch the takeoffs and landings on the night of 6 December. Other high-ranking observers included General Ridgway, temporarily back from the 82d Airborne Division in England, and Brig. Gen. Leo Donovan, the new commander of the Airborne Command. Additionally, there were several teams of high-ranking inspectors from the War Department, Army Ground Forces, and Army Air Forces.

At the five departure airfields the paratroopers and glidermen made ready for takeoff. The troopers trucked up to their planes, each truck loaded for a specific plane. Once beside their planes, the paratroopers struggled into their main chutes; adjusted their loads of field gear, weapons, and ammunition; and then clipped their reserves across their chests. The jumpmaster of each plane checked each of his men for proper adjustment of parachutes and field packs; fully rigged for jumping, each man was bent over from the tightness of the parachute harness and the weight of his personal gear. Then they lined up in reverse order of jumping, waddled to the planeside, and climbed laboriously up the steps. They sat down on the canvas benches along the bulkheads of the planes and tried to get as comfortable as the harnesses would allow. They did not relish the long ride and would have far preferred to take off and jump as soon as they reached proper altitude. But that was not to be this time.

The glidermen dismounted from their trucks near their assigned gliders. The artillerymen shoved their pack 75s into the gliders through the front of the CG-4A, whose nose, containing the pilots' compartment, was swung upward. Other glidermen loaded jeeps, small bulldozers, communications equipment, medical paraphernalia, trailers, and the whole range of supplies, weapons, and equipment needed by the division in the field for a sustained operation. Then the glidermen, without parachutes but loaded down with their own personal gear, filed into the gliders, sat down on flimsy canvas seats along the sides of the gliders, and tensely awaited the hookup to their tug aircraft and ultimately their liftoff.

The night takeoffs from the five airports were timed so that each serial would join the column in the proper place in line as the fleet of planes carrying the entire division became airborne. The planes were in a V of V's, nine ships wide. The long column headed east across the North Carolina shoreline out over the Atlantic, turned north, and finally headed back west toward the designated DZs and landing zones (LZs) located in an area to the west of the Fort Bragg reservation. The DZs and LZs included golf courses around Pinehurst and Southern Pines, open fields outside the towns, and areas adjacent to the Knollwood Airport. At 2300 on the moonlit night of 6 December, the first paratroopers in the lead ships jumped into the dark onto the DZs marked by pathfinders who had jumped earlier. As each successive V of V's droned over its assigned area at about 1,200 feet, the sky filled with paratroopers floating silently to the ground. The CG-4As, suddenly cut off from their tug ships, dropped rapidly on a sharp glide path to their LZs. The drop and landing zones were soon covered with spread-out parachutes, opened equipment bundles, and empty gliders, in a scrambled and helter-skelter pattern, with their noses swung up and open. Fortunately, almost all of the paratroopers and glidermen were on their proper DZs and LZs. There was one exception—the division chief of staff and his glider landed on a road on the Fort Bragg artillery range.

As soon as they landed and were out of their parachutes the infantrymen located their bundles, dug out crew-served weapons, assembled on the DZs, and then formed into their tactical echelons for the attack on their assigned objectives. The artillery paratroopers searched out their loads for the pack 75s, assembled them, and then moved out to their firing positions, tugging their weapons behind them. In this maneuver, the prime mover for a pack 75 was eight "redlegs." The glider elements unloaded their gliders and joined their units for movement to assigned areas and missions. In a few hours, the division was reasonably well assembled as a unit and was in pursuit of its primary mission—the capture of Knollwood Airport. By dawn, the airport was in the hands of the 11th Airborne Division.

On the following day a steady succession of troop carrier aircraft, this time loaded with all classes of supply, commenced landing at the airport, where the division had established an airhead. For the next five days, the division waged simulated combat against the defenders over the dunes and hills of North Carolina. By evening of the sixth day, Army Ground Forces declared the Knollwood maneuvers over. General Swing ordered his troops back to Mackall. That night, in a cold, driving rain from which the jump suits and fatigues offered little protection, the men mounted up for the freezing ride back to the tar paper shacks they called home.

Once back at Mackall, the division staff reviewed the operation from start to finish and, with input from all subordinate commanders, prepared a postoperational report for General Swing. In turn, on 16 December, he submitted his report to General McNair. In reply, General McNair wrote:

> I congratulate you on the splendid performance of your division in the Knollwood maneuver. After the airborne operations in Africa and Sicily, my staff and I had become convinced of the impracticability of handling large airborne units. I was prepared to recommend to the War Department that airborne divisions be abandoned in our scheme of organization and that the airborne effort be restricted to parachute units of battalion size or smaller. The successful performance of your division has convinced me that we were wrong, and I shall now recommend that we continue our present schedule of activating, training, and committing airborne divisions.

That ended the debate. The airborne division concept had been tried and tested, and found credible, workable, and functional. The five U.S. airborne divisions were safe from further cuts, doubts, and controversies. The remaining battles of World War II and the use of airborne divisions would prove the validity of the decision.

8: Airborne in the Pacific: The 503d Comes of Age at Nadzab

By the summer of 1942, the Japanese had succeeded in expanding their empire through Asia and the Pacific with the subjugation of the Philippines, Hong Kong, French Indochina, Burma, Singapore, Java, and parts of New Guinea and almost all of the Solomon Islands. In July of 1942, the Japanese decided to extend their reach in the Pacific with the occupation of the rest of New Guinea and Guadalcanal.

General MacArthur had arrived in Darwin, Australia, after a hectic trip—more properly an escape—by sea and air from Corregidor, in the Philippines. At 2115 on the night of 11 March 1942, fifty-six days before Gen. Jonathan M. Wainwright surrendered the U.S. forces in the Philippines to General Homma, General MacArthur, his wife, son, the Chinese amah, A Cheu, and seventeen staff officers got on board four PT boats at the South Dock of Corregidor. On the dock, MacArthur paused and looked back at Corregidor. "On the dock I could see the men staring at me," MacArthur wrote in his memoirs. "I had lost 25 pounds living on the same diet as the soldiers. . . . What a change had taken place in that once beautiful spot! My eyes roamed that warped and twisted face of scorched rock. Gone were the vivid green foliage, with the trees, shrubs, and flowers. Gone were the buildings, the sheds, every growing thing. . . . Darkness had fallen. . . . I stepped aboard PT-41. 'You may cast off, Buck,' I said, 'when you are ready.'"

"Buck" was Lt. John D. Bulkeley, U.S. Navy, and the commander of the four PT boats. His daring, skill, and good fortune had permitted him to lead the boats on a harrowing trip on the open sea through a Japanese minefield, past a Japanese destroyer and a cruiser, and, thirty-five hours later, land at Cagayan on the north coast of Mindanao. Brigadier General William F. Sharp, the commander of the 25,000 U.S. troops on Min-

danao, met them and moved General MacArthur and his party to the
Del Monte airfield where, a day later, they boarded two B-17s for the
1,579-mile trip to Darwin. But as they were approaching Darwin,
MacArthur's pilot learned that Japanese Zero fighters were raiding the
airfield. After five hours in the air, the U.S. planes headed instead to
Batchelor Field, fifty miles from Darwin. Shortly thereafter, MacArthur
and his party made their way to Darwin where, almost immediately, he
became the commander of the Southwest Pacific Theater Area Command, Adm. Chester W. Nimitz being the commander of the Pacific
Ocean Area Command.

On arriving in Darwin, and in spite of losing the Philippines,
MacArthur had lost none of his self-confidence or flamboyance. He
made a speech in which he said: "The President of the United States ordered me to break through the Japanese lines and proceed to Australia
for the purpose, I understand, of organizing the American offensive
against Japan, a primary purpose of which is the relief of the Philippines.
I came through and I shall return." It would take some time, but he did
have some airborne units to help on some difficult missions.

Airborne units are, by their very nature, subject to many operational
alerts over the course of a campaign. In the Pacific theater, MacArthur
eventually had both the 11th Airborne Division and the 503d Parachute
Regimental Combat Team (RCT) at his disposal. Because an airborne
unit has the inherent potential for entering combat any place in a circle whose radius is the range of the transport aircraft, for a number of
reasons it is a valuable asset to a commander even while sitting uncom-
mitted near an airbase. First, the enemy commander undoubtedly knows
where the airborne unit is, but he has no idea where or when the airborne unit might drop. Therefore, he must deploy combat forces that
he might otherwise employ in a current campaign to guard his rear or
his flanks against a possible airborne assault. Second, once the commander commits his airborne units, the enemy commander must deploy
his forces to meet the airborne threat wherever it occurs—many times,
in his lightly defended rear. Third, the enemy commander never knows
when another airborne attack might be launched. And even if the airborne attack scatters its troops far and wide, as happened in Sicily, the
enemy, as he did in Sicily, may think that the airborne force is far greater
than it is in actuality.

MacArthur was a great believer in the potential and value of the threat
of airborne forces. He planned to use them on a number of occasions,

even though some of the operations never came off. For example, when the 11th Airborne Division was in its base camp at Dobodura, New Guinea, in the summer of 1944, MacArthur alerted the division for a possible jump farther up the island. But the alert was canceled even before the troops were aware that they might be entering combat for the first time. But MacArthur did use his other airborne force, the 503d RCT, in two parachute operations, one at Nadzab and one at Noemfoor, before he committed them to the formidable task of jumping on Corregidor and wresting the island from the Japanese occupiers.

In October 1942 the War Department ordered the 503d Regiment, still without its third battalion, to the Pacific Theater. Colonel Robert F. Sink (West Point class of 1927) had left the regiment to form the 506th Parachute Regiment at Taccoa, Georgia; Col. Kenneth H. Kinsler, then commanding the 501st Battalion in Panama, was ordered to Fort Bragg to take over the 503d Regiment. In short order, the War Department ordered him to fly ahead to Australia to prepare for the regiment's arrival. Lieutenant Colonel John J. Tolson III (class of 1937), the executive officer of the regiment, led it overseas. With him, in addition to the regimental staff, were two infantry battalions and A Company of the 504th Infantry Regiment from the newly formed 82d Airborne Division at Fort Bragg.

The trip to Australia began with the inevitable train ride across the United States, which, on a crowded, hot troop train from Fort Bragg to San Francisco, seemed endless. On these trips the troops gambled, read, commiserated with each other, and got into trouble. The 503d was no exception. When the train stopped in Elko, Nevada, one afternoon to take on water and food, the sharp-eyed troopers saw a liquor store across the tracks. They enlisted the aid of some passersby, tossed money to them out the windows, and urged them to race to the liquor store for whatever libations were available. Even as the train was pulling out, the helpful civilians were still running back and forth, hauling booze. That evening on the train was far more uproarious than the previous boring ones. Even a shakedown by the regimental officers failed to produce many contraband bottles. (Perhaps some were even dissuaded from a more painstaking search with a drink or two.)

The train finally arrived at Camp Stoneman, near Pittsburg, California, where the troops unloaded and made ready for the next leg of their trip to an unknown destination—unknown, at least, to the majority of the men in the 503d. Stoneman, situated in a beautiful part of California, is flanked by scenic hills and lies in a fertile green valley about thirty-five miles northeast of San Francisco. It was designed for a specific purpose: readying a unit for overseas movement. Stoneman and its hundreds of administrators and logisticians received a unit, supplied it with odd items of equipment that it might have been unable to procure previously, gave the troops their preembarkation inoculations, fed them better than they had been in many months, and entertained them with various movies, stage shows, and band concerts—all in a routine, expeditious, and gracious manner. Even some of the slow learners among the troops said that "they were being fattened for the kill."

For a few days, the out-processing soldiers were indoctrinated on such important matters as how to leave a sinking ship; how to climb up and down a rope ladder; how to find, wear, adjust, and operate individual life belts; where to find liferafts; and what was in the liferaft kit and how to operate it. Censorship of the troops' letters, with their amazingly minor gripes, began at Stoneman and would continue throughout the war. Finally, the 503d troops boarded the converted Dutch freighter, the *Poelau Laut,* on the night of 19 October 1942.

The SS *Poelau Laut* was by no means a luxury liner. The ship was registered in Batavia, Java, and had been built in Amsterdam in 1929. She was 494 feet long and powered by an eight-cylinder oil engine. The crew was Indonesian. The 503d troopers, each loaded down with nearly a hundred pounds of personal gear, climbed up the steep gangplank, looked around for their designated holds, and pushed their way down into the cramped areas that would be their home for the next month or more. The holds, formerly for cargo, had been outfitted with bunks four and five tiers high. Air conditioning was nonexistent. Even a nonclaustrophobic soldier could begin to feel a bit crushed down.

At dawn on 20 October, the *Poelau Laut* steamed down Suisun Bay, through Carquinez Strait, through San Pablo and San Francisco Bays, and under the fabled Golden Gate Bridge. Even the hardened paratroopers felt pangs of nostalgia as they watched the orange bridge pass overhead and then fade from sight. They knew only that they were on their way—somewhere.

The 503d's destination was still a mystery to most of the men. If one of them had had a compass, he might have been surprised to find that the ship was headed due south and not southwest or west, which he might have thought was the direction of combat.

On 1 November, the ship docked off Balboa in the Panama Canal Zone. No troops got off, but the 501st Parachute Infantry Battalion, less

C Company, got on board. The 503d Parachute Infantry Regiment was now complete. The 501st, under Lt. Col. George M. Jones (class of 1935) would become the 2d Battalion, 503d; and A Company, 504th, already aboard the *Poelau Laut,* would become D Company, 503d.

The month-long trip on the crowded, hot, smelly troopship, wallowing across the vast stretch of the Pacific at twelve knots, could have been a disaster if the troops had not been kept busy and if discipline had not been enforced. Lieutenant Colonel Jones, now the senior officer on board because he outranked Jack Tolson, became the commander of all the 1,939 men and officers. He insisted on a full daily schedule of activities. Their heterogeneous tasks and pastimes included performing the inevitable KP duty, sweating through paratrooper calisthenics, swabbing the decks, cleaning personal equipment, standing inspections, and following the usual off-duty pursuits of reading, writing letters, and practically unavoidable gambling. Training continued. The regimental S-2 officer conducted classes on the size and intelligence of the Japanese soldier, which the troops later learned was understated by about 50 percent. They would have to learn the hard way that the fighting Japanese soldier was bigger and smarter than they had been led to believe.

The medics continued their inoculations against smallpox, yellow fever, diphtheria, and tetanus. More than one soldier passed out when he received shots simultaneously in both arms and under his shoulder blade.

As the days aboard the *Poelau Laut* passed in seemingly endless monotony, the officers and men were becoming a little more familiar with Lieutenant Colonel Jones. By the time of the Corregidor jump, Colonel Jones would command the 503d RCT.

In November 1942 George Jones was thirty-one years old. He was well built at five feet eleven inches and weighing about 180 pounds. He liked to say that he had graduated near the top of his class at West Point, but that was true, he added, only if you turned the graduation roster (arranged by class academic rank) upside down. He also liked to say that he was in the upper 93 percent of his class.

After six years in the peacetime regular army, he got wind of a new concept in warfare—the paratroopers then being tested at Fort Benning, Georgia. In March 1941 he signed up, became the thirty-first officer qualified as a U.S. Army paratrooper, and joined the newly activated 501st Parachute Infantry Battalion. In September 1941 Captain Jones moved to Panama with the 501st as a company commander. In March 1942, Major Jones became the commander of the 501st and was promoted to lieutenant colonel in October 1942.

The man the 503d troopers saw aboard the *Poelau Laut* as their commander was a boyish-looking man whose looks belied his stern and no-nonsense approach to matters, particularly military and disciplinary ones. For example, some officers of the 503d had the temerity to purchase several cases of beer from the ship's steward and then to drink them—contrary to the standing order of no drinking aboard ship. Colonel Jones ordered the beer drinkers to the confines of their crowded quarters for a week, allowing them out only to march to meals. From that incident and because the troops had heard that somewhere in his past, presumably in Panama, he had served as a military police officer, he was dubbed "The Warden."

Finally, after a forty-two-day trip, hardly what one might term a cruise, the ship docked at Cairns, North Queensland, Australia, on 2 December 1942.

Colonel Kinsler resumed command of the regiment when it docked in Australia. Once there, the paratroopers settled down to building their camp with pyramidal and squad tents. Once that chore was over, they trained, parachuted, and staged mass parachute jumps for visiting VIPs, including Generals MacArthur, Krueger, and Eichelberger, and various Australian generals and dignitaries. The great heat and humidity of their area of Australia acclimatized them for later combat in New Guinea and the Philippines.

On 7 August 1943, the regiment received orders to move to New Guinea in preparation for combat operations. The troops left Australia by air and sea in the middle of August and moved into a large bivouac area near Port Moresby on New Guinea's southeastern tip.

The first combat test of the 503d was a jump on the Nadzab airfield in connection with the Lae operation. In General MacArthur's words:

> My plan to advance in northeast New Guinea and to seize the Huon Peninsula was entrusted to what was called the New Guinea Force. It was largely composed of Australian troops under the command of General Blamey. My order to the force was to seize and occupy the sector that contained Salamaua, Lae, Finchafen and Madang. Lae was the first major objective—its capture would breach the vital gate into Huon Peninsula. The advance pushed the

enemy back toward Salamaua with the purpose of deceiving him into the belief that it, and not Lae, was the pioneer objective.

General MacArthur continued:

On September 4th, the attack on Lae was launched by the Australians moving along the coast to strike from the east. At the same time, another Australian column was being prepared to fly in overland by way of the Markham Valley to strike from the west. The success of this second column depended upon the seizure of an unused prewar airfield at Nadzab. With this field in our possession, and made usable, we could land troops, close the gap, and completely envelop Lae and the enemy forces there.

It was a delicate operation involving the first major parachute jump in the Pacific War. The unit to make the jump was the United States 503 Parachute Regiment. I inspected them and found, as was only natural, a sense of nervousness among the ranks. I decided that it would be advisable for me to fly with them. [Obviously he was not going to jump with them.] I did not want them to go through their first baptism of fire without such comfort as my presence might bring to them. But they did not need me. [I suspect that the paratroopers did not know he was airborne with them.]

At Port Moresby, a week before the drop, Colonel Kinsler assembled his battalion commanders and staff at his regimental CP and briefed them on their mission, which was to drop on, seize, and hold the abandoned Nadzab airstrip. Australian engineers would come in and upgrade the strip to permit the landing of planes bringing in a complete Australian division. That division, he continued, would attack Lae from the west, and the 503d would continue to secure the Nadzab airstrip.

He told Lt. Col. John W. Britten to jump his 1st Battalion directly onto the airfield and clear it of all enemy troops, although the intelligence available indicated that there were relatively few Japanese on the strip. He directed Lt. Col. George Jones to jump his 2d Battalion north of the field to provide flank protection for Britten's battalion. He assigned Lt. Col. Jack Tolson and his 3d Battalion the task of jumping east of the field and securing the village of Gabmatzung.

In August of 1943 the 503d had no attached or organic artillery. To make up for this deficiency, one week before the drop, MacArthur's headquarters attached to the regiment thirty-one non-jump-qualified but volunteer artillerymen of the Australian 2/4 Field Artillery Regiment and their two 25-pound artillery pieces. To Lt. Robert W. Armstrong of head-quarters of the 1st Battalion fell the formidable task of training the Australians in the basic skills of jumping from an aircraft: plane-exiting procedures, parachute checks, reserve parachute operation, body positions in the door and on landing, prelanding checks, landing falls, and chute control on the ground, especially in the wind. The Australian artillery-men learned to disassemble the 25-pounders and pack them in parachutable bundles. By 5 September they were ready to go.

Three days before his D day, Colonel Kinsler had arranged for his staff and battalion commanders to make a high-altitude aerial reconnaissance of the target area. When they returned to Port Moresby, he gathered his company commanders and briefed them on the mission. The troops, however, had not yet been told about the pending operation, but they sensed something was up: their officers were going to secret meetings, and C-47s kept landing on the airstrip outside Port Moresby. Finally, on 4 September, the day before the drop, the company commanders assembled their companies and spelled out their missions in some detail.

On 4 September, the 9th Australian Division under Maj. Gen. G. P. Wooten landed amphibiously twenty miles to the east of Lae in the Bula River area against light opposition. However, by midmorning Japanese bombers attacked the congested beaches. The bombers returned in late afternoon and, in spite of being interrupted by U.S. fighters, managed to damage two ships and kill more than one hundred Australian and U.S. seamen. That evening, the 9th Division moved out to the west against the Japanese in the Lae area.

Predawn conditions at the Port Moresby airstrips, Ward and Jackson, on 5 September, the day of the planned airborne assault, threatened to abort the mission. As the troops were getting out of their bedrolls and trying to eat the usual soggy pancakes with a sugar-and-water syrup, the weather started to turn bad. By the time they had been trucked to the departure airfields, the rains came and the airstrips were socked in with fog. Takeoff had been scheduled for 0530, but at that time the fog and the light rain completely enveloped the strips. By 0730, however, the fog began to dissipate rapidly. A weather plane over the Owen Stanley Mountains radioed back an all clear. The mission was on. The troopers strapped themselves into their parachutes and about eighty pounds of combat gear and climbed aboard their assigned aircraft. At 0825, the first of seventy-nine C-47s of Col. Paul H. Prentiss's 54th Troop Carrier Wing roared down the runway; in less than thirty minutes seventeen hundred men of the 503d were airborne, in the literal sense.

Lieutenant General George C. Kenney, Fifth Air Force commander, made certain that the troop carrier convoy would not be defenseless en route to the Nadzab airstrip. He assigned 100 fighter aircraft to protect the slow-moving and necessarily bunched-up transports. Ahead of the troop carrier column General Kenney placed six squadrons of B-25s, each armed with eight .50-caliber machine guns and 120 fragmentation bombs in their bomb bays. The mission of the B-25s was to strafe the DZs just minutes before the jump. Six A-20s followed the B-25s to lay smoke alongside the DZs just before the drop to screen the descending paratroopers from snipers.

Flying high above these three hundred or so massed aircraft were three heavily armed B-17s—one carried Kenney and one carried MacArthur, with the third flying protection for the first two. And above the three bombers flew six P-47s, ready to pounce on any Japanese aircraft that might have the temerity to attempt to infiltrate this armada. The C-47s flew across the saddle of the Owen Stanley Range at an altitude of 9,000 feet and then descended to 3,500 feet as they approached the U.S. airfield at Marilinan. Above Marilinan the transports rearranged their flight into three columns, each six planes wide. There were twenty-six C-47s in each column, and each column carried one battalion of the 503d. As the planes approached the DZs, they descended to tree-top level and hedge-hopped toward the DZs. The bumpiness of the last part of the ride, the heat at the low altitude, and the traces of the soggy breakfasts did little to improve the airworthiness of the paratroopers jammed together on the canvas benches along the walls of the C-47s. By the time they reached Nadzab they were ready for the green light.

As the columns crossed over the Markham River, they ascended to their proper jump altitude of between 400 and 500 feet, a relatively low altitude for a mass drop but low enough to limit a paratrooper's time in the air and being a possible target for a sniper on the ground. At 1009 the red warning lights flashed on near the jump doors. The jumpmasters shouted the standard orders. At the instruction to "close in the door," the men bunched together as closely as possible for rapid jumps and tight landing patterns. At 1021 the troopers were ready to jump. At 1022 the green lights flashed on, and the first man in each of the three battalion columns swung out of the door to his left, grabbed his reserve, tucked his head into his chest, and waited for the opening shock—often a neck-snapping but welcome jolt. In rapid succession the twenty or twenty-one men in each of the sticks followed the lead jumper. In four and a half minutes the entire regiment was on its way to the ground. The pilots of Colonel Prentiss's 54th Troop Carrier Wing had, for the first time in the war, dropped a regiment of paratroopers with pinpoint accuracy on the assigned DZs. High above the drop MacArthur watched the proceedings with gleeful enthusiasm and ardent approval. "One plane after another poured out its stream of dropping men over the target field," he reminisced. "Everything went like clockwork. The vertical envelopment became a reality.

"We closed in from all sides and entered the shambles that had been Lae on September 6th.

"To my astonishment, I was awarded the Air Medal. Like all ground officers, this exceptionally pleased me, even though I felt it did me too much credit." Some of the troopers on the ground might have agreed.

Jack Tolson's 3d Battalion was the lead battalion in the regimental column; he was, of course, the jumpmaster of the lead ship in that formation. Fortunately, he had been over the DZ a few days before in a B-25 that had been on a bombing mission over Lae. He was fortunate to have some idea of where his DZ was because, while he was standing in the door of the plane after having been given the red light by the pilot, the red light went off but the green jump light did not come on. He immediately glanced back out the door and recognized that he was, in fact, over the proper DZ. Therefore, he decided to jump without the green "go" light. Not only did his stick of jumpers follow him out, but so did the rest of the battalion because all the jumpmasters took their cue from the lead ship. Tolson had wasted a few seconds checking for the green light and, so, landed a bit farther down the DZ than he had intended. He remembered that "as a result of this delay of a few seconds, a large number of my men landed in the trees on the far end of the DZ." But fortunately, the mass of his battalion was with him. Later, he checked with the plane's pilot and found that when the copilot switched off the red light, he had left the switch in the neutral position, thinking that he had turned on the green light. Tolson's quick thinking and previous trip over the DZ had saved the day. He thought that "[the] jump in the Markham Valley was a classic airborne operation."

MacArthur obviously agreed with him. Kenney later wrote to Gen. Hap Arnold that during the jump MacArthur was "jumping up and down like a kid." MacArthur told Kenney that the drop was "the most perfect example of training and discipline he had ever witnessed."

Once on the ground and surrounding the airfield, the paratroopers were faced not so much with Japanese resistance, which was negligible, but with the suffocating heat, the enervating humidity, and the eight-foot-tall, razor-sharp kunai grass that covered the drop zones and through which the men had to hack their way with machetes to get to their assembly areas. From the air, the kunai grass had looked short and inoffensive; on the ground, it was a formidable obstacle—not unlike a field of the notoriously sharp Spanish bayonet.

The high grass proved a minor disaster for the men of the 1st Battalion. On 7 September, they had set brush fires to clear the perimeter for better observation: the fires swept through the area and wiped out most of their parachutes and drop bundles.

In short order the three battalions were on their assigned objectives, and the Australian engineers moved to the Nadzab strip, so that by the next day the strip had been sufficiently cleared to permit the landing of C-47s carrying the lead elements of the Australian 7th Division. By 10 September the Aussies had relieved the 503d of its mission of defending the Nadzab airfield.

Because bad weather prevented the arrival of all of the Australian 7th Division and because the aggressive Australian 25th Brigade, attacking down the Markham River toward Lae, had its rear exposed, Gen. Sir Thomas Blamey, division commander, asked for and got permission to use the 3d Battalion, 503d, to protect the tail of the 25th. On 14 September, Jack Tolson led his 3d Battalion down the Markham Valley to the Jalu village area, about halfway between Lae and Nadzab. There he set up a base of operations and sent out numerous patrols in all directions to prevent the Japanese from attacking the 25th from the north and the west, and to keep open the 25th's supply lines from Nadzab. The 3d Battalion ran into small groups of Japanese who were escaping to the north from the Lae area. Under General Vasey's orders, the battalion also sought to cut off large numbers of the Japanese Imperial 541st Division.

On 15 September, I Company of the 3d Battalion ran into a large group of Japanese north of Log Crossing village. The lead elements of the company, especially Lt. Lyle Murphy's platoon, had a fierce firefight with the enemy. The firefight lasted from 1600 until almost dark; Jack Tolson sent forward additional companies from the battalion, and they dug in for the night around the village. Throughout the night, there were occasional cracks of rifle fire as the Japanese tried to break through Tolson's defenses.

Even nature gave the 2d Battalion a jolt. Before dawn on 16 September a severe earthquake rocked the area where the troops were dug in; this knocked down large trees and shook the area. The rumble and the quivering did little more, however, than keep the troops alert. The man-made quakes they were to feel later on Corregidor were much more formidable and deadly. By midmorning of the same day, a patrol of Australians operating from the Lae area moved across the stream below Company H's outposts. With this linkup, General Vasey relieved the 3d Battalion of its mission, and the battalion returned to Nadzab for departure by air.

On 14 September, Australian engineers had completed two parallel, 6,000-foot runways at Nadzab. And by 16 September, Lae had fallen to the two Australian divisions converging from the northwest and the east. On the next day the 503d was relieved of its mission at Nadzab and started its flight back to Port Moresby. By 19 September the regiment was closing its base camp.

Even the Japanese admired the work of the 503d. After the war Colonel Shinoara, intelligence officer of the Japanese Eighth Army, which was defending the Lae-Salamaua area, said: "We were retreating from the Salamaua area over the Finistere Mountains toward Reiss Point when Allied paratroopers landed at Nadzab, which was one place where we thought the enemy would never attack. The remaining elements of our 51st Division were virtually cut in half by this surprise pincer movement."

The 503d in its first taste of combat had had a number of casualties. Three men were killed on the jump, two when their chutes malfunctioned, and one when he landed in a tall tree and then fell to his death after sliding part of the way down on his jump rope. Thirty-three men were injured on the jump. Eight men were killed and twelve were wounded in fights that followed the jump. Most of these were from Tolson's 3d Battalion. But on 19 September 1943, Lieutenant Millican of E Company was killed when he ran through one of his company's booby traps outside the perimeter. And Private Rivas of A Company was killed by a Japanese grenade inside the company's perimeter on the edge of the airstrip.

MacArthur showed his pride in the 503d with a radio message to Colonel Kinsler.

"Now that the fall of Lae is an accomplished fact, I wish to make of record the splendid and important part taken by five nought three parachute infantry regiment stop under your able leadership, your officers and men exhibited the highest order of combat efficiency stop please express to all ranks my gratification and deep pride."

The 503d's successful jump on Nadzab impressed the higher-ups in Washington and was a strong factor in continuing the growth of airborne units and their insertion into combat at an increasing pace. Secretary of War Henry Stimson sent a message to commanders in the field urging them to give the 503d's Nadzab jump "effective application in prospective operations." Translation: Use airborne forces to increase the power and diversity of future military operations.

At Nadzab, the 503d had exhibited its prowess as an airborne regiment and proved that it could mount a parachute operation with skill, discipline, and speed. These were qualities the 503d would need in abundance when it made its airborne assault on Corregidor—an assault unique in the history of airborne warfare. But before it would be called upon to test its mettle, competence, and courage on Corregidor, it would have to undergo other tests by fire: Noemfoor was the next airborne operation on its schedule.

9: Back to Europe

The question the Allied chiefs of staff were pondering during the summer of 1943 was "What's next?". They had become optimistic: the Allies had eliminated the Axis powers in North Africa; the Sicily campaign had been a success; the Red Army had stopped the German offensive; the Allied bombers were weakening German industries; the Japanese were at last on the defensive in the Pacific, reeling back from the Allied attacks in New Guinea and New Georgia and withdrawing from the Aleutians. Only in the China-Burma-India theater were the Allies somewhat less powerful and successful.

At the Arcadia Conference in December 1941, the Allies had agreed on a "Germany first" policy. In January 1943, President Franklin D. Roosevelt and Prime Minister Winston S. Churchill had met at Casablanca to develop global strategy for the ultimate defeat of the Axis. The intricacies of consummating that strategy were far from clear at Casablanca. The British wanted to expand operations in the Mediterranean. Roosevelt wanted to continue the massive buildup of men and equipment for the eventual and "as soon as possible" cross-Channel invasion of France. Stalin wanted battles, somewhere, to draw the Germans away from Stalingrad. At Casablanca, the Allies agreed to invade Sicily to draw Germans away from the Eastern Front and to force Italy out of the war.

For two weeks in May 1943, with the defeat of Axis forces in North Africa, the Allied Combined Chiefs of Staff held the Trident Conference in Washington to clarify their strategy. By that time, the U.S. planners were on a par in experience with the British. With some reluctance, the Americans agreed that a cross-Channel invasion of France was not in the cards for 1943 and reaffirmed the strategy of driving Italy from the war by invading Sicily. The combined chiefs directed General Eisenhower to develop an ongoing strategy for continuing the war in southern Europe after knocking out Sicily,

Eisenhower's staff, working around the clock in its CP in St. George Hotel in Algiers, looked at three possible courses of action. The first, liked by the U.S. planners, was to move from Sicily to Corsica and Sardinia, and then into southern France. This plan had a disadvantage: it would probably not drive Italy from the war. In the second plan, the British planners wanted a drive through Italy into the Adriatic region to support Tito's Partisans in the Balkans, entice Turkey into the war, shorten the routes to the Soviet Union, require the Germans to commit more troops, and save the Balkans from the Soviets. The third option was attack up the boot of the Italian peninsula, push through the German forces, seize airfields for attacks against southern Germany and the highly important Romanian oil fields, and probably drive Italy out of the war. (In actuality, the Italians, fed up with losing men, territory, and facilities, had been looking for a safe way out of the war well before the end of the Sicily campaign.) And if Italy bolted from the Axis, twenty-nine Italian divisions in the Balkans and five in France would be out of action. Obviously, Germany would have to deploy comparable forces to replace the Italians.

General George C. Marshall had his own plan. On 16 July, based on the success of the Sicily campaign and on reports of the disintegration of the Italian army, he proposed a bold plan codenamed Avalanche: seize the port of Naples on the Italian mainland and the airfields at Foggia, about fifty miles to the northeast, and then move on Rome.

Eisenhower's staff whittled down its own plan to a two-pronged attack on the Italian mainland: one prong, Operation Baytown, between 1 and 4 September, would be an assault by the British Eighth Army across the Strait of Messina into the Calabria region to tie down Axis forces that might otherwise be free to attack an amphibious landing farther north; the second prong, Operation Avalanche, approximately one week later on 8 September, would be an amphibious landing by Lt. Gen. Mark Clark's Fifth Army near Naples. His mission was to push north and take Naples. To assist Clark, Eisenhower assigned him his 1917 West Point classmate, Matthew Ridgway, and his 82d Airborne Division to use as he saw fit.

Upon closer analysis, Eisenhower's planners realized that they had to look elsewhere than Naples for an amphibious landing. Naples was beyond Allied fighter aircraft range from Sicilian airfields, the beaches were unsuitable for a landing, defenses on Mount Vesuvius would dominate the landing area, and the roads inland were heavily fortified. As an alternative, the Allied planners selected the Salerno area, some fifty miles south of Naples for Clark's part of the invasion. Salerno was lightly defended in comparison with Naples, was within fighter range, had wide, accessible beaches, and was connected to highways leading inland to Naples and Rome. And its Montecorvino airfield, when captured, could handle four fighter squadrons. It had drawbacks that would come to haunt the attackers: the Sele River with its steep banks divided the plains around the city into two sectors, requiring bridges to connect forces on either side; the mountains around Salerno would limit the depth of the landings and bring the attacking force under enemy fire and observation.

On 25 July the Allies received a very welcome gift from Italian King Victor Emmanuel III: he ousted Benito Mussolini from his twenty-one-year reign as Duce and premier of Italy and appointed in his stead the aging Marshal Pietro Badoglio. The strutting and bombastic Mussolini made one last, and futile, visit to the king, who informed him that the vote of the state council was final. Mussolini left the palace in a fury, expecting to get into his limousine, only to find himself surrounded by Carabiniere officers who whisked him to the island of Ponza in the Gulf of Naples and locked him up.

Hitler was beside himself with rage. He ordered the Germans in Italy to seize the capital, the king, Marshal Badoglio, and the pope. Later he rescinded the orders when Col. Gen. Alfred Jodl told him that such actions would jeopardize the German units still fighting in Sicily. Instead, in mid-August Rommel, with Hitler's approval, moved five infantry and two panzer divisions from Germany into northern Italy. Two more elite units—the 2d Parachute and the 3d Panzer Grenadier Divisions—moved into defensive positions outside Rome, making a total of 40,000 troops near Rome. These forces were equipped with plenty of vehicles, some two hundred tanks, and abundant, well-supplied artillery, deployed and ready to fire for effect. Not only was Rome well defended because of these deployments, but since the Allies had not blocked the Germans from moving from Sicily to the mainland, a few days later some 102,000 Axis troops were able to move across the Strait of Messina to the mainland.

"Immediately after the battle of Sicily," wrote General Gavin, "the 82d Airborne returned to North Africa, arriving there on August 20, 1943."

It received reinforcements and equipped and prepared itself for
the coming invasion of Italy. For the Division Commander and for
the staffs of the division, this was an extremely busy period. Plans
were made, and then there were changes, and more plans and
more changes. Yet all that was typical of what usually happens in
the planning stages of an airborne operation.

The final plan for the amphibious invasion of Italy . . . was to be
known as operation AVALANCHE, named, one can suppose, for
the avalanche of combat troops soon to swarm onto the war-weary
Italian Peninsula. But to some of the wags on the staff of the 82d
Airborne Division, the name was more indicative of the avalanche
of airborne plans and papers that engulfed them in the days that
followed.

During the planning stages of Avalanche, the 82d's parachute battalions were bivouacked around the Tunisian city of Kairouan, on the same
airfields from which they had taken off five weeks earlier for the
parachute assault on Sicily.

General Ridgway pressured General Clark's staff to give the 82d Airborne a decisive role in the invasion of Italy. The result was Ridgway's
first assignment: the seizure of the towns of Nocera and Sarno at the exits of the passes leading northwest from Salerno with the objective of covering the landings of the Fifth Army. Available for the airborne operation were 319 troop carriers planes and 319 gliders. On 2 August, at the
division CP at Trapani, Sicily, General Ridgway briefed his regimental
commanders on the operation.

Intensive additional study with the Air Force determined that the paratroopers would have to be dropped in Nocera Pass on the Sorrento Ridge
at altitudes of 4,500 to 6,000 feet, in moonlight. But there were big problems: the airborne operation would be at the extreme limit of fighter aircraft range, there were many enemy fighter aircraft and antiaircraft guns
in the area, and the DZs were totally unsuitable. On 12 August Clark's
staff decided to dump the plan and drop the 82d farther inland. Gavin
agreed with the decision. "As I look back on it now, it seems to me that
this first plan contemplated the use of our airborne units merely to gain
a temporary tactical advantage. Their use according to this first plan
would hardly have had a decisive bearing on the outcome of the operation as a whole. It was a good thing that the plan was dropped."

On 18 August, still at his CP in Trapani on Sicily, Ridgway got a new mission, codenamed Giant One: conduct an airborne operation at the key road hub of Capua on the Volturno River, twenty miles northwest of Naples and some forty miles from the beach landings at Salerno, destroy all crossings of the Volturno from Trifliscoto to the beaches, and block the enemy from crossing the Volturno and moving to the south. The airborne operation supported the amphibious landings south of the mouth of the Volturno. The plan held that the 82d and the British 46th Division landing at Salerno would make contact within five days.

Ridgway named Gavin to be the airborne task force commander. At all levels, the staffs immediately dug into detailed planning. Gavin's task force was two parachute regiments, a parachute artillery battalion, two engineer companies, two batteries of 57mm antitank guns, and medical, signal, and reconnaissance forces to balance the team. After the parachute assault, Lt. Col. Harry L. Lewis and his 325th Glider Infantry Regiment were slated to move from Sicily by boat and land at the mouth of the Volturno, fight inland sixteen miles, and link up with Gavin's paratroopers in their airhead. Gavin concluded that he would need 175 tons of supplies delivered by parachute daily to keep the isolated task force fighting continuously. "At the very least," he wrote, "the airborne task force would need regular supplies for a period of five days—until contact was made between our force and units of the British 46th Division, which would have landed at Salerno. . . . Any serious failure in the resupply of the 82d Airborne Task Force could only mean its loss." Another dilemma presented itself: shortly after the detailed planning for Giant One began, the U.S. Navy announced that the beaches selected for the amphibious landing were unsuitable and this phase was dropped from the plan.

The staffs planned the airborne operation down to its smallest details. The longer Gavin, Tucker, and Ridgway studied the plan, the more they were convinced that it would result in a disaster for the 82d. In meetings with the Fifth Army staff, Ridgway emphasized the enormous resupply problem requiring some 145 air transports to drop in the daily supplies. Furthermore, simultaneously with the drop of Gavin's task force, the veteran 509th Parachute Infantry Battalion, now attached to the 82d, was slated to drop somewhere behind the Salerno beachhead—at Battipaglia, Avellino, Nocera, or Sarno, to stop the Germans from reaching Salerno.

On 31 August, a star-studded array of Allied brass, including General Eisenhower, Admiral Hall, Air Chief Marshal Tedder, General Clark, all British and U.S. corps commanders, and some division commanders, including General Ridgway, assembled in the headquarters of Fifth Army at Mostaganem in Algeria to review the invasion plans. In keeping with his relatively low rank and in the presence of the pompous Clark, Ridgway was allowed only three minutes to discuss the Volturno River plan. In his brief summary Ridgway made his point: Giant One was tactically unsound and could wipe out the 82d Airborne Division. After considerable discussion and with strong supporting views from Tedder, Eisenhower canceled the mission.

Ridgway and his staff returned to the division CP at Kairouan. Only thirteen days remained until D day for Avalanche, but the 82d Airborne Division, in spite of the various, ill-conceived plans and the ardent desire of Ridgway, did not have a mission.

The 82d's staff continued to plan for any eventuality. The G-3 section (operations) of the division staff worked on devices and procedures to obviate the most pressing problem of an airborne operation made clear by the previous two combat jumps: how to get the paratroopers to the right DZ at the right time in the dark. The solution was to drop in— ahead of the main body—pathfinders equipped with small Rebecca-Eureka (mark II) radar sets to guide the lead pilots to the proper area; thirty-three-pound radio beacons (5G); and Krypton lamps, small devices that emitted a blinding one-second flash visible even in daylight from 10,000 feet up. The tests proved satisfactory, and thus were born the first highly trained and well-equipped pathfinder units.

On the evening of 2 September, Ridgway, Taylor, and the 82d's G-3 staff flew to Fifteenth Army Headquarters at Syracuse on Sicily. They moved into a conference room and listened in awe to a briefing by a British colonel. "On the night of 8–9 September," he told the astonished group, "you will air-land your maximum airborne force on three airfields just north of Rome and seize the city." Ridgway had not been consulted in advance about such a preposterous plan.

"It was to be the seizure of Rome," wrote General Gavin, "one of the most interesting plans of the war, a plan that was extensively discussed and argued about many years after the war."

This operation, known as GIANT TWO, called for landing the strongest airborne task force that the available aircraft could carry on three airfields immediately east and northeast of Rome. Because of the distance of Rome from the take-off airfields in Sicily, there was no possibility of fighter support. The date for GIANT TWO was the night of September 8–9. The mission was to secure Rome by operating in conjunction with the Italian forces in the Rome area. The airborne lift was to be repeated the next night and as directed thereafter until the mission of the 15th Army Group was accomplished. The airborne part of the operation was to be supported by a landing at the mouth of the Tiber River, also staged by troops of the 82d Airborne Division.

At a secret meeting in Spain in August, Italian representatives had assured Gens. Walter Bedell Smith and Kenneth Strong that Italian forces would cooperate fully once the mission was under way. But Ridgway realized that the Germans might make it impossible for the Italians to be of any help. By the time of the Salerno landings, the Germans had stripped the Italians of most of their ammunition and gasoline, immobilizing and defanging them. There were other problems with GIANT TWO: Rome was beyond fighter and glider range, and air-landing troops at night was slow and dangerous.

The plan kept changing. The latest version called for Tucker's 504th to jump on the night of 8 September on the Fubara and Cerveteri airfields near the seacoast and then push inland to Rome. Gavin's 505th was slated to jump on the second night on Guidonia, Littorio, and the Centocelle airfields, nearer the center of Rome, followed by division headquarters, support units, and Harry Lewis's 325th Glider Infantry Regiment air-landing in C-47s.

By early September, the 82d had moved from North Africa and was based on airfields in Sicily. On the afternoon of 8 September, the 504th went ahead with "suiting up" for the operation, as ordered. The troopers checked orders and plans, loaded their paracontainers, and made last-minute checks on ammunition, rations, and weapons. The division's teams of pathfinders, based at the field at Agrigento, were to precede the main landings by some thirty minutes. On the evening of 8 September, the pathfinders were fully rigged and their planes were on the runway with engines running ready to take off. Minutes before launch the mission was postponed for twenty-four hours.

Giant Two's actuality depended on a unique subterfuge. As the days wore on, General Eisenhower became increasingly concerned that the attack on Rome as planned, with a small, lightly armed airborne force, was headed for disaster, given the pathetic state of the Italian army and the strong buildup of German forces around Rome. He decided to infiltrate two senior officers into Rome to determine whether the Italians would and could live up to their end of the bargain agreed upon earlier in Spain. Selected for the risky scheme were the brilliant Brig. Gen. Maxwell D. Taylor, the 82d's artillery commander, well versed in five languages, and Col. William T. Gardiner, the commander of a troop carrier squadron based in Sicily. Gardiner, fifty-three, was a former governor of Maine and had been a prominent lawyer in civilian life; he also was fluent in French. Eisenhower told Taylor that he was to assess the situation and, if he thought the operation should be amended or that it was virtually impossible to carry out, he had the authority to communicate from Rome by concealed radio any alterations to the plan or to cancel it outright by radioing the codeword "Innocuous." Later Eisenhower wrote that "the risks he [Taylor] ran were greater than I asked any other agent or emissary to undertake during the war—he carried weighty responsibilities and discharged them with unerring judgment, and every minute was in imminent danger of discovery and death."

At 0200 on the morning of 7 September, the two unusual emissaries in summer dress uniforms devoid of rank insignia and ribbons went by a British torpedo boat to the island of Ustica and transferred to an Italian navy corvette *Ibis*, which landed them at Gaeta. As they hustled down the ramp, the Italians doused them with salt water and treated them as captured airmen. They were then loaded into an Italian ambulance for the seventy-five-mile hazardous ride to Rome. Through windows in the ambulance, Taylor could see a number of German roadblocks and increasing numbers of German soldiers marching along the road as the ambulance neared Rome. At about 2030, Taylor and Gardiner reached the Palazzo Caprara in Rome. Once there, an elegant Italian dinner and endless small talk convinced General Taylor that the Italians were not ready to discuss business seriously. Taylor finally met with Gen. Giacomo Garboni, commander of the Italian troops in the area and, at about midnight, with Marshal Badoglio in his villa. Speaking in French, Badoglio told Taylor and Gardiner that the Germans had moved some 120 tanks and 36,000 troops to both the north and south of Rome. He also said that he could not guarantee that the airfields would be in Italian hands and that the airborne landings would cause the Germans to take drastic action against the Italians. Therefore, he reasoned realistically, the operation would be a disaster.

General Taylor radioed Algiers, reported that "Giant Two is impossible," and asked for new instructions. General Eisenhower received the message at 0810 hours on 8 September. Taylor and Gardiner waited anxiously for a reply; none came. At 1135, just ten hours before Rube Tucker and his 504th were due to parachute onto the airfields near Rome, Taylor took matters into his own hands and radioed Algiers again: "Situation innocuous." Eisenhower canceled the mission. To ensure that his decision was clear to Ridgway and would not be garbled in a radio message, Eisenhower sent a staff officer, Brig. Gen. Lyman Lemnitzer, to Sicily to hand-carry the cancellation order to Ridgway. Lemnitzer took off from Bizerte in a light plane for the night flight to Licata on the southern shore of Sicily.

Meanwhile, at 1830, Eisenhower began reading on Radio Algiers, the announcement of the Italian armistice. The message included the statement that "all Italians who now act to help eject the German Aggressor from Italian soil will have the assistance and support of the United Nations." This announcement was the prearranged signal to launch Giant Two. Hundreds of paratroopers, who had in the previous two hours assembled in stick order by their planes, began a boarding their C-47s. Shortly thereafter, the pathfinder planes and some of the troop aircraft roared down the runways and headed for Rome.

General Lemnitzer's pilot had missed Sicily initially but finally made it to the runway at Licata. In a rush, Lemnitzer found Tucker and delivered the message to cancel the mission. Sixty-two planes already en route to Rome were called back. Once again, the 82d was without an airborne mission in the invasion of Italy. As General Gavin put it: "D-day came and H-hour struck, and despite the many plans and the days and nights of staff work, the airborne troops found themselves sitting and waiting on their take-off airdromes. Patience is an essential attribute of a good airborne trooper."

At 0430 on 3 September Operation Baytown was under way. The British Eighth Army crossed the Strait of Messina against very light opposition. After the formal announcement of the Italian surrender on 8 September, the Germans moved quickly to disarm their former allies. On 9 September, in a hastily readied operation, Slapstick, 3,600 paratroopers of the British 1st Airborne Division landed unopposed at the port of Taranto, on the heel of the Italian peninsula.

At 0330 on the morning of 9 September, some 450 ships gathered off the coast of Salerno to launch the main effort in the invasion of Italy, Operation Avalanche, about 150 miles to the north of the British invasion and 100 miles south of Rome. Some of the ships had sailed as early as 5 and 6 September from Sicily and some from Tripoli, Oran, and Bizerte in North Africa.

General Sir Harold Alexander commanded the Allied 15th Army Group made up of Montgomery's British Eighth Army and Clark's U.S. Fifth Army. Clark was a World War I veteran, had been Eisenhower's deputy for Operation Torch, and now commanded the invasion force. The Fifth Army was composed of the British X Corps, commanded by Lt. Gen. Sir Richard L. McCreery, and the U.S. VI Corps, commanded by Maj. Gen. Ernest J. Dawley (West Point class of 1910). He had served with Pershing against Pancho Villa and with Marshall in World War I. In 1943 he was fifty-seven years old, seven years older than Clark. The age difference, and the fact that Dawley was a close friend of Lt. Gen. Lesley J. McNair, created a difficult relationship between Clark and Dawley.

The assault force consisted of two British divisions, the 46th from Bizerte and the 56th from Tripoli. Only one U.S. division from VI Corps, the untested 36th Infantry Division (Texas National Guard) commanded by Maj. Gen. Fred L. Walker, could land. There was a shortage of landing craft, so the division had sailed from Oran. Other assault elements included in the Avalanche force were three U.S. Ranger battalions commanded by Lt. Col. William O. Darby and the 2d and 41st British Commandos. Two regimental combat teams (RCTs) from the U.S. 45th Division (Arizona National Guard) commanded by Maj. Gen. Troy Middleton, made up a floating reserve. General Clark's intelligence team told him to expect some 39,000 enemy troops on D day and about 100,000 some three days later when German reinforcements rushed to Salerno. Clark hoped to land some 150,000 Allied troops.

The British X Corps on the left was to land two divisions abreast south of Salerno and north of the Sele River. The U.S. Rangers and the British Commandos were to come ashore on the beaches west of Salerno to secure the left flank by seizing mountain passes through the Sorrento Peninsula between Naples and Salerno. On the right, the green 36th Infantry Division was to land, followed as soon as possible by the 45th Division and other U.S. units. The 36th would land south of the Sele River, leaving a formidable ten-mile gap and the Sele River between the British and the Americans.

The amphibious assault began early on the morning of 9 September. At 0310 the Rangers, twenty minutes ahead of the main assault, waded ashore unopposed and seized Sorrento because the Germans had not had time to take over the defenses from the Italians. The Commandos were less fortunate, and had to fight a vicious three-day battle before they captured the town of Salerno. The two divisions of the British X Corps on the left landed after a heavy naval gunfire preparation and fought against heavy opposition as they dug in close to the shore. On the right, the 36th Division came ashore with no naval gunfire support. The advanced elements took severe losses, but by 0610 all six waves of the 36th, dubbed the "Texas Army," were on the beach and began to move inland. Gavin wrote that "despite the presence of strong detachments of the German 16th Panzer Division, the 36th did exceptionally well. Driving inland, it seized the high hills at Altavilla, Albanella, and Rocca d'Aspide. After the first forty-eight hours there was considerable satisfaction in the higher command with the good work of the 36th, despite the gap of almost ten miles between the U.S. divisions and the nearest British division to the north."

General Heinrich von Vietinghoff, commander of the 16th Panzer Division, had been moving his division toward Rome well inland from the beach. When he learned of the invasion, he asked Kesselring's permission to turn around and attack to the south. Kesselring did not reply, so Vietinghoff made his own decision and turned back. After his reconnaissance forces reported the ten-mile gap between the U.S. and British divisions, Vietinghoff attacked the northern flank of the 36th on the morning of 12 September. His tanks and infantrymen poured through the gap. The 36th's flank collapsed, and Vietinghoff's force overran the high ground and the villages nearby, and very soon his forces were within six miles of the beach. Vietinghoff was elated and reported to his commander that he was about to drive the retreating Americans back into the sea. On 13 September the Germans launched a major counterattack with over four divisions, overrunning a battalion of the 36th, threatening the rear of the Allied position, and moving to within three miles of the beach. Clark became so concerned that he told his chief of staff, Gen. Alfred M. Gruenther, to plan the evacuation of one of the two beachheads and land its forces on the other. When General Dawley heard about a possible withdrawal, he protested strenuously. He did not want an American Dunkirk.

But Clark and his airborne advisor, Lt. Col. William Yarborough, recently transferred to Clark's staff from the 82d, had another plan—bring in the 82d Airborne Division. Yarborough recommended dropping two RCTs teams directly onto the beachhead behind Allied lines and one battalion at Avellino, a small town twenty miles north of Salerno. He pointed out that Avellino was a bottleneck that had to be broken because the Germans moving south by rail or road from Rome had to pass through the town. The shortage of C-47s would require that the RCTs be dropped a day apart and at night because of the strong daylight presence of the German Luftwaffe.

At about 1330 on 13 September an exhausted and begrimed fighter pilot, Capt. Jacob R. Hamilton, landed his P-38 on the airstrip at Licata on Sicily. He told Colonel Gavin, who happened to be on the runway, that he had an urgent message for General Ridgway and he would not give it to anyone else. Ridgway was in the air on the way to Termini to check the Salerno situation on the ground. Gavin had the division chief of staff, Col. Ralph P. "Doc" Eaton, radio Ridgway, who in turn had his pilot turn around in the air and land back at Licata. As soon as Ridgway got out of his plane, Hamilton handed Clark's message to Ridgway. It was an appeal for immediate reinforcement of the beachhead based on the recommendations by Bill Yarborough. Clark also guaranteed that the airborne force would not be attacked by "friendly" antiaircraft fire as had happened in Sicily. Ridgway was so adamant that the antiaircraft guns at Salerno not fire on his planes that that afternoon, after his jump plans had been hastily developed, he sent a few staff officers to the beachhead to check it out.

At Licata the 82d and the troop carrier staffs went into a huddle. "They reallocated the departure airfields, reshuffled troops as necessary, and prepared flight plans," wrote Gavin.

An immediate check was made to insure that our own ground troops and our Navy received clear warning of our routes and times, with descriptions of our flights. The messenger with General Clark's letter also delivered a plan for marking the drop zone prepared by a Fifth Army airborne staff officer (Colonel Yarborough). The troops already in the area would use cans of sand soaked with gasoline, laid out in the form of a large letter "T" (each leg a half mile long). They would light them up on the first flight of transports over the drop zone, and douse them out with dirt when the transports had gone.

In addition, special pathfinding homing equipment was to be dropped on the Sele River beachhead drop zone with the stick from the first airplane. This would then be used to assist the following airplanes to home accurately on the drop zone. All pilots and jump-masters were carefully briefed on the plan.

All plans were complete eight hours after the request for rein-forcements came from General Clark, and the troops were loaded with their complete equipment, rations, and ammunition, and the C-47s were rolling down the runways on the way.

At about 2310, at 800 feet over the DZ, Lt. William B. Jones, leader of the newly formed pathfinders, craned his head out the door of his C-47, piloted by Lt. Col. Joel Crouch, operations officer of Brig. Gen. Hal Clark's 52d Troop Carrier Wing, and spotted the burning "T." When Yarborough heard Jones's C-47 arrive on schedule, he fired a flare from his Very pistol, and his well-rehearsed team on the ground lit the gaso-line-filled jerry cans that formed the flaming marker. Jones then led his team out the door of his C-47; two other C-47s carrying the rest of the fifty pathfinders followed them. On the ground, in a matter of minutes the pathfinders set up their homing devices and had their radios in con-tact with the oncoming armada of C-47s. So far things were going well.

At about 2325, C-47s from the 61st, 313th, and 314th Troop Carrier Groups, carrying the first battalion of the main body of the 504th RCT, flew over the DZ at only 600 feet, an altitude low enough to ensure ac-curacy. The DZ was on a strip of sandy terrain two and a half miles south of the Sele River near Paestum. Major Dan Danielson led his 2d Battal-ion, 504th, out the doors of the planes: in a few minutes the night air was filled with the white parachutes of the battalion. Most of the troop-ers landed within 200 yards of the DZ; none of the jumpers came down more than a mile away. The troops rapidly doffed parachutes, gathered their gear, mounted trucks provided by the forces already in the beach-head, and headed for combat.

The second wave, carrying Rube Tucker, his command group, and the 1st Battalion, 504th, commanded by Lt. Col. Warren Williams, was not as fortunate. Tucker's fifty-one planes were ready to take off at 2100, but they had been delayed on the runways because of repairs to some of the planes. Tucker finally ordered the planes to take off in single or double flights. It was not until 0230 that Tucker's first planes dropped Williams's troopers on the DZ, marked once again with Yarborough's flaming "T." And not one plane had been fired on by "friendly" antiaircraft em-placements. One hour after the last plane had dropped its paratroop-ers, Tucker had assembled his 1,300 men, and he reported to General

Dawley that they were all assembled and ready. Dawley sent the 504th to bolster the battered 36th Division. By sunrise, Tucker had his two battalions of the 504th in place and ready to fight. The paratroopers' arrival through the air, filling the sky with parachutes, bolstered the morale of the 36th Division soldiers, who cheered from their trenches when they saw the chutes in the air.

Tucker's first mission was the seizure of the town of Altavilla. He marched the rest of his paratroopers on the double and had them on the line by dawn. He told them that there would be no retreat. Gavin said that although "the 504th has had little sustained combat in Sicily; it was commanded by a tough, superb combat leader, Colonel Reuben Tucker, probably the best regimental commander of the war."

Altavilla was located at the foot of a hill, which Tucker and his two battalions took from the Germans, who left batches of soldiers behind. At dawn the reinforced Germans counterattacked, and Tucker's stalwarts held. This was the second time that the Americans had seized the hill, important as it was for its field artillery observation posts. The 36th had taken it once, only to be driven off by German panzers. For two days, the 504th held, and then Ridgway told Tucker to withdraw. He refused and asked for his third battalion that Ridgway had held in division reserve. He got it and stayed in place.

The next day, 14 September, Clark canceled the 505th's drop on Capua, ordered Ridgway to drop the 505th on the DZ at Paestum, team up the two regimental combat teams at Salerno, and attack. That night, Gavin's 2,100 paratroopers loaded up in their 131 C-47s and took off into the moonlit night on schedule. "Soon after we left the northwest corner of Sicily," wrote Gavin, "the Italian mainland came into view off to the east."

We crossed a peninsula jutting into the Tyrrhenian Sea. In the plane the red warning light came on to tell us that we were approximately four minutes out from the drop zone. We seemed to have been flying over the peninsula forever when a white beach and a river mouth appeared. The scene looked exactly like that in the photos of the correct drop zone. The green light flashed on. There was no burning T on the ground as we had been told there would be, but the area appeared to be correct in every way, so out we went.

The first parachutes had barely opened when the great T did light up directly under us. To the Germans who occupied the hills, the operation must have appeared bizarre. Units began to reorganize; they assembled without any interference. A combat team was in action by daylight.

Yarborough met Gavin on the DZ and took him to General Clark's headquarters, where General Gruenther told Gavin to defend the southern sector and tie in with Tucker near Albanella. "Your line will extend to the sea near Agropoli," he said. Gavin loaded his men into the waiting trucks and headed out. By dawn the 505th was on line. In just over twenty-four hours, with only eight hours advance notice, some 3,400 superbly trained and led paratroopers had been airlifted and dropped directly onto the target DZ and were in the fight.

With the arrival of the paratroopers and their solid defense against the charging Germans, the morale of the troops on the beachhead soared. The battle was turned around. On the afternoon of 15 September the British force was still fifty miles to the south, so Kesselring ordered one final assault against the beachhead. It did not succeed. The failure of his attacks on 15 and 16 September caused him to withdraw to the north. On 16 and 17 September the Allies pushed ahead against the withdrawing enemy.

As early as 15 September Clark had announced that "our beachhead is secure and we are here to stay." Later that day, the 325th Glider Infantry Regiment and one attached parachute infantry battalion landed on the beach after a two-day sail from Sicily. The 325th went north of Salerno to help clear the Sorrento Peninsula, and Tucker's paratroopers marched to join the regiment at Albanella. On 18 September General Vietinghoff began a gradual withdrawal of his troops from the beachhead area.

The use of the 82d Airborne Division to reinforce the Salerno beachhead was not the sort of airborne mission initially envisaged by the original paratrooper commanders. At Salerno the paratroopers dropped onto friendly territory, on a DZ marked by U.S. ground troops. But the next phase of the airborne operation near Salerno was more typical of what the early planners had in mind—a drop well behind enemy lines with a mission to block, confuse, and scatter the enemy.

On the evening of 14 September, Lt. Col. Doyle R. Yardley, Colonel Raff's replacement as commander of the 509th Parachute Infantry Battalion, jumped his battalion into the start of a hazardous operation, the seizure of Avellino, the place that Bill Yarborough called a bottleneck, a crossroads through which flowed vast numbers of German combat units going or coming from the beachhead. The 509th was to be the cork in that bottleneck.

This was to be the riskiest of the three combat jumps by the 82d around Salerno (the 509th now being attached to the 82d). With about an hour's advance notice, Ridgway had arrived at Yardley's CP in an olive grove near Licata at about 1600 on 14 September. Ridgway told Yardley and his assembled staff and company commanders that the "Fifth Army is in serious trouble over at Salerno. You and your men will be jumping tonight well behind the lines, at a place called Avellino . . . Your mission there will be to occupy, prior to daylight, a large crossroads area at the south edge of town and deny its use to enemy units moving through it down to Salerno. This is going to be an especially dangerous mission, gentlemen." Ridgway also told Yardley that the 509th was to hold the crossroads "until relieved by Fifth Army." He added that "the Fifth Army's fate is in your hands, Good luck and Godspeed."

The mission gave Colonel Yardley more than a gentle jolt. Gavin described Avellino as "the junction of several important roads, to Salerno and Battipaglia to the north, and toward which German reserves were likely to come from farther south where hard-pressed German divisions were withdrawing under pressure of the British Eighth Army. . . . There were, however, no suitable drop zones in the area; what few flat cleared areas the photographs showed were too small, and the mountains were so high that it was impossible to jump at proper low altitudes."

For the next six hours, Yardley, his staff, and the staff of the 64th Troop Carrier Group tried to work out the details of this combat jump, which would have been difficult enough when they had had days to plan it. When the meeting with Ridgway broke up, Yardley ordered the company commanders to move their troops to the aircraft at Comiso airfield. The fighting soldiers in the ranks had little knowledge of the details of their mission, but after going through all the standard procedures of readying themselves for combat jump and boarding their planes, they realized that they were taking off and assembling in the air for the flight to Avellino. (Yardley also had a demolition section attached to his battalion.)

For the first hour or so the C-47s managed to hold a V of V's formation. But as the column moved up the coast, it began to break apart. At midnight, the planes were climbing to avoid the mountains around the so-called DZ. And, as time wore on, the C-47s drifted farther and farther apart. The pathfinders, Lts. Fred Perry and Henry F. Rouse and their team, were in a single C-47 that had preceded the main body by half an hour. Near the selected area Perry, with his head out the door, thought he was over the DZ. He jumped, and his team followed him out the door. But he had picked the wrong crossroad and was a mile south of the designated DZ. Once on the ground, he realized that he could not get to the proper DZ in time, so he marked the area where his pathfinder team had landed. But his 5G radio beacon and Aldis lamp were useless in the mountains. The scattered C-47s carrying the 509th droned on. Finally, the jump began over what some of the jumpmasters thought was the proper area. The result was a disaster. Just as they had been scattered over a wide area in North Africa, the paratroopers were spread over almost 100 square miles around Avellino. Fifteen planes dropped their jumpers within four miles of the DZ; twenty-three scattered them between eight and twenty-five miles from the DZ; two planeloads were lost.

In spite of the widespread dispersion of Yardley's men, some of them were able to join up in small groups. Over the next few days, in scattered teams they mined roads, blew up bridges, and cut telephone lines in the area, knocking out German communications. They ambushed enemy patrols, shot up convoys, and attacked German outposts. The German leaders thought there were far more paratroopers in their rear area than there really were and sent many patrols out looking for them. The paratroopers' actions reduced the potential of a regiment of the 15th Panzer Grenadier Division that had been deployed around Avellino during the preceding two days.

Colonel Yardley was in one of the ten planes that had managed to find the proper DZ. On the ground, Yardley gathered what men he could find along a road and got them ready for the three-mile march to Avellino. A little after 0100 on the morning of 15 September, he had gathered about 30 of his 641 men and decided to move out to the crossroads—his mission. About two miles down the road, a German machine gun opened fire on them and sent them jumping into ditches and behind trees along the road. Yardley could see many German tanks in the crossroads. He and his men tried to shoot their way out of their trap, but it was useless. The Germans used flares to pinpoint the crouching paratroopers and hit them with 88mm artillery shells. Yardley and a number of his men, including Lt. Jack Pogue, the battalion communications chief, were wounded, captured, and hauled off in a German ambulance. They spent the rest of the war as POWs.

Others, including Capt. Carlos "Doc" Alden, the battalion surgeon, took to the hills in the dark. Shortly afterward Doc Alden found some wounded troopers near a house in the woods; he stopped to treat them, but a number of Germans found them and took them prisoner. A few minutes later a lone paratrooper saw the group, thought they were enemy, and opened fire. In the melee that followed Doc Alden led his patients out of the area and away from the Germans.

Sergeant Levi W. Carter also managed to escape from the German tank park. He had earlier tried to hide in a ditch during daylight but was captured, and the Germans had made him and another paratrooper, Corporal Sabat, Yardley's radio operator, bury their dead comrades.

For the next few days and nights, bands of 509th paratroopers prowled the area harassing the enemy as far as forty miles deep into German territory. Captain Edmund J. Tomasik, two other officers, Sgt. Sol Weber, and about sixteen men blew a bridge over which was moving a German truck convoy loaded with Germans, the blast blowing one truck into the air. The group of troopers escaped into the dark. In another area, Capt. Archie Birkner and some fifteen men set up an ambush site and took out staff cars and any other unfortunate German going by, amassing a total of fourteen of the enemy. But Birkner's luck did not hold out: a strong patrol found them and took them prisoners. Birkner survived the war as a POW.

Over the next couple of weeks, 532 troopers out of the 640 who had parachuted behind the German lines filtered back to U.S. lines. Many others had been killed or made prisoner. "The battalion had accomplished what General Mark Clark had had in mind," wrote Gavin. "It disrupted German communications and partly blocked the Germans' supplies and reserves. It also caused the Germans to keep units on anti-parachute missions that otherwise could have been used at the point of their main effort at Salerno."

By D day plus 9, 18 September, German combat formations were moving to the north. And on 23 September the Fifth Army followed, fighting toward Naples thirty miles ahead. Naples, with its excellent port and airfields around Foggia was a superb jumping-off point for the inevitable Allied attack on Rome. But the Fifth Army's delayed attack gave the Germans time to set up defenses using the nearby mountainous terrain. The British X Corps led the assault against the defenses, and at first gained some nine miles. But then the attack wilted in the face of the rugged terrain, German demolitions, and a dug-in rear guard.

To speed up the attack, Clark formed a British and U.S. force with the 82d Airborne Division, the British 23d Armored Brigade, and a battalion of the U.S. Army Rangers. He put Ridgway in command of this combined force with its mission of passing through the X Corps and taking Naples.

On the evening of 27 September, Ridgway's combat command moved out and moved through Chiunzi Pass against relatively light opposition. Leading the attack were the British and Gavin's 505th Parachute Infantry. They rumbled and marched past the ruins of Pompeii and the base of Mount Vesuvius, the paratroopers gaping in awe at the smoldering volcano. Three days later, on the morning of 1 October, Gavin's lead scouts and a few British tanks reached the outskirts of Naples. Later that morning, Maj. John Norton, first captain of the West Point class of 1941 and now Gavin's operations officer, arrived from the rear. He told Gavin that he was to halt on the outskirts and wait for Clark and Ridgway until a "triumphal entry is organized." Gavin did as ordered, but the "triumphal entry" never materialized. Thousands of Italians crowded Piazza Plebiscito the traditional reception point for arriving "conquerors." But at midafternoon Gavin, riding in a jeep followed by Clark and Ridgway standing in a halftrack and Gavin's 3d Battalion in trucks, drove into an empty Garibaldi Square, about a mile away. Nonetheless, for the benefit of the accompanying press, Clark gave a short message to the advance guard duly noting the capture of the first large European city by the Allies. Later Clark wrote in *Calculated Risk,* "There was little that was triumphant about our journey. I felt that I was riding through ghostly streets in a city of ghosts. We didn't see a soul. . . . It was still that way as we drove out of Naples."

Clark gave Ridgway the task of cleaning up the smoking city and restoring law and order. The latter set up his command post in the Naples police chief's office and started to work, dividing the city into three zones of occupation, one for each of his regiments. The Germans had ruled Naples with traditional brutality, rewarding collaborators and executing resisters. The Allies had bombed Naples heavily, but most of the damage to the city had been caused by the Germans. Kesselring had forbidden attacking churches and monasteries, but the rest of the city was left open for ravaging. Before they left, the Germans had tried hard to gut the city, destroying communications, transportation, water, and electricity facilities. They burned hotels, broke down bridges, ripped up railroad tracks, and set fire to huge dumps of coal. They left time bombs and booby traps that later blasted buildings throughout the city, and they sank additional ships in the harbor. On 7 October the main post office building blew up, wounding some seventy-five people, half of whom were troopers of the 82d. On 11 October another bomb blew up in the 307th Engineer Battalion barracks, killing eighteen and wounding another fifty-six. Naples had become a city in chaos, with some 200,000 Neapolitans depending on the Allies for basic survival. But the troopers went about the task of rebuilding the city, and by the end of October nearly 7,000 tons of supplies were coming into the city daily. Meanwhile, there were new recruits to fill out the 509th. The paratrooper pioneer, Lt. Col. Bill Yarborough, moved from Clark's staff and assumed command of the battalion to replace the captured Doyle Yardley. Yarborough's new mission was to guard Fifth Army headquarters, and for that assignment, the 509th was detached from the 82d Airborne Division.

By 3 October, British patrols were at the Volturno River as the German forces withdrew behind that barrier. Four days later most of the British X Corps had closed on the river; the U.S. VI Corps fought its way through sixty miles of mountains and rugged valleys and occupied its south bank. Clark ordered a general assault on the Volturno for 13 and 14 October.

After Naples was secured Gavin and his 505th continued to attack toward the river. He claimed that "the fighting was not too costly, and the Germans were obviously withdrawing. They would usually make a stand by late morning, and after we drove them back and prepared for a heavy attack the following morning, we invariably found that they had withdrawn during the night."

The 505th's mission was to secure crossings on the Volturno. Gavin ordered his 2d Battalion commander, Maj. Mark Alexander, to take the town of Arnone and the five canal crossings nearby. Lieutenant Colonel Walter Winton's 1st Battalion was kept in reserve, while the 3d Battalion stayed in Naples on occupation duty. On the night of 4 October, the 2d Battalion attacked and within twenty-four hours seized five canal bridges. Arnone, however, was staunchly defended by the Germans. But on 6 October, after a bloody two-hour battle with intense German artillery fire, and using British artillery on German counterattacks, the 2d/505th overran the town. Two days later the 505th returned to Naples and police duties in the city. During the fight, Gavin was in the process of turning his regiment over to his executive officer, Col. Herbert F. Batcheller (class of 1935) because Gavin had been notified that he was being promoted to brigadier general.

"Just before we reached the Volturno," Gavin wrote, "General Ridgway called me back to division headquarters and informed me that I was to be the Assistant Division Commander.... On Sunday October 10, General Ridgway arranged a brief star-pinning ceremony in front of the Questura, the city police station, which we had been using as a headquarters." Gavin thus assumed the other brigadier general position in the 82d that had been vacated when Brigadier General Keerans was killed on Sicily.

By the night of 14 October the assault divisions of Fifth Army had crossed the Volturno. The Germans pulled back to their Gustav Line, a series of heavily defended positions built by an army of Italian laborers; it stretched forty miles inland, halfway between Naples and Rome, and was anchored on Monte Cassino. On the other side of Italy, the British Eighth Army attacked to the north. In between the two armies a gap was developing along the mountainous spine of the Apennines. Clark asked Ridgway for a regiment to plug the gap, and he got Tucker's 504th. The weather had by now turned brutal—rain, cold, and freezing mud were the norm. Trucks, jeeps, and even halftracks slid and churned through the muck.

Tucker pushed his regimental combat team into the mountains and moved twenty-two miles ahead of the Fifth and Eighth Armies. After crossing the Volturno River, the 504th fought into the rail and road center of Isernia. Tucker kept up the offensive and took over the towns of Colli, Macchia, Fornelli, Cerro, and Rochetta. Clark had also committed three other airborne units to the rugged, strength-sapping attack through the hills: Bill Yarborough's restored 509th, Brig. Gen. Robert T. Frederick's U.S.-Canadian 1st Special Service Force, and a part of Bill Darby's Rangers.

On 11 November Yarborough's 509th, attached to Maj. Gen. Lucian K. Truscott's 3d Division, marched out of Venafro to attack Mount Croce, a steep, boulder-laden 3,205-foot peak. On top of Croce, the German artillery forward observers were directing artillery on the troops, convoys, and CPs in the valley around Venafro. After a seven-hour climb, the men of the 509th reached the summit and killed or chased off the Germans at the top. The Germans reacted with artillery and mortar barrages, the 509th hung on in spite of enormous casualties. Doc Alden's medical detachment was hit by "bouncing Bettys" as it scrambled up the ridgeline. Four of his men were injured, including Sgt. Gordon Hahn and a surgeon, Dr. Bill Engleman, whose right arm was mangled in a blast. Others were killed.

In the face of gusty winds and penetrating cold the 509th dug in. Many men succumbed to heavy colds, pneumonia, and trench foot and had to be carried down off the mountain. On 13 December, after thirty-four days of freezing cold, mortar and artillery fire, and no shave or a chance to remove clothes or boots, the 509th's bedraggled troopers were relieved by a regiment of the 3d Division. Yarborough's men slid and struggled off the mountain on numb and bloody feet.

As assistant division commander, Gavin visited Tucker and his regiment on 3,950-foot Mount Sammucro. It was "an unbelievable situation," Gavin wrote.

The mountains were very high, totally rocky, and generally devoid of trees and cover. One hill they fought over was 1205 meters high. It was very cold at night, frequently rainy, and soon the first snow appeared. Unfortunately, most of the troopers were still wearing their summer jumpsuits. The fighting was extremely difficult, with frequent personal encounters and surprises for the unwary combatant. All supplies had to be brought up by mule. There was a chronic shortage of water, food, ammunition, and, of course, the wounded had to be taken out by mule. But Colonel Tucker was a combat leader of extraordinary ability. Again, one of his troopers later described a situation that evolved about the defense of Hill 1205: "About eleven o'clock the little colonel with one man as a bodyguard came down from 1205 wanting to know why in hell the attack had failed. . . . The little colonel took two men, walked to the pillbox, caught the Nazis cleaning the machine gun, and took eleven prisoners without firing a shot. He made us look silly."

On 10 December, in the rain, Tucker set up his CP at Venafro. He sent G and I Companies to relieve elements of the 3d Ranger Battalion on Hill 950. The I Company troopers moved up the hill in the face of a German counterattack. For the next twelve hours the 504th withstood seven German attacks. In the next twelve hours, I Company had 46 wounded but held its hill. The next morning, the 2d Battalion climbed up Mt. Sammucro (Hill 1205) and relieved the 143d Infantry. Even though Tucker's 1st Battalion was supposed to be in reserve, he used it to haul water, ammunition, and food up the rocky trails under German artillery fire. Ten days later the 504th was holding five hills and had patrols on two others. Its assaults took one hill after another even though the unit was surrounded on three sides by the Germans. During the nineteen days the 504th was near Venafro, Tucker's men suffered a total of 54 dead, 226 wounded, and 2 missing in action. Half the 504th's combat strength had been obliterated. The supporting 376th Parachute Field Artillery Battalion, commanded by Lt. Col. Wilbur M. Griffith, and Company C, 307th Engineers, also lost men, mostly to German artillery. To get his twelve pack 75mm howitzers to the top of the mountain, Griffith had had to break the howitzers down into nine pieces and use a platoon of mules and the sturdy backs of his "Red Legs."

On 27 December, Tucker's troopers were relieved and hauled themselves off the mountain and moved to a new camp in the vicinity of Pignataro. The 504th had fought so courageously and aggressively that German commanders groused that they were barbarians and that most of them had been released from prison simply to serve out their sentences as frontline fighters.

Later, Rube Tucker read the translation of a diary of a German soldier who had fought the 504th. "American parachutists—devils in baggy pants—are less than 100 meters from my outpost. I can't sleep at night; they pop up from nowhere and we never know when or how they will strike next. Seems like the black-hearted devils are everywhere."

In mid-November, Ridgway had a conference with Gavin about the forthcoming landings on Normandy. "They were to take place in the spring of 1944 and they would have a large parachute and glider contingent," Gavin wrote about the conference. "In response to a request from General Eisenhower, he decided to send me to London to participate in the planning for OVERLORD, the code name for the Normandy landings. At the same time he told me that I would be returned to the division to participate in the battle—a most welcome assurance." And at about the same time, Ridgway told Gavin, that ultimately he wanted him to command the 82d. Gavin wrote that he thought "he was a bit young for it" at the age of thirty-six. On 16 November Gavin left Italy and flew to Algiers and then to Marrakech. From there he flew in a four-engine airfreight flight out over the Atlantic to avoid the German fighters. He arrived in Prestwick, Scotland, at 1100 on 18 November and then flew to London. That evening, he registered at Grosvenor House in a billet provided by the European Theater of Operations, U.S. Army. In the days

following, Gavin would become embroiled in the detailed planning for
the airborne part of the invasion of Normandy and find himself exposed
to the complicated machinations of dealing with the British officers, particularly Lt. Gen. F. M. Browning, the senior British airborne officer, who
seemed determined to take command of the total airborne effort.

Even though Gavin had spent many days in combat in Italy, he kept
in his mind the need in the future for trained and efficient pathfinders
to mark drop and landing zones for airborne assaults, especially at night.
He gave the 82d's G-3, Lt. Col. Whitfield Jack, two pages of questions he
wanted answered. Jack formed an experimental pathfinder team of 125
officers and men and had them moved back to Comiso on Sicily to train
and develop pathfinding techniques. Jack put Capt. Jack Norton, Gavin's
S-3, in charge.

The team used a modified and lighter form of the British ninety-
pound Rebecca and Delta lanterns for marking glider LZs. Captain
Frank Boyd of the 376th Parachute Field Artillery Battalion was with the
team. "The entire group performed beautifully together," he wrote
later. "We had assigned eight C-47s and eight CG4A gliders, and the pilots entered right into the spirit of things. The glider pilots happily
smashed up their gliders. At the end of two weeks, top brass came for a
demonstration, including a mass jump by the 456th Parachute Artillery
Battalion. We got most of General Gavin's questions answered."

On 18 November, while the 504th and the other airborne units were
making a name for paratroopers with their rugged battles along the cold,
rainy Apennines, the 82d Airborne Division, minus Tucker's 504th RCT
and Yarborough's 509th, sailed for Northern Ireland to get ready for the
massive assault across the English Channel.

Major Robert M. Piper was the S-1 of the 505th in 1943. "We, the
505th," he wrote recently, "sailed from Naples on the USS *Frederick Funston* [an attack transport-type ship] and anchored in Oran Harbor on 22
November after the 7-day 'run' in the 'Med.'"

Here we waited for the convoy and escort ships to assemble and
sailed through the Straits of Gibraltar on 1 December '43. Because
the *Funston* was a newer and faster ship, we broke from the convoy
and arrived in Belfast, North Ireland on 9 Dec.

This was a great and welcome change from the Italians in Naples
and the Arabs in Oran. The people in Ireland were friendly, jovial,
spoke English, were white and most cooperative. There were Pubs,

dances, many young girls and the troops really appreciated the change. There had been some US troops in Northern Ireland so there were Quonset huts in many locations.

Division was north of Lough Neagh in Ballymera and other locations, and the 505th moved from Belfast to the area in and near Cookstown, County Tyrone, west of the large Lough Neagh.

Regt'l Hqtrs was in a hutment camp on the outskirts of Cookstown, Service Company was in Cookstown, and the three battalions were nearby—one at Killymoon Castle, one at Drum Manor and one at Desertcreat (all Irish Estates).

Some Reg't Hqtrs officers were billeted with Sv. Co. officers in the M'Gucken Commercial Hotel on the main street of Cookstown across the street from which was a small café and although wartime rationing was very much in effect throughout most of the British countryside, in rural towns, away from Belfast that were primarily agricultural, we could get ham and eggs, bacon and eggs, good bread, milk, etc, that we had not seen since leaving the US some 8 months/2 campaigns and 2 combat jumps before.

Regt'l strength was down so the short daylight days were primarily P.T. days. (It was dark, with the dimmed street lights on from 4 PM to 9 AM each day.)

The nights were long, cold and often rainy and the peat (that was issued for fuel in some pot-bellied stoves) burned slowly, reluctantly, and put off little or no heat. . . . One stayed warm trying to keep this peat showing any red color at all—not as a result of any heat it put out.

Despite the discomforts, I think we all enjoyed the brief stay in N. Ireland for the change of pace; the people; the first Christmas outside the US; and the chance to bring the unit up to the fighting level we had when leaving the US.

We also had some great reunions with the troopers of the 507th and 508th PIRs [Parachute Infantry Regiments] who landed at Port Rush, N Ireland and went to England in February '44 to get ready for Normandy.

Clark protested bitterly the loss of the 82d. He had wanted the division to land amphibiously up the Italian peninsula. But he would finally get one airborne regiment—the battle-weary 504th finally pulled out of the mountains after Christmas to get ready for another nonairborne operation—the landing at Anzio. On 4 January 1944, Tucker received orders to move his 504th RCT to Pozzuoli, a suburb of Naples. Tucker's "devils in baggy pants" did not know it at the time, but they were going amphibiously to a popular resort town, whose beaches would soon be crowded with tourists of a different nature—soldiers wading ashore, not in swimsuits but in combat attire, loaded for battle. They were to be involved in an operation known as Shingle. D day was to be early on the morning of 22 January 1944.

10: Anzio

While the 82d Airborne Division and the 509th Parachute Infantry Regiment were fighting as "straight legs" in Italy, the development and buildup of U.S. airborne forces continued apace. On 8 January 1944, Brig. Gen. George P. Howell and his 2d Airborne Brigade headquarters arrived in Belfast, Northern Ireland. Initially, War Department plans had Howell picking up the 501st and 508th Parachute Infantry Regiments and their eventually fighting in Europe as a brigade. But after a couple of months Eisenhower's planning staff disbanded the 2d Brigade, turned Howell, his staff, and the 508th over to the 82d, and added the 501st to the 101st Airborne Division, already training in England.

The senior command situation in the Mediterranean had changed in January of 1944, when Eisenhower relinquished command of Allied forces in the Mediterranean to British Gen. Sir Henry M. Wilson. Before the switch, Marshall had controlled the strategy in the Mediterranean and frequently communicated directly with Eisenhower. With Eisenhower's departure for London, the strategy planning passed to Britain's Sir Alan Brooke and the British chiefs of staff, under the strong influence of Churchill. Their immediate plan involved a large Mediterranean thrust into the "soft underbelly" of Italy. Churchill felt that the rapid liberation of Rome was an absolute necessity. To permit such a strategy by the end of January 1944, on Christmas Day 1943 Churchill sent Roosevelt a telegram asking the president to delay sending landing craft (LSTs, or landing ships, tank) to Britain as previously decided at the Washington Conference. Churchill wanted LSTs held in the Mediterranean area so that the Allies could mount an assault on Anzio, thirty miles south of Rome. Churchill promised that once the assault was over, the LSTs would move to Britain.

By this time the Allied forces in Italy, Mark Clark's Fifth Army and Montgomery's Eighth Army, both under the command of British General Alexander, had ground to a halt against the third German defensive line across Italy. This was the formidable, concrete Gustav Line that stretched across Italy from coast to coast at the narrowest point of the peninsula. It was under the control of the German Tenth Army commanded by Gen. Heinrich von Vietinghoff. The Tenth Army had some fifteen divisions deployed and entrenched in interlocking positions along the Gustav Line, using the high ground of the rugged Apennine Mountains that rose above Italy's rain-soaked valleys, swamps, and rivers. The Germans intended to defend its every inch tenaciously. The winter was frigid and harsh and unsuitable for air assaults. The terrain was naturally highly defensible and unfriendly to armor. Field Marshal Kesselring, commander of all German forces in Italy, promised Hitler that he would hold the Gustav Line for at least six months. The Gustav Line prevented the Fifth Army from moving up the Liri Valley, the Allies' most direct approach to a major Allied objective—Rome. As Geoffrey Perret so aptly put it in his book, *There's a War to Be Won,* "For the men who had to break through it, the Gustav Line was a Calvary, a grisly martyrdom brought upon them not by failings of their own but by the mistakes of others."

Churchill pressured his chiefs of staff to order Alexander to land an amphibious force north of the west end of the Gustav Line and south of Rome. When Alexander received the directive in January 1944, his staff dug out a previously drafted but shelved plan codenamed Shingle. On 8 November, Alexander passed to Clark an order to develop a plan to land a single division at Anzio, thirty miles south of Rome and fifty miles north of the Gustav Line, on 20 December 1943, as part of a three-pronged Allied offensive. The other two prongs included massive frontal attacks by the U.S. Fifth Army over the Rapido River near Cassino and by the British Eighth Army on the eastern end of the Gustav Line. But because of a lack of shipping and a shortage of troops, the plan was mothballed on 18 December.

On 27 December, Reuben Tucker received an order relieving the 504th RCT of its combat role in the Venafro sector and moving the frozen, battle-scarred troopers down out of the ice and snow-covered, thousand-foot-high mountains to a new camp in the vicinity of Pignatoro.

On 4 January, Tucker received a new directive: move his combat team—the 504th Infantry, Lt. Col. Wilbur M. Griffith's 376th Parachute Field Artillery Battalion, and Company C of the 307th Parachute Engineers—to Pozzuoli, near Naples. "The devils in baggy pants" did not know it yet, but they had been selected for an amphibious operation as part of Operation Shingle. And the 504th's troopers were still in their jump suits, "baggy pants" ill-suited to winter warfare, because the troops wanted to be clearly distinguishable from "leg" outfits.

After the 509th's ruinous, almost suicidal parachute jump at Avellino in the Salerno operation, Lt. Col. Bill Yarborough took over the battalion, brought it up to strength with replacements from home, guarded Fifth Army headquarters for a brief interlude, and then moved his men into the cold and icy mountains to fight with Colonel Darby's Rangers. Near the end of December, he received orders to move his 509th back to Naples for R&R (rest and recreation) and to get ready for Operation Shingle.

Shingle was more than just an amphibious landing at Anzio. It was to be supported by a 15th Army Group general offensive one week before the 22 January date set for the Anzio landings. Thus on 15 January the U.S. Fifth Army, composed of the U.S. II Corps, the British X Corps, and the French Expeditionary Corps, would launch a massive attack on the Gustav Line, cross the Garigliano and Rapido Rivers, and strike the German Tenth Army in the area of Cassino, break through the German line, fight up the Liri Valley, and link up with the forces coming ashore at Anzio. On the other side of the Italian peninsula, the British and Commonwealth forces of Eighth Army would break through the Adriatic front to tie down and prevent the shift of German forces to Anzio.

General Alexander and Churchill were supremely optimistic about the value and success of the Anzio operation. Alexander felt that the capture of Rome, theoretically a positive outgrowth of the Anzio landing, would eliminate the need to make the cross-Channel landings in France. Unfortunately, Anzio would become a time-consuming, casualty-heavy battle that ground on for months but had one major advantage: immobilizing thousands of German troops in Italy.

Alexander had selected the coastal resort of Anzio as the landing site because it was within striking distance of Rome and within the range of Allied aircraft operating out of Naples. The beachhead was fifteen miles wide and seven miles deep. Anzio's surrounding terrain was rolling, wooded farm country on a narrow coastal plain that ran from the town of Terracina to the Tiber River. "The entire region was part of an elaborate reclamation and resettlement project that had been undertaken by Mussolini to showcase Fascist agricultural improvements and was studded with pumping stations and farmhouses and crisscrossed by irrigation ditches and canals," wrote Clayton D. Laurie in *Anzio*, a U.S. Army Center of Military History brochure. The land behind Anzio sloped gently uphill to the Alban Hills twenty miles inland. Southeast of the Alban Hills ran Highway 7, a major north-south road. From the Alban Hills, a field artillery forward observer or other sightseer (enemy, of course, or friendly) could see Anzio and the nearby town of Nettuno. About twelve miles to the east of Anzio was the Mussolini Canal.

To lead the invasion of Anzio, General Clark selected Maj. Gen. John P. Lucas, "Foxy Grandpa," (class of 1911) and his U.S. VI Corps. The fifty-four-year-old General Lucas was reputedly a mild-mannered, white-haired, corncob pipe–smoking leader. In his diary after the rigorous battles in the Italian mountains, he wrote that "I am far too tender-hearted to be a success at my chosen profession; my subordinates do all the work and most of the thinking."

His VI Corps contained the U.S. 3d and the British 1st Infantry Divisions. Both divisions were combat tough, the 3d having fought in North Africa, Sicily, and the mountains of Italy, and the 1st having been used as a reserve in Italy. Added to VI Corps were the 46th, the Royal Tank Regiment, the U.S. 751st Tank Battalion, two battalions of British Commandos, three battalions of Darby's U.S. Rangers, Tucker's 504th RCT, and Yarborough's 509th Parachute Infantry Battalion. The U.S. 45th Division and Combat Command A of the U.S. 1st Armored Division would land as reinforcements once the beachhead was established. The U.S. XII Tactical Air Command, the British Desert Air Force, the Coastal Air Force, and the Tactical Bomber Force, some 2,600 Allied aircraft, would conduct major air assaults, gain air superiority, provide close air support for the landings, and destroy enemy airfields and communications. In addition, the U.S. 64th Fighter Wing would protect the landing area from some 2,000 German aircraft in the area.

Alexander felt that Lucas's mission was to go ashore at Anzio and, moving rapidly (the key word in the mission statement) inland, capture the Alban Hills, forcing Kesselring to withdraw forces from the Gustav Line and move them to the north of Rome. When General Clark gave Lucas his orders, however, he gave him two missions. The first was to go ashore and divert enemy strength from the south and prepare defensive positions. The second mission was vague: move toward the Alban Hills to link up with the rest of the Fifth Army on D day plus 7. Clark's directive, unfortunately, did not specify the immediate capture of the Alban Hills. Both Clark and Lucas thought that VI Corps would have to fight its way ashore against heavy German resistance and that the immediate capture of the Alban Hills was too optimistic, so Clark left it up to Lucas to decide when to attack out of the beachhead. The Allied intelligence network had failed to discover that only about 1,000 German troops were anywhere near the Anzio beaches for the scheduled time of the landing.

Initially, part of the Anzio operation involved an airborne mission dubbed Sun Assault. On 12 January Tucker was briefed on the plan—the 504th RCT would take off from airfields around Naples aboard 178 C-47s of Brig. Gen. Hal Clark's 52d Troop Carrier Wing and drop onto fields about eight miles north of Anzio, near the town of Carroceto. But on the morning of 15 January, Lucas canceled Sun Assault for a variety of reasons: green pilots, no full moon, and the proximity of the DZs to Allied naval gunfire that would be preparing the invasion beaches. Tucker and his 504th thus became waders instead of jumpers.

The ships to carry the amphibious force came from six nations. United States RAdm. Frank Lowry's Task Force 81 had 250 cargo vessels and assault craft. He also commanded the seventy-four ships of Task Force X-Ray, whose mission was to support the landing. Royal Navy Adm. Thomas H. Troubridge headed up Task Force Peter with its fifty-two ships to land and support the British forces in the operation. Instead of a long battlefield preparation with naval gunfire, the Allies decided to gain surprise with a short, ten-minute barrage with 1,500 five-inch rockets by two British assault ships.

Operation Hinge actually began on 12 January when the French assaulted Cassino and the British X Corps tried to cross the Garigliano River. On 20 January the U.S. II Corps launched an attack in the center of the Fifth Army front in an attempt to cross the Rapido River. The 36th Infantry Division fought a bloody battle, taking heavy losses, before it halted its attack. The Gustav Line was not breached—it was only dented.

On 21 January Lucas's VI Corps set sail from Naples under a cloudless sky in a fleet of 375 ships. The armada sailed south toward Africa until nightfall to mislead German observers on shore and in aircraft overhead; then it headed north to Anzio. By 0130 on 22 January the fleet was about twelve miles offshore and ready to launch the assault. Shortly after midnight, thousands of troops began crawling out of the holds of the ships and swarming down rope ladders to the landing craft. At 0150 two British rocket ships broke the quiet of the night, firing on the landing beaches. There was no return fire from shore. At 0200 the waves of landing craft began, and the attack on Anzio was under way.

The British 1st Division and Commandos landed unopposed on Peter Beach, three miles north of Anzio. The U.S. 3d Division debarked on X-Ray Beach, four miles to the south of Anzio, as if it were simply a training exercise. And in the center, aimed at the heart of the city, Colonel Darby's 1st and 4th Ranger Battalions landed abreast, unopposed, and spread out around the resort city. The landing craft returned to the ships and picked up the 3d Ranger Battalion and Yarborough's 509th.

In a post–World War II interview, General Yarborough talked about Rangers and paratroopers.

I had known Darby before and had a high regard for him. But mixing Rangers and paratroopers was like mixing oil and water. I just can't tell you what the differences were between our two units. Here, we went for the traditional esprit of the soldier based on the customs of the service, even in shell holes. Every man shaved every day no matter what. . . . Our men looked sharp. I required it and they took pride in the parachute uniform and the badge they had and the whole bit. Darby's guys looked like cut-throats. They looked like the sweepings of the bar room. And they wore stubble beards, they wore any kind of a uniform . . . some of them had tanker uniforms on; some had well, just anything they wanted. And Darby and I used to sit around and talk about this phenomenon and we both agreed that one should approach leadership from two points of view. . . . One was the traditional one, which I preferred and the other one was his approach which offered only blood, sweat and tears for the right kind of a guy. It could offer you nothing except the hardest bloody job and the smallest recognition.

On shore, the paratroopers formed up and made a swift, one-mile march to the south along a coastal road to their objective, the town of Nettuno. By daylight, Lucas's two divisions and the paratroopers had landed unopposed and, by noon, had carved out a beachhead three miles deep and fifteen miles wide. All of Lucas's objectives had been seized. The Allied air forces had flown some 1,200 sorties in and around the beachhead; the U.S. 36th Engineer Combat Regiment had bulldozed exits, laid log roads, cleared mines, and readied the Anzio port to receive its first LST. Unfortunately Lucas did not break out of the beachhead.

At 0700 Rube Tucker and his 504th RCT began landing on the beach. When the LCIs (landing craft, infantry) carrying the 504th were about 300 yards offshore, six Luftwaffe dive bombers screamed out of the sky and began dropping bombs in and around them. Only one made a direct hit, and that was fatal. The bomb hit a fully loaded LCI of C Company, wiping out an entire platoon, and the LCI sank to the bottom of the sea. The 504th carried on. Tucker led his men ashore through the icy, oil-covered waters, and marched them inland for two miles to a bivouac area in the Padiglione Woods. By midnight over 36,000 men and 3,200 vehicles were ashore, 90 percent of the invasion force, and the Allies had captured 227 Germans.

Lucas was totally surprised at the lack of German opposition; the German high command was deceived by the Anzio invasion. On 18 January, the Germans has evacuated their regional reserves to the south to counter the Allied attack on Garigliano, leaving only a company to defend a nine-mile-wide strip of the Anzio beach. The reason that Anzio was undefended was singularly odd: it stemmed from advice that Adm. Wilhelm Canaris had given to Kesselring a few days before the initiation of Shingle. Canaris, the head of German Armed Forces Intelligence Service (the Abwehr), had visited Kesselring in Rome and told him that Anzio was no problem, that "nothing is going to happen there." What Kesselring did not know was that Canaris was a zealous anti-Nazi and, since 1939, had been in close contact with British intelligence.

It was only at about 0500 on the morning of the invasion that Kesselring became aware of the invasion. He had few troops in the immediate vicinity of Anzio, but he called the commander of the 4th Parachute Division north of Rome and ordered him to move as rapidly as possible to the beachhead area. Then Kesselring told the commander of the 26th Hermann Göring Tank Division, whose unit was in reserve behind the Gustav Line, to move rapidly to a perimeter around Anzio. By the evening of D day, Kesselring had built a shallow defensive line behind the town. And by 24 January, Kesselring had three divisions in a ring around Anzio and more combat forces on the way from France, Germany, and Yugoslavia. His new mission was to drive the Allies back into the Tyrrhenian Sea.

Kesselring and his chief of staff, Brig. Gen. Siegfried Westphal, were amazed that the Allies had not pushed rapidly inland, given the scarcity of the defensive force. Westphal later said that there were scant German forces between Anzio and Rome and that an aggressive strike by Lucas could have had his forces charging up Highways 6 and 7 to Rome. As Clayton D. Laurie wrote, "General Lucas was neither bold nor imaginative, and he erred repeatedly on the side of caution, to the increasing chagrin of both Alexander and Clark."

Over the next few days after the landing, Lucas pushed inland for about seven miles against increasing German strength. On 24 January, in the center of the beachhead, the British 1st Division moved up the Anzio-Alban Road toward Campoleone. On that same date, Reuben Tucker's combat team was defending the VI Corps right flank along the banks of the Mussolini Canal. Tucker was ordered to attack and take over the town of Borgo Piave, some two miles east of the canal. In a few hours, with three battalions abreast, Tucker occupied the town. But the Germans were ready. Counterattacking with armor and artillery, before nightfall they drove Tucker's troops back across the canal, where they stayed until relieved on 28 January by the 179th Infantry Regiment of the 45th Infantry Division.

Meanwhile, on 24 January, Kesselring moved Gen. Eberhard von Mackensen and his Fourteenth Army Headquarters from Verona, in northern Italy, to Anzio. Mackensen soon had eight divisions in place, with five more on the way. By 1 February he had 70,000 men deployed in forward areas around Anzio, with several thousand also moving to the area. Kesselring intended to throw the Allies back into the sea.

On 30 January Lucas planned a two-pronged attack to thwart the expected German counterattack. One force would cut Highway 7 at Cisterna and then move on to the Alban Hills, and the other would move northeast up the Alban Road through Campoleone, and then to the west and southwest. Lucas thought that he could make a quick linkup with Fifth Army in the south (both the Fifth and Eighth Armies having planned to renew their stalled battles and fight to the north). But Lucas was wrong: the Germans had securely hemmed in the Anzio beachhead. The Allies would fight for four more months to extract themselves from the Anzio battleground, a scene of close combat in cold, rainy weather, with high casualties on both sides. From their observation posts in the Alban Hills, the Germans could direct their incessant 88mm artillery fire onto the Allied forces in the beachhead.

For Lucas's initial attack on Cisterna, he sent the 3d Division and Col. William O. Darby's 1st, 3d, and 4th Ranger Battalions. The 1st and 3d Rangers led the assault by infiltrating the German lines and overrunning

Cisterna and holding it until the 15th Infantry, 3d Division, and Darby's 4th Battalion came to their rescue via the Conca-Cisterna Road. At 0200 on 30 January, the 3d Division's 7th Infantry was ordered to attack on the left to cut Highway 7 above Cisterna while the 15th Infantry moved to the right and took over the highway south of the town. Meanwhile, as a diversion, the 504th attacked along the Mussolini Canal. Poor intelligence did not alert Lucas to the fact that his attack was aimed directly at thirty-six German battalions massing for their 1 February assault.

Darby's Rangers launched their attack at 0130 to the right of the Conca-Cisterna Road and, with hand-to-hand fighting and point-blank shooting, they came within 800 yards of Cisterna at dawn. Their success was to be short-lived. The Germans of the 715th Motorized Infantry Division found the lightly equipped Rangers during the darkness and hit them with devastating firepower at dawn. The Rangers could not move out from the overwhelming firepower. The 4th Rangers and the 15th Infantry tried to get to the beleaguered troopers but failed, the 4th Rangers fighting for an hour and suffering 50 percent casualties. Armored units of the Hermann Göring Division pushed the Rangers into the open where their grenades and bazookas were totally useless against the German armor. As the Rangers in small, scattered groups tried to crawl and then run out of the merciless rain of fire, they were cut down with brutal efficiency. Of the two battalions of 767 men who attacked Cisterna that morning, only six finally returned to the Allied lines.

The 3d Division made some progress against the German buildup of forces, fighting to within one mile of the village by nightfall of 31 January, but could not break through. By noon the next day, after three days of heavy casualties, it was clear that the Americans were not going to capture Cisterna any time soon. Furthermore, Allied intelligence reported on 2 February the arrival of new German units in the Anzio area and the strong possibility of a heavy German counterattack. Clark and Lucas ordered Truscott to dig in. While the Germans prepared their counterattack, the German artillery on high ground above Anzio, with a clear view of the entire beachhead, relentlessly blasted the whole area. The constant shelling made one man wish for "a good clean wound": Michael S. Davison (class of 1939), a battalion commander in the 45th Division, who would later become a four-star general and commander in chief of U.S. Army, Europe. The German attack came as predicted. On the night of 3 February the Germans launched a determined and strong counterattack, mainly against the British 1st Division. General von Mackensen and his heavy forces pushed the Allies back to the original beachhead perimeter.

Lieutenant Colonel W. L. Freeman commanded the 3d Battalion, 504th. During the German assault, his battalion was in a defensive position with the British 1st Division and was ordered to withdraw to the town of Aprilia, which had been one of Mussolini's pet projects. Between 8 and 12 February, Freeman's paratroopers were blasted repeatedly with heavy artillery and tank fire, reducing the battalion to companies of twenty to thirty men each. But in spite of the heavy fire, the icy rain, howling wind, and reduced strength, the troopers of the 3d Battalion, 504th held their ground. For its heroic efforts, the battalion received the Presidential Unit Citation, the first U.S. paratrooper unit to be so honored.

During these gruesome days of German assaults with superior firepower, Yarborough's 509th was in a dug-in defensive position near the town of Carano, between the 3d and 45th Divisions. And like the other lightly armed paratroopers, his battalion took heavy German fire as it held its ground. Lieutenant Kenneth Shaker had a platoon on line whose men were being killed or wounded every day. He sent a runner back to the company CP to find out if he could move out. The runner came back with the grim news that both the company commander and his executive officer had been killed in the same foxhole by a mortar round.

On 8 February the Germans tried to jam a wedge between the 3d and the 45th and ran into the 509th, which had sent out small patrols ahead of its positions to try to learn the strength and exact location of the enemy. One patrol was led by Cpl. Paul B. Huff from Cleveland, Tennessee, who was a great admirer of Sgt. Alvin C. York, the well-known American hero of World War I. At 0730 Huff led his six-man team out of their foxholes into the no-mans-land between the lines. A hundred yards from their lines, the men of the patrol were blasted with accurate and heavy fire from two machine guns and a 20mm flak cannon, but Huff was up to the task. He loaded his submachine gun and started to crawl through a minefield, and then his instincts took over. He stood up and charged the German position, firing from the hip as he raced forward. His charge wiped out the five-man German crew. Then he raced back to his original position and withdrew his patrol to his own lines.

That afternoon Colonel Yarborough was still looking for the Germans. Sergeant Kelly C. Bath led a large patrol back out into the area that Huff had charged through in the morning. Huff went along. In a fierce firefight, Huff again took the lead and with Bath and a few others demolished a German company of 125 men, 27 of whom were killed and 21 captured. The patrol had three men killed. For his conspicuous gallantry in these two actions Huff was awarded the Medal of Honor.

On 16 February, the Germans launched a counterattack down the Anzio-Albano Road on a four-mile front. The attack hit the 45th Division between the 179th and 157th Infantry Regiments, and the enemy moved through the gap with three regiments and sixty tanks. By dawn, the Germans had jammed a two-by-one-mile wedge through the 45th Division and were ready to break through to the beach. The Allies repositioned 90mm antiaircraft guns for use as ground artillery in this battle, and blasted the area with naval gunfire and 730 ground-support sorties by the XII Tactical Air Command. At dawn on 18 February, the Germans increased their attack against the 45th, and by midmorning had destroyed one battalion of the 179th and driven the rest of the regiment a half mile into Lucas's final defensive line. Feeling that the 179th needed a boost, Lucas sent Darby to take over the regiment with orders to hold fast. The regiment held and piled up nearly 500 German casualties in front of its positions. By midday, Allied artillery, air, and massed mortar, machine gun, and tank fire slowed the German attack. By 22 February, the U.S. VI Corps had gone over to the offensive and succeeded in retaking some lost ground.

The Germans lost 5,389 men killed, wounded, and missing during the five-day counterattack. By 23 February, the German 65th Infantry Division had dropped to 673 fighters, and one regiment of the 715th Motorized Infantry Division had fewer than 185 men. The Allies lost 3,496 men killed, wounded, or missing in addition to 1,637 noncombat casualties due to trench foot, exposure, and combat exhaustion. To appreciate these figures, it should be noted that on 12 February, 96,401 Allied soldiers were holding the thirty-five-mile perimeter against some ten German divisions of 120,000 men.

Before the Germans launched a new attack against the 3d Division in the Cisterna sector on 29 February, Clark had replaced Lucas with Lucian Truscott as commander of VI Corps on 23 February. He had reinforced his line with additional artillery and made certain that each unit had a battalion in reserve with additional support from corps. The attack began with a massive artillery barrage, but the Allies were ready. On 29 February alone, the VI Corps and 3d Division artillerymen fired over 60,000 rounds, about twenty rounds for every one that the Germans fired. The Germans dented the perimeter in some places, but the well-dug-in U.S. troops, supported by artillery, air, and armor, held their ground. Between 1 and 4 March, the 715th and 16th SS Panzer Grenadier Divisions attacked the 7th and 15th Infantry regiments and the 509th Parachute Infantry Battalion. All three units held their ground but suffered heavy losses. For its part in the brutal battle the 509th earned the Presidential Unit Citation. The Germans continued their assault on 5 March but without notable success. The second five-day counterattack cost the Germans some 3,500 troops and thirty tanks, and it had failed to wipe out the beachhead. Then the 3d Division counterattacked and regained much of the lost terrain, and the Germans went on the defensive.

After six weeks of relentless fighting, artillery bombardments, and armor attacks, the men of VI Corps were as exhausted as the enemy. On 4 March a three-month slowdown began: both armies defended their positions, made very limited raids and assaults across the lines, and waited for a renewal of the offensive on the southern front. The VI Corps, meanwhile, reorganized. At the end of March, Col. Reuben Tucker received his marching orders to leave the area of the Mussolini Canal and go to England. After seventy-three days on the line in the bloodiest of battles and the harshest of weather conditions, Bill Yarborough received orders to move his remaining 125 men from Anzio and to get ready for the invasion of southern France in Operation Dragoon.

"During March, all of April, and the first part of May 1944 the Anzio beachhead resembled the Western Front during World War I," wrote veteran Clayton D. Laurie. "The vast majority of Allied casualties during this period were from air and artillery attacks, including fire from 'Anzio Annie,' a 280mm German railway gun which fired from the Alban Hills. During March, shrapnel caused 83 percent of all 3d Division casualties, and other units experienced similar rates. The Anzio beachhead became a honeycomb of wet and muddy trenches, foxholes, and dugouts. Yet the Allied troops made the best of a bad situation, and one soldier recalled that during these months the fighting was light and living was leisurely."

On the night of 11–12 May, the Allies finally launched their all-out offensive against the seemingly impregnable Gustav Line. Initially there was little success. But by 15 May, the Polish forces, the French Expeditionary Corps, and U.S. II Corps broke through and the Germans abandoned Monte Cassino. On 24 May, the II Corps drove north and took Terracina and then sped on to Anzio. The German resistance was deteriorating and the Germans withdrew toward Rome.

On 25 May, soldiers from the 91st Reconnaissance Squadron, 85th Division, II Corps, met men of he 36th Engineer Combat Regiment at Anzio, finally linking up Fifth Army forces. The beachhead disappeared. Then General Clark split Truscott's forces and sent the 3d Division, the U.S.-Canadian 1st Special Service Force, and parts of the 1st Armored Division toward Valmontone. Unfortunately most of the German Tenth Army fled north, ready to fight again. The Fifth Army, with the 45th and 34th Infantry Divisions in the forefront, made a rapid pursuit of the Germans toward Rome, thirty miles away. On 4 June 1944, several hundred battle-hardened soldiers from the 1st Special Service Force under Brig. Gen. Robert T. Frederick, led the march on Rome. They were followed by tanks from the 1st Armored Division. Frederick (class of 1928) was thirty-seven years old and shortly would become a major general, one of the youngest in the army at the time. He received his second Distinguished Service Cross, and several more wounds, in this battle. Churchill allegedly said that Frederick was "the greatest general of all time."

The next day Clark and the 36th Division marched through Rome as the remainder of his forces were pursuing the Germans. The Italian campaign was not over.

During the Anzio campaign the VI Corps had some 29,200 combat casualties, of whom 4,400 were killed in action and 6,800 taken prisoner or missing in action. German Fourteenth Army losses were estimated to be 27,500, of whom 5,500 were killed and 4,500 missing or captured.

The Anzio campaign remains a subject of controversy. It failed to outflank the Gustav Line and slowed the march on Rome. But it took place behind the German main line of resistance, was close to Rome, and tied up 135,000 soldiers of the German Fourteenth Army. It was a costly battle for both adversaries; the Allies could hardly call it a success. And Churchill, who had strongly advocated the strategy of landing at Anzio, outflanking the German formidable lines of resistance in Italy, and racing on to the prize of Rome, was decidedly unhappy with the cost and duration of the battle. He is reputed to have said, "I had hoped that we would be hurling a wildcat ashore, but all we got was a stranded whale."

But on the night of 4 June, when the Americans had reached Rome, Churchill telegraphed Roosevelt: "How magnificently your troops have fought!"

11: Normandy

O n the evening of 5 June 1944, darkness had just fallen over the airfield at North Witham, England. Shortly thereafter, C-47s of the IX Troop Carrier Command carrying the pathfinders of the 82d and the 101st Airborne Divisions, roared down the runways and headed toward Normandy. "The airborne battle of Normandy, history's largest airborne assault," wrote General Gavin, "had gone into the decisive stage."

The pathfinders, loaded down with combat gear, automatic direction-finding radios, Eureka sets, Holophane lights, homing devices, rifles, ammunition, and parachutes, were jammed beside each other on the C-47s. Corporal Frank Brumbaugh, a 137-pound pathfinder of the 508th Parachute Infantry Regiment, was carrying the 65 pound Eureka plus all his other gear. He now weighed about 315 pounds. When the pathfinders crossed the English Channel, they did not know it and could not see it, but they would fly over the largest armada of ships ever assembled. Below them were 9 battleships, 23 cruisers, 104 destroyers, and 71 large landing craft of various sizes and descriptions. Included in the armada were hundreds of transports, mine sweepers, and merchant ships—a total of some 5,000 naval craft of every type. The C-47s roared on; the pathfinders were slated to drop one hour before the main body of paratroopers.

While still in Sicily, Gavin had seen to it that pathfinders were trained in new procedures developed as a result of the haphazard scattering of airborne troops in drops in the Sicily campaign. The training of the pathfinders, all double volunteers, was continued at a hectic pace in England. The new procedures had the pathfinders learning to mark the

DZs with a series of five lights placed in a T-shape, with the Eureka-Rebecca radar beacon at the head of the T sending a signal up to the lead C-47 in each flight. Pathfinders were to mark glider LZs with a line of seven pairs of Holophane lights, with pairs of lights every 50 yards along 200-yard-long strips in the French fields. After a number of tests, Gavin was finally convinced that large-scale glider landings could be conducted at night. He also changed his mind about the way his paratroopers should fight. Before the battle in Sicily, the airborne troops had been trained to attack in small groups whenever and wherever they found the enemy. But, based on lessons learned in Sicily, General Gavin and his team decided that it would be far more effective for small groups of paratroopers to avoid contact with large enemy formations and to head for the objective area where they could form up into bigger combat units. "This proved both realistic and helpful in the Normandy operation," he wrote later.

"The attack had been long in coming," wrote William M. Hammond in *Normandy,* a U.S. Army Center of Military History brochure. "From the moment the British forces had been forced to withdraw from France in 1940 in the face of an overwhelming German onslaught, planners had plotted a return to the Continent. Only in that way would the Allies be able to confront the enemy's power on the ground, liberate northwestern Europe, and put an end to the Nazi regime."

As early as September 1941, three months before Pearl Harbor, the British high command had directed Adm. Lord Louis Mountbatten to study the possibility of amphibious landings in the European Theater, and sometime earlier, Adm. Sir Roger Keyes had considered possible commando raids. But Churchill wanted a lot more. He made his position clear to Mountbatten: "You are to prepare for the invasion of Europe. You must devise and design the appliances, the landing craft, and the techniques. . . . The whole of the South Coast of England is a bastions of defense against the invasion of Hitler; you've got to turn it into the springboard for our attack."

In December 1941, shortly after Pearl Harbor, U.S. and British planners agreed on the overall strategy: in a two-theater war, they must first defeat the Germans and the Italians and then take on the Japanese. In 1942 and 1943, in a series of conferences at Casablanca, Quebec, Cairo, and Teheran, the Allies agreed to continue to build up a million-man assault force for a 1943 cross-Channel invasion, codenamed Bolero. The plan for 1942 was to erode the German power with relentless air attacks, to conduct campaigns along the North African coast, and to help to the Soviet Union.

In August of 1943 the Allies had not yet decided who would be the Allied commander in chief. If the invasion had occurred early on, the commander would unquestionably have been British. At the time of the Quebec Conference in August 1943 Churchill had assured Gen. Sir Alan Brooke, who had long aspired for the job, that he would be the commander. On 9 August, prior to the conference, Churchill went to Hyde Park and conferred with Roosevelt. Roosevelt convinced him that the job should go to an American, and on 15 August Churchill gave Brooke the sad news. Brooke wrote in his diary: "I felt no longer necessarily tied to Winston and free to assume this Supreme Command which he had already promised me on three separate occasions. It was a crushing blow to hear from him that he was now handing over to the Americans."

But which American? Secretary of War Henry L. Stimson had written to Roosevelt before the Quebec Conference: "I believe that the time has come when we must put our most commanding soldier in charge of this critical operation at this critical time. . . . General Marshall already has the towering eminence of reputation as a tried soldier and as a broadminded and skillful administrator. . . . I believe that he is the man who most surely can now by his character and skill furnish the military leadership which is necessary."

But after the Quebec Conference and in late fall, Roosevelt began to feel that Marshall's presence in Washington to oversee the entire global war effort was an absolute necessity. At the conference in Cairo in December 1943, therefore, Roosevelt suggested to Churchill that they substitute Eisenhower for Marshall. Churchill concurred. On his way home Roosevelt stopped in Tunis and gave Eisenhower the surprising news. Roosevelt and Churchill also decided to move Montgomery to London, where he would assume command of the Allied 21st Army Group, and thus command all the ground troops in the Normandy invasion.

Before leaving Naples on 16 November 1943, Gavin had a final session with Ridgway. In the meeting, Ridgway warned Gavin about the "machinations and scheming of General F. M. Browning, the senior British airborne officer." Gavin remembered that this was good advice.

For although the Americans had provided most of the troops and airlift, the British seemed determined to take command of the total Allied airborne effort. General Browning had not been in a command position so far but had been promoted to Lieutenant General; thus, because of his rank, he would automatically be given command of any combined British-American airborne force. I do not believe that he had any sinister design on our resources, but the British seemed to be convinced that they were better at planning and employing airborne forces than we were.

Gavin arrived in London on 18 November and went directly to Norfolk House on St. James Square. There he met with Maj. Gen. Ray Barker, the deputy chief of staff of the Chief of Staff Supreme Allied Command (COSSAC). COSSAC had been established in Norfolk House to draw up the initial plans for Overlord, the massive Allied cross-Channel invasion. Barker escorted Gavin into the office of British Lt. Gen. Frederick E. Morgan, the chief of staff of COSSAC. Morgan was a "quiet, scholarly type of officer, and an excellent chief of Staff," according to Gavin. He told him that he was to be the senior airborne advisor on the COSSAC staff.

While Gavin was meeting with Barker and Morgan, Gen. "Boy" Browning walked pompously into the office. After a few minutes of idle conversation, he told Gavin that Ridgway should have parachuted into Sicily with his troops, that going in amphibiously was "badly done." Gavin kept his composure and replied that Ridgway had handled the division properly and that he had far more to worry about than just the parachute assault. Later, General Barker told Gavin that Browning was "an empire builder."

Just before Christmas of 1943, Eisenhower moved up to London and became the supreme commander of the Allied Expeditionary Force. He brought along Lt. Gen. Walter Bedell Smith to be his chief of staff. Smith made COSSAC the supreme headquarters for the invasion and brought in General Morgan as his deputy. Eisenhower's principal commanders were British: Air Chief Marshal Sir Arthur Tedder became the principal coordinator of the theater air forces; Adm. Sir Bertram Ramsay was the naval commander; and Gen. Sir Bernard Law Montgomery was the commander of the ground forces. An American, Lt. Gen. Carl "Tooey" Spaatz (class of 1914) commanded the U.S. Strategic Air Forces in Europe while a British officer, Air Chief Marshal Sir Arthur T. Harris, commanded the Royal Air Force's Bomber Command. Air Chief Marshal Sir Trafford Leigh-Mallory directed the tactical air support.

As the pro tempore overall ground commander for the initial phases of Overlord, Montgomery was tasked with developing the final plans for and coordinating the early phases of the invasion. Under Montgomery were two commanders: Lt. Gen. Omar N. Bradley who would command the U.S. force, the U.S. First Army, and Gen. Sir Miles Dempsey who would command the British and Canadian units, as well as a small French force, the British Second Army. Lieutenant General George S. Patton, commander of the U.S. Third Army was slated to come ashore with his troops after the Allies had secured a strong foothold on the Continent. Then Patton's forces would join with the First Army, by then to be under the command of Lt. Gen. Courtney Hodges, to form the 12th Army Group under Bradley. Lieutenant General Henry D. G. Crerar's First Canadian Army would team up with Dempsey under Montgomery.

The most important problem facing COSSAC was the location of the beachhead on the French coast. The obvious solution was to land in the Pas-de-Calais area, directly across the English Channel from Dover and the shortest route from England, some twenty miles of water. But the Germans also recognized the potential of that crossing and had built heavy fortifications directly along the Pas-de-Calais coast, a fact recognizable through aerial reconnaissance to the COSSAC staff.

The Allied planners developed and set up an elaborate deception plan to convince the Germans that the invasion was indeed aimed at the Pas-de-Calais. The British strewed dummy gliders all over the southeast coast of England, near Kent, to give the impression that a vast airborne invasion was being built up there. The COSSAC staff also created the imaginary 1st Army Group, with a vast order of battle. The plans went beyond mere imaginings. Construction crews built dummy installations of plywood and canvas and dotted the area with inflated rubber tanks and vehicles. A large armada of rubber landing craft filled the Thames River estuary, well within view of German reconnaissance aircraft. General Patton became the commander of the phantom 1st Army Group. The COSSAC staff made certain that known enemy agents were well aware of the ruse. "Allied naval units conducted protracted maneuvers off the Channel coast near the location of the shadowy army," wrote William M. Hammond, "and components of Patton's fictitious command indulged in extensive radio trafficking to signal to German intelligence analysts that a major military organization was functioning."

A careful plan of aerial bombardment complemented the ploy. During the weeks preceding the invasion, Allied airmen dropped more bombs on the Pas-de-Calais than anywhere else in France.

Although American commanders doubted that their ruses would have much effect, their schemes succeeded far beyond expectations. The Germans became so convinced that the Pas-de-Calais would be the Allied target that they held to the fiction until long after the actual attack had begun. As a result, nineteen powerful enemy divisions, to include important panzer reserves, stood idle on the day of the invasion, awaiting an assault that never came, when their presence in Normandy might have told heavily against the Allied attack.

Amazingly enough, Hitler himself was not deluded about the location of the main thrust of the massive amphibious landing. He felt that the Allies would, in fact, land on the Cotentin Peninsula, but, for a change, he did not push his intuition upon his staff.

The planners then looked farther west, along the coast near Caen and the Cotentin Peninsula. Here the major ports of Cherbourg and Le Havre offered an opening to the interior of France. In the end, COSSAC decided on that area for the invasion.

After Gavin had spent some time with COSSAC, he went to General Bradley's headquarters in Bryanston Square and discussed the current COSSAC plan with him. Both Bradley and Gavin, and later Eisenhower and Montgomery, recognized that the current COSSAC plan of a three-to-five-division assault was "on too small a scale on too limited a front."

Montgomery argued for a broad attack to the west of Caen, but Morgan's planners said that an attack of that scope would require far more assault forces than were available. Montgomery would not relent, saying that the Allies would have to find the troops or get another commander.

On 2 January Montgomery arrived in London, and Overlord planning was moved from Norfolk House to St. Paul's School in Hammersmith. "There," wrote Gavin, "we got down to the realities of what had to be done."

Through January and early February of 1944, Gavin worked with the Overlord planning staff, determining the objectives of the amphibious assault and then exhaustively analyzing the man-made and natural obstacles to the landings, German defenses and troop locations, and suitable port sites. The Army Air Corps and the RAF made daily photograph runs to aid the planners.

By 23 January the planning staff had decided on a basic plan for the invasion of Normandy. The U.S. forces would land on the western flank of the beachhead nearest to Cherbourg, a large and vital port. The British would land to the east, on the approaches to Caen. What determined that arrangement of Allied forces was sheer logistics. The U.S. forces had debarked in Britain's western ports and had built up depots in that area. But, in addition, given the congestion in Britain's other ports, the U.S. logisticians had decided to load resupply ships in the United States and send them directly to Normandy. The western flank was thus closer and more adaptable to the U.S. resupply effort.

To Gavin, the most important part of the planning was how, where, and when to use the airborne forces. General Marshall made one unusual and surprising suggestion: in a letter to General Eisenhower he recommended strongly that all three airborne divisions—two United States and one British—parachute en masse, deep inland near Paris. He envisioned a drop simultaneous with the amphibious landings in Normandy, theoretically making the capture of Paris speedy and perhaps not too costly. Eisenhower replied with haste, logic, and diplomacy. He suggested, instead, that dropping the airborne forces behind the shoreline and using them to secure causeways through the swamps, knocking out German gun positions behind the beaches, and blocking German reserves was a more expeditious and economical use of airborne forces. He also concluded that an airborne force dropped near Paris could be isolated and destroyed if the amphibious forces could not reach them in a reasonable time. Marshall withdrew his suggestion.

Early in February, Gavin had attended a planning conference at 21st Army Group headquarters at Bentley Priory, where, he remembered, someone made the suggestion that the paratroopers be used "in small packets—platoon size, for example—to land on all the large gun sites on the bluffs overlooking the amphibious assault and engage the Germans at the water's edge. General Butler [the senior U.S. officer in Air Chief Marshal Leigh-Mallory's headquarters] remarked, 'This is like sending Michelangelo to paint a barn.'"

Gavin was quite disturbed that Leigh-Mallory rambled on for several hours about the ineffectiveness of the U.S. airborne forces and the superiority of the British. Even as the U.S. forces were moving to takeoff airfields in 30 May 1944, Leigh-Mallory personally called on General Eisenhower to protest the use of U.S. airborne forces, "the futile slaughter of two fine divisions." In his book, *Crusade in Europe,* Eisenhower stated that "Leigh-Mallory believed that the combination of unsuitable landing grounds and anticipated resistance was too great a hazard to overcome." Leigh-Mallory did not think that these conditions existed in the British area but that the Americans would suffer some 70 percent losses in glider strength and 50 percent in paratroop strength even before they touched down.

In discussions between Gavin and Bradley, an airborne enthusiast, along with the latter's staff, in December and January the two generals broadly agreed on the use of the two U.S. airborne divisions: dropping the 82d west of St-Sauveur-le-Vicomte and the 101st farther south near Ste-Marie-du-Mont. The final plan would vary as studies of the areas uncovered problems.

One issue made visible by the aerial photos of the possible landing areas showed a clever, and widespread, obstacle to glider and paratrooper landings: *Rommelspargel,* German for "Rommel's asparagus." Rommel had ordered his commanders to sow possible landing areas with upright wooden poles, six to twelve inches in diameter and eight to twelve feet long, planted two feet into the ground and about thirty yards apart. When he inspected the German defenses, the so-called West Wall, in the spring of 1944 he was delighted with what he found. "The construction of antiparatroop obstacles has made great progress in many divisions," he wrote. "For example, one division alone has erected almost 300,000 stakes, and one corps over 900,000. Erecting stakes alone does not make the obstacles complete; the stakes must be wired together, and shells and mines attached to them. The density must be about a thousand stakes per square kilometer. . . . It will still be possible for tethered cattle to pasture underneath these mined obstacles."

During their stationing and training in Northern Ireland and England in the early months of 1944, some major changes occurred in both the 82d and the 101st Airborne Divisions. The 82d's 504th had, of course, been left to fight in Italy after the bulk of the 82d moved to Northern Ireland. When the 504th did arrive in England early in May, it was far under strength from battle losses and did not make the final cut for the drop on Normandy with its parent division. Early in January, the 82d's major fighting units were the 505th Parachute Infantry Regiment, commanded by Col. William E. Ekman (class of 1938), and the 325th Glider Infantry Regiment, commanded by Col. Harry L. Lewis.

But then came the buildup. Joining the 82d was Col. George V. Millet's 507th Parachute Infantry Regiment. Millet was a 1929 West Point graduate and a classmate of Gavin. Millet had been commanding the

507th from the date of its activation at Fort Benning. He trained the regiment in Alliance, Nebraska, and in December 1943 brought it to Northern Ireland and in March 1944 to Nottingham, England. Also joining the 82d was Col. Roy E. Lindquist's 508th "Red Devils" Parachute Infantry Regiment. Lindquist(class of 1930) had formed the regiment at Camp Blanding, Florida, and then brought it to England. Just two years before, Lindquist, Millet, and Gavin had all been captains at Benning on the staff of the Provisional Parachute Group.

A significant change in the command structure of the 101st occurred on 9 February 1944, when Maj. Gen. William C. Lee, the "Father of Airborne," suffered a near-fatal heart attack. Ten days later he got more bad news: he had to return to the United States for treatment. His logical replacement would be his assistant division commander, Brig. Gen. Donald F. Pratt or, perhaps, the 101st's division artillery commander, Brig. Gen. Anthony C. McAuliffe (class of 1919). But Ridgway persuaded Bradley to turn the "Screaming Eagles" over to his own division artillery commander, by now a seasoned combat veteran, forty-two-year- old Brig. Gen. Maxwell D. Taylor. Taylor flew to England and on 14 March took over the division.

In September 1943, the 101st had arrived in England with two parachute and two glider infantry regiments. In January 1944, the previously independent 501st Parachute Infantry Regiment joined the 101st as its fifth infantry regiment. The commander of the 501st was the dashing Col. Howard R. "Jumpy" Johnson, an unusual officer in many respects. He had graduated from the U.S. Naval Academy but joined the army as an infantry lieutenant. He was a hard-charging officer who expected the same dash and courage from his men. After he formed the regiment at Camp Toccoa, Georgia, he took it to Fort Benning for jump training. To demonstrate his own spirit and boldness, he would often make three to five jumps a day. Pretty soon he had amassed more than one hundred jumps, more than any other soldier in the 101st. "We are the best!" was his battle cry to his regiment. (His bravery, however, would do him in on 6 October 1944, in Holland, when an artillery round found him standing bravely but unnecessarily exposed. His spine was shattered. En route to a hospital in Nijmegen, he told one of his officers "to take care of my boys." Shortly thereafter he died.)

Colonel George Van Horn Mosely Jr. commanded the 502d Parachute Infantry Regiment of the 101st. He was a West Pointer, class of 1927, and both his father and grandfather were graduates. Mosely was the driving force that built the 502d into a top-notch combat regiment. Unfortunately, on his first day in combat in Normandy, he broke his leg and had to give up command of the regiment he loved so well.

Colonel Robert F. Sink (class of 1927) was another hard-charging commander who worked his regiment, the 101st's 506th Parachute Infantry, into one of the most physically fit outfits in the army. His regiment "passed in review" on the double and marched great distances in the shortest times.

The 327th Glider Infantry Regiment was commanded by Col. George E. Wear, at age forty-six somewhat older than the other regimental commanders; the 401st Glider Infantry Regiment was commanded by Col. Joseph Harper (class of 1922, University of Delaware).

As initially designed, the glider infantry regiment had only two battalions in contrast to the parachute regiment's three. Given the numerous crash landings of the flimsy gliders, their occupants were not ecstatic about their assignments.

In February 1944 Harper's 401st Glider Infantry Regiment was broken up. The 1st Battalion went to the 101st's 327th Glider Infantry and the 2d Battalion to the 82d's 325th Glider Infantry. Harper, unhappy about losing his regiment, joined the G-3 Section of the 101st. Later, in Normandy, he would command the 327th.

The planning for the massive D-day operation in Normandy continued unceasingly. After months of study, analysis, intelligence gathering, and debates, Operation Neptune—the final amphibious assault plan of Overlord—had Bradley's First Army coming ashore, with the VII Corps landing the 4th Division on Utah Beach near Les-Dunes-de-Varreville. To the east the V Corps, made up of the 1st Division and a part of the 29th, would wade ashore on Omaha Beach near the town of Vierville-sur-Mer. Once firmly ashore, the V Corps would expand to the south while VII Corps cut across the Cotentin Peninsula and then swung north to capture Cherbourg. With Cherbourg in U.S. hands, the VII Corps would turn south and move toward Saint-Lô. Once Bradley had captured Saint-Lô and the road from Saint-Lô to Périers, he would be able to bring in mechanized forces. With that accomplished, Patton could bring in his Third Army, advance into Brittany, seize Brest, and cover the south flank of First Army's attack toward Paris.

In the east, the Second British Army was slated to land in the area between Bayeux and Caen, an area selected because it had suitable sites for airfields and the route out of the beachhead to Paris was presumably lightly defended. The British 6th Airborne Division would land before dawn on the northeastern flank of the British beachhead near Caen and the Orne River. At H hour, the British XXX Corps would land on Gold Beach near Bayeux; I Corps would make a two-pronged attack to the east. The British 3d Division was one prong that would land at Sword Beach near Lion-sur-Mer; the other prong was the 3d Canadian Division that would land at J Beach near Courseulles.

In the overall strategy, the Allies intended to force a lodgment between the Seine and the Loire Rivers. The Allies assumed that the enemy would put up a strong resistance initially and then withdraw slowly behind the Seine River. The Allied planners estimated that that phase of the most massive, cross-water invasion in history would take about ninety days.

The airborne plan to support the amphibious landings went through a number of gyrations. Bradley was a strong defender of the maximum use of airborne forces; he and Gavin agreed wholeheartedly on their overall tactics. But part of the problem was the changing strength and disposition of the German forces in the landing areas generally suitable for airborne operations behind the beaches. Originally the Germans had the 243d and 709th Divisions, plus some coastal defense groups, deployed in the region. But in May, intelligence operators found that the German 91st Infantry Division had been deployed in the Carentan–St.-Sauveur-le-Vicomte–Valognes area, right in the middle of the planned landing areas of the 82d and the 101st. Originally the 82d was slated to land Task Force A, a three-regiment combat team task force commanded by General Gavin, twenty miles inland behind Utah Beach, in a fortified area and beyond immediate relief from the amphibious forces, and to stay on the defensive until the arrival of the ground forces. The 101st would land by parachute and glider behind Utah Beach, capture the town of Ste.-Mère-Eglise, hit the German coastal defenses from the rear, and capture four causeways over flooded areas behind the beach, permitting the amphibious forces to get off the beaches and out of the direct range of German fire. Then the 101st was slated to join up with land forces and capture Cherbourg from the rear.

The mission of the airborne forces, particularly the 101st, was derived from General Eisenhower's deep concern about the ability of the amphibious forces to get off the beaches. In *Crusade in Europe* he wrote:

The only available beach on the Cotentin Peninsula was, however, a miserable one. Just back of it was a wide lagoon, passable only on a few narrow causeways that led from the beaches to the interior of the peninsula. If the exits of these causeways should be held by the enemy, our landing troops would be caught in a trap and eventually slaughtered by artillery and other fire to which they would be able to make little reply.

To prevent this, we planned to drop two divisions of American paratroopers inland from this beach, with their primary mission to seize and hold the exits of the vital causeways. The ground was highly unsuited to airborne operations. Hedgerows in the so-called "bocage" country are big, strong, and numerous. The coast lines that the vulnerable transport planes and gliders would have to cross were studded with anti-aircraft. In addition, there were units of mobile enemy troops in the area and these, aside from mounting anti-aircraft fire, would attempt to operate against our paratroopers and glider troops before they could organize themselves for action.

The whole project was much argued from its first proposing, but Bradley and Major General Ridgway, our senior American airborne general, always stoutly agreed with me as to its necessity and its feasibility.

With the German 91st Division in the area of St.-Sauveur-le-Vicomte, General Gavin wrote that "the situation did not look promising for the U.S. 82d. Indeed, it looked so uncompromising that it was decided to change our landing areas. On May 26 we received new orders, moving the division farther east."

All plans had been completed for the 82d Division to carry out its original mission. Field and administrative orders for our D-day preparations had been published and distributed. And in a series of map maneuvers on a special large-scale map, regimental and battalion commanders of the division had outlined their plans in order that all commanders, down to those of the smallest units, could be made thoroughly aware of all plans of maneuver.

The seaborne echelons of the 82d had already departed for the marshaling yards. They were scattered along the coast of Wales and southern England. It was just five days until Y-day (Ready Day).

The new lineup was as follows: The 82d Airborne Division was to land on both sides of the Merderet River. It was then to seize, clear, and secure the general area of Neuville-au-Plain, Ste-Mère-Eglise, Chef-du-Pont, Etienville, and Amfreville. It was to destroy crossings over the Douve, and the 82d Division was then to be prepared to advance to the west on Corps order. The mission of the 101st remained generally unchanged, except that responsibility for capturing the bridges over the Merderet was given to the 82d. The mission of the British 6th was also the same as before.

We received the new plan without a single regret. . . . We assigned regimental missions to conform to the new division mission merely by sliding the regimental drop zones the necessary number of miles to the east. We left unchanged the relative location of the drop zones. Consequently, no change had to be made in the assignment of units to take-off airfields and troop carrier units.

Despite the late change, all airborne troops were fully briefed and on their take-off airfields, ready to go on June 4.

The several dry runs of Y-day and D-day that had been held during the preceding month had taken the novelty out of the staging and sealing process. The cover plan for the D-day operation had apparently worked very well.

"As the day of the invasion approached, the weather in the English Channel became stormy. Heavy winds, a five-foot swell at sea, and lowering skies compelled Eisenhower to postpone the assault from 5 to 6 June," wrote William M. Hammond. "Conditions remained poor, but when weathermen predicted that the winds would abate and the cloud cover rise enough on the scheduled day of the attack to permit a go-ahead, Eisenhower reluctantly gave the command. Expecting casualties of up to 80 percent among the airborne forces, he traveled to an air base at Newbury to bid farewell to the members of the 101st Airborne Division before their tow planes and gliders carried them off to battle." A newspaperman who accompanied Eisenhower later told friends he had seen tears in the general's eyes.

The weather actually worked to the Allies' advantage. When the BBC broadcast the lines from Verlaine's poem indicating commencement of the attack—Blessent mon coeur d'une longeur monotone ("[The violins of autumn] wound my heart with monotonous languor")—the 15th Army in the Pas-de-Calais went on alert, but Rommel's Army Group B headquarters in Normandy did nothing. The weather was so foul that no one believed an invasion possible. Indeed, many commanders of 7th Army had already left for Brittany to participate in an exercise designed, ironically, to simulate an Allied landing in Normandy. Rommel himself was in Germany celebrating his wife's birthday.

Despite the D-day delay caused by the weather and the realignment of the drop and landing zones, the airborne forces were ready to go on the night of 5 June. "Calm and quiet prevailed," wrote Gavin.

But that surreal atmosphere, on the night before the greatest amphibious and airborne invasion in history, was not to last.

12: Normandy—The Onset

By early May 1944 some 1,500,000 U.S. soldiers, double the number who were there in January, had arrived in England and were bivouacked in makeshift camps all over the island.

Earlier in the spring, the military traffic on the island had reached such a level that, on 10 March, all civilian traffic except for medical or other emergencies was restricted. On 6 April all military leaves were halted and mail censorship was enforced. The entire island was a scene of nonstop, feverish activity—750,000 tons of U.S. materiel each month piling up at hundreds of docks; vessels of all sizes being built and modified in shipyards, alleys, and streets; military traffic of all kinds jamming the roads and highways; and military planners at headquarters of all levels working frantically to understand their missions, pick their objectives, plan their tactics and deployments in minute detail, set up schedules timed to the minute, and brief all their commanders down to squad level on charts, maps, and sand tables. The airborne troopers were still able to get an occasional pass, make it to town on army trucks, check out the local pubs and young ladies, and take a bus back to camp. When they weren't training they could get up a game of tackle football—without pads—or baseball with a few odd gloves. Boxing between units was still an outlet for unit and individual spirit. And the troopers were certainly not above gambling their small incomes at poker, on boxing matches, or even on the date of the "big day."

The base camps and airfields for the 82d and the 101st were in clusters all over southern England. On 16 February, for example, the 325th Glider Infantry Regiment had moved down from Northern Ireland to a meadow near the village of Scraptoft. "From then on through early spring," wrote Charles J. Masters in *Glidermen of Neptune,* "the weather was windswept, rain soaked, gray, and bleak."

Despite the weather, the nearness to Leicester afforded the men the chance to enjoy the local British hospitality.

During these months housing accommodations consisted of floorless pyramidal tents. Nissen huts were constructed to serve as mess halls and kitchens, and several other comparable structures housed battalion and the regimental command post. Other improvements were made as time passed, including the building of fences and roads. By the time spring arrived, the 325th camp, which was similar to other airborne camps, had benefited from a significant amount of American "spit and polish."

In some of the past chronicles of World War II airborne operations, the glider riders or "those who were roped in" have not gotten the recognition they so rightly deserve. To start with, they were not volunteers, but simply assigned to glider units from the stream of incoming draftees. Paratroopers received jump pay of $100 per month for officers and $50 for enlistees. (Eventually, all ranks would receive the same jump pay.) Glidermen did not receive hazardous duty pay until July of 1944. At about the same time, they finally received a glider badge—similar to jump wings—with the front-end view of a CG-4A glider replacing the parachute in the middle and a round patch for their caps identifying them as glidermen.

But there was more to the plight of the glider riders. Glider pilots were not normally as well trained as the C-47 pilots, they had had no infantry training, and they were slated to remain on the ground in the battle zone, without a job, until they could somehow be evacuated. And the glidermen knew that their chance of landing safely in the combat zone was far from certain.

"Aldermaston, Ramsbury, Greenham Commons, Membury, Welford, Upottery, and Merryfield: These were the names of the airfields, taken from nearby towns and villages, from which the glidermen would take off to spearhead the attack on Hitler's fortress Europe," wrote Masters.

Almost 4,000 men, fully laden with their own weapons, ammunition, and supplies, would attack in their gliders. Loaded up with them they would bring the necessities of modern war to the battlefield. They would attempt to glide through the air carrying scores of howitzers, jeeps, trailers, mortars, machine guns, hundreds of tons of ammunition, antitank guns, mines, grenades, cans of water, and medical supplies—virtually everything they could squeeze into their gliders that could be utilized to penetrate the Fuhrer's Atlantic Wall.

Individual glidermen were so loaded down with personal equipment—weapons, packs, ammunitions, grenades, rations, first aid equipment, lifejackets—that they needed help to climb into the gliders. And they were still wearing obsolete lace-up canvas leggings around their shins, while the paratroopers proudly wore their spit-shined jump boots beneath baggy pants.

Each Waco CG-4A glider could carry some 3,750 pounds—fifteen combat-loaded men or a jeep and a couple of soldiers. The bigger British Horsa glider could carry some 6,900 pounds. But after some calculations and discussions about availability, the Americans ended up with Wacos. Another problem was the timing of the landing. Originally the gliders were slated to land during the hours of daylight, in early dawn. But the final plan had them landing during the hazardous hours of night. When the troop carrier and glider commanders found out about it, they complained to General Montgomery. His final word was decisive: "We'll have to suffer it." Lieutenant Colonel Mike Murphy, the senior U.S. glider pilot, made the grim prediction that night crash-landings would mean a 50 percent loss of men and extremely important equipment.

The final plans for the glider portion of the airborne assault of the 82d and 101st called for six glider missions. The 82d's battle-hardened 325th Glider Infantry Regiment had four of the missions, and the 101st's 401st Glider Infantry Regiment the other two. The 325th would glide or crash land around Les Forges, in the western end of the sector; the 401st would land near Hiesville, in the east. Some of the glider units landed shortly after H hour; many of the units crashed into Normandy during the daylight and evening hours of D day.

Sergeant J. A. (Jack) Crosscope Jr. was a nineteen-year-old paratrooper assigned to the 508th Parachute Infantry Regiment stationed in the "beautiful countryside of Nottingham, England," he wrote many years later.

On May 26, 1944, all parachute units were moved under secrecy to staging areas in Southern England and in the area of Bristol. My regiment was assigned to a tent city compound which we shared with the Canadian Queen's Own Rifles Regiment. After several days of rest and being fattened on the finest of food, things began to fall into place.

One morning at about 2:00 AM, the barracks door opened and the loud voice of Sgt. Bill Kreye awakened us all: "Everyone!! On your feet and line up."

We formed two lines in the center of the barracks. One was for the purpose of obtaining escape kits and the other was for money exchange to receive French francs.

On the following morning, the final equipment inspection was conducted, ammunition was issued, and special assignments were made.

On the night of June 5, the order was given for all personnel to report to the airfield and prepare to load on planes. We had distinguished visitors to see us off—General Eisenhower, General Collins, and British Prime Minister Winston Churchill each gave us a pep talk, wished us luck, and told us they would see us in the fields of Normandy.

D day was originally scheduled for 5 June. But the fierce weather and the roaring storm that hit England and the Continent forced Eisenhower to postpone the momentous date by one day. Ships already on the way to the French coast had to return. But at 2130 on the night of 4 June, Group Captain J. M. Skagg ("a dour but canny Scot," according to General Eisenhower), the senior weatherman for Supreme Headquarters, Allied Expeditionary Force, also known well as SHAEF, optimistically told a top-level group of Allied brass in Eisenhower's headquarters at Southwick House that the weather would clear on 5 June and hold for the next twenty-four hours. Leigh-Mallory was not enthusiastic; he wanted to postpone landing operations until 19 June. Tedder thought it was "chancy." Looking at Montgomery, Eisenhower asked, "Do you see any reason for not going Tuesday?" Montgomery looked directly at Eisenhower and said. "I would say, Go!" At 2145 Eisenhower made the decision. "I am quite positive that the order must be given," he said. That set the date for the immense invasion, as well as setting the date for the airborne assault—the night of 5 June and the early hours of 6 June.

During the afternoon of 5 June, the paratroopers of the 82d and 101st marched out of their tent and Quonset hut cities, headed for their departure airfields, and began checking their gear. Each infantryman carried an M1 rifle either disassembled and in a padded Griswold container or already assembled and slung in front under his parachute harness. He also carried 160 rounds of ammunition, two hand grenades, a Gammon grenade (two pounds of plastic explosive), a knife, three days worth of field rations, a gas mask, cartons of cigarettes, a first aid kit with sulfa tablets and two morphine syrettes, and a toy cricket for challenges—one click-click was answered with a double click-click. Machine guns, mortars, bazookas, radios, and extra belts of ammunition were crammed into A-5 equipment containers, each with its own cargo chute.

That evening, Eisenhower had dinner with General Taylor at the airfield near Greenham Common, one of the departure fields for 101st Division paratroopers. Later the two visited the men who had covered their faces with Apache-style war paint and were putting on their parachutes and combat gear. Eisenhower moved slowly among the men, talking to them, and asking some of them where they came from. Later Eisenhower told Taylor, "I don't know if your boys will scare the Germans but they sure as hell scare me." One trooper called out: "Now quit worrying, General, we'll take care of this thing for you." When Eisenhower finished his visit, he shook hands with Taylor and said, simply, "Good luck, Max."

(In the famous prejump picture of Ike talking to a small group of unnamed paratroopers in jump suits, helmets, and part of their field gear, the man in the front, second from the right, was twenty-two-year-old Lt. Wallace C. Strobel, from Saginaw, Michigan. He became one of the most famous "unknown" soldiers of the war after the picture appeared in many books and on a U.S. postage stamp. Strobel died in September 1999 at the age of seventy-seven.)

At the various takeoff airfields, before the paratroopers boarded their assigned aircraft, the commanders gathered their men around them and gave them pep talks, some highly spirited. "Jumpy" Johnson, the hard-charging commander of the 501st, stood on the hood of a jeep and gave a fiery talk, emphasizing his shouted comments by pulling his knife out of his boot and waving it overhead, yelling that he fully intended to stick it in the "foulest Nazi belly in France. Are you with me? We're the best!" he shouted. Then he had the men line up, so he could go down the line shaking hands with each one of them.

Lieutenant Colonel Edward "Cannonball" Krause, commander of the 3d Battalion, 505th, gathered his men around him at Spanhoe airfield, stood on his jeep, and raised a U.S. flag over his head. He bragged that "tonight we're going to march on Ste. Mère Eglise and fly this flag from the tallest building in town."

Companies gathered around their company commanders and platoon leaders for a final briefing, emphasizing challenges, passwords, and replies. Some of them were things like "Flash," "Thunder," and "Welcome," selected because a German might say "Velcom" and perhaps get shot.

The stage was set. The troops were ready. The airborne concept was about to get tested in a fierce examination—battle.

13: Operation Neptune: Airborne Invasion of Normandy

By 2200 on the night of 5 June, the paratroopers and glidermen of the U.S. 82d and 101st Airborne Divisions and the British 6th Airborne Division were ready to jump or glide and fight in France. On their departure airfields throughout southern England, as the troopers were clambering aboard their C-47s and Waco and Horsa gliders, some of the pilots and flight crews were finishing their checklists around the outside of their planes, while others were in their cockpits checking instruments. To carry the paratroopers and tug the gliders, 1,086 planes were warming up.

At 2300, eighteen planeloads of pathfinders rolled down the runways and lifted off into the black night. The pathfinders were in six serials of three planes each. At 0021 on 6 June, the first planes of the main bodies of paratroopers began lifting off from nine different airfields. For the next two hours, hundreds of C-47s roared off their airstrips and formed a 300-mile-long column of planes in a nine-ship-wide V of V's formation—three planes to a V. The 6,418 paratroopers of the 82d were in 378 C-47s. The 6,638 paratroopers of the 101st were in 490 C-47s of Col. Hal Clark's 52d Troop Carrier Wing.

The majority of the pilots were novices in this massive airborne operation. For most of them, it was their first combat mission. The tight formation they would fly, only a hundred feet from wing tip to the adjacent wing tip, and with no guidance lights except a small blue light in the tail of the plane in front, made flying hazardous in the extreme. These pilots were not the barnstorming, superbly qualified "Blue Angels" types of later years. They were young, relatively inexperienced pilots, each with only a few hundred flying hours. Their worst fear was a midair collision. But they were resolute and uncommonly brave, like the men they were carrying in their ships.

Inside the planes, the troopers were strapped tightly in their parachutes and equipment, hardly able to move. Once settled, they talked, said their prayers, fingered their rosaries, or even opened and read a Bible, sometimes aloud. One trooper even asked his next seat buddy to lend him his rosary when he had finished with his own five Our Fathers, fifty Hail Marys, and five Glory Bes.

"The atmosphere during that time aboard the plane was a fantastic mix of gloom and laughter," wrote Jack Crosscope, a young sergeant in the 508th Parachute Infantry Regiment. "We took the opportunity to smoke the last cigarette and the talk was of wives, families and sweethearts. We were all hoping and praying that all would go well."

The 513 gliders that would eventually crash-land in Normandy in the following two days were being towed by the 9th Troop Carrier Command's seven groups operating from bases throughout southern England. Each group had some fifty-two C-47s, and each C-47 tugged one CG-4A Waco glider with a 300-foot towrope. When it came time to separate, the glider pilot pushed a release arm that cut the glider loose from the tug ship. Communications between the glider pilot and the C-47 pilot initially had been by telephone cable wrapped around the towrope. The line frequently shorted or snapped, so eventually two-way radios were installed. Frequently these did not work, either. "The glider assault plan was, by any standard, remarkable in its degree of detail and complexity," wrote Charles J. Masters in his book *Glidermen of Neptune.* "Glidermen from the 82d and 101st Airborne Divisions were to attack in a precisely timed sequence of six separate glider missions. The 82d Airborne, with the battle-hardened glidermen of the 325th Glider Infantry Regiment, would bear the burden of four of the missions, while the Screaming Eagles of the 101st Airborne would strike with the other two. The six glider missions were code-named Chicago, Detroit, Keokuk, Elmira, Galveston, and Hackensack."

At 0100 the first glider serial, Mission Chicago, fifty-three Wacos towed by C-47s from the 434th Troop Carrier Group carrying 155 men of the 327th Glider Infantry of the 101st, lumbered down the runway at Aldermaston in Berkshire. At the same time, Mission Detroit, made up of fifty-two C-47s of the 437th Troop Carrier Group, each pulling a Waco glider, lifted off from Ramsbury in Wiltshire and carried 220 fully equipped men from the 325th Glider Infantry Regiment of the 82d Airborne Division. The gliders were crammed with sixteen 57mm antitank guns, crates of ammunition, twenty-two jeeps, five trailers, cans of water, medical supplies, and ten more tons of other equipment and supplies. Throughout D day and D plus 1, additional flights of hundreds of Wacos and Horsas landed in Normandy to bring in additional troopers, ammunition, medics, jeeps, and 75mm pack howitzers.

In the British zone, shortly after midnight, 4,000 paratroopers and 4,000 glidermen of the 6th Airborne Division were to drop and glide onto landing zones northeast of Caen near the mouth of the Orne River. Once in place, the 6th would anchor the British eastern flank by seizing bridges over the river and the Caen Canal. In their landings the British would be more fortunate than the Americans because they would land on flat, wide-open fields with no marshes or thick hedgerows to impede their landing and assembly. Also, the British began their attack with glider troops: at 0015 on 6 June, the British tug ships cut loose six Horsa gliders at about 5,000 feet over the Orne River—the glider troops they carried would pave the way for the paratroopers.

The U.S. pathfinder planes flew across the Channel between the islands of Alderney and Guernsey and crossed the west coast of the Cotentin Peninsula. Because the main body of the 101st preceded that of the 82d, the 101st pathfinders jumped ahead of the 82d pathfinders.

Eight minutes after crossing the coast at 0015, Capt. Frank L. Lillyman, the lead pathfinder of the 101st, stepped out of his plane 450 feet above ground, made a rough parachute landing when he hit the ground, and became the first U.S. paratrooper to land in occupied France. Lillyman had torn ligaments in his leg in a jump four days earlier but told no one about it—he did not want to miss this gut-wrenching, once-in-a-lifetime, main event. He landed near the village of St-Germain-de-Varreville. Farther to the east, the lead pathfinder of the British Red Devils, Capt. Ian A. Tate, jumped near Caen to mark the landing zones for the British gliders. The invasion of France was under way.

In one of the C-47s carrying the main body of his men, General Ridgway stood in the door watching his flight of planes disappear into a dense cloudbank. And in his plane, General Gavin ordered his men to chute up as soon as his plane crossed the coast, figuring that if his plane were hit, they could at least bail out over land and not get dumped into the English Channel.

Because of the cloud cover, most of the pathfinder plane pilots failed to find the proper DZs. One planeload from the 101st was lost; the men jumped early and were lost in the Channel. Only one pathfinder team from the 101st found its proper DZ. In the 82d only the 505th pathfinders dropped accurately onto their target, DZ O. Once on the ground and after checking for any kind of landmarks, most of the pathfinders knew they had been scattered and were not on their proper DZs. Therefore, to avoid further confusing the pilots and jumpmasters of the follow-on echelons, they did not turn on their guidance equipment.

Another problem that helped scatter the main body of troopers was heavy fire from German antiaircraft guns once the air armada arrived over the coastline. One plane took a direct hit and crashed. After the planes were deeper inland German machine guns took them under fire. The pilots could see tracers slashing through the sky around them and veered off course to avoid the bullets. A few pilots, lost and out of formation, headed back to England with their troops still aboard. The clouds, the antiaircraft fire, and the misdropped pathfinders all added to the wide dispersion of the thousands of the main body of paratroopers of the 82d and the 101st.

Stephen Ambrose, in *D-Day,* wrote about the troop-carrying C-47s crossing the coastline where the planes hit a cloudbank.

The pilots instinctively separated, some descending, some rising, all peeling off to the right or left to avoid a mid-air collision. When they emerged from the clouds, within seconds or at the most minutes, they were hopelessly separated. Lt. Harold Young of the 326th Parachute Engineers recalled that as his plane came out of the clouds, "We were all alone. I remember my amazement. Where had all those C-47s gone?"

They could speed up, which most of them did. They were supposed to throttle back to ninety miles per hour or less, to reduce the opening shock for the paratroopers, but ninety miles per hour at 600 feet made them easy targets for the Germans on the ground, so they pushed the throttle forward and sped up to 150 miles per hour, meanwhile either descending to 300 feet or climbing to 2,000 feet and more. They twisted and turned, spilling their passengers and cargo. They got hit by machine-gun fire, 20mm shells, and the heavier 88mm shells. They saw planes going down to their right and left, above and below them. They saw planes explode. They had no idea where they were, except that they were over the Cotentin.

At 0130, the main body of paratroopers of the 101st began dropping in a spread-out circle southeast of Ste-Mère-Eglise. After landing in the black of the night, commanders at all levels could gather quickly only a few of their men. The 377th Parachute Field Artillery Battalion, for example, lost eleven of its twelve pack 75s and their crews in a marsh cunningly flooded by the Germans just before the invasion. Throughout the DZs, hedgerows, four or five feet high and three to four feet thick, covered with thick vines and embedded with tall trees, separated farmers' small lots and seriously aggravated the problem of assembling units. In the 101st some 1,500 troopers landed outside their designated areas; a great many were killed or captured.

Because the 82d followed the 101st across the Cotentin Peninsula, the German antiaircraft gunners were far more alert when the 82d Division's planes flew over. The 82d's order of flight was Colonel Ekman's 505th, Colonel Lindquist's 508th, and Colonel Millet's 507th, along with two pack 75 howitzers and crews of Lt. Col. Wagner J. D'Allessio's 456th Parachute Field Artillery Battalion. Once they were over land, they were hit with very heavy antiaircraft fire and were scattered widely. Only one of the 82d's three parachute regiments, the 505th, landed even close to its assigned DZ.

General Taylor landed in a pasture, struggled out of his parachute harness, and looked around. He found quickly that he was alone. But about twenty minutes later he met up with a rifleman from the 501st. They hugged each other. Shortly after, more men from the 501st showed up from behind the hedgerows. Brigadier General Anthony McAuliffe, Taylor's artillery commander, appeared with some of his men. Then his chief of staff, Col. Gerald J. Higgins (class of 1934), and his division engineer, Lt. Col. John Pappas, appeared out of the darkness. Finally more staff officers appeared. With this small group, consisting of more officers than enlisted men, and hardly a formidable assault force, Taylor moved out toward the Marie-du-Mont–Vierville road. He later claimed that "never in the annals of warfare had so few been commanded by so many."

Father Francis L. Sampson, the chaplain of the 101st, landed in a deep swamp and sank into water over his head. His parachute stayed open above him and, with the wind, acted like a sail pulling him around the swamp, finally, and fortunately, into some shallow water. He cut away his parachute harness and his other gear including his Holy Mass kit. He laid low for about twenty minutes, gathering his strength and senses, and then began to look for his equipment, especially his Mass kit. On his fifth dive into the swamp he found it. Much later he remembered that he thought he had prayed the Act of Contrition, his final prayer as he tried to survive in the swamp. In actuality he realized that he had said Grace Before Meals.

Gavin was in command of Task Force A, made up of the 82d's three parachute regiments, the 505th, 507th, and 508th. "Our operation was launched by pathfinder teams followed by the 505th Infantry," he wrote later. "It had the farthest to go and had the mission of seizing Ste-Mere-Eglise. I flew in the lead plane of the 508th Parachute Infantry. The 507th Parachute Infantry followed the 508th. Altogether, it took 378 C-47 airplanes to lift the parachutists. These were to be followed by 375 gliders a day later carrying troops of the 325th Glider Infantry. Fifty-two gliders carrying antitank weapons and heavy communications and other equipment were to land with the parachute echelon during darkness the first night."

His flight had taken off from Cottesmore, England, "exactly on schedule." But soon his plane ran into a dense fog. "I felt increasingly disturbed and quite alone," Gavin wrote.

> About seven minutes after we crossed the coast, the clouds began to clear. As they did, I could see a great deal of heavy flak coming up off the right of our flight. I had studied the antiaircraft gun dispositions, and the only town in that part of the peninsula that had heavy antiaircraft guns was Etienville. . . . We began to receive small-arms fire from the ground. It seemed harmless enough; it sounded like pebbles landing on a tin roof. . . . We were at about 600 feet, the green light went on, and I took one last precious look at the land below. We were about thirty seconds overtime. About three seconds after the green light went on, I yelled, "Let's go," and went out the door with everyone following.

Gavin was finally in France, and he set about the almost impossible task of rounding up his scattered regiments and getting on with his mission.

"Within minutes of sighting the Normandy coast," wrote Jack Crosscope, "the pilot put on the red light and the jumpmaster gave his command: 'Stand up and hook up. Check equipment. Sound off for equipment check.'"

The green light came on and the jumpmaster gave the command, standing at the door: "Go!" Within seconds, the sky was filled with thousands of young American paratroopers jumping from hundreds of transport planes, falling into what would be the large battle zone.

There are some moments of humor in all military operations. In my case, I had my first lesson in how to prune trees. I fell through an apple tree, pruning it from top to ground. I heard my buddy Sal, from Brooklyn, calling for help. When I got to him, he asked me to "please get me out of this mess." He had fallen into a fresh pile of doo-doo.

Even at the lowest levels, the troops knew what they were supposed to be doing. Crosscope wrote that "our job was to prevent the German Army units from assaulting the Allied forces landing on the beaches west of us, or to slow them down enough for our forces on the beach to establish firm positions."

Unit commanders from the squad to the regiment level tried to assemble their men by whatever means available and head toward their assigned objectives. Some were more successful than others. In spite of the dispersion of his troops, General Taylor was able to gather a large group and take quite quickly some of his immediate objectives, including St-Martin-de-Varreville and Pouppeville. But far more important, he and his few men were able to secure some vital exits from the beaches, allowing the amphibious forces a cleared route inland.

Taylor's 506th, commanded by Colonel Sink, landed about twenty miles from its assigned DZ. Its mission was twofold: capture causeways 1 and 2 and seize two wooden bridges over the Douve River.

Of Sink's two battalions slated to land on DZ C, only nine planeloads hit the target. Lieutenant Colonel William L. Turner (class of 1939), commander of the 1st Battalion, could find only fifty of his men two hours after the drop. A few hours after landing, Lt. Col. Robert Strayer, commander of the 2d Battalion, 506th, found himself leading a disparate group of 300 troopers from his own battalion, the 3d Battalion, 506th, and the 508th from the 82d. He led them on to capture one of the important causeways from the beach.

Lieutenant Colonel Robert G. Cole, (class of 1939), and only twenty-nine years old, was the commander of the 3d Battalion, 502d. He and a portion of his battalion landed on the outskirts of Ste-Mère-Eglise. He knew this was an 82d objective, so he headed for St-Martin-de-Varreville, a 502d target. By the afternoon of D day, Cole had gathered about 250 men and had made contact with advanced troops of the 4th U.S. Division coming across Utah Beach. So, the mission was partly accomplished.

In an operation studded with catastrophes, the fate of the 3d of the 506th stands out. On landing, the troopers ran into Germans who were primed and ready. The enemy had recognized that the area designated as DZ D, assigned to the 3d Battalion of the 506th, was a likely airborne DZ. Around it the Germans had cleared fields of fire and had soaked nearby wooden barns with oil, and then they ringed the area with machine guns and mortars. When the 3d Battalion, 506th, planes neared the area the Germans ignited the barns, and the bright fires illuminated the paratroopers floating helplessly to the ground. Many were shot as they swung beneath their chutes or struggled after landing to get out of their harnesses. In a little less than ten minutes the Germans had killed the battalion commander, Lt. Col. Robert M. Wolverton (class of 1938), his executive officer, Maj. George S. Grant, and a large number of defenseless paratroopers. The only lucky members of the 3d Battalion, 506th, were two planeloads that were dropped a few miles from DZ D. In a couple of hours, in an action of sheer determination and leadership, Capt. Charles Shettle, Wolverton's S-3 officer, assembled five officers and twenty-nine men and captured two bridges over the Douve, accomplishing an important part of the battalion's mission.

The first contact with the rear area in England came from an unlikely source. The 326th Airborne Medical Company parachuted and glided onto their turf and set up a hospital in the Château Colombières near Hiesville. Three NCOs of the 101st Airborne Signal Company joined them and dragged in a large radio; they made the first communication of the morning with England.

But the radio was not the only means by which the airborne troopers tried to contact their home bases in England. Jack Crosscope remembered another system, dredged up perhaps from the Civil War. "We could not depend on radio contact during the first hours of the invasion, and our company clerk jumped with the carrier pigeon who would carry the initial report of our landing back to England. When he landed, the clerk was leaning forward. . . . When we got to him, he told us that the landing had almost killed the pigeon. He was in the process of giving it artificial respiration. The pigeon recovered and was soon released for its long flight back to England."

At 0400 on D day the 101st's first fifty-three gliders, in Mission Chicago, began landing on LZ E, two miles west of Ste-Marie-du-Mont. The gliders carried 155 glidermen of the 327th Glider Infantry Regiment. Six gliders landed on their target LZ, and fifteen others came down a half-mile away near Les Forges. All but one glider were within two miles of the LZ.

The first glider, *The Fighting Falcon,* was flown by Lt. Col. Michael Murphy, who had been one of the nation's top stunt pilots before the war and was now the senior U.S. glider pilot. Seated next to him in the copilot's seat was Brig. Gen. Donald F. Pratt, the assistant division commander of the 101st. Pratt was a paratrooper and had wanted to jump in, but Taylor ordered him to glide in for two reasons: one, to give some status to the underglamorized glider troops and, two, to command the second echelon of troops—some coming by glider and some by ships across the channel.

At 0400, Murphy spotted the marked LZ and made as perfect a landing as a glider pilot could make—given the darkness, the hedgerows, and the lack of a motor. After he slid the glider onto the pasture, it skidded roughly and rapidly across the field and crashed into a hedgerow, and was demolished. The crash threw Murphy out of the glider with two broken legs. But General Pratt was far less fortunate. He was smashed against part of the metal frame of the glider and killed instantly. He was the second U.S. general, so far, to die in the war.

When Taylor heard of Pratt's death, he made his chief of staff, thirty-four-year-old Col. Gerald Higgins the new assistant division commander, bypassing two more senior officers, Colonels Sink and Johnson.

The other glider operation on the morning of D day was Mission Detroit. It took off, as scheduled, at 0100 on 6 June from Ramsbury in Wiltshire and flew along the east coast of the Cotentin Peninsula. (The paratrooper planes had flown down the west coast.) Over the Channel the visibility was about ten miles, but as the planes neared Normandy they ran into the usual banks of clouds. Seven gliders were accidentally released, and German antiaircraft fire blasted them. The C-47 pilots dropped down to 500 feet, and seven more gliders were released over swampy fields west of the Merderet River. German antiaircraft shells and bullets pierced the canvas skin of many gliders, wounding the unprotected glidermen and heavily damaging thirteen C-47s, as well, causing one to crash. Twenty-five others also took hits.

In spite of the enemy fire and the clouds, the pilots of the remaining gliders in the column held fairly steady and released their gliders in two columns at 400 to 500 feet. The glider pilots flew straight ahead and down, crashing into the hedgerows, trees, Rommel's asparagus, other gliders, and even a herd of cattle. Some twenty gliders landed on the intended LZ. Almost all the gliders and eleven of the twenty-two jeeps were destroyed. The glidermen did their best to gather equipment, find their artillery pieces, and get organized. By noon the artillerymen were firing their pack 75s at the Germans.

The British glider assault was far more effective.

Starting at about 0300, sixty-nine Horsas brought in a glider regiment and the commander of the 6th British Airborne Division, Maj. Gen. Richard Gale. The force landed near Ranville. Forty-nine of the Horsas landed safely on the targeted LZ and brought in jeeps and antitank weapons.

Finally, by the evening of D day, Generals Taylor and McAuliffe had trekked through the rugged terrain to Colonel Sink's 506th CP at Coloville. With his regiment badly scattered and caught in the German antiparatrooper defenses, Sink had to report that the highway and railroad bridges on the Douve Highway had not yet been taken. That became an objective for D plus 1.

The 82d had a multiple mission: seal off the Cotentin from the south; destroy bridges over the Douve River at Pont-l'Abbé and Beuzeville; occupy and hold both banks of the Merderet River; protect the southwest flank of VII Corps by holding the line of the Douve River; and, most important, seize Ste-Mère-Eglise.

The landing of the 82d was even more hazardous than that of the 101st. The 82d had dropped near the Merderet River. Ridgway and his staff landed near their target DZ in an orchard that Ridgway had personally picked weeks earlier as his CP. But, unfortunately, a large portion of the 82d had landed in an area of ersatz swamps, the land having been flooded by the Germans just days before. The dispersion of the 82d had been so broad that, by D plus 2, he had only about 2,100 of his scattered paratroopers under command control. He had contact with only one battalion of Colonel Lindquist's "Red Devils" 508th Infantry and half a battalion of Colonel Millet's 507th that had dropped near the Merderet. Both the 507th and 508th had landed very near the German 91st Division.

Gavin and his plane of troopers landed about three miles off course in an orchard. "My aide had landed near me," wrote General Gavin, "and together we began to assemble the troopers from our plane as per plan."

I heard someone across a hedgerow, and we challenged each other at about the same time. It was Captain Carl M. Price of the Division Intelligence. He joined me. I moved quickly, and as I left the field, I came on a small, worn country road going to the right. I followed it and in about 400 yards came to a vast expanse of water.

By that time about fifteen troopers were with me. Bundles had landed in the water. It was important that we rescue them, because they contained our bazookas, radios, mines, everything critical to our survival. One man in our group, Lt. James H. Devine, at once took off all of his clothing and waded out into the swamp to retrieve the bundles. I can see him now, pale white as a statue standing out against the swamp background; at the moment I was concerned that he would be a sure target if the Germans attacked. So far, they had not; we heard only an occasional shot some distance away. Along the marsh I found prepared fox-holes. Evidently the Germans had prepared the bank for defense in the event of an attack coming from the other direction, from the English Channel.

Shortly after he had landed, across the swamp Gavin saw red and green lights, the assembly signals of the 507th and 508th. He sent his aide, Capt. Hugo Olson, to cross the swamp and find out "what was going on." Olson came back in about an hour and reported that he had waded through the swamp at shoulder depth and found the railroad that ran along the bank of the Merderet. Gavin decided that he was about two miles north of the La Fière Bridge, the objective of the 505th. By daylight Gavin had gathered about 130 troops, some of whom had been injured in the jump.

At about the same time Gavin also learned that a glider had crashed about a quarter of a mile away. He sent Lt. Thomas Graham and a patrol from the 505th to check out the glider. Shortly after, Graham reported that the area was surrounded by Germans, that it would take an organized attack to get to it, and that the attack would probably be futile because the glider was deep in the swamp and the gun aboard it could not be dragged through the swamp and underbrush.

By this time, Gavin had about 200 troopers and ordered them to follow him through the swamp. "It was quite light then, and we started across, widely deployed," he wrote.

We must have covered an area several hundred yards across, with troopers 15 to 25 yards apart, holding their rifles and sometimes their equipment over their heads as they went into the marsh. Soon we were almost shoulder deep and the going was extremely difficult. . . . By then the Germans had reached the bank and were firing at individuals. Occasionally troopers would be hit and go down. . . . Finally we made the railroad embankment. It was about six feet high, firm and dry, and we crawled up on it. Evidently the Germans did not have weapons capable of reaching that far. We reorganized, helped those who were wounded, and started a column down the railroad track toward La Fiere.

The 2d Battalion of the 505th had probably the best landing of any of the 82d's battalions. Its pathfinders had found its DZ near the road connecting Neuville-au-Plain with Ste-Mère-Eglise and had set up their Eurekas and lights. The pilot of the lead C-47 carrying the battalion commander, Lt. Col. Benjamin Vandervoort, saw the lighted "T" where he expected it. At 0145, some twenty-seven of the thirty-six sticks of the battalion landed on the correct DZ or within a mile of it. Even though Vandervoort's planes had also been widely scattered, some of the pilots managed a difficult maneuver: they circled back over the DZ that the pathfinders had been able to mark. On four of the six other 82d DZs, the enemy scattered around the area and the wide dispersion of the pathfinders had made it impossible for the pathfinders to mark the zones.

Like a number of his men landing on the very hard turf of the DZ, Vandervoort had a bad landing—he broke his left ankle. Captain Lyle Putnam, Vandervoort's battalion surgeon, happened upon Vandervoort in the dark. "He was seated with a rain cape over him, reading a map by flashlight," Putnam remembered. "He recognized me and, calling me close, quietly asked that I take a look at his ankle with as little demonstration as possible. His ankle was obviously broken. He insisted on replacing his jump boot, and we laced it tightly." Vandervoort got up, using his rifle as a cane, and said to Putnam, "Well, let's go." He moved out, sent up his green flares as identification, and, within thirty minutes, had assembled some six hundred of his troopers. That was the record for the fastest assembly of a battalion that morning.

Lieutenant Colonel Edward Krause commanded the 3d Battalion of the 505th. His battalion landed outside DZ O in an area fortunately free of Germans. After he had assembled about half of his battalion, he started toward Ste-Mère-Eglise, his D-day objective. Krause had with him a French guide who led them almost unnoticed into the town, but once inside, the battalion's troopers ran into German patrols and guards—of whom they killed ten and captured thirty. Before dawn the next morning the 3d of the 505th had captured Ste-Mère-Eglise, and, over the town square, Krause mounted a U.S. flag that he had packed in with him. Ste-Mère-Eglise was the first town liberated on the Western Front.

Vandervoort's mission had been to set up blocking positions in Neuville-au-Plain, a village just north of Ste-Mère-Eglise. After he gathered his men he started moving toward his objective. The crippled Vandervoort rode in an ammunition cart pulled by two of his NCOs. En route to Neuville-au-Plain, he got a message from his regimental commander, Col. William E. Ekman, telling him to halt where he was and set up a blocking position. Ekman wanted to send Vandervoort to Ste-Mère-Eglise in the event that Krause could not get there. What Ekman did not know was that Krause was already in Ste-Mère-Eglise and had established a sturdy defensive position in the city.

But at 0930 the Germans, with a mixed force of armored vehicles and elements of the 6th Parachute Regiment, attacked Krause's defenses on the south edge of the city. Ekman sent a radio message to Vandervoort, north of the city, to march south and attack. Vandervoort moved out, but sent Lieutenant Turnbull and his reinforced rifle platoon, forty-seven men, to move north into Neuville-au-Plain and block to road leading down to Ste-Mère-Eglise. Turnbull set up a defensive barrier but was attacked almost immediately by a large force from the 1058th Infantry Regiment. Turnbull's men fought with paratrooper intensity and in four hours of fierce, close combat drove off the Germans who thought, incorrectly, that they were outnumbered. Turnbull's gallant stand cost him thirty-two men killed or wounded. But he held the position and saved the troops in Ste-Mère-Eglise from having to defend both ends of the town.

Inside the town, Krause rounded up several small bands of stray paratroopers from other regiments who had dropped erratically there during the night. With these strays from Vandervoort's battalion and his own men, he was able to hold off the German tanks and paratroopers. Krause lost several men and, although he was hit twice, he stayed in command of the battle.

Major F. C. Kellum commanded 1st Battalion, 505th. His mission was to secure a bridge across the Merderet River at La Fière. Kellum gathered a force from his A Company and attacked a series of buildings around the east end of the bridge, but his attack was futile. Before his troops got to the buildings, the Germans blasted them with machine gun fire and drove them back. In a second attack on the buildings Kellum was killed. The 1st Battalion, 505th executive officer, Maj. James McGinty took over the company and later that day made a third unsuccessful effort to take the bridge. It cost him his life.

With Ste-Mère-Eglise under control, Ridgway and Gavin concentrated on their other two primary objectives: the two key bridges over the Merderet River at La Fière and the one near Chef-du-Pont. During the morning of D day, Gavin walked the area between La Fiere and Chef-du-Pont, leading the battle for the two bridges. His hastily assembled band of troopers captured the Chef-du-Pont bridge after a heavy fight, but he could not dislodge the Germans from La Fière.

For the airborne effort, portions of the 101st and the 82d glider forces also came across the channel in navy ships. Colonel Edson D. Raff, who had commanded the 509th in the North African invasion, brought in amphibiously a diverse group of ninety glidermen from the 82d's 325th Glider Infantry Regiment, units of the 82d's glider field artillery, and a company of tanks from the 746th Tank Battalion. Raff landed on Utah Beach on D day and joined General Ridgway at the 82d's CP near Ste-Mère-Eglise.

Colonel Millet's 507th's target was DZ T, west of the Merderet River, and its mission was to set up a defense facing north and west along the northwest side of the division's area. But the regiment had a disastrous drop, which had some of its origins in the 507th's pathfinder drop that was itself a catastrophe. The 507th's pathfinders, commanded by Capt. John T. Joseph, had landed in the middle of heavy enemy fire, and two officers broke their legs. After the pathfinder drop, Joseph could find only two of his men, one of whom had a Eureka that by 0220 was operating. In a short time, Joseph saw twenty of the eighty-three C-47s carrying the 507th fly overhead and then drop their men miles from DZ T. The Eureka had malfunctioned. Only two planeloads landed in the proper DZ; twelve loads landed twenty miles to the west. The other 507th planes flew over the DZ and dropped their troopers into the Merderet River and adjacent swamps. And some planes even dropped their unfortunate troops at speeds of 175 miles per hour, about sixty miles an hour faster than planned. Because of their heavy loads, many troopers drowned in the neck-deep swamps, unable to extricate themselves from their gear.

Only a small fraction of one of the 507th's battalions could operate as a team on D day. The 2d Battalion, 507th commander, Lt. Col. Charles J. Timmes, was able to assemble some fifty men and move out to Cauquigny, a small town just west of the Merderet River. He ran into a force of Germans and lost four of his men. Outnumbered, Timmes pulled back into an apple orchard north of Cauquigny and dug in. That afternoon, Capt. Ben Schwartzwalder joined him after he and his men had fought across the La Fière bridge.

Captain Clarence Tolle commanded D Company of the 507th, and after the drop he ran into Lt. Lewis L. Harris, one of his platoon leaders. Other men of D Company also dropped in the vicinity. For instance, 1st Sgt. Barney Hopkins landed in a tree near a group of buildings a few hundred yards west of Amfreville. Almost immediately, some Germans had begun firing at him from one of the buildings, but he climbed out of the tree, cut off his chute, and escaped.

Harris and Tolle got together and decided to unload the part of their gear not needed immediately—entrenching tools, first aid packets, K-rations, raincoats, and dispatch cases. Tolle had lost his M1 carbine, so Harris gave him his pistol. They moved out and ran into their commander, Colonel Millet, and together tried to determine where their men were. They walked carefully through an apple orchard, but not carefully enough: when they came out of the trees, a German with a Schmeisser automatic pistol opened fire. They ran back into the orchard, took some more German fire, and hit the ground. Harris fired back, but his carbine jammed. The German patrol then disappeared, and Millet decided to wait for daylight before moving out.

At dawn, they spotted a German patrol, but it faded out of sight before they could attack it. Millet then decided to ambush the Germans. At this time, Tolle heard some firing and found Sergeant Hopkins and about thirty men shooting at another German patrol. Millet then saw Amfreville ahead and led his small band toward it. As he neared the town, they ran into Germans and were quickly in a heavy firefight with them. After assessing the situation, Millet moved his men west of the village and there decided that he and his thirty men were no match for the German force they had run into. They set up a defensive position and for the next two days stayed immobile. Germans often passed by within twenty yards, but Millet's group held its fire and went unnoticed.

On the second day Maj. Benjamin Pearson of the 2d Battalion, 507th arrived with thirty more men, and Millet's men captured a German convoy of seven trucks and a motorcycle. The convoy provided them with food and water and, amazingly, two cases of Hennessey brandy. Millet's mission was to capture Amfreville, so he decided to stay where he was; by the evening of that day, he had about a hundred men gathered in his defensive position. On the third day Capt. Allen Taylor arrived with 250 men he had found on the DZ waiting for orders. During that day Millet and his men fought small skirmishes with the enemy, with no men lost to enemy mortar rounds but two to rifle fire and one to a machine gun.

That evening Millet finally made contact with the 82d Division. He was ordered to move out and join Colonel Timmes. So, at about noon the next day Millet and his men moved out of their defensive position. They soon ran into German bicycle patrols, and Millet's column was split and then broken. In addition, fire from Germans in the hedgerows was overwhelming. Millet and his small group were finally captured.

The 508th Red Devils landed more compactly than the 507th had but still had a difficult time accomplishing its mission—securing the left-most portion of the 82d's airhead, most of which bordered the banks of the Douve River, and seizing its bridges. DZ N was designated for the 508th, and 124 paratroopers in seven planes actually hit it, but nine planeloads landed in the 101st's across Causeway 3, one of the 101st's objectives. The latter jumpers were lucky because they landed 500 yards from the English Channel, where they would have drowned in their heavy gear if they had been dropped ten seconds later. Five other planes dropped their men fifteen miles north of DZ N. The bulk of the Red Devils, 2,056 paratroopers, ended up scattered across the landscape.

Lieutenant Robert M. Mathis was a redheaded, freckle-faced, hardmuscled Irishman who led the 2d Platoon, E Company, 508th. At age twenty-eight he was somewhat older than other paratrooper lieutenants, but he was in superb physical condition and a champion boxer and longrange marcher. He was tough on himself and his men, whom he trained to the ultimate in all phases and possibilities of combat. He led them with rough kindness, hard but fair, making certain that they were ready for battle. He studied military history and was an expert on all of the weapons in his platoon as well as many German weapons. He spoke German very well and had some proficiency in French. At the loading zone the night before the jump, in a typical gesture, Mathis had shaken hands with all his men and given them words of encouragement. His regimental commander, Col. Roy E. Lindquist, said of him that "he will either earn the Medal of Honor or be the first 508th man killed in action." Colonel Lindquist was prescient.

At about 0200 on 6 June, Lieutenant Mathis was standing in the door of his C-47 waiting for the red and then the green light over the jump door. Below the planes the Germans antiaircraft guns were active. Flakvierling 38s (20mm four-barreled antiaircraft guns) were spewing flak all over the fleet, and machine gun bullets peppered fuselages. The jumpers could hardly wait to get to the door and go. Just as the red light in his plane went on, a burst of flak hit Mathis in his reserve chute and went into his chest, making him fall to the floor of the plane. The green light went on in the door over his head. He climbed groggily to his feet and stood in the door, hanging on to its sides. Badly wounded, he could have rolled out of his stick's way and flown back to England with the C-47, but he did not. He raised his arm, yelled, "Follow me!" and leaped out the door. His men found his body about thirty minutes later. How he had died, was not clear—excessive bleeding, rough landing, or opening shock. But it was judged that Mathis was the first U.S. officer killed by German fire in Normandy.

Colonel Lindquist had an unusual landing: he arrived on the east side of the Merderet River, while his entire 508th landed haphazardly to the west. He found his orderly, and together they started along the edge of the river toward La Fière. Shortly afterward Lindquist spotted a blue light, his regimental assembly point. But there were only twenty of his 1,980 men there. He kept moving toward La Fière and by chance ran into Ridgway, who ordered him to seize the bridge near La Fière. First, though, Lindquist had to round up a sizable portion of his Red Devils.

Lieutenant Colonel Thomas J. B. Shanley (class of 1939) commanded the 2d Battalion of the 508th. He and a group of his men were the only force from the regiment able to accomplish a part of the Red Devils' mission on D day, which was to capture a bridge over the Douve River near the town of Pont l'Abbé. In the two hours after the drop Shanley had been able to gather about two companies of men, some from other regiments. He decided to move on toward the bridge. A mile from Pont l'Abbé Shanley ran into a German battalion that halted his march. Knowing that he was under serious attack by a much larger force, Shanley gathered his wounded and moved back to Hill 30, where for the next two days he held off several strong enemy attacks on his position.

In one small but successful battle, SSgt. Raymond J. Hummel of the 508th gathered together some thirty-six troopers near Picauville. For four days they were on their own, but they fought the Germans near their position and killed forty and knocked out a tank. Hummel lost only six men.

The other four glider missions began arriving on the afternoon and evening of D day. Mission Keokuk, the smallest of the six glider missions and the first done in daylight, was made up of thirty-two Horsa gliders, "English coffins." It took off from the steel runway at Aldermaston at about 1830 on D day, some seventeen hours after the launch of Mission Chicago from the same airstrip. The gliders arrived over the LZ at about 2100, some seven minutes early. The Germans in strongholds near St-Côme-du-Mont and Turqueville waited until the gliders were released before opening fire, but fortunately most of the circling gliders were out of range. Even so, a number of them took direct hits that killed and wounded some of the men jammed inside. On landing, the survivors grabbed the dead and wounded and hauled them out of the wrecks. Then they searched for their howitzers and other gear. Five gliders had landed on target, and fourteen skidded to crash landings two and a half miles away. There were fourteen men killed, thirty seriously wounded, and ten missing and presumed captured.

The largest glider operation of Neptune was Mission Elmira, an 82d operation involving 176 Horsa and Waco gliders taking off from four different airfields in two echelons—one of 100 gliders and the other of 76. Starting at 1640 on 6 June, the gliders lifted off in serials from airfields in Ramsbury, Greenham Commons, Membury, and Welford. In the first serial, the aircraft pilots cut the gliders loose six miles inland, directly over German antiaircraft guns. Few glider pilots found their target LZs. The fire from the ground ripped into the canvas of the gliders and into the helpless men inside (one C-47 alone took sixty-five bullets). After their crash-landings against trees, poles, and hedgerows, the glidermen had to fight in close combat with the Germans dug in around the LZ. Eighty percent of the Horsas and half the Wacos were destroyed. There were five glider pilots killed, seventeen severely wounded, and four missing and undoubtedly captured. Of the 82d's glidermen, five were killed and eighteen were seriously wounded.

The second serial of Mission Elmira was more accurate than the first. Most of the gliders crash-landed within a mile of the LZ. But fifty-six of the eighty-six Horsas were wrecked, and all fourteen Wacos were demolished. But the glidermen, after fighting off the Germans, were able to recover forty-two jeeps, twenty-eight trailers, and twenty-four pack 75 howitzers. Ten pilots were killed and 29 seriously injured. Seven were captured. The glidermen lost 28 killed and 107 seriously wounded. The remainder of the force of 955 glidermen, many wearing bloody bandages, formed into their fighting units and got on with the battle. Mission Elmira was the last U.S. glider assault on D day.

The last two glider missions of Operation Neptune were Galveston and Hackensack, slated to bring in the bulk of the 82d's 325th Glider Infantry Regiment on D day plus 1. By 0330 on 7 June the troops had checked equipment, formed into units, and lined up in front of their gliders. At Ramsbury, for Mission Galveston, the first serial was made up of 50 gliders, 32 Wacos and 18 Horsas, carrying 717 troopers and 17 vehicles, 9 howitzers, and 20 tons of combat equipment. The second serial, leaving from Aldermaston, was composed of 50 Wacos, carrying the headquarters of the 325th, the 82d's Reconnaissance Platoon, 11 howitzers, 24 vehicles, and 5 tons of ammunition. At about 0400, the first planes and gliders roared down the runways slashed by rain and strong winds. The wind was so strong that one overloaded Horsa had to be cut loose, one was accidentally released, and two Horsas were unable to make the formation. Aboard the gliders, some of the boxes of equipment broke loose and injured the troopers belted to their canvas seats inside. Once the aircraft were over the coastline the weather improved and the rain stopped, but rifle and machine gun fire from the Germans slammed into the gliders.

In the first serial ten Horsas were destroyed and nine Wacos were wrecked, with most gliders missing their LZs. But in the second serial, the gliders cut loose at a higher altitude and landed more accurately. Sixteen Wacos were wrecked and twenty-six damaged. Seventeen of the 325th glidermen were killed on landing and eighty-five severely wounded.

The final glider assault in Operation Neptune was Mission Hackensack, in which over 1,300 glidermen of the 325th came into Normandy two hours later than Mission Galveston. Serial one, of thirty Horsas and twenty Wacos carrying 968 men from the 2d Battalion of the 325th and 401st, left from Upottery at 0647. Thirty minutes later the second serial of Hackensack left from Merryfield. It was composed of fifty Wacos carrying 363 troops from the support units of the 325th and the 401st. This serial carried twelve 81mm mortars, twenty jeeps, six tons of ammunition, and another eighteen tons of mines and antitank grenades. Over the water one gliderman, in feigned desperation, yelled out, "Is this trip really necessary?" A number of his buddies laughed in agreement.

The two serials of Hackensack began their landing assaults around 0900. The glider pilots cut loose at about 600 feet, and the gliders immediately came under intense fire. The rounds knifed through the floor-boards of the gliders and into the glidermen. The gliders landed with the usual crashes, slamming into the hedgerows, trees, antiglider poles, houses, and other wrecked gliders. Some landed in waist-deep water, drowning some troopers. The uninjured men scrambled out of their aptly named "flying coffins" under heavy machine gun fire and mortar blasts to try to save injured buddies.

In the first serial fifty-eight gliders landed in an area from one to five miles apart. The second serial was much more accurate: twenty-five hit the target LZ and twenty-five others came within a mile. "Although the scene on the ground gave the appearance of a massacre," wrote Charles J. Masters, "Hackensack turned out to be a remarkable success. Most of the glidermen were delivered to the battlefield, as well as much of the other cargo of ammunition, mortars, and supplies. Ten Horsas were damaged and sixteen others were demolished. Ten Wacos were damaged, while four were destroyed. Hackensack casualties included two pilots killed and eleven others severely injured, plus fifteen glidermen killed and fifty-nine others severely wounded. Many of the rest sustained multiple injuries but were considered able to continue their engagement with the enemy."

In spite of the widespread landings and injuries in the crashes, Col. Harry L. Lewis was able to assemble about 90 percent of his 325th Glider Infantry Regiment within a few hours of landing. By 1015 all three battalion commanders had checked into his communications network. He moved his regiment to Chef-du-Pont, in an area that the Germans had already left. Ridgway gave Lewis the mission of forcing a crossing over the Merderet River. Lewis decided that the best way to accomplish this was to move north of the La Fière bridge to an area where a ford appeared on the map. Lewis sent his 1st Battalion, commanded by Lt. Col. Terry Sandford, across in the dark. Once across, Sandford was to attack south and destroy the German force defending the bridge. Then Lt. Col. Charles J. Timmes's 2d Battalion of the 507th would join him.

By the morning of D day plus 2, Sandford's battalion was almost completely across the river and moving south against sporadic resistance. C Company's mission was to attack a stronghold near the bridge and then join B Company in dislodging the Germans there. At dawn, C Company was getting ready to join B Company for the final attack on the bridge but, in moving out, one of C Company's platoons became separated from the rest of the company. The Germans attacked that platoon, which was cut off.

Private First Class Charles N. DeGlopper was a member of that platoon. He was a huge young man, twenty-two years old, and, at six feet seven inches tall and 240 pounds, towered over his buddies. He was a veteran of the Italian campaign. In the heat of the battle in Normandy, as the Germans confidently increased their fire on the separated platoon, he stood up and began firing at the Germans with his BAR (Browning automatic rifle). Enemy return fire wounded him. Bleeding but still erect, he reloaded and continued blasting the enemy. He was hit a second time and fell to his knees, bleeding profusely from a number of wounds; from the kneeling position he continued to fire. Finally the Germans were able to kill him. Meanwhile, as the Germans were occupied with wiping out the American giant, the rest of the platoon broke off and headed for the La Fière bridge. DeGlopper was awarded the Medal of Honor posthumously, the only member of the 82d Airborne Division so honored in Normandy.

However, the La Fière bridge remained in German hands. Ridgway ordered Colonel Lewis to attack the bridge with his other two battalions still on the east bank of the Merderet. At 1015 on 9 June, a heavy U.S. artillery barrage paved the way for the 2d, 325th, followed by the 2d, 401st, to attack the bridge. But the Germans were not knocked out by the artillery fire. They continued to fire as the glidermen moved slowly across the bridge and the adjacent causeway. At last, the glidermen prevailed and overcame the German defense. That afternoon, the 90th Infantry Division, which had just landed on Utah Beach, advanced through the glidermen on its way to cut off the Cotentin Peninsula.

By the evening of D day plus 3, the surviving troopers of the 82d and 101st Airborne Divisions had been in deadly, unrelenting combat for four days with little sleep, meager food, and constant German fire. Because of the wide dispersion of the drops, units were a mixed bag of soldiers, NCOs, and officers from other outfits. Everywhere were leaders and soldiers who had never worked together before, and naturally some outfits took on the objectives of other units. But the airborne troopers grouped together with determination and skill, and relied on their past training to make up for the existence of their newly diverse units.

The 82d fared worse than the 101st because of the scattered drops. Even though it was able to accomplish its D-day mission of capturing Ste-Mère-Eglise, Ridgway was without radio communication with his commanders on D day and he could not account for about 4,000 of his men and most of his supplies.

Taylor was able to accomplish his most important mission—clearing the exits from Utah Beach so that the 4th Infantry Division of the VII Corps could get ashore relatively unimpeded. He also maintained radio contact with his superior, Lt. Gen. J. Lawton Collins, the VII Corps commander. But at the end of D day, Taylor could account for only some 2,500 of his paratroopers.

Both the 82d and the 101st suffered high casualties because of the dispersed landings, the irregular drops at high speeds and from wrong altitudes, the enemy's presence in unexpected locations, and the crashes of the gliders. On D day, the 82d had 1,259 troopers killed, wounded, or listed as missing—these last probably captured, killed, or wounded. The 101st had a similar number of casualties—1,240. The supply situation was almost a disaster: 60 percent of the 101st's gear, including howitzers, jeeps, and tons of ammunition, was lost or wrecked.

In 1944, only four years after the initiation of the U.S. airborne effort, and after the largest airborne assault in history, this question arose: Was the airborne effort in Normandy worth the numbers of dead and wounded and the costs of lost equipment? One answer is to look at the results of the U.S. amphibious landings at Utah and Omaha Beaches. Here Bradley's demand for airborne forces dropping behind Utah seems to vindicate the forces' use. When the VII Corps forces began to land on Utah at 0630 on 6 June, there was insignificant enemy opposition except for a few long-range artillery shells. By the end of D day, 23,000 troops and 1,800 vehicles had come ashore. The U.S. forces landing at Utah Beach had 197 casualties, 60 of whom were killed in the Channel when their boats sank.

On Omaha Beach, however, behind which there was no U.S. airborne force, slaughter took place. Men of Maj. Gen. Leonard T. Gerow's V Corps were killed in the water and were pinned against the cliffs by intense, initially unopposed German machine gun crossfire. Soldiers laden with heavy packs and weapons waded through water that was sometimes up to their necks. Under relentless fire, they had to fight and crawl across the beach and up the cliffs. During the day, enemy mortar and artillery batteries poured devastating fire onto the landing craft and the almost helpless infantrymen. Wrecked watercraft on the beach piled up and blocked the landing of the vessels behind them. Many boats grounded on sandbars 50 to 100 yards offshore; only about a third of the first wave reached dry land. By the end of the day, the 1st and 29th Infantry Divisions had forced their way only a mile and a half inland. D day on "Bloody Omaha" saw 2,374 men killed, wounded, or missing.

Were U.S. airborne forces responsible for the huge difference in casualties between the Omaha and Utah landings? It was the German seventh Army that had opposed the amphibious landings in Normandy. On 10 June its chief of staff reported to his headquarters that "the superior navy and air force have given the enemy advantages which cannot be compensated for, even through strong fortifications. The operation of the 'new weapon,' the airborne troops, behind the coastal fortifications, on the one hand, and their massive attack on our own counterattacking troops, on the other hand, have contributed significantly to the initial success of the enemy."

Lieutenant Colonel Günther Kiel was captured west of Cherbourg, later in the campaign. He told his captors that the U.S. 4th Infantry Division drove inland from Utah Beach far faster than the Wehrmacht commanders had thought possible. Kiel complained that "each time we tried to assemble behind Utah Beach on D-Day, we were disrupted by bands of American paratroopers."

In the days following 6 June, the 82d and 101st Airborne Divisions remained in Normandy to fight the battle alongside the Allied forces that had come ashore amphibiously. The 82d did, in fact, succeed in seizing the La Fière bridge and then moved westward with airborne guts and determination to cut off the Cotentin Peninsula. "The final attack of the 82d Airborne Division was launched on July 3," wrote General Gavin. "Attacking with three parachute regiments abreast and the 325th Glider Infantry, the division swung south through Etienville, across the Douve River and the Prairies Marecageuses for several miles, then turned to the southeast, finally capturing the high ground overlooking the town of La-Haye-du-Puits. There it remained in a defensive role until it was relieved and withdrawn into Army reserve on July 11, 1944. It was to be its last battle in Normandy. Shortly thereafter it was withdrawn to the United Kingdom to its old billets."

On 25 July, Ridgway sent a message to the supreme commander, General Eisenhower, in which he wrote:

> Landing during darkness, beginning at H-4 hours on D-Day, this division participated in the initial operations of the invasion of WESTERN EUROPE for thirty-three consecutive days without relief and without replacements. It accomplished every assigned mission on or ahead of the time ordered. No ground gained was ever relinquished and no advance ever halted except on the order of

Corps or ARMY. It sustained an aggregate loss of 46 percent in killed, missing, and evacuated wounded. Prior to launching its final offensive, its infantry had sustained a loss of 45 percent. At the conclusion of its operation, it went into ARMY reserve, with fighting spirit as high as the day it entered action.

After seizing its D-day objectives, the 101st received the town of Carentan as its next objective in an effort to link up with V Corps units that had landed on Omaha. Carentan was the junction for the U.S. forces from Utah and Omaha Beaches. After a bloody three-day battle in which it took many casualties, the 101st seized Carentan, and thereby reduced the German 6th Parachute Regiment to ineffectiveness.

Lieutenant Colonel Robert G. Cole, (class of 1939) was commander of the 3d Battalion of the 502d. On 11 June, on the way to Carentan, a few miles out from the city limits his battalion ran into a strong German defensive position some 300 yards from Bridge 4. The core of the position was a stone farmhouse, with enemy machine gunners dug in around it. With the Germans starting to mow down his troops, Cole halted his battalion and had his artillery forward observer blast the farmhouse and the dug-in enemy, all to no avail. Cole knew he had but two courses of action: stay where he was and wait for some direct-fire weapons or launch a frontal attack with bayonets fixed. Cole opted to charge.

To get ready, Cole yelled to his executive officer, Maj. John P. Stopka: "Tell everyone to fix bayonets. When I blow my whistle, I want everyone to charge the farmhouse." After telling his mortar men to cover the farmhouse with smoke, he blew his whistle and in the lead, took off running under heavy fire for the farmhouse. He turned around about fifty yards from the farmhouse to find that only about twenty of his men were running behind him. But to his left, he saw Major Stopka, firing his pistol and leading another fifty men. Cole was alarmed that so few of his men were charging. But the problem was that most of his men had not heard his shouted order to charge. Besides that, the Germans were dropping many mortar rounds on the battalion, killing a large number of men along the line. Obviously the injured and the dead could not pass along the order to charge.

When Cole and Stopka were about halfway to the farmhouse, some of the rest of the uninjured men in the battalion saw them attacking, fixed bayonets, and ran through the open field toward the building. Cole and his men stormed through the German defenses and wiped out the defenders of the farmhouse. This was the U.S. Army's only bayonet charge in World War II. For this daring exploit, Cole received the Medal of Honor and Stopka earned the Distinguished Service Cross. Later, in Holland, Cole was killed by a sniper; at Bastogne Stopka was killed two weeks after he had his award pinned on him.

The 101st moved against Carentan on 12 June in an assault headed by Brig. Gen. Anthony C. McAuliffe. The troops attacked from the northeast and southwest. "The 17th SS Panzergrenadier Division attempted to break through and drove the paratroopers southwest of the town back nearly half a mile," wrote Geoffrey Perret in *There's a War to Be Won.* "Suddenly, roaring through them from behind like Tinseltown cavalry, came Combat Command A of the 2d Armored Division, expeditiously dispatched, thanks to Ultra." With combined attacks by Combat Command A, close air support from the Air Corps, and the 101st, Carentan fell on 12 June and was the last battle for the 101st in Normandy.

On 26 June General Collins, with three U.S. infantry divisions (the 9th, 79th, and 4th) attacking to the north abreast, captured Cherbourg, the objective of the Overlord campaign. The Germans had so destroyed Cherbourg's docks, breakwaters, and harbors that the Allied engineers needed to apply two months of intensive work to reestablish the port as a useful facility. Fortunately, the Germans had failed to destroy the fuel tanks at Cherbourg: the fuel saved helped the Allies break out across France.

The second week in July marked the end of Operation Neptune for the brave hearts of the 82d and 101st Airborne Divisions. The price of the campaign was expensive: of the nearly 12,000 All-Americans dropped or glided into Normandy, 5,245 were killed, wounded, missing, or captured. Of the nearly 13,000 Screaming Eagles who entered the Normandy combat zone, 4,670 were casualties.

The airborne troops moved back to England aboard LSTs. They debarked in Southampton and were met with brass bands and throngs of happy Britons who greeted them with "God bless you, Yanks." Trains took them back to their old billets in the same towns they had left just five weeks earlier. The troops took a ten-day R&R and then got back to training for their next mission. In the next few months, the airborne establishment went through some major changes. The army established the XVIII Airborne Corps, and Ridgway became it first commander. Gavin got his second star at age thirty-seven and took over the 82d on 15 August 1944. Because of the buildup of airborne forces in the European

Theater, on 21 August 1944 Eisenhower established the 1st Allied Airborne Army under the command of Gen. Lewis H. Brereton. It was made up of the XVIII Airborne Corps and its three U.S. airborne divisions, the 82d, 101st, and the 17th. Also included were the British 1st and 6th Airborne Divisions, the Polish 1st Independent Parachute Brigade, and the U.S. 9th Troop Carrier Command.

While the combat-hardened airborne troops enjoyed the peace of the British countryside, with its welcoming pubs and smiling and affable young ladies, they knew that the war was far from over for them. The units were being refilled with replacements from the United States, and the equipment was being restored to TO&E standards. The training went on even more rigorously, for many more airborne operations were yet to come.

14: Noemfoor

After a few weeks back at Port Moresby the troops were restless. The weather was hot, humid, and wet. Many of the paratroopers were suffering from the usual tropical diseases—jungle rot, a fungus infection of the skin, especially the feet, from wearing wet socks and boots for days at a time; malaria; scrub typhus; Japanese river fever (the ague); and dysentery. In addition, the food was barely edible—nothing fresh, bully beef often, dehydrated potatoes that the cooks managed to reduce to rocklike pebbles, dehydrated eggs that bore a resemblance to the real thing only in color, and jungle butter, which was advertised not to melt in the tropics. It did not—nor did it melt in the troopers' stomachs. But the regiment licked its wounds; trained replacements; fired weapons; trained "in the field"; and, in their off-duty hours, went to outdoor movies, played cards, talked endlessly, drank an occasional beer (usually warm), and reveled in the infrequent USO shows that made their way to the area.

Colonel Kenneth H. Kinsler, the 503d regimental commander, was personable, smart, and a "staff officer type," according to one officer who knew him well. He was an introvert, a man "improperly assigned as a leader of a Parachute Regiment." He made frequent parachute jumps because he was afraid of losing his nerve to jump. But before each jump he had the regimental surgeon, Maj. "Jock" Gall, tape his ankles; both of them "made a big thing about preparations" for a jump. Behind his back, the troops referred to him as "Egg Shell." Apparently he was not a "soldier's soldier."

In October of 1943 Gen. Walter E. Krueger, the commanding general of the Sixth Army, sent his inspector general to the 503d base camp to investigate the condition of the regiment. The inspector general spent three days interrogating various officers and men and looking at the records of the regiment. After that was all done, he debriefed Colonel Kinsler and then left.

The evening of that day, 22 October 1943, Colonel Kinsler invited his four lieutenant colonels—the executive officer and three battalion commanders to his tent "for a drink." "Liquor was pretty scarce," General Jones remembers, "so we didn't turn down the invitation. We had a drink and a friendly conversation." It was an ordinary evening with the five officers talking and ruminating about what was next. Colonel Kinsler seemed not at all tense or under any strain; he had undoubtedly already made up his mind to take the drastic final action.

Sometime after the four officers had left Kinsler's tent, he walked to a nearby gravel pit just outside the base camp at Port Moresby and, in the dark New Guinea night, killed himself. No one ever found a note that might have explained this extreme solution to whatever problems he thought he had.

Word of the suicide got to Lt. Col. Joe Lowrie, the 503d executive officer, the next morning. He immediately sent for George Jones, the senior officer in the regiment, who was in the field with his battalion. At about noon Jones arrived at the 503d CP and assumed command.

The commander of the Sixth Army ordered Colonel Jones to report to him at his CP on Good Enough Island. At this meeting Krueger asked Jones how old he was. Jones told Krueger, thirty-two. To that Krueger remarked, "I had more years of service than that before you were born." Then he continued with his welcome to the new 503d commander: "Jones, I don't know anything about you. You have assumed command of the 503d because you are the senior lieutenant colonel. I am not going to recommend your promotion. Of course, if you do well at some future date, I will recommend your promotion. If you don't, I'll be forced to relieve you." As Jones later observed, "To the point, eh?"

And Krueger was as good as his word in waiting for Jones to prove himself: Jones finally got to put his eagles on in July 1944.

Shortly after Jones assumed command of the 503d, he called for Maj. Jock Gall's reassignment because he felt that Gall was not giving the proper leadership to the other medical officers in the regiment. Three or four months later, in an unusual coincidence, Major Gall committed suicide.

Jones was a positive, strong-willed, self-possessed commander. In a letter to the author he spelled out his leadership style: "My philosophy of command was to put out as few orders as possible. To simplify the task of seeing that they were carried out, ascertain by roll call that everyone got the word. After 48 hours has passed, find an officer who was not obeying the order and promptly courtmartial him for disobedience of orders. I found after doing this a couple of times, that I got excellent responses and compliance to my few orders."

For the next couple of months, the 503d carried on its training mission in and around Port Moresby. Krueger, meanwhile, was developing plans for the capture of Rabaul, on the eastern tip of New Britain Island. "Rabaul," said MacArthur, "was the primary goal in 1943." He wanted "to cut off the major Japanese naval staging area, the menacing airfields, and the bulging supply bases at Rabaul." In 1943, this town alone was manned by more than 135,000 Japanese soldiers, sailors, and airmen.

To seize New Britain and Rabaul, MacArthur assigned to Krueger the 1st Marine Division, the 32d Infantry Division, the 503d Parachute Infantry Regiment, and the 632d Tank Destroyer Battalion. This became the Alamo Force. On 22 September, MacArthur directed the Alamo Force to seize the Cape Gloucester area on the western tip of New Britain, to establish airfields on Cape Gloucester, and to take a role in the reduction of the huge Japanese naval and airbase at Rabaul.

Krueger assigned the 503d to the Backhander Task Force under U.S. Marines Maj. Gen. William H. Rupertus, commander of the 1st Marine Division. Backhander's mission was to seize Cape Gloucester airfields and establish control over the western end of New Britain. In addition to the 503d, Rupertus had parts of his own division and the 12th Marine Defense Battalion. Rupertus intended to drop the 503d near the Cape Gloucester airfields in conjunction with the amphibious landing of marines on Cape Gloucester beaches on 26 December.

Once again, however, circumstances over which the 503d had no control canceled its participation in an airborne operation for which it had been alerted. General Kenney told General Krueger that to make room for enough transport planes at Dobodura to lift the 503d to Cape Gloucester, he would have to move a heavy bombardment group from Dobodura to Port Moresby on the western side of the Owen Stanley Range. Krueger realized that "the frequent heavy-weather fronts over the Owen Stanley Range raised doubts as to the effective support from

Moresby; and to assure this support, the group was kept at Dobodura and the 503d deleted from the Backhander troop list."

General Krueger could have committed the 503d to the Cape Glouces- ter area piecemeal, using a few transports that could have squeezed onto the Dobodura airfields. But he decided against that option, which would have had two strikes against it from the start.

The marines invaded Cape Gloucester, and the air forces pummeled the shipping in the harbor and the airfields at Rabaul. By the end of Jan- uary 1944, the marines had established a comfortable perimeter around Cape Gloucester, Rabaul was isolated, and Japanese aircraft that ventured out from Rabaul, some seventy to eighty at a time to attack the advanc- ing Allied forces, were shot down "by the dozens" by U.S. P-38s. Rabaul, that once formidable bastion of the Japanese in the South Pacific, was now no longer a threat. More than 135,000 Japanese were still dug in at Rabaul, but they were isolated and impotent—and they were still there at the end of the war.

Also in January 1944 Colonel Jones, sensing the boredom and frus- tration of his regiment, requested that General Krueger either commit the unit to combat or send it back to Australia for R&R. For some rea- son Krueger decided to send the 503d to Australia, where it spent the next eight weeks at Camp Cable, about thirty miles outside of Brisbane.

Camp Cable had been a jungle warfare training center for Australian units and for the U.S. 32d Division. Once they were at Cable, Jones gen- erally granted leaves to his men to the nearby villages and cities. The usual training, jumping, and integration of new men into the regiment were the order of the day at Cable.

In the spring of 1944 MacArthur's Allied offensive was moving rapidly up the coast of New Guinea, and Admiral Nimitz's forces waded ashore and fought on the islands of the central Pacific. By early April, the 503d was on its way back to the combat zone. It left Camp Cable on 8 April aboard another Dutch liner, the SS *Van Der Lijn*. The ship put in at Milne Bay, New Guinea, but the troops did not debark. The following day, 16 April, the ship pulled into Oro Bay and the troops unloaded in the Do- bodura area. The 503d set up a base camp at Cape Sudest and settled down to the usual life of troops waiting for a combat mission. They were hot, the weather was humid and rainy, and the days in the field were bor- ing. Soon, however, they were to be back in combat in the Hollandia op- eration.

On 22 April, Lt. Gen. Robert Eichelberger with two divisions—Maj. Gen. Horace H. Fuller's 41st, and Maj. Gen. Frederick A. Irving's 24th— launched his two-pronged attack, Operation Reckless, against Hollandia in Humboldt Bay and, to the west, against Tanahmerah Bay, about twenty-five miles west of Hollandia. There were some 11,000 Japanese troops at Hollandia, only five hundred of whom were combat soldiers. The Japanese had no plans for the defense of the areas or even enough arms for the service troops who garrisoned the towns. The Allied landings completely surprised the Japanese, who fled into the interior when warships supporting the landings opened fire.

Between Humboldt Bay and Tanahmerah Bay were the Cyclops Mountains. West of the Cyclops the Japanese had built three substantial airfields bordering narrow Lake Sentani. Eichelberger's two divisions double-enveloped the mountains, and by 26 April all three of the airfields were in U.S. hands, but thousands of Japanese combat and service troops were still at large.

MacArthur had launched the attack on Hollandia using his highly effective strategy of leapfrogging enemy strong points, setting up his own bases and airfields, and then allowing the Japanese to "wither on the vine," to be subdued later by follow-up forces—usually Australian—moving up the vast reaches of the island. He needed the Hollandia area to base heavy bombers in support of his drive toward the Philippines and Nimitz's operations in the Mariana Islands and Palau. Unfortunately, the soil near Hollandia was too soft to support heavy bombers until the engineers had done extensive work. Though behind schedule, Hollandia would eventually become a major air and naval base.

On 2 June the 503d boarded C-47s at the Dobodura strip and flew into Cyclops Field, one of the three airstrips captured from the Japanese in the early assault on Hollandia. After landing, the 503d moved to a bivouac area about seven miles to the south. The 503d's mission was to guard the airfield, protect Krueger's advanced Sixth Army CP at Hollekang, patrol the area to a radius of about fifteen miles, and, according to Krueger, "be ready for employment on Biak if that should become necessary." As events turned out, it would not.

The 503d met little resistance, and the Japanese they did meet were demoralized and sick. The greatest enemy for the men of the 503d was the jungle, with its thick canopy, enervating heat, and stifling humidity. During the month-long patrolling action, the 503d killed fifty-six

Japanese, mostly stragglers, and captured twelve men, eleven of whom were Formosan (Taiwanese) laborers and one who was a crewman of a Japanese merchant ship. The regiment suffered only one slightly wounded soldier. The entire Hollandia-Aitape operation had cost the Japanese some 12,153 killed in action and 819 taken prisoner. "Our own losses were disproportionately lower," read Krueger's modest report.

As General MacArthur wrote of the invasion, "The Hollandia invasion initiated change in the tempo of my advance westward. Subsequent assaults against Wakde, Biak, Noemfoor, and Sansapor were mounted in quick succession, and, in contrast to previous campaigns, I planned no attempt to complete all phases of one operation before moving on to the next objective. I was determined to reach the Philippines before December, and consequently concentrated on the immediate utilization of each seized position to spark the succeeding advance."

On 27 May, General Fuller's 41st Division waded ashore on the beaches of southern Biak near Bosnek against relatively light opposition. But that light Japanese reaction to the invasion gave no hint of what was to come. The enemy was to use the peculiar terrain of Biak to devise a brilliant defense. Colonel Naoyuki Kuzume, the commander of the 11,000 Japanese military personnel on Biak, a third of whom were combat forces, positioned the bulk of his units in the rugged coral hill masses and caves of the island and waited patiently for the U.S. forces to move up into the hills. Then his units poured deadly artillery and machine gun fire onto the beaches and airfields. The caves held thousands of men, amply supplied with ammunition, food, and, most important of all, water. Each advance of the Americans was met with accurate and heavy fire from the crevices and creases in the hills. On one occasion, the Japanese even surprised the attacking forces by using five-ton tanks, which, however, were no match for the U.S. Shermans.

The tenacity and strength of the Japanese on Biak surprised and puzzled Eichelberger, who had arrived on Biak on 15 June. (Later Eichelberger discovered that the Japanese had been bringing in replacements at night by barge from Noemfoor Island.) On top of this, a raging and frustrated Fuller reported to him and asked to be relieved of command of the 41st Division. He had had enough of "stupid, insulting" messages from Krueger telling him how to fight the battle. Eichelberger turned the division over to Col. Jens Doe, commanding officer of the 163d Regiment.

It was only after persistent aerial reconnaissance found the entrance to the caves that the attacking U.S. troops were able to defeat the tenacious enemy. Units of the 41st then poured hundreds of gallons of gasoline into the entrances of the main tunnel complex and set them ablaze. The engineers lowered a charge of 850 pounds of TNT into the cave and detonated it. Hundreds of Japanese died in the fire and explosion. This kind of warfare was a limited preview of what the 503d would be subjected to on Corregidor.

By 21 July the defenders were desperate. On that day Colonel Kuzume presided over a ceremony in which the Japanese flag was burned, and then he directed all men able to walk to evacuate the caves in which they had been hiding for a final assault against the U.S. Biak Task Force. He distributed hand grenades to the wounded and then set the example by committing hara-kiri. It was only on 22 July that the fight for Biak was finally over.

Even while the fight for Biak was still raging, Noemfoor became MacArthur's next target in his relentless and determined drive toward the Philippines. Seizing Noemfoor would not only stop the flow of Japanese replacements to Biak, but would give him two or three more airfields along his path to vindication—a return to Manila.

Noemfoor Island, only fifteen miles long and twelve miles wide, lies about seventy-five nautical miles due west of Biak. On it, the Japanese had partially developed three airfields, Kornasoren, Kamiri, and Namber. Kamiri, with a strip about five thousand feet long and ample side taxiways for parking and dispersal areas, was the most developed. It was on the northwest corner of the catcher's mitt–shaped island. But Kamiri field was to prove a terrible DZ for the 503d. Even so, it was far more forgiving than the two postage stamp–sized DZs on Corregidor ever would be.

Operation Tabletennis, codename for the seizure of Noemfoor, really got under way on 20 June when the Allied air forces began to bomb the small island, particularly the airfields. By H hour, 0730 on 2 July 1944, the Fifth Air Force had pounded the island with more than 8,000 tons of bombs. Beginning at H-80 on D day, three cruisers, twenty-three destroyers, and three LCIs armed with rockets opened fire on the Kamiri beach area and on enemy fortifications near Namber. At H-15, the naval gunfire shifted to the flanks of Kamiri beach, and thirty-three A-20s on call strafed and bombed enemy positions on the high ground south of and near the ends of Kamiri airfield. Krueger's G-2 had estimated that the Japanese had about 2,750 troops on the island, but might be able to increase that number to 3,250 before the landing. He estimated that most of the Japanese were combat troops of Shimizu's 219th Infantry Regiment. Krueger later wrote that "considering the presumably weak enemy forces on Noemfoor, the preliminary bombardment may seem heavy. But I felt it was better to use gunfire and bombing liberally than expose any ground troops, in particular my infantry, to unnecessary losses."

Nor was Krueger going in with the odds against him as far as the size of the assault force was concerned. The Noemfoor task force, under the command of Brig. Gen. Edwin D. Patrick, was composed of the 158th RCT (Reinforced). In all he had 8,069 combat troops, 5,495 service troops, and about 10,000 Air Corps men. Patrick also had the 503d and the 34th Infantry Regiments in reserve.

The prelanding softening up of Yellow Beach on the northwest corner of the island and the landing of the 158th RCT went like clockwork on D day, 2 July:

0500. Forty LCMs carrying the combat elements of the 158th lay 3,000 yards offshore. The LCMs were surrounded by twenty-one Australian and American warships for protection.

0640. Escorting cruisers and destroyers unleashed a barrage that thundered over the crouching figures of the infantrymen in their landing craft (LCMs).

0745. Naval gunfire shifted to the flanks of Kamiri field and Yellow Beach.

0746. Thirty-three B-24 Liberators from Nadzab dropped 108 tons of antipersonnel fragmentation bombs directly on the high ground behind Yellow Beach where the G-2 estimated that the bulk of the Japanese defenses were dug in.

0747. The LCMs began their run to the beach over the wide coral reef that lay offshore; B-24s dropped 500-pound demolition bombs behind Kamiri airfield; A-20s strafed the area behind the landing beach; an LCI loaded with 800 rockets fired a salvo; the rockets flared and whooshed over the LCMs and rained down with pulverizing, widespread effect on the entire landing area.

0800. Exactly on schedule, the troops began to land but not without difficulty—not from the enemy, who had withdrawn under the devastating prelanding air and naval firepower but from the coral reef that they had to cross get to the beach. The reef was pitted with deep depressions totally hidden from the aerial photos and from the LCMs. Initially, shallow-draft Buffaloes and DUKWs (both amphibious utility vehicles) unloaded equipment and supplies, but shortly afterward the demolition teams blasted channels through the coral and the deeper-draft ships came ashore. Fortunately, the Japanese had not planted any underwater obstacles or mines.

The first waves of wading infantrymen found no Japanese opposition on the beaches. There was sporadical mortar and artillery fire from the hills, some of which hit the beaches, but the few enemy who were around the airfield were so stunned by the heavy prelanding fire that they were totally ineffective. Others fled to the caves in the coral terrace south of Kamiri.

0900. The infantrymen of the 158th quickly put up a perimeter defense and sent out some patrols to the nearby caves; immediately after they came ashore three combat and airfield engineer battalions, equipped with bulldozers, heavy trucks, and graders started to improve the Kamiri runway. Infantrymen along the perimeter of the airfield ran into a small detachment of Japanese. After a brief firefight, a few wounded Japanese were taken prisoner, and one told his interrogator that a week before the U.S. landing 3,000 Japanese reinforcements had arrived on Noemfoor.

1115. General Patrick, concerned about the report and under orders to secure the other two airfields on the island, radioed Krueger and requested the prompt dispatch of the 503d to reinforce his troops. "Late on D-day" [Krueger's estimate], he received his request and immediately ordered the 503d to proceed by air to Noemfoor.

Krueger's order to Colonel Jones did not take him by surprise. As soon as he had learned that the 503d was in reserve for Operation Tabletennis, Jones ordered 2,200 freshly packed personnel parachutes to be sent by air from the 503d's rear base near Gordonvale, Queensland, Australia. By 1 July the chutes arrived at Hollandia. In addition, he had proceeded on the assumption that the 503d would drop (rather than air-land) on Noemfoor. He arranged for sand tables, maps, and briefings to inform his men of the pending operation. He also arranged to have his battalion commanders and some of his staff fly over Noemfoor in four separate reconnaissance flights.

On the afternoon of 30 June, thirty-eight planes of the 54th Troop Carrier Wing arrived at Hollandia. The next day the wing commander ordered a practice flight to stress formation flying and proper airspeed and altitude for dropping paratroopers. The jumpmasters for the first day's drop flew along. Lieutenant Larry Browne, the 503d operations officer, supervised the preparation of the planes for the jump—removing cargo doors, taping sharp protuberances near the doors, setting up a parking plan, and arranging for thirty-eight trucks, each numbered the same as a jump plane, to assemble at the 503d CP if and when the regiment was ordered to drop.

0300, 3 July. The trucks reported to the CP. Major Cameron Knox, commander of the 1st Battalion, 503d, supervised the truck loading of his battalion, slated to drop first on Kamiri. Major John R. Erickson's 3d, 503d, would drop on 4 July, and Lt. Col. John W. Britten's 2d, 503d, on 5 July.

0505. The 1st Battalion, 503d arrived at Cyclops airfield, Hollandia. The men detrucked, finished their final checks for the jump, and climbed aboard the C-47s at 0615.

0630. The first C-47, with Colonel Jones as jumpmaster, left for Noemfoor. The rest of the planes took off and formed V's in trail, a three-ship-wide formation. The plan was for the planes to form into a column two planes wide, echeloned to the right rear, for the drop itself. Kamiri was only 200-feet wide, dictating the odd alignment of the planes. But even two planes wide proved to be too much. A Canadian paratroop officer assigned to Tabletennis staff had advised General Patrick that the planes should fly in single file because of the narrowness of the area, but, unfortunately, this message did not get to the Fifth Air Force until the planes were airborne and well on their way to Noemfoor. It was by then too late to change the formation.

0930. George Jones stood in the door of the lead C-47 and watched the water beneath the plane. Noemfoor was not far ahead. Jones thought to himself that they seemed "pretty low for a drop" but attributed it to the fact that they were over smooth water and that he could have been deceived; his jump altitude, after all, was only 400 feet.

1000. Jones's pilot gave him the green light. He jumped. Oscillating only once, he hit the runway with a bone-breaking crash. He smashed his head against the coral and was saved from a crushed skull by his steel helmet. The headache lingered for several days.

His premonition was correct: his pilot had failed to adjust his altimeter and, as a result, dropped Jones and his stick from a height of 175 feet, a radically unsafe paratrooper jump altitude.

The remainder of the formation, fortunately, was at 400 feet—a barely safe jump altitude. In twenty minutes 739 men of 1st Battalion, 503d and the regimental staff landed on Kamiri. There were seventy-two jump injuries sustained by the paratroopers who landed hard on bulldozers, parked LCMs, trucks, and other military construction equipment. The most seriously injured were the men who jumped from the first two planes. Of the eighteen men in Jones's plane, nine were critically injured from their bone-jarring landings with chutes barely open. Jones's enlisted aide broke both legs. Knox suffered a broken foot and had to be evacuated a few days later. A radio operator broke his back.

0955, 4 July. The 3d Battalion, with Erickson in the first plane, began its jump. In this flight the planes were in single file at 400 feet, and Patrick ordered the military vehicles pulled back off the runway and into the jungle. The coral runway, the DZ, was like concrete. The T-5 parachute had a twenty-eight-foot canopy and lowered a man none too gently under the best of conditions. But coral is not grass. The 3d Battalion suffered fifty-six jump casualties—more than 8 percent—a totally unacceptable jump injury rate. Of the 1,424 men of the 503d who jumped on Noemfoor, 128 suffered severe injuries. The 503d lost one battalion commander, three rifle company commanders, the regimental communications officer, and several squad and platoon sergeants.

On the ground, Jones had had enough of watching his regiment shatter itself on the coral of Kamiri. He told Patrick that John Britten's 2d Battalion, 503d should not jump in but should be brought in by landing craft. Patrick agreed and notified Krueger of his request, which Krueger approved, and ordered the 2d Battalion to fly from Hollandia to Biak and then sail by LCI to Noemfoor.

In retrospect, one must question the wisdom of dropping paratroopers onto a coral runway lined with heavy equipment—and completely in friendly hands—especially when a fully and heavily equipped 34th Infantry Regiment was on Biak and could have been on Noemfoor in ten hours, ready to fight before midnight of D day. It took two full days for two lightly armed parachute battalions to land on the island, with an unacceptable jump casualty rate, to boot. Besides that, when the 158th landed on Noemfoor, Japanese strength was only about 2,500; the Japanese prisoner who had reported 3,000 more either did not know better or had lied.

After the 1st and 3d Battalions of the 503d closed in on the Kamiri airfield, they and the 158th extended the perimeter with vigorous pa-

trolling, especially to the south and southwest. The 1st Battalion, 158th
had set up a night perimeter around a Japanese garden area, which was
overgrown with fruits and bushes, near Kamiri village. On the night of
4 July the Japanese launched their only offensive operation of the Noemfoor campaign. The 158th called for protective fires on the incline that
approached the garden area. The 631st Tank Destroyer Battalion and
the 147th Field Artillery Battalion responded with mortars and artillery
fire. But the Japanese in the area were undaunted. In the dark of the
morning of 5 July, Colonel Shimizu ordered an attack by his 219th Infantry Regiment against the 158th's garden perimeter. The forward observers for the artillery and the mortars and the machine gunners of the
158th were ready. Their concentrated fire broke the attack, and the
perimeter held. The Japanese offensive cost the attackers more than 400
casualties. Thereafter the enemy broke contact and drifted to the south
of the island.

On 6 July, based again on information from a Japanese prisoner that
Namber airfield was virtually abandoned, Patrick ordered the 2d Battalion, 158th to land on the southwest corner of the island. At the same
time a detachment of the 2d Battalion, 503d went ashore on Namin Island, three miles west of Namber, to put in a radar installation.

Because the paratroopers had reinforced Patrick's command, he was
able to get ahead of schedule with the task of clearing the island. For
three days, starting on 7 July, he expanded his perimeter around the
Kamiri airfield. His patrols ran into little opposition, so he correctly concluded that the Japanese had withdrawn into the interior of the island
to make their usual last-ditch stand.

On 11 July Patrick called a meeting of his senior subordinate commanders. His G-2 officer briefed them on the enemy situation as best he
knew it, concluding that the enemy had gone to the interior of the island. Then Patrick spelled out his plan for clearing the island. "The
158th Infantry," he said to its commander, Col. J. P. Herndon, "will patrol the northern half of the island. And your regiment," he told Colonel
Jones, "will work the southern half." Jones did not know it at the time,
but his lightly equipped parachute regiment had just been assigned the
toughest half of the island—overgrown with thick jungle and punctuated
with high peaks. The northern half of the island was flat and generally
clear, so, naturally, the enemy had selected the southern half in which
to hide.

On that same day, the 2d Battalion, 503d was finally committed to
combat on Noemfoor after its jump on 5 June had been canceled. On

the afternoon of 10 July, Krueger's headquarters ordered Britten to move his battalion by LCI from Biak to Namber. By midnight, he had loaded his battalion aboard the LCIs for the ten-hour trip, landing at 0930 on 11 July. Patrick's headquarters ordered Britten to move his 2d Battalion overland on foot to the native village of Inasi on the east coast of the island and to patrol the area from there. The battalion arrived in Inasi on 13 July.

On 11 July, Colonel Jones and the 1st and 3d battalions had begun patrolling and clearing the southern half of the island. Patrick had assigned to Jones one battery of the 147th Field Artillery Battalion, a tremendous asset because the heaviest weapons the 503d had were 81mm mortars.

For the next two days the patrolling produced no decisive results. But on 13 July the 1st, 503d, now commanded by Maj. Robert H. Woods, reached the foot of Hill 670 in the west-central part of the island and about five miles southeast of Kamiri airfield. Patrick's G-2 believed that Colonel Shimizu and a large detachment of the 219th Infantry were dug in on top of that hill. Woods sent C Company to contact the main portion of the enemy and force it toward 2d, 503, which had just reached Inasi. At 1400, the lead element of C Company came under intense small-arms, mortar, and machine gun fire from the slopes of Hill 670. Captain John Rucker, C Company commander, knew that he was in trouble. After subtracting his jump casualties he could muster no more than ninety men. And from the firepower the enemy was throwing at him, he guessed he was facing a force of at least 400 Japanese. A prisoner later reported that Rucker had grossly underestimated the enemy force facing him—there were more than 1,200 Japanese on Hill 670, and they were commanded by Shimizu. In the next few weeks Shimizu would prove a most elusive foe.

For three and a half hours C Company fought fire with fire, but their light weapons were no match for the entrenched Japanese armed with heavy machine guns, screened and abetted by a line of snipers. Rucker ordered his company to withdraw 300 yards to the north and radioed Woods about his tight situation. Woods ordered him to dig in for the night. But he also sent A and B Companies to join C Company in its defensive position at the foot of Hill 670. At 1845 A and B Companies arrived.

The next day, "Pug" Woods sent patrols onto and around Hill 670 to try to find the dimensions and location of Shimizu's main positions. He discovered shortly that the Japanese had not abandoned the position, heavy machine gun fire and snipers forcing the patrols to withdraw. The artillery forward observer with the 1st, 503d called in an accurate and intensive artillery barrage against the enemy positions so far located on the hill. For the rest of the day Pug Woods probed the Japanese positions with patrols.

At 0700 the next morning A Battery, 147th Field Artillery Battalion, fired a concentration in front of B and C Companies before they moved up the slope of the hill. They ran into only slight opposition; then they found out that the main body of Shimizu's command had left the area. Woods set up a perimeter defense on the crest of Hill 670 and sent patrols on a sweep of the area around the hill to try to find the Japanese.

The troopers of the 503d were beginning to realize the difficulties of jungle fighting—they gained expertise only through trial and error and sometimes bitter experience. Roads were nonexistent in the thick, vine-entangled jungle and had to be hacked out at times with machetes and axes. An advance of 400 yards seemed like a mile. Medics had a tough time getting to the wounded and an even more arduous task carrying them by litter to an area where they might be moved to an evacuation airstrip. Toting just one wounded man required four litter bearers plus a few riflemen to guard them. Field telephone wire was almost impossible to get to work beyond eight miles, thus operational and intelligence information was rarely available in the field. Resupply of food, water, and ammunition was sometimes available by drops from small planes, but their capacity was limited. An occasional C-47 drop was possible, but it was rare and often inaccurate. Coupled with the jungle diseases—malaria, scrub typhus, dysentery—life in the jungle, aside from clashes with the enemy, was far from pleasant.

Jones tried to keep in touch with his widely scattered battalion elements by flying over them in a small Cub artillery spotter plane and calling for colored smoke grenades to mark their positions. He could thus check the accuracy of patrol location reports and inform patrol leaders on just where they were. He also used the Cubs to drop blood plasma, ammunition, messages, and other pertinent supplies.

For a week after 15 July, neither the 1st Battalion, 503d, patrolling south and southeast of Hill 670, nor the 2d Battalion, 503d, patrolling to the north and northwest of Inasi, could pin down Shimizu and the remnants of his 219th Infantry. But on 23 July, patrols of 2d Battalion, 503d operating four miles north of Inasi finally ran into the bulk of the enemy. During an intense firefight a platoon of D Company was cut off.

D Company's commander ordered Sgt. Roy E. Eubanks and his squad to try to relieve the pressure on the trapped platoon.

Eubanks led his squad toward the Japanese position. Within thirty yards of the enemy position they came under Japanese fire. Ordering the rest of the squad to take cover, Eubanks and two scouts crawled through a shallow ditch toward the enemy. Within fifteen yards of the Japanese stronghold, the three men came under even heavier machine gun fire. Eubanks took a BAR from one of the scouts, stood up, started firing on automatic, and raced toward the Japanese position. He had almost reached the machine gun nest when he was knocked down by a burst of fire and dropped the BAR. Dazed and bleeding, Eubanks picked up the BAR and, using it as a club, succeeded in killing four of the Japanese before they killed him. He was awarded the Medal of Honor posthumously.

Distracted by the one-man charge by Sergeant Eubanks, the Japanese temporarily halted their fire, and the isolated platoon managed to return to the company perimeter. D Company resumed its attack and pushed the Japanese back from their dug-in position. When they reached the enemy position they found forty-five bodies, but most of the Japanese force had once again eluded the Americans. The 2d Battalion, 503d returned to its base for resupply. For more than two weeks, the 503d had no further contact with Shimizu even though Jones sent out numerous patrols from their bases at Inasi, Menoekwari, and Namber.

On 10 August, a patrol from 3d Battalion found a trail about two miles southwest of Inasi that looked as if a large body of men had recently traveled over it. Major Erickson, commander of 3d, 503d, sent G Company to try to find the enemy. It found the remnants of Shimizu's men—probably now down to 200 effectives—poised atop Hill 380, three miles south of Inasi.

As usual, the Japanese were well dug in and armed with machine guns and mortars. G Company spread out and took them under fire in a fight that lasted all afternoon, and then withdrew so that the artillery and air could blast the position the next day. The next morning, after a rolling barrage and air strikes by B-25s operating out of Kornasoren airfield, five companies of the 1st and 3d Battalions moved up Hill 380 shortly after dawn. They found many dead and wounded, but once again Shimizu and his main body had taken off in the darkness to escape to yet another hilltop and yet another assault by increasingly frustrated paratroopers. Colonel Jones was more than ever determined to find Shimizu and his men and annihilate them.

The Japanese, elusive and wily, skilled at camouflage and stealth, were being worn down. They had been cut off from all supplies for over a month by Jones's patrols, the strafing fighters, and naval gunfire. Stoic and dedicated to their no-surrender vow, they were reduced to eating whatever they could find—insects, birds, weeds, and leaves. In their final desperation they were reduced to cannibalism. In early August patrols of the 503d found corpses from which large slices of flesh had been hacked. At first the unbelieving and puzzled paratroopers thought that the wounds were the result of artillery fire. But a Japanese medical officer, captured later, confirmed the desperate acts when he admitted openly that he had used surgical instruments to slice flesh from both Japanese and U.S. dead. Some of the patrols of the 503d found human flesh in the knapsacks of dead Japanese, as well. When Jones's staff reported the details to Patrick's staff, they were not believed. Finally, they sent photos of butchered bodies and samples of flesh in the socks of slain Japanese to convince them.

The 503d continued its extensive patrolling of the south half of Noemfoor. About 1730 on 14 August, A Company contacted what the company commander thought was the main body of Japanese troops. For two days both sides fought a close battle south of Inasi. Finally, on 17 August, near the town of Pakriki on the southern shore of Noemfoor, the 1st and 3d Battalions cornered what was left of Shimizu's force in a pocket formed when the paratroopers surrounded the Japanese on three sides; the ocean formed the fourth. Even at the end, twenty Japanese escaped the trap—the unbelievably slippery Shimizu among them. Neither Shimizu's 300-year old samurai sword, long sought by the 503d, nor the colors of the 219th were ever found.

Just before the close of the operation, the 503d's S-2 received a report that a small boatload of Japanese soldiers had slipped away in the night from the southern shore near Pakriki and seemed to be heading toward a small island about twenty-five miles away. Jones immediately took off in one of his artillery spotter planes, armed with hand grenades, a Thompson submachine gun, and many magazines of ammunition. "The Warden," as he had been dubbed by his troops way back in the days aboard the *Poelau Laut,* was determined to "get" Shimizu; he was convinced that the elusive Japanese commander was on the boat.

Jones and the pilot searched the area for a long time, the pilot finally reporting that the plane was getting low on fuel and that they should head for home. But, just then, Jones and his pilot spotted a small boatload of naked men about a mile and a half away. "That's when the fun began," Jones remembered. The small Cub plane flew over the boat, and each time it made a pass, the Japanese in the boat dove overboard. Jones dropped grenades and strafed the bodies with his submachine gun on each low-level pass. Finally a small U.S. J-boat appeared on the scene. Jones had killed one of the escapees, and the J-boat picked up eleven. The fate of Shimizu, however, is still unknown.

On 31 August Sixth Army declared the Noemfoor operation over. The 158th Infantry had killed some 611 of the enemy, captured 169, and liberated 209 Javanese slave laborers. These laborers were all that was left of more than 3,000 Javanese captives the Japanese had abducted and forced to work on the three airfields on the island. The 158th had lost only six men killed and forty-one wounded. The 503d had killed more than 1,000 Japanese and captured 82 prisoners; as well, it liberated 312 Formosans and 9 Javanese slave laborers. The 503d lost 38 killed in action and 72 wounded, but had almost 400 noneffectives from various jungle diseases. On 28 August the 503d moved to a base camp near the Kamiri airfield.

While the 503d was fighting in the jungles a dramatic transformation had taken place on the airfields. By 20 July, the Kamiri airfield had been extended to 5,400 feet and been paved with coral. On 6 July a squadron of Australian P-40s was operating from Kamiri; by 9 September there were two fighter groups there. In July Namber had been dropped from the construction program. By 25 July one fighter group of fifty P-38s was flying out of Kornasoren; by the next day a B-25 had landed on the strip; and on 27 July 2,000 additional feet of runway became operational. The airfields at Noemfoor moved bombers and fighters increasingly closer to the heart of the Japanese empire. From Noemfoor, bombers could support the upcoming invasion of the Vogelkop Peninsula and Moratai Island and could attack the large Japanese petroleum resources on Borneo.

Near the end of the Noemfoor campaign, the 503d added two elements that were to become an integral part of the 503d and make it a regimental combat team: the first was the 462d Parachute Field Artillery Battalion, equipped with twelve 75mm pack howitzers and commanded by Lt. Col. Donald F. Madigan; the second was C Company of the 161st Parachute Engineer Battalion, commanded by Capt. James Byer.

During the late summer and early fall of 1944, the paratroopers of the 503d RCT settled into their base camp at Kamiri. At the same time, General MacArthur had pushed his New Guinea campaign to the maximum. On 30 July, the U.S. 6th Infantry Division landed amphibiously at Sansapor on the Vogelkop Peninsula supported by bombers and fighters operating out of Kamiri airfield. The 6th then pushed rapidly inland and cut off more than 8,000 Japanese on the south side of the peninsula. With this operation the battle for New Guinea was virtually over.

Early in August, it suddenly occurred to General Marshall in Washington, D.C., that little had been said about the disposition of the thousands of enemy troops who had been bypassed by MacArthur's progress up the coast of New Guinea and those far away in the Solomon Islands. So he queried MacArthur about it. "The various processes of attrition will eventually account for their final disposition," MacArthur replied. "The actual time of their destruction is of little or no importance."

Fortunately the Australians were unaware of this exchange of radio messages, for in mid-July MacArthur had directed Gen. Sir Thomas Blamey, the overall commander of the Australian forces, that henceforth he was responsible for the "continued neutralization" of the bypassed Japanese, a task the Australians had already been performing. His directive to Blamey indicated Australian responsibility for the area from the northern Solomons to New Britain to Australian New Guinea, with the exception only of the Admiralty Islands.

By 16 September U.S. forces were ashore at Moratai, MacArthur's most advanced base, and only 300 miles from the Philippines. Only two hours after the invasion, MacArthur arrived. "He gazed out to the northwest," one aide remembered, "almost as though he could already see through the mist the rugged lines of Bataan and Corregidor. 'They are waiting for me there,' he said. 'It's been a long time.'"

The 503d RCT did not know it yet, but it was to become an integral and active part of MacArthur's dream to return to Bataan and Corregidor.

So far the combat history of the 503d had been mixed—some being relatively easy and some of it hellish. But all of it had trained the RCT and readied its mettle for what the Japanese commander on Corregidor thought was impossible: an attack on Corregidor by airborne assault.

15: Invading Southern France

The invasion of Southern France in the summer of 1944 was a successful but highly controversial operation. And because it was sandwiched between the operations in Normandy and Italy, on both the calendar and the map, it has been somewhat ignored by historians and battle analysts.

In the summer of 1943 the Allied planning staffs drew up plans for the invasion of Western Europe. Included were two monumental amphibious landings—one along the Riviera, Operation Anvil, and the invasion of Normandy, Operation Overlord. Anvil was designed to pull the Germans down from the north of France to ease the Allied landings along the Normandy shores. Originally, the planners scheduled Anvil to take place either just before or simultaneously with Overlord so that Anvil would immediately drain the German defenses in France or keep the Germans in the south from moving north to counter Overlord. But the lack of ships, planes, and combat equipment precluded launching both operations at the same time.

In the summer of 1944, the Allied campaign through the mountains of Italy was turning into a torturous, costly uphill fight in which the German defenders were at a distinct advantage. Neither the Anzio invasion nor the capture of Rome eased the deadly combat in Italy's rugged mountains.

General Eisenhower wrote that "the complementary attack against southern France had long been considered—by General Marshall and me, at least—as an integral and necessary feature of the main invasion across the Channel."

In the planning of early 1944, I supposed that all principal commanders and the Combined Chiefs of Staff were solidly together on this point. Our studies in London, however, soon demonstrated that, even with a June date of attack, the Allies did not have enough landing craft and other facilities to mount simultaneously both the cross-Channel and the Mediterranean attacks in the strength we wanted.

The United States was at that time committed to offensive action in the Pacific and the necessary additional craft could not be diverted from that theater. In the face of this, General Montgomery proposed the complete abandonment of the attack in southern France, which had the code name of Anvil. He wrote to me on February 21, 1944: "I recommend very strongly that we now throw the whole weight of our opinion into the scales against Anvil." I refused to go along with this view. But it became clear that there was no other recourse except to delay the southern attack for a sufficient time to permit ships and craft first to operate in Overlord and then to proceed to the Mediterranean for participation in that battle.

The Marshall-Eisenhower side of the alliance felt that the capture of Marseille, France's largest port, and the rehabilitation of the Rhone Valley rail and road network were highly important in the defeat of Germany. Proof of the validity of that reasoning is that after the invasion of Southern France and the rehabilitation of the port of Marseille and until the capture of Antwerp in December 1944, the Rhone Valley supply route carried one third of the Allied logistics in northern France.

But while the British accepted Overlord with some hesitation, they never bought Anvil. The British, encouraged by Churchill, developed many staff studies to prove the stupidity of Anvil and that it would fail. Later in the war they published a book, *The Castigation of Anvil,* describing it as an idiotic operation. In a lengthy telegram, Churchill even appealed directly to Roosevelt to cancel Anvil, citing the fact that just the threat of an invasion of southern France was enough to tie down scores of German units. Roosevelt did not agree, emphasizing that the objective of the war was the occupation of Germany, not the Balkans. With that incentive, the Allied command officially brought Anvil back to life on 24 June. On 2 July the combined chiefs directed the theater commander, Gen. Sir Henry Maitland Wilson, to execute Anvil "as soon as possible."

It was not until 11 August, four days before Dragoon's D day, however, that Wilson received final approval for the invasion of southern France.

During the planning phase for Anvil the operation's name was changed to Dragoon because, as Allied intelligence had determined, the Germans had discovered the codename Anvil, although apparently they were unaware of what it meant exactly. Axis Sally on Radio Berlin did tell the U.S. troops that "our courageous boys in southern France know how to deal with you vicious gangsters from Chicago." A rumor started that the name was changed to Dragoon because Churchill had groaned, "I was dragooned into it." The quip was Churchillian but not true.

The Germans were well aware of the possibility of an invasion of Southern France from pure logic: the port of Marseille could handle 20,000 tons of supplies a day. And in the United States, Marshall had thirty divisions ready to ship to the European Theater of Operations; Marseille, not ports in Brittany, could handle them.

Lieutenant General Alexander M. Patch (class of 1913), fifty-four years old, was the commander of U.S. Seventh Army. He had recently arrived from the Guadalcanal campaign in the Pacific. "Marshall had not been overly impressed by Patch's performance on Guadalcanal," wrote Geoffrey Perret in *There's a War to be Won*. "Eighteen months after that campaign ended, Patch was still a major general. He was chosen to command the Seventh Army mainly because his friend Walter Bedell Smith urged Ike to ask for him. Patch got a third star only a week before the invasion was mounted."

Patch's staff drew up the Dragoon plan. The major element was the U.S. VI Corps under the command of Maj. Gen. Lucian Truscott. It included Maj. Gen. John W. "Iron Mike" O'Daniel's U.S. 3d Infantry Division, Maj. Gen. John E. Dahlquist's U.S. 36th Infantry Division, and Maj. Gen. William W. Eagles's (class of 1917) U.S. 45th Infantry Division. In the plan, and as shipping schedules would permit, the three U.S. divisions would be followed ashore by seven French divisions under the command of Gen. Jean de Lattre de Tassigny. In the overall scheme of things, the VI Corps and its three divisions had been battle-hardened in the North African, Sicilian, and Italian campaigns, while many of the French units were colonial outfits only recently organized in French North Africa.

The airborne element of Dragoon was ad hoc and provisional, a British-U.S. unit of airborne-division size, with 9,732 officers and men. (Airborne divisions in World War II were considerably smaller than the standard infantry division.) It was named 1st Airborne Task Force (FABTF) and commanded by Maj. Gen. Robert T. Frederick (West Point class of 1928), thirty-seven years old. During the Italian campaign, Frederick had been a one-star general in command of the 1st Special Service Force, a U.S.-Canadian infantry unit, highly trained in night fighting and mountain warfare techniques, and outstandingly aggressive in battle. Frederick was a "lead from the front" commander, as evidenced by the eight Purple Hearts he earned during the Italian battles in the mountains and at Anzio. Eventually he earned two Distinguished Service Crosses and two Distinguished Service Medals. At Anzio Frederick's command had been dubbed "The Black Devils of Anzio." He was honored by his troops with the title of "Head Devil." After the fall of Rome, General Clark had wanted Frederick to take over the 36th Division, but the feisty Frederick wanted an airborne command. He got the FABTF.

The FABTF assembled near Rome on 11 July, and Frederick set up his CP at the Lido di Roma airfield outside Rome. He had no staff officers, so the army quickly flew in from the United States thirty-six officers from the 13th Airborne Division that had been activated at Fort Bragg on 13 August 1943, and a few from the Airborne Center at Camp Mackall, North Carolina.

Frederick went on to get ready for airborne combat. In checking his command's combat gear, Frederick found a shortage of cargo delivery chutes and other equipment critically needed for the all-important aerial resupply. The army logisticians sent him 600,000 pounds of air delivery equipment on D day minus 4.

The units that would make up the FABTF were a mélange of independent parachute and glider outfits hastily brought together outside Rome on 11 July—five weeks prior to Dragoon's D day. The British turned over Brigadier Frederick C. H. V. Pritchard's 2d Independent Parachute Brigade with the attached 2d Mortar Battalion (4.2-inch mortars). The rest of the FABTF, codenamed Rugby Force, was made up of a number of separate U.S. airborne units rounded up from the Mediterranean Theater. They included Lt. Col. Rupert D. Graves's (class of 1924) 517th Parachute Infantry Regiment with these attachments: Lt. Col. Raymond L. Cato's (class of 1936) 460th Parachute Field Artillery Battalion, the Antitank Company of the Japanese-American 442d Infantry Regiment, the 596th Airborne Engineer Company, and Company D of the 83d Mortar Battalion (4.2-inch mortars); Lt. Col. Bill Yarborough's combat-hardened 509th Parachute Infantry Battalion with Lt. Col. John

Cooper's 463d Parachute Field Artillery Battalion attached; Lt. Col. Wood Joerg's (class of 1937) 551st Parachute Infantry Battalion; Lt. Col. Edward I. Sachs's (class of 1930) 550th Glider Infantry Battalion; a platoon of the 887th Airborne Engineer Company; and the Canadian-U.S. 1st Special Service Force.

The 517th had been activated at Camp Toccoa, Georgia, in March of 1943 and originally had been slated to be part of the 17th Airborne Division. But when the regiment was at Camp Mackall, it added the 460th Parachute Field Artillery Battalion and became the 517th Parachute Infantry Combat Team. The 517th sailed for Italy aboard the *Santa Rosa* in May of 1944, docking two weeks later in Naples. It was attached to the 36th Division and received two weeks of battle training in combat near Grosseto. Then it withdrew to Rome and geared up for Dragoon with intensive physical training, equipment checks, and plane-loading practice.

The 550th Glider Infantry Battalion was activated in Panama in July 1941, but in August 1943 it had moved to Laurinburg-Maxton Army Air Base in South Carolina for glider training. In April 1944 the 550th boarded the Liberty ship *James Whitcomb Riley* and sailed to Oran in Algeria as part of a 100-ship convoy. In Oran the 550th busied itself with guarding the docks for three weeks, then sailed to Italy and bivouacked at Bagnoli, ten miles north of Naples.

The 551st , under Lt. Col. Wood Joerg, was the other unit of FABTF with no combat experience. The 551st had also been formed in Panama to replace the 501st that had been made part of the 503d and moved to Australia. In May 1943 the 551st was alerted for a surprise attack on Martinique, a Vichy French island in the West Indies. But in June 1943 the French admiral commanding at Martinique surrendered to a U.S. Navy admiral. In August 1943 the 551st went to Camp Mackall, and in April 1944 it landed in Naples. By July 1944 the 551st had joined the FABTF outside Rome.

One significant deficiency in Frederick's command was that some units (among them field artillery, antitank, engineers, signal, chemical mortar, ordnance, and medical units) had become glider units overnight with, of course, no previous glider training. Frederick assembled them at his airborne training center outside Rome and put the glidermen (who were not volunteers) through an abbreviated training program.

At the center, the pathfinders also went through a brief joint-training period with troop carrier serial leaders. They flew over naval vessels carrying navigational aids so that the pilots and pathfinders could have a short rehearsal in what was in store for them. Some of the parachute units made skeleton jumps of two or three men from each of some of the planes that would drop them later.

The original plan for FABTF's part in Dragoon, drawn up by Seventh Army in Naples, scattered the elements in small units all over southern France. Frederick recognized the inherent tactical weakness of such a foolish plan and promptly sent Lieutenant Colonel Yarborough to Naples to assist Seventh Army planners in the proper use of airborne troops. Soon after, Yarborough returned with the new plan—mostly his. When Frederick saw it he was delighted.

The very next day Frederick briefed his commanders on the revised plan. He pointed out that the town of Le Muy, fifteen miles inland, was an intersection of roads from the west, north, and east, a primary, tactical objective.

Then Yarborough took over the briefing and, pointing to Le Muy on the map, said: "My 509th will jump at oh-four-one-five on D day, land in the south and southeast of Le Muy, and capture the high ground overlooking the town. Colonel Graves and his 517th will jump fifteen minutes later and seize the hills west and north of Le Muy and block the main roads leading west into Toulon and [north] to Draguignan, where a Kraut corps headquarters is located." Then he added, with a wry smile, "Maybe with a little luck, we'll be able to personally invite a Wehrmacht general at Draguignan to be a guest of the U.S. government." He did not know how prescient his remark was. He also did not add that at Le Muy the Germans had 1,000 officer candidates in training, an infantry battalion, a tank destroyer battalion, 500 labor troops, and a couple of assault gun platoons. He had to figure out what he was going to do with all the prisoners that would be taken. So he had sixty of his men trained as military police.

On 29 July, General Patch spelled out for his assembled staff and commanders his final plan for Dragoon. During the night of 14–15 August, he explained, French commandos would land and block the coastal roads leading to Toulon and Cannes. At the same time, the Canadian-U.S. 1st Special Service Force would assault the offshore islands of Port-Cros and Levant to knock out the German coastal guns that were capable of bombarding the landing beaches. Then, just before dawn, Frederick's troopers would jump and glide into the Le Muy sector to block the enemy from moving to the invasion beaches. H hour for the amphibious invasion was 0800. The VI Corps would hit the beaches from Cavalaire to St-Raphaël and then move inland to seize airfields in the area. Then the French I and II Corps would land, move through VI Corps, and liberate Marseille and Toulon.

"With the clock running," Jeffrey J. Clarke wrote in *Southern France,* a U.S. Army Military History publication, "the Allied land and naval staffs supervised the massive loading requirements of the D-day convoys, their departure from a variety of ports, and their subsequent rendezvous off Corsica during the night of 14–15 August. Together they comprised approximately 885 ships and landing vessels sailing under their own power and carrying nearly 1,375 smaller landing craft, about 151,000 troops (the bulk of the French were in follow-on convoys), and some 21,400 trucks, tanks, tank destroyers, prime movers, bulldozers, tractors and other assorted vehicles. The campaign for southern France was about to begin."

On 14 August Frederick's hastily assembled combat team was ready. All his subordinate units had been briefed on sand tables and maps on the mission, their battle plans, their battle area geography, and the enemy situation in as much detail as possible in the time and with the resources available. That evening the troopers were standing by their aircraft and gliders on ten airfields, which had been carved out of hard flatland soil north of Rome by U.S. engineers. The entire airlift of 526 C-47s and 452 Waco and Horsa gliders was part of Maj. Gen. Paul Williams's 50th, 51st, and 53d Troop Carrier Wings. At the Marcigliana airfield, the three pathfinder teams were going, once again, through the details of their crucial mission and the loading of their gear, including radar guidance devices. Upon their young shoulders rested the success of the airborne operation. The takeoff was slated for 0100.

The airborne operation actually got under way at about 0100 on D day, when six C-47s, en route to false DZs north and west of Toulon, dropped huge bunches of aluminum foil strips to create the impression of a massive airlift on German radar. Then, over the false DZ, the planes dropped 600 parachute dummies and noise simulators. Later, German radio reported the parachute attack as a reality. In another preliminary attack shortly after midnight, the 1st Special Service Force successfully assaulted the islands of Levant and Port-Cros, taking the German defenders by surprise but discovering that the coastal artillery guns were dummies. Simultaneously, French commandos landed along the coast to set up blocking positions around Cape Negre.

Exactly on schedule, at 0100 on D day Frederick's pathfinders in three C-47s took off from Marcigliana's airport. At about 0330 the planes flew over the coast of southern France through a thick layer of fog. The pilots could not find the DZs, so they flew out to sea and tried again and again. On their fifth attempt, German antiaircraft fire caused the lead pathfinder pilot to turn on the green "go" lights—but the proper DZ was fifteen miles to the east. Lieutenant Dan DeLeo, a veteran of two previous combat jumps, was the lead pathfinder for the 509th's twelve-man team. He and his team went out the doors on the green light. In midair DeLeo was hit on the helmet by a flak shell fragment and knocked unconscious. The rest of his men landed safely. But it was not until nearly a half hour later that one of DeLeo's men, Pvt. Vincent Kluystuber, saw DeLeo hanging from a pine tree, still unconscious. Kluystuber and two other pathfinders pulled him out of the tree and revived him. Once he regained his senses he realized that they were far from the DZ.

Shortly after midnight the marshaling of the aircraft was under way, with the troops being loaded and the engines warmed up. During the marshaling phase several aircraft were damaged and one was destroyed. Two more collided while taxiing to the runway, and one plane from the 439th Troop Carrier Group crashed and burned on takeoff.

The nine serials of 396 C-47s lifted off from the ten improvised airfields around Rome at about 0330 and thereafter flew in a V of V's formation of forty-five planes in each serial for the 500 miles from takeoff to the coast. En route they were guided by radio, radar, Eurekas, and other markers set up on their departure fields, on naval vessels, and on Giroglia Island (off northern Corsica) and the northeast tip of Elba. They met no antiaircraft fire from the enemy or, fortunately, from Allied naval ships. Because a thick haze blanketed the coast, the pilots were flying blind, and the pathfinders, far from the DZs, had not been able to set up their guidance gear. But by dead reckoning and the occasional sighting of a peak or a mountain, the lead pilots were able to make the most accurate U.S. mass combat jump so far in the war. In about an hour and a half some 75 percent of the jumpers landed on or near the proper DZ.

Years later Lt. Gen. Bill Yarborough reminisced about his jump: "For the south of France, we picked our own drop zone."

I was sick of having people pick them for me and I picked the one at Le Muy above the village because it was rugged and I didn't want to have the German anti-parachute outfits on my back when we got in. . . . And really, I had a little task force with the 551st, Wood Joerg's battalion, and the 460th Artillery which was commanded by a classmate of mine, Ray Cato. . . . That operation was one to remember, because we took off from ten airdromes. And if you can imagine ten airdromes jammed with C-47s and gliders loading at night, marshalling at night. You had to get the right squads on the right airplane when you see a whole line of airplanes as far as the eye can reach in a war situation where the lighting around the field is zilch at night, with jeeps coming and going and three quarter tons full of bundles that have to get to the right place.

The flight into the south of France was made more difficult by a change in weather. The weather was very overcast and cloudy. And the wind changed about 180 degrees from predicted.

But his flight hit the drop zone near Le Muy. "We did it, we did it," he recalled.

I remember jumping out into what appeared to be black as a pocket; you couldn't see a bloody thing. Nothing. Not even the sensation of falling. . . . And the first thing I knew that I was on the ground was when the ground hit me. You know that feeling at night. I came crashing down through some trees and found that the trees had been burned over for some reason and became rather sharp and pointed. The next thing was to assemble the command group, and I couldn't hear a bloody thing except my heart beating, see, real loud.

At about 0430 the main body of paratroopers began arriving over the southern coast of France. The 396 planes of the 442d Troop Carrier Group carried 5,607 paratroopers. The remainder of Frederick's force, some 3,400 men, would jump and glide into southern France later in the day. Yarborough's 509th led the 100-mile-long parade of planes, followed by Col. Rupert Graves's 517th Parachute Infantry Combat Team. The jump altitude had been raised to about 1,800 feet—far above the normal jump altitude of 400 feet—so that the planes would not smash into nearby mountain peaks.

Although a large number of Yarborough's and Graves's paratroopers hit near their three DZs, there were some mistakes and crucial errors. One of Yarborough's serials, of forty-five planes and carrying his B Company, and serials of two planes of the 463d Parachute Field Artillery were dropped near St. Tropez. "In true paratrooper style," remembered Yarborough, "instead of crying about being in the wrong place, they went to work on the krauts, assisted the sea landings, and became invaluable, joined the French forces of the interior and together had a task force over there." The task force liberated that resort town. "But the tragedy of the erroneous drop," Yarborough said, "was that two airplanes got the wrong signal and went into the Mediterranean and were never heard from again." One of the planes carried Capt. Ralph Miller, commander of B Company, and fourteen of his men.

Another error was the misplaced drop of Lt. Col. Melvin Zais's 3d Battalion, 517th Parachute Infantry. Zais's battalion was dropped in three echelons, each about four miles apart, near the village of Callien, about twenty-five miles east of his target DZ near Le Muy. By daybreak, Zais had gathered up his scattered troops and began, at paratrooper double time, to march to Ste-Rosseline, 517th's CP.

At 0800 Truscott's three divisions began going ashore. On the right the 36th landed near St-Raphaël, in the center the 45th waded ashore at Ste-Maxime, and the "elite" 3d Division beached southwest of St. Tropez. The 36th was the only amphibious force that ran into strong defenses. But by the night of 15 August Truscott had 95,000 troops and 11,000 vehicles in southern France, two hundred of his men being killed or wounded. The Germans had lost far more: already 2,000 had become prisoners.

At about 0800 thirty-nine C-47s of the 436th Troop Carrier Group, each tugging two Waco CG-4A gliders, flew across the Ligurian Sea and headed toward the beachhead. The gliders were loaded with antitank gunners and mortarmen, plus their weapons and ammunition. The gliders slid and crashed to stops on the landing zone around Le Muy with a minimum of injuries. The only tragedy in this echelon was one glider's having its right wing torn off during the flight. The glider flew apart in the sky and crashed into the sea, killing all of the men aboard.

By noon of D day, Truscott's VI Corps had slowly wiped out almost all resistance along the beachhead and started a drive to the east and west along the coast roads and north into the interior. The French II Corps was fighting toward Marseille and Toulon.

In the hills around Le Muy, Frederick's paratroopers had accomplished almost all their initial missions. The 517th—with the exception of Zais's 3d Battalion, which was still on the march—was in control of two key towns in the northwestern sector of their area. Major William J. Boyle (class of 1939) and his 1st Battalion had Les Arcs only partly under control. But Lt. Col. Dick Seitz and his 2d Battalion had cleared the Germans out of La Motte and had met up with the British paratroopers on the right flank.

At 1800 on D day, Joerg and his 551st jumped in broad daylight and landed without enemy opposition in a parachute landing perfect enough to be a model for an airborne field manual.

At about 1900 Joerg's men, leaving their DZ, heard the roar of a seemingly endless column of C-47s, each tugging a glider on a 300-foot tow line, approaching DZs A and O, the areas they had just left. DZ A was to the west of Le Muy and DZ O to the north. The air armada carried Lt. Col. Edward Sachs's 550th Glider Infantry Battalion plus additional artillery and resupplies. Sachs's task force was designated Dove and was the last glider operation of Dragoon. It had been delayed until the evening of D day so that Joerg's men could knock down as many of Rommel's antiglider poles as possible. Most of the landings, even at ninety miles an hour and smashing without brakes into poles, trees, rocks, and other gliders, were successful—even though there were some fatalities: eleven pilots were killed and thirty more were hurt. But, surprisingly, none of the glider troopers was killed, although many were obviously shaken up. Colonel Sachs himself, while trying to help one of his men with his seat belt, was injured on landing when the unbelted man smashed against him, making him hit a piece of aluminum tubing on the glider frame and break three ribs. Nonetheless Sachs stumbled—painfully—out of the glider and got on with his mission.

"During the morning and afternoon of the 15th" wrote Jeffrey J. Clarke, "the armor-supported American infantry slowly eliminated almost all resistance along the shoreline and began pushing east and west along the coastal road and north into the interior. By the following day they had secured the two hill masses overlooking the beaches, while tank destroyers from the 45th Division had penetrated north to assist the paratroopers in a final assault against Le Muy."

By noon of D plus 1 the combined attack against Le Muy was a complete success.

At Draguignan, a small town a few miles to the northwest of Le Muy, German Maj. Gen. Ludwig Bieringer had his CP and district staff. On the evening of D plus 1, Wood Joerg and his 551st were moving toward the town on orders from General Frederick to attack and seize it and liberate some French *maquisard* units that had been captured when they came out to fight in the open too soon. He moved out in the darkness with Capt. Marshall Dalton's A Company and Capt. James "Jungle Jim" Evans's B Company in front. Against light opposition Joerg's men marched through the town, freed the French prisoners, and, after crashing through the doors of the huge building that housed the German commander, captured General Bieringer and his staff.

Les Arcs had not yet been taken. On the evening of D plus 1, Colonel Graves ordered Dick Seitz and his 2d Battalion to assist the 1st Battalion in clearing the town. When Mel Zais and his 3d Battalion arrived at Ste-Rosseline after a long twenty-five-mile march from their drop far off target, Graves gave them a short rest in the woods and then sent them toward Les Arcs. At 1800 Zais led his battalion up the valley toward the town. When Lieutenant Freeman's H Company moved across some railroad tracks, it was hit by a fusillade of German machine gun fire; Freeman and the first sergeant were wounded. After a fierce firefight, Zais led the battalion through the woods and forced the Germans back into the hills above Les Arcs. On the evening of D plus 1, with tanks from the 45th Division joining up with Frederick's troops, the airborne phase of Dragoon was over. But on the morning of D plus 2, the battle for Draguignan was still not "mission accomplished." Finally, by late afternoon, Joerg was able to radio General Frederick that he had secured the town.

Within two and a half days, Frederick and his airborne troops had seized all their objectives, confounded the Germans behind the coastal defenses, cut German telephone communications out of the area, and blocked any attempt to reinforce the German troops on the coast.

During Operation Dragoon the Provisional Troop Carrier Air Division had flown 987 sorties, towed 407 gliders, and carried over 9,000 airborne troops, 221 jeeps, 213 artillery pieces, and over 2 million pounds of equipment and ammunition. Eleven glider pilots were listed as killed in action, and sixteen were injured seriously enough to be hospitalized. The other 746 glider pilots returned to their units.

Of the airborne forces, initially 873 U.S. troopers were listed as killed, captured, or missing in action. But by 20 August that figure had been reduced to 434 still listed as killed, missing, or captured.

After Truscott began his attack up the Rhone Valley, General Patch assigned Frederick a new mission: attack east along the Riviera to free Cannes and Nice and then move into strategic locations in the Maritime Alps along the Italian border. For this mission, Frederick gained the 1st

Special Service Force and lost the British 2d Independent Parachute Brigade that was redeployed to Italy. Frederick's troops liberated Cannes on 24 August and five days later marched into Nice, where Frederick set up his CP in a hotel. The FABTF continued its assault through Grasse and into the Maritime Alps.

Yarborough described the move into the mountains:

> Well, we came down from the heights above Le Muy and started to push up the coast toward the Italian border. We had real fights in front and in back of each of the towns we uncovered. The first one was just short of Cannes. We'd deploy; attack; and the Germans would put up a real tough rear guard operation, and then phase through the town and we'd see them on the other side. This continued right up the coast. The 509th was doing fine along the coast. . . . But I was ordered presently to turn north up the valley of the Var River into the French Maritime Alps. And this started screening the right flank of the 7th Army that was moving north. And the 1st Special Force then was given the coastal route and went up toward Menton. But as we got into the Maritime Alps, we got into the most intriguing, interesting terrain from a military point of view and from, I guess you'd say, a psychological point of view. My lines, if you can call it a line, stretched ultimately over a length of some 35 miles and there was no way to keep it intact. The German mountain troops would therefore come through this line selectively and we'd chase them as best we could, and they'd go back into the mountains and we'd do the same thing to them. And in the most beautiful country you could imagine, where in the morning you could hear the tolling of the bells in the little villages around the pastoral beauty of the Maritime Alps, this deadly game of cops and robbers was going on along this extended front.

For the rest of August and on into September, Frederick's troopers moved and fought limited battles through the Maritime Alps. Toward the end of October, the 14th Armored Division and the French 1st Algerian Rifle Regiment began to take over the missions of the FABTF. Slowly, Frederick's troops came out of the mountains and set up camps along the Riviera. The 517th was the last down and, on 16 November, went on a thirty-mile march from Sospel to Nice.

Shortly after Thanksgiving the FABTF, on order, disbanded. General Frederick took over the 45th Division. The diverse units of FABTF moved to Antibes and took trains that churned their way through the winter snows to Soissons. There the paratroopers spread out and bunked in French barracks. The 550th moved to Aldbourne, England, with its immediate fate unknown.

The overall success of Operation Dragoon was phenomenal. In just two weeks the Allies had taken 57,000 prisoners and opened Marseille and Toulon; the Allies themselves had suffered some 7,000 casualties.

They called it the "Champagne campaign," this war in the Maritime Alps, because of the way the champagne flowed in the celebrations by the liberated people at Antibes and Cannes and Nice during the pursuit of the Germans.

Howard Katzander, a *Yankee* staff correspondent, wrote: "True, the men of the Airborne Task Force that liberated the Cote d'Azur could still get 24-hour rest periods in Nice, an hour's drive away, and those who wanted to risk the MPs and a stiff fine could still filter into Monaco to walk with the girls of Monte Carlo in the royal gardens of Prince Louis II.

"But when they went back into the mountains, to their foxholes on the terraced hillsides under the shelter of the OD olive trees, they returned to a full-fledged war—an infantryman's war."

After his retirement as a four-star general, Mel Zais had this to say: "They talk about the Champagne Campaign, but it wasn't that to the people like us who did the fighting. Our regimental combat team had no more than approximately twenty-five hundred men on the flank. Out of these, we suffered a hundred killed and perhaps seven hundred wounded during the time we were involved in this action. So it wasn't a Champagne Campaign while we were on the lines, although I'll have to admit that it was delightful to be able to stop every once in a while and go down and enjoy a day or two's rest and recreation in Nice."

As usual, there are two sides to a story.

16: Market Garden: The Bridges

By early September 1944, the atmosphere in Gen. Dwight Eisenhower's Supreme Headquarters, Allied Expeditionary Force (SHAEF) bordered on the euphoric. Three Allied Army groups, the result of Overlord and Dragoon, were moving steadily eastward across France from the English Channel to Switzerland in a powerful armored and infantry assault. The Red Army was relentlessly attacking west toward the German frontier. Allied air power dominated the skies above the Wehrmacht and was devastating German factories and road and rail net.

"Optimism was pervasive in the highest headquarters," wrote General Gavin. "As early as 11 August, Major General Kenneth W. D. Strong, Eisenhower's Chief of Intelligence, thought that the war would be over in three months. Most astounding, post-exchange officials distributed a memorandum saying that they were arranging to return Christmas presents—already in the mail—to the United States. According to Captain Butcher, General Eisenhower's aide, Maj. Gen. Bedell Smith, Eisenhower's chief of staff, told members of the press in early September, 'Militarily, the war is won.'" A U.S. 1st Army intelligence officer was even more confident and stated that German resistance would fizzle by 1 December 1944. But not all intelligence officers were unanimously optimistic. Colonel Oscar W. Koch, the Third Army G-2 officer, speculated with some precision that the German army was hanging on valiantly and was ready for a "last-ditch struggle in the field at all costs."

General George Marshall was so delighted with the march across France and with the success of the airborne operations in Normandy and southern France that he pressured SHAEF to expand the use of this new vertical arm of warfare and create an airborne army. The British agreed, but they hoped that command of the army would fall to their top airborne strategist, Lt. Gen. Sir Frederick A. M. "Boy" Browning, a forty-seven-year-old Grenadier Guards officer. But that was not to be. On 2 August 1944 the Allies activated the Allied First Airborne Army, and the command fell to Lt. Gen. Lewis H. Brereton, of the U.S. Army Air Forces. The U.S. part of the First Allied Airborne Army was composed of the 82d, 101st, and 17th Airborne Divisions. The British contributed a smaller force: their I Airborne Corps, made up of the 1st and 6th Airborne Divisions, reinforced by the Polish 1st Brigade. The aviation elements of the First Allied Airborne Army included Gen. Paul Williams's U.S. 9th Troop Carrier Command (50th, 52d, and 53d Wings) and the British Troop Carrier Command (38th and 46th Groups).

General Brereton, at age fifty-five and five-feet-six-inches, was a hard-driving, highly motivated officer who had had an odd military career. He had graduated from Annapolis in 1911 but immediately transferred to the army and went to flight school. He was a fighter pilot in World War I and shot down a German plane, earning a Distinguished Service Cross. Later, he became a staff officer for Gen. Billy Mitchell and was a part of Mitchell's staff that drew up the incredible plan for dropping the 1st Infantry Division by parachute behind the German lines in November 1918. Fortunately, the war ended before such a risky plan could be given any more than a cursory look. To compensate for Brereton's lack of airborne experience and planning ability and to appease the British, Eisenhower gave him General Browning as his deputy.

With the creation of the First Allied Airborne Army, soon to be dubbed the First Triple A, or FAAA, came the birth of the XVIII Airborne Corps. After the formation of FAAA, Eisenhower appointed Ridgway to command the newly created corps, composed of the 82d and 101st Airborne Divisions, as well as the recently arrived 17th Airborne Division. The 17th was commanded by one of the earliest airborne legends, Maj. Gen. William M. Miley. Ridgway had felt that he himself was highly qualified to command the airborne army; but, instead, Eisenhower gave him the corps as a consolation prize.

Ridgway's departure from the 82d left the commander's position vacant. General Gavin, by virtue of his outstanding record as a combat commander of a regiment and an airborne task force, was the obvious choice to succeed Ridgway, which he did. After assuming this command, Gavin was promoted to major general, and, at age thirty-seven, was the youngest U.S. Army two-star general in World War II.

"By the third week of July, the 82d Airborne Division was back in its old billets in mid-England," wrote General Gavin.

Division headquarters and three infantry regiments were near Leicester, and other divisional troops were in Nottingham and Market Harborough. Immediately following their return from Normandy, all troopers were given short furloughs. On their return, we settled down to dealing urgently with the problems of taking in new volunteers and giving them parachute training, welcoming back our wounded, re-equipping—and finally intensive training. Our casualties had been heavy; some infantry companies lost more than 50 percent killed, wounded, or missing. Offsetting those losses was the extensive battle experience gained by the survivors.

On the Continent the Allies continued to move with power and speed. Progress was so rapid that, on 1 September, Eisenhower moved SHAEF headquarters to France and took direct command of all the Allied ground forces.

In the European Theater, Montgomery's 21st Army Group had overrun the V-1 rocket sites that were pounding England and then had pushed into the Netherlands. Bradley's 12th Army Group stayed neck and neck with the 21st Army Group. Patton and his Third Army raced through the Argentan-Laval-Chartres sector; Lt. Gen. Courtney J. Hodges's First Army trapped a large German contingent in the Mons pocket and then drove speedily into Belgium. By the middle of September, Eisenhower's massed forces had reached the German frontier on a line running from the Netherlands south to Trier and Metz. This wide distribution of Allied ground forces along the front was symptomatic of the Eisenhower strategy of spreading out, keeping the enemy widely deployed so that he could not concentrate and blast a hole through a reasonably undefended area, and having a wide and deep secure area behind the front to handle the massive logistical organization needed to support the final thrust into Germany.

Through all his planning, General Eisenhower kept the airborne potential in mind. "It appeared to me that a fine chance for launching a profitable airborne attack was developing in the Brussels area, and though there was divided opinion of the wisdom of withdrawing planes from supply work because of the uncertainty of the opportunity, I decided to take the chance," he wrote in *Crusade in Europe*. "The Troop Car-

rier Command, on September 10, was withdrawn temporarily from supply missions to begin intensive preparation for an airborne drop in the
Brussels area. But it quickly became clear that the Germans were retreating so fast as to make the effort an abortive one. Except with rear
guards, the Germans made no attempt to defend in that region at all."

On 11 September, Patch and his Seventh Army linked up with Third
Army after a 400-mile drive up the Rhone Valley in less than a month.
This linkup created a solid wall of Allied forces stretching from Antwerp
to Switzerland. On 15 September, Operation Dragoon forces, at the time
under the command of British Gen. Henry M. Wilson, were reorganized
into the 6th Army Group under Lt. Gen. Jacob L. Devers (class of 1909),
who at fifty-seven years of age was one of the older commanders in the
field. He got his fourth star in 1945.

The battlefield situation was as follows. In the north, Montgomery's
21st Army Group was made up of Lt. Gen. Henry D. G. Crerar's Canadian First Army and Gen. Miles C. Dempsey's British Second Army. In
the center, General Bradley's 12th Army Group had Lt. Gen. William H.
Simpson's newly formed Ninth Army, Hodges's First Army, and Patton's
Third Army. In the south, General Dever's 6th Army Group comprised
Patch's Seventh Army and Gen. Jean de Lattre de Tassigny's French First
Army. As Eisenhower put it:

> All along the front we pressed forward in hot pursuit of the flee
> ing enemy. In four days the British spearheads, paralleled by equally
> forceful American advances on their right, covered a distance of
> 195 miles, one of the many fine feats of marching by our forma
> tions in the great pursuit across France. By September 5, Patton's
> Third Army reached Nancy and crossed the Moselle River between
> that city and Metz. Hodges' First Army came up against the
> Siegfried defenses by the thirteenth of the month and was shortly
> thereafter to begin the struggle for Aachen.
>
> Pushed back against the borders of the homeland, the German
> defenses showed definite signs of stiffening. On 4 September,
> Montgomery's forces entered Antwerp and we were electrified to
> learn that the Germans had been so rapidly hustled out of the place
> that they had had no time to execute extensive demolitions. Mar
> seilles had been captured on August 28 and this great port was be
> ing rehabilitated.

But by mid-September, in spite of the massive attacks all along the front, Eisenhower was convinced that Germany could not be defeated in 1944. In a 14 September letter to General Marshall, Eisenhower wrote that, in spite of the rapid advance across France he did not envision the feasibility of an all-out advance to the German border without regrouping. He felt that a "rush right on to Berlin" was not possible and "wishful thinking."

Montgomery was insistent on reaching the Rhine before Hodges got there. His original plan was to drop Maj. Gen. Robert Urquhart's British 1st Airborne Division, supported by Maj. Gen. Stanislaw Sosabowski's Polish Airborne Brigade, at Arnhem in the Netherlands, seize the huge concrete-and-steel highway bridge over the lower Rhine, and then air-land an infantry division in the airhead. Thereafter, he would send the British Second Army on a sixty-five-mile race toward Arnhem from the south.

Eisenhower met Montgomery in Brussels on 10 September and listened to his bold plan. After some deliberation, Eisenhower approved the plan, which showed Montgomery's aggressiveness, something he had not displayed up to this point. But intelligence reports indicated a German buildup in the area. One report from Holland indicated that "battered panzer formations have been sent to Holland to refit." General Dempsey's intelligence officer, Maj. Brian Urquhart (no relation to General Urquhart), estimated that there were at least two panzer divisions in the Arnhem area. The aerial photos of the area proved him right: there were tanks around Arnhem.

The estimated increase of German defenses in the area demanded that Montgomery increase his airborne force and use the 82d and 101st Airborne Divisions. Eisenhower agreed, and his staff integrated them into the bold thrust. Given the new size of the operation, Brereton appointed General Browning to command the largest airborne assault in history.

After Eisenhower left Brussels, Montgomery took General Browning aside and on a map outlined his planned use of the three and a half airborne divisions. Browning immediately saw the stretching of the First Airborne Army—seizing five major bridges across the Maas, the Waal, and the Lower Rhine—a stretch of some sixty-four miles between the Belgian-Dutch border and Arnhem. The airborne force had also to keep the narrow corridor open to permit the rapid advance of Second Army's armor. Browning was not exuberant about the plan. He pointed to the most northern bridge over the Lower Rhine at Arnhem and asked Montgomery: "How long will it take the armor to reach us?" Montgomery replied, rather sharply, "Two days." Browning kept looking at the map and said, "We can hold it for four." But then, almost foretelling the future, he said, "But, sir, I think we might be going a bridge too far."

"Eisenhower directed that Montgomery, recently promoted to field marshal, take his 21st Army Group along with part of the U.S. 12th Army Group and the First Allied Airborne Army, and push over the Rhine to the north," wrote Ted Ballard in *Rhineland*.

> He charged the 12th Army Group with capturing Brest (in western France) and executing a limited attack to divert German forces southward until Montgomery had established his bridgehead over the Rhine. After the northern bridgehead was secured, the Third Army would advance through the Saar and establish its own crossing sites. Eisenhower also tasked Montgomery to clear the approaches to Antwerp, thereby opening that vital port for Allied use. After securing the bridgeheads across the Rhine, the Allies would seize the Ruhr and concentrate forces for the final drive into Germany. The Combined Chiefs of Staff approved Eisenhower's plan. . . . The Allies dubbed this operation, the first in the Rhineland Campaign, MARKET GARDEN.

When General Gavin was in London visiting "some friends" one Sunday afternoon, on 10 September, he got a phone call from Brereton's headquarters in Sunningdale, about an hour's drive away. Gavin was told to be at FAAA headquarters as fast as he could because another airborne operation was imminent. He arrived at 1800 hours and found that the meeting was already under way, with General Browning holding the floor. Besides Brereton, present were General Taylor from the 101st, Gen. Robert F. Urquhart from the British 1st Airborne Division, and all the British and U.S. troop carrier commanders. Ridgway's absence was not explained.

"General Browning continued to outline the plan for the proposed operation," wrote Gavin. "It envisioned seizing bridges over the five major waterways, as well as a number of other tactical objectives extending from the present front of the British 2d Army along the Albert Canal, 64 miles into Holland, to the farthest bridge, over the lower Rhine into the town of Arnhem." One of the more important decisions Browning made was to launch the operation in broad daylight, keeping in mind the wide scattering of paratroopers in the pitch black of Normandy.

But it turned out that the most important decision Browning had made was where each division would land, based on where the divisions were located in England. The carpet of airborne forces would extend from Arnhem in the north, the deepest of the landings, to Nijmegen in the middle and Grave in the south. As Gavin put it:

> The British 1st Airborne was best positioned for the Arnhem drop, the 82d Airborne Division for the operation between Nijmegen and Grave, and the US 101st Airborne Division for all the southern bridges. . . . The mission assigned to the 82d Airborne Division was to seize the long bridge over the Maas River at Grave, to seize and hold the high ground in the vicinity of Groesbeek, to seize at least one of the four bridges over the Maas-Waal Canal, and, finally, to seize the bridge over the Waal at the city of Nijmegen.
>
> The US 101st Airborne Division had the mission of seizing the bridges of several canals and rivers south of Grave. Finally, the British 1st Airborne Division was to seize the bridge over the lower Rhine at the town of Arnhem.

There is some question as to why the British 1st Airborne Division drew the most dangerous mission of Market Garden. General Gavin thought it was because of location of the base camps in England. But in 1954 Gen. Anthony McAuliffe, the 101st Airborne Division's artillery commander in World War II, wrote a letter to the U.S. Army's chief of military history and explained the basis of the decision. He stated that the original plan had the 101st attacking the Arnhem bridge, but the British 1st Airborne staff had already planned a drop in that area (Operation Comet) that had been canceled. So Browning felt, wrote McAuliffe, that the British were more ready for that drop than the U.S. 101st.

The commanding general of the British 1st Airborne Division, Maj. Gen. Robert Urquhart, was a giant of a Scot, six feet tall and 200 pounds. But he had never made a parachute jump or ridden in a glider—in training or in combat. The previous commander, Gen. Eric Down had been hurriedly transferred to India so that Urquhart, a seasoned warrior in previous WW II battles, got the mantle of the British 1st Airborne.

Operation Market Garden was actually two plans in one: Market was the airborne phase; Garden was the ground operation. Montgomery was indeed anxious to get across the Rhine over the bridge at Arnhem, but first he had to seize the canal and river bridges between Eindhoven and Arnhem with airborne forces. Then, over this carpet of parachutes and gliders, Montgomery could send the British Second Army spearheaded by Lt. Gen. Brian G. Horrocks's XXX Corps, advancing from a bridge-head across the Maas-Scheldt Canal south of Eindhoven to the Ijs-selmeer River, about ninety miles to the north, in two to four days. Supporting Horrocks's flanks would be the British Second Army's VIII and XII Corps. The strategy of Market Garden was to cross the Rhine at Arn-hem before the Germans could react decisively and in strength. It was clear to Montgomery's planners that if the Germans foresaw the thrust across the Rhine, they would blow up all the bridges. Hence the need for a rapid airborne assault.

Market Garden was a bold and courageous, but foolhardy, plan. First, Montgomery's intelligence network reported, inaccurately, that the Germans in the Eindhoven-Arnhem corridor were second-class, poorly trained soldiers. Second, Montgomery's planners estimated mistakenly that the narrow road network was suitable for supporting the advance of the 20,000 vehicles of Horrocks's XXX Corps. Third, the planners felt, incorrectly, that the weather in northeastern Europe in September would permit the necessary resupply of the airborne forces for a few days. With these misassumptions, the planners went ahead, feeling that the opportunity to cross the Rhine and outflank the Siegfried Line was worth the odds. But the odds changed considerably when the Germans increased their buildup in the area—to a force Montgomery seemed unwilling to recognize.

After they had studied the plans for the operation, Generals Urquhart and Sosabowski had doubts about its success. Because of marshy terrain around Arnhem, Urquhart had to select drop zones six to eight miles from the Arnhem bridge, and Sosabowski realized that it would take five to six hours after landing to reach the bridge. When he told Browning of his doubts, he received this answer: "But, my dear Sosabowski, the Red Devils and the gallant Poles can do anything."

The makeup of the 82d had changed from the days of the Normandy campaign. Colonel Reuben Tucker's 504th Parachute Infantry Regiment, weakened at Anzio, had missed Normandy. But now it was back to full strength and replaced Col. Edson D. Raff's 507th that had been attached to the 82d for Normandy. "Raff's Ruffians" remained in England during Market Garden and joined Miley's 17th Airborne Division. But Gavin kept Colonel Lindquist's 508th Parachute Infantry Regiment.

For Market Garden, Taylor's 101st Airborne Division had the same structure as in Normandy. There was only one change, and that involved the command of the 502d Parachute Infantry. Because Col. George Mosely, commander of the 502d, had broken a leg on the Normandy jump, Taylor gave command of the regiment to Col. John H. Michaelis, a thirty-two year old (class of 1936).

The U.S. 17th Airborne Division ("Golden Talon"), only recently arrived in England from the United States, was not ready for Market Garden. The division was still sorting out its gear at Camp Chisledon when the campaign began. Later in the war it would be committed to battle, but as ground-pounders—"leg infantry," in airborne jargon.

In simple terms the airborne portion of Market Garden was this: the 101st would seize the bridges around Eindhoven; the British would capture Arnhem; and the 82d would take Nijmegen. For the U.S. airborne division commanders two points were notable: the highest land in Holland was near Nijmegen and had to be controlled immediately; and the Nijmegen bridge across the Rhine needed to be captured intact almost on landing. The most important of these two missions was the capture of the Nijmegen bridge, and whoever did it had to be on the alert for Germans moving from the flat terrain on the east side of the city. Gavin gave the job to Lindquist and his 508th. On Friday, 15 September, Urquhart trucked his troops to his eight departure airfields, and Gavin and Taylor moved their men to their sixteen fields. By dark, the troops were sealed in, allowing them almost a day for final preparations. Gavin and Taylor assembled their regiment and battalion commanders on Saturday and went over the plans for the operation in minute detail. They used charts, photographs, sand tables, scale models, road maps, and diagrams to clarify and point out assembly areas, assembly and recognition signals, details of unit missions, and other assorted tasks. The regiment and battalion commanders went back to their own fields and carried on the briefings and orders down to the lowest levels—most important, to the platoon and squad leaders. Then the troopers went back to their huts and tents and spent time writing letters, playing poker, packing their gear, and even sleeping.

At 1900 on Saturday evening, 16 September, Browning held a final session with his commanders in the FAAA headquarters war room. In a short session, he told the commanders that the weather experts expected good flying conditions the next day. Given the situation Brereton made his final decision: launch the next day.

At 0945 on Sunday, 17 September 1944, the skies over the British coast began to fill with various types of Allied aircraft; 1,500 C-47s, some 500 gliders—Wacos, Horsas, and the massive Hamilcars—1,250 fighters, and about 1,000 bombers. By 1115 the entire airborne armada carrying 20,000 men, 511 vehicles, 330 artillery weapons, and 590 tons of ammunition, rations, and other equipment was in the air and on its way to Holland. The mass of planes flew along two routes: to the north flew the British 1st Airborne Division, followed by the 82d. To the south flew the planes carrying the 101st. General Ridgway rode in a B-17 at the head of the 82d's column. Although he had had no part in planning the operation, he insisted on watching his 82d Airborne launch itself into yet another airborne operation. In the British operation, once again, the gliders landed before the paratroopers, and General Urquhart was in one of the lead gliders.

Even before the fleet crossed the British coast, there were accidents. Thirty gliders were lost, some because of tug ship engine failure, some from broken tug lines, and some because of heavy cloud cover. Twenty-three of the lost gliders were from the British 1st Airborne. Then, once over the English Channel, Urquhart lost five more gliders.

Over the Continent German antiaircraft defenses filled the sky with flak. Pieces of shrapnel pierced the C-47s' thin fuselages; some passed through the sides of the gliders. The escorting fighters flew out of their flank positions, subjected the German guns under heavy fire, and silenced most of the coastal flak guns. But over Schouwen Island, an 82d C-47 and its glider were shot out of the sky, with the tug crashing on landing and killing all on board. The glider broke up in midair, spewing the troopers and their gear across the landscape.

The 101st pathfinders were first over their target area. Over Belgium one pathfinder C-47 was shot down, and only four troopers were able to jump. But the men of the second pathfinder unit hit DZ A perfectly, and shortly had the homing radio operational. They marked the DZ with burning letters, T and A. The pathfinders for the other two DZs were also on target and soon had their gear ready. At 1300, the main body of the 101st in 500 C-47s and seventy gliders came over their DZs and LZs and landed successfully against little German opposition. But after the C-47s discharged their troopers and gliders, German antiaircraft fire shot down sixteen departing C-47s. The planes were relatively easy targets because the intrepid pilots held steady to proper jump altitude and speed, a discipline that had been wanting in some previous air assaults. With their planes damaged some pilots could justifiably have turned away— but did not, and two planes crashed and burned only after dropping their paratroopers. In all, the pilots were successful in dropping 80 percent of the 101st paratroopers on the proper DZs.

The landing of 7,250 men of the 82d from 479 C-47s was equally successful. The pathfinders who dropped near Grave were met with heavy antiaircraft fire, but the escort fighters attacked those positions and silenced the guns. The 82d's pathfinders hit the 505th and 508th DZs accurately, and then came the main bodies of paratroopers led by General Gavin in the first plane. With him was his G-3, Lt. Col. John Norton. The paratroopers hit their DZs and began to assemble. Next came eighty-eight gliders carrying Lt. Col. "Tex" Singleton's 80th Antiaircraft Battalion, Browning and his British Airborne Corps staff, headquarters units, and more supplies and equipment. Thirty-eight gliders landed about a mile from their LZ but the troops quickly assembled and moved out.

The British 1st Airborne Division jumped and glider-landed some 6,000 men eight miles northwest of Arnhem. Urquhart's plan had about two-thirds of his men guarding the DZs and LZs and three battalions attacking into town and seizing the bridge over the Rhine. Four hours after landing, Urquhart sent three battalions into the Arnhem area. Only A Company of Lt. Col. John D. Frost's 2d Battalion, 1st Parachute Brigade was able to get to the north end of the bridge at first. Frost's men tried to get to the south end but were driven back by the Germans there. The standoff was to continue into the night and beyond.

General Taylor and his 6,769 101st paratroopers flew in on 424 C-47s. The planes carried Jumpy Johnson's 501st, Iron Mike Michaelis's 502d, and Bob Sink's 506th Parachute Regiments. The planes ran into the heavy flak over the Dutch coast, but the pilots held their course and dropped their men on the DZs. Within an hour Taylor has assembled his troops and moved them out on the assigned missions. Jump casualties came to less than 2 percent. Although a glider landing under any circumstances is hardly routine, in only one hour seventy of the division's gliders arrived and fifty-three landed safely. The others crashed on landing, some landed behind German lines, two had to abort the flight in England, and one crashed in the Channel.

By 1500 on D day, the entire British and U.S. airborne forces in the initial flight were assembled on the ground and moving out toward their objectives. (The 82d and the 101st landed and moved with the speed and efficiency usually found only on daylight maneuvers in the States.)

In spite of the Allied preparatory bombings and the steady noise of the transports flying over Holland, the Germans were taken by surprise. General Kurt Student, the commander of the First Parachute Army, was in his office in Vucht, about seven miles from the 101st's DZs. When he heard the planes coming closer, Student got up on the roof and watched General Taylor and his 101st drop along "Hell's Highway." Nearest to Student's CP was Colonel Johnson and his 501st. Lieutenant Colonel Harry W. O. Kinnard Jr., (class of 1939), twenty-nine years old, was the commander of the 1st Battalion, 501st. His battalion and one other were the only two to miss the 101st's airhead. Kinnard and his troopers landed west of Veghel, about six miles from Student's CP. He assembled his battalion in short order and took over two railroad bridges to the west of Veghel; the other battalions took a bridge intact over the Wilhelmina Canal and another one over the Aa River.

Taylor's 502d and 506th landed six miles farther south between St. Oedenrode and Best. Moving out rapidly and with the Germans still unprepared after the shock of the airborne assault, Lt. Col. Pat Cassidy, commander of 1st Battalion, 502d, seized the road bridge over the Dommel River at Saint Oedenrode. In the firefight with the Germans his troops killed twenty of the enemy and captured fifty-eight. The 3d, 502d attacked Best but was held up by stiffening enemy defenses.

Colonel Sink's 506th did not fare as well as Taylor's other two regiments. His troops landed on DZ C along the edge of the Zonsche Forest. He gave Maj. James L. LaPrade (class of 1939), thirty years old, the mission of capturing the main road bridge and two smaller bridges over the Wilhelmina Canal at Zon. When LaPrade had taken the bridges, Sink's plan was to move south with his other two battalions and take Eindhoven, including four smaller bridges over the Dommel River. The seizure of the Eindhoven bridges was essential to Taylor's mission because the overall plan had Taylor meeting British armor units on D day as they fought their way north to Arnhem. Unfortunately, his troops were held up by German roadblocks and arrived at the Zon Bridge just as the Germans blew it up. Undaunted, the troops found some small boats, ferried themselves across the canal, and spent the night in foxholes three miles outside Eindhoven.

That evening, Taylor and his G-3 checked the Screaming Eagles's situation. Jumpy Johnson and his troops had the bridges around Veghel. John Michaelis's 502d had taken St. Oedenrode and were fighting near Best. Sink was across the Wilhelmina Canal and was awaiting daylight to attack Eindhoven. The British armor supposed to cross into Eindhoven on D day was in a fight with the Germans six miles away.

Lieutenant Colonel Robert G. Cole (class of 1939), age twenty-nine, was the commander of the 3d Battalion, 502d. On the battalion's approach to the canal at Best on 18 September, he was killed by a sniper. He had won the Medal of Honor leading a bayonet charge in Normandy, but he would not live to wear it.

In the 82d's area, Gavin remembered that "early indications were that the drop had been unusually successful. Unit after unit reported in on schedule, and with few exceptions, all were in their pre-planned locations."

One of the first of the 82d's units to land was Lt. John S. Thompson's E Company, which landed south of its objective, the 1,100-foot bridge over the wide Maas River, not far from Grave. After assembling his men he broke his company into two teams. They worked around to the end of the bridge and cut all the wires leading to it, then they marched across. Soon after, Thompson met up with other men of the battalion who had seized the other end of the bridge. All together they captured the flak towers on the northern end and then cut the rest of the wires, putting the bridge into the hands of the 82d. To Gavin, this was the most important bridge because it ensured a linkup of the 82d Division and the British XXX Corps.

Colonel Reuben Tucker's 504th Parachute Infantry landed almost precisely as planned—between the Grave Bridge over the Maas and the Maas-Waal Canal. Tucker immediately sent patrols to his two objectives: the main road from Grave to Nijmegen and the bridges over the Maas-Waal Canal. The patrols at the bridge found and cut all the wires to the explosives. In short order they captured the long, low nine-span bridge at Grave with some ease because they had dropped at both ends of the bridge. This success permitted the British armor to cross over and race northward toward Nijmegen and Arnhem. The capture of this bridge was probably the most important airborne D-day event. Late that afternoon Gavin continued to receive favorable reports from his commanders. "Both glider troops and parachute troopers landing behind the Germans were, in most cases, able to fight their way back with little difficulty," he wrote.

Then Gavin got a jeep and drove to Groesbeek. While en route he ran into Lt. Col. Wilbur M. Griffith (class of 1936), the twenty-nine-year-old commander of the 376th Parachute Field Artillery Battalion. Griffith was being pushed about in a wheelbarrow, having broken his ankle on the jump. Griffith reported to Gavin, "General, the 376th Field Artillery is in position with all guns ready to fire." Before the operation Gavin had considered that dropping the 376th was an experiment; he now concluded that it was successful. In the first twenty-four hours after landing, the 376th fired 315 rounds from their pack 75s and had kept a large force of Germans away. In addition the 376th captured eight German officers and 400 enlisted men.

Back at his CP the night of 17 September, Gavin got reports from each of his regimental commanders. "Colonel Tucker with the 504th had captured the big Grave bridge and helped capture bridge No. 7 at Molenhoek," he remembered.

He was patrolling aggressively toward the west, expecting a major German reaction from that direction. Colonel William W. Ekman and the 505th, with two battalions, was organizing a defensive position from Mook through Horst, swinging back toward the town of Kamp, approximately a mile out of Groesbeek. Patrols had been sent to the Reichswald. The 2d Battalion, 505th under Lt. Col. Ben Vandervoort, was in division reserve on high ground about a half mile from the Division Command Post. Colonel Lindquist's 508th organized a defense from Kamp to Wyler and established several roadblocks along the south of the high ground at Bergen-en-Dal.

As we had seized all our other bridges in the division area the key to the success of the battle was now the Nijmegen Bridge. It absolutely had to be seized and its destruction prevented as well. . . . When I went to the 508th Command Post, the report was grim. My heart sank. They had failed to get the bridge.

At dusk on D day Lindquist had ordered Lt. Col. Shields Warren Jr. (class of 1939), twenty-eight years old, to reconnoiter the defenses of the bridge. Warren sent a reinforced rifle platoon into Nijmegen in the hopes of finding some Dutch civilians who might know the location of the German defenses. When the platoon leader failed to report back, Warren moved toward the bridge with his A and B Companies. A patrol from A Company, led by a Dutch guide, moved to the main post office building, where the patrol found a device rigged by the Germans to blow the bridge. The patrol cut all the wires leading to the building. But the two companies were stopped by a fierce firefight with the Germans defending the bridge, and the Germans continued to hold the bridge for the next five days.

On the morning of 18 September, Gavin was worried about the arrival of his glider troops. He told Lindquist to free his 3d Battalion and move it back to clear the LZ of Germans, who were in the woods between Bergen-en-Dal and Wyler, and on the attack.

The 3d Battalion, 508th, commanded by Lt. Col. Louis G. Mendez Jr. (class of 1940), twenty-nine years old, had been fighting most of the night and now was under orders to move seven miles back to Wyler, search out and clear the Germans from the woods, and then get to the LZ and clear it for the glider landings. Gavin was deeply concerned about clearing the LZs before the 82d's glider units arrived in the early afternoon of D day plus 1. The only immediately available reserves he had were two companies of engineers under the command of Capt. William H. Johnson, which he sent through Groesbeek and toward Kamp. He ordered Johnson to clear the LZ before the gliders arrived. Gavin even went with the small force for several miles through broken country.

"Shortly before 1400 hours the great air armada could be seen approaching from England, 900 aircraft in all, 450 gliders and 450 C-47 tugs," Gavin wrote.

The drone of the engines reached a roar as they came directly over the landing zones. I experienced a terrible feeling of helplessness. I wanted to tell them that they were landing right on the German infantry. Soon they were overhead, and the gliders began to cut loose and start their encircling descent. As they landed, they raised tremendous clouds of dust, and the weapons fire increased over the area. Some spun on one wing, others ended up on their noses or tipped over as they dug the glider nose into the earth in their desire to bring them to a quick stop. Glidermen could be seen running from their gliders and engaging the Germans. Others were attempting to extricate their artillery and jeeps.

It seemed almost a miracle when the battle was over and a count was taken of the men and equipment. The 319th Glider Field Artillery Battalion recovered 12 of its 12 howitzers and 26 of its 34 jeeps; the 320th Glider Field Artillery Battalion recovered eight of its 12 howitzers and 29 of its 39 jeeps. The 456th Parachute Field Artillery Battalion recovered 10 of its 12 howitzers and 23 of its 33 jeeps. Some of the glider units landed far behind the drop zones in Germany, but most of them fought their way back. In addition, the medical battalion brought in 26 jeeps. The 307th Engineer Battalion had 100 percent recovery, five out of five jeeps, the Signal Company eight out of ten jeeps. And finally, most important of all, eight of eight 57mm antitank guns and eight out of nine jeeps were recovered by Battery D of the 80th Airborne Antiaircraft Battalion. A highly creditable performance and one that I never would have thought possible as I watched them approach the landing zone. The landings had begun at 1400 hours, and the last glider had landed by 1430 hours.

We were still very short of infantry, but we expected the 325th Glider Infantry to land the following day, 20 September. It took an hour or so to get everything arranged; then I moved once again to the 508th sector in which combat was the most intense in the division area.

Lieutenant Edward L. Wierzbowski was a platoon leader in H Company of the 502d. At about 1100 on the morning of D day plus 1, he led his platoon of only fifteen men in an attack on the Germans defending the bridge at Best. They stopped the platoon within a hundred yards of the bridge and blew up the structure. That afternoon the Germans attacked Wierzbowski's position, seriously wounding Pvt. Joe E. Mann for the second time that day and killing Pvt. Onroe Luther. Then, for some reason, the Germans stopped their attack. The next morning at dawn, Wierzbowski and his platoon were attacked by the Germans throwing "potatomasher" grenades. When they got to within twenty yards of the paratroopers' position, Sergeant Betras and some of his men got out of their holes and, in return, threw grenades at the enemy. The Germans continued their attack. Private Vincent Laino was blinded by a grenade but managed to find another one in his foxhole and throw it back.

The Germans kept throwing grenades at the paratroopers, who were by now almost without ammunition. One grenade landed in a hole near Pvt. Joe E. Mann, who had been severely wounded and had both arms in slings. He saw the grenade, yelled "Grenade!" and jumped on it as it exploded, killing him and wounding three others. He received a posthumous Medal of Honor.

By now Wierzbowski's platoon was reduced to three unwounded men and no ammunition, so he was forced to surrender to the Germans surrounding the remnants of his platoon. But, incredibly, later that afternoon he and his few men were freed by other paratroopers.

On the afternoon of D day plus 1, Col. Joseph H. Harper arrived with the 428 gliders carrying his 327th Glider Infantry Regiment consisting of 2,579 glidermen, 146 jeeps, and 109 trailers, as well as ammunition and food. One of the reluctant glider riders was Brig. Gen. Anthony McAuliffe, whose glider had been shot up just before landing. When they met later, he told General Taylor that in the future he would jump in.

In the Arnhem area, at 1500 on 18 September, the second half of the British Airborne Division landed by parachute and glider on the same DZs and LZs that the British had used the previous day. But even with these reinforcements, Urquhart was unable to link up with the intrepid Colonel Frost and his men holding the north end of the Arnhem bridge. That day, one message from a Dutchman in the Arnhem area reported that "the Germans are winning over British in Arnhem." Urquhart pulled his men into a close defense near Oosterbeek to await the arrival of the Polish 1st Parachute Brigade due to parachute in on D day plus 2, 19 September.

Early on the morning of 19 September, tanks of the British Guards Armored Division rumbled into Col. Reuben Tucker's 504th position near Grave, ending one phase of Market Garden. But heavy fighting for all the airborne troops was still in the offing.

On the same day, Generals Brereton and Ridgway decided to see for themselves how the battles across the airborne carpet were progressing. They landed at Antwerp and then went by jeep to Eindhoven, which was occupied by the 101st's 506th. During one of their road trips they found themselves under a Luftwaffe bombing run and they were both thrown into a ditch. Brereton lost his pistol, a memento he had taken with him when the Japanese had forced his departure from the Philippines. Confusion followed; they did not see one another again until their return to England.

In the 82d's area the 508th had not taken the southern end of the Nijmegen bridge. The senior Allied generals were deeply concerned about the problems facing the operation and the lack of progress in some areas of the battlefield. In midafternoon of 19 September Gavin had a top-level meeting on the sidewalk in front of his CP, the Malden School-house, with British Generals Horrocks, commander of the XXX Corps, Browning, commander of the Allied First Airborne Army, and Allan Adair, commander of the Guards Armoured Division. At the time, they did not know that General Student, the commander of the German forces opposing them, had a copy of the Allied attack order an hour after the 17 September D-day landings. A German soldier had taken the order from a wrecked glider. The order told Student exact plans of unit missions and routes of attack, letting Student set up counterattacks in several critical areas.

Gavin outlined for Horrocks his plan to seize the Nijmegen bridge that would permit the British armor to drive on to Arnhem. In an hour, the 2d Battalion, 505th under Lt. Col. Ben Vandervoort, in whom Gavin "had great confidence and commanded one of the best battalions in the division," would attack the south end of the bridge. Horrocks then said that, to assist in this effort, he would supply a company of British infantry and a battalion of tanks from the Guards Armoured Division. Gavin went on to say that he wanted to send another force in small boats across the river to attack the bridge from the north "as quickly as possible." But, Gavin said, he had no boats. Horrocks offered him thirty-three engineer assault boats for the river crossing, but, unfortunately, they would not be available for twenty-four hours.

At 1500 that afternoon, Vandervoort's 2d Battalion and the British troops moved into Nijmegen and attacked the south side of the bridge. The Germans were ready with an 88mm gun that knocked out the lead tank and stopped the attack. The Germans riddled the infantry with machine guns along the route and by dark were still in control of the Nijmegen bridge. Gavin was getting desperate because he knew that the British armor had to cross the bridge to get to the British airborne elements at Arnhem. He made plans on the almost spur of the moment for a radical amphibious operation. He sent for Colonel Tucker that night and told him to cross the river in British engineer boats that would be available the next day. For fire support Tucker would have about eight British and U.S. artillery battalions, one squadron of British tanks, and British aircraft to bomb and strafe just before H hour, which Gavin set for1400 on 20 September.

"Thus," wrote Gavin, "20 September turned out to be a day unprecedented in the division's combat history. Each of the three regiments fought a critical battle in its own area and won over heavy odds, but the most brilliant and spectacular battle of all was that of the 504th to get across the Waal River."

Tucker decided to give Maj. Julian A. Cook (class of 1940), twenty-seven years old, and his 3d Battalion, 504th, the "boat" mission. Once he had made the crossing, Maj. Willard E. Harrison and his 1st, 504th, would follow. The men of the 3d Battalion, were ready at 1300 on the river line, but what turned out to be twenty-six boats, not the expected thirty-three, were twenty minutes late. And the boats were hardly made for assault river crossings. They were nineteen feet long with canvas sides, each weighing about 200 pounds, and capable of carrying about thirteen paratroopers and three engineer crewmen to row them across. The river crossing was about a mile downstream from the bridge, about 400 yards wide, and with a flow of about ten miles per hour. It would be an extraordinary river trip.

"Twenty-six boats were assembled, someone yelled 'Go,' and there was a rush for the water's edge." Gavin wrote.

The troopers had a hard time getting the boats into deep water while they climbed over the sides with their weapons. To add to their difficulties, German small arms fire began to intercept the fragile flotilla. Never having rowed together, the troopers sometimes worked against each other, and boats were spinning in the river. The German fire steadily increased, heavy artillery fire joining the machine gun and mortar fire.

Nevertheless, as we expected, the 504th kept battling its way across the bloody river. There were many individual acts of courage, many casualties, and later, the troops told me of stuffing handkerchiefs in the bullet holes to keep the water from pouring into the boats, and using their helmets to bail out water, while all around them men were being killed and wounded.

To those watching the crossing, it seemed forever before the first boats touched down on the northern bank. Men struggled out of the boats, waded and made their way through the mud, and ran forward. Some of them said later that they were so glad to be alive that they had only one thought: to kill the Germans along the embankment who had been making the crossing so difficult. As reported by Cornelius Ryan in *A Bridge Too Far*, Lieutenant Colonel Giles Vandeleur, who had been watching the landings, later said, "I saw one or two boats hit the beach followed immediately by three or four others. Nobody paused. Men got out and began running toward the embankment. My God, what a courageous sight it was! They just moved steadily across that open ground. I never saw a single man lie down until he was hit." Then, to Vandeleur's amazement, "the boats turned around and started back for the second wave." Turning to Horrocks, General Browning said, "I have never seen a more gallant action."

Lieutenant Delbert Kuehl, chaplain with the 504th, was in the first wave across. He remembers the boat ride this way:

Then we asked the fatal question, When would we cross? Obviously at night, under the cover of darkness. Still wrong. We learned that the bridge was so strategic to save the British paratroopers to the north and for our advance into Germany that we would cross the river in the afternoon of September 20 in broad daylight. So in short, we were on a suicide mission and my men didn't even have the choice to volunteer. Since they had to go, I chose to go too. I remember how one officer reacted to this information. He took a cigarette from his pack and threw the rest in the river. He lit it with his lighter and then threw it in the river as well. His comment: "I won't be needing those anymore." His premonition was right. He was killed in midstream.

Then our moment of truth arrived. As we loaded up into 26 canvas skiffs and pushed off into that 300 yard wide river, we must have surprised the Germans. Few military leaders in their right minds would attempt what we were doing under the conditions we faced. As we got to midstream, the bullets splashing on the surface made it look like it was raining. Men were getting shot and falling overboard. The boats were getting peppered with holes and sinking and troops drowning. The man next to me had the middle of his head blown away so that his skull dropped on what was left of his lower face.

Just twelve of the 26 boats reached the far side of the river, and then we who had survived the crossing had many meters of open river flats to charge to reach cover and repulse the Germans defending their positions. Some were killed or wounded doing that while those who were still able charged the German positions with fixed bayonets, and killed the German machine gunners, secured the highway and railroad bridges and prevented them from being demolished by German explosives at the last minute. Our tanks, artillery and infantry crossed the bridges and moved inland.

My role was to tend the wounded and move them to the water's edge for transfer to the other side. While giving first aid to a man who had a serious stomach wound, I was hit in the back by shrapnel and fell on top of him. I'll never forget the concern he showed me when he cried out, "Oh, Chaplain, did they get you too?" Here's a trooper with his belly torn open and he's sorry about me. That's what made the 504th the unit it was. Never was I prouder than then to be a member of such a fighting force of diehards.

On 13 December 1944, General Gavin awarded Chaplain Kuehl the Silver Star for his gallant behavior in tending to the wounded troopers under fire on the north bank of the Waal River.

Two hours after the boat operation, Cole and his men had seized control of the northern end of the bridge, and the Germans were running desperately across it. The Germans lost many troops, some killed jumping into the river, others shot out of the bridge girders. The Allied soldiers found 267 dead Germans on the bridge alone.

By 1800 at the other end of the bridge, Vandervoort's men and the British Grenadier Guards were moving against the Germans in their foxholes and then swarming across the bridge to link up with Cole and his pseudo-beachers. An hour later both ends of the bridge were in Allied hands. The cost of seizing it had not come cheap: Tucker lost some 200 of his paratroopers.

The Americans had expected to hear and see the British armor rolling across the Nijmegen bridge as soon as they had secured it. But by dark, no tanks had yet appeared. At dawn on D day plus 4, 21 September, Tucker's troops were still building up their defensive positions. The British armored units sat idly by, waiting for reinforcements of infantry and gasoline to build them up for the push to Arnhem.

At about noon a German force of about 100 infantrymen, two tanks, and a halftrack attacked the 504th's position near the bridge. With extraordinary courage for even a paratrooper, Pvt. John R. Towle, a bazooka man in C Company, 504th, climbed out of his foxhole, ran across an open field, knelt, and fired two bazooka rounds at the tanks. He got two direct hits and forced the tanks to back off. Still in no-man's-land by himself, Towle saw nine Germans race to a nearby house. He ran up to the house, fired a bazooka round through the door, and killed all nine. Towle had one target left—the halftrack. He ran toward the vehicle and, in plain sight, got down on one knee and took aim. Unfortunately, just at that moment, a mortar round landed right beside him and killed him. For his unusual valor, Towle was awarded the Medal of Honor posthumously.

Finally, on 22 September, two days after the capture of the Nijmegen bridge, the British armor, along with infantrymen from the 43d Division, began to roll toward Arnhem. German Gen. Heinz Harmel was in a bunker beyond the bridge and saw the British tanks driving across it. Near him was an engineer with a detonator box connected to the explosives the Germans had placed on the bridge months before. Harmel therefore ordered the engineer to blow up the bridge. After the engineer pushed the detonator's plunger down twice with no result, Harmel realized that the wires had been cut. The Grenadier Guards' tanks continued to roll across, blasted two German 88mm guns at the other end to climax their success, and moved on.

Earlier, on 20 September, the British were involved in one of the most "courageous actions of the battle," wrote Gavin. " It was being fought by a handful of British troopers at the northern end of the Arnhem Bridge." The British 1st Airborne Division had landed eight miles to the west of the Arnhem bridge, and Urquhart had sent three battalions on three separate routes to seize it. Lieutenant Colonel John Frost and his men of the 2d Battalion, 1st Parachute Brigade, worked their way along the northern bank of the Rhine. His men quickly knocked out small German units along the way, and in seven hours, they were at the northern end of the bridge. Frost deployed his battalion at about 2000 hours. The Germans attacked from their position at the south end of the bridge through the night. By then Frost had been badly wounded, and some 200 of his troops were casualties. He had tried to save them by having them carried into the cellars of nearby buildings, but the Germans surrounded the buildings and set them afire. As the buildings collapsed and beams fell on his helpless and injured men, Frost realized the futility of his situation. He sent out a Red Cross flag and asked for a truce. This was a tragic loss of gallant troops.

To the west of Frost's position, near Oosterbeek, Urquhart had moved the rest of the 1st Airborne Division into a pocket two and a half miles from the Arnhem bridge. Near the town of Driel, on the evening of 21 September Major General Sosabowski's Polish 1st Parachute Brigade began landing after bad weather in England had delayed their departure. The Polish brigade had the mission of crossing to the north side of the Lower Rhine to reinforce Urquhart, now dug in near Oosterbeek. But the plan did not work out well: more bad weather forced half of the planes to return to England without dropping their troopers. Sosabowski and the remainder of his troops made the drop but, on landing, found that the Germans were on the far side of the Rhine and had sunk the ferryboat. That night, about fifty of the Polish troops managed to get themselves across the river in small boats but they were too late to help the beleaguered British. On D day plus 5, 22 September, British tanks did link up with the Polish soldiers, but the Germans were in control of the river. There could be no crossing.

In Oosterbeek, the British airborne troops had dug into their perimeter and suffered constant attacks by a much larger German force that shelled the perimeter constantly with mortars and artillery. "The more the perimeter shrank," wrote Lt. Col. Walter Harzer, commander of the Hohenstaufen Division, "the more stubbornly the British troops defended every heap of ruins and inch of ground." "Hour by hour new German infiltrations into the British positions were reported," wrote Cornelis Bauer in *The Battle of Arnhem.* "House by house, ruin after ruin, yard after yard was lost. Ammunition, water, food—everything was running short." The situation inside the British perimeter was becoming critical and desperate. A British artilleryman near Oosterbeek-Lang wrote in his diary: "A considerable force of enemy penetrated between the gun area and Div HQ cutting the Div area in two."

On Sunday, 24 September, Brereton decided that there was no way to relieve Urquhart and what was left of his British airborne troops. Brereton ordered Urquhart to evacuate what was left of his command. At 1030 on 25 September Urquhart radioed that he agreed. Brigadier Hicks, commander of the British 1st Airlanding Brigade, wrote this later in his battle report: "13.30. Order for Operation 'Berlin' issued, ie for evacuation to the other side of the river during the night (25–26 September)."

On the night of 25–26 September, ferries brought out about 2,000 of the 9,500 men who had landed around the Arnhem bridge. Urquhart had lost 6,986 of his men, killed, wounded, or captured. The troops were brought to Nijmegen where the 82d supplied them with food, blankets, and shelter. "We in the 82d," wrote Gavin, "had a lasting regret that we had not reached them. They were brave men and they had done all that human flesh and human spirit could accomplish. Thus, the great gamble to end the war in the fall of '44 came to an end."

In the 101st's area the Germans started an attack on 22 September and cut the highway above Veghel. They held it until 26 September. On 22 September, as well, a German artillery shell hit a tree underneath which were some senior officers of the 101st. Colonel Michaelis, the commander of the 502d, took shrapnel in his arms, stomach, and both legs. His orderly, Pfc. Garland E. Mills, was killed. Also wounded were Michaelis's S-2, Captain Bisuke, his S-3, Captain Clemens, and his assistant S-3, Captain Plitt. Hit as well were the division G-2, Lieutenant Colonel Danahy; the division G-3, Lieutenant Colonel Hannah; the commander of the 377th Parachute Field Artillery Battalion, Maj. Luke Elkins; and the commander of the 1st Battalion, 501st, Lieutenant Colonel Cassidy.

Michaelis was forced to turn over his regiment to Lt. Col. Steve Chappuis, commander of the 2d Battalion. And with the loss of Lieutenant Colonel Hannah, the 101st got a new G-3 officer, Lt. Col. Harry W. O. Kinnard previously commander of the 1st Battalion, 501st Parachute Infantry.

The U.S. airborne forces suffered their share of the casualties of Market Garden. The 82d had 1,432 killed and missing, while the 101st's ranks were depleted by 2,110. Combat for the 82d and 101st was not over when the drive to Arnhem was halted and the British had withdrawn from the cauldron around the bridge. The Germans continued their pressure against the Market Garden salient, and the Allies felt the need to use the 82d and 101st men as ground troops. The 82d continued its defensive action on the Groesbeek Heights, and the 101st moved to a new defensive position between the Waal and the Rhine. The lengthy ground battles in those areas brought additional losses of 1,682 casualties to the 82d and 1,912 to the 101st. One historian reported that the Allied losses in Market Garden were greater than those in Normandy. On 6 June 1944 the Allies lost an estimated 10,000 to 12,000 troops; in the nine days of Market Garden the combined airborne and ground losses totaled more than 17,000.

By mid-October, General Brereton began to press for the release of his two U.S. airborne divisions. But the fighting was still intense, and General Eisenhower continued to support Montgomery's offensive, giving him logistical priority. Montgomery was fighting to keep the territory in Holland that the British had taken at great expense and to wipe out the Germans blocking the seaward approaches to Antwerp. The U.S. airborne divisions continued their fight with their usual determination, handicapped only by their having only the airborne's usual light weapons. Finally, on 11 November some of the 82d units were pulled off the Groesbeek Heights. The rest of the division left on 13 November, D day plus 57. The 101st, until relieved in position by Canadian forces, stayed on the line on the south bank of the Rhine until 25 November 1944.

One of the 101st's losses was Jumpy Johnson, a leader renowned for his bravery, bravado, ability to inspire his troops, and fearlessness in combat. He had activated the 501st Parachute Infantry Regiment and led it through all its battles. Having gotten his nickname by jumping three or four times a day while training his regiment at Fort Benning, in combat he fought and led his troops as if he were indestructible. On 8 October Johnson was in one of his usual positions, checking his front lines and talking to his troops. In the 2d Battalion area he met with Major Pelham, the battalion executive officer, and Captain Snodgrass, D Company's commander. At that moment a German artillery shell came roaring into the area. Pelham and Snodgrass heard it coming and dove for cover, but Johnson, whose ear had been wounded earlier, did not. After he was blown off his feet, medics carried him to an ambulance that was about to leave for the hospital at Nijmegen. He died en route to the hospital.

The troopers of the two U.S. airborne divisions pulled their weary bodies onto trucks and trains and headed for Reims in France. Here the XVIII Airborne Corps pulled itself together. In the area, in addition to the 82d and the 101st, General Ridgway had the 517th Parachute Infantry Regiment, the 509th and 551st Infantry Battalions, and the 463d Parachute Field Artillery Battalion. These last four units had been in combat in southern France.

About twenty miles from Reims at Sissonne, to the north, and Suippes, to the east, the troops moved into old French army billets that had been used by the Germans before they left. As Gavin put it, the quarters "did not offer much in the way of comfort, but they were far better than the foxholes in the fall and winter in Holland."

Once they settled into their new barracks, the veteran troopers of the 82d and the 101st spent their time cleaning or being issued new battle gear, weapons, and clothing, going on passes into Reims, and causing countless ruckuses in the bars and other houses of amusement. Recruits from home joined the combat veterans of the divisions and were integrated into the battle-depleted units. Training and occasional parachute jumps kept the edge on the troopers. Of course they did not know what was next for them. They did know that the Germans were far from beaten, and that there would be other battles ahead now that they had proven their extraordinary value as airborne troops, capable of flying over the enemy forces and landing en mass in vulnerable rear areas.

An analysis of the value of Market Garden shows a mix of success and failure. The U.S. airborne divisions accomplished their missions and won all their battles from Nijmegen to Eindhoven. They had liberated and returned to the Dutch many valuable areas. The British airborne operation was a costly failure, so tragic and disjointed that the British 1st Airborne Division never fought again as a unit.

As Ted Ballard, a historian with the U.S. Army Center of Military History, wrote: "To General Eisenhower the ramifications of Market-Garden were abundantly clear. The failure to reach Arnhem dashed any hope of seizing a bridgehead over the Rhine and outflanking the Siegfried Line before the onset of winter. Additionally, the annihilation of the 1st British Airborne Division, coupled with the need to retain the 101st and 82d Airborne Divisions in the field, denied SHAEF the immediate option of further airborne drops along the Rhine. Finally, the failure of Market-Garden reinforced in Eisenhower's mind the wisdom of his broad-front strategy."

On 9 July 1943, paratroopers of the 82d Airborne Division's 505th Parachute Infantry Regiment load up for their combat jump on Sicily. Note the M-1 rifles slung over their shoulders. (National Archives)

In July 1943, on Operation Husky in Sicily, 82d Airborne Division paratroopers patrol along a highway at a railroad crossing. (National Archives)

One paratrooper inspects another's reserve parachute prior to boarding a C-47 for the D-day drop on Normandy. (National Archives)

Normandy kickoff. On the eve of the Allied invasion of Normandy, General Eisenhower, the Supreme Allied Commander, offers his best wishes for a successful landing to Lt. Wallace C. Strobel and his platoon from the 502d Parachute Infantry Regiment. (National Archives)

One 82d Airborne Division paratrooper checks his sergeant's parachute prior to mounting a C-47 for the drop on Normandy. Note the bayonet on the boot of the trooper on the right. (82d Airborne Division Museum)

Troopers from the 82d Airborne Division board a C-47 for their drop on Nijmegen in Operation Market Garden, 17 September 1944. (82d Airborne Division Museum)

Holland is the next stop for this glider, shown being towes from as airport in England by a C-47 troop carrier of the 1st Allied Airborne Army. (82d Airborne Division Museum)

A heavily laden 101st Airborne Division paratrooper climbs aboard a C-47 headed for a drop zone near Eindhoven, 17 September 1944. (82d Airborne Division Museum)

Paratroopers crammed aboard a C-47 en route to a drop near Nijmegen, Holland. Note the rifle packs on the knees of the troopers. (National Archives)

A trooper of the 82d Airborne Division one second after he stepped out of the C-47 jump door over Holland in September of 1944. His static line is pulling his main chute out of its backpack. (82d Airborne Division Museum)

Paratroopers of the 82d Division set up a firing position on a street in Nijmegen. (82d Airborne Division Museum)

General Ridgway (on the left) commander of the newly formed XVIII Airborne Corps and General James Gavin, newly appointed commander of the 82d Airborne Division, meet in the fall of 1944. Note Ridgway's hand grenades on his harness. They were his trademarks, always worn on his battle uniform, even during the Korean War when he was the Eighth Army Commander. General Gavin at age 37 was the youngest U.S. Army major general since George Armstrong Custer. (Gerald M. Devlin)

Major General Gavin, commander of the 82d Airborne Division, armed as usual with his M1 rifle, on a personal recon during the Battle of the Bulge, December 1944. (Gerard M. Devlin)

Troops of the 325th Glider Infantry Regiment of the 82d Airborne Division make their way through the deep snow near Bastogne, January 1945. (National Archives)

In Belgium in January 1945, a bazooka team of the 325th Glider Infantry Regiment of the 82d Airborne Division set up a firing position. (National Archives)

An 82d Airborne Division paratrooper moves along a roadway near Bastogne, January 1945. Note the bazooka on his left side and his bayonet on his right ankle. (82d Airborne Division Museum)

Troops of the 101st Airborne Division leave Bastogne after the Battle of the Bulge, January 1945. (National Archives)

On 3 February 1945 at Elmore airstrip on Mindoro Island in the Philippines, troopers of the 511th Parachute Infantry Regiment of the 11th Airborne Division chute up for their drop on Tagaytay Ridge, south of Manila on Luzon. Tagaytay Ridge was some twenty miles east of Nasugbu where the two glider regimental combat teams of the 11th Airborne Division had waded ashore on 31 January 1945. (U.S. Army photo)

Corregidor under attack. Left, is the "mile-long barracks" and the parade ground drop zone to its front. Right, is the nine-hole golf course drop zone. Center, Lt. Col. Edward M. Postlethwait's 3d Battalion of the 34th Infantry Regiment land on Black Beach. (U.S. Army photo)

Corregidor regained. On 2 March 1945, Gen. Douglas MacArthur and staff (in khakis) watch men of the 503d Parachute Regiment raise the flag on a battered Corregidor. (U.S. Army photo)

A parking lot outside XVIII Airborne Corps headquarters in Diesford, Germany on 26 March 1945. (VIII Airborne Corps historian)

In a significant ceremony on a roof top at Duisberg, Germany, men of the 17th Airborne Division raise the American flag. Note the soldier with hand salute. (National Archives)

On Good Friday, 23 March 1951, 3,447 troopers of the 187th Airborne Infantry Regimental Combat Team and the 4th Ranger Company drop from 80 C-119s and 55 C-47s on Munsan-ni, North Korea, twenty miles northeast of Seoul in Operation Tomahawk. Shortly after the drop, General Matthew B. Ridgway, Eighth Army commander, landed in an L-4 liaison plane and met up with Brig. Gen. Frank Bowen, the 187th's commanding general who had jumped in. (Fort Campbell historian)

In October of 1950 at Sukchon-Sunchon in Korea, a C-119 aircraft drops supplies to the troopers of the 187th Airborne Infantry Regimental Combat Team already on the ground. (Fort Campbell historian)

While the Munsan-ni drop is still in progress, F. Company of the 187th ARCT attacks along a ridgeline. (Fort Campbell historian)

In March of 1966, "Sky Soldiers" of the 2d Battalion, 503d Infantry of the 173d Airborne Brigade (Sep) board helicopters for Operation Silver City near the Song Be River in War Zone D. (XVIII Airborne Corps historian)

In March 1968, troopers of the 82d Airborne Division set up an M 60 A1 machine gun position in Quang Tri Province in Operation Carentan 1. (XVIII Airborne Corps historian)

In February 1985, female paratroopers of the 1st Corps Support Command of the XVIII Airborne Corps check parachutes. Currently, in the 82d Airborne Division, there are 459 female paratroopers assigned. (XVIII Airborne Corps historian)

In March of 1988, during Operation Golden Pheasant, an 82d Airborne Division trooper, armed with an M16 A2 weapon, stands guard in Honduras. (XVIII Airborne Corps historian)

On Green Ramp at Pope Air Force Base, N.C., troops of the 82d board a C-130 for a training jump. (XVIII Airborne Corps historian)

A communications team from the 101st Airborne Division (Air Assault) sets up its gear in Desert Shield/Desert Storm. Note the weapons as well as the commo gear. (XVIII Airborne Corps historian)

During the Desert Storm victory march in New York City in April of 1991, Lt. Gen. Gary Luck, XVIII Airborne Corps commander, leads his troops. (XVIII Airborne Corps historian)

17: The Bulge

O n 16 December 1944 General Montgomery sent to his command, the 21st Army Group, his estimate of the current situation: "The enemy is at present fighting a defensive campaign on all fronts; his situation is such that he cannot stage major offensive operations." General Omar Bradley, commanding the U.S. 12th Army Group, held much the same view based on reports from his intelligence staff.

Exactly three months earlier in his "Wolf's Lair" headquarters in East Prussia, Hitler listened to Col. Gen. Alfred Jodl present a discouraging briefing on the general situation on the fronts in the east and the west. In September, Jodl explained carefully, well aware of Hitler's distaste for bad news, German forces were withdrawing all across France and were being attacked and pursued relentlessly in the east. Present at the briefing were three other top-level generals from Hitler's General Staff. Soon Hitler stopped the briefing. For a few moments there was dead silence. Then he said, "I have just made a momentous decision." He stood, pointing at the map. "I shall go over to the counterattack, that is to say, here, out of the Ardennes, with the object being Antwerp." The German officers could not believe what they were hearing. They knew the extent of their tremendous losses on both fronts and, given their almost hopeless situation in the east, could only hope, at best, for some sort of a negotiated peace in the west.

In *Mein Kampf* Hitler had written, "Strength lies not in defense but in attack." He was ordering his commanders to carry out that principle. In October, as he continued to oversee his General Staff's planning for his bold, offensive strategy, he recalled seventy-year-old Field Marshal Gerd von Rundstedt to organize and implement this mission that seemed impossible to the minds of his senior generals.

Rundstedt himself was dumbfounded by the order. It required assembling a vast force, moving it over fifty miles to the Meuse (Maas) River, and then pushing it more than 110 miles to Antwerp. But Rundstedt, ever the Prussian, obediently and resolutely followed what he presumed were suicidal orders. He pressured the staff to force into high gear Germany's wartime factories making planes, tanks, and guns, and he began to collect the men, the armor, the ammunition, the fuel—all the necessary stuff of battle, now in shorter and shorter supply. He was unbelievably successful. He amassed 200,000 men in thirteen infantry and seven panzer divisions with almost 1,000 tanks and some 2,000 artillery pieces. Hitler had initially planned to launch the attack in November, but Operation Market Garden had upset his schedule. By early December, Rundstedt had deployed his force along a sixty-mile front in heavily wooded areas inside Germany behind the Siegfried Line. For a second wave, Rundstedt had five more divisions ready to attack. And, in reserve, he had another formidable force bolstered with 450 tanks.

Hitler's overall plan was to drive an armored wedge of three armies between Montgomery's British force and Lt. Gen. Courtney Hodges' U.S. First Army. The SS Sixth Panzer Army was on the German right, the Fifth Panzer Army in the center, and the Seventh Army on the left. The Fifth Panzer Army's mission was to secure the road network hubs at St-Vith and Bastogne in Belgium. The Sixth's mission was to reach the Meuse on D day plus 3 and then continue the blitz to seize Antwerp, cutting off a most important harbor for much needed Allied supplies.

To accomplish his mission, Rundstedt had first to seize St-Vith and Bastogne, both major road and rail hubs. Then he would press on and take Antwerp, at which time, the German high command reasoned, the Allies would negotiate a peace. The path of the attack followed much the same route that the Germans had used in 1870, in 1914, and in Hitler's overwhelmingly successful 1940 blitzkreig.

On the Allied side, Eisenhower's broad-front strategy had stretched his troops farther and farther and thinner and thinner the deeper they advanced toward the German homeland. By mid-November, the Allied offensive had slowed almost to a halt. On 15 December, the U.S. VIII Corps situation report stated simply, "There is nothing to report." The VIII Corps lay directly in the path of the massive German onslaught.

The U.S. sector in the Ardennes Mountains was quiet. Some of the overly relaxed commanders referred to it as a "ghost front," and one company commander even described it as a "nursery and old folk's home." By mid-December the Allies were almost at rest, with many experienced troops on leave, and replacements filling many ranks.

Some of the senior officers of XVIII Airborne Corps were also "at ease." General Ridgway was in England—not at his advanced CP in Reims. Major General Taylor was in the United States, discussing with the army staff the reorganization of the airborne division based on recent combat realities. Colonel Higgins, the assistant division commander of the 101st, was in England with five of his senior unit commanders, lecturing on the lessons learned in Holland.

Lieutenant General Courtney Hodges's U.S. First Army was on line in what would become the center of the German assault. His VIII Corps, commanded by Maj. Gen. Troy H. Middleton, covered an eighty-eight-mile front north of the Ardennes. Middleton had three divisions, two of which were green. The 99th Division had been in Europe for only a month, and the 106th had had little combat experience. The third, the 28th, had fought tough battles in the Hürtgen Forest and was in the process of reequipping and absorbing new troops. The 14th Cavalry Regiment, attached to the 106th Division, was the most combat-ready force in VIII Corps.

Essentially, the Allies were deployed along the front in a series of strongpoints connected by intermittent patrols. No ground reconnaissance probed deeply into the German sector. The weather was another factor that lulled the Allied high command into believing that all was quiet along the front. The Ardennes were knee-deep in snow and mud, the temperature was low one day and high the next, and the skies were laden with fog and clouds, making aerial reconnaissance sporadic at best. The Allies did not expect an attack in such miserable weather. To further complicate the situation, the Germans enforced strict radio silence and security measures. On the Germans' *Null-Tag* (Zero Day), 16 December, the front they shared with the Allies exhibited nothing but tranquility, which was about to be shattered.

From 0530 until almost 0700, SS Lt. Gen. Josef "Sepp" Dietrich's Sixth Panzer Army's 1,000-plus artillery guns laid down barrage after barrage along Middleton's front. Dietrich concentrated his attack along a front about thirteen miles wide. With its ninety Tiger tanks the Sixth Panzer Army was the strongest force deployed. The other two German armies bombarded along their fronts with similar heavy concentrations of artillery. While the shocked U.S. troops were suffering from the blasts and digging into their defenses, German storm trooper battalions marched forward through the mud and snow. Among the forward elements of some of the attacking columns, English-speaking Germans rode in captured U.S. jeeps and wore U.S. uniforms taken from U.S. prisoners of war (POWs). (However, some of the U.S. POWs ordered to strip in the prison camps, the *stalags*, had cut their uniforms into shreds rather than turn them over.) Many of these Germans in U.S. combat gear managed to pass undetected through outlying guard posts; the storm troopers were immediately followed by tanks and armored columns. Because of this deception practiced by the Germans, Allied commanders ordered all guards on forward posts to challenge everyone—including high-ranking U.S. officers.

In the area of Maj. Gen. Allen Jones's 106th Division and the 14th Cavalry regiment, the defense was uncoordinated. On 18 December, three German divisions converged on St-Vith and surrounded the 106th's 422d and 423d Infantry Regiments' positions on the Schnee Eifel. On 19 December, the Germans pounded the two units with artillery throughout the day and drew a tighter and tighter circle around them. A desperate attempt to air-drop ammunition and rations to the beleaguered regiments was unsuccessful. By 1600 on 19 December, unable to break out of the tight encirclement, almost all personnel of the two regiments and their support forces—over 7,000 men—surrendered. One battalion did manage to escape until 21 December, and one company-sized group from the 422d made it out safely.

In the early hours of 17 December, the Sixth Panzer Army had broken through along the U.S. V Corps–VII Corps boundary. Through the Losheim Gap between Germany and Belgium, an advance element of the SS 1st Panzer Division, Combat Group Peiper, commanded by Col. Joachim Peiper, marched with grim determination with the advancing infantry. Combat Group Peiper had 2,200 men, 100 tanks and self-propelled assault guns, and orders to spearhead the main assault to the Meuse River without regard for boundaries, defenses, or time. Peiper followed his orders to the letter—and indulged his unit in the traditional SS order to terrorize as it advanced. South of the main panzer attack, his men moved through the Losheim Gap and entered the Belgian town of Büllingen (Bullange), three miles behind the U.S. lines. Peiper's troops refueled their tanks with captured gasoline and proceeded to murder fifty U.S. POWs. Then, just after noon, Peiper's group

overran a 7th Armored Division field artillery observation post southeast of Malmédy and slaughtered another eighty U.S. prisoners. Before
his murderous offensive action was over, Peiper had killed at least 300
U.S. POWs and 100 unarmed Belgians in a dozen different locations.
"Word of the Malmedy Massacre spread," wrote Roger Cirillo in *Ar-
dennes-Alsace*, "and within hours units across the front realized that the
Germans were prosecuting the offensive with a special grimness. American resistance stiffened."

Peiper's group was halfway to the Meuse when it ran into a unit from
the U.S. 9th Armored Division that stopped it and hit it hard at the bridge
at Stavelot. Then an engineer squad from the 9th blew up the bridge.
So Peiper headed for Trois-Ponts, literally "three bridges," one of which
he desperately needed. Here, though, with speed and courage under
fire, men of the U.S. 51st Engineers blew up two of them, and men of
291st Engineer Battalion did the same to the third. Peiper was stopped
cold. By 20 December Peiper's force was out of fuel and surrounded.
During the night of 23 December Peiper ordered his men to destroy
their equipment, abandon their vehicles, and walk out to escape capture.
In spite of its murderous attacks, his force was badly beaten, with only
800 surviving of the original 5,000 men in the combat group. Peiper left
behind a fifty-man suicide squad, many wounded, and 131 prisoners.

The Germans pulled out all the stops in their blitzkrieg, including the
use of paratroopers. During the night of 17 December, 1,200 German
paratroopers and 300 dummies were landed behind the U.S. lines on
the Hohe Venn's high point at Baraque Michel. A separate special operation, led by the legendary Lt. Col. Otto Skorzeny, also used small
teams of English-speaking German soldiers in U.S. uniforms to create
diversions. The paratroopers landed in a widely dispersed pattern and
then hid in the woods in small groups. In reality, though, neither of the
special operations had much of an impact, one report having it that the
dummies were more effective than the live paratroopers.

By 17 December 1944, Eisenhower's intelligence had become more
aware of the German strength and objectives. It was obvious that the Germans had to reach the Meuse quickly and then turn north. But the German divisions were being slowed down in jammed-up columns trying to
pass through the narrow Losheim Gap. Even though the area was still
controlled by U.S. VIII Corps, the center of it had been overrun. Thus
it fell on Middleton to slow the German drive to the west, gaining time
for Eisenhower to bolster the shoulders north and south of the salient
and to prepare a counterattack.

Middleton committed his only reserves, Combat Command Reserve of the 9th Armored Division and seven battalions of VIII Corps and other army engineers at critical road hubs. But in the snow and mud of the area, the German tanks rolled through the immobilized U.S. forces. By dawn of 18 December, defenses had been shattered and three divisions of the XLVII Panzer Corps were charging toward the town of Bastogne.

On the afternoon of 17 December, at the request of Hodges, Eisenhower decided to commit his theater reserves—the XVIII Airborne Corps. With the absence of Ridgway and Taylor, Gavin was the corps's senior officer. He was at dinner with his staff the night of 17 December when he got a phone call from Col. "Doc" Eaton, the corps chief of staff. Eaton told Gavin that the corps had been alerted to move to the front after daylight the following day. Gavin told Eaton to pass the alert on to Brigadier General McAuliffe, the acting commander of the 101st Airborne Division, with Taylor and Higgins absent. Gavin's staff immediately went into action to alert the 82d Airborne Division's unit commanders, round up the trucks to move the division, and plan the details of the move. At 2100, Gavin got another call from Eaton telling him that the situation was now even more compelling. The XVIII Airborne Corps would be attached to Hodges's First Army, said Eaton, and the corps was ordered to move "without delay" toward Bastogne. There, Gavin would receive a more specific mission. Gavin gave his staff orders to move the division by truck toward Bastogne one hour after daylight the next morning, 18 December. He also told corps headquarters to move the 101st out at 1400 the afternoon of the same day. At 2330 on 17 December, therefore, after Gavin was satisfied that his orders were clear and were being implemented, he left for Hodges's First Army Headquarters in Spa. That same night, the troopers of the 82d and 101st got ready once again for combat—this time well aware of what they would need to carry and wear. But there were no parachutes: they were being committed as standard ground troops.

At 0200 on 18 December, one of Eisenhower's staff officers told Ridgway the details of his corps's commitment in the sudden action. Ridgway ordered up all C-47s available and, at dawn, left for France with his entire staff in fifty-five planes. He also alerted General Miley to get his 17th Airborne Division ("Thunder from Heaven") from England and to France as soon as possible. Unfortunately, fog and thick clouds were to ground the 17th in England for a week.

Gavin reported to Lieutenant General Hodges at 0900 on 18 December and informed him that the 82d and the 101st were in trucks on the way from Reims. Hodges and his staff briefed Gavin on the enemy's tactical situation. Hodges had been personally affected profoundly by the German onslaught but was well enough collected to tell Gavin that he was attaching the 82d to V Corps. Gavin's mission was to deploy his units to the vicinity of Werbomont, northwest of St-Vith, and to block the Sixth Panzer Army's advance. Hodges then laid out the plan for the 101st, assigning it to VIII Corps, whose headquarters were in the hub town of Bastogne. This arrangement scenario set up one of the best known battles of World War II.

The advance elements of the 82d started to arrive in Werbomont at about 2000 on 18 December. By the next morning, after a long truck march through wretched ground conditions, the entire division arrived in the area and began to trudge for miles along muddy, snowy roads to their defensive positions.

McAuliffe had received his marching orders at 2030 on the night of 17 December, and mounted his 11,840 troops in ten-ton, open-bay trucks, hastily gathered from Rouen and Paris. The 101st then bumped and slid its way over 107 muddy miles to Bastogne. When the division arrived there, they found that the Germans were already overrunning the light defenses around the town. McAuliffe directed Julian Ewell, the 501st's commander, and the first to arrive, to move his regiment east in the direction of Longvilly. The rapid deployment of the 501st made it possible for McAuliffe to set up the defenses of Bastogne before the Germans could mount a strong attack.

Ridgway had arrived in Werbomont the night of 18 December and established his headquarters in an old farmhouse. As the German attack continued, Ridgway's corps grew stronger with the addition of the U.S. 3d Armored Division and the U.S. 30th Infantry Division. He and his staff then planned the defense of the northern flank of the "bulge" so far produced by the German operation.

The German armored assault continued with force and speed. On 19 December German formations cut the north-south road from Bastogne to Werbomont in the vicinity of Houffalize and surrounded St-Vith in the north. By 20 December Bastogne was also encircled, the Germans' having already thrust thirty miles into Allied defenses in Belgium. The bulge was deepening, but north and south of St-Vith and Bastogne U.S. units held their ground.

Ridgway was ordered to hold along the line Stoumont-Stavelot-Malmédy and counterattack toward Trois-Ponts to stop the Germans in the northwest. He assumed command of the sector generally south of the Amblève River, including Houffalize. Based on his orders, Gavin sent Rube Tucker's 504th to seize the high ground northwest of Rahier, Bill Ekman's 505th to take the high ground in the vicinity of Basse-Bodeux, and Roy Lindquist's 508th to occupy the high ground near Chevron. Lindquist moved one company to the crossroads one mile east of Bra. Charles Billingslea's 325th Glider Infantry held on in Werbomont, with the 3d Battalion near Barvaux and one company at the road hub at Manhay. The commanders relayed the orders down the ranks, and the troops trudged through the mud and snow, occupied their positions on the night of 19–20 December, and immediately sent patrols out to reconnoiter the enemy.

"Shortly after daylight December 20," wrote General Gavin, "I met Colonel Reuben Tucker, 504th commanding officer, in the town of Rahier at which time he had just received intelligence from civilians that approximately 125 vehicles, including approximately 30 tanks, had moved through the town that afternoon before moving in the direction of Cheneux. If this were the case, the seizure of the bridge over the Ambleve River at Cheneux was imperative if their further movement was to be blocked.

"Initial contact was made at the western exit of Cheneux by a patrol which had been sent from Rahier by the 1st Battalion of the 504th. They were engaged at once and a heavy fight took place, lasting all day long. This German force, we know now, was the advance guard of a reinforced battalion of the SS 1st Panzer Division. The 1st of the 504th drove them back into Cheneux." Gavin ordered Tucker to move toward Rahier and Cheneux and link up with the 505th at Trois-Ponts. The 1st Battalion of the 504th had orders to take the towns of Brume, Rahier, and Cheneux.

Captain Helgeson, B Company commander, 1st Battalion, sent a patrol from Rahier and made contact with the Germans at the western exit of Cheneux. The patrol ended up in a heavy firefight all day long. Helgeson moved the rest of the company up and, after another firefight, captured a German 77mm self-propelled howitzer, which his men used to knock out two enemy machine guns. Near Cheneux, he ran into strong enemy forces, so he sent two platoons along the sides of the road, so that as one advanced, the other covered it with fire. But in Cheneux the Germans were ready. They shelled B Company with fire from a heavy mortar and two 20mm flak wagons, with antiaircraft guns lowered to fire flat across the ground. Six of Helgeson's men died in this attempt. Helgeson brought up the captured halftrack with its 77mm gun, but intense 20mm fire drove it back. His third platoon tried to advance but was stopped just ten yards from the enemy line, which was a formidable position with two heavy machine guns and the 20mm gun, all surrounded by barbed wire. At 1700 Helgeson pulled his troops back about 200 yards and set up a defensive position in the woods.

Later Helgeson met with his battalion commander, Maj. Willard E. Harrison, who had had a session with Colonel Tucker, in which Tucker had ordered Harrison to make a night attack on Cheneux. Harrison gave the mission to his B and C Companies. Company B led the attack and, after a seemingly easy march across some open terrain, got to within about 200 yards from Cheneux but then was caught in a barrage of 20mm, machine gun, rifle, artillery, and mortar fire. Staff Sergeant James M. Boyd remembered that the men began to fall "like flies." Fire support never materialized, and the first two assault teams were almost wiped out.

B and C Companies fought a bitter, close-in, and, in some cases, hand-to-hand battle with the Germans in the town: at a roadblock riflemen managed to kill twenty Germans, and Private Barkley of C Company, who had no ammunition left, climbed up the side of a flak wagon and slit the German gunner's throat with his knife. By 2200 that evening of 20 December the battalion held the edge of the town, while the Germans holed up inside some buildings. But Harrison's losses were heavy. For instance, SSgt. Clyde Farrier had become B Company's commander because all its officers were killed or wounded. Finally, Colonel Tucker sent word that G Company of his 3d Battalion would attack through the 2d Battalion and take the town.

What was left of B and C Companies, plus a platoon from the 307th Engineers, dug in on the high ground around the town. Some Germans crawled out of Cheneux at about 2300 on 20 December. At 0300 the next morning, the 3d of the 504th arrived and took over the town. In B Company there were no officers, and only eighteen men were left; C Company had three officers and thirty-eight men. But the 1st Battalion's fight and the arrival of the 3d Battalion 504th, secured the town and the bridge across the Amblève River. In addition, the 3d Battalion took over fourteen flak wagons, four 105mm howitzers, and many vehicles. When

Gavin showed up the next day, he was impressed with the contraband but very distraught at the loss of his men.

The German force here, as noted by General Gavin, was the advance guard of a battalion of the SS 1st Panzer Division; the rest of the 3d Battalion 504th had come up on line and driven this advance guard back into Cheneux. In the same period, by 0900 on 19 December the entire 82d had already arrived in Werbomont and began to set up defensive positions and roadblocks. By this time, as well, the 101st had dug in around Bastogne.

By 22 December McAuliffe found himself in command of an odd assortment of U.S. forces. In addition to his four airborne regiments, he had the 969th and 755th Field Artillery Battalions, both armed with 155mm howitzers, which were far more powerful than the pack 75s of airborne division artillery. McAuliffe also had Combat Command B of the 10th Armored Division and Combat Command R of the 9th Armored Division, but the two combat commands had a total of only forty combat-ready tanks. The 705th Tank Destroyer Battalion was also in the perimeter. All such nonairborne units played a decisive role in the defense of Bastogne.

On 20 December, the Germans completed the isolation of Bastogne by cutting the last road out of town. The continued success of the German attack depended on capturing Bastogne, which was a potential prime obstacle to the push west. Powerful German armored and infantry units tried to break through the 101st's lines on the north, then the south, and finally the west, but were thrown back in each attack. One of the encircled, veteran troopers of the 101st made the wry comment that "the Germans have us surrounded—the poor bastards."

At noon on 20 December, with the Germans increasing the size of the bulge, Eisenhower divided the battlefield. In the north, Montgomery took over the U.S. Ninth and First Armies. In the south, Patton assumed command of Middleton's VIII Corps and its Bastogne garrison. Patton moved forces from as far as 120 miles to attack positions south of the German salient. On 21 December, McAuliffe received an order from Middleton to hold Bastogne "at all costs."

Lieutenant General Hasso von Manteuffel, the commander of the Fifth Panzer Army, attacked into the center of the U.S. VIII Corps. He had ordered two of his divisions to bypass Bastogne and speed toward the Meuse and he hoped to encircle Bastogne. On 22 December, Manteuffel's 26th Volksgrenadier Division and the XLVIII Panzer Corps' artillery closed around Bastogne, confident of forcing the surrender of the U.S. forces caught there.

At 1130 that same day Manteuffel's emissaries, a major, a captain, and two privates, one of them carrying a white flag, arrived at the front lines of the 101st, at a defensive position held by F Company of the 327th Glider Infantry Regiment. They were met by three 101st troopers, Sgt. Oswald Butler, Pfc. Ernest Premetz, and one other. Premetz, a medic, could speak some German. For this meeting the German captain at first spoke in English. He said to Butler, "We are parlementaires—we wish to speak to the American commander of Bastogne." Premetz helped in the discussion that followed. The German privates were held under guard, and the two officers were blindfolded and taken to the commander of the 2d Battalion, 327th, Maj. Alvin Jones. One of the officers handed Jones the surrender ultimatum, dated 22 December 1944 and signed by Lt. Gen. Heinrich von Leuttwitz, the XLVII Panzer Corps commander. It read:

To the USA Commander of the encircled town of Bastogne.

The fortune of war is changing. This time the U.S.A. forces in and near Bastogne have been encircled by strong German armored units. More German armored units have crossed the river Ourthe near Ortheuville, have taken Marche and reached St. Hubert by passing through Hompre-Sibret-Tillet. Libramont is in German hands.

There is only one possibility to save the encircled U.S.A. troops from total annihilation: In order to think it over, a term of two hours will be granted beginning with the presentation of this note.

If this proposal should be rejected, one German Artillery Corps and six heavy A. A. Battalions are ready to annihilate the U.S.A. troops in and near Bastogne. The order for firing will be given immediately after this two hours' term.

All the serious civilian losses caused by this artillery fire would not correspond with the well-known American humanity.

The German Commander

Jones took the ultimatum to the 101st Division CP and handed it to Brigadier General McAuliffe, who asked him what it was all about. "They want us to surrender," was the reply. McAuliffe's immediate reaction was a curt, "Aw, nuts," and he laughed. He knew that he had to reply, but how, he wondered aloud. At the division CP with McAuliffe were Lt. Col. Harry Kinnard, the 101st's G-3 officer and the rest of the division staff. "Well, sir," opined Kinnard, "that first remark of yours would be hard to beat." The rest of the staff heartily agreed. And so McAuliffe became renowned in airborne history when he wrote in pencil on the German ultimatum, "To the German Commander, NUTS! The American Commander." He gave the paper to Col. Joseph H. Harper, commander of the 327th, who had just arrived at the CP, and told him to take the message back to the German officers in the woods at the 327th's perimeter.

Harper met the German officers and said, "I have the American commander's reply." "Is it written or verbal?" asked the German captain. "Written," said Harper. "Is the reply in the negative or the affirmative? If it is the latter, I will negotiate further," continued the captain. "The reply is decidedly not affirmative," he said. The German major nodded as if he understood.

Harper took the two officers back to the main road in his jeep, had the blindfolds removed, and then told them, "If you don't understand what 'Nuts' means, in plain English, it is the same as 'go to hell.' And I will tell you something else: If you continue this attack we will kill every goddam German that tries to break into this city." The captain saluted Harper sharply and said: "We will kill many Americans. This is war." "On your way, Bud," said Harper. And then added to his later regret: "And good luck to you." The four Germans took off toward their lines, and Harper walked back to his jeep. It was 1350 hours.

Later Kinnard reminisced: "We had absolutely no idea sending back 'Nuts' would have the kind of impact it did. But I'm not surprised, because 'nuts' is a typical American word, and it was exactly how we felt about surrendering. It was also a huge morale boost for the public back in the States hearing about our desperate situation of being surrounded at Bastogne."

Robert Wright, a medic with the 501st, remembered how bitter the weather was, with subzero temperatures, the countless injured soldiers, and the dearth of medical supplies. As he recalled it: "We were trained to be successful. So we all agreed that was as good an answer as anybody could come up with, because that was how everyone felt."

Allison Blaney was a medic with the 326th Medical Battalion. He said the "Nuts" reply was "a priceless memory." "It provided the motivation needed to show the Germans just how determined and dedicated we were. And I don't believe anyone knew or could have guessed to the outcome that one word would have on the world. It was just fantastic."

It was out in the field that Tom Splan, a forward observer with the 377th Parachute Field Artillery Battalion, heard about the "Nuts" reply. "I said it's a damned good thing McAuliffe said that," he remembers, "because I wasn't about to give in. And while I didn't fully realize that we were surrounded with such force against us, it didn't matter, because that answer fired everybody up." For the rest of the day, he and two of his buddies remembered they laughed and said what a great way it was to say "go to hell." "It was a standing joke among us, and all day long we had conversations like 'nuts to you' and 'nuts to the weather' and 'nuts' to everything else. . . . And even though so many years have passed, I still think and laugh about it."

(Today, Bastogne proudly hosts a NUTS museum and a NUTS café. Many stores and shops in town sell NUTS t-shirts, coffee mugs, and other items.)

The massive German artillery fire did not materialize as promised. At 1600, and again an hour later, some fifty Germans made feeble forays against F Company's position, but they were beaten back both times. Later that night, however, and for the next four nights, the Luftwaffe blasted the city with heavy bombing.

"For four days fighting raged in a clockwise rotation around Bastogne's southern and western perimeter, further constricting the defense within the low hills and patches of woods surrounding the town," writes Roger Cirillo.

> The infantry held ground, with the armor scurrying to seal penetrations or to support local counterattacks. Once the overcast weather had broken, the defenders received both air support and aerial resupply, making it imperative for Manteuffel to turn some of his precious armor back to quickly crush the American defense, a large deadly threat along his southern flank.
>
> Meanwhile, as Bastogne held, Patton's Third Army units streamed northward. Maj. Gen. John B. Millikin's newly arrived III Corps headquarters took command of the 4th Armored and 26th and 80th Infantry Divisions, in a move quickly discovered and monitored by the Germans' effective radio intercept units. In response,

Bradenberger's Seventh Army, charged with the crucial flank guard mission in Hitler's offensive, rushed its lagging infantry divisions forward to block the expected American counterattack.

The situation inside Bastogne was becoming more and more desperate. "Christmas Day was a pig," remembered a 101st sergeant. The 101st's division history recorded that "to the men of the division it seemed that the end was at hand. On Christmas night, many of them shook hands with their comrades. They said to one another that it would probably be their last night together." But relief was at hand. The 4th Armored Division, with Lt. Col. Creighton W. Abrams's 37th Tank Battalion in the lead, was on the way. On Christmas night, Abrams and his tanks and the 53d Armored Infantry Battalion were six miles from Bastogne. By noon the next day they had fought their way to Clochimont, a small hamlet three miles from Bastogne. As Abrams deployed his tanks and moved forward, his lead company ran into entrenched Germans firing *panzerfausts* at his tanks. Abrams advanced with some infantrymen and captured all the Germans.

Abrams got back in his tank and pulled up alongside the tank of Capt. Jimmie Leach, his B Company commander, and told him to knock out an antitank gun in the next town that was firing on A Company. Leach sent a platoon forward to get into a better position, but Abrams became impatient. He moved his tank up next to Leach's, and barked a command to his crew. Abrams's gunner, John Gatusky, scored a direct hit. Leach remembers the occasion clearly. "One round, one antitank gun in the air, by Creighton W. Abrams, Lieutenant Colonel, Cavalry. . . . I tell you, it was a sight to behold."

Lieutenant Colonel "Jigger" Jacques was the commander of the 53d Armored Infantry Battalion. At 1630 on the day after Christmas, Abrams and Jacques stood on the side of the road discussing their next attack. From the road, they could see hundreds of C-47s dropping supplies among the troops in Bastogne. Captain Bill Dwight, Abrams's liaison officer, remembered the drops. "I saw those damn C-47s coming in to drop their colored parachutes for the 101st. They . . . were taking one hell of a beating. We trembled standing there and watching it. . . . After Abe watched that, he said, 'Well, if those fellows can take that, we're going in right now.' And that was it."

What Abrams had done was switch his mission without asking his boss, the Combat Command R commander. His original orders had him en

route to seize Sibert, a well-defended town. Abrams now had only twenty
Sherman tanks left in his battalion, a few more than one of his companies would normally have. Harold Cohen remembered that Abrams
knew that he was taking a great personal risk and that he could have been
court-martialed for disobeying orders. Abrams himself "realized that it
was then or never. And he took the calculated risk."

Abrams gave the orders for the change in mission. He gave Captain
Dwight command of the two units that would lead the attack—Company
C of the 37th Tank Battalion and Company C of the 53d Armored Infantry. Abrams told Dwight to contact the 101st and let them know he
was coming. He also called for heavy artillery concentrations on Assenois,
just south of Bastogne. At 1610 Abrams told Dwight, "This is it." Dwight's
force moved out with his tanks in the lead.

Lieutenant Charles Boggess, commander of Abrams's C Company,
and in the lead tank, led the charge on Assenois with all guns blazing
and throttles wide open. Thirteen batteries of artillery blasted Assenois,
and the U.S. tanks and the infantry halftracks roared forward. Four tanks
made it through safely, but a halftrack took a direct hit and slowed down
the column. Another was stopped by a fallen telephone pole. After
Abrams and his tankers got out and cleared the road, the rest of the column went forward. Some infantrymen even dismounted and fought the
Germans in Assenois in hand-to-hand fights. Abrams left the infantry in
Assenois and pressed ahead with his four tanks.

In the woods along the road ahead of this small column of tanks
Boggess saw some Germans. His tanks sprayed the area with machine gun
fire. "I saw the enemy in confusion on both sides of the road," remembered Boggess. "Obviously, they were surprised by an entry on this road,
as some were standing in a chow line. They fell like dominoes." Then
Boggess found some foxholes. He yelled, "Come on out, this is the
Fourth Armored." No one moved. "I called again and again, and finally
an officer emerged from the nearest foxhole and approached the tank.
He reached up a hand, and with a smile, said. 'I'm Lieutenant Webster
of the 326th Engineers, 101st Airborne Division. Glad to see you.'" The
road to Bastogne was cut at 1650 on the day after Christmas. A *Yank* correspondent wrote that "as dusk started to come down, Col. Abrams rode
through—a short, stocky man with sharp features—already a legendary
figure in this war."

Patton wrote in his diary that "It was a daring thing and well done."
He wrote to his wife, Beatrice, that "the relief of Bastogne is the most

brilliant operation we have this far performed and is in my opinion the outstanding achievement of this war."

The parachute drops that Captain Dwight witnessed while he was on the road to Bastogne were part of a relief effort requested by General McAuliffe. The 101st and the surrounded troops had taken a relentless pounding from German artillery and the Luftwaffe and were in desperate need of medical and other supplies. On 26 December, a team of pathfinders parachuted into a DZ south of the division's perimeter, and a half hour later, eleven gliders, shot through by German antiaircraft fire, landed on target and brought in 32,000 pounds of medical supplies and five teams of combat doctors. While landing, three surgeons were killed by the antiaircraft fire. The next day another glider relief operation ended badly: Fifteen of the fifty gliders and seventeen tug ships were shot down.

The first aerial resupply of the 101st took place as early as 23 December, by which time the artillery had become woefully short of ammunition. For instance, the 463d Parachute Field Artillery in support of the 327th was down to 200 rounds. By 1600 of the same day, 241 C-47s dropped 1,400 bundles, totaling 144 tons, and the troops on the ground recovered 95 percent of them.

Meanwhile, as the besieged 101st was fighting gallantly in the much publicized Bastogne defense, the 82d was engaged in tough combat along the northern shoulder of the bulge.

On 21 December the encircled armor forces in St-Vith withdrew through the lines of the 82d. On the afternoon of 22 December, the German SS 2d Panzer Division following the retreating U.S. armor hit the 504th and 325th. The 325th's outposts gave some ground, and Colonel Billingslea finally ordered his men out of the outpost line (only 44 of the 116 men who had been holding the crossroad outpost made it back). Even though it took a severe pounding, the 504th, through its ardent and costly defense, won its second Presidential Unit Citation.

Along the northern border of the bulge, the 509th Parachute Infantry Battalion and the 517th Parachute Combat Team were attached to the 3d Armored Division, fighting on the right of the 82d. (Major General Maurice Rose, commander of the 3d Armored, met a bloody death when he was captured and killed in cold blood by a German tanker on 31 March 1945.)

Private First Class Melvin B. Biddle, B Company of the 517th, was a lead scout when his battalion was ordered to move toward the town of

Hotton to root out some Germans holed up there. When he was 400 yards from the town, three snipers fired at Biddle. He checked the location of each one and then proceeded to kill them all. Just a few hundred yards farther along the road, he ran into a machine gun nest. He crawled through the snow to within hand grenade range and killed the German crew with one throw. When a second machine gun took him under fire, he ran toward the gun and killed all five Germans. However, the company had not yet taken Hotton.

At dusk B Company halted and dug into the snow; during the night Biddle scouted the woods and found a direct route into Hotton. The next morning, the company resumed its attack, and Biddle, who was later awarded the Medal of Honor, knocked out another machine gun nest on the road to town. The battalion secured the town that afternoon, 24 December.

By late December, the German offensive had begun to lose its initial impetus and slowly came to a halt. In one last attempt to penetrate the northern shoulder of the U.S. defenses, Rundstedt thrust his SS 9th Panzer and 62d Volksgrenadier Divisions against the 82d on 27 December. In this desperate and fierce attack, the 3d Battalion, 508th was literally run over by German armor: when the paratroopers saw the tanks coming they ducked into their foxholes and let the tanks pass over them. After this impressive action Lt. Col. Louis G. Mendez Jr., the 3d Battalion's commander, obtained the reserve company of the 2d Battalion, 508th, on his left and counterattacked and drove the SS 9th Panzer from its position, restoring his main line of resistance. According to General Gavin, "The Storm Troopers' losses were extremely heavy. From one field alone, 62 bodies were later removed."

By 3 January 1945 the Allies were ready to attack and punch through the bulge. Part of Hodges's First Army on the northern boundary was the XVIII Airborne Corps. Collins's VII Corps was to the west. By this time Ridgway had under his command the 1st, 30th, and 84th Infantry Divisions and the 82d Airborne with the 551st Parachute Infantry Battalion and 517th Parachute Combat Team attached. In the attack, Ridgway would cover the northeastern flank of VII Corps and attack toward St-Vith. His plan called for the 1st Infantry Division and the 82d to make the main attack eastward and then later leapfrog the 30th and 84th.

The 82d's 551st had a difficult time: battling through forests, the battalion came under heavy German artillery fire that decimated it. On 7

January 1945 Lt. Col. Wood Joerg was killed by a shell that hit the tree under which he was standing, the command of the battalion falling to Maj. William N. Holm, twenty-eight years old (class of 1940). The 551st charged on.

At Holzheim, a village in the 508th's zone, 1st Sgt. Leonard A. Funk of C Company had his rank and position validated by his action there. West of Holzheim eighty German POWs were being guarded by six U.S. soldiers, the rest of their company having pushed ahead. The POWs and the paratroopers guarding them were all wearing white snow camouflage over their uniforms. At a quick glance, it was difficult to tell German from American. Suddenly four armed Germans with a Luftwaffe officer came out of the woods and disarmed the U.S. troopers. Just then, Sergeant Funk came around a building with some other paratroopers and moved up to this odd group, Funk being under the impression that the POWs were still under U.S. guard. But suddenly, the German major pulled his Schmeisser machine gun pistol, stuck it in Funk's ribs, and demanded his surrender. Funk began very slowly to remove his tommy gun that hung by its strap from his shoulder. With a flipping motion usually reserved for action movies, Funk in one lightning stroke grabbed the tommy gun in midair, pulled the trigger, and killed the major. Then, like an action movie hero, he sprayed the other armed Germans while the suddenly freed paratroopers used their knives to kill the closest Germans. Funk's heroic action restored the POWs to POW status. Later, in a White House ceremony, President Harry Truman would award Funk the Medal of Honor. With his other awards, including three Purple Hearts, the Distinguished Service Cross for heroism in Holland, and a Silver Star for valor in Normandy, First Sergeant Funk became the most highly decorated paratrooper and his decorations for valor equaled those of better known Lt. Audie Murphy of the 3d Division.

The 82d's next battle was launched on 3 January. As Gavin remembered it, "The Division attacked, completely overrunning the 62d V.G. Division and the 9th SS Panzer Division, and capturing 2,500 prisoners, including five battalion commanders. It regained its former position on the Their-Du-Mont heights.

"From here, the division withdrew to a rest area from which it was later committed to the attack east of St. Vith, attacking through deep snow over thickly wooded mountains and overrunning a considerable group of German defensive forces in a constant day and night attack lasting for six days. Ultimately, they drove into the Siegfried Line to seize Udenbreth and the ridge extending south."

On 6 February the 99th Infantry Division came on line and relieved the 82d, and Gavin moved his troopers to reserve positions near Vielsalm. When Ridgway's XVIII Airborne Corps occupied the Hürtgen Forest sector, Gavin moved his division to that area. A few days later the XVIII Corps advanced toward the Roer River. On 17 February, Gavin was ordered to take his men back to their home base in camps at Sissone and Swippes near Reims.

Going back to 27 December 1944, the day after Colonel Abrams and his tanks broke through to Bastogne, General Taylor arrived by jeep. The Germans were then continuing to attack the 101st. On 3 January, the Germans launched a strong infantry-tank attack on the northern sector of the 101st's perimeter. The next day the Germans hit the 327th's position but here the airborne troopers prevailed and drove the Germans back. On 13 January the 101st went on the attack toward Bourcy, a small town five miles northeast of Bastogne and four days later Bourcy was in the hands of the division.

On 26 January 1945, Taylor received orders to move his division south into the French province of Alsace along the French-German border. The 101st was attached to the Seventh Army and assigned a defensive role. One month later, with new orders the division was relieved and ordered back to its home base in Camp Mourmelon near Reims.

Back on 18 December 1944, Ridgway had ordered General Miley to move his 17th Airborne Division to France as soon as possible. Bad weather prevented the movement by air until 23 December, when the division air-landed in France and moved to an assembly area near Reims. On Christmas Day, the division was attached to Third Army and ordered into a defensive position thirty miles long along the Meuse River near Charleville, France. When the threat to that area had eased by New Year's Day, the division moved by truck to the town of Neufchâteau, southwest of Bastogne, and then marched to the battered village of Morhet, on the south side of the bulge, arriving there on 3 January. Miley and his troops relieved the 11th Armored Division and became part of Patton's Third Army. The next day, Patton ordered the 17th and the 87th Infantry Division to attack a number of towns to the west and rear of Bastogne and clear the Germans out of the area. Patton told Miley that "there's nothing out in front of you." Miley wondered who had cut up the 87th and the 11th Armored when they fought over the same terrain just hours be-

fore. But he had the mission—and no time to send out patrols or reconnoiter the area.

At 0815 on 4 January, the troopers of the 101st began their march
north from Morhet through heavy snow drifts, thick fog, and bitter cold.
On the left flank of the 101st the 17th moved out. Miley planned his attack with two regiments in the assault. On the right was the 194th Glider
Infantry Regiment, commanded by Col. James R. "Bob" Pierce (class of
1922), forty-five years old. Attached to his regiment was the 550th Glider
Infantry Battalion commanded by Lt. Col. Ed Sachs (class of 1930),
thirty-seven years old. On the left was the other regiment in the assault,
the 513th Parachute Infantry Regiment, commanded by Col. James
Coutts (class of 1932), thirty-five years old. In reserve, to meet any German armored counterattacks, were the 193d Glider Infantry Regiment,
commanded by Col. Maurice Stubbs, and the 507th Parachute Infantry
Regiment, commanded by the battle-hardened Col. Edson D. "Little Caesar" Raff. For artillery support, Miley used his three pack 75mm howitzer
battalions: Kenneth L. Booth's 466th Parachute, Paul F. Oswald's 680th
Glider, and Joseph W. Keating's 681st Glider Field Artillery Battalions.

Once the attack was under way, the Germans launched dozens of tanks
and artillery barrages at the advancing infantrymen. "The 2,250 yards of
narrow, high-rimmed road northeast of Bastogne rightfully earned its
nickname of 'Dead Man's Ridge,'" according to Lt. Col. Bart Hagerman,
the 17th's historian. "Attacking in a driving snow storm, the Division battled for control of the ridge. It was a bitterly fought battle that saw the
17th suffer close to a thousand casualties during the three-day battle."
Noted military historian S. L. A. Marshall later wrote "that no other
American division suffered as brutal and as high a casualty rate in their
baptism of fire."

During the battle, Lt. Col. Allen C. "Ace" Miller and his unit, the 2d
Battalion, 513th Parachute Infantry Regiment, ran into a heavy barrage
from German mortars. E Company lost three company commanders
at the very start of the attack. Lieutenant Samuel Calhoun, platoon
leader in F Company, formed a skirmish line with his platoon and began a brave attack over some flat terrain. The Germans raked his line
with machine gun fire. Calhoun managed to slide back to his takeoff
point and tried to round up his men. Of the twenty-eight who started,
he could find only fourteen. Behind an embankment, he ordered these
men to fix bayonets and charge across the snow to the edge of the
woods where the Germans were in foxholes. As Calhoun and his men

reached the area, some thirty Germans rose out of their foxholes with their hands in the air.

In the area near Flamierge, the 513th had a run-in with Germans in a defensive position that flamed into a bloody battle. Sergeant Isadore S. "Izzy" Jachman was a twenty-year-old squad leader in B Company. He had been born in Berlin of Jewish parents; his father had fought for Germany in World War I. His mother had brought Jachman to the United States when he was only nine months old. Seven of his aunts still in Germany had been sent to concentration camps. At the start of World War II, Jachman volunteered for the paratroopers in hopes of helping to defeat Hitler. In the course of the battle near Flamierge, German tanks rumbled down the road toward Jachman's company, firing their machine guns as they came. The fire knocked out some of B Company's bazooka teams before they could reply. Under this fire, Jachman ran across an open field to the bazooka teams, picked up a bazooka, loaded it, fired, and knocked out the first tank. He loaded again, ran up the road, all the time under heavy automatic-weapons fire, and knocked out a second tank. The rest of the panzer column broke off and withdrew. But while Jachman was firing at the second tank, a burst from a nearby German machine gun killed him. For his extraordinary valor Jachman was awarded a posthumous Medal of Honor.

On 7 January, with Stubbs's 193d and Raff's 507th in the vanguard, the 17th broke the Germans' line and sent them into retreat. In blizzard weather and with no air support, the "Thunder from Heaven" Division pushed ahead to seize Flamierge, Flamizoulle, Renaumont, and Héropont. Raff's patrols reached the Ourthe River and made contact with the British 51st Highland Division coming down from the north. As Hagerman put it, "The 'nose' of the Bulge had been pinched off and a large bag of prisoners fell to the advancing troops."

Attached to a special armored task force, the 193d drove to take Houffalize, while the rest of the Division moved on through Flamizoulle to take Gives, Bertogne, Compogne, Limerle, Watermal, Hautbellain, and Espeler.

After the capture of Espeler, the Division was again relieved and this time trucked to Luxembourg where they closed in an assembly area in the vicinity of Eschweiler. This action marked the end of the Ardennes campaign and the beginning of the Rhineland Campaign.

Miley's new mission was to drive the Germans back into Germany. With the 193d and the 507th in the lead, the division attacked across Luxembourg to the Ourthe River where the 507th, the 513th, and the 193d launched aggressive patrols across the swollen river. The 507th skirmished and advanced against the German 5th Airborne Division and was the first of Miley's units to set up on German soil.

Patrols from the division probed toward the Siegfried Line. "But," as Hagerman wrote, "as the snow began to melt and the river ran wide and swift, the launching of an attack had to be delayed." On 10 February 1945, the Division was relieved by the 6th Armored Division.

After the Battle of the Bulge and the advance into Germany, some airborne units suffered deactivation while others were strengthened by reorganization. On 1 March 1945, XVIII Airborne Corps closed down the veteran 509th Parachute Battalion, and Maj. Edmund Tomasik and his few survivors became "All Americans." Writing about the final disposition of the battalion, Morton N. Katz, the battalion historian said:

In bloody fighting at Sadzot the troopers accomplished their mission of holding the Manhay-Grandménil-Erézée supply lines at all costs and thoroughly defeated the 1st and 2d Battalions of the 25th SS Panzer Grenadier Division. This fighting from December 22–30, 1944, resulted in the unit's second citation. The men hung the Oak Leaf Cluster on their Distinguished Unit Badges, and the men of Company C on their second cluster.

Attached to the 7th Armored Division, the Battalion captured Born on January 20, 1945, and later captured Hunningen and cleared the woods north of St. Vith, to let the 7th Division roll through unopposed. After this action, seven officers and 43 men came down the hill on January 29, 1945, from the last action. All others were dead or hospitalized. Men released from hospitals came to the final CP in Trois-Ponts to face the bitter news that the 509th was to disband. Units were to be consolidated for the final push on Germany, and special units were no longer needed.

On March 1, 1945, the 509th Parachute Infantry Battalion was officially disbanded. Officers and men of this great outfit were assigned to the 82d Airborne Division, which was then at Stavelot, and some to the 13th Airborne Division.

This was also the case for about 100 officers and troopers of Major Holm's 551st Parachute Infantry Battalion. Colonel Graves and his

517th Parachute Combat Team joined the 13th Airborne Division, which had arrived in Europe in late January and was commanded by Maj. Gen. Eldridge Chapman, an early parachutist. Its three regiments were the 513th and 515th Parachute Infantry Regiments and the 326th Glider Infantry Regiment. Although the 13th had been alerted for combat jumps during the Battle of the Bulge, it was never committed.

When General Miley and his 17th Division were pulled off the line, they went back to their base camp at Châlons-sur-Marne. During early March, the decimated 193d Glider Infantry Regiment and the 550th were deactivated. The remaining men of the 193d were absorbed by the 194th and the men of the 550th became the 3d Battalion of the newly constituted 194th Regimental Combat Team. General Miley also took on the 464th Parachute Field Artillery Battalion. The 17th ended up with two parachute infantry regiments and one glider infantry regiment.

The airborne enthusiasts on Eisenhower's staff had yet another exciting plan in mind for the airborne troopers of the British 6th and the U.S. 17th and 82d Airborne Divisions. The two U.S. divisions and one brigade from the 6th were to be dropped in daylight on DZs in and around Berlin to capture Hitler and end the war. These thinkers were so positive that commanders had been briefed and maps issued. The capture of Berlin was part of Operation Eclipse, a SHAEF plan in formulation since the fall of 1944. By March of 1945 commanders began to take it seriously. Gavin wrote that "the 82d planned to land two parachute regiments just south of Tempelhof airfield. These regiments were to move to defensive positions well south of Tempelhof and block any German efforts to recapture the airfield." The 17th and the British 6th drew up similar plans. "But on March 28," wrote General Gavin, "Eisenhower sent a message to Marshal Stalin by way of our military mission in Moscow, which was headed by Major General John R. Deane. He outlined his plans for the immediate future and his intention to drive directly east to Leipzig. Implied was the abandonment of Berlin." That ended Eclipse and foiled an Allied attempt to beat the Russians to Berlin.

Hitler's great gamble in Ardennes and Alsace had been costly even though it had delayed the Allied advance by six weeks. But the Germans suffered. "In one month," according to Geoffrey Perret, "the equivalent of twenty full-strength Germans divisions, including all their equipment, had been destroyed."

The Wehrmacht's armor reserve had been expended. The hundreds of thousands of dead, crippled and captured German soldiers, the 1,500 shattered tanks, the hundreds of wrecked artillery pieces that littered the Ardennes would have helped make the Rhine a daunting barrier. A destroyed tank or gun on this side of it was worth three on the other shore. . . .

For all the initial shock, despite the loss of many good men and irrespective of the strains it placed on the Allied high command, the Bulge proved to be an unlooked-for blessing, albeit in a feld-grau disguise.

18: Across the Rhine: Varsity

The final defeat of Germany seemed inevitable to the Allies by the early spring of 1945. Hitler's December attack in the Ardennes had been thrown back with disastrous German casualties. Subsequently the Germans suffered more heavy losses in the Rhineland. By the middle of March, the British and the Americans had powerful forces all along the western bank of the Rhine, had seized a bridge at Remagen, and had a small bridgehead on the eastern bank. On the Eastern Front, Soviet forces were in Hungary and Czechoslovakia and were deployed along the Oder-Neisse line. Hitler's catastrophic losses on both fronts had weakened his potential for a strong defense of the Rhine.

By March of 1945 Eisenhower had under his command ninety full-strength divisions: twenty-five armored, five airborne, and sixty infantry. No commander in any war in history had ever commanded such a formidable force. Eisenhower's deployed command stretched along the Rhine some 450 air miles from the North Sea in the Netherlands to Switzerland. In the north, Montgomery's British 21st Army Group, including Lt. Gen. William H. Simpson's U.S. Ninth Army, covered a line from the North Sea to Cologne. On Montgomery's right flank, Bradley's U.S. 12th Army Group occupied a line from ten miles north of Cologne to a point about fifteen miles south of Mainz. On Bradley's right flank, Devers's U.S. 6th Army Group covered the rest of the area down to the Swiss border.

Eisenhower assigned to the scrupulous Montgomery the mission of making the main assault across the Rhine, far to the north.

"Montgomery was always a master in the methodical preparation of forces for a formal, set-piece attack," wrote Eisenhower.

In this case he made the most meticulous preparations because we knew that along the front just north of the Ruhr the enemy had his best remaining troops, including portions of the First Paratroop Army.

His assault was planned on a front of four divisions, two in the Twenty-first Army Group and two in the attached Ninth Army. Supporting these divisions was an airborne attack by the American 17th Airborne Division and the British 6th Airborne Division.

And to prove that Eisenhower had eventually changed his mind about the use of airborne forces in combat, he went on:

> Normal use of airborne forces was to send them into battle prior to the beginning of ground attack so as to achieve maximum surprise and create confusion among defending forces before the beginning of the ground assault. In this instance Montgomery planned to reverse the usual sequence. He decided to make the river crossing under cover of darkness, to be followed the next morning by the airborne attack. It was also normal to drop airborne forces at a considerable distance in the rear of the enemy's front lines, where the landing would presumably meet little immediate opposition and so give them time to organize themselves, to overrun headquarters, block movement of reserves, and create general havoc. But in this operation the two divisions were to drop close to the front lines, merely far enough back so that they would not be within the zone of our own artillery fire. From those positions they were to wreck the enemy's artillery organization and participate directly in the tactical battle. Elaborate arrangements were made for the use of smoke to provide artificial concealment for the river crossing and a great array of guns was assembled to support it.

D day for Montgomery's crossing of the Rhine, codenamed Plunder, was 24 March. Montgomery's command was loaded with troops and supplies. Ready for the assault, he had thirty full-strength divisions and supporting outfits, amounting to more than 1.25 million troops and 256,000 tons of supplies.

Montgomery's plan called for Dempsey's British Second Army to make the main crossing of the Rhine at three locations: Rees, Xanten, and Rheinberg. To assist Dempsey, Montgomery gave him the U.S. XVIII Airborne Corps and the U.S. 17th Airborne Division and the British 6th, now commanded by Maj. Gen. Eric L. Bols. In the southern sector of Operation Plunder, Montgomery had the assault divisions of the U.S. Ninth Army crossing the Rhine along an eleven-mile front south of Wesel and the Lippe River. In preparation for the crossing, he planned to pummel the area for several weeks with aerial bombing, concentrating on rail yards, bridges, communication centers, and industrial sites, followed by a final, intensive artillery barrage just hours before the assault. His overall plan had his advanced elements joining up with the U.S. First Army as it made a secondary advance northeast from below the Ruhr River, forming a pincer movement that would envelop the Ruhr industrial area, neutralizing the largest remaining concentration of German industrial might.

Operation Varsity was the code name for the airborne phase of the Rhine crossing. Originally, Gen. Lewis H. Brereton, commander of the First Allied Airborne Army, had included the U.S. 13th Airborne Division in the operation, but a lack of aircraft precluded its use.

The 13th was the fifth World War II U.S. airborne division. It had been activated at Fort Bragg, North Carolina on 13 August 1943 under the command of Maj. Gen. George W. Griner Jr. In December of that year he had been replaced by Maj. Gen. Eldridge G. Chapman, former head of the Airborne Command, who brought the division to France in February 1945. His chief of staff was Col. Hugh P. Harris (class of 1931), thirty-six years old, who in 1964 would wear four stars as the Commanding General of the Continental Army Command. The division arrived in France in January 1945, and camped in billets at Sens, Joigny, and Auxerre, about seventy miles southeast of Paris. The 13th had one parachute regiment, the 515th, commanded by Col. Harvey J. Jablonsky (class of 1934), thirty-six years old, a former All-American football player, and a football Hall of Fame member. Initially the 13th had two glider regiments: the 88th commanded by Col. Samuel Roth (class of 1930), thirty-nine years old, and the 326th commanded by Col. William Poindexter. On 1 March, Col. Rupert D. Graves (class of 1924), forty-four years old brought his separate 517th Parachute Regimental Combat Team, fresh from battles in Italy, Southern France, Belgium, and the Ardennes, to Joigny to join the 13th. Shortly after the 13th's arrival in France, the 88th was deactivated and its troops assigned to the 326th Glider Infantry Regiment. With the addition of the 88th's men the 326th became a three-battalion regiment. In the original TO&Es for airborne divisions glider regiments had only two battalions.

The 13th Airborne Division had an incredibly frustrating history. After the lack of aircraft dropped it from a role in Varsity, it "geared up for Operation CHOKER, the landing across the Rhine at Worms," wrote Col. James E. Mrazek, in a history of the 13th.

The day before the division was to take off, the 13th paratroopers and glider troops again moved out of the barbed wire enclosed assembly areas. Paratroopers marched to the airfield, found the C-47s, climbed in the ones they were assigned and secured drop loads. Glidermen loaded and lashed ammunition, pack howitzers, Jeeps and trailers into the gliders ready to take off at dawn. They woke up the next morning to the news the mission had been cancelled while they slept. Gen. Patton had captured Worms while they were loading up the day before!

Next came Operation EFFECTIVE, which was to deny part of the Alps to the Nazis to prevent them establishing a last ditch stronghold there. New intelligence, however, indicated that this operation was no longer necessary, and it was cancelled. Finally, as the days of the Third Reich were drawing to a close, elements of the 13th were scheduled to land at Copenhagen, Denmark, on a classified mission. It, also, was cancelled. Shortly thereafter, First Allied Army Headquarters announced that the division would be redeployed to the Pacific to participate in the invasion of Japan after a stopover in the United States. The division arrived at the New York Port of Embarkation on August 23, 1945 and moved to Fort Bragg, NC.

(The 13th Airborne Division passed into history after Japan's surrender in September 1945. On 26 February 1946, the division was inactivated at Fort Bragg and its troops transferred to the 82d Airborne Division.)

Dempsey's overall plan for crossing the Rhine assigned Ridgway's XVIII Airborne Corps the mission of seizing the Diersfordter Forest plus several small bridges across the Issel River, parallel to and about ten miles to the east of the Rhine. Ridgway's staff developed a plan to drop the British 6th Airborne in the northern half of the corps zone and the 17th Airborne in the southern half. The staff worked out the details of the drop and selected four parachute drop DZs and six glider LZs, all of which were crowded in an area of five by six miles. The total glider and parachute force, all dropped or landed on D day, added up to 21,680 men—a force larger than Market Garden's. And all DZs and LZs were within artillery range from the west shore of the Rhine.

"The assault on the night of March 23–24, was preceded by a violent artillery bombardment," wrote General Eisenhower.

On the front of the two American divisions two thousand guns of all types participated. General Simpson and I found a vantage point in an old church tower from which to witness the gunfire. Because the batteries were distributed on the flat plains on the western bank of the Rhine every flash could be seen. The din was incessant. Meanwhile, infantry assault troops were marching up to the water's edge to get into the boats. We joined some of them and found the troops remarkably eager to finish the job. There is no substitute for a succession of great victories in building morale.

With the arrival of daylight, I went to a convenient hill from which to witness the arrival of the airborne units, which were scheduled to begin their drop at ten o'clock. The airborne troops were carried to the assault in a total of 1,572 planes and 1,326 gliders; 889 fighter planes escorted them during the flight, and 2,153 other fighters provided cover over the target area and established a defensive screen to the eastward.

Fog and the smoke of the battlefield prevented a complete view of the airborne operation but I was able to see some of the action. A number of our planes were hit by anti-aircraft; generally, however, only after they had dropped their load of paratroopers. As they swung away from the battle area, they seemed to come over a spot where anti-aircraft fire was particularly accurate. Those that were struck well inside our own lines, and in nearly every case the crews succeeded in saving themselves by taking to their parachutes. Even so, our loss in planes was far lighter than we had calculated. Operation Varsity, the name given to the airborne phase of this attack, was the most successful airborne operation we carried out during the war.

The airborne operation that General Eisenhower, Prime Minister Churchill, and Field Marshal Brooke watched so eagerly had begun some seven hours earlier. At twelve airfields in northern France and Belgium, Miley and his men of the "Thunder from Heaven" 17th Airborne Division ate a superb precombat jump breakfast including steak and apple pie, then marched to their 903 planes and 897 gliders and loaded up for a combat jump and glider landing. Major General Paul Williams's IX Troop Carrier Command carried all the paratroopers of both divisions and tugged the 17th Airborne's gliders. The gliders of the British 6th were "roped in" by two groups of the Royal Air Force. At sixteen fields in southern England, the British 6th went through a similar procedure, getting aboard 699 planes and 429 gliders. There was one hitch: because of the size of the Varsity operation, seventy-two C-46 aircraft, in addition to C-47s, had to be used for the first time in combat. The C-46 carried thirty-six troopers in contrast to the C-47's eighteen and had jump doors on both sides of the plane, permitting a simultaneous exit of the two sticks of jumpers. But the C-46 had a deeper main section than the C-47's, and its wing tanks were so located that if punctured by antiaircraft fire, they would spew gasoline down the fuselage, setting the whole plane on fire.

At 2100 on the night of 23 March Montgomery's ground assault began at Rees, the northern crossing site, by elements of the British Second Army's XXX Corps whose mission was to distract the Germans from the main crossings at Xanten in the center and from Rheinberg in the south. This force met only slight opposition. Two miles north of Wesel, a Second Army commando brigade boated across the river and stopped a mile from the city while the RAF bombers pulverized it with 1,000 tons of bombs. Late on the morning of 24 March the commandos secured Wesel.

At 0200 on the same day the Second Army's XII Corps and the U.S. Ninth Army's XVI Corps began the main effort. The lead divisions of XVI Corps were the veteran 30th Infantry Division, commanded by fifty-three-year-old Maj. Gen. Leland S. "Old Hickory" Hobbs (class of 1915, Eisenhower's class), and the 79th Infantry Division, commanded by fifty-eight-year-old Maj. Gen. Ira T. Wyche, (class of 1911). The main effort was preceded by a massive aerial bombardment and artillery barrage so devastating that the 30th and the 79th crossed the river against relatively weak opposition. On the east bank both divisions charged ahead and, supported by heavy equipment ferried across the Rhine, penetrated three to six miles into the German defenses before nightfall.

The Varsity phase of the operation began at 0950 on 24 March, as well. Colonel Edson Raff's 507th Parachute Infantry Regiment led the assault by the 17th Airborne Division. As was his wont, Raff was in the lead airplane. His target was DZ W, two miles north of Wesel at the southern edge of the Diersfordter Forest. But pilot disorientation caused a split in Raff's drop. He and some 690 of his troops dropped onto an area about two miles northwest of DZ W, near Diersfordt Castle. The rest of his regimental combat team, including Lt. Col. Edward S. Branigan's 464th Parachute Field Artillery Battalion ("Branigan's Bastards"), landed on target. Raff assembled his misdropped men rapidly and led them south through the woods to DZ W. Just a short distance away he and his men then surrounded a large German force, taking it under direct small arms fire and killing 56 and capturing 300. Near Diersfordt, he and his men found a German 155mm artillery battery firing at the ground troops crossing the river. He personally led an attack on the artillerymen and killed or scattered them. To close the deal his men wrecked the guns with thermite grenades in the barrels.

Private First Class George J. Peters, a youngster from Cranston, Rhode Island, was a rifleman in Raff's G Company. He and ten men from his stick had landed on the edge of DZ W, near the small town of Fluren. As they were getting out of their chutes and readying their weapons, they were fired on by a German machine gun about seventy yards away. The fire raked them and forced them to flatten themselves on the ground—except for Peters. He got up and charged, armed with his rifle and a few grenades. The Germans spotted him, fired bursts at him, wounding him and knocking him down. But, with uncanny bravery, he crawled to his feet and charged again. Fifteen feet from the German machine gun crew, he lobbed two grenades and then collapsed on the ground. His grenades killed the crew, but he died in front of the position. He was awarded a posthumous Medal of Honor.

General Miley landed far from his target DZ. And none of his staff who jumped with him, landed near him. When he got out of his parachute harness he spotted three privates nearby. He also saw a container so marked that he knew it contained a machine gun. He yelled to the privates to meet him at the bundle. They then assembled the gun, moved toward enemy soldiers who were firing at them, and set up the gun and blasted away. It was an odd machine gun team—a two-star general and three privates. Shortly thereafter, Miley found part of his staff and set up a skeleton CP under some trees on the edge of the DZ.

Behind the 507th came the 513th Parachute Infantry Regiment commanded by Col. James W. Coutts. The troopers of the 513th were crammed into seventy-two C-46s, with Coutts and his staff in the lead plane. Behind them came Lt. Col. Harry Kies and his 1st Battalion, Lt.

Col. "Ace" Miller and his 2d Battalion, and Lt. Col. Morris Anderson and his 3d Battalion. Ground fog confused the C-46 pilots, and all of Coutts's men missed their target, DZ X. The 513th landed near Hamminkeln, a British glider LZ. The 513th's greatest misfortune was that its column flew over a very active belt of German antiaircraft defenses. Twenty-two C-46s succumbed to their flawed gas tanks and went down in flames, but not before the valiant pilots kept the planes aloft long enough for the troopers to leap out both doors of the planes. The crews were not so fortunate. Coutts's plane, piloted by Col. Bill Filer, the air group commander, was one of the planes hit. It began to drop, and at 542 feet of altitude the green light came on. Coutts led his men rapidly out the doors. The plane exploded shortly after the jump. Thirty-eight other planes were hit but kept flying. "Ace" Miller's plane was also hit, and he led his troopers out the doors into a fusillade of automatic-weapons fire from the ground. Once on the ground himself, Miller got out of his harness and ran to a nearby barn. He crouched at a corner, and looked around it to spot a German machine gun set up ten feet away. He killed the gunners with four accurate shots from his Colt .45 pistol. Nearby was a farmhouse from whose windows two machine guns were firing. Miller tossed a grenade into each window and wiped them out. Then he raced away from the farmhouse.

The bulk of the 513th landed in a German stronghold—a dug-in artillery battery guarded by infantrymen. Coutts rapidly gathered enough troopers to attack the position. In the middle of his attack the British gliders began to land. As soon as the glidermen were assembled, they joined with Coutts and his men, cleared the area, and moved on to Hamminkeln. The British then seized two bridges over the Issel River.

Lieutenant Colonel Harry Kies's E Company/513th, landed to the west of its DZ, near railroad tracks that passed along the edge of the Diersfordter Forest. After assembling his men, he led them toward the rest of the 513th engaged in a battle near Hamminkeln. But as the company marched past some concrete buildings along the railroad near Wesel, it came under fire from Germans in one of the buildings. A platoon spread out and made a frontal attack on the buildings. They had raced only about fifty yards when the Germans peppered them with heavy machine gun fire and forced them to hit the dirt. Private Stuart S. Stryker decided on his own to attack. He got up, ran to the front of the platoon, and found the dead bodies of his platoon leader and platoon sergeant. Stryker's reaction was pure intestinal fortitude. He stood up and yelled to the rest of the platoon: "Come on, you guys! Follow me." Stryker ran toward the building, firing his carbine; the platoon got up and followed him, blazing away with their weapons. Stryker ran on, still firing as he went. But some twenty-five yards from the building, he was riddled with machine gun fire and fell dead. The rest of the platoon charged on, storming into the building and subduing the Germans. They rounded up some 200 Germans and freed three U.S. bomber pilots who had been held captive inside. Stryker received the Medal of Honor posthumously.

By 1400 on 23 March, Coutts reported to General Miley that the 513th had accomplished all its missions and seized all its assigned objectives. The regiment had wiped out two artillery batteries, destroyed two tanks, and captured 1,152 Germans.

Lieutenant Colonel Kenneth L. Booth was the commander of the 466th Parachute Field Artillery Battalion, which was in direct support of the 513th and followed it in the long line of C-47s. On its drop, the 376 men of the 466th and twelve howitzers hit their target, DZ X, on dead center. The 466th had along two unusual part-time gunners: Brig. Gen Josiah T. Dalbey (class of 1919), forty-seven years old, commander of the Airborne Training Center at Camp Mackall, North Carolina, and Brig. Gen. Ridgely M. Gaither, head of the Parachute School at Fort Benning, Georgia. The two generals had said that they wanted to get the authentic sense of a combat jump. And they did. Along with the other troopers in their stick, they were raked with machine gun fire during their drop and shot at as they struggled out of their harnesses. But the two generals returned the fire, and Dalbey even gathered a few troopers and wiped out a German antiaircraft battery.

Fifteen minutes after the last stick of paratroopers "hit the silk," a seemingly endless flow of gliders floated over the LZs and began, mostly, to crash-land, their almost inevitable method of landing. But they did hit LZ S accurately. The 194th Glider Infantry Regiment was commanded by Col. James R. Pierce (a classmate of Maxwell D. Taylor). Pierce's mission was to land his regiment a mile and a half from Wesel, seize a bridge over the Issel, and guard the division's right flank. In the 194th Lt. Col. Frank L. Barnett commanded the 1st Battalion, Lt. Col. William S. Stewart, the 2d Battalion, and Lt. Col. Robert L. Ashworth, the 3d Battalion. Integral parts of the 194th Regimental Combat Team were Lt. Col. Paul Oswald's 680th Glider Field Artillery Battalion, Lt. Col.

Joseph W. Keating's 681st Glider Field Artillery Battalion, and Lt. Col. John W. Paddock's 155th Glider Antiaircraft Battalion.

Nine hundred ten Waco gliders carried the regiment, some being double-towed by the workhorse C-47s. The approach flight of the glider column became hazardous in the extreme: before they were cut loose, the gliders were slashed with machine gun and small-caliber antiaircraft fire. At least two-thirds of the gliders were hit, and twelve C-47s, though hit, kept on course, unleashed their gliders, and then crashed. Another 140 tug ships were hit but managed to keep on course. The landings, many at eighty miles an hour, were calamitous. Many gliders hit obstacles and were crumpled, killing and wounding many of their trapped and helpless riders. Thirty-two glider pilots were killed and 106 were wounded.

But Pierce and his men were fighters. They landed in an area of German artillery pieces that were still firing at the troops crossing the Rhine in boats. When the Germans saw the gliders crash-landing and skidding across their front, they lowered their guns and fired at them. But the 194th's soldiers struggled out of their "flying coffins," got organized, and attacked. Part of F Company, commanded by Capt. Robert Dukes, saw an opportunity. Spotting a German CP they quickly got organized for a charge and overran the CP and captured a German colonel and his staff. They also recovered very helpful maps and overlays of German defenses in the Wesel area.

By 1400 on the afternoon of D day, the airborne part of Thunder—Varsity—had finished as a complete success. The U.S. 17th Airborne Division and the British 6th Airborne Division had paved a wide path for Montgomery's ground forces to drive deep into the German homeland. Major General Eric L. Bols and his Red Devils had cleared the northern part of the drop and landing zones, captured thousands of prisoners, and made contact with Montgomery's ground forces on the eastern shore of the Rhine.

Early on the evening of D day, General Ridgway, who had crossed the Rhine in a boat, arrived at General Miley's CP near Fluren. Miley was able to report on the success of his operation but pointed out that the 513th, which had landed in the middle of a large German concentration, was still fighting. A few hours later, he reported that Coutts and his troops had marched into the division perimeter escorting some 1,100 German prisoners.

At about 2000 hours on 23 March Ridgway and Miley, accompanied by aides and some troopers in a couple of jeeps, made their hazardous way to Bols's CP. They arrived at about 2300 hours and went into a fast map study of the situation in his area. By midnight, they were on their way back to Fluren, when the three-jeep convoy ran into a few Germans. Ridgway fired his Springfield '03 rifle at the shadowy figures and believed that he got at least one. In the brief shoot-out, however, he was slightly wounded in the shoulder by a grenade that landed just a few feet way. Back at Miley's CP a doctor examined him and said that he would have to perform surgery to take the fragment out of his shoulder. Ridgway declined the surgery and carried the fragment in his shoulder for the rest of the war.

The success of Varsity was more expensive than the commanders had first estimated. Bols lost 347 men and another 731 wounded. Miley suffered 393 men killed in action or on landing, another 934 wounded, and 164 missing in action. The U.S. IX Troop Carrier Command had 41 killed, 153 wounded, and 163 missing in action. There were twenty-two C-46s shot down in flames. The C-46 had proved so dangerous that Ridgway eliminated them from any future airborne operation. The glider loss was extensive: salvageable were only 24 British Horsas and Hamilcars and 148 Wacos. The rest of the 1,305 gliders used in Varsity were wrecked or shot up so badly that they were left to disintegrate on the field of battle.

On 26 March Montgomery launched his assault into the German homeland. Leading the attack was the XVIII Airborne Corps with Brigadier C. I. H. Dunbar's 6th Guards Armoured Brigade and the British 1st Commando Brigade attached. Miley's paratroopers were in a new role—they rode on the British tanks against faint resistance and made an advance of 3,000 yards.

The next day, the 194th Glider Infantry Regiment ran into strong German defenses near the town of Lembeck. I Company was deployed and made a frontal attack on them, but it was thrown back three times with heavy casualties. One of the bravest of the brave, Tech. Sgt. Clinton M. Hendrick, grabbed a Browning automatic rifle (BAR) and charged. The survivors in I Company inspired by this action, rose to their feet and followed Hendrick. Hendrick ran toward six Germans who tried to counterattack and mowed them all down with his BAR.

Some Germans escaped and ran back toward Lembeck and piled into a castle with a moat and a drawbridge. Hendrick charged across the drawbridge up to the courtyard. A German appeared and shouted in English: "We wish to surrender." Hendrick and four of his men walked into the courtyard and a trap. The Germans fired on the men under fire, riddling

Hendricks, who was in the lead. He shouted to his men to "get the hell out of here!" The troopers fled, but he kept firing and moving forward toward the Germans, who shot him up. When the firing stopped, other I Company men moved in to find a bleeding Hendrick lying on the courtyard pavement. He had wiped out the German contingent, but he died as the medics were carrying him across the moat. He was awarded a posthumous Medal of Honor.

The U.S. and British airborne troops continued their advance into Germany riding on or in any kind of vehicle they could find or steal; one enterprising British paratrooper used a steamroller to move ahead. Others rode bicycles, trucks, and even horses. In a letter to author William B. Breuer, Colonel Coutts wrote:

"I rode on the tank of the 6th Guards Armoured Brigade's commander, Brigadier Dunbar, holding tight to my tommy gun. Sometimes it was like a jaunt through a peaceful park; then all hell would break loose. When we were halted by heavy fire, my paratroopers would jump off the tanks and dig out the enemy from foxholes and buildings in towns. Sometimes I got into the action with my tommy gun. Then we'd all scramble back onto the tanks and, with a mighty roar, off we'd go again."

By 28 March Montgomery and his Allied force had moved some thirty miles from the Rhine. In the march to the east, the XVIII Airborne Corps had collected some 7,000 POWs and overrun Haltern and Dulmen. On Easter Sunday, 1 April, Coutts and his 513th were on the outskirts of Münster, fifty miles from the Rhine. In heavy fighting in that city, Coutts was seriously wounded by a mortar round and knocked out of the rest of the war. The next day Münster fell to the paratroopers.

After the U.S. 2d Armored Division had blasted through Haltern and Dulmen, Gene Simpson ordered a combat command from the 2d Armored to make a fifteen-mile southeast advance to Lippstadt, midway between Beckum and the halted 3d Armored Division spearhead. Early on 1 April, units of the 2d and 3d Armored Divisions met at Lippstadt, forging a link between the Ninth and First Armies and encircling the prized Ruhr industrial complex, along with 350,000 German troops of Field Marshal Walther Model's Army Group B.

While the armored forces were reducing the Ruhr pocket, Ridgway ordered the 17th Airborne to Essen, the hub of Germany's industries, and the site of the Krupp arms complex, Germany's greatest producers of weapons of war. Ed Raff's 507th drove into the city and into the man-

sion of Alfred Krupp von Bolen und Halbach, the head of the arms empire. Raff's men took Krupp out of his mansion, in spite of his reluctance,
and housed him in his gardener's small villa.

Other important Germans fell to the U.S. troops. Near Hirschberg,
east of Essen, Col. Jim Pierce's glidermen nabbed Franz von Papen,
Hitler's longtime diplomat and erstwhile envoy to Turkey and the United
States just as he was about to sit down to dinner in his secluded palatial
home. Also captured in the Ruhr by British soldiers was Gen. Kurt Student, the developer of Germany's airborne forces.

Field Marshal Model, one of the Nazi's most famous and successful
commanders, being caught in the Ruhr pocket, refused to surrender.
Ridgway sent one of his German-speaking aides under a white flag to reason with Model and ask him to surrender honorably. The aide returned
with a German colonel who told Ridgway that Model refused to surrender and that he, the colonel, wished to become a prisoner of war. Two
days later Model went into the woods near his command post and, with
his Lüger, put an end to his army's defeat. He was buried secretly by his
aides near Wuppertal.

Thousands of prisoners were captured daily by the advancing Allied
forces, the Germans surrendering in droves. In the Ruhr alone 325,000
surrendered, far beyond the estimates of the Allied high command. In
the field, tactical commanders simply set up open spaces surrounded by
barbed wire to house the POWs. In addition, the Allies liberated many
forced laborers and Allied POWs seeking shelter. The U.S. logistical system quickly became strained.

On 1 April, General Taylor deployed his 101st Airborne Division in a
defensive position along the Rhine opposite Düsseldorf. On 6 April,
Gavin brought the 82d across the Rhine by boat and occupied positions
along the Rhine north and south of Cologne. About the third week in
April, Gavin received an alert to move north and rejoin the British Second Army under Ridgway's XVIII Airborne Corps.

"I was directed to assemble the division on the west bank of the
Elbe River, well south of Hamburg, near the small German town of
Bleckede," wrote General Gavin. "Once the division was withdrawn
from its front and organized for the move, I hurriedly went to the
new area to learn what our next mission would be."

On the afternoon of April 20 the 82d Airborne Division was
strung out, moving by truck and rail, more than 200 miles from

Cologne. By darkness the 506th Parachute Infantry, less one battalion, was expected to arrive at the Bleckede ferry site. General Sir Miles Dempsey . . . and Lieutenant General Ridgway . . . came to my command post to discuss the proposed crossing with me. General Dempsey was most anxious that the crossing be made as soon as possible in order to cut off the Russian advance toward Denmark. About twenty miles to our left the British has established a bridgehead over the Elbe, but if we used it, it would delay our meeting the Russians by another five or six days, and we most certainly would be too late to intercept them. We had to make a hasty crossing and establish our own bridgehead at Bleckede.

In the south the Allies were marching rapidly toward the Alps. Montgomery in the north drove north and northeast. On 19 April the British Second Army reached the Elbe River southeast of Hamburg. A week later it captured Bremen. On 29 April the Second Army made an assault crossing of the Elbe, supported by XVIII Airborne Corps. Ridgway now had the following divisions in his corps: the British 6th Airborne, the U.S. 82d Airborne, and the U.S. 7th and 8th Infantry Divisions, and the U.S. 7th Armored Division. Ridgway's mission was to attack to the north to the Baltic Sea to seal off the Danish peninsula. The bridgehead expanded rapidly, and by 2 May the Allies had captured Lübeck and Wismar, some 45 miles beyond the Elbe, effectively sealing off the enemy forces in Jutland in Denmark. Before that, on 30 April, patrols from the U.S. 82d and the British 6th had made contact with Red Army tankers at the Elbe.

"Within twenty-four hours I met the Russians," wrote General Gavin.

Earlier I had sent an armored cavalry unit that had been attached to the 82d Airborne Division, under the command of Captain William Knowlton, to find the Russians. It was a hair-raising experience for him, but he made his way through the skeptical Germans and finally established contact with the Russians and was able to communicate to me that he had done so. The day after the surrender of Tippelskirch, I made my way with a Russian interpreter, a sergeant from the 82d, toward the Russians lines. . . . As I entered the town square of Grabow, I saw that Russian soldiers had a hogshead of wine in the square. They had fired into it with their pistols, and as the wine spurted out, they caught it in their helmets and drank it.

On 2 May the Russians were in Berlin.

It was reported that there were still some Germans unwilling to surrender and who had holed up in the "national redoubt" in Berchtesgaden in Bavaria. Therefore, the U.S. 101st Airborne and 3d Infantry Divisions were ordered to follow French tanks in an attack on the village. The German last stand turned out to be bogus. The 3d Infantry Division and two battalions of the 506th entered Berchtesgaden on 4 May. Troopers of the 506th captured Field Marshal Kesselring, by then the German commander in chief in the west.

"By the end of April the Third Reich's twilight was turning to night," wrote Edward N. Bedessem.

> Its armies in tatters, Germany retained only a small fraction of the territory it had captured a few years before . . . With his escape route to the south severed by the 12th Army Group's eastward drive and Berlin surrounded by the Soviets, Adolf Hitler committed suicide on 30 April, leaving to his successor, Admiral Karl Doenitz, the task of capitulation. After attempting to strike a deal whereby he would surrender only to the western Allies—a proposal which was summarily rejected—on 7 May Doenitz granted his representative, General Alfred Jodl, permission to effect a complete surrender on all fronts. The appropriate document was signed on the same day and became effective on 8 May. Despite scattered resistance from a few isolated units, the war in Europe was over.

But the war in the Pacific was not. Ridgway's XVIII Airborne Corps and the 13th and 82d Airborne Divisions were alerted for redeployment to the Pacific. But the two atomic blasts in Japan in August made certain that the Japanese were about to give up. The 17th continued occupation duties until relieved by the British on 15 June. Then the division began to be split up, and some of its troopers moved to the 82d or to the 13th, at that time slated for reassignment to the Pacific. The final echelon of the 17th returned to Camp Myles Standish, and on 16 September 1945 was deactivated. In August the 13th Airborne Division was shipped home and deactivated. In July, Gavin and his All Americans moved to Berlin to occupy the U.S. occupation zone in the city. The 508th was detached from the 82d and sent to occupy Frankfurt.

The Screaming Eagles occupied southern Germany and parts of Austria. "While at Berchtesgaden," wrote Col. Robert Jones, the division historian, "the 101st received the surrender of the German XIII SS and

LXXXII Corps. Several prominent Nazis were also captured. The 502d Parachute Infantry Regiment captured Julius Streicher, the anti-Semitic editor of *Der Sturmer,* and Obergruppenfuhrer Karl Oberg, the chief of the German SS in occupied France. Colonel General Heinz Guderian, a leading armor expert, was also captured. . . . On 1 August, the 101st Airborne Division left Germany for Auxerre, France, to begin training for the invasion of Japan." That same month, General Taylor left the 101st to become the superintendent at West Point. Brigadier General Stuart Cutler became the acting commanding general.

Shortly after the surrender of Japan, the War Department announced the deactivation of the 82d Airborne Division and the movement of the 101st to its permanent base at Fort Bragg, where Maj. Gen. Anthony McAuliffe awaited its arrival and assumption of its command. The War Department had also planned a grandiose arrival ceremony for the 101st: parade up Fifth Avenue in New York City after its arrival by ship from France in December 1945. The 101st commanders went all out to ready the troops for the parade. Each man got a new pair of jump boots and a silk parachute scarf to wear in the parade. The 101st's Parachute Maintenance Company went so far as to make a fifty-foot-square banner, highlighting the division's shoulder patch and its battles, to hang from the ship when it sailed into New York harbor.

But that extraordinary gala for the Screaming Eagles did not happen. The War Department, after reviewing the battle and combat records of the 101st and 82d, decided that the 82d should be honored with the Fifth Avenue parade. To finish the mortal wound to the 101st, the War Department also announced that the division would be deactivated in France on 13 November and that the 82d would take up permanent residence at Fort Bragg.

On occupation duty in Berlin the 82d played host to many visiting dignitaries. General Gavin formed an honor guard of his most highly decorated soldiers, all of whom were over six feet tall. They wore spit-shined jump boots with white laces, parachute scarves, and gloves and were drilled to perfection. After a visit and watching the honor guard, the authoritarian General Patton said: "In all my years in the Army and of all the Honor Guards I've seen, the 82d Berlin Honor Guard is the best." Since that time, the 82d has been known as America's Guard of Honor.

In December 1945, the 82d moved from Berlin to Camp Lucky Strike near Le Havre in France and shortly thereafter sailed for the United

States aboard the *Queen Elizabeth*. On 3 January 1946, the division docked in New York and boarded ferries for the trip to Camp Shanks, their departure point for Europe a couple of years earlier. For over a week, the division got ready for its march down Fifth Avenue. Just after noon on 12 January, General Gavin stood proudly at the front of his troopers standing erect in their pressed uniforms, shiny jump boots, and jump helmets. The parade signified the ultimate victory of the Allies, more specifically the United States, over their despised enemies. Gavin, standing in the arch at Washington Square, gave the order, "Forward march!" and stepped out to lead his proud All Americans up Fifth Avenue before thousands of cheering fans including New York governor, Thomas E. Dewey; New York City mayor, William O'Dwyer; and Gen. Jonathan M. Wainwright, back from his three-year ordeal as a prisoner of the Japanese. "Gavin swung, slim and erect, up the pavement in the cold," wrote T. Michael Booth and Duncan Spencer, in *Paratrooper, the Life of Gen. James M. Gavin,* "disguising the pain from his broken vertebrae, as well as the pain he felt for the dead; 60,000 men had passed through the division, and many of them were gone and more were wounded and crippled. He would march with his enviable luck intact, but with only twelve of his peers, men like him who had made all four combat jumps. He was a hero, and almost a national figure. The war had made him 'Slim Jim, Gentleman Jim, Jumpin' Jim.'"

The departure of the 82d left only one airborne outfit in Europe—the 508th in Frankfurt. But its stay would be short lived—in November 1946 the 508th sailed home to Camp Kilmer, New Jersey, and met its fate: deactivation.

The many airborne operations made the pages of history in Europe, but such history was also being written in the Pacific.

19: The 11th Airborne: Heading for the Pacific

In the Pacific there were only two U.S. Army airborne outfits—the 503d Parachute Regimental Combat Team and the 11th Airborne Division—two completely separate units.

The 11th Airborne Division was organized according to the original airborne division TO&E: one parachute infantry regiment with three battalions, two glider infantry regiments each with two battalions, and the supporting arms to back up that odd organization. (Glider regiments could not execute the time-honored, often misused military plan of attack of "two up and one back.") The parachute artillery battalion, for example, had three batteries of four pack 75s each; the glider field artillery battalions had only two batteries but with six pack 75s each. The service and support units were about one-third paratrooper and two-thirds glidermen. The division strength was 8,321 men, just slightly more than half of a standard infantry division. But in combat in the Philippines, later on, the senior commanders under whom the 11th fought, took no notice of the size of the division and assigned Maj. Gen. Joseph M. Swing, the commander of the 11th from its birth, the same sort of grueling missions they would allocate to a standard infantry division.

General Swing, initially an artilleryman, was forty-nine years old, a member of the famous West Point Class of 1915, the class "the stars fell on," which included Generals Eisenhower, Bradley, Van Fleet, Harmon, and Stratemeyer. Of the 164 men who graduated in that class, fifty-two became generals. Swing was a tall, ramrod-straight, slender, white-haired professional officer who demanded the best of himself and his troopers. His father-in-law was Gen. Peyton C. March, a former U.S. Army chief of staff.

Except for the field officers, the officer cadres for the glider units in the division came from the 76th Infantry Division at Fort Meade, Maryland. Special Orders Number 149, headquarters 76th Infantry Division, dated 11 December 1942, and in the arcane language of adjutants general, ordered the cadres to report to the commanding officer of Laurinburg-Maxton Army Air Base, Laurinburg, North Carolina on 27 December 1942 to "pursue sp course of instrn. Upon completion of the course o/a 8 Jan 1943 these O's WP from Laurinburg, NC to Ft Benning, Ga rptg to Comdt The InfSch on 10 Jan 1943 for further temp dy to pursue a course of instrn. Upon compl of this course o/a 5 Feb 1943 these O's WP fr Ft Benning, Ga to Hoffman, NC rptg thereat for dy not later than 8 Feb 1943."

The enlisted cadre for the 11th Airborne Division glider units came from the 88th Infantry Division at Camp Gruber, Oklahoma. The officers and men of the parachute units came from the parachute school at Fort Benning, and cadres from other parachute units already on board. The division's activation date was 25 February 1943 at Camp Hoffman, North Carolina, soon to become Camp Mackall.

On 8 November 1942, just a few weeks after the army chief of engineers had selected the Hoffman site for a new camp, civilian work crews began building it on 51,971 acres in the middle of the North Carolina–South Carolina maneuver area. In six months the camp, such as it was, was complete. It contained some 1,750 buildings, mostly tar-paper-covered huts built of green lumber that cracked and split as the days wore on; sixty-five miles of hastily paved roads (which many months later were still rough and either dusty or muddy); a 1,200-bed hospital; five theaters; six beer gardens; and three 5,000-foot all weather runways formed in a triangle. The first plane touched down on one of the new runways on 8 February 1943 and brought in Maj. Gen. E. G. Chapman Jr. and the first elements of the airborne command staff that had moved from Benning to Bragg only a few months earlier. On that same date, 8 February 1943, the War Department published General Order Number 6, which officially changed the name of the camp from Camp Hoffman to Camp Mackall.

Camp Mackall was a prime example in World War II of the very difficult problem of constructing barracks, mess halls, hospitals, supply sheds, and other basic installations on a "crash and money-saving" basis. In going to this "theater of operations" type of construction, the engineers had planned to double-bunk the men in the barracks. Then they built the mess halls, latrines, dayrooms, and recreation buildings based on the number of barracks, not on twice the number of men who would occupy them.

When Swing noticed the dearth of support buildings because of the engineers' miscalculation, he immediately contacted the chief of engineers in the Pentagon and reported the intolerable situation. The chief reacted promptly and gave orders to alleviate the problem, at least in part. But throughout the 11th's stay at Mackall, many officers and men lived in winterized pyramidal tents and jammed themselves into small, inadequate mess halls because of a shortage of barracks and bachelor officers' quarters.

Within a very few weeks after the activation of the 11th, the troopers would see their general in unlikely places, checking the motor pools, the messes, the barracks, and the sick calls—the general condition of his men in all aspects of their lives. He would continue his dedication to his troopers through the rigors of battle in the Philippines, an "up front" commander.

As described earlier in this book, the 503d Parachute Infantry Regiment, less one infantry battalion, sailed from San Francisco on 10 October 1942, stopped in Panama to pick up its third infantry battalion, the 501st Parachute Infantry Battalion, and, after a seemingly endless voyage, landed at Cairns in Australia on 2 December 1942.

So far, the combat history of the 503d had been mixed—some relatively easy campaigns and some difficult and hard-fought. But all of its battles trained the paratroopers of the 503d and hardened their mettle for what the Japanese commander on Corregidor thought was an impossibility: attacking Corregidor by airborne assault.

20: The Angels in Combat

In January of 1944, the 11th Airborne Division moved by train from Camp Mackall, North Carolina, to Camp Polk, Louisiana, for four weeks of maneuvers and final tests in the Calcasieu Swamps before moving overseas to combat. While there, General Swing received approval from Army Ground Forces to establish his own jump school. He was an ardent proponent of the need to train all his troops as both paratroopers and glidermen, and he wanted it done with speed. His candidates became qualified paratroopers in less than a week. He continued setting up his own jump schools throughout the career of the 11th whenever it was out of combat.

On 20 April 1944 the division boarded trains for its trip to the port of embarkation (POE) and on 28 April unloaded at Camp Stoneman, California. On 2 May the first units of the division marched out of Camp Stoneman, moved to Pittsburg, California, and then boarded inland boats for the trip to San Francisco, the division's POE. On 4 May, the division set sail for New Guinea and waved goodbye to the Golden Gate Bridge. In early June the division arrived at its new base camp in Dobodura, an abandoned U.S. airfield. The troops set about erecting pyramidal and squad tents, getting acclimatized to the stifling heat and humidity, training in the nearby jungle, and parachuting into the kunai grass around the airstrip.

From July to September, the division and the 54th Troop Carrier Wing conducted a combined airborne–troop carrier program, operating with a different troop carrier squadron each week. The program provided valuable training in formation flying and dropping paratroopers for the troop carrier pilots, whose main mission to date had been hauling cargo. The wing and division established a joint standard operating procedure for airborne–troop carrier operations that would prove its value in the days ahead. The division also practiced amphibious landings at Oro Bay in New Guinea. One trooper wrote that "it became an invariable and fiendish custom of higher headquarters to give the 11th Airborne amphibious training whenever possible." The 11th troopers would rather jump and glide than wade.

On 11 November 1944, the division left Oro Bay in a convoy of nine attack transports and attack cargo ships escorted by nine destroyers and arrived at Bito Beach, on Leyte, in the Philippines, "unopposed," according to one trooper. Once there, it built yet another base camp of canvas and bamboo on the beach and waited for a summons to combat. In the interim, the troops watched U.S. fighters shoot Japanese planes out of the sky and a kamikaze dive into the bridge of a transport unloading off the beach and sink the ship. But the idle days were soon over.

On 22 November, Swing received orders from Sixth Army to relieve the 7th Infantry Division along the Burauen–La Paz–Bugho line across the narrow southern waist of Leyte and destroy all the enemy forces in the area.

The 511th Parachute Infantry Regiment was the first unit committed to combat. Within days, however, the entire division would find itself strung out across the mountains of southern Leyte, fighting a dug-in, tenacious enemy along uncharted trails and in the middle of torrential rains that made the dirt roads impassable swamps and jungle trails slippery and knee deep in mud. In November alone, more than twenty-three inches of rain inundated Leyte.

Major General Swing set up his division CP near Burauen, about ten miles inland from the Bito Beach. Burauen was the hub for three airfields—San Pablo, Buri, and Bayug. All the division's Cub planes, the dozen or so L-4s and L-5s that ordinarily flew artillery forward observers near and over enemy lines, were based at San Pablo. Soon they were to become far more useful.

The farther the 11th's troopers advanced and fought across the Leyte hills to the west, the more difficult the terrain and resupply efforts became. Major General Swing decided to use his fleet of Cub planes most creatively by having the pilots rig them for dropping supplies along the jungle trails. After hundreds of resupply flights the planes came to be called "biscuit bombers." Eventually, they were fitted with stretchers over the back seats and used to evacuate wounded from a makeshift jungle clearing at Manarawat, halfway across the southern part of the island. More original uses for the Cubs were yet to come.

The conditions for the troops in the hills, searching for and wiping out the tenacious, strong, and suicidal bands of enemy soldiers scattered across the mountains and throughout the jungles, were treacherous. The steady rains and low clouds frequently grounded the "biscuit bombers," with the result that the soldiers were constantly without sufficient food, ammunition, and medical supplies. For long periods three men would have to make do with only one K-ration per day. Platoon leaders rationed ammunition, which the riflemen counted by the bullet rather than the clip. In the incessant mud, the troops' fatigues became soaked and rotten, and that mud sloshed over the tops of boots whose soles had disintegrated after a few days of forced marches. The night air was penetratingly cold, especially for the troops who slept or stood guard in their foxholes in wet boots and clothes. Men off guard duty wrapped up in ponchos and "steam-dried" themselves while they tried to sleep. Some of the troopers endured days without taking off their fatigues or boots: dry socks were a luxury; and a shave and a hot bath were what dreams were made of.

On 2 December C Company of the 187th Glider Infantry Regiment, commanded by Lt. Charles "Pop" Olsen, received orders to move into the hills from its San Pablo airfield bivouac area. But Lt. Col. George Pearson, his battalion commander, startled Olsen by telling him that Major General Swing wanted one of his platoons to parachute into Manarawat ahead of the company that would still be strung out on the mountain trails. Following orders, Olsen told Lt. Chester J. Kozlowski, who had been with the 503d on the Noemfoor jump and then been transferred to the 11th, to report to Swing at division headquarters. Swing told Kozlowski that he had heard of him and wanted to drop his platoon into Manarawat. By this time, of course, many of the men of the 187th Glider Infantry had become qualified for parachute jumps. Kozlowski was surprised but, of course, was ready to go. Swing took Kozlowski to the airstrip where the L-4s and L-5s were parked and had one of the pilots brief Kozlowski on how to jump out of a Cub plane. "Slide into the back seat, sit with your feet out the door, hook up the static line to a D ring on the floor of the plane, and roll out the door when I give you the hand signal," the pilot told him.

That afternoon Kozlowski was the first to load up. Of the six planes at the strip, Kozlowski and his runner were in the first two planes. After a fifteen-minute flight, they were over the DZ at 400 feet. On the pilot's signal, a tap on the leg, Kozlowski slid out the door. "There was no opening shock, and it was a smooth landing," Kozlowski remembered. His platoon had twenty-four men, so it took four trips to drop all of them. Thus was developed and initiated probably the first combat jump from Cub planes. A number of staffers and commanders later used the same technique to get into the hills rather than trudge for hours through the soggy jungle.

The troopers in the hills were in dire need of artillery support and were out of the pack 75s' range. But the troopers of the 457th Parachute Field Artillery Battalion, fit as they were, could not break down their pack 75s into the usual loads of more than 200 pounds and carry them along the mountainous jungle trails as mules once might have. Even the *carabao,* the local beasts of burden, were not willing to perform the task. The solution was another 11th Airborne innovative parachute entry into combat.

On 3 December 1944 Lt. Col. Nick Stadtherr, the battalion commander, told Lt. Milton R. Holloway that he wanted him to jump his A Battery into an area near Manarawat. But when Capt. John Conable, the battalion S-4 officer, got to San Pablo airstrip to find some aircraft larger than the Cubs to drop the artillery, he found a large problem. All the C-47s in the area were urgently needed for the aerial resupply of the troops in the hills throughout Leyte. Obviously the Red legs could not use the Cubs for their mission. Conable persuaded the pilot of an air-sea rescue C-47 to take on the mission. He ordered parachutes, parachute racks for the C-47, and equipment containers from the Quartermaster Company at Bito Beach. With surprising speed the equipment arrived that evening. Holloway, meanwhile, had brought his battery up from the beach in DUKWs, an amphibious wheeled vehicle. But that day, Conable was ordered to division headquarters to become the new assistant division quartermaster, and it fell to Lieutenant Colonel Stadtherr to supervise rigging the plane and the entire operation.

Ordinarily a pack 75 battery needs twelve C-47s to drop its four howitzers, ninety or so men, ammunition, and support gear. Stadtherr had to do with one C-47, but would use it thirteen times because of the need for short sticks of five men each. By the morning of 4 December, the C-47 had been rigged for the first drop. Stadtherr loaded the plane and personally acted as jumpmaster over the Manarawat DZ, which was small and surrounded on three sides by high hills. He dropped the troops and their loads right on target from 300 feet, and flew back to San Pablo to repeat the operation twelve more times. Holloway assembled his Red legs, assembled his pack 75s, and got ready to fire. The 457th's A Battery stayed in the hills until the end of the campaign, almost a month later.

On the evening of 6 December Major General Swing and his staff were near his CP, having just eaten what passed for dinner. They heard the drone of aircraft engines, ran out of the mess tent, and were surprised to see some thirty-nine Japanese transports, much like C-47s, with fighter and bomber escorts, roar over Burauen at low altitude. The bombers dropped several incendiary bombs on the San Pablo airstrip, and the fighters strafed up and down the area. Eighteen of the planes were shot down by antiaircraft guns protecting the airstrips. But then came the jumpers. The commander of the Japanese 3d Parachute Regiment managed to jump with about sixty of his men onto the Buri strip. Between 250 and 300 Japanese landed near San Pablo. There they ran up and down both sides of the runway, burning five Cubs, a pile of ammunition, several tents, and a gasoline dump.

With most of his infantry committed to the operations in the Leyte hills to the west, Swing assembled near San Pablo an ad hoc task force of troopers from the 674th Glider Field Artillery Battalion without their howitzers, the 127th Engineer Battalion without their small, airborne bulldozers, and various service and support troop units without their typewriters. The task force, led by Swing personally, swept across the strip with Civil War tactics and cleared the area. At Buri, 1st Battalion, 187th, fought across the strip in a heavy firefight. In about a week most of the Japanese paratroopers, who were huge men by normal Japanese standards, had been wiped out or swept into the hills.

By late December, the 11th Airborne had fought its way across the island and joined the 7th Division on the west coast. By 15 January 1945, the entire 11th returned to Bito Beach for the six R's—rest, recuperation, reorganization, reequipping, remanning, and retraining.

On 22 January 1945, General Swing received Eighth Army Field Order Number 17 that alerted the 11th to taking part in an impending division operation on Luzon. The order directed that the "11th A/B will land one regimental combat team on X-Day at H-Hour in the Nasugbu area, seize and defend a beachhead; 511th PRCT will be prepared to move by air from Leyte to Mindoro bases, land by parachute on Tagaytay Ridge, effect a junction with the force of the 11th A/B moving in-

land from Nasugbu; the 11th A/B reinforced, after assembling on Tagaytay Ridge will be prepared for further action to the north and east as directed by the Commanding General, Eighth Army." One of the original
scenarios for the 11th was a parachute-and-glider attack by the entire division on Clark Field, fifty miles north of Manila. This plan fell apart
when it became evident that there were not enough planes for the operation, and the CG-4A gliders in the theater were still in crates on some
remote island. Another part of the plan attached the 503d Parachute
RCT to the 11th Airborne for operations on Luzon, but this plan evap-
orated when the general headquarters staff began to plan the recapture
of Corregidor using the 503d.

The amphibious units of the 11th (i.e., the glider units) boarded their
ships on 26 January and set sail the next day. With them in the LCIs was
part of the 511th Parachute Infantry Regiment that would be dropped
off on Mindoro. The remainder of the 511th, the 457th Field Artillery
Battalion, and a platoon of medics from the 221st Medical Battalion, flew
by C-46 from Leyte to Mindoro.

At dawn on 31 January 1945, the amphibious convoy carrying most
of the glider units of the 11th arrived off Nasugbu's shore in southern
Luzon. The sea was calm, the sky clear, and the visibility superb. At 0830,
after navy ships shelled the beach and eighteen A-20s and nine P-38s
strafed it, Lt. Col. Ernie LaFlamme (class of 1937), who had spent many
weekends at Nasugbu when he was a young lieutenant stationed at Fort
McKinley before the war, waded into the surf and led his 1st Battalion,
188th Glider Infantry ashore. The amphibious assault was under way.
The rest of the 188th and then the 187th Glider Infantry completed their
landings against minor opposition.

Between 31 January 1944 and 3 February 1945, the 188th and 187th,
with their artillery and support troops behind them, fought their way up
Highway 17 from Nasugbu, through strong Japanese defenses in the Aga
Defile, and on toward the heights of Tagaytay Ridge where the 511th
Parachute RCT was slated to land. Lieutenant General Eichelberger, the
Eighth Army Commander, had hoped to bring in the 511th on 2 February to give him an extra day in which to beat General Krueger and the
Sixth Army to Manila. (Earlier, on 9 January, the Sixth Army had gone
ashore on Luzon in a major amphibious landing at Lingayen Gulf, 120
miles north of Manila, in the same area where the Japanese had invaded
in December of 1941.) But because the prolonged and brutal fight at
the Aga Defile had slowed the advance of other 11th Division units,

Eichelberger had to put off the jump until the morning of 3 February. Moving by air and water, the 511th had already by 30 January 1944 arrived in marshaling areas on Mindoro and gotten ready for this drop. On 1 February the commander of the 511th, aptly named Col. Orin D. "Hard Rock" Haugen (class of 1930), thirty-seven years old, and his three infantry battalion commanders, the artillery battalion commander, the regiment's S-3 officer, and Col. John Lackey, commander of the 317th Troop Carrier Group, flew to Luzon and made an aerial reconnaissance of the selected DZs. On their return, they briefed the units down the line on the details of the operation, using maps, aerial photos, and sand tables. The operation began to take on a definite shape.

Because there were only forty-eight C-47s available, the drop had to be made in three lifts. The regimental staff, 2d Battalion, 511th, and half of 3d Battalion, 511th, made the first lift; the rest of the regiment was in the second lift; and the 457th was in the third.

At 0300 on 3 February, the troops in the first lift climbed aboard trucks and headed for the San Jose airstrip on Mindoro. Each truck had been appropriately chalk-marked with the same chalk-marked number on the plane to which it was headed.

At 0700 the first plane, piloted by Colonel Lackey and on which Colonel Haugen was jumpmaster, started its takeoff. By 0715, the forty-eight planes were in a V of V's over the airstrip, with P-61 Black Widow night fighters covering them. En route, however, they were escorted by P-38 Lightnings. The column flew north over Mindoro, then headed for Batangas Bay, and then on to Lake Taal, which bordered the southern edge of Tagaytay Ridge. Finally the planes few along Highway 17, parallel to the long axis of Tagaytay Ridge.

The ridge itself was an excellent DZ for a mass jump. It was open, about 2,000 yards wide and 4,000 yards long, and plowed in some places. Best of all, the local guerrillas had cleared it of most of the Japanese. The most serious danger to a paratrooper was the possibility of being blown by the wind off the ridge over its steep side, and down into Lake Taal.

Just a few minutes before 0815 Colonel Haugen stood in the door of the lead plane, sticking his head out the door as far as he could. He was looking for the green smoke signal that would indicate that Lt. David Hover and his pathfinders had made their way overland ahead of the ground elements of the 11th fighting up Highway 17 and had gotten to the ridge. As a precaution, Lt. Col. Douglass P. Quandt (class of 1937), the division G-3 officer, was in a Cub plane over the DZ ready to drop smoke grenades if Hover had not made it. But Hover and his men were on the DZ. When Haugen saw the smoke, he gave the word and led his men out the door. He was followed by the 345 men in the first eighteen planes of the first lift, all of whom hit the DZ. But the second echelon of the first flight, 570 men in thirty planes, were six miles and three minutes behind the first planes. This group jumped prematurely about 8,000 yards east of the go point. One theory had it that a jumpmaster saw another plane inadvertently drop an equipment bundle and then jumped. Pilots and crew chiefs tried unsuccessfully to block the jumpers, but to no avail.

At about 1210, the second lift approached Tagaytay Ridge from the east and met with some difficulty in hitting the proper DZ. Some 425 jumpers landed on the ridge; but another 1,325 jumped early and landed four to six miles to the east and northeast. The cause of the premature jump was probably because some pilots saw chutes of that morning's early drop and turned on their green lights ahead of schedule. In spite of the scattered drops, the 511th got itself assembled in about five hours.

By 1300 the afternoon of the same day, the 188th had moved up the ridge and made contact with the 511th. At about 1515 hours, Major General Swing moved his CP to the Manila Hotel Annex on the ridge overlooking Lake Taal, and Lieutenant General Eichelberger joined him there. In actuality, at this time the Eighth Army consisted only of the 11th Airborne Division and some minor support units. Fortunately Philippine guerrillas had cleared a large portion of the Tagaytay Ridge area, and the 11th could get ready to attack Manila from the south. The division's original mission had been to clear southern Luzon, but Eichelberger changed its mission to an attack on Manila from the south: he desperately wanted to beat Krueger to Manila, another "pearl of the Orient."

By midafternoon of 3 February, the 11th's quartermaster had brought seventeen 2.5-ton trucks up from Nasugbu. At the 11th CP on Tagaytay Ridge, Haugen reported to Major General Swing, who checked on the status of the 511th and then told Haugen to get ready to move up Highway 17 to the north, toward Manila.

Ahead of the 511th, Lt. George Skau and his reconnaissance platoon made a reconnaissance of the highway by jeep during the evening of the same day. At 2300, Skau radioed to the division G-2 officer, Lt. Col. Henry J. "Butch" Muller, that he had gone some fifteen miles toward Manila without running into any opposition. At 0400 the next morning, 4 February, Skau reported again and said that the road was clear as far as Imus, where the Japanese had blown a bridge and set up a defensive line. Haugen ordered Lt. Col. Frank S. "Hacksaw" Holcombe and his 2d Battalion, 511th to move out at dawn and move up along Highway 17 as far as Bacoor. Holcombe, in turn, told Capt. Steve Cavanaugh to mount up his D Company in 2.5-ton trucks and head up Highway 17. When Cavanaugh got to Imus, the attack on Manila from the south began.

At 0815 on 4 February the third serial of the 511th, consisting mostly of Lt. Col. Nick Stadtherr's 457th Parachute Field Artillery Battalion, parachuted onto Tagaytay Ridge. Meanwhile the trucks that had carried 2d Battalion, 511th forward returned to the ridge and picked up Lt. Col. Ed Lahti (class of 1938), thirty-one years old, and his 3d Battalion, 511th and moved them up the highway as far as it was clear. Lieutenant Colonel Henry Burgess and his 1st Battalion, 511th marched on foot the entire thirty-six miles from Tagaytay Ridge to the cathedral in the town of Paranaque.

By the night of 4 February, the 511th had advanced as far as the Paranaque River bridge, on the southern boundary of Manila. The 187th and the 188th Regiments had also begun their moves north. Because the Japanese, in their early planning for the defense of Manila, had concluded that the U.S. main attack would be from the south, they had set up the defends of Manila with the formidable Genko Line, 6,000 yards deep, that stretched east from the Manila Polo Club across Nichols Field and Fort McKinley and was anchored on the high ground at Mabato Point along Laguna de Bay. The Japanese had used thousands of Filipino laborers to build the fortifications. The Genko Line consisted of blockhouses two and three stories deep, naval guns embedded in concrete, 150mm and 300mm mortars, 120mm antiaircraft guns sighted horizontally, machine guns by the score, and naval bombs rigged as booby traps. The defense complex was manned by some 6,000 Japanese sheltered in about 1,200 pillboxes. The Japanese commander in the area, General Yamashita, had originally concluded that Manila was untenable and ordered it declared an open city. But after some orders and counterorders, the local naval commander, Admiral Iwabuchi, decided to stay even though General Yokoyama, the area commander, had ordered him twice, on 19 and 21 February, to evacuate the city. The entire 11th Airborne Division was now poised for its most critical and bloodiest combat, which would last until 3 March, when General Krueger finally decided that all organized Japanese resistance in Manila had ceased.

21: Corregidor

One of the most difficult, yet most successful, parachute operations of World War II was the assault by the 503d Airborne Regimental Combat Team (Rock Force) on Corregidor.

After an uneventful tour of duty on Leyte in late January 1945 the 503d Airborne RCT paratroopers shipped out to Mindoro and set themselves up in a fairly comfortable base camp near San José on the banks of the Bugsanda River. During that month, Lt. Col. George Jones and his staff melded new recruits into the 503d, trained the unit rigorously, spread the combat-experienced leaders among the units, and got reequipped for a possible airborne operation. Lieutenant Colonel Jack Tolson had been transferred from his 3d, 503d, to the G-3 section of the Sixth Army staff, and his major mission was to plan for the Corregidor operation.

By the end of January the Sixth Army plan for retaking Corregidor was pretty well set. On 4 February the plan went to Douglas MacArthur's headquarters. The next day, after a careful briefing by the Sixth Army staff, he approved the mission and set 12 February as the target date. (With MacArthur's approval, the Sixth Army later changed D day to Friday, 16 February.) On 6 February Jack Tolson flew to Mindoro and gave Colonel Jones a "heads up" for an airborne operation that was to seize Corregidor.

The drama of the return to Corregidor was thus set up by the methodical, grimly efficient staffs at the headquarters of the Southwest Pacific Theater Area Command and the Sixth Army. The actors had their scripts; now they began to study their roles and the stage. The men of the 503d, gearing up for their third combat jump in the Pacific, wanted to play their parts like the seasoned professionals they had become. They

were soon to learn, however, that the stage and the scenery their supe-
riors had selected for them were, to say the least, extraordinary for a paratrooper cast.

Corregidor is a tadpole-shaped island of volcanic rock in Manila Bay.
It is one of four fortified islands in the bay and lies some twenty-five miles
southwest of Manila Harbor. It is only 3.5 miles long and 1.5 miles wide
at its broadest point, which lies at Topside (the head of the "tadpole"),
which is also the highest part of the island, rising sharply to 550 feet. Toward the tail, the terrain slopes off to a small plateau known as Middle-
side. Here it drops to the waist of the island, 300 yards wide, Bottomside.
Malinta Hill to the rear of Bottomside rises to 390 feet. Years earlier, U.S.
Army engineers had dug a tunnel 1,450 feet long, 30 feet wide at the
base, and 20 feet high at the arched ceiling through Malinta Hill.
Branching off from the main tunnel were twenty-five laterals each 200
feet long. The walls, floors, and overhead arches were of reinforced concrete. Before the war improvements to the tunnel had continued, and
by the time of U.S. involvement in the war in December 1941, the tunnel housed a 300-bed hospital, a storage area, barracks, and eventually
MacArthur's headquarters before he left for Australia in 1942. Behind
Malinta Hill stretched the long, narrow tail of the island on which was
located Kindley Field, with its 2,000-foot runway, and another tunnel.

Before World War II, the United States had built Corregidor into a
seemingly impregnable fortress bristling with twenty-three batteries of
coast artillery guns. Some were monsters, including the twelve-inch
guns of Batteries Wheeler and Crockett and the twelve-inch mortars of
Batteries Geary and Way. There were also six batteries of three-inch antiaircraft guns, twelve batteries of .50-caliber machine guns, and one battery of five sixty-inch searchlights. The troops lived in the "Mile-Long Barracks" on Topside. The officers and their families were housed in
concrete bungalows around the parade ground and the nine-hole golf
course. Filipinos who worked for the army lived in a village near Bottomside.

By February 1945, there was probably no strategic or tactical need to
retake Corregidor—it could probably simply "die on the vine." But it was
a thorn in the side of U.S. forces because many ships sailing in the narrow straits around the island toward Manila were repeatedly fired upon
by Japanese emplacements on the island. Its occupation by the Japanese
probably rankled General MacArthur more than anyone else because it
was the place from which he had left ignominiously.

The Sixth Army plan called for a combined amphibious-parachute attack on the island. The airborne portion of the assault force, Rock Force, was the 503d Parachute RCT; the amphibious element was the 2d Battalion, 34th Infantry Regiment, part of the 24th Division, commanded by Lt. Col. Edward M. Postlethwait (class of 1937), thirty-three years old.

On 6 February, Col. George Jones flew to Sixth Army Headquarters and contacted Jack Tolson, who briefed him on the plan. Tolson pointed out that the Sixth Army staff had decided that there were few areas suitable for an amphibious landing and that an airborne operation would, therefore, probably have fewer casualties. Tolson also pointed out the obvious fact that there were relatively few decent DZs on Corregidor and asked Colonel Jones, at General Krueger's request, to fly over the island, reconnoiter it, and recommend possible DZs. Tolson also gave Jones the latest aerial photos and maps of the island. The Sixth Army G-2 officer told Jones that, to the best of his knowledge, there were about 850 first-line Japanese troops, marines, on the island. This estimate would later prove to be devastatingly inaccurate. Jones flew back to his CP on Mindoro, gathered his staff, and briefed them on the situation as he understood it.

On the next day, he flew over the island in the machine gunner's seat in the nose of a B-25. He had the pilot make a few low-level runs over the island and was dismayed at what he found. For the previous twenty-five days, the navy and the Fifth Air Force had been pounding the island night and day. During that time, 3,125 tons of bombs had blasted an area of just over one square mile: Topside was littered with debris, downed trees, shattered concrete buildings, innumerable bomb craters, blasted rock outcroppings, and tangled undergrowth. There were only two clearings there for possible DZs: the rubble-strewn parade ground in front of the old concrete barracks, 325 by 150 yards, and the old, sloping, bomb-pitted, nine-hole golf course, about 350 by 165 yards, which was surrounded by wrecked officers' quarters. The edges of these two areas fell off sharply into ravines and were bordered by steep, rocky cliffs on the west and the south. Colonel Jones considered these two areas for DZs hazardous, at best. When he flew over the airstrip on the east end of the island he felt that it was the best DZ on the island, but even that was marginal. He returned to Mindoro and radioed his recommendation to Jack Tolson at Sixth Army, who in turn presented it to General Krueger—who promptly vetoed it. He felt that a drop on Kindley Field would expose the paratroopers to heavy, accurate fire from Malinta Hill and Topside. Krueger personally made the decision that the 503d would drop on the old parade ground and the golf course. Like the good soldier that he was, Jones did not debate the decision.

He and his staff then went about developing the Rock Force assault plan: Lt. Col. John Erickson's 3d Battalion, the RCT staff, C Company of the 161st Engineer Battalion, and A Battery of the 462d would drop on both DZs at 0830 on D day and secure them. At 1030 on D day, Postlethwait's 3d Battalion, 34th, would storm ashore on Black Beach, on Bottomside's south shore. On the same afternoon Maj. L. B. Caskey would jump his 2d Battalion, 503d, plus B Company, 462d, on both DZs. Caskey's initial mission was to help Erickson clear Topside. At 0830 on D day plus 1, Maj. Pug Wood's 1st Battalion, 503d, plus C Company, 462d, would parachute onto the island using the same two DZs. Colonel John Lackey and his 317th Troop Carrier Group would provide the jump aircraft.

Because of the size of the DZs and the prevailing twenty-five-knot wind across the island, Lackey knew that it would be difficult to put all the jumpers safely onto the tiny DZs. Each plane would be over the DZ for only six seconds, he calculated, and each trooper would drift about 250 feet to the west during his twenty-five-second descent. Given these considerations, Lackey and Jones estimated that the jump casualties would be in the neighborhood of 50 percent, almost unthinkable.

Lackey finally decided on his plan: his fifty-eight C-47s would fly over the DZs in a flight pattern of single ships in trail with twenty-five-second intervals between planes; the planes over the parade ground would fly in a counterclockwise circle; the planes over the golf course would fly in a clockwise circle; the drop altitude would be 1,150 feet over Topside and thus 600 feet above the ground; each plane would drop eight troopers per pass. And Jones and Lackey decided that Jones would fly in the lead plane in the cockpit so that together they could monitor the details of the operation and make tactical decisions and changes on the spot.

At dawn of D day, fourteen U.S. Navy destroyers and eight cruisers, plus thirty-six B-24 bombers, began blasting Corregidor. Just as the lead jump plane came into view, thirty-one A-20s strafed the island. Unfortunately, the bombing and strafing killed few Japanese because they were safely ensconced in the many tunnels and caves on the island.

At 0833 on 16 February, just three minutes behind schedule, John Erickson led his stick of eight men out of the lead plane in his serial. The last jumper barely got onto the parade ground. Colonel Jones, hovering in the plane over the rock with Lackey, saw the problem and immediately radioed the other pilots to reduce their jump altitude to 400 feet and to cut the sticks to six men each. Later Jones said that "this did the trick pretty well . . . we had no people who landed in the water." One hour and forty-five minutes after Erickson jumped, his last jumper landed on Topside. Casualties were high: 25 percent of the force either injured on landing or killed in initial skirmishes with the enemy.

Because of the strong prevailing winds, twenty-five men of I Company, assigned to land on the golf course, drifted over the cliff near Breakwater Point and landed in some scrub-covered hillocks 200 feet or so above the water's edge. They got out of their chutes and started to move along a trail to Topside, but at a turn in the trail the lead man saw about eight or nine Japanese standing near the trail staring intently to the south over Geary Point. The lead paratrooper waved his arms to those behind them, quietly motioning them to deploy. Then on signal they started shooting and throwing grenades at the Japanese, who scattered but returned fire. But that was too little and too late. In short order the I Company men killed most of the Japanese.

With almost unbelievably good fortune, one of the dead was Captain Itagaki of the Imperial Japanese Navy, the commander of all the Japanese on Corregidor. He and his staff had been watching the landing of the 3d Battalion, 34th RCT coming ashore at Black Beach just after the 3d Battalion, 503d had finished jumping on Topside. (Meanwhile, Postlethwait and his troops swarmed out of their LSMs and started their climb up to Malinta Hill.)

After Colonel Jones got reports on the injuries his men had suffered in the drop, he considered calling off the afternoon jump phase and bringing the rest of the 503d in by boat. But since he did not know the real enemy situation on the island, he permitted the second drop to go in as planned, which began at 1240. The second drop was more accurate, but the Japanese were now coming out of their caves and holes and firing at the descending troopers. With the arrival of the second lift, Jones had some 2,050 men. Fifty others were shot and killed in midair and eight were killed from jump injuries: another 210 were out of action with wounds and other injuries. The injuries and deaths in action were serious, but amounted to only about half the predicted 50 percent losses. The 3d Battalion, 503d spent most of D day securing the northern half of Topside and succeeded in knocking out the Japanese communications center that housed all the terminals for wire communications throughout the island, thus severing the enemy's ability to send messages and orders; meanwhile, the 2d Battalion, 503d worked at clearing the southern half of Topside. At about sunset Jones made the decision to fly Pug Woods and his 1st Battalion, 503d, to an airfield near Subic Bay and then ship them by LCM to Corregidor rather than risk dropping them on the island the next morning. But Woods had already rigged the C-47s to drop his heavy equipment and ammunition boxes. To save the trouble of reloading, he decided that he would simply drop these items from the C-47s as they flew over Corregidor. On the afternoon of 17 February Woods and his battalion landed on Black Beach and moved up to the fight.

Meanwhile, at midnight on 17 February, fifty wildly screaming Japanese Imperial Marines launched a surprise banzai charge against K Company of the 34th Regiment, dug in on top of Malinta Hill, and got themselves killed. At dawn K Company troops counted thirty-six dead Japanese at the foot of the hill. At 0800 on the 18th the Japanese charged up the hill again and again. In the ensuing bloody battle, the Japanese lost 150 dead and the 3d Battalion, 34th counted sixty-eight dead and wounded.

At 0500 on 19 February, Lieutenant Endo led 600 Imperial Marines in a banzai charge from Cheney Ravine and Wheeler Point on Topside against the dug-in 2d, 503d. Armed with grenades, rifles, and even bayonets strapped to sticks, the Japanese stampeded against the paratroopers with diabolical fervor. Private Lloyd McCarter of F Company, 2d Battalion, fought so valiantly that he was later awarded the Medal of Honor, the only one awarded to a trooper on Corregidor. The men of the 2d Battalion, fought with courage and heart from their foxholes and then charged out to fight hand to hand with bayonets against the swarming Japanese. When the fight was over in about thirty minutes, some 500 dead Japanese marines littered the area. The 2d Battalion, 503d, had thirty-three killed and seventy-five wounded in action.

For the next two days the paratroopers hunted the Japanese survivors of the banzai attack. The latter were found in caves and had to be killed because they would not surrender.

Some 2,000 Japanese had holed up in Malinta Tunnel directly below the 3d Battalion, 34th Regiment. Bombardments by U.S. forces had caused rockslides and closed the tunnel's exits. Inside, the trapped Japanese decided to blast open an exit and charge out of it against Lieutenant Colonel Postlethwait's men. At 2230 on 20 February, a fuse leading to the explosives stacked against a tunnel door was lit. Massive sheets of fire shot from both ends of the tunnel, rocks and dirt cascaded throughout the immediate area, and six men of the 3d Battalion, 34th, were killed in a resulting rockslide. But the Japanese plan backfired: flames from the initial explosion set off tons of other explosives stored in the tunnel, and all but 600 Japanese were killed. The survivors ran to their deaths off the side of the island.

On 24 February Colonel Jones decided to clear the tail section of the island. He ordered Pug Woods to lead his battalion, accompanied by tanks from the 3d Battalion, 34th, toward that area and secure it. By late afternoon of that day Woods's troops had wiped out 101 Japanese. The battalion dug in for the night but was hit by a Japanese counterattack shortly after dark. The enemy troops were beaten back, but in the close-in fighting Woods and three of his troopers were killed.

The 1st Battalion, 503d, continued pushing toward the eastern edge of the island. By the morning of 26 February the battalion was on Monkey Point, a small hill overlooking Kindley Field. Directly below Monkey Point was the radio intercept tunnel in which the Japanese had stored tons of explosives. At noon, troopers from A Company, 1st Battalion, standing on the hill were blown into the air by a blast so strong that it turned over a thirty-five-ton Sherman tank and threw Maj. John Davis, the new battalion commander, through the air. Although he was unharmed, fifty-two of his men were killed along with 150 of the enemy in the tunnel.

Colonel Jones ordered the 3d Battalion to move through the battered 1st Battalion and continue the attack toward the airstrip. By 27 February, the battalion had reached the tip of the tail of the island. With that, all organized resistance on Corregidor ceased.

By actual body count, 4,500 Japanese had been killed and 20 taken prisoner. This was a far cry from the original Sixth Army G-2 estimate of 850 Japanese on the island. MacArthur wrote that "virtually the entire Japanese garrison of approximately 6,000 men were annihilated." Total U.S. losses were 1,003 men, of whom 210 were killed and 450 wounded in action, 340 were injured, and 3 were missing

At 1000 on 2 March General MacArthur, in his typical style, returned to Corregidor. "There are moments of drama and romance in every life, and my first visit to recaptured Corregidor was one of these," he wrote in *Reminiscences*.

I borrowed four PT boats from the Navy and gathered all those who had originally left Corregidor with me. We went back to the Rock the same way we had left it. We had departed in the dark of a somber night. We came back in the sunlight of a new day. In the background, the ragged remnants of our parachutes dangled from the jagged tree stumps, the skeleton remains of the old white barracks of "Topside" gleamed down on us, and a smart-looking honor guard rendered us a salute.

I was greeted by Colonel George Jones, the young man who had commanded the troops that had so recently retaken the island in such gallant fashion. I congratulated and decorated him.

"I see that the old flag pole still stands," I told him. "Have your troops hoist the colors to its peak, and let no enemy ever haul them down."

22: The Los Baños Raid

After the return of U.S. forces to Luzon, one of General Mac-
Arthur's most urgent missions was the rapid liberation of POWs
and civilian internees taken by the Japanese and incarcerated in
various camps around Luzon. "I was deeply concerned about the thousands of prisoners who had been interned at the various camps on Luzon since the early days of the war," he wrote in *Reminiscences.*

> Shortly after the Japanese had taken over the islands, they had
> gathered Americans, British, and other Allied nationals, including
> women and children, in concentration centers without regard to
> whether they were actual combatants or simply civilians. I had been
> receiving reports from my various underground sources before the
> actual landings on Luzon, but the latest information was most
> alarming. With every step that our soldiers took toward Santo
> Tomas University, Bilibid, Cabanatauan, and Los Baños, where
> these prisoners were held, the Japanese soldiers guarding them had
> become more and more sadistic. I knew that many of these half-
> starved and ill-treated people would die unless we rescued them
> promptly. The thought of their destruction with deliverance so near
> was deeply repellent to me.

The Los Baños camp was located on the sixty-acre site of the Agricultural College of the Philippines on the south shore of Laguna de Bay,
a large fresh-water lake, forty miles southeast of Manila and, in February 1945, twenty-five miles behind U.S. lines. Shortly after the 11th Airborne Division had waded ashore at Nasugbu and parachuted onto
Tagaytay Ridge, MacArthur alerted Eichelberger to the pressing need to

rescue all the prisoners in the various camps throughout the U.S. Eighth Army's area of operations but set no timetable for their release.

On 3 February 1945, as the 11th Airborne was battling its way toward Manila in a series of vicious battles, Eichelberger first passed to Maj. Gen. Joseph Swing, the 11th's commander, the mission of rescuing the civilian interned at Los Baños. But in the next few weeks, the division would be too heavily engaged in attacking the Genko Line south of Manila and the defenses of Nichols Field and Fort McKinley to do anything about those in Japanese captivity.

In the interim Swing tasked his G-2 officer, Lt. Col. Henry "Butch" Muller, to gather all the information he could about the Los Baños camp. Muller worked with the guerrilla forces in the area, and particularly with Maj. Jay D. Vanderpool, the U.S. liaison officer with the guerrilla command in southern Luzon. Liaisons between Vanderpool's guerrillas and Major General Swing and his staff were fairly easy and direct. The 11th Division headquarters at Paranaque had a rudimentary officers' mess (airborne units were not given to luxurious trappings), where Lieutenant General Eichelberger and his staff (until they returned to Leyte and Eighth Army headquarters on 8 February), Swing and his principal staff officers, and Vanderpool and some of his guerrilla staff members ate together. At least once a day Vanderpool and his staff briefed the 11th Airborne's staff on the conditions around Los Baños. Vanderpool's G-2 officer was Col. Marcelo Castillo, a 1938 graduate of the U.S. Naval Academy. His G-3 officer was Col. Bert Atienza, who had had military experience with the U.S. forces and spoke fluent English. Thus Muller could keep up with the latest intelligence from the guerrillas, and Lt. Col. Douglass P. Quandt, thirty years old, the 11th's brilliant G-3 officer, could keep abreast of the current operational planning and continue to work on a plan of his own.

Muller got information not only from Vanderpool and his staff, but also directly from guerrilla headquarters in and around Nanhaya through Sgt. John Fulton, a member of the division's 511th Signal Company. Muller volunteered to join the guerrillas via a hazardous, nighttime *banca* (small boat) trip along the south shore of Laguna de Bay. Muller also had detailed maps and aerial photos of the area. One piece of intelligence was most troubling: the Japanese Tiger Division, the 8th, with about 9,000 battle-hardened troops, was located in the Santo Tomas-San Pablo area, about an hour-and-a-half march away for one of its battalions.

At Los Baños the internees themselves were not idle. The younger and stronger of them occasionally escaped at night to hunt for food and information. On the night of 12 February, Freddie Zervoulakos, nineteen years old, son of a Greek father and a Filipino mother and fluent in Tagalog, made his way to Tranca and the home of Mrs. Espino, wife of Colonel "Price," a pseudonymous guerrilla leader. There he met Colonel Ingles from Vanderpool's staff, who told Zervoulakos that the guerrillas were planning a raid on their own to liberate the camp. Zervoulakos hurried back to the camp and told Peter Miles and Ben Edwards about the plan. (Ben Edwards, twenty-four years old, had been a mechanic for Pan Am World Airways and had arrived in the Philippines in October of 1941.) Miles and Edwards immediately talked to the camp secretary, George Gray, who had been on the legal staff of the U.S. High Commissioner for the Philippines before the war. Gray called a meeting of the camp committee, most of whom were reluctant to pursue the matter. Gray, Edwards, and Miles, however, were not. On the night of 14 February George Gray and Freddie Zervoulakos left camp again and met Ingles at Mrs. Espino's home. Gray briefed Ingles on the camp's guard posts, routines, and the almost desperate condition of the internees. Gray and Ingles agreed that without transportation for the sick and infirm, the guerrillas' plan would not work. Gray went back to camp and talked again to the committee, which decided that it could do nothing and was forced to leave the rescue up to U.S. forces. Gray would not accept that restriction. He talked it over with young Zervoulakos, Miles, and Edwards, who decided that the latter three should meet again with Ingles on the night of 18 February.

At 2100 on that night, with Miles feigning sickness, the trio wandered as inconspicuously as possible to the Los Baños hospital and slipped out again under the nearby rolls of barbed wire. They arrived at Tranca about 2300. There they met with Colonel "Price" and John Fulton, who decided that Miles should go to the 11th Airborne's CP at Paranaque, and Zervoulakos and Edwards should go to Nanhaya, ready to go to Paranaque if Miles failed in his attempt. With three young guerrillas, Miles made the trip to Paranaque by about 2300 on 19 February. The next day, he met with Muller and gave him information and intelligence that no other source could have provided.

From Miles, an engineer with an almost encyclopedic memory, Muller learned many intricate details of the camp and the internees. The 2,122 civilians were in four categories: Protestant missionaries and their families; Roman Catholic priests and nuns; doctors, engineers, and other professionals and their families; and a few hundred wives and children of U.S. servicemen. Among the other nationalities were British, Canadians, Dutch, and Norwegians. Miles helped Muller develop a detailed map of the camp and, most important, the daily routine of the prison guards. Each morning at 0700, he told Muller, all prisoners are lined up and counted. At the same time, all the guards, except for a skeleton crew in the watchtowers, began a thirty-minute exercise program with their weapons some distance away in arms racks.

Over the next few days the 11th Airborne staff, principally Muller and Quandt, developed a plan to liberate Los Baños. The one certainty was that H hour would be at 0700, when the guards were exercising and away from their weapons and the prisoners assembled, making the evacuation of the latter more manageable.

The final plan had four phases. First, the 11th's thirty-one-man reconnaissance platoon, under Lt. George Skau, would travel in *bancas* across the lake two nights before H hour, go ashore about five miles from the camp, move in the dark to the outskirts of the camp to await H hour and, in addition, secure a large open field abutting the camp for a DZ. Second, at H hour a company of paratroopers would drop next to the camp, eliminate what guards remained, and organize the internees for evacuation. Third, at the shore of Laguna de Bay two other companies would come ashore in fifty-four amtracs (tracked amphibious utility vehicles), debark and secure the beachhead area while the amtracs and some guards moved to the camp, got the internees on board, and brought them back to Mamatid. In a second operation the strike force would be returned by the same method. Finally, a reinforced infantry battalion task force with two artillery battalions and a tank destroyer battalion would come down Highway 1 to block any enemy forces moving up on the southwest side of the camp.

By 20 February, Major General Swing felt that he could pull troops from the attack on Fort McKinley to launch the raid. He told Col. Edward H. Lahti, commander of the 511th Parachute Infantry Regiment, to select the battalion. Lahti told Lt. Col. Henry Burgess that he and his 1st Battalion, 511th, would make the assault. Burgess selected B Company, commanded by Lt. John M. Ringler, to make the drop. Lahti, Burgess, and Ringler reported to Swing at the division CP on 20 February, and Muller and Quandt briefed them on their mission. In more detail, Ringler's company was to drop 200 yards from the camp, assemble, kill the guards, and gather the internees for their evacuation. Ringler was also to move his company out of combat and get to the departure airfield, Nichols Field, on 22 February. Burgess's mission was to move the rest of his battalion to Mamatid on the western shore of Laguna de Bay, load it in the amtracs of the 672d Amphibious Tractor Battalion at 0500 on D day, sail across the bay to a beachhead at Mayondon Point near San Antonio, some two miles from the camp, secure the beachhead with two companies, move the amtracs into the camp, load up the internees, move them to Mamatid, and then return to pick up his men in the second lift of the amtracs. The ground attack force became the Soule Task Force, named after Col. Robert H. Soule, the commander of the 188th Glider Infantry Regiment. The task force was composed of the 1st Battalion, 188th, two artillery battalions, and a tank destroyer battalion.

After dark on 21 February, Lieutenant Skau and his platoon left the northern shore of Laguna de Bay and headed across the lake in three *bancas:* Skau and six men were in one, Sgt. Martin Squires and six men in the second, and the rest of the platoon and the bulk of their gear in a larger third. At Nanhaya, Lieutenant Skau and Sergeant Squires met with the guerrilla leaders, Ben Edwards and Freddie Zervoulakos, in the Nanhaya schoolhouse. Ben drew a sketch of the camp on the school blackboard and briefed Skau, Squires, and the guerrillas in detail on the terrain around the camp, the location and size of the guard posts, and the location of the fences and barbed wire. Then Skau made his final plans and asked Ben Edwards to accompany Sergeant Squires, six reconnaissance men, and twenty guerrillas to hit the guard posts on the northwest corner of the camp. He assigned other teams to locations around the camp and one team to mark the DZ for the parachute drop. After dark on 22 February, the various reconnaissance/guerrilla teams made forced marches as secretly as possible to their designated attack positions.

At 0700 the following morning the guards, as promised, routinely checked the assembled prisoners. Off in the distance, two columns of white smoke set off by Skau's team rose through the jungle foliage. The C-47s flew over the area, and Lt. John Ringler jumped out the door of the lead ship. He was quickly followed by the rest of his company. Skau saw Ringler's chute open, the signal for the attack on the guards. He tapped the shoulder of one of his men who fired a bazooka round at the pillbox beside the main entrance to the camp. The rest of Skau's team and the guerrillas opened fire on the guard towers. Sergeant Squires and

Ben Edwards were near the fence opposite the YMCA building at the northwest corner of the camp.

"When the first chute opened," Edwards recalled, "we threw grenades over the fences toward the spot I had told everyone was the location of the guard post. Unknowingly, I threw a phosphorous instead of a frag-mentation grenade, but it landed in the guard post. We cautiously climbed over the swali-covered fence, then jumped down and crawled under the inner fence." He and Squires's team went on inside the camp looking for other Japanese. On schedule the rest of Skau's teams hit their assigned posts and towers. With only one of his men having been injured in the jump, Ringler had his men assembled and moved toward the camp at 0715 on 23 February. They raced into the camp, hunted down some stray Japanese, and then started to round up the prisoners.

The prisoners were in a state of shock. Recent rumors throughout the camp had held that because of the deteriorating situation on Luzon, the Japanese had intended to kill them all. A large ditch that had been dug by the prisoners outside the camp, possibly their graveyard, reinforced that horrific view. When the internees saw the parachutes floating down right next to the camp and heard the shooting, they realized that it was all over and that they had been saved. They milled wildly and happily about the camp, oblivious to the need for getting organized and out of the area. In the near chaos some internees fell to the ground to avoid the firing, and some of the women grabbed their children and headed back to their huts. Others tried to gather their meager possessions. Meanwhile, in less than twenty minutes Ringler's men, Skau's recon-naissance platoon, and the guerrillas wiped out almost all of the 243 camp guards.

The amtracs lumbered into the camp, and Hank Burgess now had the formidable task of rapidly organizing the evacuation, well aware of the proximity of the Japanese Tiger Division. The prisoners were delirious and thought that their problems were over now that the paratroopers had arrived, and saw no need for haste. Ringler noted that some of the barracks were on fire, and that the prisoners were moving away from them toward the amtracs now assembled on the ballfield. He suggested to Burgess that they start some more fires to herd the internees toward the amtracs. Burgess agreed. The new fires and smoke drove the in-ternees toward the amtracs where Burgess and his men started to put them on board.

As best he could, Burgess gave priority in the amtracs to the women, children, and disabled men. Some men, however, refused to leave their wives and children, so Burgess simply loaded everyone as they arrived. Those who could walk started the two-mile trek to the beachhead at San Antonio. Burgess used part of Ringler's company to form a perimeter around the camp and the rest of B Company to make certain that all the internees had left their dwellings and were on the way to the beach by amtrac or on foot. By 1130 the evacuation of the camp was complete. By then Burgess knew that the camp had been cleared, none of the internees had been lost, all the Japanese had either been killed or dispersed, none of his troops had been killed and only two had been wounded, and two guerrillas had been killed and four wounded.

The first shuttle of amtracs left San Antonio at about 1000 hours, each carrying thirty to thirty-five internees, their baggage, and a few paratroopers to guard them. The amtracs beached at Mamatid well behind U.S. lines, rapidly unloaded the internees, and at about 1300 returned to San Antonio to evacuate the rest of the paratroopers and former prisoners. By the time Burgess and the last six amtracs pulled out of San Antonio at about 1500, the Japanese had moved close to the beachhead and were shelling it with artillery fire and spraying it with machine guns.

The Soule Task Force had attacked across the San Juan River early on the morning of 23 February and had run into some opposition near the Lechería Hills, where one of the men was killed. The commander of the 637th Tank Destroyer unit was also killed when he attempted to inspect a gun emplacement at a road junction still manned by a Japanese soldier. By midmorning the task force cleared the area and was marching down the road toward Los Baños. And by this time Colonel Soule could see the amtracs on the lake moving back to Mamatid. He ordered his task force to reestablish a bridgehead near the San Juan River. John Ringler credits the Soule Task Force with greatly contributing to the success of the raid because it engaged and diverted the enemy in the Lechería Hills–Rock Quarry area and blocked the road from Santo Tomás to Los Baños. Without their help, it is very possible that the Tiger Division could have sent a force to attack the internee rescue column. The raid would have turned into a disaster if the Japanese had made such a move.

At Mamatid the internees, safely behind U.S. lines, were in one large group in a small, constricted area and carrying a minimum of baggage. Thus Burgess had somewhat better control of the situation. The internees wandered about, looking for close friends, hugging one another, and embarrassing the paratroopers of the 511th with the warmth of their gratitude and congratulations. But in about an hour, they were loaded into trucks and ambulances and moved out on Highway 1 for the fifteen-mile ride to Muntinlupa and the New Bilibid prison, which would be their home for the next few weeks before their evacuation to the United States. At New Bilibid they ate heartily but carefully. One of the rescued nuns, Sister Maria, remembers: "When we landed here [at New Bilibid] they took our names and checked us off as 'released' from the Los Baños Internment Camp. Then, a smiling soldier boy handed me four Hershey bars. How good they were! Went to the kitchen and got bean soup. Oy, bean soup, real bean soup!"

On the day after the raid, 24 February 1945, General MacArthur sent a special communiqué to the men of the 11th Airborne Division: "Nothing could be more satisfying to a soldier's heart than this rescue. I am deeply grateful. God was certainly with us today."

And for once, the 11th could count a victory by the number of people saved rather than the number of men killed or miles of ground gained.

(In 1947, after he had been discharged from the army, Martin Squires saw a newspaper article that referred to one of the Los Baños internees, Margaret Whitaker. After a courtship of some weeks, Squires married the young lady he had helped rescue at Los Baños.)

23: Aparri and the Occupation of Japan

The last airborne operation of World War II was the 11th Airborne Division's assault by parachute and glider near Aparri, on northern Luzon, on 23 June 1945.

By then Japanese General Yamashita had concentrated his fourteenth Army area of 150,000 men in three defensive positions in northern Luzon. As early as December 1944, he had realized that the most he could accomplish with his forces was to delay Allied progress toward Japan by tying up in battle as many U.S. divisions as possible. He concentrated his best group, the Shobu, in the north because it provided the best opportunity for delaying action. General Krueger, commander of the U.S. Sixth Army, committed four infantry divisions, an armored group, a large force of guerrillas, and a separate RCT against the Shobu Group. By mid-June, Krueger estimated that if the U.S. 37th Division, attacking up the Cagayan Valley toward Aparri, could continue its fast drive north, it might be able to end the Luzon campaign then and there.

On 17 June the 37th continued its advance up Route 5 in the Cagayan Valley. Two days later the 37th ran into elements of the Yuguchi Force, which was still trying to move south along Route 5. Over the next four days, the 37th killed more than 600 Japanese, captured 285 more, and destroyed fifteen light tanks in a fifteen-mile stretch of the highway. By 25 June, the remnants of the Yuguchi Force were in full flight toward the untracked wilds of the Sierra Madre, which separated the Cagayan Valley from the east coast of Luzon.

Although the 37th Division was successful in its drive north, Krueger felt it necessary to assist Maj. Gen. Robert Beightler, the 37th's commander. Krueger's plan was to land an airborne force near Aparri on the

northern tip of Luzon and then have it attack to the south to link up with
Beightler's 37th. The joining of the forces would, in effect, seal off the
Cagayan Valley and the northern part of Luzon, the only area still in-
fested with large numbers of combat-ready enemy forces. On 21 June he
ordered Major General Swing to land a battalion combat team near
Aparri on 25 June.

On 23 June, Maj. Robert V. Connolly and his truck-mounted Connolly
Task Force (800 men, including a reinforced company from the 33d Division, a Ranger company, and a battery of artillery) entered Aparri from
the west. The next day, elements of Connolly's task force and the 2d Battalion of Col. Russell W. Volckmann's 11th Infantry of the Philippine
Army were ten miles south of Aparri along Route 5 and had secured the
Camalaniugan airfield, three miles from Aparri. Despite the success of
the Connolly Task Force and 2d Battalion, 11th Infantry, Krueger decided to go ahead with the airborne operation.

Because of the rapid advance of the 37th, Krueger advanced the air-
borne operation to 23 June. This meant that thirty-six hours after Sixth
Army had alerted the 11th Airborne for the operation, the Connolly Task
Force would be in action. Swing formed the Gypsy Task Force to accomplish the Aparri mission and assigned the command to the executive officer of the 511th Parachute Infantry Regiment, Lt. Col. Henry
Burgess. His task force of 1,030 men consisted of the 1st Battalion and
G and I Companies of the 511th; C Battery of the 457th Parachute Field
Artillery Battalion; a composite platoon of C Company, 127th Engineers;
the 2d Platoon, 221st Medical Company; and teams from the 511th Signal Company, the Language Detachment, and the 11th Parachute Maintenance Company.

On the afternoon of 22 June, Krueger arrived at Lipa to inspect the
preparations for the next day's drop. As he and Swing walked through
the men, who were loading their gear on the planes and checking
parachutes, Lieutenant Colonel Burgess reported to General Krueger,
who asked Burgess how old he was. He replied that he was "twenty-six."
Then Krueger asked Swing whether he had an older officer to command
the force. General Swing said, "Yes, Colonel Lahti, who is thirty-one, but
in the event the Gypsy Task Force has trouble, Lahti would have to take
the rest of his regiment and reinforce the troops." On that date, Colonel
Lahti was the oldest officer in the 511th and older than all but two of
the enlisted men.

The departure strip for the Aparri operation was the concrete airfield at Lipa, built by Japanese engineers in 1942. It is ironic that when the Japanese had launched their parachute attack on 11th Airborne units around the strips at San Pablo on Leyte in December of 1944, they used Lipa as their departure airfield.

At Lipa, Col. John Lackey and his veteran 317th Troop Carrier Group assembled fifty-four C-47s and thirteen C-46s, and, for their first combat use in the Pacific Theater, seven gliders—six CG-4As and a larger CG-13. The Gypsy Task Force began loading at 0430 on 23 June with Krueger and Swing present for the 0600 takeoff.

The first plane off the strip was a C-46 piloted by Colonel Lackey. One after another, the rest of the transports followed, assembled in the air, and went on course in a V of V's, with the seven gliders and their tug ships bringing up the rear of the column. The flight course was northwest to a checkpoint at Santa Lucia on the west coast of Luzon above the Lingayen Gulf, then to the northeast directly to the Camalaniugan airfield, the DZ. Bombers and fighters of the Fifth Air Force flew cover, and other planes laid smoke screens to the east and south of Camalaniugan to conceal the drop from the Japanese in the hills to the east.

On 21 June, two days before the drop, the 11th's pathfinders had flown up to the area, contacted Colonel Volckmann's Philippine 11th Infantry on the west bank of the Cagayan River, and then, the night before the drop, had slipped across the river and moved to the Camalaniugan DZ.

Precisely at 0900 on 23 June the pathfinders set off colored smoke to mark the DZ. Colonel Lackey picked up the signal, turned on his green jump light, and the first V of nine planes dropped their jumpers onto the field. As the rest of the flight flew over the go point in succession, the pilots turned on their green lights, and the jumpers exited the planes in precisely the proper area. But the jump casualties were high: two men were killed when their parachutes malfunctioned, and seventy men—a very high rate of about 7 percent—were injured on landing. Contributing to the high rate of jump casualties were a wind of twenty to twenty-five miles an hour and rough terrain, much of which was flooded rice paddies along the airstrip, *carabao* wallows, and bomb craters hidden by thick kunai grass. Colonel Volckmann remembers that he had his 11th Infantry and his engineer battalion fill shell holes on the strip and, just before the drop, chase *carabao* off the DZ.

Once on the ground and after checking his troops, Lieutenant Colonel Burgess contacted both Colonel Volckmann and Major Connolly, whose forces had remained in the vicinity of Aparri. Burgess led his Gypsy Task Force south along Route 5 and the Cagayan River to contact the 37th Division. Burgess wrote later: "The Aparri operation was one long, hot march, but militarily it was not difficult. A drop of flamethrowers and Lt. Ken Murphy along the route were of great assistance in taking out pillboxes encountered. We continued the march without interruption." On 26 June, Burgess's point men ran into the lead elements of the 37th Division near the Paret River, thirty-five miles south of the Camalaniugan airfield. Burgess remembers:

At the end of the march we met the 37th Division under the command of General Beightler . . . General Ennis Swift, the Corps Commander, was travelling with the lead of the 37th Division. . . . I saluted and reported to the generals. General Beightler turned and remarked to General Swift that his division had "rescued the 511th." My temper flared at that, as I deemed the remark an insult, and pointed out that we thought we were rescuing the 37th, as we had out-marched them and their armored column. . . . General Swift laughed and said, "Well, you sound like one of Joe Swing's boys." That remark ended the conversation.

Later that day, Burgess went to the CP of the 37th, set up along a small stream, to call the 11th's CP for permission to bring the Gypsy Task Force back to Lipa on the C-47s that were bringing in supplies at Tuguegarao, a nearby strip. A Sixth Army staff officer had showed up on one of the C-47s in response to Burgess's request and told Burgess to countermarch his troops to Aparri. Burgess wrote:

There we would have been picked up by Naval shipping which would take us to Manila, some eighty miles from Lipa, which would mean a truck ride and a week or more delay in returning to the division. There was no way I was going to march that battalion back up the valley some fifty-five miles in midday heat of 120 degrees and sit in the shade for three days if we could ride those airplanes. So I talked to the pilots as they came in, and they began flying my men "home" to Lipa in exchange for some mementos . . . Japanese guns, uniforms, helmets, etc. . . . Within two days we were all back at Lipa. . . . I landed in the last plane.

• • •

Major John Conable, the 11th Division's G-4 officer, also had a part to play in the return of Gypsy Task Force to Lipa. He had intended to jump from an L-5 near Lt. Jack Hayes's C Battery of the 457th Parachute Field Artillery to help arrange the return of the task force. But Swing found out about Conable's "combat jump" proposition and ordered him to land on the highway instead. Conable wrote that "I landed properly on the highway and got everyone back to Lipa safely."

For Sixth Army, the meeting up of Gypsy Task Force and the 37th Division marked the end of the campaign on northern Luzon. But there was still much fighting for the Eighth Army when it took over responsibility for northern Luzon from the Sixth Army. In April, Major General Swing had pleaded with Sixth Army to drop the whole 11th Airborne Division near Aparri when the Sixth Army was having such a difficult time in Balete Pass. But he was turned down, permitting the Japanese, according to Swing, to withdraw the greater part of their garrison to the northern end of the Cagayan Valley.

During June and July the 11th was totally involved in retraining, R&R, and reorganization. In May the division had shifted to a new TO&E, which in effect gave three battalions to the glider regiments, converted the 188th and 674th to parachute units, made the 472d Field Artillery Battalion organic to the division, upped the 2.5-ton truck count from 100 to 250, and increased the strength of the division from 8,600 to more than 12,000 men. In late June, Col. Ducat McEntee arrived in the Philippines with his 541st Parachute Infantry Regiment aboard the USS *Johnson*. He had organized the 541st from scratch in 1943, but had seen it lose personnel time and again to provide replacements for the heavily depleted European airborne divisions. This time, he thought that his beloved regiment would remain an entity and become a regiment of the 11th Airborne. But that was not to be. As soon as he and the 541st debarked in Manila, Colonel McEntee received orders deactivating his regiment and assigning his men to the 11th as replacements.

At Lipa the 11th instituted training for the troop carrier pilots, who were more accustomed to delivering supplies than dropping troopers or tugging gliders. The pilots even practiced "snatch pickups," whereby a C-47 flying about fifteen feet above the ground with a hook at the end of a cable wrapped around a drum in the plane and protruding from the door, would hook onto a glider's tow rope looped and erected on a vertical frame next to the nose of the glider. To the pilot of the C-47 it might not have been too much of a challenge; but to the glider pilot and the men in the glider it was an interesting phenomenon to be sitting still one moment and be airborne at 120 miles an hour a few seconds later.

The intensity of the Air Corps troop carrier groups' training and the establishment of the 11th's third parachute school at Lipa started rumors flying throughout the division area. The more practical savants had the division jumping ahead of the forces invading Japan; others thought China a more obvious choice; and still other amateur strategists thought that Formosa would make a DZ. But, of course, none of these speculative courses of action was the right one.

On 6 August the *Enola Gay* dropped an atomic bomb over Hiroshima; on 9 August *Bock's Car* dropped a second bomb on Nagasaki; on 10 August Japan decided to surrender. After a few days of negotiations, on 14 August Emperor Hirohito took the unprecedented step of addressing his nation on radio to inform his people that Japan had accepted the Allies' surrender terms.

On 15 August Washington received Japan's acceptance of the surrender terms, President Truman announced the end of the war in the Pacific, and General MacArthur was appointed supreme commander for the Allied forces in the Pacific.

At 0430 on 11 August, the 11th Airborne duty officer awoke Major General Swing with a long, top secret message that alerted him to be prepared to move all combat elements and equipment by air on forty-eight hours' notice to a staging area on Okinawa for the eventual occupation of Japan. The message, in short, meant that MacArthur had selected the 11th Airborne Division to lead the Allied forces in occupying Japan. The division's G-3 air officer (the author, a twenty-three-year-old major at the time) flew up to Far East Air Force (FEAF) headquarters at 0530 that Saturday morning, 11 August. When he first arrived about midmorning, the FEAF operations officer, Col. Francis C. Gideon (class of 1940), confirmed that the planes would start arriving in forty-eight hours. A few minutes later, Colonel Gideon told the G-3 air officer to get back to the 11th's CP because the planes were already on their way to Lipa and some would be arriving that afternoon.

The 11th Airborne started its move to Okinawa on 12 August 1945, and by 15 August the bulk of the forward echelon of the division had arrived on Okinawa. For the flights, the 54th Troop Carrier Wing had rounded up 99 B-24s, 351 C-46s, and 151 C-47s to airlift 11,100 men; 120

all-purpose jeeps for communications, command, and supply; and 1.16 million pounds of equipment.

The airlift was not without its disasters. At Lipa, a C-46 carrying men from the 11th's command group was about to taxi for takeoff. Lieutenant George Skau, the gallant and superb commander of the 11th's Reconnaissance Platoon, quite properly wanted to be the first man of his platoon to land on Okinawa. There was no room for him on the plane, so he told his platoon sergeant, Sgt. Martin Squires, to get off and give him his seat. Reluctantly, Squires got off.

As that C-46 approached the Naha strip on Okinawa, Japanese kamikazes were hitting the ships in the harbor below the Naha strip, which was located on a cliff above the harbor. For their own protection, the ships in the harbor were belching smoke that rose up and obscured the edge of the Naha runway. On its third landing attempt, the C-46 crashed into the cliff and killed all thirty-one men aboard.

The troopers of the 11th Airborne Division settled down on Okinawa in crude encampments of pup tents on the sides of hills and waited for their next mission. It came in the form of the 11th's Field Order Number 34 stating that the division would land on Atsugi Airdrome outside Yokohama, starting on Z day, 28 August 1945, seize and secure Atsugi, remove all Japanese from the airfield to a distance of three miles, occupy Yokohama, and prepare for further occupation operations on northern Honshu.

By 28 August, Gen. William O. Ryan, commander of the Air Transport Command–Pacific, had assembled on Okinawa every C-54 transport from around the world, thereby obviating the need for any other type of plane to carry the 11th to Atsugi and the occupation of Japan. The final phase of the beginning of the occupation of Japan was under way. At 0600 on 30 August, Major General Swing's C-54 touched down on Atsugi, the first plane in a seemingly endless string of transport aircraft ferrying the 11th into Japan for the start of peaceful occupation, an event that the troopers of the division had thought impossible just days ago.

The full division closed at Atsugi on 7 September. In the previous nine days, General Ryan and his Air Transport Command–Pacific had moved 11,708 men, 640 tons of supplies, and more than 600 jeeps and trailers of the 11th. It was the longest (1,600 miles) and largest air transported troop movement ever attempted and completed. And it made the 11th Airborne Division the first force to occupy Japan and started the next phase in the division's chronicle.

The morning of 2 September 1945 (3 September in Japan) was yet another momentous and significant date in the annals of the world's history. On that morning, the U.S. battleships *Missouri* and *South Dakota* and the British battleship *Duke of York* and hundreds of other warships were at anchor in Tokyo Bay.

With the signing of the surrender documents on the *Missouri*, the greatest disaster in recorded history was over. After six years of war the loss of 55 million civilians and soldiers; the destruction of untold and uncounted cities, factories, transportation facilities, and ports; and the loss of countless billions of dollars' worth of minerals and materials was ended. The guns, grenades, bombs, rockets, artillery, and rifles were finally silent. "Fix bayonets" became a command reserved for the parade grounds. The truly global World War II was over.

24: On to Korea

For the airborne forces of the U.S. Army, the period between the end of World War II and the beginning of the Korean War was filled with turmoil.

The 13th Airborne Division, alerted a number of times for combat in the European Theater of Operations, was frustrated each time. Possible missions included joining with the 17th Airborne Division for an airborne assault at Wesel, Germany. That mission was canceled due to a lack of aircraft for both divisions. The next canceled mission was Operation Choker, the drop across the Rhine at Worms. The day before the landing the paratroopers and glidermen of the division went to the airfield, loaded C-47s and gliders with their gear, and got ready to take off the next morning. When they woke up to move to the departure airfield, they found out that the mission had been scratched: Patton had captured Worms the day before while they loaded and lashed.

Three other missions for the 13th loomed on the horizon. One was Operation Effective, a plan to get to the Alps before the Germans could establish a base for a last holdout in the mountains—but Allied intelligence decided that the trip was not necessary, and the commander of the First Allied Airborne Army canceled it. Toward the end of the war the 13th received another top secret mission: land at Copenhagen—and another frustration when it was called off. Then the commander told the division commander, Maj. Gen. Eldridge G. Chapman, to get his division ready to go to the Pacific to take part in the invasion of Japan. The division sailed home on 23 August 1945, docked at the New York port of embarkation, and moved down to Fort Bragg. Japan surrendered on

2 September 1945, and the 13th Airborne Division was deactivated on 25 February 1946 and its men transferred to the 82d Airborne Division. Thus ended the saga of the 13th, perhaps confirming the putative unluckiness of its designation.

The 17th Airborne Division had had only sixty-five days in combat in three campaigns in Europe: the Ardennes, the Rhineland, and Central Europe. But it had suffered 1,314 men killed in action or who had died of their wounds and 4,904 men wounded or injured in action. After the surrender of Germany on 7 May 1945, it continued its occupation duties until relieved by British troops on 14 June 1945. Many of the 17th's troopers were transferred to the 82d in Berlin and to the 13th, which was supposed to be getting ready for the airborne invasion of Japan. After Japan surrendered, the division moved to Camp Myles Standish and on 16 September 1945 was deactivated. The 17th was reactivated from 6 July 1948 until 19 June 1949 as a training division but, thereafter, Thunder from Heaven was phased out of the army's register.

In July 1945, the 82d Airborne Division moved to Berlin for five months of occupation duty and welcomed hundreds of VIPs of all nationalities and such military leaders as Eisenhower and Patton, Soviet Marshal Zhukov, and British Field Marshal Montgomery.

In December 1945 the 82d left Berlin and returned to the United States. After its parade up Fifth Avenue in New York City on 3 January 1946, it moved to Fort Bragg, where, on 15 November 1948, it was designated a regular army division. Today it is still America's Guard of Honor in fact as well as in title. A current book describing the units making up the XVIII Airborne Corps puts it this way: "The 82d Airborne Division is stationed at Fort Bragg, NC. Three airborne infantry brigades and an aviation brigade make up the 82d with a full complement of supporting arms and equipment.

"This division is capable of rapid deployment, anywhere in the world. All of its ground equipment can be air-dropped. Thus the entire division can be delivered by air to any theater or area the Air Force can reach. The airflow of the division can start within 18 hours of notification to deploy."

Major General Joseph Swing continued to command the 11th Airborne Division in Japan until January of 1948. He was succeeded by Maj. Gen. William Miley, who commanded the division until 23 March 1949, when he was followed by Brig. Gen. Lemuel Mathewson, the former division artillery commander. In May 1949, the division was relieved of occupation duties in Japan and moved to Fort Campbell, Kentucky. After the move, the 188th Airborne Infantry Regiment was inactivated. On 1 September 1950, the 187th Airborne Infantry Regiment and the 674th Airborne Field Artillery Battalion were broken out of the division as a separate airborne RCT and ordered to Korea. The 187th was then replaced by the reactivated 188th.

From September to December 1950, the 11th trained, processed, and prepared 13,000 recalled reservists for shipment to Korea. In December 1950 Maj. Gen. Lyman Lemnitzer took over command of the division. On 2 March 1951, the 503d Airborne Infantry Regiment was reactivated and became an organic part of the 11th at Fort Campbell. At that time, the division consisted of the 188th, 511th, and 503d Airborne Infantry Regiments; the 544th, 89th, 457th, and 675th Airborne Field Artillery Battalions; the 88th Airborne Antiaircraft Artillery Battalion; the 127th Airborne Engineer Battalion; the 76th and 710th Tank Battalions; the 11th Medical Battalion; and other special troops.

THE RAKKASANS IN KOREA

"It was early morning Sunday, June 25, 1950, when the telephone rang in my bedroom at the American Embassy in Tokyo," wrote General MacArthur in *Reminisces.*

It rang with the note of urgency that can sound only in the hush of a darkened room. It was the duty officer at headquarters. "General," he said, "we have just received a dispatch from Seoul, advising that the North Koreans have struck in great strength south of the 38th Parallel at four o'clock this morning." Thousands of Red Korean troops had poured over the border, overwhelming the South Korean advance posts, and were moving southward with a speed and power that was sweeping aside all opposition.

I had an uncanny feeling of nightmare. It had been nine years before, on a Sunday morning, at the same hour, that a telephone call with the same note of urgency had awakened me in the penthouse atop the Manila Hotel. It was the same fell note of the war cry that was again ringing in my ears. It couldn't be, I told myself. Not again! I must be asleep and dreaming. Not again! But then came the crisp, cool voice of my fine chief of staff, General Ned Almond, "Any orders, General?"

On 30 June 1950, in what was to be a United Nations action, President Truman authorized MacArthur to use all U.S. forces available to stem the North Korean advance. Initially, the United States and the Republic of Korea (ROK) forces were beaten back into what came to be so well known as the Pusan perimeter. But on 15 and 16 September, Maj. Gen. Edward M. Almond, now commanding X Corps, made up of the 7th Infantry Division and the 1st Marine Division, landed at Inchon on the west coast of the peninsula, more than 200 air miles from Pusan. In two weeks after that the X Corps recaptured the capital, Seoul, from the North Koreans. On 16 September, Lt. Gen. Walton H. Walker, commanding Eighth Army, launched an attack out of the Pusan perimeter with two U.S. corps and two ROK corps abreast. Walker's forces originally ran into heavy opposition. But when General Chai, commander of the North Korean forces, recognized that his forces could be squeezed and totally smashed between the Eighth Army and X Corps, he ordered a retreat to the north. The retreat was, in fact, a rout. But a large portion of the North Korean People's Army (NKPA) escaped the trap. By 1 October, most of the NKPA survivors had retreated north of the 38th parallel that divides the two Koreas or had escaped into the mountains of South Korea. The stage was thus set for the pursuit of the remnants of the North Koreans above the parallel and for the possible use of an airborne force to parachute behind the retreating NKPA, cut off their escape, capture high-ranking military and civilians fleeing north out of Pyongyang, and rescue UN POWs presumably being taken north.

On 1 August 1950, in Theater 3 at Fort Campbell, Col. Frank S. Bowen Jr. (class of 1926), forty-five years old, announced to his assembled 187th Regiment troopers that the unit had been alerted for overseas movement. By 27 August, the 187th officially became the 187th Airborne Regimental Combat Team with the addition of the 674th Airborne Field Artillery Battalion, A Company of the 127th Airborne Engineer Battalion, A Battery of the 88th Airborne Antiaircraft Battalion, and detachments of military police, quartermasters, parachute maintenance riggers, and medics.

(In June 1951, the 187th Airborne Regimental Combat Team moved to Camps Chickamauga and Wood on Kyushu Island, Japan, their home bases between combat tours in Korea. In short order, the Japanese around the camps began referring to the 187th troopers as "Rakkasans," a translation of the Japanese term for "umbrella men.")

On 22 September, after a trip from Fort Campbell by rail, sea, and air, the first element of the 187th began landing at Kimpo Airfield in South Korea, seven days after the Inchon landings. Kimpo was the major airfield in South Korea, about ten miles west of Seoul, across the Han River. The 187th had moved by truck from Moji Port to Ashiya Air Force Base in Japan and then almost immediately was flown to Korea by the 314th and 21st Troop Carrier Wings. Lieutenant Colonel Delbert E. Munson (class of 1940), thirty-two years old, commanded the 3d Battlion, 187th, Airborne RCT, the first battalion to land at Kimpo. It was too late for the 187th to be a part of General MacArthur's well-calculated surprise, the eminently successful end run around NKPA forces that severed their lines of communication into the south.

Next to arrive was Lt. Col. Arthur H. "Harry" Wilson Jr. (class of 1937), thirty-eight years old, and his 1st Battalion, 187th. Harry Wilson had commanded the 2d Battalion, 187th, Glider Infantry in the Leyte and Luzon campaigns of the 11th Airborne Division and, later, the regiment in Japan and at Fort Campbell. Following was the 2d, 187th, commanded by Lt. Col. William J. Boyle, (class of 1939), thiry-three years old. By 26 September, the entire 187th Airborne RCT was in Korea except for a small rear detachment at Ashiya and the Parachute Maintenance Company and the Personnel Section at Camp Kashii, Japan. After the 187th landed at Kimpo, it was given the mission of clearing the Kimpo Peninsula that ran between the Han River and the Yellow Sea. By 2 October, the 187th and a battalion of ROK marines had cleared the area and re-assembled at Kimpo, but not without losses to the RCT.

Fred J. Waterhouse, the 187th's historian, wrote that "at 1230 on the 27th, Company L was ambushed by an estimated enemy force of four hundred men."

The enemy allowed the Rakkasan truck column to advance halfway through a small village before opening fire. The fight continued for four hours with the Rakkasans inflicting heavy losses on the enemy, during which Lt. William E. Weber was wounded and later awarded the Silver Star for action during the battle. Withdrawing in orderly fashion, L Company carried out their dead and wounded without losing a single piece of equipment. Sgt. First Class Bailey, Sgt. Kenneth E. Stevenson, and Pfc. Clark Bradford were among the first battle deaths suffered by the regiment.

On 7 October reconnaissance patrols of the 1st Cavalry Division crossed the 38th parallel, and by 20 October, the 5th Cavalry Regiment of the 1st Cavalry Division had entered Pyongyang against light resistance.

With the Eighth Army's rapid advance north, MacArthur decided to drop the 187th at Sukchon-Sunchon, north of Pyongyang on 21 October. But when the ROK 1st and 7th Divisions entered Pyongyang on 19 October, they found that the ruler of North Korea, Kim Il Sung, his government, and most of the NKPA had fled north. To try to block these forces, MacArthur advanced the time of the 187th's jump to dawn on 20 October. He saw the 187th in a classic airborne maneuver—dropping behind enemy lines, attacking him from an unexpected direction, blocking his escape routes, and crushing him between the paratroopers and the advancing ground forces.

The plan for the 187th was simple: parachute onto two DZs astride two major highways and railroads running north from the Pyongyang to block the main NKPA routes of escape. One DZ was at Sukchon, about twenty-five miles north of Pyongyang; the other was at Sunchon, about thirty miles to the northeast of the city and seventeen miles east of Sukchon. The plan for the drop had Colonel Bowen and his command group, the 1st and 3d Battalions, plus a part of the 674th Airborne Field Artillery Battalion (about 1,500 troopers) jumping at Sukchon to block the two highways and railroad leading north from Pyongyang. On 21 October the British 27th Commonwealth Brigade, attached to the U.S. 24th Division, would link up with the Sukchon team. For the second part of the operation, troopers of the 2d Battalion, 187th, plus some artillerymen from the 674th, (a total of about 1,300 men) would jump on Sunchon to block another highway and railroad. The 70th Tank Battalion would attack north from Pyongyang and link up with 2d Battalion, 187th, the day after the jump.

At 1900 on 18 October pilots and jumpmasters went through a final, detailed briefing at Kimpo. A heavy drizzle that continued throughout the day dampened the spirits of the keyed-up troopers. One of the staff briefers announced that if the weather worsened, the jump would be delayed in three-hour increments. At 0230 on 20 October, in heavy rain and darkness, the 187th's troopers fell out for reveille, ate the traditional hearty, prejump breakfast, and then were trucked by stick loads to their assigned planes on the ramps at Kimpo. At 0400 the troops drew their chutes and began to adjust them. The rain still came; the jump was postponed again for three hours.

By late morning the skies had begun to clear, and at 1030 the order came down the line to "chute up." In short order the troopers, carrying M1 rifles or carbines, .45-caliber pistols, packs, canteens, radios, ammunition, rations, personal gear, and reserve parachutes, climbed awkwardly into their planes—seventy-three C-119s (a Fairchild-made cargo plane, successor to the old C-82 of the late 1940s) of the 314th Troop Carrier Wing from Ashiya Air Force Base on Kyushu and into forty C-47s (the old workhorse of World War II days) of the 21st Troop Carrier Wing from Brady Air Force Base, Kyushu. A typical C-119 load was forty-six men in two sticks, fifteen monorail bundles, and four door loads, two for each of the two jump doors. The planes were so crowded that, once it was loaded, some of the jumpers had to sit on the floor.

At noon the first plane, carrying Colonel Bowen, riflemen, unit guides, part of the RCT staff, and thirteen pathfinders, was airborne, headed for DZ William southeast of Sukchon. As the troop carriers approached DZ William, U.S. fighters rocketed and strafed the area. At 1400 Bowen's pilot flipped on the green go light, and Bowen was out the door. The 187th's first combat jump in Korea was under way.

Lieutenant Colonel George H. Gerhart (class of 1934), thirty-eight years old, executive officer of the 187th, led the jumpers from a second serial of nineteen C-119s onto the rice paddies of the DZ. His force included Harry Wilson's 1st Battalion, 187th, and support troops. The first two serials dropped 1,470 men and seventy-four tons of equipment. During the drop, one soldier was killed in his parachute by enemy fire and twenty-five were injured on landing, but both serials landed fairly accurately in the DZ. Shortly thereafter, Munson's 3d, 187th, jumped onto the same DZ.

After the troop drop on DZ William came the heavy equipment drop on both DZs. The total drop included twelve 105mm howitzers (the successor in airborne artillery to the old pack 75), thirty jeeps, four three-quarter-ton trucks, thirty-eight quarter-ton trailers, four 90mm antitank guns, a mobile radio transmitter, equivalent in weight to a two-and-a-half-ton truck, and 584 tons of ammunition and other supplies. The 674th Field Artillery Battalion, (minus B Battery) under the command of Lt. Col. Harry F. Lambert, who jumped from the first plane with Colonel Bowen, dropped seven 105mm howitzers and 1,125 rounds of ammunition. The 674th recovered six of the howitzers. The heavy drop—the first time in combat—was made possible by the configuration of the C-119, which could lower a ramp in the rear, permitting the heavy loads to slide into the air when static lines immediately pulled open the huge cargo chutes.

After landing and assembling quickly, the 3d Battalion, 187th, headed south of Sukchon, and set up roadblocks across the highway and railroads in their area. By 1630 it had secured its objectives, killed five enemy soldiers, and captured forty-two with no losses to itself. Munson was prepared to resume the attack south along the railroad and highway toward Pyongyang. He spread out his battalion along the high ground 3,000 yards south of the Sukchon. Company I was on the left, and Company K, commanded by Capt. John E. Strever, was on the right and set up a blocking position along the Sukchon-Pyongyang road.

The 1st Battalion, 187th, had the mission of clearing Sukchon, securing the high ground to the north, and setting up a roadblock to block enemy withdrawal to the north. Lieutenant Colonel Wilson sent patrols to the river in the vicinity of Naeman-ni. Brigadier General Bowen, who was notified of his promotion after the jump, also ordered him to be prepared to move south of Pyongyang.

"The first platoon of the Engineers reached the town of Songnani-ni at 1530 hours, where they were delayed forty-five minutes by enemy fire," wrote Arch Roberts in *Rakkasans*. "Fifteen prisoners were taken by SFC Marcuso and his squad, and these were impressed as porters to move the engineer equipment on handcarts." When the platoon reached Namil-ni, it captured an additional sixteen North Korean troops and killed five.

By late afternoon, Bowen had set up his regimental headquarters along the dikes of the Choeryong River and his CP at Chany-ni on Hill 97.

DZ Easy, the other drop zone, was two miles southwest of Sunchon. At 1420, Lt. Col. William J. Boyle led his 2d Battalion, 187th, reinforced with B Battery of the 674th; 2d Platoon, Company A; 127th Engineers; 4.2-inch mortar platoon of Support Company; a pathfinder team; one section of 90mm antitank guns; and a forward air control party, onto DZ Easy. Twenty jumpers were injured in landing.

By nightfall the 2d Battalion had secured its objectives against feeble resistance. "As the Rakkasans marched into Sunchon in a column of twos," one trooper, Private First Class Kirksey of F Company, remembered that "the Koreans tossed rifles and other weapons out onto the streets. The din was terrific."

Clay Blair, in *The Forgotten War*, wrote that "compared with most World War II airborne operations, the jump was outstanding—indisputably the best combat jump the Army ever staged."

The airborne operation, of course, had not gone unnoticed by General MacArthur; in fact he and Generals Stratemeyer, Wright, and Whitney had flown in from Japan to watch the air drop from the air. After he saw the success of the drops MacArthur flew into Pyongyang, where he told reporters that the airborne operation had apparently taken the enemy completely by surprise. He suggested that some thirty thousand enemy troops, about half those remaining in the north, were trapped between the 187th and the 1st Cavalry and the ROK 1st Division at Pyongyang to the south, and he had every expectation that they would be trapped and captured or wiped out. He said that the airborne operation was an "expert performance" and that "this closes the trap on the enemy." The next day, back in Tokyo, MacArthur, flushed with the success he had witnessed over the 187th's DZs, predicted too optimistically that "the war is very definitely coming to an end." Unfortunately the Chinese would think otherwise.

A large portion of the surviving NKPA had moved north of Sukchon before the 187th's drop. No important NKPA or government officials were cut off, killed, or captured. Civilians in Pyongyang reported that the principal officials had left Pyongyang on 12 October for Manpojin on the Yalu River. And, unfortunately, most of the U.S. and South Korean POWs had been successfully moved into a remote part of North Korea.

On the morning after the drop, 1st Battalion, 187th, seized dominating terrain directly north of Sukchon to set up a blocking position on the main highway running northward. That afternoon, patrols from the 1st and 2d Battalions made contact at Sunchon.

The most significant combat action after the drop involved the 3d, 187th on 21–22 October about eight miles south of Sukchon near Opa-ri. At about 0900, Lieutenant Colonel Munson started his battalion in two combat teams south toward Pyongyang from its roadblock positions. His mission was to meet the advancing 27th Commonwealth Brigade.

At about 1300, I Company reached Opa-ri and was hit by an enemy battalion supported by 120mm mortars and 40mm guns. The NKPA formation had caught the company in an ambush and laid heavy grazing fire into the company's position. Master Sergeant Melvin Stawser, a platoon sergeant in I Company, remembers the heavy enemy fire hitting his platoon, but he managed to pull troops back—a squad at a time. For two and a half hours, I Company held out in a heavy firefight. But then the NKPA overran two platoons and forced the company, with ninety men missing, to move back to Hill 281 west of the railroad. Fortunately, the NKPA soldiers did not take advantage of the situation and withdrew to their former defensive positions on the high ground around Opa-ri.

Private First Class Richard G. Wilson was a medic attached to I Company. During the battle at Opa-ri, Wilson moved among the wounded, doing his best to give them first aid. In so doing, he exposed himself constantly to the heavy enemy mortar, 40mm gun fire, and rifle fire. When Munson ordered what was left of I Company to pull back, Wilson helped the wounded to safety and made certain that no wounded were left behind. Later he found out that one of the men, previously believed to be dead, had been seen moving and attempting to crawl to safety. In spite of his buddies' protests Wilson returned to the battlefield to search for the wounded man. Two days later a patrol found Wilson lying beside the man he had returned to aid: Wilson had been shot several times while trying to shield and administer aid to the wounded trooper. Wilson was subsequently awarded the Medal of Honor for his self-sacrifice.

While at Sunchon, Lieutenant Colonel Boyle's troops had heard rumors that the NKPA had massacred many U.S. POWs nearby. Unfortunately the rumors were true. On 20 October a trainload of these POWs had been northbound when the 187th parachuted into the area. The train pulled into a tunnel to hide, and there sixty-six POWs were murdered. Brigadier General Frank Allen, the 1st Cavalry assistant division commander, had led a search party for the POWs. His team found the bodies as well as seven other Americans who had died of starvation or disease. In the area, his team also found twenty-three emaciated U.S. POW survivors, many badly wounded, two mortally. Of the estimated 2,500 U.S. POWs being held by the North Koreans, these ninety-six were all that could be found.

On 23 October, troopers of the 3d Battalion, 187th, moved back into the Opa-ri area to search for any men who might have survived the battle. En route to the area they captured fifty NKPA soldiers wearing civilian clothes, and shortly after, the 3d's troops found several wounded paratroopers. On the same day a patrol captured yet another fifteen NKPA soldiers. "These people," Sgt. Edward R. Gasperini remembered, "were wearing pile jackets and jump boots taken from I Company dead. We stripped them, shooting two who tried to escape. One of them, wearing the clothing of Pfc. Wilson, I Company's medic, was shot while trying to escape. Later, we found 50 North Korean uniforms discarded by the Reds, who had donned American clothing."

"Prisoners of war proved a difficult problem for the 187th," wrote CWO John Hudson later. "After being cut off, the enemy troops would change into civilian clothes, stand in front of houses in Sukchon waving South Korean flags. Sometimes the evaders would hide in the homes while women and children of the town would wave the flags. At night, the 187th had to dodge the bullets of these 'civilians.' The MPs had the job of mopping up and rounding up the North Koreans."

During the Sukchon-Sunchon operation, the 187th had battled against some 8,000 NKPA troops, killing an estimated 2,764 and capturing 3,818. The total RCT casualties were forty-eight killed and eighty wounded in action, with one man killed and fifty-six injured in the jump.

Late in the afternoon of 23 October, the 2d Battalion, 187th, left Sunchon on foot and was picked up by a truck convoy about six miles away. The battalion moved toward Pyongyang and arrived there about midnight, followed by the 1st and 3d Battalions. All the other RCT units had already arrived. Shortly thereafter, the 187th reverted to theater reserve with the ancillary mission of guarding Pyongyang, Chinnanmpo, the Pyongyang airfield, and the main supply route. It waited for its next airborne mission, which was not long in coming.

By the end of October 1950, brief clashes with Chinese troops in the sectors of both the Eighth Army and X Corps that had landed on 26 October, well behind schedule, at Wonsan, on the east coast of North Korea, posed a new and ominous, but as yet unappreciated, threat to the UN forces. In fact the senior commanders in Korea, from General MacArthur on down, believed that the war in Korea was virtually won. On 3 November, MacArthur's veteran G-2 officer, Maj. Gen. Charles A. Willoughby, estimated that the Chinese Communist Forces (CCF) in North Korea at between 16,500 and a maximum of 34,000. On 6 November, he upped his guess to 34,500 Chinese facing both the Eighth Army and X Corps. The UN strength on that date was 250,000 men.

Optimism was running high in the UN ranks. The Department of the Army and MacArthur were making plans to redeploy Eighth Army units from Korea, with the 2d Division slated to go either to Europe or the United States. Many troopers of the 1st Cavalry Division thought that on Thanksgiving Day they would be on parade in the Tokyo Plaza, proudly wearing their yellow cavalry scarves. The 1st Cavalry even started turning in equipment in preparation for its return to Japan. The *New York Times* said editorially that "except for unexpected developments along the frontier of the peninsula, we can now be easy in our minds as to the military outcome." More death and destruction, however, were yet to come in the "forgotten war."

Major General Willoughby's figures missed the mark widely. By early November the total CCF forces in North Korea had grown to thirty infantry divisions, a force of over 300,000 men. By late November the CCF had struck Eighth Army. On the evening of 25 November, Gen. Lin Piao unleashed his hordes along the Eighth Army's front. On 26 November the CCF struck again. In the west the CCF hit the 2d, 24th, and 25th Infantry Divisions and the 1st Cavalry Division with heavy and relentless attacks. Three CCF divisions assailed the Marines in the center of North Korea near the Chosin Reservoir. In the northeast, two CCF divisions attacked and encircled three regiments of the 7th Division. With these attacks and the complete rout of ROK forces on the Eighth Army's flank, Lieutenant General Walker's situation became desperate, and he faced a monumental decision. The Chinese had encircled many of his units and had seized the high ground to their rear. By 28 November the situation was clear: he was forced to order a general retreat from the north and fall back into a solid enclave around Pyongyang.

The 187th moved through Pyongyang to set up blocking positions in the Sukchon area. On 10 December, the 187th closed out of Pyongyang and set up a new CP at Sohung. Like the rest of the retreating U.S. forces, the 187th blew up supplies left behind and fought a series of battles to keep the withdrawal route open. Brigadier General Bowen's new mission was to provide security across the Han River, conduct operations in the Hoengsong, Wonju, Chechon, and Chungju areas, and protect and assist in the evacuation of the Kimpo airport and Inchon.

For the next few days, the 187th blocked CCF probing attacks north of Wonju. Holding the Ranyang-Punji Pass, Brigadier General Bowen deployed the regiment with the 1st and 3d Battalions on line and the 2d in reserve. According to Bill Weber, "This was particularly severe duty as the temperatures hovered in the twenty to thirty-below range [with wind chill] and we were without winter equipment. Weapons would not function and men would become almost lethargic from the cold. The CCF were only about a hundred yards from our positions but, except for intermittent firing, they were suffering as much, if not worse, than we. This type of operation [all battalions involved] continued through 19 January 1951, when we were relieved by the 38th Infantry and passed to corps reserve."

On 23 December the Eighth Army commander, Lt. Gen. Walton H. Walker (class of 1912), sixty-one years old, was killed in an accident on an icy road leading from the 24th Division CP when his jeep was hit by an ROK weapons carrier. At 1130 on 24 December, in an incredibly fast change of command, Lt. Gen. Matthew B. Ridgway landed in Tokyo to succeed Walker. The next day, after a long discussion of the Korean situation, MacArthur told him, "The Eighth Army is yours, Matt. Do what you think best." And what he did was a success.

The CCF launched a massive assault across the 38th parallel at daybreak on New Year's Day, 1951. On 4 January 1951 Seoul fell again to the enemy. By 14 January, the UN lines were back along the 37th parallel in South Korea. But on 25 January the UN forces resumed the offensive under the brilliant, aggressive, and untiring leadership of General Ridgway. In early January, the 187th, now under Major General Almond's X Corps, fought as standard infantrymen in heavy fighting in the defense of the Tanyang-Punji Pass.

On 3 and 4 February, thousands of charging CCF hit Harry Wilson's 1st, 187th, dug-in perimeter. On the night of 3 February B Company, the hardest hit, had six men killed in action; the battalion lost fifty men killed and wounded in action. But Wilson's troopers held their position, inflicting heavy casualties on the Chinese. In the fight the 1st Battalion lost three first lieutenants: Robert B. Coleman (class of 1947), David B. Spellman (class of 1946), and Robert M. Garvin (class of 1947). They had all been with a tank company attached from the 1st Cavalry Division.

On 28 February the 187th closed into its rear area assembly area at Taegu, and throughout the first half of March remained in administrative bivouac at K-2 airstrip near Taegu. Rumors were rampant that the RCT was getting ready for another combat jump. The rumors proved correct. Munsan-ni was to be another chapter in the storied history of the Rakkasans.

Just after the jump at Sukchon, Bowen was restored to his World War II rank of brigadier general, which he had earned as the G-3 officer of General Eichelberger's Eighth Army from 1944 to 1946; he retained command of the 187th RCT. Lieutenant Colonel George Gerhart became the commander of just the regiment. Lieutenant Colonel Harry Wilson retained command of the 1st Battalion, 187th; Lt. Col. William J. Boyle, who had won the Distinguished Service Cross in the Battle of the Bulge, had a clash with Bowen after the Sukchon-Sunchon jump and was replaced by Lt. Col. John P. "Poopy" Connor (next to last man in the class of 1937); later Lt. Col. Delbert Munson recovered from his wounds and resumed command of the 3d Battalion, 187th.

In early March Ridgway went on the offensive. On the night of 14–15 March, a patrol from the ROK 1st Division probed the outer defenses of Seoul and found to its surprise that the enemy had virtually deserted the city. Once UN troops moved in, Seoul had now changed hands for the fourth time since July 1950. Within a matter of hours, once again the ROK flag flew above the National Assembly building. The UN troops found a city devastated by the enemy: no utilities were operational; the Bun Chon shopping district had been flattened; wires dangled loosely from the telephone poles; and the city's population had shrunk from 1.5 million to 200,000 ragged and mostly homeless civilians.

By 19 March, Ridgway's forces had fought northward and had established a new line across Korea just below the 38th parallel, approximately where the war had started some nine months earlier. The enemy was not idle, however. General Piao had assembled more troops and equipment for a resumption of his offensive. In typical airborne reasoning Ridgway decided that his best strategy was the offensive. On 22 March he presented his plan, Operation Courageous, to MacArthur. This offensive would move Eighth Army to a line that was just above the 38th parallel, except for a short part in the west, and generally between the confluence of the Han and Yesong Rivers on the west coast and the village of Yangyang on the Sea of Japan. On 22 March Eighth Army launched its attack and advanced all along the front. According to General Ridgway, "The spirit of the Army was at its peak."

Hoping to set a trap, the Eighth Army alerted Bowen to drop the 187th behind the enemy forces near Chunchon on 22 March. But by 19 March, when UN armored patrols from the 1st Cavalry Division entered the Chunchon Basin, it became apparent that the enemy had withdrawn and that a massed parachute assault would be unprofitable. Ridgway canceled the drop, but, meanwhile, on 21 March, the eighty C-119s and fifty-five C-46s planned for the drop arrived at Taegu from Brady and Ashiya airfields in Japan. The huge air fleet, parked wingtip to wingtip, completely filled the dusty graveled parking area and thus forced the fighters normally based there to fly to other strips.

Ridgway now wanted to bring the U.S. I Corps forward from the Seoul area to the Imjin River at Munsan. The plan included the following operations:

The 187th, with the attached 2d and 4th Ranger Companies, would spearhead the I Corps attack and jump at Munsan-ni (about twenty miles northwest of Seoul) in Operation Tomahawk behind the NKPA I Corps; two large armored task forces, Growdon and Hawkins, would attack to the north through Uijongbu and Munsan-ni, the latter to link up with the 187th within forty-eight hours and trap the North Koreans between the two forces. The ROK 1st Division and Maj. Gen. "Shorty" Soule's U.S. 3d Division would follow the armored task forces.

For almost the first half of March, the 187th had been in an "administrative" bivouac in an apple orchard at K-2 Airstrip near Taegu. Brigadier General Bowen, always alert to the need to jump-qualify his new replacements, set up a parachute school. To practice for Tomahawk, and because most of his veterans had not jumped since the Sukchon-Sunchon drop, on 8 and 9 March Bowen led 4,033 men of the RCT in a mass training jump hear Taegu. Unfortunately one trooper was killed on the jump.

On the afternoon of 21 March, Brig. Gen. John P. "Jock" Henebry, commanding general of the 315th Air Division, Col. R. W. Henderson, commander of the 314th Troop Carrier Group, Col. John W. Roche, commander of the 437th Troop Carrier Wing, Bowen, and key members of their respective staffs, made an aerial reconnaissance or the Munsan-ni area. On this low-level flight they selected two small DZs near Munsan-ni.

At the CP at Taegu the 187th's staff and commanders reviewed maps and photos of the area, outlined the DZs, drew up the battle plan, and briefed the troops down to squad level. "At the briefing by our platoon leader," remembered Sergeant Gasperini, "he told us that we were going to jump at Munsan-ni, the same area where we had dug in on 15 December in the retreat south. The forty-eight hour linkup plan sounded good to me."

Sergeant First Class William Ignatz, injured in the Wonju action, reported back from the hospital on 19 March. "Our pathfinder team leader, Lt. Maloney, put me in the first wave," he recalled. "I had the same beat-up white panels and a supply of colored smoke grenades. This was Sukchon all over again."

For a brief time, Ridgway had considered jumping in with the 187th but he said later that it would have been a "damned fool thing to do." To dissuade himself, he had visions of a broken leg or strained back requiring him to give up command of Eighth Army. He opted to have his veteran liaison plane pilot, twenty-three-year-old Capt. Mike Lynch, fly him over the DZ during the operation.

On the morning of 23 March MacArthur sent Ridgway a startling message. He was authorized to cross the 38th parallel in force and attack northward to Ridgway's proposed new line, codenamed Kansas. MacArthur had made the decision on his own; the Joint Chiefs of Staff had not given him authorization. He was beginning to overstep his bounds and get into the political arena, much to the U.S. administration's annoyance.

At 0300 on the morning of Good Friday, 23 March, under a full moon the troopers of the 187th rolled out of their sleeping bags and started the precombat jump rituals—eating a great breakfast, forming into planeloads, putting on their combat gear, moving to their assigned aircraft, and strapping on the parachutes they had checked the previous day and had left at their planes.

The troopers of the 187th and the men of the 2d and 4th Ranger Companies climbed aboard the eighty C-119s and fifty-five C-46s. Fortunately the weather was "paratrooper perfect"—with clear visibility and low breezes. By 0700, the planes were loaded with troopers crammed along the walls of the planes and monorail bundles were in place. The planes revved their engines, creating huge clouds of dust, the jumpmasters checked their troops, and the long line of planes began to taxi slowly in line to the airstrip, churning up even thicker blankets of dust that soon obscured much of the flight strip area. At 0730 the first plane roared down the runway and took off. Thereafter, at ten-second intervals the rest of the planes followed in dust so thick that the pilots flew blind until after liftoff.

The air force commander and Brigadier General Bowen and his staff had selected two DZs, one to the north of Munsan-ni and one to the south. Onto the northern DZ would jump the bulk of the combat team: Bowen and his staff; Munson's 3d Battalion, 187th, in the lead; Connor's 2d Battalion, 187th; the two Ranger companies; and Harry Lambert's 674th Airborne Field Artillery Battalion. Harry Wilson and his 1st Battalion, 187th, would jump on the southern DZ to provide an early-on linkup with the armored forces moving north. Munson, who had been wounded by "a stray round in the small of his back," had come back to the 3d Battalion, 187th, in December 1950 after a two-month hospital stay in Japan. Major Rye Mausert had been the commander of the 2d Battalion, 187th, in his absence.

Ahead of the troop carriers flew a C-54 Skymaster, the command ship piloted by Brigadier General Henebry. The FEAF filled the skies between Seoul and Munsan-ni with fighters that bombed and strafed the road network. Sixteen F-51 Mustangs circled the troop carriers in broad sweeps, ready to attack ground fire or enemy aircraft. The troop carriers flew a flight path out over the Yellow Sea and then directly back east to Munsan-ni.

During the flight over the Yellow Sea, one troop carrier developed engine trouble and crashed into the sea. Shortly after that, Harry Wilson's plane developed engine trouble and was forced to return to Taegu, where Wilson promptly demanded another airplane. He got it, but he and his staff lagged considerably behind his battalion.

At about 0900 the lead serial, Munson and his 3d Battalion, 187th, and the 4th Ranger Company, jumped onto the north DZ. Directly behind them came Connor's 2d Battalion, 187th, the 2d Ranger Company, and Bowen and his staff, engineers, medics, and others, including the Eighth Army assistant G-3 officer, Lt. Col. Hank Adams, who had overseen the planning for Tomahawk. None of the troopers was hit in the air, but on the ground the troops drew some light NKPA machine gun and mortar fire. As they floated down the troopers could see burning buildings around the DZ.

In an effort to speed things up, Wilson's deputy in the second plane in the 1st Battalion, 187th, serial skipped a landmark and headed directly for the southern DZ. But because of a "navigational error," he missed the south DZ and led the battalion directly onto the north DZ. Munson, already on the ground, recalled that "all those unscheduled people dropped on top of us, on a DZ that was already badly congested. It was like a Chinese fire drill. But what was more serious was that we didn't have a force on the south DZ, which was the linkup point for the armored task force."

When Harry Wilson arrived over the south DZ, he was startled to find no parachutes on the ground where his battalion had supposedly jumped. "There was nobody there," he recalled. "We thought that they must have picked up their chutes and moved on. So we jumped anyway." When they jumped, Wilson and the twenty-nine men of his battalion staff were greeted with machine gun fire from some nearby hills. Fortunately the NKPA stayed in the hills, and later in the day patrols from his own B Company rescued Wilson and the men.

"My serial was airborne at 1000 hours," MSgt. Willard W. Ryals remembers.

One plane had engine trouble and crashed into the sea during the flight. Another was lost from the preceding serial. We flew out to sea for our rendezvous, then flew north in column. Crossing the coast, I could see Chinese Communist forces dug in trenches surrounding the DZ. The air force, prior to the jump, had reported the enemy, in groups of a thousand men, moving in on Munsan-ni valley. USAF pilots called Munsan-ni "Holiday Valley," because of the large number of targets. . . . The village of Munsan-ni was burning in the near distance. Farmhouses ringed the DZ.

In some amazement, I saw that the green light had flashed on. Flipping out my door bundle, I followed after. As the engine noises subsided, I could hear a considerable amount of small arms fire below. Landing in soft ground, I cleared my parachute harness and headed for my assembly area on the southwestern section of the DZ. A few minutes after we had secured the high ground in our sector, the heavy drop arrived and, with it, the attached medical unit from India.

The Indian unit comprised twelve members of the 60th Parachute Field Ambulance Battalion, including surgeons, anesthetists, and medical technicians, under the command of Lt. Col. A. G. Rangarai. Among the members was a surgeon, Capt. V. Rangaswami, who retired as a major general.

William "Fuzzy" Moore, assigned to the 4th Ranger Company, jumped with the company on the northern DZ. He recalls that "loading the aircraft and jumping seemed to be a blank."

This was Munsan-ni via parachute. I remember seeing the Indian medics with red turbans and large black beards. I don't remember how many days later Paddy Purchell (an Irishman and member of the 4th Ranger Company) related to us that on hitting the DZ he was knocked out and when he came to "here was a large Indian medic cutting his harness off" and what Purchell related to us was "sure and bejesus I knew I was going to meet my maker but I didn't think that he would be black." The jump was made on 23 March

1951. I remember thinking—Good Friday—no better time to be in the sky close to God.

In the jump, of 3,447 paratroopers eighty-four men were injured with broken ankles or legs or severe bruises. Half returned to duty. Eighteen were wounded and one man was killed on the ground. The C-119s and the C-46s dropped a total of 220 tons of equipment and cargo, including twenty-seven jeeps and trailers, two weapons carriers, four 105mm howitzers, twelve 75mm pack howitzers, and fifteen load-bearing platforms each carrying 600 pounds of supplies.

During the drop General Ridgway had been circling overhead in his L-4 Cub. At 1000 he asked Lynch to land. "We were right in the middle of everything," Lynch remembered.

The next battalion jumped almost on top of us. I had to land to get out of the way! I said, "Hold on. We're going in." I made a bouncy landing on a piece of raised straight road—like a dike— about a hundred yards long. Ridgway went to find Bowen; I turned the plane around by its tail. Then a group of about fifteen or twenty [enemy soldiers] began to take the "landing strip" with machine guns. I had to dive over the embankment. I led a charge of paratroopers to get [them]. The paratroopers got them.

After he landed and moved to the CP area the commander of the 187th, Lt. Col. George Gerhart, saw Ridgway. "At first I thought he had jumped with us," he wrote later, "but apparently he was there checking on the drop."

At about midmorning army and air force helicopters landed on the DZs to evacuate the wounded. The helicopters ferried the wounded and injured men to airstrips near Seoul, where Kyushu-based Gypsy C-47s were waiting to move them to army hospitals farther south.

During the drop several troop carriers were hit by bullets, but only one was shot down. After making the drop, the pilot of another C-119 reported that his engines were smoking badly and that he thought his plane had been hit by ground fire. Shortly after his message, both engines burst into flames and he ordered the crew to bail out. Five crewmen parachuted safely, but then the C-119 blew up in midair and both the pilot and copilot were killed.

After landing and reassembling, the battalions of the 187th moved on toward their assigned objectives. The 1st Battalion took the high ground to the north, the 2d moved on to a hill on the east of the DZ, and the 3d took the northern side of a hill to the west. "The 1st Battalion marched all night," according to Sgt. W. B. Alexander, a rifleman with A Company, "to reach the 2d Battalion which was heavily engaged. We immediately went into the attack and took the critical terrain to establish blocking positions to cut off the retreating Chinese and North Korean forces.

"The enemy was well dug in around Munsan-ni. It was later learned that the CCF were withdrawing in that sector in order to draw the UN forces north, so that an envelopment by enemy forces could be accomplished and thereby cut off friendly units. Later reports revealed the Chinese Communist forces had been in the area for two or three days before the drop."

While the 187th was still landing on the DZ the two armored tank forces, Growdon and Hawkins, were rumbling forward from Line Lincoln toward Munsan-ni and Uijongbu, respectively. Growdon's march was not without difficulty. One of the armored troopers said that "the road along its route of march is the most extensively mined area yet encountered in Korea." Growdon's forces lost four Patton tanks, two jeeps, and a scout car to the mines and two Pattons to NKPA artillery. Task Force Growdon took twelve hours to travel fifteen miles, but the lead element linked up with the 187th at about 1830 hours on 23 March. The bulk of the force arrived in the area at 0400 on 24 March. Task Force Hawkins had an easier run and was in Uijongbu in about two hours.

Once the tanks from Task Force Growdon entered the 187th's area, Brigadier General Bowen mounted some of his troopers on the tanks and moved out on a new mission, which was to move to the east and north of Uijongbu and attack across seventeen miles of broken and heavily defended terrain toward Uijongbu Valley to link up with the U.S. 3d Division moving north. The 3d had run into strong CCF defenses and was advancing very slowly, hampered by the enemy and the heavy rains. Task Force Growdon reinforced the 187th's attack to the east toward Uijongbu.

Because of the muddy roads, lack of fuel for the tanks, and no logistics tail, the RCT depended totally on aerial resupply for the basics of combat: ammunition and food. In fifty-six airdrops between 24 and 27 March, air force cargo planes dropped 264 tons of critical supplies to the 187th RCT.

The 187th's attack up the Uijongbu Valley to link up with the 3d Infantry Division was a series of battles up and down hills with narrow crests and steep slopes. The paratroopers had to get out of the valley and attack up these hills and crests because the enemy, knowing the value of holding "the high ground," had had time to dig deep holes and trenches and build defenses along the crests. They had also zeroed in their artillery and mortars. The Rakkasans also found that the CCF and NKPA were somehow supplied with an endless number of grenades.

In one fight up the valley, E Company came under a fierce counterattack by horn-blowing, flare-throwing Chinese. Crossing a stream on a makeshift footpath, Capt. Jack B. Shanahan, E Company commander, was killed as he tried to cross the levee.

"The Chinese counterattacked one of the airborne companies with bugles blaring and screams of 'Banzai' filling the air," wrote Capt. W. T. Crawford. "Medal of Honor winner MSgt. Jake Lindsey rallied his platoon and they met the charge with a countercharge. Cutting into the Red attackers, the troopers were shouting, 'Airborne,' and burying bared steel bayonets in fleeing, shrieking Communist soldiers."

In its sector, in the midst of rain and sleet so heavy that weapons and machine guns jammed, G Company ran into a strong defensive position. Master Sergeant Ervin L. Muldoon, the Machine Gun Platoon leader in H Company, arrived in the area as all this was taking place (he had been in Japan and missed the jump). Lieutenant Jones N. Epps, platoon leader in G Company, pointed H Company's location out to him—and that was the last he would see of his old friend from Fort Benning days. Muldoon was killed that afternoon leading an attack with such personal bravery that he was awarded the Distinguished Service Cross posthumously.

G Company lost two platoon leaders in the battle, who were wounded and evacuated. Ten G Company soldiers were killed in action, including Sfc. James A. Vandergast, whose wife became a war widow for the second time, her first husband having been killed in World War II.

On 26 March, as his 2d Battalion moved up toward Uijongbu, "Poopy" Connor sent F Company to occupy Hill 178, a low hill on the flank of the battalion. Once again the enemy was dug well into defenses on the hill. F Company made a strong attack but needed G Company's 3d Platoon to help in the counterattack. F Company's commander, Capt. Thomas H. Agee, and Lt. Robert D. Hammond were casualties. First Lieutenant Samuel Morse became the company commander, and all platoons were now commanded by NCOs.

The 2d Battalion next attacked Hills 507 and 519, rising above the valley. "At 0600 28 March," wrote Lieutenant Epps, now the G Company executive officer, "the 1st and 3d Battalions attacked east. By 0830, the 3d Battalion had seized Hill 299, but the 1st Battalion, meeting greater resistance, was still heavily engaged fighting for Hill 322. At 1200 hours, the 2d Battalion attacked in column through the 3d Battalion on Hill 299. Company E, leading, met stiff resistance the entire way along the razorback ridge from Hill 299 to the junction of the higher hill mass 507–519. As the attack of E Company began, enemy mortar fire landed on the reverse slope of Hill 299. Capt. Jack Miley, commanding G Company, was down, seriously wounded."

The 2d Ranger Company had landed near an orchard on the east end of its DZ. From his position, First Sergeant West could see two enemy machine guns about to fire into his company. He grabbed a few of his men already in the assembly area, charged the gunners, and captured them before they could fire a round. The 2d Ranger Company was the first of the 187th team to turn in prisoners and weapons. At about 1030, the 2d Rangers cleared the village of Sangdokso-ri, killing six enemy soldiers and capturing twenty. Its next objective was Hill 151. Lieutenant James Queen, the company executive officer, directed F-51 fighter attacks and 81mm mortar fire onto the hill. The attack was successful, but the Rangers lost Pfc. William Van Dunk, killed in action, and Sergeant First Class Boatwright and Sergeant Robinson, wounded in action.

"The entire RCT attacked the final hill on the sixth day [29 March]," wrote Captain Crawford.

The mountain was a huge honeycomb of entrenchments. In some places the Chinese had dug right through the mountain so they could bring up supplies and replacements for the front slope without crossing the ridgeline.

The attack pushed off after daybreak as three battalions of determined paratroopers started up the seventy-degree slopes. Tanks and artillery fired hundreds of shells into the hilltop above them. The heavy weapons companies fired every weapon they could muster into the slopes teeming with entrenched Chinese troops. Shells, bullets, and rockets tore through the air, pounding into the hills and rocks. "The fire was so heavy," said Sfc. Leo Kropka, "that anyone who exposed part of his body was hit."

Climbing the steep slopes, the paratroopers were hit by a rain of concussion hand grenades . . . Probing through the rocks and caves, the troopers dug out the Chinese with grenades and bayonets. Pfc. Norman Fullerton leaped into a hole, tossed a grenade into the recesses, dug into the mountainside, and routed a half dozen enemy grenadiers. . . . Some holes had Chinese soldiers with whole boxes of grenades, throwing them as fast as they could be uncrated.

The 4th Ranger Company had as its objective Hill 205, described by one Ranger as "a hill upon a hill." The well-dug-in enemy was stubborn and resistant and, on 23 March, beat off two attacks by the 4th Rangers. Air attacks softened the enemy positions, and on the next day the 4th Rangers took the hill.

As the rest of the 187th neared the top of their objective, Chinese soldiers began to flee down the opposite side. Troops of A Company, who could see part of the north side of the hill, mowed them down as they fled. A machine gun operated by Sgt. Charles Ferguson fired 10,000 rounds of ammunition in an hour. At five in the afternoon some of the 187th were on the top. But by sundown the troopers held the entire top, commanding the main supply route of what had been a Chinese field army.

During the battle a Chinese radio operator cut into the U.S. radio net to say, "We'll return tonight to retake the hill. You're crazy to fight us." They never lived up to that boast.

The 187th's medics and a field surgical team of twelve men from the 60th Indian Field Ambulance Unit worked around the clock. Their "bloodshot eyes and blood-caked clothes told their story at a glance," wrote Captain Crawford. "Helicopters cut through the rain with their flailing rotors spilling water in sheets across the gray sky. Five at a time they came into the isolated command post and carried out the wounded. There was no other way out."

In the fight for Hills 507–519, the 187th's troopers had broken the CCF 234th Regiment and seized commanding terrain in the area. On 29 March, the 187th linked up with the 3d Division and cleared the last vital route north along the Uijongbu-Chapmon axis. In Operation Tomahawk, the 187th suffered heavy casualties, 782 killed and wounded in action. After the linkup with the 3d Division Bowen moved the RCT back to Taegu to reorganize, reequip, reman, and retrain.

For the next three months the Rakkasans fought as ground troops in battles from Munsan-ni to the battle of "Bloody Inje." "The 187th Airborne RCT engaged in heavy fighting at Inje supported by the 9th, 23d, and 38th Infantry Regiments," wrote Rakkasan historian, Fred J. Waterhouse. "Meanwhile, units attacking to the left of the Hwachon Reservoir had done well taking 6,000 prisoners. The 187th was now preparing to continue the attack from Inje to the sea fifty-two miles away. Van Fleet was extremely satisfied with the results of the offensive. He was aware that the 187th had taken heavy casualties. The Rakkasans lost 286 killed and wounded in running the gauntlet to Inje. He cancelled the 187th push to the sea and ordered all units to dig in and defend their hard won real estate. For the 187th, the battle of 'Bloody Inje' was over. The Regiment was relieved by US Marines."

On 11 April 1951, President Truman relieved General MacArthur of his Far East command, named General Ridgway to succeed him, and appointed Gen. James A. Van Fleet (class of 1915), fifty-nine years old, to command the Eighth Army.

General Ridgway had made it clear to his staff that he did not favor using the 187th Airborne Regimental Combat Team in a strictly ground role. He felt that the highly trained paratroopers should be used primarily in airborne missions—dropping deep behind the enemy's lines and boxing him in while UN ground troops moved forward for the kill.

Generally speaking, the airborne operations in Korea were smaller and more accurate than those of World War II in Europe. In Europe most airborne operations had been massive drops of division-sized units, entering combat by both parachute and glider over wide areas. Many of the drops were at night, and many of the flight formations were scattered by enemy ground and antiaircraft fire, inaccurate navigation, and, as in Sicily, by "friendly" fire from our own navy and shore-based antiaircraft guns. The airborne units in Europe accomplished their missions against great odds, scattered as they were and fighting with the light weapons of the paratroopers/glidermen, against formidable, heavily equipped and armed enemy concentrations.

The airborne operations in Korea, conducted during the daylight hours and unhampered by any concentrated enemy aircraft and antiaircraft fire, were more precisely executed. The airborne effort in Korea had some other advantages. General MacArthur was a staunch supporter of the airborne capability, and, of course, General Ridgway had been the XVIII Airborne Corps commander in Europe. The use of the

C-119 cargo plane permitted the dropping of heavy equipment. Speaking of the Musan-ni operation, Ridgway wrote: "It was a good drop. We had improved our techniques some since World War II. We were dropping jeeps now, under big cargo canopies, and 105 howitzers, a heavier gun than we'd been able to take in on our drops in Europe."

He summed up the situation this way: "The American flag never flew over a prouder, tougher, more spirited and more competent fighting force than was 8th Army as it drove north beyond the Parallel. It was a magnificent fighting organization, supremely confident that it could take any objective assigned to it."

The 187th Airborne Regimental Combat Team and its attached Ranger companies were proud and gallant fighting members of that Eighth Army.

In late June and early July of 1951, the 187th moved to camps in Japan. Two infantry battalions settled into Camp Chickamauga near Beppu and the 1st Battalion, 187th; the 674th Airborne Field Artillery Battalion; and A Battery of the 88th Airborne Antiaircraft Artillery Battalion took up residence across the island of Kyushu at Camp Wood, near Kumamoto. Brigadier General Frank Bowen injured his back on a jump at Oita near Beppu, and on 27 July 1951, Brig. Gen. Thomas J. Trapnell (class of 1927), forty-nine years old, took over the command. Trapnell had been captured on Bataan and survived the Death March and three years of Japanese imprisonment.

On 17 May 1952 Trapnell received a new type of mission for the 187th. Move the RCT to Koje-do, an island off Korea, and restore order in a camp housing some seventy thousand extremely unruly North Korean POWs. By 15 June the Rakkasans had the compound in order; the Koje-do operation was "mission accomplished" for the 187th. But it was not back to the "heaven" of Beppu and Kumamoto for the Rakkasans. It was back to the Korean War and to the Iron Triangle sector, along the current defensive line. And the Rakkasans got a new commander. On 5 July Trapnell was assigned to head the Military Advisory and Assistance Group in French Indo-China, and on 29 July Col. William C. Westmoreland, (class of 1936), thirty-nine years old, who was promoted to brigadier general on 7 November 1952, flew into Taegu and took over command. The RCT stayed on line. According to Fred Waterhouse, "It was outpost battles, trench raids, artillery duels, and nightly ambush patrols into the valley. On a daylight reconnaissance patrol at Kumwha Valley, Corp. Lester Hammond, radio operator, A Company was posthumously awarded the Medal of Honor after calling in artillery fire on top of his own position after an enemy ambush. In so doing, he saved his patrol but gave his life in the effort. The battle escalated into an all-day fight with thousands of Chinese rushing into the valley. The 674th Field Artillery used all available guns including corps artillery to decimate the enemy who finally withdrew in a rout." The 187th stayed on line until the middle of September 1952 and then returned to its bases in Japan.

In June of 1953 the Rakkasans returned once more to the Korean War and, between 20 and 22 June 1953, were deployed along defensive positions in the Chorwon Valley, the "Bowling Alley," leading to Seoul. Here, the Chinese had launched a major assault against the Eighth Army defensive line in the last major offensive of the Korean War. The war ended with an armistice on 27 July 1953, and the Rakkasans went into a new defensive position and built a formidable barrier of bunkers and trenches, the "Blackjack Bastion." On 1 October, Westmoreland received orders to move the RCT back to home bases in Japan. On 19 October 1953 Westmoreland was ordered to the Pentagon, and Brig. Gen. Roy E. Lindquist (class of 1930), forty-six years old, took command.

Until the spring of 1955 the 187th stayed in Japan, training, jumping, and even opening a jump school for officers in the Japanese Self-Defense Force. But in May 1955 the first elements of the 508th Airborne RCT began to arrive under Operation Gyroscope to replace the 187th, and the first contingent of the 187th returned to Fort Bragg and became part of the XVIII Airborne Corps. By 17 July the Rakkasans' airlift was complete. The Rakkasans' days in combat in Korea were over, but ahead of them were many more reconfigurations, mass jumps, strenuous field training, upgrading of equipment (including parachutes), more overseas moves, and combat.

25: After Korea

I n the post–Korean War period, the army was in the throes of a major reorganization. The Cold War was descending into glacial conditions, and the U.S. Army was preparing to meet the era's challenges. Gyroscoping (The movement of one army division from the continental United States to replace another division in Germany, which returns home. The program is no longer in effect.) units were switched back and forth across the Atlantic and Pacific. "Massive retaliation" became a policy and resulted in drastic cuts in the end-strength of the army during the Eisenhower years. The army attempted to cope with the new strategy with two major reorganizations of its divisions that caused turmoil in the ranks and command structure. "First came the pentomic [or pentana] plan of 1957–1959, then the Reorganization Objective Army Divisions (ROAD) plan of 1962–1964," wrote Mary Lee Stubbs and Stanley Russell Connor in *Armor-Cavalry*, in the Army Lineage Series.

Underlining these reorganizations were developments in nuclear weapons—without the loss of massed firepower—mandatory characteristics for military forces. Combat areas of future nuclear wars were viewed as much broader and deeper than battlefields of the past, requiring small, self-contained fast-moving units. Speed was imperative, not only for the concentration of forces but also in dispersion for defense. On the other hand, the Army had to retain its ability to fight limited or non-nuclear wars, where the requirements for mobility or dispersion were not as important.

The 187th Airborne RCT and other airborne units found themselves caught in the middle of these substantial changes.

In the spring of 1949 the 11th Airborne Division had arrived at Fort Campbell, Kentucky, after combat in the Philippines and after almost four years of occupation duty in Japan. Then, early in the spring of 1956, the 11th gyroscoped to Germany. Rumors among the troops had it that the 101st Airborne Division was about to be reactivated and that the 187th would have a major part in forming the "born again" division. They were right on.

At Fort Bragg, in January of 1956, Col. Joseph F. Ryneska, who had assumed command of the 187th in August 1955, got the order to move the 187th to Fort Campbell. By bus and truck convoys in a move appropriately dubbed Operation Gypsy, the Rakkasans left Fort Bragg on 19 January and then settled into the barracks only recently vacated by the 11th Airborne Division.

"Training continued for the Rakkasans," wrote Bob Domitrovits. "Green recruits were to be molded into new Rakkasans, double timing, push-ups, sit-ups, were the name of the game. Jump school would have been tough enough, but taking Advanced Infantry Training by airborne cadre made the next eight weeks feel like eight weeks of jump school."

On 27 March, the 187th formed Test Group Neptune and began a series of training exercises and tests in the army's new pentomic concept. There were four tests over a period of some four months, during which the 187th rarely left the field. The tests included a parachute assault and a linkup with an armored force, an air transportability test, and a raid in which the paratroopers parachuted into a DZ, destroyed enemy installations, and then were extracted by air transports. The fourth test was a final examination testing all aspects of ground combat.

On 19 June 1956 the 187th felt the changes brought on by the new pentomic mode—it was deactivated as an RCT and faded temporarily from the active army roster. On the same day, the three battalions of the 187th were assigned as cadre to the 101st Airborne Division, reactivated on 21 September at a ceremony attended by the secretary of the army, Wilbur M. Brucker, and the army chief of staff, Gen. Maxwell D. Taylor. At the ceremony, General Taylor, commander of the 101st in the Normandy invasion and later in the fight across Europe, presented the colors of the Screaming Eagles to its new commander, Maj. Gen. T. L. Sherburne Jr. (class of 1929), fifty-one years old. With its reactivation, the 101st became a pentomic division, a poorly conceived organization structure centered on a pentagonal concept: to replace the normal three infantry regiments, the pentomic division had five infantry battle groups of five companies each (no battalion-sized unit in the infantry units), plus separate battalions dedicated to command and control, communications, engineer formations, and artillery. The concept was doomed almost from its start. On that same date, the 187th Airborne Regimental Combat Team was designated the 187th Airborne Regimental Combat Group.

On 1 March 1957, the 1st Battalion of the 187th emerged from the dusty army record bins and was reactivated as the 1st Airborne Battle Group, 187th Infantry, under the command of Col. Norman G. Reynolds, and assigned to the 11th Airborne Division in Germany. It left Fort Campbell in the spring of 1957 and remained overseas for the next fourteen months.

On 25 April 1957 the 2d Battalion of the 187th became the 2d Airborne Battle Group, 187th Infantry, under the command of Col. Melvin Zais, a renowned paratrooper in World War II and later commander of the 101st in Viet Nam. Later he achieved the rank of four-star general.

The 1st Airborne Battle Group, 187th Infantry, joined the 11th Airborne Division in Augsburg, Germany, and moved into Gablingen Kaserne. For almost a year, the battle group trained with the division in the rugged and scenic hills of the Hohenfels training area. On 15 March 1958 at a formal parade at the kaserne, Lt. Col. Thomas W. Sharkey (class of 1941), thirty-nine years old, took over command from Colonel Reynolds.

In the spring of 1958 U.S. interests in the Middle East were compromised when rebel uprisings, aided and sponsored by Nasserite and Soviet agents, threatened pro-Western governments. In May of 1958, troubles sprang up in Jordan, Iraq, Lebanon, and Syria. On 14 July President Eisenhower, reacting to the murder of King Faisal and the overthrow of his government in Iraq, alerted U.S. forces, including the 1st Airborne Battle Group, 187th, in Germany, for deployment. On 15 July Eisenhower sent the Ninth Air Force, the tactical strike force, and air transports from Donaldson Air Force Base in South Carolina to Europe. The Sixth Fleet, which included a naval task force of seventy-four ships with three carriers and two cruisers, and 45,000 men counting among them 5,000 marines, moved into the eastern Mediterranean. The marines landed and occupied the airport at Beirut, Lebanon, a state torn by violence, "to help preserve that country's government in the wake of internal revolts and a coup in neighboring Iraq." The mission was to show support for Lebanese President Camille Chamoun's government.

In Germany, on 1 July 1958, the 11th Airborne Division was deactivated and the 1st Airborne Battle Group (ABG), 187th, was assigned to the 24th Infantry Division (Pentomic). In the 24th Division there were now two airborne battle groups, the 1st ABG, 187th, and the 2d ABG, 503d Airborne Infantry. Sharkey still retained command of the 1st ABG, 187th.

On 14 July, the 1st ABG, 187th, returned to Gablingen by airdrop after two weeks of rugged training at Hohenfels. On 15 July, Sharkey got orders to move his battle group from Germany to Adana, Turkey. On 16 July, it began a massive air movement from the Fürstenfeldbrück airbase near Munich to a staging area in Turkey, and then to the Beirut International Airport. By the time the lift was over on 19 July, some 1,800 paratroopers and all of their combat equipment, including rifles, machine guns, jeeps, ammunition, and artillery, had flown to Beirut in some seventy-six C-119s, C-124s, and C-130s. With this buildup, there were now 7,200 combat troops in Beirut, including three battalions of marines and the 187th's paratroopers. The Rakkasans set up camp, named Camp Zeitoune, in an olive grove near the airport and manned a perimeter defense around the airport. Along with the marines the Rakkasans made a show of force in and around the area.

The summer passed under a baking Lebanese sun. As the political situation cleared a bit, the U.S. forces trained the Lebanese forces in the use of U.S. arms and ran a combined land-sea-air training exercise on the shore adjacent to the historic ruins of Byblos. The Rakkasans continued to man the roadblocks, patrol the mountains, and occasionally jump on a DZ named "the Sahara."

Five members of the West Point class of 1956 were lieutenants in the 1st ABG, 187th, in Lebanon. Before their careers were over, they had achieved substantial rank: John W. Nicholson and Arvid E. West became brigadier generals; Michael J. Conrad, a major general; Robert D. Hammond, a lieutenant general; and John W. Foss II, a four-star general.

By October 1958, after three and a half months in Lebanon, the situation eased enough to permit the return of the Rakkasans to Augsburg, Germany. Later, on 20 November 1958, Colonel Sharkey turned over the battle group to Col. Donald C. Clayman at a change-of-command ceremony at Gablinger Kaserne. This was Clayman's second tour with the Rakkasans: in 1951 and 1952 he had served as the 187th's deputy commander. A graduate of Cornell in 1935, he had served in World War II as a battalion commander in both the 47th and 60th Infantry Regiments.

Shortly after its return to Germany, it was the 187th's turn to gyroscope. On 9 February 1959, the battle group arrived in New York harbor aboard the USNS *Buckner,* staged through the Brooklyn Navy Yard,
and entrained for a trip to Fort Bragg. In March 1959, the 1st ABG,
187th, reassembled at Fort Bragg and joined the 82d Airborne Division
as part of XVIII Airborne Strategic Army Corps. Units of the 187th now
had the distinction of being or having been part of the 11th, 82d, and
101st Airborne Divisions.

Another member of the West Point class of 1956, Lt. H. Norman
Schwarzkopf, twenty-three years old, had joined the 2d ABG, 187th Infantry, with the 101st at Fort Campbell. "When I reported for duty at the
101st Airborne Division at Fort Campbell, Kentucky, in early 1957," he
wrote in his book, *It Doesn't Take a Hero,* "I was the typical West Point graduate—eager to serve my country, hungry for glory, filled with the wish
to be a leader of men. . . ."

"The army that I entered was suffering from the after effects of Korea, officers and noncommissioned officers were in short supply and bud-
gets had been cut so severely that there weren't enough funds for day-
to-day operations. In the age of massive retaliation, the army believed
itself in danger of being completely overshadowed by the air force. Despite this pessimistic outlook, my friends and I were not discouraged. . . .
Who had ever seized and held territory with an airplane? Our job was to
be ready when called upon."

In June of 1958, Maj. Gen. William C. Westmoreland became the commanding general of the 101st. He concentrated not only on combat
readiness but also on improving post maintenance and administrative
services. But during his stay with the 101st he became disillusioned with
the pentomic division. He wrote in *A Soldier Reports:*

> Under the concept, infantry and airborne divisions would have
> five battle groups of 1,400 men each, each one therefore larger
> than a battalion but smaller than a regiment, which could be em-
> ployed in battle singly or in combination. Since the battle group
> replaced both the battalion and the regiment, one echelon of com-
> mand was eliminated in the organization, which cut down on staff
> overhead. . . .
>
> As I prepared to relinquish command of the 101st Airborne in
> 1960, I recommended abolishing the pentomic division, primarily
> because I had found the control of the five separate battle groups

by the division headquarters and five companies by a battle group headquarters was difficult. I recommended reestablishing a regimental-level headquarters, additional artillery, and better communications as necessary to give the division staying power. That was what the army eventually adopted.

On 21 December 1960 Col. Arndt L. Mueller, a World War II combat veteran with the 6th Infantry Division in the Pacific, assumed command of the 2d ABG, 187th. For the next two years, the battle group trained, trained, and trained. In late 1962, to prove that this had not been in vain, it went on full combat alert as a reactionary strike force during the Cuban missile crisis.

The army was in the throes of initiating another major development in tactics and organization—the "air assault" theory.

AIR ASSAULT

In the early 1960s, some forward-looking savants in the Pentagon were urging the army to explore new ways to fight wars in which battles might not always be fought with massive fleets of tanks, scores of artillery battalions, and hundreds of bombers and fighters. In the future, they reasoned, all wars might not be unlimited. Even President Kennedy, whose massive retaliation strategy was his answer to the immense and continued military buildup by the Soviet Union, encouraged the army to search for a "new look."

In January 1960, the army chief of staff established the Army Aircraft Requirements Board, chaired by Lt. Gen. Gordon B. Rogers (class of 1924), fifty-eight years old, deputy commanding general of the Continental Army Command (CONARC). The board met at Fort Monroe from 29 February to 6 March. It reviewed the Army Aircraft Development Plan, discussed roles and missions of army aviation, projected army funding, assessed combat surveillance requirements, and examined procurement plans. "With historic hindsight," wrote Lt. Gen. John Tolson in *Airmobility—1961–1971*, "it is apparent that the scope of the Rogers Board review was limited. It obviously did not constitute a major advance in tactical mobility for the army. But in comparison with the advances made during the 1950s, the board's objectives, if obtained, would have represented a substantial gain in mobility through the use of aviation."

But at least one part of the army was making some progress in imaginative and visionary use of army aviation. In 1960, Lt. Col. Russell P. Bonasso (class of 1942), the aviation officer of the 101st Airborne Division, persuaded Westmoreland to centralize control of all aviation assets in the division. As a result, Westmoreland authorized the formation of the 191st Combat Aviation Battalion, the first such organization in the U.S. Army.

The army continued to study and forward its aviation requirements to the Defense Department. During January and February 1962, analysts in the office of the secretary of defense reviewed the army's submissions. "Their review was extremely critical of the army's so-called caution," wrote General Tolson. On 19 April 1962, Secretary of Defense Robert S. McNamara sent the army a strong, pointed, and "now famous" message in which he concluded that the army's current program was "dangerously conservative." He prodded the army to open its mind to innovation and break away from the tactics and equipment of the past. He directed the army to investigate enhanced "land warfare mobility" and that the examination be conducted in an "open and free atmosphere."

The result of the secretary's memo was the Army Department's directive to Gen. Herbert B. Powell, commander of CONARC, to establish the Tactical Mobility Requirements Board. He appointed as its president one of the army's most open-minded senior officers, Lt. Gen. Hamilton H. Howze (class of 1930), fifty-four years old, the commander of the XVIII Airborne Corps at Fort Bragg. The board's secretary was Col. John Norton (class of 1941), forty-four years old, who had been the G-3 officer of the 82d Airborne Division in World War II under Gen. James Gavin. Both Howze and Norton were army aviators. There were six other officers and six top-level civilians named to the board that eventually became known throughout the army as the Howze Board. General Powell, under guidance from the Department of the Army, directed Howze to look to the future and determine the army's aircraft requirements and tactical organizations for the years 1963 to 1975. A shorter version of General Howze's mission was to determine whether "ground vehicles could be replaced by air vehicles and, if so, to what extent?" The army did not know it at the time, but these would be the years of buildup, combat, and withdrawal from Vietnam, the place where the army's air mobility and air support would be put to the ultimate test.

The Howze Board reached out to the army, air force, and industry for new ideas, equipment, organizations, and tactics. The board developed many recommendations that used army helicopters and fixed-wing air-craft in close-support roles and as battlefield transportation and tank killers. The board conducted a series of forty tests in basic flying tech-niques, small-unit deployment, and air support with helicopters. Its rec-ommendations were so extreme that the army decided to test them rad-ically, unrelated to current organization and tactics. The Department of the Army (DA) organized an entirely new division to be the test bed. On 1 February 1963 the 11th Air Assault Division (Test) was organized at Fort Benning under the command of Maj. Gen. Harry Kinnard, the veteran G-3 officer of the 101st Airborne Division. In theory, the 11th was to be a "light" division capable of air movement by air force and/or army air-craft. The planners scrubbed previous TO&Es, made many innovative changes, and came up with a "lean" division.

In December 1960, based on recommendations from Westmoreland and other dissatisfied pentomic division commanders, the Army De-partment directed CONARC to reevaluate the pentomic concept. In April 1961, the secretary of the army approved the CONARC study, *ROAD (Reorganization of Army Divisions),* basically returning the army di-visions to the triangular concept, with three infantry brigades or battle groups per division. In February 1962 the ROAD reorganizations began. By June of 1964 all fifteen regular divisions had been reconfigured ac-cording to the ROAD plan.

On 1 February 1963, the 3d ABG, 187th, was resurrected from the Army's dusty record books and on 7 February was activated as the 3d Battalion, 187th Infantry, of the 11th Air Assault Division at Fort Ben-ning as a relatively standard nonpentomic infantry battalion. In the 11th the 3d Battalion, 187th, was joined by the 3d Squadron, 17th Cavalry (minus B Troop), and the 10th Transportation Brigade, composed of several battalions of both fixed- and rotary-wing aircraft. At its initial manning the 11th had only 3,023 men but was at full strength by 1964. In July 1963, the 1st Airborne Brigade of the 11th was fleshed out with the activation of the 1st Battalion, 188th Airborne Infantry, and the 1st Battalion, 511th Airborne Infantry. With these additions the 187th, 188th, and 511th, the original glider and parachute regiments of the original 11th Airborne Division formed in February of 1943, were once again on the rolls of the 11th—this time an "air assault division." In ad-dition to the standard infantry, artillery, and support units, the division included an aviation group with enough aircraft to lift one-third of the division simultaneously.

In July of 1963 Lt. Gen. William Westmoreland, former commander of the 187th Airborne Regimental Combat Team in Korea and Japan and of the 101st Airborne Division, became the commander of XVIII Airborne Corps.

For over two years, Major General Kinnard and the 11th Air Assault Division developed, tested, refined, and retested the division's equipment, organization, and tactics. Test sites were sited in the low country and swamps of Florida and the hills of Georgia and North Carolina. The 187th and other battalions of the 11th tested the helicopter in numerous combat roles, command and control, attack formations, scouting and screening, reconnaissance, aerial resupply, and air assault tactics. During the trials, the air force and army argued about which had the role of "close support" on the battlefield and which had the mission of tactical air mobility.

The 3d Battalion, 187th, stayed with the 11th as an air mobility test bed for a year. On 3 February 1964, it was relieved of assignment to the 11th Air Assault Division and reassigned as an organic unit of the 3d Brigade of the 101st at Fort Campbell, where its air mobility expertise was put to good use training the rest of the 101st. From 1964 until 1971, the other two infantry battalions of the 3d Brigade, 101st, were the 1st and 2d Battalions of the 506th Infantry.

Following activation in 1964 the 3d Brigade took part in Exercise Desert Strike in the Mojave Desert. In a 1965 exercise, the 2d Brigade participated in the 101st's CPX (Command Post Exercise) Gold Fire and Eagle Jump. In May of 1966, the 3d Brigade took part in the division's exercise Eagle Prey I designed to teach the troopers the methods of countering guerrilla warfare. During September of 1966 the 3d Battalion, 187th, flew to Norway, where it participated in NATO Operation Bar Frost.

On 1 February 1964 the 2d ABG, 187th Infantry, 101st Airborne Division, was deactivated. On 6 March 1964 the 1st ABG, 187th, that had served in Germany, Beirut, and Fort Bragg, was designated the 1st Battalion, 187th, relieved of assignment to the 82d Airborne Division at Fort Bragg, and transferred to the 11th Air Assault Division at Fort Benning for training and testing.

On 17 March 1964, the 2d Brigade of the 2d Infantry Division at Fort Benning was added to the roster of the 11th Air Assault Division for additional air mobility tests. Additional changes, in the division began with the additional units. In one major organization change three battalions of thirty-six helicopters each were added. The helicopters were armed with 3.5-inch rockets and constituted the division's aerial rocket artillery.

Colonel (later Brigadier General) B. K. "Igor" Gorwitz, once with the 187th's 674th Airborne Artillery Battalion in Korea, was the 11th division artillery commander. He wrote about the army's wisdom in keeping conventional artillery. "We had three battalions of 105mm howitzers that had the capability of firing around the clock, in all weather, on station at all times, and a reload capability unattainable by helicopters. The air force did see the armed helicopters as an attempt to take over their close-in support role."

Once more the Pentagon brass decided that the colors of the 11th Air Assault Division should be cased. In June 1965, the colors of the 1st Cavalry Division in Korea were put on a plane and flown to Fort Benning. In a simple ceremony the colors were presented to the 11th Air Assault Division (Test). On 29 June 1965 the 11th Air Assault Division and the 1st Battalions of the 187th, 188th, and 511th were inactivated. The next day the 1st Cavalry Division (Air Mobile) was officially activated pursuant to General Order Number185, headquarters 3d Army. The men for the new division came from the 11th Air Assault Division and the 2d Infantry Division at Fort Benning. It was a formidable force, with 15,847 officers and men, six Mohawk fixed-wing aircraft, 287 Huey helicopters, and forty-eight CH-37 Mojaves.

In a letter to the author in which he discussed his tour as commander of the 11th Air Assault Division, Lieutenant General Kinnard wrote:

> I focused from the outset, and until the very end, on recreating in the 11th Air Assault Division (and then in the 1st Cavalry Division) the spirit and esprit of the paratrooper. From the moment I received my marching orders from on high, I felt that an 'Airborne state of mind' was a sine qua non for realizing the maximum potential of the helicopter force. . . . At the end of our testing period—in my final report—I strongly recommended that all the combat arms of the division should be jump-qualified. This recommendation stood up pretty well as the report was staffed—on up through CONARC—but was regarded a bit nutty by H. K. Johnson [class of 1933, age fifty-four], then Chief of Staff. He did, however, discuss my recommendation with Buzz Wheeler (the chief of staff who had given me my marching orders, and who at the time was Chairman of the Joint Staff). Wheeler rather liked my idea and the result was

as strange compromise in which one of our three brigades was designated airborne. This was the structure which we transposed into the 1st Cavalry. Our 1st Brigade, under Elvy Roberts [class of 1943, age forty-eight], was authorized to be parachute-qualified with a complement of other units in the division (one FA battalion, and so on).

My bias was evident, as well, in the key officers and NCOs which we assembled at Fort Benning. I won't go into the arguments here; to you I'd be preaching to the choir. Suffice it to say that nothing in our Testing Phase, or later in our combat experiences, changed my original thought that the assault by air requires a special breed of cat, whether the mode is parachute, glider, or helicopter.

During the early and middle 1960s, the army lived—sometimes struggled—through major changes in the tactics, organization, and equipment—its very essence. The 187th Infantry, like other units in the army, also felt the reverberations—at times earthquake-like. The battalions of the regiments became battle groups and then went back to being battalions; they were activated, transferred across the Atlantic, and then sent back; then they were made inactive. By 1965, the sole identity of the 187th Airborne Infantry Regiment rested with the 3d Battalion, 187th Infantry, one of the three relatively standard battalions (no longer forced into the aborted pentomic concept) in the 3d Brigade of the 101st Airborne Division at Fort Campbell.

Very soon, though, the 3d Battalion, 187th, and many other battalions and units of the U.S. Army would prove their fighting mettle once again, this time in Vietnam.

26: Vietnam

In May of 1965, the 173d Airborne Infantry Brigade was the first U.S. Army unit to be deployed to Vietnam. Its other distinction was the singularity of its concept, organization, mission, and tactical employment.

In the spring of 1963, Brig. Gen. (later Maj. Gen.) Ellis W. Williamson met with Army Chief of Staff Gen. Harold K. Johnson.

In his meeting with Johnson and several of his staff officers, Williamson learned about the new air mobile concept and that he would "move to the island of Okinawa," Williamson wrote later, "where I would organize, train, command and commit to combat if necessary, a unique organization. He was told that this unit would be the only one of its kind in the U.S. Army. It would be prepared to respond to emergencies in any of the countries around the 'Pacific Rim.' The unique aspect of this specific unit was that it would be an especially tailored separate airborne brigade. It would have all of the elements of a complete division, except in lesser numbers. Its capability to project throughout its vast area of responsibility would be in close coordination with both the U.S. Air Force and U.S. Navy." Johnson told Williamson, "You have my personal support in assembling your team of good people."

On Okinawa over the next two years he lived up to his commitment and orders with personal dedication. Brigadier General Williamson was already a distinguished warrior, his awards included the Distinguished Service Cross, three Distinguished Service Medals, six Silver Stars, two Legions of Merit, four Bronze Stars, five Purple Hearts, the Distinguished Flying Cross, and twenty-four Air Medals.

"The 'Sky Soldiers,' as the Nationalist Chinese paratroopers called the 173d," wrote Brigadier General Williamson, "made thousands of parachute jumps in a dozen different Pacific-area countries. They experimented with the use of all types of aircraft, submarines, aircraft carriers, and assault boats. They even had their own private jungle training island far south of Okinawa. Within the parameters of safety, all junior leaders were told to be rapid, flexible, and pragmatic, i.e., 'try anything that might work better.' Often platoon-sized units were left on the island, completely by themselves, with no commander looking over the leader's shoulder."

When the 173d was deployed to Vietnam, most of the brigade landed at Bien Hoa airfield and, on the same day, the troopers moved into the jungle and set up patrol bases. Shortly after the arrival of the 173d in country, troops from New Zealand and Australia arrived and were put under Williamson's command until the summer of 1966.

During the Vietnam War, a number of airborne and air assault units in addition to the 173d were sent to Vietnam. On 29 July 1965 the 1st Brigade of the 101st arrived at Cam Ranh Bay, where it was met by two former commanders of the 101st, Maxwell D. Taylor, U.S. ambassador to Vietnam, and General Westmoreland, commander of the Military Assistance Command Vietnam (MACV). At Fort Campbell, in November and December 1967, the 2d and 3d Brigades of the 101st took part in Operation Eagle Thrust. Later, according to Col. Robert Jones, the 101st's historian, the division "made military history as the only Army division to be completely airlifted into combat. In 41 days, 10,536 troops and 5,118 tons of equipment were airlifted to Vietnam." By 13 December, the division commander, Maj. Gen. Beverly E. Powell (class of 1936), fifty-five years old, reported that his CP at Bien Hoa was up and running and ready for missions. With the start of the Tet offensive of 1968, combat missions flowed into the CP. In February of 1968, for example, a thirty-five-man platoon from the 101st defended the U.S. Embassy in Saigon and knocked off the attackers.

The unit designation of the famous Screaming Eagles had undergone some changes. First it had been the 101st Airborne Division. In Vietnam it became the 101st Air Cavalry Division. Then, on 29 August 1968, it became the 101st Airborne Division (Air Mobile), emphasizing a shift from parachute assaults to air mobility. Finally, it received its present designation: 101st Airborne Division (Air Assault).

The 1968 Tet offensive launched by the North Vietnamese Army on 25 January created the need for additional U.S. troops in Vietnam. One of the few units still available in the United States for deployment was the 82d Airborne Division at Fort Bragg. General Johnson elected to send the 3d Brigade of the 82d. It was not an easy deployment: the brigade was short of airborne-qualified troops and, in early February, trained paratroopers were moved in from other units in the division as well as from Special Forces units at Fort Bragg. On 14 February, Col. (later Maj. Gen.) Alexander R. Bolling, (class of 1943), forty-six years old, led his 3,650-man brigade to Chu Lai, Vietnam, by way of Alaska and Japan and some 140 aircraft sorties.

According to the division historian, SSgt. Steven Mrozek, "Once 'in-country,' it was discovered that a majority of the brigade personnel did not meet the requirements for overseas combat deployment. Over 2,500 troopers accepted the option to return to Fort Bragg. Once again replacements were desperately sought. Being less particular this time, most of the new replacements were nonairborne qualified." But the brigade retrained and fought so valiantly that it became known as the "Golden Brigade." In March of 1968, for example, it fought with the 101st in Operations Carentan I and II and in Quang Tri and Thua Thien provinces. The brigade suffered some 43 killed and 270 wounded in action, while killing 727 enemy soldiers and capturing 18. After twenty-two months of combat the brigade returned to the United States in December 1969.

Vietnam was the proving ground for a new use of army rotary-wing aircraft—the air mobility concept. The introduction of the helicopter in a combat role—carrying men into battle and supporting them with medical evacuation with helicopters, helicopter gunships, and helicopter command and control ships—opened the way for the rapid insertion of air mobile troops behind enemy lines or in battle areas where other troops already in a fight required reinforcement. The nature of the Vietnam battles, the combat tactics, and the political limitations on the objectives of U.S. forces almost entirely ruled out the traditional use of massed "airborne" forces. There were some examples, however.

In the early stages of the war, a number of small covert South Vietnamese teams parachuted into North Vietnam to foment guerrilla warfare against the Communists. Unfortunately most of these teams were immediately wiped out, and a few were even "doubled" against South Vietnam.

Standard South Vietnamese parachute units were also used a number of times in combat in the south. In January 1963, for example, the

South Vietnamese dropped a battalion of their elite airborne division at Ap Bac. But the DZ was badly chosen; the battalion landed in an area from which it could have little effect on the outcome of the battle.

The one and only major U.S. parachute assault in Vietnam occurred on 22 February 1967, when the commander of the 173d Airborne Brigade, Brig. Gen. John R. Deane Jr. (class of 1942), forty-seven years old, and eventually a four-star general, led his 2d Battalion, 503d Airborne Infantry Regiment in a jump that marked the beginning of Operation Junction City Alternate. The 2d, 503d, was commanded by Lt. Col. Robert H. Sigholtz, described by the 173d historian, Michael E. Creamer, as "a charismatic leader. . . . An aggressive fighter, he had given his unit the unofficial nickname, 'We Try Harder.'"

The overall operation employed the largest contingent of forces so far in the war: the 1st and 25th Infantry Divisions, the 196th Light Infantry Brigade, elements of the 4th and 9th Infantry Divisions, South Vietnamese units, and the 173d Airborne Brigade. The target of this seemingly overwhelming force was to locate and obliterate the Central Office, South Vietnam (COSVN), the supreme headquarters of the Viet Cong. Some intelligence had it located north of Tay Ninh City in War Zone C. The decision to use paratroopers was based on the need to get a large number of men on the ground as soon as possible and still have enough helicopter assets to make a large heliborne, immediate follow-up.

The exact location of the DZ was a closely guarded secret. One previous parachute assault had been canceled because the location of the DZ had been compromised. Lieutenant General Jonathan O. Seaman, (class of 1934), fifty-five years old, commander of Second Field Force, Vietnam, and Jack Deane designated another area, a "notional" drop zone, twenty-five kilometers east of Katum in the center of eastern War Zone C, as the intended target. George L. MacGarrigle wrote in *Taking the Offensive:*

> Not until 21 February, the day before the jump, after all who were to participate had been sealed in a marshaling area at Bien Hoa Air Base, did Deane reveal that the parachute assault was to be made on a large savanna four kilometers north of Katum. Although Deane had notified MACV headquarters the previous night of the true drop zone site, Westmoreland's aide did not get the message, and he guided the MACV commander to the decoy area instead. Westmoreland, who had led the only airborne regimental

combat team in the Korean War, saw only the last of the jumpers landing. [The author was in the plane with General Westmoreland.]

"Several hours after daybreak on February 22d 1967," wrote Michael E. Creamer, "thirteen C-130 aircraft droned in formation to the small clearing near the Cambodian border."

Seated inside, burdened by heavy loads of weapons, ammo and equipment, were 780 men of the 2d Bn., C Battery, 319th FA [Field Artillery] Regiment, and a support contingent of engineers and MPs. They were in high spirits, astounding the aircrews and accompanying journalists by singing the lusty Airborne theme song, "Blood on the Risers." Jumpmasters leaned out the open doors scouting the area, the powerful slipstream distorting their faces into bizarre masks. The planes began their descent to the jump altitude of 1,000 feet, the red lights came on, and the familiar jump commands began . . . finally came GO GO GO. For the first time since the Korean War, American paratroopers hurtled in a rush from their aircraft. . . . There was some sniper fire as the men descended but, all things considered, resistance was light. . . . The next pass of the C-130s brought howitzers, mortars and ammo. . . . A half hour later, the big Herky Birds came in once more using the Low Altitude Cargo Delivery System to slingshot more supplies to the men on the ground. . . . It had all gone off without a hitch. . . . Not one piece of the 60 tons of equipment or one case of the 40 tons of supplies had been lost or wrecked.

The 173d was under the operational control of the commander of the 1st Infantry Division, Maj. Gen. John H. Hay. The battalion dropped on schedule at 0900, and by 0920 the 780 men were on the ground. Eleven had sustained only minor injuries. The heavy equipment drop from eight C-130s began at 0925 and continued throughout the day. The 1st Battalion, 503d, part of the 173d, began landing by helicopter at 1035 on the 2d Battalion's DZ. These units made no contact with the Viet Cong during the early hours of 22 February. Another of the 173d's battalions, the 4th Battalion, 503d, made a helicopter assault in seventy choppers into two nearby LZs at 1420. This operation essentially completed phase one of Junction City Alternate.

During the operation, the 173d was supported by the 11th, 145th, and 1st Aviation Battalions, which flew over 9,700 sorties, lifting 9,518 troops and a daily average of fifty tons of cargo. Some operational problems did result, though, from mixing parachute and heliborne assaults on the same terrain. One accident and several near accidents occurred when helicopters tried to land on DZs littered with personnel chutes. In World War II this had not been a problem. Personnel parachutes strewn about a DZ did not cause a problem for the gliders sliding across the fields. Trees, ditches, and hedgerows were far more dangerous and destructive.

Operation Junction City Alternate, begun with the drop by the 2d Battalion, 503d, continued into May 1967. The campaign netted some 2,700 dead Viet Cong along with vast quantities of ammunition, 800 tons of rice, and masses of medical supplies.

In summing up the role of airborne versus heliborne assault forces, Lt. Gen. John J. Tolson, commander of the 1st Cavalry Division in Vietnam and later commander of XVIII Airborne Corps, wrote that "the employment of the airborne parachute force is historically visualized as a theater-controlled operation aimed at achieving tactical surprise. Although parachute delivery of troops and equipment is a relatively inefficient means of introduction into combat, the very existence of this capability complicates the enemy's planning and offers the friendly commander one more option of surprise."

That airborne techniques were not used more often in Vietnam can be attributed to many factors. "The most obvious restraint was the time lag inherent in airborne operations in responding to intelligence on the elusive enemy," Tolson continues.

The relatively unsuccessful French airborne operations [in Vietnam] already had pointed this out to us. A much more important restraint was the nature of the war and the limitations imposed on US forces. From a strategic point of view, the US posture in Vietnam was defensive. US tactical offensive operations were limited to the confines of South Vietnam. Had the rules been changed, the parachute potential could have been profitably employed by planning and executing an airborne assault into enemy territory at a distance within the ferry range of the Huey. This would have allowed the parachute force to secure a landing zone and construct a hasty strip. Fixed-wing aircraft would have air-dropped or air-landed essential fuel and supplies. Then the helicopters could have married up with this force, refueled and immediately given them tactical mobility out of the airhead. These circumstances never came about.

In summary, the one major airborne operation in Vietnam was a follow-up to World War II–style airborne operations but on a much smaller scale, with more accuracy, with more concentration on the DZ because of the larger personnel-carrying aircraft, with much longer sticks jumping out of both sides of the plane, with heavier equipment drops, and under more favorable conditions of daylight and generally lighter enemy response with antiaircraft and fighter plane fire.

The airborne operations in Vietnam were a totally different from those of either World War II or Korea because of tactical situations, limited objectives, dispersion of U.S. forces throughout the country, size of the country, and proliferation of mobile, ready, rapidly reacting, trained, heliborne assault forces able to concentrate on and flood a landing zone not far away.

In late 1971 and early 1972, the 101st left Vietnam for Fort Campbell. The division was the last U.S. Army division to leave the country. In a homecoming ceremony on 6 April 1972, Vice President Spiro T. Agnew and General Westmoreland welcomed the Screaming Eagles home. The division had returned at 20 percent of its original strength, but by June of 1973 it was back at full strength. On 1 February 1974 the last paratrooper unit of the 101st, the 3d Brigade, lost its jump status. And on 4 October of that year "Air Mobile" was dropped from the division's title and replaced by "Air Assault."

When the colors of the 173d Airborne Brigade (Sep) "were furled at Fort Campbell, Kentucky in January 1972," wrote General Williamson, "a unique chapter in the Army's combat history was closed. Created to 'quickly snuff out small brush fires in the Pacific,' the 173d Airborne Brigade (Sep) spent its combat operational life at the cutting edge of the Army's Vietnam Campaigns."

During its tour in Vietnam, the 173d had twelve Medal of Honor recipients and was involved in seventy-three operations from Bien Hoa to Binh Dinh Province. The 173d paid an enormous price, however, losing 84 officers, 2 warrant officers, and 1,526 soldiers to combat. Another 8,500 officers and men were wounded in action.

"The United States cannot afford to put itself again at such strategic disadvantage as we found ourselves in Vietnam," concluded Gen. Bruce Palmer Jr. (class of 1936) in his book *The 25-Year War*. "How deep Vietnam has stamped its imprint on American history has yet to be determined. In any event, I am optimistic enough to believe that we Americans can and will learn and profit from our experience."

27: After Vietnam

The post-Vietnam doldrums were over. The military forces of the United States—all volunteers—had proved in a number of situations, some involving combat, that they were highly trained, superbly equipped with the latest and best arms and equipment available to any military force, and dedicated and disciplined professionals who knew their business.

As Will and Ariel Durant wrote:

> War is a constant of history. In the last 3,451 years of recorded history, only 268 have seen no war. In the 215 years of its history, the United States has been involved in 11 major wars and over 171 battles. The U.S. armed forces have lost over 650,000 men and women in battles and have had nearly 2½ million wounded. Since World War II, worldwide, there have been almost 400 revolts, coups, and small wars, and 69 major wars, including Afghanistan, Iran-Iraq, the Falklands, the Yom Kippur War, and the Vietnamese invasion of Kampuchea.

Since World War II, the United States has been involved in six major engagements including those in Korea, Vietnam, Panama, and the Persian Gulf, and has resorted to the use or threat of force for political effect some 219 times. These include, among others, the air attack on Libya, the stationing of forces in the Sinai, the *Mayaguez* affair, and the dispatch of marines to Lebanon.

The road back from the victories of World War II was long, difficult, and circuitous. The Korean War started with a weak army, part of which was accustomed to the easy life of occupation duty. By the end of the Korean stalemate, the army had regained some stamina, discipline, and esprit. But the politically designed end of the war—an armistice—left the army with a feeling of frustration and skepticism about the worth of its sacrifices and losses. In Vietnam the army started out with a will and determination, and an "ask not what the country can do for you" enthusiasm. It found itself with another political solution and army-wide frustration. But the army was coming back with skill, determination, and new tactics.

On 20 November 1970, a group of carefully selected Green Berets led by the stalwart and battle-experienced Col. "Bull" Simon raided the Son Tay camp in North Vietnam that allegedly was holding U.S. prisoners of war. The raid was carried out with surprise, skill, and courage by a singularly well-trained, disciplined, well-led group of volunteers. Unfortunately, however, the North Vietnamese had moved the POWs, and the raiders found the Son Tay camp empty.

In April 1980 the U. S. Joint Chiefs of Staff, with the full knowledge and approval of President Jimmy Carter, planned an airborne (really, helicopter-borne) raid, codenamed Operation Blue Light, to rescue the U.S. Embassy personnel being held hostage in Teheran by the new regime in Iran. It was a joint operation involving U.S. Army Special Forces, Marine helicopter crews, and Air Force C-130s and crews. The commander of the Blue Light unit was Col. "Charging Charlie" Beckwith, an experienced, combat-wise infantry and Special Forces commander.

"The operation called for ninety Special Forces and ninety Air Force helicopter crewmen to fly from Egypt to a desert landing strip called 'Desert One,' some 350 miles southeast of Teheran," wrote Charles M. Simpson III in *Inside the Green Berets*.

There they would rendezvous with eight Sikorsky RH-53 helicopters, flown in darkness from the U.S.S. *Nimitz* somewhere in the Arabian Sea, said to be 530 miles from Desert One. All aircraft would fly low to escape radar detection. There in the desert the helicopter crews that practiced with the Blue Lights would take over the choppers, load the SF [Special Forces], and fly to an undisclosed landing site outside Teheran. Details of the plan have never been released, but presumably Blue Light force would make its way to the U.S. compound, release the hostages, and call in the helicopters to lift them all out. The retrograde movement would probably have been a reversal of the approach, with rendezvous with the C-130s at some point and withdrawal out of Iran's air space.

On the night of 24 April the plan for Desert One disintegrated. A blinding dust storm made helicopter navigation difficult, the marine Sea Stallion helicopters arrived late, two already having been scratched due to mechanical problems. Eventually there were only five helicopters, not enough to complete the mission successfully and carry out the hostages, raiders, and helicopter crewmen. Colonel Beckwith decided then and there to recommend abandoning the attempt, and President Carter approved his recommendation.

Then came another disaster. In the night departure from Desert One, one helicopter pilot lifted up to twenty feet and tried to go around a C-130 on the ground. He banked, and his rotor blade smashed into the C-130, causing it to burst into flames, killing the five air force crewmen aboard the plane and the helicopter's four marines. "Beckwith ordered the other four helicopters abandoned," continued Colonel Simpson, "and the C-130s took off, leaving eight American bodies behind. The danger of spreading fire and explosions motivated Beckwith's decision to leave behind four operable heavy-lift helicopters."

OPERATION URGENT FURY

The island of Grenada is remote and generally unknown to most Americans, who could not describe its location or size or give a reason why U.S. forces should invade it. But on 25 October 1983 U.S. military forces, led by the 1st and 2d Battalions of the 75th Infantry Regiment (Rangers) did land on Grenada, some by parachute and some by air-landing. The Cold War was not yet over, and the Communists were still trying to expand their interests and influence.

Grenada, the southernmost of the Windward Islands in the West Indies, 90 miles from Trinidad, is oval in shape and only 120 square miles in area. In 1974, Grenada had attained independence from Britain, causing dissent inside Grenada. After much bickering and election rigging, the New Jewel Movement, under Maurice Bishop took over, with Bishop becoming prime minister. Bishop leaned more and more toward a form of government that emulated that of Castro's Cuba, and civil rights were coming to be totally suppressed. One hundred Cuban advisors and workers had arrived in Grenada by 1980, and Bishop had also been in negotiations with the Soviet Union and North Korea. Dissent was rampant in the island, and on 19 October 1983 Bishop and a number of his cabinet members were murdered. A revolutionary council was set up under army Gen. Hudson Austin, who imposed a strict curfew and isolated the island from the rest of the world. Included in the isolation on the island were almost 1,200 Americans and some 595 medical students at the St. George's University of Medicine.

By this time, the Organization of Eastern Caribbean States (OECS) felt that Grenada was becoming a threat to the other island countries in the Caribbean and officially requested help from the United States to assist in resolving the dangerous situation and in restoring the legal government of Grenada. By 24 October Austin had tightened his grip on the island, the American students were not being allowed to depart, and violence and brutality were widespread. Some 680 Cuban construction workers were expanding the airport's runway and converting the island into a fortress. Cuban Col. Pedro Tortolo took command of the military forces on the island.

President Reagan acted promptly and decisively on the request from OECS. He ordered the Joint Chiefs of Staff to launch an assault on the island, counter the incumbent regime, rescue and evacuate the American medical students and other U.S. citizens, eliminate Cuban and communist influence, and restore democracy and stability to the island. Operation Urgent Fury was born under Adm. Wesley McDonald, head of the U.S. Atlantic Command. He set up Joint Task Force 120 to implement the operation. Admiral Joseph Metcalf III was the overall commander, and he designated the targets for the army, navy, marine, and air force components. The actual command and control of the ground forces was through Lt. Gen. Jack V. Mackmull, the commander of the XVIII Airborne Corps.

"In the early hours [0536] of October 25th, Air Force Combat Controllers [airborne-qualified and today's version of the World War II pathfinders] rushed to the island on USAF aircraft," wrote Don Lassen and Richard Schrader in *Pride of America*.

Right behind them were Army Rangers aboard a formation of C-130s. Riding with them were two engineers from the 82d Airborne Division who were to help clear the runway of obstructions. . . .

Lt. Col. James L. Hobson of the 1st Special Operations Wing was in command of the MC-130E leading the formation of Rangers. He led the way to the designated Drop Zone at Point Salines.

The men were to jump at 500 feet on account of high winds and the DZ's close proximity to the ocean. Suddenly a searchlight illuminated his aircraft and enemy gunfire erupted. Lt. Col. Hobson maintained his composure and held his Hercules straight and level to enable a safe jump for all of the Rangers aboard. His courage under fire allowed the first shock troops to parachute into Grenada and spearhead the assault. For his action he was awarded the Mackey Trophy for the "most meritorious flight of the year."

The Rangers aboard the plane were part of the 1st Ranger Battalion commanded by Lt. Col. Wesley Taylor.

The remainder of the two Ranger battalions followed shortly thereafter and parachuted onto the DZ from an altitude of 500 feet, fortunately below the 23mm antiaircraft fire from Cubans in the hills around the airfield. Their eighteen C-130s came from the 317th Tactical Airlift Wing stationed at Pope Air Force Base, adjacent to Fort Bragg. The 2d Battalion of Rangers dropped without reserve chutes because of the low altitude. Lieutenant Colonel Taylor assembled his troops and, with the two engineers from the 20th Engineer Brigade, XVIII Airborne Corps, commandeered some bulldozers and began to clear the airfield for the air-landing of 82d Airborne Division troopers. While the Rangers were in the air on the way to Grenada, the 82d's Ready Brigade at Fort Bragg had been alerted and was in the process of getting ready for takeoff from Pope.

On the ground, the Rangers fought skirmishes with the Cubans and secured the airhead. "But the job was not quite complete," wrote Hans Halberstadt in *Airborne, Assault from the Sky*, "and would not be until the opposition no longer wanted to come out and fight. Bravo Company, 1st of the 75th, assaults toward the western end of the ridge while mortar rounds drop around them. Their first sergeant and three of his Rangers charge into a Cuban platoon, kill two and capture twenty-eight. Their snipers take out the mortar gunners from 1,000 meters with rifle fire. The first sergeant convinces another 175 Cubans to surrender."

Some Rangers raced toward the medical college, the True Blue Medical Campus. By 0850, they had succeeded in rescuing the first of the students by blasting through defensive barriers set up by the Cubans. One of the Rangers burst into the men's dormitory in the compound and shouted: "American soldier. We're here to take you home."

By 1000 hours the airfield had been bulldozed clear of obstacles, with AC-130 gunships, and helicopters provided air cover, strafing the Cuban guns along the airfield. The first troopers of the 82d, under the command of Maj. Gen. Edward L. Trobaugh, began to air-land safely in C-141s. Halberstadt quotes the following from the platoon leader of the lead element from the 82d:

> We were airlanded rather than airdropped; we didn't know what it would be until two hours out. We had parachutes in the aircraft. We didn't know the situation on the runway. General Trobaugh was with our platoon; we were the first plane. He had a TACSET [tactical satellite radio] and had communications with the Rangers on the ground. We based our plan on a set situation, but this situation was changing while we were in the air. As we were going down there he got the word that the runway was clear. Now the runway was clear of obstructions—but it was not clear of the enemy! There was still enemy fire that could be directed on the runway.
>
> There is an advantage in control when you airland in that you get off the plane together, and you have a little more control initially, but the disadvantage was that the runway could handle only one C-141 at a time, so we took longer to assemble our combat power on the ground by airlanding than if we had jumped. Plus, we didn't get our gold star on our jump wings!

The AC-141 Starlifters continued to air-land 82d troopers. The first 82d unit to deploy was a task force of the 2d Battalion, 325th Airborne Infantry Regiment. On 26 and 27 October, the 1st Battalion, 505th Infantry, and the 1st Battalion, 508th Infantry, with support units landed in Grenada. It is important to note that the first plane carrying Major General Trobaugh and his staff touched down at Point Salines only seventeen hours after first alert at Fort Bragg.

As rapidly as possible, the units assembled, relieved the Rangers securing the airfield, attacked the Cuban defenders around the airfield, and commenced patrolling from the southwest of the island through to the north. In their operations, they captured an additional 812 Cuban and Grenadian People's Revolutionary Army troops. At 1900 on 25 October the 82d had relieved the Rangers, and the Rangers headed for home. Then the troopers from the 82d liberated the remainder of the students from the dorms where they had been incarcerated during the preinvasion curfew and the fighting and guarded them until they could be air-evacuated.

During the invasion aircraft from the carrier USS *Independence* provided air cover. The firefights and the battles throughout the island were not without casualties. In a battle with Soviet-built BTR-60 armored personnel carriers near the Calliste compound, a Ranger lieutenant was killed. In another battle, B Company, 325th, assaulted an area known as Little Havana. The B Company commander, Capt. Michael F. Ritz, decided on his own to make a reconnaissance before the assault. At 0430 on 26 October Captain Ritz and his patrol were ambushed. He was killed, but the rest of his patrol, some of whom were wounded, survived. B Company soon discovered large caches of weapons and equipment. Staff Sergeant Gary Epps, a squad leader, found a loaded recoilless rifle and decided for the sake of safety to remove the round. The round exploded as he was removing it, and he was killed in the explosion. In the end, Ranger and 82d losses amounted to twelve killed and 120 wounded in action; the navy had four killed in action, and the marines had three wounded in action.

Over the next couple of days, the entire 82d Airborne Division, men from the 4th Psychological Operations Group at Fort Bragg, the U.S. Army Reserves 358th Civil Affairs Brigade from Norristown, Pennsylvania, and the 7th Special Forces Group were flown into Grenada to take part in the final stages of Urgent Fury.

One important and unexpected discovery was an arms depot holding 10,000 rifles and machine guns, 40 crew-served weapons, more than 5 million rounds of Soviet-manufactured ammunition, 9,000 mortar rounds, 120,000 rounds of machine gun ammunition, more than 2,250 grenades, and 2 armored fighting vehicles.

During the invasion the Grenada commercial radio station was knocked out. The 4th Psychological Operations Group took it over and broadcast messages to calm the civilian population. After the fighting died down, the 82d went about the task of clearing some of the towns and villages of suspected Cuban and People's Revolutionary Army holdouts, and managed to capture Gen. Hudson Austin. The Cubans, living and dead, but including Colonel Tortolo, were shipped back to Cuba—where a disgusted Castro demoted him to private. In early November 1983 the 82d left the island.

After the departure of the 82d, mobile training teams from the 7th Special Forces Group remained on the island and helped train the local militia. The 4th Psychological Operations Group and the 96th Civilian Affairs Group put their training and mission to the test and helped the local legitimate government resume control and reestablish a peaceful and healthy environment. Thus ended Urgent Fury.

OPERATION JUST CAUSE

The climactic year in the dictatorial reign of Manuel Noriega, the belligerent, power-crazed, and fanatical tyrant of Panama was 1989. He had assumed complete control of the Panama Defense Force (PDF) and organized and armed the so-called Dignity Battalions, bands of young civilian hoodlums who were intensely loyal to him. (Later U.S. troopers disparagingly referred to them as the "Dingbats.") Among many other acts of corruption and belligerence, Noriega was involved in the protection of drug runners. In January 1988 Stephen M. Kalish, a convicted American drug smuggler, testified before a U.S. Senate committee investigating Noriega and admitted that in exchange for help in his own drug business, he had bribed Noriega with millions of dollars. On 4 February 1988 two grand juries, in Miami and Tampa, returned indictments in which the U.S. Department of Justice charged Noriega with violation of U.S. racketeering and drug laws.

His relations with the United States declined markedly in 1989. On 13 January, the Panamanian government reported that the Soviet Union and Panama had signed a trade agreement that would result in the first Soviet mission in Panama. On 16 January, Noriega opened his own bank in Panama City in what was reported to be a move "to expand his control over the economy and to launder drug money." On 2 March 1989, the first major rally of political forces opposing Noriega drew fifty thousand demonstrators. On 3 March, the Panamanian traffic police stopped twenty-one U.S. Department of Defense school buses and ticketed the drivers for operating vehicles with U.S. Navy license plates. On 21 March Panamanian President Delvalle, who was still recognized by the United States as the legitimate head of state, announced that he had taken up residence in Miami. On 5 April Kurt Muse, a U.S. citizen, was arrested and charged with violating state security. Noriega suspected him of operating a clandestine communications network that interfered with PDF and police transmissions and even became sophisticated enough to override the state radio network and broadcast opposition messages to the Panamanian people. His rescue became very important to the Bush administration: apparently Muse was no ordinary U.S. citizen playing communications games with his fellow Rotarians. Noriega had him incarcerated in the Carcelo Modelo.

On 18 April 1989, the Panamanian government announced that henceforth U.S. citizens would require visas to travel to Panama. On 22 April the U.S. Southern Command, the senior headquarters for all U.S. forces then in Panama, announced that it planned to move its headquarters to the United States as part of the "phased withdrawal" of the forces from Panama, a move dictated by the 1977 Panama Canal treaties that required the United States to end its military presence in Panama by 1999.

On 18 May, the U.S. Defense Department reported that there had been more than twelve hundred violations of the Panama Canal treaties in the preceding fifteen months, enumerating specific incidents of harassment of U.S. military personnel. On 18–19 May, Panamanian security forces detained seventeen members of the Panamanian company that provided security for the U.S. Embassy. On 8 June, a U.S. State Department representative disclosed that in recent months Nicaragua had sent planeloads of military weapons to Panama in anticipation of a possible U.S. military attack.

On 8 August U.S. officials arrested twenty-nine armed Panamanians, including nine soldiers, in a restricted area during a U.S. military training exercise. In retaliation the PDF on 9 August detained two U.S. soldiers. In response the United States had Fort Amador, which was jointly occupied by the PDF and U.S. forces, and where the two soldiers were being held, sealed off. The United States lifted the closing after Panama agreed to release the two soldiers and the United States agreed to release two men seized during the 8 August arrest. In the following days, similar arrests occurred. On 11 August, Noriega took his complaints to the United Nations and, charging treaty violations, asked the world body to send observers. The United States, not to be outdone, held a "major contingency operation" in Panama City on 17 August.

On the last weekend in September 1989, two significant changes in the hierarchy of the U.S. military occurred: Gen. Colin L. Powell, fifty-two years old, a former national security adviser to President Reagan, assumed the military's number one position, chairman of the Joint Chiefs of Staff. In Panama, Gen. Maxwell R. Thurman, fifty-eight years old, assumed command of the U.S. Southern Command. Thurman was a dedicated, hard-working bachelor who had, from 1979 to 1981, run the army's recruiting command and transformed it from a "dead end of the world for an Army officer," in the words of an officer who worked for Thurman, to a vital and rewarding element of the army. "Be All You Can Be" was Max Thurman's personal philosophy.

Some three days after the two changes, on 3 October 1989 a small group of rebel PDF officers staged a coup with some initial success. The rebels seized the Commandancía and, at about 1130 on the day of the coup, announced that Noriega was in their hands. But the apparent success of the coup was short-lived. At about 1000 the elite PDF Battalion 2000, a well-equipped and well-trained unit (many of its members being Cuban trained), left its base at Fort Cimarron, near the Torrijos-Tocumen Airport, about fifteen miles northeast of the Commandancía. Once it arrived at the Commandancía, Battalion 2000, led by Maj. Francisco Olechea, encircled and attacked the rebels with rifle fire, grenades, and mortars. By 1400 the battle was over. Ten rebels, including Maj. Moíses Giroldi Vega, in charge of security of the Commandancía, died in the firefight.

On 15 December, the 510-member, Noriega-appointed National Assembly of Representatives voted to elevate Noriega to head of government and "maximum leader of the struggle for national liberation." At that same session, echoing Noriega's bellicosity and chest-thumping egotism, the National Assembly approved a resolution stating that "the Republic of Panama is declared to be in a state of war" with the United States as long as "aggression" in the form of economic sanctions imposed in 1988 continued.

The next day, Saturday, 16 December, some PDF guards stopped a private car bearing Michigan license plates and carrying four off-duty U.S. soldiers at a roadblock outside PDF headquarters in the old section of Panama City. PDF soldiers tried to drag the men from the car, but the Americans attempted to drive away through a mob that had gathered. A PDF soldier opened fire with an AK-47 and mortally wounded marine Lt. Robert Paz, twenty-five years old, and wounded another officer in the ankle. Later the other men in the car explained that they had gotten lost; the PDF claimed that they were on an unauthorized reconnaissance.

Shortly after that incident the PDF arrested Adam J. Curtis, a navy lieutenant, and his wife, Bonnie, who had been stopped at the same roadblock about a half hour earlier and had witnessed the shooting of Lieutenant Paz. The PDF personnel present blindfolded both of them with masking tape and held them in custody, interrogating them repeatedly. They beat Lieutenant Curtis brutally, kicking him in the groin and the head, and threatened to kill him if he did not give them information about his unit and his activities. These PDF members threatened Mrs. Curtis with rape—fondling her neck and the backs of her legs—and then cut her head when they slammed her against a wall to emphasize their point. She collapsed on the floor. When Curtis protested the treatment of his wife, the PDF interrogators shoved wads of paper down his throat. One of them put a gun to his head and kicked him repeatedly in the groin. After four hours of interrogation and beatings, the PDF personnel abruptly escorted the Curtises to an avenue that led back to the U.S. area and released them. They made their way back to the U.S. Naval Station at about 0215.

The Bush administration had initially taken little public notice of the Panamanian National Assembly's "state of war" declaration. At a news conference, President Bush said only that "I've taken note of [the] statement." White House spokesman Marlin Fitzwater said that the declaration "may have been a license for harassment and threats." One top administration official described the president as "deeply disturbed" by the events in Panama. Former assistant secretary of state Elliot Abrams said that "the scuttlebutt I hear is that the sexual abuse of the Navy officer's wife sent Bush up the wall."

Some 330 days into his administration, President George Bush was faced, for the first time, with a decision to commit U.S. troops to battle—and with it the unavoidable casualties that would result. But Noriega's imperious conduct in Panama and his blatant thumbing his nose at the United States had escalated degraded relations to the stage where a serious response was called for. Negotiations, third-party emissaries, liaison visits from White House staffers, and empty public rhetoric were no longer viable courses of action for the president. The national objectives in Panama were obvious: restore democracy and capture Noriega. Those national objectives translated into four military objectives: protect U.S. citizens; defend the Panama Canal; restore democracy; and capture Noriega.

By 17 December Colin Powell was fully prepared to recommend a course of action, Operation Just Cause, that would answer the president's needs decisively. Powell converted the broad military objectives into this mission for General Thurman: "Conduct joint offensive military operations to neutralize the PDF and other combatants, as required, to protect the US lives, property, and interests in Panama and to assure the treaty rights as accorded by international law and the US Panama Canal treaties."

The Joint Chiefs of Staff developed the basic concept for the operation into a threefold approach: phase one comprised combat operations at the onset designed to neutralize and fix the PDF in place, capture Noriega, install a new government, and protect and defend U.S. citizens and key facilities; phase two would set in action stabilization operations to ensure law and order and begin the transition to support a newly installed government; phase three would initiate nation building to support the anti-Noriega government headed by Guillermo Endara and his two vice-presidential running mates, Ricardo Arias Colderon and Guillermo "Billy" Ford. This last phase would eventually be turned over to the State Department.

In more specific terms, General Thurman's operational tasks were to protect some thirty thousand U.S. citizens; defend 142 key facilities along the Panama Canal; neutralize the PDF forces, which were spread out in thirteen key objective areas; neutralize the Dignity Battalion hoodlums; and find and capture the elusive Noriega who slept in a different house each night.

Before he took over the U.S. Southern Command, and to get ready for the job, Thurman flew into Fort Bragg to review the Joint Special Operations Command and the XVIII Airborne Command contingency plans for Panama, codenamed Blue Spoon. In early September 1989 Maj. Gen. William A. Roosma, the XVIII Airborne Corps deputy commander, visited Panama, met with the Southern Command staff, reconnoitered the area in detail, and met with the commanders of the U.S. troops already in Panama. Back at Fort Bragg, Col. Thomas H. Needham and Col. William H. Walters, respectively the corps G-3 and G-2 officers, worked long hours with their staffs and a special "core planning cell" to upgrade Blue Spoon into Just Cause. On 9 October, at Thurman's request the XVIII Airborne Corps commander, Lt. Gen. Carl W. Stiner, and his key staff officers flew to Panama for a contingency planning summit. Because security was tight, the visitors wore civilian clothes. For three full days and nights, the two staffs worked together to develop the details of the plan.

After the assaults on U.S. military personnel in December, General Powell, Secretary of Defense Dick Cheney; Secretary of State James Baker, National Security Advisor Brent Scowcroft, and other senior officers went to the White House on 17 December and met with the president who was hosting a Christmas party. After the guests had left, in the president's living quarters Powell briefed Bush on the plan for Operation Just Cause. After getting specific answers to many questions the president said without hesitation, "Okay, let's do it."

On 18 December 1989, a small element of the XVIII Airborne Corps Assault CP flew into Panama and set up an emergency operations center with General Thurman's Southern Command staff. Carl Stiner would become Thurman's "war fighter," the commander in charge of all operations. Under his cammand for Just Cause, Stiner had nearly the entire 7th Infantry Division (Light), one parachute brigade of the 82d Airborne Division, a mechanized battalion from the 5th Mechanized Division, a battalion-sized task force of marines, the three battalions of the 75th Ranger Regiment, task forces of navy SEALs, special forces from Naval Special Warfare Group 2 and the army's 7th Special Forces Group, and the 193d Light Infantry Brigade in place in Panama.

Stiner was faced with neutralizing the PDF stationed throughout the country. Not every position could be attacked simultaneously. The majority of the critical command and control nodes and the majority of the U.S. citizens and interests were in Panama City. Southern Command planners thought of the old Canal Zone and Panama City as the center of the target—the bull's eye. In October, the PDF demonstrated its ability to reinforce the Commandancía rapidly from Rio Hata and Fort Cimmaron. These two locations fell into the ring of the target closest to the bull's eye and could be ignored only at the peril of the rest of the operation. The rest of the country fell into the fourth or fifth ring out and could be handled at a later date.

Stiner's plan called for a number of simultaneous attacks at various locations around the country according to the following scenario:

Task Force Bayonet was made up of Col. Michael G. Snell's 193d Infantry Brigade (Light), permanently stationed in Panama and reinforced with 5th Battalion, 87th Infantry, 1st Battalion, 508th Infantry (Airborne), and 4th Battalion, 6th Infantry (Mechanized). Snell's mission was to isolate the Commandancía in the *barrio* of Chorillo, about 400 meters south of Ancon Hill and Southern Command headquarters; seize and secure the Curundú-Ancon Hill-Balboa areas; and air-assault into Fort Amador and neutralize the PDF's 5th Company stationed there.

Task Force Semper Fi, composed of Col. Charles E. Richardson's Marine Forces Panama, a reinforced brigade with units in Panama, was to block the western approaches to the city and secure the Bridge of the Americas.

Task Force Atlantic, which comprised Col. Keith Kellogg's 3d Brigade of the 7th Infantry Division (Light) plus Lt. Col. Lynn Moore's 3d Battalion, 504th Parachute Infantry Regiment, already in Panama since 10 December 1989 on a training mission, and Lt. Col. John Brooks's 4th Battalion, 17th Infantry, of the 7th Division. Kellogg's mission was to isolate Colón; neutralize the PDF 8th Company and naval infantry company; protect Madden Dam; and free a number of political prisoners at Gamboa, midway across the Isthmus of Panama.

Joint Special Operations Task Force was Maj. Gen. Wayne A. Downing's command composed of Col. William F. Kernan's 75th Ranger Regiment, four SEAL platoons, and Lt. Col. Roy R. Trumbull's 3d Battalion of the 7th Special Forces Group. This task force's mission was to parachute-assault onto Rio Hato; neutralize the PDF 6th and 7th Companies; disable PDF patrol craft in Balboa Harbor and a television tower at Cerro Azul; deny the use of Paitilla Airport; and mount operations to capture Noriega or rescue American hostages, as required.

Task Force Pacific, led by Maj. Gen. James H. Johnson Jr., commander of the 82d Airborne Division, was made up of Col. Jack Nix's 1st Brigade, the 82d's Division Ready Brigade. Task Force Pacific's mission was to parachute-assault onto Torrijos-Tocumen Airport and then air-assault onto Fort Cimarron, Tinajitas, and Panamá Viejo. More specifically, the 82d's objectives were the UESAT Cav Squadron at Panamá Viejo (objective one); the PDF 1st Infantry Company ("Tigers") at Tinajitas (objective two); and Battalion 2000 at Fort Cimmaron (objective three). In addition, after "taking down" these objectives, the 82d was to move into Panama City and to neutralize the Dignity Battalions' staging at three different locations.

The initial attacks of Operation Just Cause were launched by the in-country U.S. forces on 19 December 1989. Thereafter, the sequence of events evolved in the order laid out by General Stiner and his staff in support of General Thurman's four objectives.

At 0155 on 20 December, the 75th Rangers arrived over their DZ and bailed out into the blackness of the morning. The 1st Battalion from Hunter Army Airfield along with part of the 3d Battalion from Fort Benning landed at Torrijos-Tocumen Airport east of Panama City. They removed their jump gear, armed themselves for an attack, formed into combat units, and quickly put down the 2d Infantry Battalion and air force troops of the PDF. Meanwhile, the Rangers's 2d Battalion from Fort Lewis, Washington, and the rest of the 3d Battalion jumped onto the Rio Hato airfield west of Panama City. These Rangers attacked and subdued the elite 2000 PDF Battalion and the 6th and 7th Rifle Companies.

On the ground, C Company of Lt. Col. William R. Fitzgerald's 1st Battalion, 508th Infantry (Airborne), part of the in-country Southern Command forces, attacked the PDF CP in the center of Panama City. The rest of the battalion moved on Fort Amador and took out the PDF in the area and set up protection for U.S. forces' dependent families in the area.

Part of General Downing's Joint Special Operations Task Force including the 75th Ranger Regiment, Navy SEALs, and the Delta Force, was in country, part air-landed in Panama and part parachuted in. Downing accomplished an assortment of missions, including storming and seizing the Pacora Bridge and neutralizing in a fierce firefight a force of armed PDF troops. United States Air Force C-130 gunships helped the troops on the ground. With some difficulty and bloodshed, Downing's Delta Force also managed to extract Kurt Muse from the Carcelo Modelo.

Back on Monday, 18 December, at about 0900 hours, the 82d Division Ready Brigade, made up of the 1st Battalion, 504th, 2d Battalion, 504th, and 4th Battalion, 325th (plus A Company, 325th), plus other support elements of the division, had been alerted for its role in Task Force Pacific for Operation Just Cause. During the early evening hours of 19 December, despite foul weather, the entire task force of 2,200 troopers, led by the 82d's commander, Maj. Gen. James Johnson, was transported with its heavy equipment to Panama from Pope Air Force Base on C-141 Starlifters.

Beginning at 0155 on 20 December, after a flight of four and a half hours, the lead elements of Task Force Pacific parachuted onto Torrijos-Tocumen Airport. The All Americans teamed up with Rangers and took control of the airport. Throughout the rest of the early morning hours of 20 December, the 82d's paratroopers continued to parachute on the airport DZ. After assembling, each infantry battalion with support elements moved by helicopter to previously assigned objectives. The 2d Battalion, 504th, moved out first and took over a PDF barracks at Panama Viejo. The 1st Battalion, 504th, took control of a small PDF post at Tinajitas. The 4th Batallion, 325th, captured the PDF's Fort Cimarron. The 3d Battalion, 504th, already in country on a jungle training mission was under the operational control of the 7th Division.

Within hours after the initial launch of paratroopers and the in-country forces, all missions assigned to General Stiner had been accomplished with one big exception—the capture of Manuel Noriega. The U.S. administration became so frustrated in trying to find him that it put a $1 million bounty on his head. Part of Wayne Downing's mission had been to use his Special Forces to track down Noriega, and the relentless tracking finally brought results, of sorts. At about 1530 on Christmas Eve, a car drove up to the residence of the Vatican's representative in Panama, the papal nuncio, Monsignor Sebastian Labora. Out of the car emerged Noriega, wearing a t-shirt and carrying two AK-47s slung on his shoulders; he entered the residence and requested political asylum.

Max Thurman tried a number of methods to extract Noriega from the residence, even going so far as to put loudspeakers outside the building and blasting it with rock music. Noriega did not emerge.

By 27 December the Panama Canal was returning to normal, and officials said that they hoped to get it into round-the-clock operations to clear a backlog of some 125 ships. After ten days of negotiations and psychological pressure from Monsignor Laboa, and after 20,000 Panamanians surrounded the *nunciatore* and shouted at him, at 2044, 3 January 1990, Noriega came out carrying a Bible and a toothbrush. He walked the twenty yards from the *nunciatore* to Avenida Balboa and surrendered to the Delta Force troops there. Forty-one minutes after he left the *nunciatore*, he was in a plane on the way to the U.S. District Court in Miami on federal drug-trafficking charges.

As word of Noriega's departure and his surrender to U.S. officials spread across Panama City, horns honked; fireworks shot into the black sky; and people laughed, yelled, and raced up and down the streets, waving U.S. and Panamanian flags. Hundreds of cars jammed Fiftieth Street, near the center of what had been a thriving international finance center.

Max Thurman had accomplished the last of his four missions.

Operation Just Cause made evident the work, the training, and the revitalization of the U.S. armed forces during the 1980s. Television shots of troops in action in Panama showed soldiers properly clad in their uniforms, wearing helmets, and handling their weapons expertly. But that was only part of the metamorphosis of the post-Vietnam U.S. military establishment. The men and women who carried out the missions in Panama were all volunteers. Almost all of them had at least a high school education because recruiters could by then be "choosy" about whom to select for enlistment. The military's leaders had reinstated discipline in the ranks; NCOs and officers were well trained in their specialties; and training was no hit-or-miss proposition. The National Training Centers at Fort Irwin, California, and Fort Chaffee, Arkansas, had forged personnel into units who knew how to fight the kind of battle specified in U.S. Army *Field Manual 24-100.*

Operation Just Cause was one of the largest and most sophisticated airborne and ground contingency operations in modern history. (The 1982 British invasion of the Falkland Islands was by far the longest.) Just Cause represented joint integrated planning and execution among the army, navy, marines, and air force. It demonstrated that the mixing of special and conventional forces was not only possible but enhanced the success of the operation as well. It showed the practicability of the use of joint communications—electronics operating instructions. It validated the necessity of small-unit drills and training in urban terrain. It showed that night operations have a great advantage, and that night-vision devices are essential for night air assaults. It certified the worth of the AH-46 Apache helicopter on night operations and the Hellfire missile as a "surgical weapon." It proved the value of using psychological operations troopers with conventional forces. And it proved that U.S. military planners could tailor and package a force of paratroopers, special forces, light infantry, mechanized infantry, marines, sailors, airmen, psychological operations units, military police, and civil affairs units for the task at hand. It proved that obedience to the oft-repeated but ignored principles of war—surprise, mass, objective, unity of command, maneuver, offensive, and economy of forces—paves the way to success in battle. The commander in chief of the U.S. armed forces, the president of the country, was able to give his commanders a job to do and then let them do it. As a spokesman for Southern Command said, "Operation Just Cause was the largest use of strategic air assets to introduce tactical forces directly into combat in the history of U.S. military. In the initial operations, it delivered the equivalent of a division minus onto tactical drop zones and had delivered an entire division within the first thirty-six hours. Strength figures peaked out at just over twenty-seven thousand soldiers, sailors, airmen and marines."

The operation was not without costs. Eighteen soldiers, four sailors, and one marine were killed, and 255 soldiers were wounded. The reported enemy losses were 314 killed and 124 wounded.

The army's commanders in the field recognized some faults. They saw the need for better "antifratricide" equipment to prevent, among other things, casualties from one's forces through "friendly fire." For example, at Rio Hato, during the hours of darkness a "Little Bird" Hughes 500 helicopter fired on a squad of men moving on the ground in the same area where it was conducting strafing operations. Two men were killed. In another case, the Spectre gunship firing near the Commandancía on D day wounded a number of U.S. personnel assaulting the building.

There were some difficulties on the ground during Just Cause. For instance, a number of paratroopers and some of the 82d's heavy-drop equipment missed the designated DZs. (In addition, the miserable weather at Pope Air Force Base had postponed the arrival of the 82d's paratroopers at the scheduled time, delaying the start of their mission.)

When they returned to Fort Bragg from Panama, on 12 January 1990, and parachuted from 800 feet from twenty C-141 Starlifters onto Sicily DZ, the 1,924 XVIII Airborne Corps and 82d Airborne Division paratroopers were led by General Stiner and General Johnson. General Carl E. Vuono, the army chief of staff and a former member of the 82d, was on the DZ to greet the troopers, who formed into five columns upon landing and marched toward the stands where over 5,000 members of their families, fellow soldiers, and friends awaited them.

By and large Just Cause was a winner, an operation executed—as planned—with vigor and daring. Obviously the Vietnam doldrums were over with. The next display of U.S. armed might, only about a year later, would be a roaring, television-centered, hero-worshipping, chest-thumping, flag-waving, parade-making, military success. Desert camouflage fatigues would become a fashion.

28: The Gulf War

This will not stand. This will not stand, the aggression against Kuwait." The president of the United States was adamant. On Sunday afternoon, 5 August 1990, three days after the armed forces and armored personnel carriers of Saddam Hussein's Iraq had rolled almost unchallenged and untouched into a virtually defenseless Kuwait on 2 August 1990, President George Bush spoke out. He had just stepped from his helicopter on the White House lawn and walked to the inevitable phalanx of photographers and reporters. Simply listening to him, one could almost see him pounding his fist into his open palm as he vowed to confront Saddam Hussein and throw this latest world's bully out of Kuwait.

Moving his Republican Guard armored forces to Kuwait's border was not a sudden, unpremeditated whim on Saddam's part. Iraq's war with Iran from 1980 to 1988 had severely depleted Hussein's supply of cash. He desperately needed more money to pay off his $80 billion in war debts. As he had in the past, he saw his superrich, minuscule neighbor to the southeast as a way out of his financial problems. And after claiming that Kuwait was stealing Iraq's oil, he could have a pretext to get closer to the vast pools of oil in a poorly defended Saudi Arabia right next door to Kuwait.

Wednesday, 1 August 1990, was a hot and steamy day in Washington, D.C. In the deserts of the Middle East the temperature was probably thirty-five degrees higher, but the humidity in Washington hovered at around 95 percent. By that evening, Saddam had finished massing 100,000 of his men, tanks and armored personnel carriers (APCs), artillery, and logistics and communications units on the border with Kuwait. Saddam's forces outnumbered the Kuwaiti forces by about five to one.

At 0200 local time in Kuwait on 2 August, Iraqi Republican Guard tanks roared across the border, past the customs buildings and a gas station at Abdaly, and headed down the six-lane highway toward Kuwait City, eighty road miles away. Kuwaitis in their ultramodern high-rise dwellings in Kuwait City could look out of their windows and see the flash of air-to-ground missiles and hear the rockets crash into the Dasman Palace of their ruler, the Emir Sheikh Jabir al-Sabah.

At 0515 Jabir al-Sabah telephoned the U.S. Embassy for help but asked that the conversation not be made "public." An hour later he called again to request U.S. help officially, and he did not care who knew it. Kuwait was in serious trouble. But all that the United States had in the country at the time was a small detachment of U.S. Marine guards at the embassy. Kuwait would have a while to wait for U.S. help.

In three and a half hours Iraqi tanks were in Kuwait City. As the tanks circled the palace, the emir loaded his family onto a helicopter and flew off in the morning's turmoil to a safe haven in Saudi Arabia.

As he flew out, he could witness the devastation in Kuwait City caused by the invader's artillery and tank fire and could see some of the 300 Iraqi tanks that rumbled and blasted their way through the city. One force had encircled the central bank building; others laid siege to the Ministry of Information, the home of Kuwait's state television and radio broadcasting facilities. By nightfall of 2 August, all of the Emirate of Kuwait and its 2 million people were under the control of Iraq's armed forces, principally the Republican Guard. Saddam Hussein's forces had overrun Kuwait in less than a day.

By July 1990, the Republican Guard had grown to twenty-eight combat brigades organized into eight divisions, including armor, mechanized infantry, dismounted infantry, and special forces, and all equipped with the best Soviet tanks and artillery. The civilized world now had a new menace on its hands, one whose atrocities in the past dwarfed those of the likes of Lt. Col. Mengistu Haile Mariam of Ethiopia, Fidel Castro of Cuba, or Manuel Noriega of Panama. It was now up to the free world and the United Nations to combat Saddam Hussein. And President Bush took the initiative to do so.

President Bush held a number of consultations with his top advisors, including the secretary of defense, Richard Cheney; the chairman of the Joint Chiefs of Staff, Gen. Colin Powell; the commander of the U.S. Central Command, Gen. H. Norman Schwarzkopf; the secretary of state, James Baker; the CIA director, William Webster; and the national security advisor, Brent Scowcroft. After Cheney and Schwarzkopf consulted with King Fahd in his summer palace on 6 August and received permission to bring U.S. troops into Saudi Arabia, President Bush was ready to act.

On the morning of 4 August the president, Vice President Dan Quayle, Cheney, Powell, Schwarzkopf, Baker, and additional advisors met in the Aspen Lodge at Camp David, Maryland. The purpose of the meeting was to sort out U.S. national interests, determine the extent to which Saddam Hussein had threatened them, and decide on a course of action.

When Schwarzkopf was called on to brief the conferees he used two charts: one showed what it would take to defend Saudi Arabia, and the other detailed the forces needed to liberate Kuwait. Schwarzkopf also gave a schedule of units and their possible deployment dates, the availability of air and sea transportation to ferry these units from their U.S. and European bases to the Persian Gulf area, the buildup timetable, the dates when troop units could be in Saudi Arabia, and the difficulties inherent in the plan. He made one point absolutely clear: ground troops were a necessity because air and naval forces alone would not suffice.

General Powell insisted that, whatever the mission, half measures would be disastrous; the United States had to send enough troops to do the job rapidly. To prove his point, Powell reviewed the experience of Operation Just Cause in Panama. In that operation, he pointed out, the United States had sent enough forces to overwhelm the Panama Defense Forces immediately with minimal U.S. casualties.

With the Powell-Schwarzkopf unified plan Bush had agreed to send what some termed a "tripwire" force: the division ready brigade (DRB) of the 82d Airborne Division, a brigade that is on twenty-four-hour alert and ready to be in the air in eighteen hours; a 16,500-man marine amphibious brigade armed with tanks and APCs aboard pre-positioned ships; two squadrons of air force F-15s; and a number of B-52 bombers moved from the continental United States to the Indian Ocean island of Diego Garcia (a British possession) to go into action against Iraq in the event that Saddam Hussein headed for the Saudi oil fields. This force would be followed by the 101st Airborne Division (Air Assault) from Fort Campbell and the 24th Infantry Division (Mechanized) from Fort Stewart, Georgia. The president was ready to send 200,000 troops to fight Saddam Hussein. President Bush told reporters after the Camp David meeting, "This will not stand, this aggression against Kuwait."

On 6 August the scenario for Operation Desert Shield began to take shape. First, King Fahd had finally and, apparently reluctantly, asked for

U.S. troops to defend Saudi Arabia. Second, the United Nations authorized economic sanctions against Iraq. Finally, the Pentagon sent out orders alerting the first units for deployment. Two squadrons of F-15 Eagles, forty-eight aircraft, from Langley Air Force Base in Hampton, Virginia, received orders to move to airfields near Riyadh and Dhahran, Saudi Arabia. The air force commander was prepared to have his pilots fight their way into Saudi Arabia, so he timed their arrival for dusk, when the Iraqi Air Force was known to be less than alert and courageous.

Arriving with the planes of the 1st Tactical Air Wing was the 82d Airborne Division's DRB of 2,300 troopers. Major General James Johnson, commander of the 82d, received orders on 6 August from the commander of the XVIII Airborne Corps, Lt. Gen. Gary Luck, to deploy his DRB (division ready brigade) of some 2,300 troopers. The brigade, plus a skeleton staff from the XVIII Airborne Corps, the U.S. first ground element to arrive in Saudi Arabia, arrived on 8 and 9 August. The first soldier, an 82d paratrooper, was on the ground in Saudi Arabia within thirty-one hours of the initial alert order. Operation Desert Shield, the first phase of the Gulf War, was under way.

For the troops of the only U.S. air assault division, the 101st Airborne, the summer of 1990 was a period of intensified training at Fort Campbell, numerous off-base specialized training exercises, and multiple commitments for training Army Reserve and National Guard troops and cadets at West Point. From the commanding general, J. H. Binford Peay III, a 1962 graduate of the Virginia Military Institute, to the newest private in the rear ranks, the 101st Airborne was busy.

On the weekend of 4 August 1990, Peay was on leave in Virginia Beach, his first break since assuming command of the 101st a year earlier. He was in a cottage on the beach when he got a call from his assistant division commander, Brig. Gen. Henry H. Shelton: "Montie Hess [the 101st's G-3 officer] just got a 'heads up' call from Tom Needham at corps," Shelton told Peay. "Needham says that there is a possibility that we might deploy a force to Saudi Arabia. He did not give us any specific numbers. He did tell us to get our DRB ready to go." After alerting Peay, Shelton remembers, "I convened the command element in the division briefing room, gave them a good rundown on what I knew to date, and started the process of getting the DRB-1, the first major force, ready to deploy."

On Monday, 6 August, Gen. Edwin H. Burba Jr, the commander of Forces Command at Fort McPherson, Georgia, called Shelton and told him, "You guys are going, and we are going to find some additional attack aviation to marry up with you."

On 8 August, advance command and control detachments from the XVIII Airborne Corps and the 82d Airborne Division arrived in Saudi Arabia. The next day Burba's headquarters issued its Operation Desert Shield deployment order to the 101st. The division followed up that order with its own Fragmented Order 90-1, providing guidance to subordinate unit commanders on canceling leaves, freezing retirements and permanent change-of-station moves, and listing deployment criteria. The 101st's assault command post (ACP) began preparing to move out.

The first two aircraft to depart from Fort Campbell were C-5s, carrying twelve AH-64 Apache helicopters; General Shelton; the aviation brigade commander, Col. Tom Garrett; the Apache battalion commander, Lt. Col. Richard Cody (class of 1972), (as of this writing commander of the 101st); and 144 troopers. The planes left at 0500 on 17 August and landed at Dhahran International Airport at noon the next day. The temperature was 128 degrees. "When I walked off the airplane," remembered Shelton, "I'll be very frank . . . I thought I was standing in an engine backwash. And as I walked across the ramp . . . away from the plane, I noticed that the backwash did not go away. It was the darndest thing I had ever seen."

After he landed, he went to the XVIII Airborne Corps command post to see Brig. Gen. Ed Scholes, chief of staff of the XVIII Airborne Corps, who had led the advance element of the corps to Saudi Arabia. According to Scholes, the lead element of the corps was the 4th Battalion, 325th, of the 82d, which had taken off from Pope Air Force Base at 0300 on 8 August. Only fifty-seven minutes later, Scholes and seventy-seven troopers, one communications vehicle, one pallet of equipment, and the ACP for the corps took off from Pope Air Force Base in a C-141 Starlifter. Shortly before 0900 the next morning he and his crew landed at Dhahran.

At 1000, on 8 August, thirty-six hours after the alert, the first troopers of the 82d's DRB also left Pope Air Force Base, followed in four days by the rest of the brigade, a total of 4,575 paratroopers and their gear, using Boeing 747s air force C-141s and C-5s. Between 13 August and 8 September, the other two brigades of the 82d, more than 12,000 troopers, arrived in Dhahran in 582 C-141 flights. By 24 August all nine infantry battalions were in Saudi Arabia.

Over the next two months the units of the XVIII Airborne Corps continued to arrive and settle into base camps. By 5 November, Lieutenant

General Luck had his corps fully combat ready. It was made up of the 82d Airborne, 101st Airborne, 24th Infantry, 1st Cavalry Divisions, and the 3d Armored Cavalry Regiment. The total combat power of the corps included 763 main battle tanks, of which 123 were the potent M1A1 Abrams; 444 howitzers and 63 multiple-launch rocket systems; 1,494 fighting vehicles and APCs, of which 596 were M3 Bradley Fighting Vehicles; 24 Patriot and 24 Hawk missile launchers; 227 attack helicopters, including 145 AH-64 Apaches; and 18 nonmechanized infantry battalions, equipped with 368 Humvees with tube-launched, optically tracked, wire-guided missile launchers (Humvee TOWs).

By 21 November units of the VII Corps in Germany began to be deployed to Saudi Arabia. Coincidentally, the first Army National Guard round-out brigades were called to active duty, a move that stressed the importance of the buildup and that began to make an impression on the American public.

The VII Corps was deployed with the 2d Armored Cavalry Regiment, the 1st and 3d Armored Divisions, and a forward-deployed brigade from the 2d Armored Division. Moving the corps from various locations throughout Germany to the ports of embarkation required 465 trains, 312 barges, and 119 ships; the move to Saudi Arabia required 578 aircraft and 140 ships. The first ships carrying the heavy equipment and vehicles reached the seaports of Dammam and Jubail on 6 December, and the VII Corps was fully in theater on 6 February, when the last elements of the 3d Armored Division arrived. The VII Corps troops were initially billeted in a complex near Dhahran Airport.

The 1st Infantry Division out of Fort Riley, Kansas, was also assigned to the VII Corps at that time. Although the division did not begin its deployment until late November, it was in place and ready for combat by early February 1991. The VII Corps was by now made up of the 1st and 3d Armored Divisions, the 1st Infantry Division, and the 1st Cavalry Division.

With the arrival of the VII Corps, the army, with support from its sister services, had in six months put in place a force equivalent to eight divisions and their supporting forces—some 250,000 soldiers—and sixty days of supplies. In theater the number of soldiers, marines, sailors, and airmen totaled 365,000. The logistics involved in deploying combat forces and their support units in Saudi Arabia was nothing short of phenomenal. The United States moved forces and supplies by air and sea over greater distances and in less time than ever before in its history, despite its limitations on "strategic lift." In the first eighty days of the deployment, more than 170,000 troops and more than 160,000 tons of cargo were moved to Saudi Arabia by air. More than 7.5 million square feet of cargo and equipment were moved by sea. By the time the coalition forces began the offensive on 17 January 1991, the United States had shipped some 560,000 tons of ammunition, 300,000 desert camouflage uniforms, 200,000 tires, and 150 million military meals to sustain 540,000 soldiers, airmen, and marines.

The logistics miracle coordinated by Lt. Gen. Gus Pagonis and the 22d Theater Army Area Command (TAAC) can be likened to moving the entire city of Atlanta—all of its people and anything movable—to Saudi Arabia and then providing it full support. Pagonis and the 22d TAAC managed this massive effort with the help of active and reserve units, civilian technicians, contractor teams, and Saudi contractors and civilian employees.

One of Saddam Hussein's major miscalculations was to discount this successful effort.

Beyond the reception seaports and the airfields, there was little permanent infrastructure in Saudi Arabia. The troops had to build up their entire support system in the fine, gritty sand of the desert and in the searing heat of the summer. This extremely harsh environment also challenged the ingenuity of the army's equipment operators and maintenance troops to keep their gear in operating condition at all times.

As 1990 was coming to a close, Central Command staffs down to squad level were working long hours and preparing the plans for an entirely new mission, Desert Storm, an attack out of Saudi Arabia to crush Saddam Hussein's forces. The coalition forces would no longer simply be "shielding" Saudi Arabia.

Earlier, in mid-November, General Schwarzkopf had briefed his subordinate commanders on the "Hail Mary" operation for the ground war. The operation was not a miracle, however; it did not come from someone's brilliant flash of intuition overnight. It had to be planned in minute detail, examined from every angle—foremost the logistical one—and briefed down the line and back-briefed up the line.

The tactics for the Hail Mary phase of the ground war came from the "Jedi Knights," a term out of the movie *Star Wars,* applied to some officers involved in the planning. According to Bob Woodward in *The Commanders,* "Key portions of the ground campaign had been developed by a half dozen junior officers in their second year at the Army Command

and General Staff College at Fort Leavenworth. . . . These majors and lieutenant colonels, nicknamed the 'Jedi Knights,' had been sent to Saudi Arabia to apply the elements of advanced maneuver warfare—probing, flanking, surprise, initiative, audacity—to the war plan."

Working in a small top-secret corner of Schwarzkopf's head-quarters, they had applied the principles of the Army's unclassified 200-page operations manual (*FM 100-5*). Chapters 6 and 7 on offensive operations were built around concepts built around Grant's 1863 Civil War campaign at Vicksburg. Instead of attacking directly into enemy fortifications, Grant sent his troops in a wide maneuver around the Confederate front line, and then attacked from the side and rear. This indirect approach was deemed the best way to defeat Saddam Hussein.

According to one of the "Jedi Knights," Maj. Terry Peck on the staff of the XVIII Airborne Corps, Woodward had it about right.

Between 18 January and 7 February 1991, the XVIII Airborne Corps moved from the vicinity of Dhahran to the northwest, in a vast sweep that was the essence of the Hail Mary plan. The corps finally lined up near the Iraqi border, well past the VII Corps. The XVIII Airborne Corps staff paper on the vast sweep to the west read as follows:

Only two routes were available to the 100,000 plus soldiers of the XVIII Airborne Corps and those had to be shared with the normal heavy traffic required of Desert Shield forces. The typical Corps unit had to travel 665 kilometers; other elements moved up to 1,100 kilometers. . . . XVIII Airborne Corps moved three full US combat divisions, an armored cavalry regiment, and nearly all of its supporting specialized groups and brigades. That translates into flying approximately 980 helicopters; driving 25,310 vehicles (20,165 wheeled and 5,145 tracked) by road; and using nearly 1,400 Air Force transport sorties to deploy an additional 2,719 vehicles, 15,876 personnel and thousands of tons of supplies, food and ammunition into both fixed airfields and XVIII Airborne Corps–constructed assault landing strips.

On G day, Sunday 24 February 1991, the U.S. and coalition forces were deployed along the northern border of Saudi Arabia. In the west, was the Central Command. It was now made up of XVIII and the VII Corps. The XVIII Airborne Corps had the French 6th Division on the left (west), and then, going east, the 82d Airborne Division, the 101st, the 24th, and then the 3d Armored Cavalry Regiment. To the right of the XVIII was the VII Corps with the 1st Armored Division, the 2d Armored Cavalry Regiment, the 3d Armored Division, the 1st Infantry Division, the 1st Cavalry Division, and the British forces. To the east of the Central Command were the Joint Forces Command North, then the Marine Central Command, and then, on the right, the Joint Forces Command East.

An e-mail from the current XVIII Airborne Corps commander, Lt. Gen. Dan McNeill, on 9 February 2001, points out the difference between General Patton's forces moving across France, under orders from General Eisenhower to relieve the pressure on the surrounded 101st at Bastogne, and Lieutenant General Luck's XVIII Airborne Corps moving from Saudi Arabia into Iraq to force the latter's forces out of Kuwait. Patton's Third Army had 9,404 vehicles of all types; General Luck had 28,029; Patton had 42 aircraft; Luck had 980; Patton's Third Army traveled 140 kilometers along four routes; Luck's XVIII Airborne Corps traveled 883 kilometers along two routes. "General Luck could easily have been commanding one of the five largest Air Forces in the world at the time he crossed the Line of Departure," Lieutenant General McNeill added.

Prior to G day, "On the left flank XVIII Airborne Corps conducted mounted and aerial raids deep into Iraqi territory to hit armor, artillery, bunkers and observation posts," reported an Institute of Land Warfare special report, *Desert Victory, The US Army in the Gulf.* "In one armed reconnaissance mission by the 101st Airborne Division on 20 February, a helicopter with a loudspeaker induced 476 frightened Iraqis to surrender after fifteen of their bunkers were destroyed by air and tube-launched, optically tracked, wire-guided antitank (TOW) missile fire. The cross-border operations were not without cost, but Iraqi resistance was generally so weak that by 22 February helicopters of the 82d Airborne Division were penetrating deep into enemy territory with impunity in daylight."

It was ten seconds before 0238 in the black, moonless morning of 17 January 1991. The 101st's Task Force Normandy's two teams of four AH-64 Apache helicopter crews hovered at fifty feet over their targets fifty miles inside Iraq. On their forward-looking infrared screens, the pilots saw the two Iraqi radar sites that were linked to four fighter bases and the intelligence operations center in Baghdad. Each radar site, separated from each other by sixty-nine miles, offered a complex of at least a dozen targets—three ZPU-4s; a tropo-scatter radar; generator buildings; Spoon Rest, Squat Eye, and flatface dish antennas; EW electronic warfare vans; and barracks.

Lieutenant Tom Drew was at the controls of AH-64 Apache number 976. "Party in ten," he said, breaking radio silence for the first time on the mission. Ten seconds later the Apaches launched a salvo of laser-guided missiles. Desert Storm had begun. Four and a half minutes later, the Apache teams of the 1st Attack Helicopter Battalion of the 101st Aviation Regiment had, in the words of General Schwarzkopf, "plucked the eyes" out of Saddam Hussein's Soviet-supplied air defense installations.

Twenty-two minutes after the "Expect No Mercy" pilots of 1st Battalion, 101st Aviation Regiment, commanded by Lt. Col. Richard Cody, had blasted the Iraqi radar sites, 100 coalition planes boomed through the deaf, dumb, and blind alley that the Apaches had carved out inside Iraq. Desert Storm was under way, with army helicopters firing the first shots of the war.

For thirty-four days, from 17 January to 24 February, the coalition air forces pounded Iraqi military targets relentlessly. In addition, U.S. ships in the Persian Gulf fired on military targets with precision. Toward the end of the third week of the air campaign—more rapidly than even the most optimistic planner had predicted—General Schwarzkopf declared air superiority, if not supremacy, after the initial targets had been virtually destroyed and Saddam Hussein's air force rendered impotent. Most of the Iraqi air force went to ground in civilian communities or in protective bunkers that were later destroyed by precision-guided missiles. The few Iraqi aircraft that took to the skies were either quickly shot down or flown across the border into Iran, where 140 aircraft were impounded. The term "bug-out" might have been used to describe the precipitous cross-border flight of part of Saddam Hussein's air fleet.

Then, Schwarzkopf shifted to around-the-clock air strikes against Iraqi ground troops and their lines of communication, command and control centers, logistics centers, and armored vehicles, especially of those Iraqi units across the Kuwaiti–Saudi Arabian border. He concentrated particularly on the Iraqi Republican Guard divisions.

The Institute of Land Warfare reported in *Desert Victory* that "on 22 January, in XVIII Corps' sector near the boundary with VII Corps, the 3d Armored Cavalry Regiment took part in the first ground encounter of the campaign."

A squad exchanged fire with an Iraqi force of undetermined size, possibly from the border police. Two Iraqi were killed and six captured at the cost of two American wounded. On the extreme left, patrols of the 82d Airborne, 101st Airborne and French 6th Light Armored Divisions screened XVIII Corps' front near Rafha, manning listening posts and conducting reconnaissance into the barren wastes. They encountered fewer Iraqi scouts this far west, but clashes nevertheless occurred.

To discover what lay behind the border berms in the north, CENTCOM [Central Command] relied partly on Army special operations forces. During the early days of the crisis, Green Berets of the 5th Special Forces Group (Airborne), in cooperation with Saudi paratroopers, manned observation posts and patrolled the Kuwaiti border to provide early warning of an Iraqi attack. Since September, almost the entire 5th Group had become involved in liaison work and combined training, and CENTCOM used a battalion of the 3d Special Forces Group (Airborne) to carry out long-range patrols north of the border. In all, Special Forces soldiers conducted twelve such operations.

Special operations personnel also conducted extensive psychological operations (PSYSOPS). To induce large numbers of enemy soldiers to desert radio and television broadcasts, leaflets and loudspeakers proclaimed the themes of Arab brotherhood, the omnipotence of Allied air power, and the utter political and economic isolation of Iraq. In other special operations, Army helicopters cooperated with those of the Air Force to rescue downed pilots, and civil affairs officers worked closely with the Kuwaiti government in its reconstruction planning. Although Desert Storm proved to be primarily a conventional campaign, special operations played important parts in the final victory.

In spite of their success in deep reconnaissance, intelligence gathering, direct-action missions, and search and rescue operations, the role of Special Forces in the Gulf, according to the U.S. Army Special Operations Command, "was coalition warfare. Special Forces soldiers were attached to the coalition forces and were their trainers and advisers. Working with nearly every battalion of coalition forces, the Special Forces would prove to be a critical factor throughout Desert Shield and Desert Storm."

Army Special Forces trained with the Saudi Arabian military and with soldiers from the United Arab Republic, Qatar, Oman, Morocco, Bahrain, Syria, Egypt and France. According to the U.S. Special Operations Command, U.S. Army Special Forces were on the border with the Saudis. "Special Forces also were assigned to US Marine Corps units, but more than 90% of their time was spent with coalition forces. The 5th Special Forces Group sent 108 teams—usually three-to-four men to a team—to work with coalition forces' forward battalions. One Special Forces battalion alone combined for 6,000 hours of training with coalition forces in a 13-week period."

Unites States Army Special Forces made up only about 1 percent of the U.S. forces in the theater. Their missions were unique, hazardous, and lengthy, consuming many weeks of operating almost alone in enemy territory or working closely with coalition forces, training them, and in combat acting as liaison with the senior levels of command. They communicated, directed air strikes, gave situation reports, and served as links between the U.S. commands and the forces they accompanied.

The air forces in Desert Storm pummeled the Iraqi forces in Iraq and Kuwait for thirty-eight days. Going on an optimistic report from General Schwarzkopf, President Bush gave him permission to launch the ground campaign, the Hail Mary wide sweep around the flank of the Iraqis.

At 0100 on G day, Luck started his offensive with patrols from the French 6th Division moving into Iraq on the far west of his line of advance. At 0400 the French started their main attack through a light rain, their forces were heading for the small town of Al Salman, about 144 kilometers into Iraq. The 2d Brigade of the 82d attacked with the French, moved rapidly across the border against no opposition, and sped to the north in the darkness. On the way to Al Salman, French patrols ran into the perimeter of the Iraqi 45th Division. General Bernard Janvier, commander of the French 6th, sent his Gazelle attack choppers against the Iraqis' dug-in tanks and bunkers; the French lost two killed and twenty-five wounded in action but they captured some 2,500 Iraqis, took control of the division area, and pushed on to Al Salman. With this operation Luck's west flank was secure.

"The 82d Airborne Division, minus the brigade attached to the French 6th Light Armored Division," reported the Institute of Land Warfare in *Desert Victory*, "trailed the advance and cleared a two-lane highway into southern Iraq—main supply route (MSR) Texas—for the troops, equipment and supplies supporting the advance north. . . . From the Saudi border, XVIII Airborne Corps support command units drove 700 high-speed support vehicles north with the fuel, ammunition, and supplies to support a drive to the Euphrates River."

By the night of G day plus 1, 25 February, General Schwarzkopf was well beyond a simple Hail Mary plan. And, with the way things were going in Iraq, he was probably ready to say a Rosary in thanksgiving.

On G day, starting at 0705, the 101st launched the largest and longest one-day air assault in military history. From the Tactical assembly area (TAA) Campbell in northern Saudi Arabia, some 2,200 men of Col. James T. Hill's 1st Brigade Task Force flew ninety-five miles in two round trips of sixty-six UH-60 Black Hawks and thirty CH-47 Chinooks into Iraq. Included in the airlift were an additional seventy-five CH-47 sorties carrying 145,000 gallons of aircraft fuel and 100 attack, scout, general-support, and command and control helicopters. Ground transport consisting of 632 vehicles brought an additional 100,000 gallons of fuel and attack helicopter ammunition. Thus did General Peay set up the forward operating base (FOB) Cobra in the middle of the Iraqi desert, 176 kilometers from TAA Campbell, the launch base.

The Iraqis were stunned and disorganized by the onslaught of the 101st deep into their territory. By midafternoon, hundreds of Iraqis turned themselves over to the troops of the 101st. In TAA Campbell, Col. Bob Clark's 3d Brigade, the Rakkasans, readied itself for the launch to the Euphrates—the most combat-oriented phase of the 101st's air assault into Iraq. By the morning of G day plus 1, 25 February, General Peay was ready to attack. It was now time to catapult the Rakkasans into the division's main effort, which was to "attack, interdict, block and defeat enemy forces operating in and through AO Eagle [i.e., Highway 8] and, on further orders, attack to the east toward the Republican Guards retreating westward from the Kuwait area and north of Basra."

By the evening of G day plus 2, the 3d Brigade had air-assaulted into AO Eagle, 270 kilometers into Iraq, astride Highway 8. Colonel Clark had deployed his troopers into a defensive setup to block any Iraqi traffic moving east to reinforce the Iraqis near the Kuwaiti border or west to escape the attack by the coalition forces in the east. As one writer in *Triumph Without Victory* put it, "As Iraqi military convoys attempted to crash through the American roadblocks, they were fired upon by soldiers from Clark's 3d Brigade of the 101st Airborne. Most deadly were the wire-guided TOW missiles fired from launchers mounted on Humvees. Seeing the carnage, some Iraqi soldiers turned their vehicles around and fled. General Peay's soldiers had seized and secured Highway 8. Nothing would move on the road without his permission."

Colonel Ted Purdom had moved the CP of his 2d Brigade (3d Battalion, 502d Infantry and 1st Battalion, 320th Field Artillery) and his support and combat service slices into FOB Cobra on G day. Lieutenant Colonel James Donald, commander of the 1st Battalion, 502d, also moved his battalion into FOB Cobra and reported to the commander of the 1st Brigade, Colonel Hill.

East of the 101st Airborne, advanced elements of the 24th Infantry Division arrived about seventy miles southeast of FOB Cobra. Colonel Ted Reid's 197th Brigade of the 24th had made it halfway to the Euphrates River and just east of FOB Cobra when it linked up with the 1st Brigade of the 101st along MSR Virginia, near the 101st's eastern boundary. Farther east, on the 24th's right, was the 3d Armored Cavalry Regiment.

"It was just like a parade," said Lt. Col. B. J. Craddock, a battalion commander in the 24th. "The only problem was the weather. We faced, in my opinion, the worst weather we had the whole time we were over there, what with the sandstorm followed by the rainstorm." And the roads that the commanders had selected from maps before moving into Iraq turned out to be nothing more than muddy "goat trails," or quagmires.

The 101st's linkup with the 82d to the west of FOB Cobra was delayed because the 82d Airborne was stuck in the traffic backup in the French sector. But by the end of G day plus 1, both the 82d Airborne and the French 6th Light Armored were in the vicinity of Al Salman airfield to the west of FOB Cobra and along the west flank of XVIII Airborne Corps sector.

By the night of G day plus 2, the coalition forces along the entire front had moved north into Iraq with unexpected speed. Because of this success, which required Luck to issue the 101st new orders and missions, Peay was forced to make rapid, almost immediate changes in his plans; he had to remain flexible. And to do so, he used the division's aerial assets to move brigades rapidly and he decentralized command and control.

On 26 February, Luck notified Peay that the entire coalition force was reorienting itself toward the east "in order to cut off the enemy's escape routes north of Basra." The division's new direction of attack, Luck told Peay, was north of the 24th Division "to further interdict Iraqi escape routes." This move required the 101st to slide under the 24th—a "by the right flank" in old infantry drill maneuvers—and then directly over the 24th for an attack to the east. Then, after he received Luck's new battle plan, Peay quickly adjusted his scheme of maneuver. He decided to establish a new FOB, Viper, ninety-three miles due east of FOB Cobra from which he could launch helicopter assaults to the northeast.

The rains finally stopped on 26 February, but the sandstorm blew on unabated. (In an interview after the war, Peay said that the sandstorms on G days plus 1 and 2 were unlike any storms he had ever seen.) But at 0830 on 27 February, G day plus 3, Col. Ted Purdom launched his 2d Brigade from FOB Cobra to FOB Viper. He used 55 CH-47 Chinook and 120 UH-60 Black Hawk sorties. "The air assault into Viper went relatively smoothly," wrote Lieutenant Colonel Cody, "when you consider all of the moving parts Division and Aviation Brigade had to juggle. At the end of the day on the 27th, the Division had the 1st Brigade at Cobra, the 3d at AO Eagle, 2d Brigade and most of the Aviation Brigade at Viper." For artillery support on FOB Viper Colonel Purdom had the eighteen 105mm howitzers from his direct-support battalion, Lt. Col. Harlan Lawson's 1st Battalion, 320th Field Artillery Regiment, and eight 155mm howitzers from C Battery of the 8th Field Artillery Battalion. Meanwhile, up with the 3d Brigade deployed along the Euphrates, traffic along Highway 8 was almost at a standstill by G day plus 2.

By the evening of that day, the coalition forces were attacking forcibly with almost maneuver-like speed across the entire Iraqi front—from the 1st Marine Division near Kuwait City in the east to the French 6th and the 82d Airborne Divisions more than 200 miles to the west.

"You guys are doing a great job," said Schwarzkopf to Luck on 26 February. "Now I want to make sure you understand your mission from here on out. It is to inflict maximum destruction, maximum destruction, on the Iraqi military machine. You are to destroy all war-fighting equipment. Do not just pass it on the battlefield. We don't want the Iraqis coming at us again five years from now."

The coalition forces were now definitely in the "exploitation and pursuit" phase of the campaign. Its objective centered on removing Iraq's offensive potential and destroying its capability for large-scale mechanical movement. With Iraqi forces escaping to the north, clearly their escape routes had to be cut and their mechanized forces destroyed.

Of the three main routes out of the Kuwait theater of operations, two had been blasted by the U.S. Navy and Air Force. Damaged and burning vehicles blocked almost all motor vehicle traffic on the roads. Only the causeway over the Euphrates was still usable. The air strikes had also blown up many vehicles on the causeway, creating a bottleneck. Reconnaissance, however, had shown that several thousand more vehicles were inching forward and waiting to snake their way through the wreckage. Around the causeway, smoke from the burning vehicles and the oil well fires in Kuwait started by the departing Iraqis reduced visibility to about 1,000 meters. On 27 February, G day plus 3, Lieutenant General Luck ordered the aviation units under his command—the 101st Aviation Brigade and the 12th Aviation Brigade—to cut this final Iraqi escape route. Three AH-64 Apache battalions—the 2d Battalion, 229th Aviation, the 1st Battalion, 101st Aviation, and the 1st Battalion, 24th Infantry— and the cavalry squadrons of the 101st Airborne and the 24th Infantry took part in the "Battle of the Causeway." Among the vehicles and other military hardware destroyed in the battle were fourteen Iraqi APCs, eight BM-21 multiple-rocket launchers, four Mi-16 helicopters, fifty-six trucks, and two SA-6 radars. Also damaged was one of the few surviving bridges across the Euphrates.

On 27 February, G day plus 3, General Schwarzkopf held a press conference. He pointed out that it was not the intent of the coalition forces to destroy Iraq. "When we were here," he said, pointing to the position of the 3d Brigade of the 101st in AO Eagle along Highway 8, "we were 150 miles from Baghdad. If it had been our intention to take Iraq, to overrun the country, we could have done it unopposed for all intents and purposes."

In actuality, earlier in the war, to give Schwarzkopf as many alternatives as possible, Gary Luck and his XVIII Airborne Corps staff had discussed informally a plan to attack Baghdad with the 82d Airborne, the 101st Airborne, the 24th Infantry, and the 3d Armored Cavalry Regiment. They suggested dropping the 82d by parachute on one side of Baghdad, air assaulting the 101st to another, and attacking the heavy armored and other defenses of the city with the 24th Infantry and the 3d Armored Cavalry Regiment. The XVIII Corps staff even had tried, unsuccessfully, to find the jump aircraft for the 82d's attack.

General Colin Powell, the chairman of the Joint Chiefs of Staff, and Schwarzkopf had a phone conversation on 27 February in which Powell relayed to Schwarzkopf the gist of the discussions going on in the Oval Office. Aides to President Bush wanted a cease-fire at 0800, 28 February, but thinking no doubt about a "hundred-hour war," they suggested terminating hostilities at 0500 and announcing a cease-fire at 0800. When Powell relayed this information to him, Schwarzkopf replied, "I don't have any problem with it. Our objective was the destruction of the enemy forces, and for all intents and purposes, we've accomplished that objective. I'll check with my commanders, but unless they've hit some snag I don't know about, we can stop."

Schwarzkopf called his major commanders. He told Gen. Chuck Horner to keep reloading his bombers but to make sure that they'd be able to stop at 0500. He told Gen. John Yeosock, the army component commander, "Until five o'clock, it's business as usual. I encourage you to do as much damage as you can with your Apaches right up till then."

I called Admiral [Stan] Arthur, General [Walt] Boomer [commander of the marines in the war] and Major General Wayne Downing, who was running the US special operations deep behind enemy lines. Nobody seemed surprised that a cease-fire might be declared.

A few hours later Powell called to confirm: "We'll cease offensive operations, but there has been a change. The President will make the announcement at nine o'clock, but we won't actually stop until midnight [Washington time]. That makes it a hundred-hour war." I had to hand it to them: they really knew how to package an historic event.

President Bush and Secretary Cheney each came on the line to offer congratulations. Finally, Powell came back on and said, "Okay, that's it. Cease fire at eight o'clock local tomorrow morning."

In a televised address from the White House on the evening of 27 February 1991, President Bush announced, "Kuwait is liberated. Iraq's Army is defeated. Our military objectives are met. . . . [This] is a time of pride in our troops. . . . And soon we will open wide our arms to welcome back home to America our magnificent fighting forces."

During the hundred-hour war the Iraqis lost 3,847 of their 4,280 tanks, more than half of their 2,880 APCs, and just about all of their 3,100 artillery guns. Of their forty-three divisions at the start of the war, only about seven were still capable of fighting at the end. Some 60,000 Iraqi soldiers surrendered. The U.S. forces lost 148 killed in action.

The U.S. Army had achieved a remarkable victory. The Gulf War proved once again the absolute need for ground forces to win battles and retain control of enemy forces and terrain. And it proved without a doubt the diverse capabilities, combat readiness, and inherent adaptability of airborne forces—parachute and air-assault—in contributing mightily to U.S. military power.

29: After the Gulf War: The Nation's Ready Force

The XVIII Airborne Corps is the nation's contingency corps. Its home base is Fort Bragg, North Carolina, home of the airborne and special operations forces. The corps's mission is clear: "To maintain the XVIII Airborne Corps as a strategic crisis response force, manned and trained to deploy rapidly by air, sea and land anywhere in the world, prepared to fight upon arrival and win."

The days of the Cold War and the potential for a global conflict are seemingly over, but according to a corps publication, "Amid the changing relationships between nations, the strategic imperative of deterrence remains valid."

War to the XVIII Airborne Corps comes in the shape of contingency operations. The Corps provided command and control for the Army's crisis response forces. This mixture of force capabilities is as versatile and lethal as it is deployable and expansible. It is not a fixed force, but can be tailored to any contingency worldwide based on factors of METT-T [mission, enemy, terrain, troops, and time available.]

Likewise, the Corps' missions range from a single show-of-force (Honduras 1988) to providing a deterrent force against a major and immediate threat (Saudi Arabia 1990). The Corps often operates in undeveloped, austere environments without in-place logistic and communications infrastructures and with little or no host nation support. Further, the most likely contingencies require the Corps simultaneously to fight in the objective area while deploying additional forces to amass the combat power necessary for decisive operations.

To accomplish its myriad missions and respond to contingencies, the XVIII Airborne Corps is made up of combat forces that run the gamut from light to heavy. The "readiest" of its combat power is the 82d Airborne Division stationed at Fort Bragg and ready to deploy in eighteen hours, day or night. The unit's mission is stated thus: "Within 18 hours of notification, the 82d Airborne Division strategically deploys, conducts forcible entry parachute assault and secures key objectives for follow-on military operations in support of national interests." Because of the range and capacity of today's aircraft, the 82d is a versatile force with a capability to act anywhere in the world. It does not have to air-land on a secure airfield or debark in a friendly port; it is ready to jump from aircraft and fight on the ground in hostile territory. And no longer does the division have to rely on small "jump" aircraft like the eighteen-man C-47s of World War II. Today, the U.S. Air Force has the C-130s, C-141s, and C-17s with much more carrying and dropping capacities. In a combat jump, the C-130 can drop sixty-two paratroopers in four sticks using four jump cables. The C-141 and the C-17, respectively, can drop 164 and 102 combat-ready troops. The carrying capacity of C-5 cargo planes allows the 82d to build up its combat power rapidly once it has secured an airfield. As well, the operational range is more than substantial: the C-130, carrying a full load of paratroopers, can fly 1,900 to 2,000 nautical miles in seven hours. The C-141 can fly 3,000 nautical miles in eight hours. (Of course, the air columns have fighter aircraft to protect them through hostile airspace en route.)

The 82d has a parachute-qualified strength of 14,341 men (and about 200 jump-qualified women in jobs not coded for "direct combat probability"—if there are such tasks in the division). Except for its helicopters and some radar, all the division's fighting gear, including its fifty-four 105mm howitzers, can be dropped by air. The 82d's helicopters are air-transportable in C-130s and air force strategic lift aircraft. A salient feature of Fort Bragg is that Pope Air Force Base, home of the transport aircraft, is adjacent.

The 82d Airborne Division Ready Force (DRF) concept requires that one battalion task force, the DRF-1, remain on a two-hour recall basis. To lift a DRF battalion task force of approximately 800 troopers and its equipment, including six 105mm howitzers, requires sixteen C-17s or an equivalent. N hour is notification—mission received. By N hour plus 4 the troops begin movement to the corps marshaling area. At N hour plus 4:30 heavy drop rigging begins. By N hour plus 8, the troops begin loading their heavy drop equipment on the planes parked at the Pope Air Force Base Green Ramp. By N hour plus 12, the DRF-1 conducts assembly and mission rehearsals. From N hour plus 15 to N hour plus 16, the air force and 82d Division commanders conduct a mission brief. By N hour plus 17:30, the troops are aboard the planes on Green Ramp. And at N hour plus 18, the lead aircraft has its "wheels up."

The division has plans for a wide variety of different contingency plans to support operations around the world. Its missions range from disaster relief and civil support to peacekeeping operations to combat. "During the 1970s," wrote the 82d's historian, " the Division was alerted three times."

War in the Middle East in the fall of 1973 brought the 82d to full alert. Then in May 1978, the Division was alerted for a possible drop into Zaire, and again, in 1979, the Division was alerted for a possible operation to rescue American hostages in Iran.

On October 25, 1983, elements of the 82d deployed to the tiny island of Grenada. The first 82d unit to deploy on Operation URGENT FURY was a task force of the 2d Battalion, 325th Airborne Infantry Regiment. On October 26 and 27, the 1st Battalion, 505th Infantry and the 1st Battalion, 508th Infantry, with support units deployed to Grenada. The first aircraft carrying division troopers touched down at Point Salinas 17 hours after notification.

In March 1988, elements of the 504th Parachute Infantry Regiment conducted a parachute insertion and air-land operation into Honduras. The deployment was a joint training exercise, but the paratroopers were ready to fight. The deployment caused the Sandinistas to withdraw back to Nicaragua. In Army lexicon, this deployment was called a "flexible deterrent operation."

In August 1992, the Division was alerted to deploy a task force to hurricane-ravaged Florida and provide humanitarian assistance. Division troopers provided food, shelter and medical attention to a grateful Florida population, instilling a renewed confidence in the military.

To carry out its many and diverse missions and responsibilities around the world, XVIII Airborne Corps has a force to fit most of today's demands. In addition to the 82d Airborne Division at Fort Bragg, there is the 101st Airborne Division (Air Assault) with three maneuver brigades at Fort Campbell, Kentucky. The 101st has the same basic organization as the 82d's but is enhanced by nine battalions of helicopters, including three battalions of Apaches, making it a powerful tank-killing force. Its Chinook and other helicopters give the division air-assault mobility. The XVIII Corps historian reports that "the night fighting capability of the 101st [cannot] be matched by any other force."

The ability to see, fly, shoot and fight at night with unerring accuracy makes the division one of the most versatile and potent forces on the battlefield.

During Desert Storm, the division covered more ground in one afternoon than many units did during the entire war. The 101st had the deepest penetration into Iraq of any conventional force in the U.S. Army, establishing a blocking position along Iraq highways within miles of Baghdad. The101st is the most versatile and flexible force in the Corps Commander's arsenal. It is capable of fighting at any level of warfare by avoiding enemy forces that it cannot immediately overpower, and by overpowering all that it cannot elude.

With its three ground maneuver brigades as its combat power centerpiece, the 3d Infantry Division (Mechanized) located at Forts Stewart and Benning and Hunter Army Airfield, all in Georgia, is the corps commander's iron fist. Its more than 17,000 soldiers make the 3d Division, the Rock of the Marne, one of the U.S. Army's largest. The division is not only intrinsically powerful, but with its Abrams main battle tanks and Bradley Fighting Vehicles, it is capable of all types of combat in many types of terrain. The 3d Division has the ability to deploy rapidly to any of the world's trouble spots and its rapid-response capability has been greatly enhanced in recent years by the army's prepositioned equipment, whether afloat or on land. Apache helicopters with this division's aviation brigade provide a significant complement to the ground maneuver units.

One could argue that the 101st and 3d Divisions are the corps commander's knockout punches.

The XVIII Airborne Corps' 10th Mountain Division (Light) is stationed at Fort Drum, New York. Even though it has only two ground maneuver brigades and is "lightly" equipped, this outfit, the Climb to Glory division, has been the most frequently deployed in the past decade. The 9,000 soldiers of the 10th Division are ready—well trained and prepared—for operations in almost any kind of warfare, and are especially suited for operations short of full war. The history of this legendary outfit goes back to the early months of World War II when it was organized and trained to counter the threat of the Axis powers' Alpine units. It is a "light" division in organization and structure but can defeat any enemy formation when it is augmented by other corps resources. All the same, this division is most at home when operating within the constraints of urban areas, jungles, and mountains.

The corps' 2d Armored Cavalry Regiment is stationed at Fort Polk, Louisiana. Although more appropriately called a light cavalry regiment because of the wheeled vehicles that replaced its tracked vehicles when it was posted back to the United States from Germany, the 2d Regiment has the organization, equipment, tactics, techniques, and standard operating procedures to provide reconnaissance and security operations for the corps commander. One of the army's oldest and longest serving units, the 2d Regiment has both the capability and elan in quantities sufficient to accomplish a host of battlefield tasks for the XVIII Airborne Corps. The twenty-four Kiowa Warrior helicopters of the regiment's air cavalry squadron greatly increase the commander's ability to see and engage enemy formations before the enemy is able to close with the corps' main battle formations.

The corps' two aviation commands, the 18th Aviation Brigade and the 229th Aviation Regiment, provide, respectively, the lift helicopters and attack helicopters. The 18th Brigade with its Blackhawks and Chinooks provides the corps the ability to move soldiers and materiel about the battlefield. The Flying Tigers of the 229th Regiment give the corps commander the ability to "shape the battlefield" by attacking enemy formations at extended ranges or in "deep operations." The XVIII Airborne Corps also has a limited number of fixed-wing aircraft assigned to the 525th Military Intelligence Brigade.

At Fort Bragg is the XVIII Airborne Corps artillery headquarters, which serve as the corps commander's force artillery headquarters and enables the commander to bring to bear all indirect fires and tactical air support on a decisive point of the commander's choosing. With more than 300 guns and launchers assigned to the corps, that firepower is massive and effective. Normally, the corps artillery controls general support and reinforcing artillery units in the corps' task organizations.

A number of other commands organic to XVIII Airborne Corps, the separaters or enablers as they are known in corps jargon, perform significant battlefield functions that not only enable the corps commander to lead the corps but greatly enhance the execution of war task requirements of the divisions assigned to the corps. The 525th Military Intelligence Brigade with its three battalions provides signals, electronic imagery, and human intelligence. Airfield maintenance, construction of fighting positions, road maintenance, vertical construction, demolitions, mine laying or clearing, bridging, and topography are a few of the missions fulfilled by the 20th Engineer Brigade. The soldiers and battalions of the 35th Signal Brigade provide the corps commander with the requisite command and control communications and computers. The 44th Medical Brigade provides medical and dental operations and logistics well forward in the battle space in support of the corps.

Air defense and theater ballistic missile defense for the corps is handled by the 108th Air Defense Brigade that is assigned to Fort Bliss, Texas. The military policemen of the 16th Military Police Brigade support the corps with enemy POW operations, battlefield circulation control, rear area defense, convoy escort, and command post security. The 18th Soldier Support Group keeps the soldiers of the corps paid and processes requisite personnel administrative actions for the soldiers of XVIII Airborne Corps.

The largest nondivisional unit of the corps is the 1st Corps Support Command, the logistic might of the XVIII Airborne Corps, that provides all classes of supply and services. The headquarters command of the XVIII Airborne Corps is the Dragon Brigade, which provides the necessary equipment and manning for the corps' CPs.

One striking example of the corps' ability to react and execute a contingency plan rapidly was Operation Restore Democracy (later Uphold Democracy).

Haiti is one of the poorest nations in the world. It is an independent republic in the West Indies, located in the western third of Hispaniola, some 556 miles from the United States. Once again, in 1949, the government went through a series of revolts and dictatorships. First came the overthrow of the democratic rule of Gen. Dumarsais Estime by Gen. Paul Magloire, who was succeeded in 1957 by François "Papa Doc" Duvalier, who set up a dictatorship enforced by his secret police, the "Tontons Macoutes." In 1971 Duvalier died and was succeeded by his son, "Baby Doc," who set up an even more corrupt and repressive dictatorship. After violent demonstrations against his rule he fled the country in 1986. In 1991 Jean-Bertrand Aristide, a Roman Catholic priest, was sworn in as the democratically elected president. But seven months later, on 30 September 1991, a military coup, carried out by relics of the Duvalier era, ousted him. He was reinstated in October 1993 by a U.S.-led multinational force under UN Resolution 940. Troubles developed, and he was ousted once more. Then the United Nations imposed an oil and almost complete trade embargo on Haiti and authorized the use of force to restore Aristide to power.

The force was the XVIII Airborne Corps, and for the operation it was converted into a joint headquarters, Joint Task Force 180, commanding U.S. Army, Navy, Marine, Coast Guard, and special forces in Operation Uphold Democracy. The major elements of the joint task force were the 82d Airborne Division and the 10th Mountain Division. Operation Plan 2370 called for a forcible entry into Haiti with the mission of neutralizing the Haitian armed forces and police in order to protect U.S. citizens and interests, restore civil order, and help the transition to a democratic government. The major element of the forcible entry was the dropping of elements of the 82d into Haiti at night on 18 September to secure the unopposed air-landing of the 10th Mountain Division. The major element of the forcible entry plan was the drop of the 504th Parachute Infantry Regiment, reinforced with the 2d Battalion of the 325th Airborne Infantry Regiment, in an assault early on the evening of 18 September 1994 to seize Port-au-Prince International Airport and to secure key objectives in Port-au-Prince and the surrounding area. The overall primary mission was to oust Haiti's military dictator. At the time, Maj. Gen. William M. Steele was the 82d's commander. In the year prior to the operation, he had put the entire division through rigorous training, developed detailed plans for each phase of the operation, and set up realistic rehearsals.

Steele assigned the 505th Parachute Infantry Regiment for the follow-up to the 504th's air assault. The mission was a night parachute assault onto two DZs, the Pegasus DZ and Papia airport, to assist the 504th in restoring order in Haiti and to clear the area for the unopposed air-landing of the 10th Mountain Division.

Another part of the operation involved a special operations forces helicopter assault into downtown Port-au-Prince to attack military CPs and kill or capture commanders and terrorists whose whereabouts were generally known. Then the 2d Battalion of the U.S. Marines 2d Regiment was scheduled to come across the beaches of the northern port city of Cap-Haïtien. Theoretically, the assault mission was basically a two-day operation. Then the 10th Mountain Division would occupy the country—unopposed.

On 16 September, on D day minus 2, as a last resort President Clinton sent a three-man delegation to Haiti to induce General Cedras, the military commander and head of the government, and the illegitimate president, Emile Jonaissant, to return power to the duly elected Aristide. The delegation was composed of ex-president Jimmy Carter, Senate Armed Forces Committee Chairman Sam Nunn, and the former chairman of the Joint Chiefs of Staff, Gen. Colin Powell.

While the delegation was meeting with Cedras, Lt. Gen. Hugh Shelton, the XVIII Airborne Corps commander, was aboard the USS *Mount Whitney* off Haiti with his joint task force headquarters staff. But at the very last moment of conversation with the Carter team on 18 September 1994, Cedras agreed to step down and turn the government over to Aristide.

At 1600 on 18 September, Shelton had a video conference call with the Norfolk Command commander, under whom Shelton's Joint Task Force was operating. Carter's team had relayed to Clinton Cedras's agreement, and he accepted it. The attack was canceled, but the first wave of nearly 3,000 paratroopers of the 504th was on the way to jump into Haiti in the early morning hours of 19 September. And the 505th was on the Green Ramp at Pope Air Force Base combat-loaded onto aircraft, ready to take off for the follow-up parachute assault.

When Shelton got the message he ordered the 504th to turn around and land back at the air force base instead of making its combat jump. Instead, the 10th Mountain Division was able to make an unopposed air-landing at the Port-au-Prince airport the next day. A planned forcible entry had become an operation other than war.

Once the 10th Mountain Division had secured the airport, Shelton headed to Port-au-Prince for a meeting with Cedras. Shelton remembered that "once Cedras realized that the invasion was under way, he folded. [I was] going to tell him to look out in the harbor. What you see is one-fourth of what we've got locked and cocked." Shelton continued to meet with Cedras in a number of frustrating sessions. He insisted that the Haitian Armed Forces comply with the Carter-Cedras accords, that U.S. citizens and interests be protected, that civil order be restored, and that a democratic government be maintained. Shelton, demonstrating the combination of warrior's skills and political savvy that would lead him to the highest military position, told Cedras that time was up and negotiations were over. He suggested that Cedras would be treated with reasonable dignity if he left freely, or, if the dictator continued to stall or resist, he would leave the country feet first.

Finally, on 15 October, Aristide was restored to rightful power over the people who had freely elected him. Once Aristide was back in the presidential palace, the operation became Operation Uphold Democracy. And, three years later, Gen. Henry H. Shelton went on to become chairman of the Joint Chiefs of Staff, serving in that capacity until October 2001.

Operation Restore Democracy, and then Uphold Democracy, is a clear demonstration of the adaptability, degree of training, wide spectrum of military power, and readiness available day and night of the XVIII Airborne Corps—the nation's ready force.

Bibliography

Adleman, Robert H., and Col. George Walton. *The Champagne Campaign.* Boston: Little, Brown and Company, 1969.

Ambrose, Stephen A. *D-Day.* New York: Simon and Schuster, 1994.

———. *The Victors.* New York: Simon and Schuster. 1998.

Anderson, Charles R. *Algeria, French Morocco.* Washington, D.C.: U.S. Army Center of Military History, 1992.

Anderson, Col. Randall J. "After Action Report of 101st Airborne Division (Air Assault) Artillery in Operation Desert Storm, January–March 1991," 5 January 1991.

Appleman, Roy E. *South to the Naktong, North to the Yalu.* Washington, D.C.: U.S. Government Printing Office, 1961.

Association of the U.S. Army. *Desert Victory, The US Army in the Gulf. An Institute of Land Warfare Special Report.* Arlington, VA: February 2001.

Ballard, Ted. *Rhineland.* Washington, D.C.: U.S. Center of Military History, 1992.

Bauer, Cornelis. *The Battle of Arnhem.* New York: Kensington Publishing Corp., 1979.

Bedessem, Edward N. *Central Europe.* Washington, D.C.: U.S. Army Center of Military History, 1992.

Birtle, Andrew J. *Sicily.* Washington, D.C.: U.S. Army Center of Military History, 1992.

Black, Robert W. *Rangers in Korea.* New York: Ivy Books, 1989.

Blair, Clay. *The Forgotten War.* New York: Random House, 1987.

Blanchard, Gen. George S. (ret.). Letter to author, 1 April 1999.

———. Letter to Gen. William C. Westmoreland, 15 June 1972.

Bolling, Maj. Gen. Alexander R. Jr. (ret.). Letter to author, 19 January 1999.

Bolt, Col. William J. "Command Report: 101st Airborne Division (Air Assault) for Operation Desert Shield and Desert Storm, 2 August 1990 through 1 May 1991," July 1, 1991.

Booth, T. Michael, and Duncan Spencer. *Paratrooper, The Life of James M. Gavin.* New York: Simon and Schuster, 1994.

Breuer, William B. *Geronimo!* New York: St. Martin's Press, 1989.

Burger, Sgt. Knox. "Reception at Atsugi." *Yank, the Army Weekly* (n.d.).

Charles, Col. A. K. Letter to author, 15 September 1995.

Cirillo, Roger. *Ardennes–Alsace.* Washington, D.C.: U.S. Army Center of Military History, 1992.

Clarke, Jeffrey, J. *Southern France.* Washington, D.C.: U.S. Army Center of Military History, 1992.

Cody, Lt. Col. Richard A. "Task Force Normandy." *Defence Helicopter* (Spring Supplement, 1972).

Crawford, Capt. W. T. Interview of Col. G. H. Gerhart, Taegu, Korea, 8 April 1952.

Deane, Gen. John R. Jr. (ret.). Letters to author, 13 and 24 February 1999.

Devlin, Gerard M. *Paratrooper.* New York: St. Martin's Press, 1979.

Eisenhower, Dwight D. *Crusade in Europe.* Garden City, NY: Doubleday, 1948.

Fehrenbach, T. R. *This Kind of War.* New York: Macmillan, 1963.

Flanagan, Lt. Gen. Edward M. Jr. *Battle for Panama, Operation Just Cause.* Washington, D.C.: Brassey's (U.S.), 1993.

————. "Hostile Territory Was Their AO in Desert Storm." *Army* (September 1991).

————. *The Angels.* Novato, CA: Presidio Press, 1989.

————. *Corregidor.* Novato, CA: Presidio Press, 1988.

————. *Los Baños Raid.* Novato, CA: Presidio Press, 1986.

————. *Lightning, The 101st in the Gulf War.* Washington, D.C., Brassey's (U.S.), 1994.

————. *The Rakkasans.* Novato, CA: Presidio Press, 1997.

Foster, Renita. "Surrender? Nuts!" *Soldiers* (December 2000).

Gavin, Gen. James M. *On to Berlin.* New York: Viking, 1978.

Gilbert, Martin. *Second World War.* New York: Henry Holt and Company, 1991.

Gorwitz, Brig. Gen. Bertram Hall. Letters to author, 20 July 1989 and 19 June 1995.

Goulden, Joseph C. *Korea—The Untold Story of the War.* New York: Times Books, 1982.

Hagerman. Lt. Col. Bart. *War Stories*. Paducah, KY: Turner Publishing Co., 1993.

Halberstadt, Hans. *Airborne, Assault from the Sky*. Novato, CA: Presidio Press, 1988.

Hallanan, Col. George H. Letter to *Army*, April 1995.

Hammond, William M. *Normandy*. Washington, D.C.: U.S. Army Center of Military History, 1992.

Hayward, Maj. Gen, Howard I. (ret.). Letter to author, 5 March 1999.

Holling, Alexander R. Jr. Letter, 19 January 1999.

Hoyt, Edwin P. *The Bloody Road to Panmunjom*. New York: Military Heritage Press, 1985.

———. *On to the Yalu*. New York: Military Heritage Press, 1984.

———. *Airborne*. New York: Stein and Day, 1983.

Huston, James A. *Out of the Blue*. Nashville, TN: The Battery Press, 1972.

Joyce, Carlton. *Stand Where They Fought*. Newman, GA: Battlefield Publishing House, 1999.

Kass, Dominick George. Letter to author, 22 April 2001.

Kenderick, Col. Robert C. (ret.). Letter to author, 9 June 1997.

Kerwin, Gen. Walter T. Letter to General Yarborough, n.d.

Kinnard, Lt. Gen. H. W. O. Letter to author, n.d., 1995.

Kroesen, Gen. Frederick J. (ret.). Letters, 2 and 7 January 1999.

Kuta, Gene. *Airborne Ranger, 50th Anniversary publication*. Paducah, KY: Turner Publishing Company, 1990.

Lassen, Don, and Richard K. Schrader. *Pride of America*. Missoula, MT: Pictorial Histories Publishing Company, 1991.

Laurie, Clayton, D. *Anzio*. Washington, D.C.: U.S. Army Center of Military History, 1992.

Liddell Hart, B. H. *History of the Second World War*. New York: G. P. Putnam's Sons, 1970.

MacArthur, Gen. Douglas. *Reminiscences*. New York: Da Capo Press, 1964.

MacGarrigle, George L. *Taking the Offensive*. Washington, D.C.: U.S. Army Center of Military History, 1998.

Mackmull, Lt. Gen. Jack V. Letter to author, 30 May 2001.

———. Letter, 18 July 1993, giving a comprehensive account of the origin of the air-assault concept.

Manchester, William. *American Caesar*. Boston: Little, Brown and Co., 1978.

Masters, Charles J. *Glidermen of Neptune*. Carbondale: Southern Illinois University Press, 1995.

McFarren, Maj. Gen. Freddy E. (ret.). Letter to author, 7 February 1999.

McNeill, Lt. Gen. Dan K. E-mail, 9 February 2001.

———. Letter to Col. R. M. Piper, 21 October 1999.

Meloy, Maj. Gen. Guy S. III (ret.). Letter to author, 15 December 1998.

Merriam, Robert E. *The Battle of the Bulge.* New York: Ballantine Books, 1947.

Miley, Col. W. M. Jr. Letter, 1 October 1998.

Mitchell, Col. Ralph M. *The 101st Airborne Division's Defense of Bastogne.* Fort Leavenworth, KS: U.S. Army Command and General Staff College, 1986.

Moore, Lt. Gen. Harold G. Letter, 6 June 1999.

Munson, Brig. Gen. Delbert E. Letters, 21 and 23 June 1995.

O'Hare, Richard F. Letter, 21 January 1999.

Palmer, Gen. Bruce Jr. Letter to author, 20 September 1999.

———. *The 25-Year War.* New York: Simon and Schuster, 1984.

Peacock, Maj. Gen. Oliver L. Letter to author, 6 April 2000.

Perret, Geoffrey. *There's a War to Be Won.* New York: Ballantine Books, 1991.

Piper, Col. Robert M. Letters to author, 1 March, 2 April, and 25 May 1999.

Porter, Capt. W. R., and Capt. T. M. Fairfull. *The History of the 3d Brigade, 82d Airborne Division.* Toronto: Image Public Relations Ltd., n.d.

Porter, Maj. Gen. Bobby B. (ret.). Letter to author, 10 January 1999.

Raff, Col. Edson D. *We Jumped to Fight.* New York: Eagle Books, 1944.

Ridgway, Gen. Matthew B. *Soldier—The Memoirs of Matthew B. Ridgway.* New York: Harper and Bros., 1956.

Ryan, Cornelius. *A Bridge Too Far.* New York: Simon and Schuster, 1974.

———. *The Longest Day.* New York: Simon and Schuster, 1959.

Sampson, Chaplain (Lt. Col.) Francis L. *Look Out Below.* Washington, D.C.: Catholic University of America Press, 1958.

Scholes, Maj. Gen. Edison. Letter to author, 26 April 1991.

Schwarzkopf, Gen. H. Norman. *It Doesn't Take a Hero.* New York: Bantam Books, 1992.

Seitz, Lt. Gen. Richard J. (ret.). Letters to author, n.d.

Simpson, Col. Charles M. *Inside the Green Berets.* Novato, CA: Presidio Press, 1983.

Smith, Col. Kenneth V. *Naples-Foggia.* Washington, D.C.: U.S. Army Center of Military History, 1992.

Soldiers, the Official U.S. Army Magazine, December 2000.

Sorley, Lewis. *Thunderbolt.* New York: Simon and Schuster, 1992.

South Carolina National Guard. Memorandum of 10 January 1992, re: retirement of Brig. Gen. John A. Crosscope Jr. on 1 February 1992.

Steele, Dennis. "The Last Battle." *Army* (April 2001).

Steele, Lt. Gen. William M. Letter to author, 1 April 1999.

Stiner, Gen. Carl W. (ret.). Letter to author, 1 May 1999.

Stiner, Gen. Carl W. Letter to author, 1 May 1999.

Stolley, Richard B. "Our Man in Haiti." *Life* (November 1994).

Strukel, Maj. Gen. Jack Jr. Letter to author, 24 February 1999.

Stubbs, Mary Lee, and Stanley Russell Connor, *Armor Cavalry,* Washington, D.C.: Office of the Chief of Military History, 1972.

Tackaberry, Lt. Gen. Thomas H. (ret.). Letter to author, December 1998.

Taylor, Allan. *Chaplain—You Didn't Have to Be on the Front Line.* Publisher and date unknown.

Thurmond, Sen. Strom. Letter to Col. Henry Durant, 1 February 1992.

Tolson, Lt. Gen. John J. *Airmobility, 1961–1971.* Washington, D.C.: U.S. Government Printing Office, 1973.

True Stories of World War II. Pleasantville, NY: Reader's Digest, 1980.

USA Airborne, 50th Anniversary. Paducah, KY: Turner Publishing Co., 1990.

U.S. Army Command and General Staff College. "The Battle of Sukchon-Sunchon." Staff paper, Fort Leavenworth, KS.

Warner, Gen. Volney F. (ret.). Letters to author, 4 and 23 February 1999.

Waterhouse, Fred J. *The Rakkasans.* Paducah, KY: Turner Publishing Co., 1991.

Weber, Col. William E. (ret.). Letter to author, 23 April 2001.

Westmoreland, Gen. W. C. Letter to author, 19 April 1989.

Woodward, Bob. *The Commanders.* New York: Simon and Schuster, 1991.

Yarborough, Lt. Gen. William P. Letter to author, 8 January 1999.

———. Oral history. Carlisle Barracks, PA: U.S. Army Military Research Collection, 19 August 1975.

———. *Bailout Over North Africa.* Williamstown, NJ: Phillips Publications, 1979.

XVIII Airborne Corps, America's Contingency Corps. Pamphlet, n.d.

173d Airborne Brigade. *Sky Soldiers.* Paducah, KY: Turner Publishing Company, 1993.

Index